$38.00

D0812354

Communication Networks
for
Computers

WILEY SERIES IN COMPUTING

Consulting Editor

C.A. Lang, *Computer Laboratory, Cambridge University*

Numerical Control-Mathematics and Applications

P. Bézier
Professeur au Conservatoire National des Arts et Métiers
and
Technological Development Manager, Renault, France

Communication Networks for Computers

D.W. Davies
and
D.L.A. Barber

National Physical Laboratory,
Teddington

Communication Networks

for

Computers

Donald W. Davies

and

Derek L. A. Barber

National Physical Laboratory, Teddington

JOHN WILEY & SONS
London - New York - Sydney - Toronto

Library of Congress Catalog card No. 73-2775

ISBN 0 471 19874 9

Reprinted April 1975
Reprinted March 1976

Printed in Great Britain
By Unwin Brothers Limited
The Gresham Press, Old Woking, Surrey.
A member of the Staples Printing Group.

To
Diane and Ann

Preface

For the first decade of its development, computer technology was concerned with single, isolated computers. People brought their problems to the machines and carried away the results. Then experiments were tried in which two computers interacted and computers were accessed from a distance. These were the beginnings of computer networks, the potential of which is still being explored.

We are seeing a convergence of two technologies, those of computers and telecommunications, and the emergence of systems which combine them both in order to provide 'teleprocessing' services. These enable data to be captured at source, processed in a timely way by reference to large stores of immediately-accessible information and the results presented to the user so quickly that a 'conversation' between the user and the machine is possible.

Our aim in this book has been to explore the new technology created by the convergence. One particular theme is in the forefront; the communication needs that are being created by computer networks. The needs are very different from those human requirements which led to the design of present-day telecommunication networks. Our present networks cannot adequately serve the great variety of 'subscribers' which must be able to intercommunicate—terminals with a wide range of speeds, and computers which can converse at the same time with many different terminals and with each other.

Convergence could go to the point where one universal network serves all purposes and carries speech, pictures, data and so forth. We think not, but the question is a controversial one. Certainly, whatever different services are provided for subscribers there will be one network in the sense that many facilities will be used in common. For example, long-distance transmission will be digital and will serve both the telephone and data networks.

The most difficult design problems today concern public data networks, which must meet a wide range of communication needs that have not yet been defined. Much of the material in the book is intended to illuminate these problems. Because the new teleprocessing systems must be designed as a whole, a new breed of engineer must be trained, and we would like this book to be a means of introduction to the new speciality.

The book divides into three parts. Chapters 1 to 4 deal with computer-communication networks as they now are, with the use of the telephone network and with private networks. From Chapter 5 onwards we go back to the principles of computer networks in order to understand the new possibilities.

Chapter 5 deals with data transmission in a more basic way than Chapter 2. Chapters 6, 7, 8 and 9 treat the use of storage, multiplexing, message switching and data switching respectively.

The final part of the book comprising Chapters 10 to 14 is concerned with the new possibilities for communication networks which have arisen because stores and processors are cheaper and data transmission is faster. In these chapters we develop the principles first introduced in Chapter 8 and called 'packet switching'. Chapter 12 introduces a new theme, which is the optimization of network geography. Chapter 13 describes the principles of software design for a modern switched network and Chapter 14 reviews some of the general themes that have been found to underlie the design of computer networks.

Terminology was a problem, and we have tried to make a mid-Atlantic compromise, choosing what are in our view the best of U.S. and U.K. terms, with a slight bias towards the terms used by CCITT. If any terms are unfamiliar, the glossary at the end of the book should help by providing a definition, or a familiar equivalent word.

Acknowledgements

Our colleagues at the National Physical Laboratory and in the U.K. Post Office have helped us a great deal to formulate the ideas described in this book, and to find some of the information we needed. Many of the ideas described in Chapter 13 are based on the work of Dr. Peter Wilkinson. We thank him particularly for his invaluable help with the preparation of this Chapter. We also had willing help from the staff of Lloyds Bank, BEA and SITA to enable us to describe accurately their pioneering work in computer networks. The many discussions we have had with the builders of the ARPA network have also made a significant contribution to the book. Prof. David Aspinall of Swansea University and Dr. Alexander G. Fraser of Bell Telephone Laboratories read the manuscript and gave us helpful advice. The computer-drawn graphics used to illustrate Chapter 5 were produced by Mr. J. H. Sexton and Miss E. C. Windridge. Where diagrams are derived from journals or other sources, the acknowledgement is given with the diagrams themselves. Our thanks are also due to Ann, Jennifer and Sheila, for their rapid and accurate typing of the manuscript.

Contents

Chapter 5. Data Transmission

Chapter 11. Protocols, Terminals and Network Monitoring

Chapter 12. Network Geography, Reliability and Routing

Chapter 13. The Software of Packet Switching Systems

Chapter 1
Computers and Communications

1.1 INTRODUCTION

In the development of technology there are three dominant themes. The first can be traced back to prehistory and is the discovery and production of new materials. The second is the finding of new sources of energy. The third is the invention of new ways of handling information. All three themes can be seen in modern technology and at the present time we are experiencing a very rapid phase of development in the third of them—in information technology.

Information handling is based on the computer, which in the 'second industrial revolution' takes a role like that of the steam engine. Not only do the computers appear as the 'main engines' of information processing, they also function as 'donkey engines' in the subsidiary tasks such as communications. The explosive development of computer technology which began in 1945 is still continuing and the cost reductions and performance improvements which are still to come will lead to the use of stored-program devices wherever logical functions are needed.

Modern information technology has been paced by the improvement of stores, and all the big developments of information systems depend on a store hierarchy stretching from small stores resembling logic to big stores, which can cost less than writing data on paper. Instead of being restricted to calculation, or the storing of valuable data, information systems can now be used for the general run of information storage and retrieval. They can handle low-valued transactions with reasonable economy. This greatly widens the scope for information handling by machine, and we can expect the use of information systems to become as frequent and casual as the use of the telephone.

But computers as local services are very restricted, because the data on which they work are hardly ever found in the computer room or destined for a user who is on the spot. The methods by which data are captured for the computer and disseminated to the end users can determine the cost of the operation. For this reason the use of computers from a distance is an important trend. Modern computers are increasingly being connected to communication networks to serve a public which is widely spaced, and already the great majority of new computers are going into such 'teleprocessing' environments.

A second trend which can now be seen is the connection of two computers by a data network so that they can collaborate in a task. This is part of the 'division of labour' in information systems which allows each unit to do its job more efficiently by specializing its function. Systems are now in operation in which one computer depends on another for its backing store, its fast processing or a range of output devices.

In this way, computers and communications have come together to produce information handling systems with a new kind of power, but the communications systems we know well are not completely suitable for the task. The main theme of this book, therefore, is the study of the *real* communication needs of computer systems and how to meet them.

1.2 EVOLUTION OF COMPUTER SYSTEMS

When the first digital computers were developed, information in digital form was already being handled by punched card equipment—invented by Hollerith in 1899—and by five-track punched paper tape in connection with telegraph message switching. This had evolved from early systems devised in the 1860s. It was natural, therefore, that one or other, and sometimes both, of these forms of recording digital information were used for the input to and output from the early computers. These machines were generally fitted with a fairly elaborate control console which allowed the operation of the computer to be monitored; many lights were provided to display instructions, and keys enabled alterations to be made to instructions and allowed a program to be obeyed instruction-by-instruction under the control of the programmer. The instructions displayed were in machine code, that is to say were merely groups of binary numbers and an expert programmer would memorize the binary instructions and would be able to manipulate the binary keys, rather like playing a piano.

In the early days of computing, it was customary to prepare a program in machine code on punched cards, or punched paper tape, and this program was then fed into the computer and the programmer sat at the console and proceeded to test and amend the program until it functioned satisfactorily. This was a tedious business, and soon the idea of a post-mortem program was introduced whereby the contents of all the stores in a computer could be punched out and taken away for examination by the programmer at a later date.

It was not long before the value of computers, and the number of people wishing to use them, increased so much that it was no longer acceptable to have the programmer sitting at the console stepping through a program instruction-by-instruction. The idea of a batch operation was introduced and programmers would provide the ready-punched program and any special instructions for trained operators to enable them to try out the program; the programmer was provided in return with either the results of his program if it had run successfully, or a post-mortem (such as a memory dump) if it had not. This made reasonably efficient use of the computer but it made poor use of programmers, who had to spend much time waiting for results.

At about this time the idea of autocodes or symbolic assembly languages was introduced. These arose at first from the use of teleprinters to prepare punched paper tape. It was fairly easy to produce programs to interpret groups of alphabetic characters and to translate these, or compile them, into the equivalent machine code instructions. Thus, the computer was made to aid the human being by taking part in the process of program preparation, and the use of mnemonic alphanumeric symbols made it easier for people to prepare the initial, or source programs ready for compilation later. Nevertheless, the time lags between successive trials of a program were still tedious for the programmers and programs took a long time to develop. For this reason, keen programmers were often prepared to work through the night if they were allowed to sit at the computer console and interact with the computer in the task of debugging, or removing the errors from, their program, even through it meant using machine code.

The next step was the connection of a teleprinter directly to the computer and the provision of a simple program to handle the input and output of information in symbolic form. This allowed a programmer to interact more efficiently during the development of his program and made much more effective the use of him; although the computer itself was certainly not being used to best advantage, when proceeding slowly at a pace suited to the reaction time of a human user.

In these early days a remarkable forerunner of teleprocessing came into operation. It was the 'Magnetronic Reservisor', built by the Teleregister Corporation and installed at La Guardia airport in 1952. It was a magnetic drum based system which handled seat reservations and was connected to American Airlines offices in the New York area. Soon afterwards, with the start of the SAGE project, defence systems became the spearhead for real-time developments, still in the days of thermionic tubes.

Towards the end of the 1950s, computer development moved in two directions. For efficient use of computers with programs that were already written and tested, the idea of batch processing under the control of a monitor program was evolved. This derived from the earlier idea of operators running programs on behalf of the users, but now various monitoring, scheduling and control programs were devised to assist them to do this efficiently. These programs were the forerunners of modern batch-process operating systems. The other direction of development was towards time-sharing systems, particularly oriented towards easing the problems of program production. The idea was to connect a number of terminals to a computer so that several people could simultaneously step through their programs, by making the computer deal with each one in turn. An operating system was required to control the sharing of the computer's resources among the several terminals; if this was done successfully, each programmer appeared to have the sole attention of the computer and could develop his programs at a rate to suit himself.

In the early 1960s an ambitious experiment known as Project Mac was undertaken at the Massachusetts Institute of Technology. Project Mac was designed to connect a relatively large number of terminals to a single time-shared computer and very successfully demonstrated the value to the user of such an arrangement, particularly when the development of a common file storage system enabled users at different terminals to cooperate with one another, by sharing programs and other facilities.

The operating systems to time-share a computer among many terminals were more complex than those required to batch-process jobs, which were usually scheduled to run to completion before the next job began. For a while arguments raged on the merits of one or the other system, and the choice was clearly dependent upon the task which had to be done. Gradually, however, the size of computers and their capability increased, while the cost of processing power was reduced. This made it possible to produce more elaborate operating systems and shifted the balance in favour of time-sharing. Meanwhile, new programmers' aids had been appearing, such as compilers, to translate high-level languages into machine-code instructions. These high-level languages like FORTRAN and ALGOL made it much easier for people to write computer programs and this allowed computers to be applied to an ever widening range of problems.

The advent of time-sharing brought new languages designed for use with on-line terminals, where the computer program monitored the user's behaviour and tried to correct errors as they were made, by 'conversing' with the user. These conversational languages made it very easy to write programs and brought the use of computers out of the specialist field. This made it possible to employ computers for a whole variety of new tasks.

The essential ingredients of a time-shared interactive system are: a means of storing information, processing capability, and a means of switching these two between a number of users, in such a way that each user is, ideally, unaware that the other users are active. Because the store may be common to all users each of them may be operating independently on a common data base. For example, in an airline automatic seat reservation system a number of geographically separated sales offices may sell tickets for particular flights by referring to a central file of available seats. As each seat is sold the file is updated, so the duplication of the sale of the particular seat is avoided.

In addition to the computer systems which are used directly by people there are many other applications where the computer system is used to control such things as industrial processes, the distribution of electricity and gas, the flow of traffic on roads. In all these applications the computer systems involved are known as real-time systems. The design of such systems is complicated by the need for them to respond as, and when, required by the external environment in which they operate. For, whereas a person at a terminal will only get annoyed if he has to wait for a reply from a computer with which he is conversing, the delay introduced by a computer in a control loop may be critical and could lead to instability if it became too long. Indeed, failure to react quickly enough to an alarm indication in an aircraft or a chemical plant could lead to dangerous situations.

Computer systems may, therefore, be divided into three broad and overlapping categories: real-time systems where there is a strict upper limit on the time within which the computer must deal with the signals from a number of different input channels, quasi real-time systems where the failure of the computer to respond causes annoyance rather than damage and batch-processing systems where the response is not at all critical and jobs may be scheduled to use the resources of the computer to best advantage. In all these categories it is a common requirement to site the various terminals or other peripheral devices which are served by the computer at sites remote and often widely separated geographically. Hand in hand with the development of these remote access systems has gone the development of communication facilities, without which it would be impossible to operate. At first, the Telex (public telegraph) and telephone networks were used to get information from remote points to a central computer, and as the sophistication of the system increased the technique for using telephone channels was developed until, eventually, expensive private networks of leased lines carrying digital information between computers and remote peripheral devices became established. The proliferation of such networks as the volume of data traffic began to increase eventually led to the idea that data networks shared between a number of computer systems would be more economic and thus to the possibility of public data communication networks.

1.3 THE DEVELOPMENT OF NETWORKS

The earliest networks were designed simply to connect a number of remote terminals to a single computer. At first, this was done using telegraph lines or telephone lines with modulators and demodulators to convert the digital signals to an analogue form for transmission. The equipment which does the conversion is called a modem or a Dataset (proprietary word of ATT). Later, automatic answering equipment was introduced by the telephone companies and it became possible to use the public switched telephone network to make connections between terminals and the computer; again, of course, it was necessary to use modems.

As the use of terminal access networks increased it began to be appreciated that there would be advantages in allowing computers to communicate with other computers as well as with groups of terminals. Depending on whether the computers connected together are identical, similar, or dissimilar, it is possible to arrange for them to share their resources to a greater or lesser degree. It is relatively easy, of course, to arrange for a group of identical computers to share programs and data, and the availability of a network connecting them makes it easy to spread the load of computing amongst them, and to reorganize the work should one or more of the computers fail. It is much more difficult to achieve any real degree of cooperation between completely independent and dissimilar computer systems; but, nevertheless, the presence of a data network connecting them enables them to, at least, exchange information. This kind of thing is becoming increasingly important as more and more companies develop computer-based information and control systems.

Although people commonly talk about communication taking place between computers it is, of course, the programs within the computers which interact with each other. More particularly, it is the *processes* in one machine that have to interact with processes in the other; ideally, this should occur in a similar manner to the way processes situated within one computer interact with each other. The future importance of the specialized networks now being developed for connecting computers lies in the facilities they will provide for efficient interprocess communication between processes situated in several computers. As techniques and standards are developed which facilitate this kind of interaction through a data network, it will be possible to build computer systems which differ markedly from those available today. For example, it will be possible to have specialist computer centres concentrating on particular tasks or providing particular kinds of service.

Already this specialization of function can be seen in collections of computers attached to one network, though at present it is in an early, experimental form. For example, at the U.K. National Physical Laboratory a data network interconnects a group of computers which provides time-sharing services, an editing service, information storage and retrieval, and a large backing store, all as specialist services produced by different computers. Furthermore the editing service makes use of the backing store. The network in question has other interesting features because it uses dynamic multiplexing and packet switching which are described in more detail in Chapters 7 and 10 of this book.

In the U.S.A., the Advanced Research Projects Agency (ARPA) network is a similar example of a network designed to share the resources of many dissimilar computers, in a research environment. Many of the detailed discussions in the book are illustrated by reference to the ARPA and NPL networks.

1.4 COMMUNICATIONS TECHNOLOGY

In a sense, telecommunications began with the earliest and most remarkable of man's achievements which produced the natural languages. Only now, when we try to mirror their structure in a computer, do we begin to understand the complexity of these languages, but in simplified forms the structures they incorporate have become part or the artificial languages which underlie the use of computers. Communication by sound has a limited range, which was stretched to its limit by drums, the war trumpets and the whistling language of Silbo. The telephone and telegraph networks are the end points of the development of man-to-man communication which began with speech and writing. They handle information in the form which people understand, so they fit without much adaption to human society in its pre-information-technology form.

Speech and writing are examples of the two fundamental ways of handling information. With speech, time is important; a severe distortion of the time scale renders it unintelligible. With writing, the structure of the information is critical, but time plays no part in its intellibigility. As we shall see, computers invariably deal in structured data. This is why data can be read, stored, manipulated and played back on many types of equipment at various speeds.

The traditional form of telecommunication networks is, naturally enough, fitted to human communication patterns such as the length of a telephone call and the transit time of a telegram. These networks have also been adapted to 'interface' them to human organizations. Private exchanges and extension plans with secretaries and local operators act as the filters and adaptors between an organization and the network.

Brought into the traditional telecommunications environment, data communication for computers can become troublesome, even disruptive, because of its different traffic pattern and interfacing requirements. Some of these problems, no doubt, will be overcome as experience grows. But computers work in a world of megabits per second and millisecond-long messages. They can be adapted by buffers to kilobits and seconds, but at a cost in performance, which is an unnecessary cost. A thousand calls can have a response over a megabit line measured either in milliseconds, by interleaving the messages, or in seconds, by interleaving the bits. The computer designer would almost always choose the former, but it needs a system design which is foreign to the switched telephone network.

The limited information handling rate of people sets an upper bound on the usefully usable bandwidths of channels, and the bandwidth-time space available is best partitioned into relatively narrow band, long duration channels. The planned future telecommunications networks based on digital transmission generally assume this same kind of division of the total available information handling space, because they must interface with existing services, and with people.

On the other hand, the natural information handling rate of the computer is so high that a different kind of division of the total available information space is required. The computer would, ideally, prefer a wide-band channel allocated to it for a very short time. The two fundamentally different ways of partitioning the bandwidth-time space to best suit people and computers are compared in Figure 1.1.

The difference in computer communication requirements appears most strongly at the interface itself, i.e. at the junction between the computers and the communication system. The computer designer is accustomed to seeing local terminals and tends to add extra equipment to adapt his input-output (I-O) interface for remote terminals. In fact, the true I-O interface is much nearer to the computer, and the process of adaption to a well-designed network consists of removing, not adding, equipment.

For all these reasons, the building of teleprocessing systems is not a matter of taking existing computers and existing networks and fixing them together by matching devices. A more radical look at the communication requirements of computers is needed, which leads, as the following chapters will show, to the description of a new kind of public data communication network. In arriving at this description we have to keep in mind all the uses to which

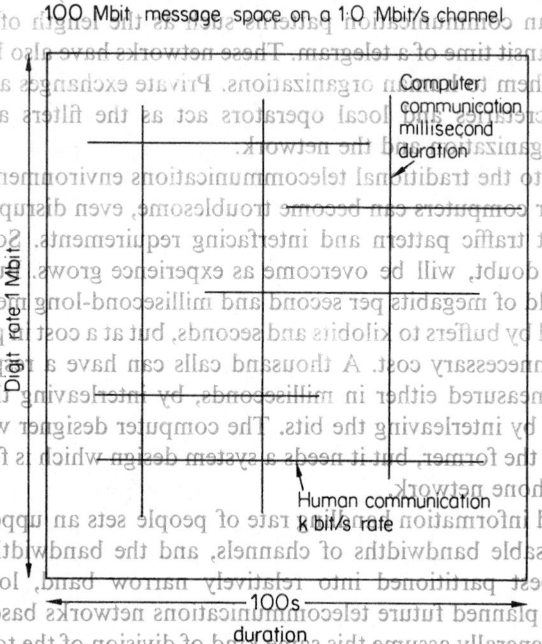

Figure 1.1. Different use of 'message space' by people and computers

computer networks will be put, and this includes both man-computer (i.e. terminal-computer) and computer-computer interaction.

1.5 TELEPROCESSING SYSTEMS OF THE FUTURE

The experience that data communication engineers acquired in the 1960s was derived from networks built around specific applications. All the design decisions could be referred back to the particular application. Only in 1972 was there much thinking about public data networks and, for the first time, it seemed likely that public data networks would be built in U.S.A.

The design of public networks requires a new attitude of mind, so the design philosophy has been evolving rather slowly. Such networks are built for an indefinitely wide range of computer applications, a range which cannot easily be guessed when the main design decisions are made.

In many countries in Europe and elsewhere a government monopoly of telecommunications has been established and the monopoly has been extended, almost without comment, to data communications. In U.S.A. telecommunication services are operated by private companies and regulated by the Federal Communications Commission. The use by a company of a dominant position in telephone communications to extend its power to data communications would clearly not be in the spirit of 'regulation' which the U.S.A. has adopted. But while data communication could still be treated as a byproduct of the telephone network this extension of franchise from telephones to data was a natural consequence. The situation had all the making of a conflict of powerful interests.

A bad effect of these regulation problems has been that the real technical issues have been submerged. A breed of engineer has evolved whose field of expertise is no wider than optimising a private network, for all the many complex tariffs of the carriers. It seems likely to be some time before a truly nationwide public data network, designed for the purpose, can evolve in U.S.A. Regulation problems are extremely complex and could merit a book of their own, and in U.S.A. it is difficult not to be immersed in them. We in U.K. are unlikely to be able to see all the issues properly from our viewpoint, so there will be no more discussion of regulation in the later chapters.

Before large investments are made in new public data networks it is pertinent to ask who will use them; but this question is as difficult to answer in a detailed way as the question 'Who will use the telephone network?' put to Alexander Graham Bell.

Attempts were made to list future computer services which needed a data network, as part of the Federal Communications Commission enquiry (Docket No. 16979) of 1967-1968. They produced lists in which 80% of all computer applications were marked as potential for teleprocessing. But this misses the real point. Computer systems such as the ones listed have grown up in an environment in which data communication was difficult, less reliable than it should be, subject to an unspecified noise (error) level and expensive because it entailed custom-design for each private network. By the end of the next decade only the cost of the terminal will decide whether an information system is viable, and this means that new services can be developed which we have not yet envisaged. In particular, the use of terminals by *untrained* people must be possible.

To illustrate this point, consider a system now operating at Glasgow General Hospital. Patients for a gastro-enterology clinic are asked if they would mind taking part in an experiment. They all agree, in practice, and are shown how to use a simple terminal with only three buttons to operate, marked YES, NO and DON'T KNOW. The interview (for that is its nature) takes place on a normal commercial time-sharing system and asks all the questions that the doctor would ask, but a little more systematically, because the program was the result of collaboration by several doctors. By careful attention to the writing of the script the interview has been 'tuned' to the Glasgow patients; but it has also been written for Urdu and Punjabi speech, which the doctor using it in Leeds would have found difficult to manage, and the appearance to the patient can be that of a teletype, a display, a voice or a voice with picture. (The audio-visual effects are locally produced, but the other terminals are controlled, as it happens, from a computer in Cleveland, Ohio.) The essential point is that the patients—an unselected group—can interact with the computer without training and they say that they prefer this method for the initial interview. This interview is a preparation for a later personal interview with the physician.

The use of the computer in Cleveland has a special significance too. Because information is handled in addressed blocks within the communications network linking terminals and computers, it matters little in terms of cost per block where the parts of the system are located. Given that a line has to be leased to provide a Europe-U.S.A. link, the more blocks it carries the better.

The medical interview is just one example of a teleprocessing application that:

1. must cost very little if it to be widely used,
2. makes no use of computation,
3. needs a big data base of scripts, when widely used,
4. will give rise to a considerable number of calls such as a possible demand for 1,000 to 10,000 simultaneous calls in U.K.

The balance between locally controlled systems (cheap but inflexible) and remotely controlled is difficult to judge, but there will always be a need for 'tailored' versions that are remotely stored, for convenience. The same kind of interaction has been applied to psychiatric medicine and to aptitude tests, and the bulk of computer-assisted instruction may be run in a similar manner.

1.6 SOME PHILOSOPHICAL CONSIDERATIONS

This book is largely concerned with the problems of information exchange between computers. When thinking about these problems, there is a natural tendency to draw analogies with the way people communicate with each other. This can be most valuable in giving a qualitative feel for the kind of factors likely to be important in the interaction between complex systems; but this does not mean that a desirable end result is a group of computers acting as if it was a group of people. In fact, it may be a very long time before computers can simulate human intellect to any useful degree, so we can regard, most valuably, a group of communicating people as a limiting situation to judge our computer systems. What is difficult to do with such a group will be well-nigh impossible with computers.

Consideration will show that it is rare for more than two people to be joined simultaneously by communication links, with the intention of interacting together. This is partly, perhaps, due to a lack of facilities for making such connections; but the major problem is that of controlling the interaction, i.e. deciding who speaks when.

If the group of people are in the same room, both aural and visual methods of communication can be used; but even so, the protocols governing multiple interactions are not very well established. Informal groups of a few people can work together, but with more members, a chairman is needed, and progress may be slow. It will be interesting to see whether conference television will be really successful, or whether the more subtle methods of information exchange, such as facial expression, and the general atmosphere—available only with personal contact—prove to be more important than we fully appreciate at the moment.

Experiments have been made in which groups of people share files on a computer and thus cooperate in some task. The results of such experiments are important, for it is clearly of great value to mankind to discover ways in which cooperative ventures of an intellectual nature may be made more effective.

The use of computers to enhance the ability of man to communicate with his fellows has not received much attention, as yet. But, as computers are used more and more for educational purposes it is very likely that interaction of several people with a common pool of stored knowledge will become important.

The widespread use of linked computers to assist man in intellectual development is both exciting and alarming. The exciting possibility is that more, and better classified and presented information will be available to decision makers, and that groups of decision makers may interact closely in solving complex problems. The alarming aspects arise from the danger of uniformity that may follow eventually. Already we see changes in the way society operates, designed to suit the limited abilities of computer systems.

Stereotyped forms and procedures, and standardized ways of structuring data of all kinds, are gradually moulding the world to be uniform and commonplace. When taken to an extreme, this process removes the variety, and adaptability, necessary for satisfactory evolution in the face of the changing environment.

Nevertheless, it is evident that the growth of human society has been dependent on man's ability to cooperate and organize himself, and it has been the greatly improved means of communication developed in recent years that make it possible to control and increase the complexity of modern communities.

We see the same principles of complex system organization in human society that we talk about in connection with our computer networks. There are hierarchies of structure, and there are protocols for behaviour and intercommunication. An interesting truism about the structure of human organizations is that they seldom function in the manner in which they have been designed. Very often unofficial communication paths and protocols are used to make an organization function properly. The difference between a good organization, and a poor one, can be difficult and sometimes impossible to define. This is usually revealed when attempts are made to apply computers within an organization and it is necessary to really understand what is going on in order to model it in some way.

As more and more large organizations come to depend on computers, and these organizations become more closely represented by their models in the computers, there will be a growing need for the computers of different organizations to intercommunicate. This will begin in trivial ways, but will grow in complexity as far as the reliability and capability of the communications facilities will permit. So, because we cannot predict what kind of communication will be required, the facilities provided must be flexible and adaptable.

The computer allows individual organizations to become more efficient, and effective communications between computers will allow groups of organizations to be successfully managed. However, the real extent of the communications facilities required is difficult to assess, and perhaps an indication is obtainable from human experience.

The use of analogy is a powerful method for conveying new ideas between people. An important factor in the learning process seems to be the analogy between new information and what is already known. It seems that a hierarchical structure of knowledge is built up, and new ideas need a certain minimum basis of knowledge before they can be understood. The analogy between people and computers is an interesting one, particularly in the area of interaction and intercommunication. The redundancy in human communication seems very high, particularly when new ideas are being discussed. If this reflects the difficulty of conveying, meaningfully, new information from one complex entity to another, we may find the amount of information exchanged between advanced computer systems—in order to achieve other than trivial interaction—much higher than might, at first sight, be supposed.

If this is so, the volume of information that must be exchanged, and the speeds of interaction required will make it essential to develop a world data communication network that is well adapted to computer systems; the kind of network which is the subject of this book. An increasingly complex society continually throws up challenges to our powers of handling information. World-wide meteorology, air transport and the policing of the nuclear test ban are examples of modern activities that depend on widespread communication between computer systems. We evidently need a very versatile world data network, and we shall achieve this not by copying the telephone system but by looking afresh at the problem of communication between computers.

Chapter 2
Data Communication and the
Telephone Network

2.1 INTRODUCTION

The world's telephone network is an enormous capital asset, and it interconnects a great and ever-increasing number of telephones. Any new telecommunication service such as data communication must, for reasons of economy, depend on some degree of commonality with the telephone network. A study of the telephone network is therefore a preliminary to any consideration of data networks.

The degree of commonality is a matter of choice. At the one extreme, a completely integrated network can be imagined, in which all transmission and switching is designed to be suitable for telephone and data messages. There are reasons why this ideal may never be achieved, basically because the data and telephone requirements are so different. There are intermediate levels of commonality such as common transmission with separate switching. It is the long distance transmission of information, whether as data or speech, that gives the greatest economies of scale, and this makes it almost inconceivable that data could justify separate transmission methods—the more so because speech will increasingly be carried in a digital form.

In the local distribution network the situation is less clear. Today's methods of connecting telephones to their switching centre by multipair cables are likely, in time, to give way to *digital* methods which employ less copper, and are easier to change and to repair. When this happens, the methods chosen should allow data to share the system and avoid the need for data to use separate pairs. But the local network is a large part of the telephone system's big capital cost, and radical changes in it are likely to be a long term matter.

Together with the telephone service we have a Telex network for carrying telegraphic messages. This is a digital network of a kind, with a limited speed which makes it unsuitable as a general vehicle for data traffic. But its development points the way that data services may develop. (Telex is used here to mean the switched public telegraph network, but different words are used for such services in particular countries.) With the exception of TWX in USA, Telex developed as a separate service, with its own switches, but using the telephone network's transmission plant. The service that is most widespread runs at 50 bit/s and has a five bit code (CCITT alphabet No. 2) but a more advanced service at 200 bit/s with the seven-bit standard data code (CCITT alphabet No. 5) is coming into use. (Information about CCITT is given on p. 32 and in reference 11, p. 62.) For the future public data service it will be important not to set the targets too low, but to allow for the higher speeds that will become commonplace. In other respects, also, the design of the new service must look to the future. Some of these features such as multiplexed interfaces with subscribers are the subject of later sections of this book. Since the Telex service is switched and digital it has much in common with a data network. The rapid increase in data communication terminals with their much more complex requirements imply that, in due course, Telex could be treated as a service carried by the data network. In some countries such a merger seems likely, but U.S.A. is moving in the direction of specialist carriers for data, voice and telegraphy.

The telephone network is the subject of the first part of this chapter. It has several points of contact with data communication:

1. At present it is the main vehicle for carrying data, because special data communication services are in an early stage of development. In order to use the telephone network for data transmission, its basic design must be understood, and also its limitations. Some of the network's characteristics which affect data were not investigated until data transmission came along.

2. The telephone network provides a fully worked out example of one of the basic designs of switched communication system, namely a 'circuit switched' network. This allows us to understand how a data network based on the same principles could be made. (But the nature of digital data and the special requirements of the users give rise to other types of switched data network which have considerable interest and are the subject of later chapters).

3. A public switched data network, however much it distinguishes its service from the telephone service, will employ equipment in common with the telephone network. The design of a telephone transmission system, its multiplexing methods and even its local network must influence the form of the future data network. It is to be hoped that the service to the users will be based on their actual requirements and not distorted to fit telephone standards but this does not prevent the adoption of the telephone networks standards *inside* the data network, where this is economically sound.

The first part of this chapter describes the telephone network in sufficient detail to relate it to data networks and data transmission. The second part treats, in an elementary way, the transmission of data over the network. The third and final part describes some of the characteristics of a telephone channel as a carrier of data.

2.2 THE TELEPHONE NETWORK

A telephone call connects two subscribers, one of whom, the calling subscriber, originates the call by indicating to the network (by dialling) the number of the telephone he wishes to call. The distinction of calling and called subscriber stays throughout the call, and in general only the calling subscriber can release, or close down the call.

We shall use the term *subscriber* also in connection with data networks, but must be careful to define it. Basically it is what is just beyond an 'interface' between the network and the outside world. In the case of the telephone the interface is partly acoustic, for transferring the voice information which is the real traffic of the network, and partly digital (in both senses of the word) for the dialling information which goes from subscriber to network. In the data network the *subscriber* could be represented by a computer or a multiplexer connecting many *terminals* to the network, and it is the *terminal* which is the ultimate point of contact with the user. Nevertheless we shall sometimes regard a computer as a terminal on the network, and indeed the distinction is observed by the existence of 'intelligent terminals' containing small computers. But where there is ambiguity we shall use the term *subscriber* to mean the thing the network is connected to in the outside world.

Telephone engineers use the telephone *call* and connection as the unit of traffic. They are therefore concerned with such statistics as the rate of calling (calls originated per hour) and the proportion of time that a line is occupied. An important characteristic of the user's behaviour is the mean hold time of a call, and the statistical distribution of call hold times. For the purpose of later comparison with a data system it can be said that on the line from a telephone subscriber the calling rate is low (a few per hour) the proportion of time that the line is occupied is low (less then 0.1) and the mean call hold time is two to three minutes.

The concept of a *call* is appropriate to a system in which a connection is made between subscribers and held for a substantial time, then broken. There are data network designs for which the concept of a call simply does not arise, though analogous concepts appear with somewhat different meaning. It is important not to carry over a familiar concept into a new kind of network, without a critical examination of its relevance.

The Telephone Switch

In earlier automatic telephone central offices, calls were routed through the switches under the control of the dial pulses. More recent developments have increased the amount of equipment which is common to the whole central office until now, in stored-program controlled offices, all the control is central-ized, using stored-program computers, and the rest of the equipment carries out its functions in response to commands from this central controller. Figure 2.1 shows such a central office in outline. Central office design has many variations, of which we shall describe just one example. The main units are the common control and the switch.

The switch is able to make a connection from any one of the common units on the right-hand side, links or junctors, registers and senders, to any of the other lines. Typically these connections are still made by metallic contacts in reed relays or crossbar switches and controlled by electromagnets. There are sufficient links, registers and senders for all the calls that are in progress or being set up. Details differ in different designs; for example a register and sender may be combined and there will probably be different kinds of link equipment or junctor for different types of call.

A local call will be routed from the local loop on the left of the figure through the switch to a link on the right and back through the switch (by a different route) to the other local loop. In this type of call, the link, in some designs of switch, carries out many functions. It can generate the ringing current, detect the raising of the handset of the called telephone that cuts off the ringing current, provide the transmission bridge which powers both telephones and so forth.

Only a small proportion of the local loops will be in use at one time, but

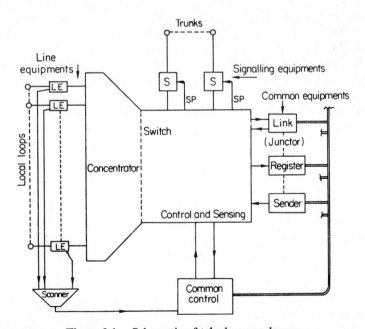

Figure 2.1. Schematic of telephone exchange

the trunks which interconnect offices are more heavily used—in the busy hour each may be in use for more than half the time. Links and registers are also used heavily because there is no need to provide many more than are needed for the busiest hour of the busiest day. The different lines coming into the switch therefore have different traffic levels, and to accommodate this conveniently the switch is sometimes separated into two sections. The part on the right in the figure would deal only with concentrated traffic. The left-hand part, which is actually larger, is the *concentrator* which connects the local loops into the right-hand part.

If the telephones in a local area are clustered, as they would be if it covered several small towns, the cost of lines could be reduced if the traffic of a cluster was concentrated on the spot. Part of the concentrator, with its scanner and line equipments and a data link to the controller, can be geographically separated from the main office, connected to it by telephone lines carrying concentrated traffic. Because the central control is a highly reliable, stored-program system, it is expensive and a remote concentrator can be more economic than a complete small switching centre.

The setting up of a call begins when the calling telephone goes 'off-hook'. This completes a DC connection over the local loop, a condition which is sensed in the line equipment. The central control operates the scanner so that it can scan each line in turn to see whether the off-hook condition has occurred. After a short delay while the scanner finds it, the condition will be reported to the control.

The control must first find a spare register to receive the dialled numbers. It then establishes a route through the switch to connect the register to the calling telephone. The register provides dial tone and receives the dialled number, which it reports to the control. If the call is local, it is set up by making further connections from calling line to link to called line and the register is then released.

When a call originated on this office is destined for a telephone elsewhere, the connection will be extended over one of the available trunks. The first part of the operation is the same as before, and the calling line is connected to a a register. The area code of the number will show that a trunk is needed, so the control must find and seize one. From this point onwards the central office acts towards the next office rather like a subscriber making a call. It must first go 'off-hook', i.e. seize a trunk, then wait for a signal to be returned which says that the far end is ready for 'dialling'. At this point, the *sender* sends the information over the trunk to the *register* in the next office. But the information sent is, strictly speaking, an indication of the route of the call, which is not the same as the dialled information. The first office carries out the process of translating the dialled number into the routing data, which contains instructions to all the offices en route. The call may then go through several offices and several trunks.

When a trunk has been seized, routing data is sent over it to the next office. This office then established a further connection, and then more routing information must be sent. So, at each stage, a signal comes back to request the next block of routing data from the sender.

Finally, in answer to a signal from the last central office the local number of the required telephone is sent.

Control Signalling

One of the key processes in setting up a telephone connection is the sending of routing information from office to office. This is digital data, and yet it is usually sent over the same channels as the voice signal. For this purpose the information is converted into voice-frequency signals with equipment marked S, 'signalling equipment' in Figure 2.1. This process is exactly like that of data transmission but it has developed in a different way and methods are used that are slow, but very reliable.

In telephone networks this particular process of digital transmission is called *signalling* and it has its corresponding process, of course, in those data networks which also switch circuits. Here, however, we have to make the distinction between the signalling to set up calls and the signalling of the subscribers' data. The correct term to be used for the former is therefore *control signalling*.

Very many, different schemes of control signalling have been devised and are in use in different parts of the same network. This is the reason why the signalling equipment in Figure 2.1 is associated with the trunk it serves rather than being built into the sender. It has the effect that the sender needs to use a special path through the switch, shown in the figure as SP, the signalling path. When the call is completed, all the extra paths can be dropped by the switch, leaving only the voice path through its link.

The arrangement we have described is the one most commonly used. It carries the control signals over the same channel as the voice and is called *channel-associated signalling*. If the control signals also fall within the speech band, this is *in-band signalling*. A problem with in-band signalling is that a voice or data signal coming from the subscriber may imitate the control signals and cause false operation. This is particularly troublesome with the signal which releases the circuit, because the equipment is expecting such a signal when the call is in progress.

But the sending of these signals over the telephone lines requires the registers and senders, plus registers at all the intermediate offices and signalling equipment on each trunk. It accounts for a major part of the cost of an office. It would clearly be better to have a direct data link between the controllers of two central offices which would handle all the signalling requirements of their connecting trunks. Such a method is called *common-channel signalling* and it will certainly come into wider use when stored-program control of central offices is widespread, but an early change to common-channel signalling will be expensive because of the cost of making it compatible with those offices which do not have stored-program control.

A recommendation has been prepared for international signalling over common channels. It is called the CCITT number 6 signalling system. In effect it is a distributed data network for handling short messages.

The signalling method varies with the line. Shorter lines which have direct electrical connection allow DC signalling. More often, the channel is capable of handling only voice frequencies, so the signals have to be tones in the voice band. But some of the simpler carrier systems used on shorter trunks allow the use of tones outside the voice band. The digital type of carrier system called *Pulse Code Modulation* which is coming into wide use has a built in, separate digital signalling channel for each speech path. This feature is described more fully in Chapter 7.

The signals over a trunk are of two kinds. Those 'line signals' needed to seize and release the line are local and pass only between the equipment at the two ends of the line. Variety of system is not so troublesome for such signals. But other signals pass through central offices. Typically these are the 'inter-register signals' which carry routing information and the responses which acknowledge them. As the network becomes more complex, speed and compatability of inter-register signalling becomes important. There is an internationally recommended method (R2) which uses 12 different frequencies, six for each direction, as follows:

forwards   1380, 1500, 1620, 1740, 1860, 1980 Hz
backwards   540,   660,   780,   900, 1020, 1140 Hz

A symbol is sent by transmitting two frequencies at a time, giving an alphabet of 15 different symbol values. This kind of signalling is called *multi-frequency* or m.f. signalling.

In normal pratice the terms signal or control signal are applied to the digital signals that pass between central offices to control the use of trunks and send routing data. Note that the control of the use of trunks is the concern only of the two offices at each end of the link, but routing data concerns the whole network. In data networks, also, signals and protocols at various levels, local and global, will be found.

But the telephone subscriber also exchanges digital signals with the network, and these can properly be called 'control signals' through they usually are not regarded as such. The main ones are the 'off-hook' signal which initiates or answers a call, the dialled number and ringing current. The dial tone and other tones also enter into the procedure of setting up or abandoning a call, but are less easily categorized as control signals. These local line signals have developed in a variety of different modes of transmission and this inhibits the further development of the local network. For data systems there should evidently be a more uniform approach, using digital signals that are distinguishable from the subscribers data. In a data system, any of these signals may have to be received by a computer or, where appropriate, generated by it. They must therefore be clearly identified as control signals, in a digital form.

The change from the rotary dial, which employs short breaks of the DC path, to push buttons which send multifrequency signals is a move towards the rationalizing of control signals in the telephone network. Figure 2.2 shows the keyboard and the set of eight frequencies agreed by CCITT. Each key, when pressed, sends the two frequencies corresponding to its row and column. The upper frequency of 1633 Hz is not yet allocated, but a hypothetical set of keys is shown for it.

According to the way the circuit is designed, pressing two keys in the same column results in sending only one frequency (the one corresponding to that column), while two keys in a row send only the row frequency .This is not part of the agreed code and it is not used in the network but it has been used to send seven additional signals to a subscriber's data receiving equipment.

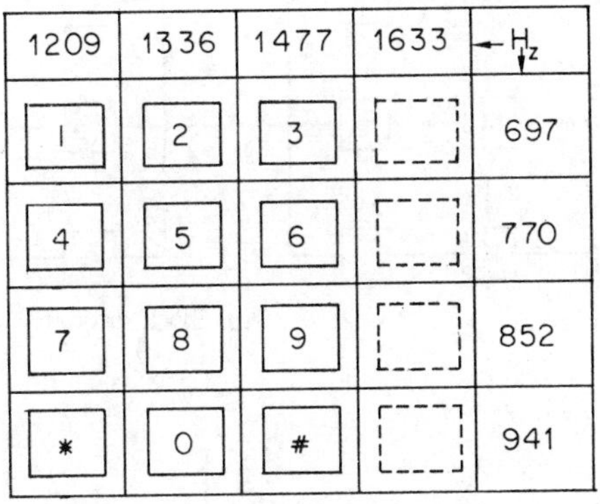

1209	1336	1477	1633	← Hz
1	2	3		697
4	5	6		770
7	8	9		852
*	0	#		941

Figure 2.2.   Telephone keyboard, with
frequencies sent

Frequency-division Multiplexing

Where many telephone channels have the same route it is higly economic to combine them on one cable. The method mostly used is *frequency-division multiplexing*, and it has much in common with the way that radio programmes are transmitted.

First, let us clarify the terminology. A multiplexer is an equipment which combines a number of channels into one transmission path in such a way that they can be separated out by a *demultiplexer* at the other end. In Figure 2.3, A is the multiplexer and B the corresponding demultiplexer. There are five constituent channels which behave as though they are entirely separate but in fact are carried by a single combined channel.

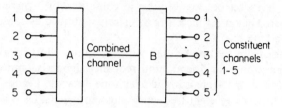

Figure 2.3. Multiplexing

In frequency-division multiplexing (FDM), the telephone channels are combined in an analogue transmission path of higher bandwidth, usually allowing 4 kHz for each of the telephone channels it carries. Thus a 12-channel system occupies 48 kHz of bandwidth. Figure 2.4 shows the principle.

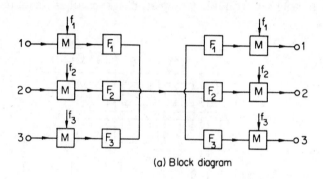

(a) Block diagram

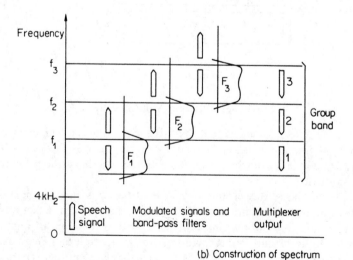

(b) Construction of spectrum

Figure 2.4. Frequency-division multiplexing

Channel 1 is modulated by a carrier at frequency f_1. This produces two sidebands, and since speech is contained in the band 0 to 4 kHz, the lower sideband fits into the range of frequencies from $f_1 - 4000$ Hz up to f_1, as Figure 2.4(b) shows. By using a balanced modulator, no component at the carrier frequency is produced. In the example, the *lower* sideband is selected by a band-pass filter which rejects signals except in the frequencies of the lower sideband. The carrier of frequency f_2 which modulates the second channel is equal to $f_1 + 4000$ Hz and f_3 is $f_1 + 8000$ Hz. When the lower sidebands of these channels, selected by appropriate band-pass filters, are mixed, the three modulated voice signals do not overlap in frequency, in fact there is a small region between them, a 'guard-band'. This is useful when the three components are to be separated at the receiving end by three band-pass filters, because the guard band accommodates the sloping edges of the filter characteristics.

In this example, lower sidebands are used, so each speech signal is frequency inverted, but an alternative technique would be to use upper sidebands throughout and not invert the speech.

The demultiplexer separates the constituent channels by the filters, then modulates them again. This returns the signals in each channel to the original 0 to 4 kHz baseband. To reproduce the three carriers at the receiver, accurate oscillators could be used, but it is also possible to send along a signal at a pilot frequency, from which the carriers can be derived. A small difference, of a few Hz, between the carriers used at each end of the channel, leaves the outcoming audio signal slightly shifted in frequency. This has been tolerated in many carrier systems, and has no perceptible effect on speech, but it presents problems for certain kinds of data transmission.

A telephone connection can carry speech either way, of course. In the pair of wires between the telephone and the central office, both directions of transmission occur over the same pair. Switching in local offices is also done with such two-way pairs. But in a carrier system such as FDM, the two directions of transmission have to be separated because the amplifiers, modulators etc. are unidirectional. Coming out of the multiplexers and demultiplexers, each direction of transmission is carried on two wires, so that telephone connection entails four wires. This *4-wire transmission* is only extended to the customers' premises if he needs it for non-voice purposes, such as data transmission.

The lowest level of FDM system in common use handles 24 channels but the real economies come with systems carrying many more channels on coaxial cables or microwave radio systems. The cables are laid up with from four to 24 tubes in each, and have repeaters to amplify the signals at spacings of from 1·5 to 10 km, depending on the bandwidth used and the cable dimensions. Bigger multiplexing schemes are also used with microwave radio transmission.

Figure 2.5 shows the economies gained by increasingly complex FDM systems in the U.K. network. As the number of channels in the carrier systems

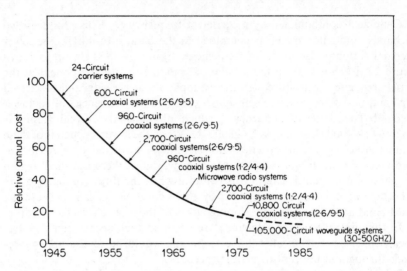

Figure 2.5. Relative line-plant costs of a 100-mile trunk circuit (Reproduced by permission of Post Office Electrical Engineers Journal)

have increased, the line plant costs per channel have reduced. For the coaxial cable systems, the figures given in brackets are the diameters of inner and outer conductors in millimetres. Some of the economies have come from the use of smaller cables. The trend of decreasing cost is expected to continue into the future.

To pack more channels into one carrier system, the scheme of Figure 2.4 is repeated, with a different set of carriers, to combine several multiplexed channels into an even bigger band. This can be illustrated by reference to a multiplexing scheme that is widely used, the CCITT modulation plan No. 2. This begins by combining 12 voice channels in the band 60 kHz to 108 kHz, using the lower sidebands so that each speech channel is inverted. This is shown schematically in the first part of Figure 2.6 where the triangles are used to show whether a sub-channel has been inverted. Such a set of 12 speech channels is called a *group* or *primary group* and is the basis of nearly all FDM schemes, but at higher levels the terminology and structure of the systems varies.

The supergroup in Figure 2.6 is made by combining five groups into the band 312 kHz to 552 kHz without inversion. It therefore contains 60 telephone channels. At the next stage, 16 supergroups are multiplexed to form a mastergroup contained in the band 60 kHz to 4028 kHz and carrying 960 voice channels. In this stage of multiplexing, all the supergroups are inverted except number 2, which is exceptional because it is the unchanged supergroup. This arrangement is used to fill the available spectrum of a coaxial system. Radio channels are also constructed from 960 voice channels and transmitted

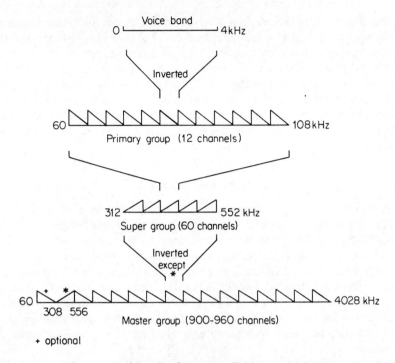

Figure 2.6.   Plan for frequency division multiplexing

in a number of bands between 1,700 MHz and 11,700 MHz. Higher frequencies of radio transmission run into the trouble of attenuation by water in the form of heavy rain. So it seems likely that the next stage of development will be waveguide systems (see Figure 2.5) and that these will use digital waveforms with only one level of frequency-division multiplexing.

When mastergroups are combined together, the lowest supergroup is not used, so there are 15 supergroups or 900 channels and these are combined, in the U.K. network, into units of 1800 channels for radio systems and 2,700 channels for coaxial cable systems. Figure 2.6 is just one FDM plan. Many other schemes are used, for example in U.S.A. a mastergroup of 600 channels contains 10 supergroups.

With these large assemblies of voice channels it is not always convenient for all circuits to take the same route. It is possible, without demultiplexing fully, to divert a block of channels of any size from a multiplexed waveform by means of a filter and replace it by a similar sized block coming from a different direction. The 'through group filters' which carry out this process introduce extra phase distortion at the edges of the bands, so the telephone channels at the ends of a group, for example, may be less suitable for data transmission than those in the middle. Switching of higher units than the telephone channel is not normally required by the customer of the telephone service, but it can help the administration of the service to deal with unusual traffic, such as that caused by a sporting event. The switching is done when the group in question has been emptied of traffic in a quiet period.

The way in which channels are combined together in several stages in FDM allows a wider bandwidth than the normal voice channel to be extended to the customer if he needs it. Usually he must accept the bandwidths used in the telephone system, which are the primary group of 48 kHz or the supergroup of 240 kHz. Special arrangements are made to bring suitable wide band connections, in the 4-wire form, to the subscriber.

The Network Hierarchy

A typical local area of the telephone system served by a local office has several thousands of telephones joined to it by multi-pair cables. The interconnection of the local offices by trunks must be done in a special way if it is to be economic and effective. A mesh of connections over the whole country would have several bad effects. There would be too many switching points in a long distance call, which would delay its setting up; the frequent multiplexing and demultiplexing would degrade the circuit and no large collection of circuits would be formed such as modern multiplexing schemes require. To avoid this, networks have switching centres at many levels, forming a hierarchy.

The detailed schemes and their terminology differ from country to country. We shall use the U.K. network as an example. The lowest level is the local office. Where these are close together and there is enough traffic, direct routes are provided between them, called 'junctions'. A junction area, over which a call can be completed entirely at this level can be quite large, for example the London region.

Calls that cannot be made in this way use the full mechanism of subscriber trunk dialling (direct distance dialling) and for this they go to the next level in the hierarchy, called a group switching centre or GSC. These GSCs are interconnected by trunks, but calls are not allowed to have more than two of these trunks in tandem, i.e. one intermediate GSC.

Calls which would break this rule use a higher part of the network called the transit network. Here they are switched as 4-wires because all the connections coming into the transit network are already on carrier systems. Whereas local offices and GSCs serve a local area to switch and concentrate telephone connections, the transit network handles only concentrated, long distance traffic. It also has two levels, main switching centres and district switching centres, making four levels in all. Main switching centres are fully interconnected, meaning that there are trunk routes from each one to each other.

The hierarchy is not rigidly enforced, and it allows connections from the GSC into any part of the transit network. The important distinction is between the local office or GSC, (which serve local loops and switch 2-wire circuits) and the transit network, which switches 4-wire and makes connections between trunks. The GSCs form the only way into the transit network.

A hierarchy of this kind will be imposed on any widespread network, in order to reduce the number of switching centres involved in a connection and concentrate traffic into main routes. But in a data network the smaller number of subscribers requires a simpler hierarchy with perhaps only two levels, local and transit, in the early years of the network.

Digital Transmission of Speech

The speech waveform can be converted to a digital representation and transmitted in digital form. This method of transmitting speech has already proved economic over short distances and is gradually coming into wider use. Conceivably it might eventually replace the analogue method of transmission, but only in the very long term.

The attractions of digital transmission are similar to those which led to the wide adoption of digital methods in other fields. Basically, the ability to restore a digital representation gives it an advantage over analogue methods. In Figure 2.7 a digital waveform is shown at (a), which has become distorted in transmission. The waveform can be restored to sharp pulses with well-defined levels by the regeneration process shown. It is first sampled at regular intervals near the middle of the distorted pulses giving waveform (b). The samples are compared with a standard level L and a decision made. The decision is used to set or clear a trigger and generate a 'perfect' waveform again (c). Such a *regeneration* process can have a very low probability of error in practical systems.

Regenerative repeaters in communication lines are particularly useful

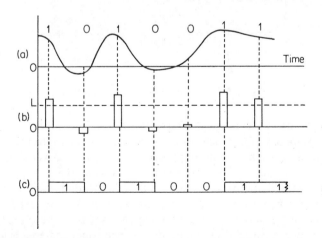

Figure 2.7. Stages in regenerating a digital waveform

because they can remove distortion before it reaches the point when a correct decision on the digital value would be difficult. But digital waveforms use higher bandwidths. Analogue systems employ linear repeaters instead of regenerators, and these must be carefully designed and maintained because their contributions to noise, distortion and gain variations add through the entire path. The various compromises in the choice of signal level, spacing of repeaters or regenerators, bandwidth etc. are coming out in favour of digital transmission for all the more advanced transmission methods. This has a special significance for data transmission because it will provide the kind of transmission plant that is very efficient for data.

There are two basically different ways to digitize the speech waveform which are called *delta modulation* and *pulse code modulation* (PCM). PCM is the method most used in telephone systems, and it sends digitized samples at regular intervals.

Delta modulation is much used in military systems. A delta modulator is shown in Figure 2.8. It signals *changes* in the signal rather than the signal itself. These changes can be measured by a feedback loop, as shown in the figure. To begin, consider the box marked 'predictor' as containing an analogue integrator. If its output waveform is more positive than the device input, the difference A will be negative. The discrimination at the sample time will transmit a negative pulse, which will push down the output of the integrator by one increment, making it come nearer the analogue input. If the input changes slowly enough the 'predictor' output will follow it. At the receiving end it is only necessary to have a copy of the predictor. The error in the output waveform will equal the signal at A, which can be small.

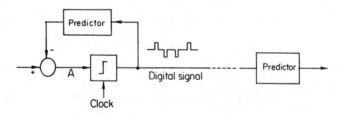

Figure 2.8.   Principle of delta modulation

A simple integrator is not the best form of predictor. Double integration has been proposed, and much inventive effort has gone into improving this part of the system. The stream of pulses (positive or negative) constitutes the digital representation which is transmitted down the line.

Delta modulation introduces two kinds of distortion to the waveform. For small levels of speech output the sampling error at A is noticeable as noise. For rapid changes of the waveform the increments cannot keep the output in step. The latter is called slope limiting and affects higher frequencies.

Delta modulation is very simple, but for the quality of transmission needed in the telephone network it is found to require a higher data rate than the alternative, PCM. Delta modulation may come into use when the voice waveform has to be digitized at the telephone instrument, and there are digital methods that can be used to convert it to PCM and back again, so that PCM could be used in the main part of the network.

Pulse Code Modulation

In pulse code modulation[1], analogue samples of the waveform are taken at a rate of 8,000 per second, then these are digitized and sent over the line. Figure 2.9 illustrates the principle. At the 125 microsecond intervals samples are taken and their amplitudes are converted to a digital representation. This is shown in the figure as a string of signed decimal numbers, but it is convenient, of course, to use the binary representation shown below. The first binary digit represents the sign. At the distant end, the sample levels can be reproduced, with a certain *quantisation error* (or noise) due to the restricted number of bits devoted to the measurement of each sample.

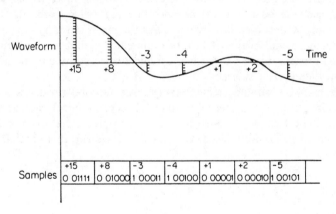

Figure 2.9.   Sampling and digiting a waveform

There are, in fact, two kinds of 'quantisation' in the PCM method of transmitting speech, quantisation in time and amplitude. The quantisation noise is due to the finite number of amplitude levels. The effect of sampling at a finite number of points and reconstructing the signal from these samples is merely to restrict the bandwidth to half the sampling frequency, and 4 kHz is completely adequate for telephone speech.

The relationship between sampling rate and bandwidth is a fundamental one which appears again in Chapter 5. It is described in the Appendix at the end of the chapter (page 60).

Direct digital measurement of the signal amplitude is not the best that can be done because the effect of quantisation noise is worse at low signal levels. By measuring the *logarithm* of the signal amplitude the noise due to quantisation is reduced for small signals. Such a law relating the amplitude to the digital representation is equivalent to *compression* applied before transmitting the speech waveform and *expansion* at the receiving end, and because it applies to instantaneous values rather than time averages it is called *instantaneous companding*. It is easier to think of it simply as a non-linear representation of the signal in digital form.

An example of a companding law recommended in a CCITT document is shown in Figure 2.10. It has been necessary to use two different vertical scales in order to show the relationship clearly. Both positive and negative signals are subject to the same law, and the binary number transmitted has one sign bit and seven bits to represent the absolute value of the signal. This gives 128 possible numerical values, on either positive or negative side, and these are shown on the horizontal axis. The vertical axis gives the corresponding signal amplitudes on a scale 0 to 4096. In effect, therefore, a 12 bit representation is compressed to seven bits. The characteristic is made up from seven straight line segments, and is designed to be easy to achieve with digital equipment, yet close to a logarithmic form. In practice there are small differences between the definition of the encoding law (which sets discrimination levels) and the decoding law (which gives the mean outputs).

A further detail of the CCITT recommended coding law is that alternate bits are inverted. In this way a silent channel does not give a preponderance of zeros in the binary pattern.

The eight-bit sample at 8000 samples per second produces a 64 kbit/s stream for each PCM speech channel. The economical rate at which to operate PCM systems, is much higher, and in practice a group of 24 or 30 speech channels is multiplexed. In the CCITT system, there are 30 channels

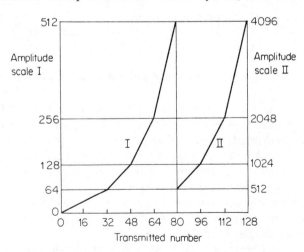

Figure 2.10.   Example of a PCM companding law

and the transmission system operates at 2·048 Mbit/s. This rate would give space for 32 channels, but two are used for signalling and other purposes. The most widely used system, at present, is the T1 carrier of the Bell System, which carries 24 channels at 1·544 Mbit/s. It differs in many details from the CCITT system just described and it is treated later on page 244.

The details of methods of interleaving will be taken up again in Chapter 7 under the heading of digital multiplexing.

PCM was introduced in the first place for use over the short trunks that connect local offices. These trunks had been constructed with multiple pairs in cables. By applying PCM transmission to a selection of the pairs in each cable, the capacity of a route could be increased without the expensive business of laying new cable.

It is not possible to use all the pairs in the cable, because of interference, or crosstalk, from one pair to another. When the same cable is used to send digital streams in both directions (representing the two directions of the telephone circuit in 4-wire form) the crosstalk from the transmitted waveforms to the received waveforms at the same end is the limiting factor. This is called *near end crosstalk*. It can be reduced by using separate cables for the two directions, a measure which is essential if higher speeds are to be sent on pairs, but is not always practicable.

These junction cables were originally installed for 2-wire audio transmission and had loading coils at intervals along them. In some systems, for example, the spacing is 2000 yards. To equip them for PCM, all the loading coils are removed from the chosen pairs and replaced by regenerative repeaters.

Such systems are not economic on very short routes because of the cost of terminal equipment, and on long routes FDM carrier systems, which carry many more channels, are at the present time cheaper. The range 5 to 50 miles was found suitable for the basic PCM systems which have 24 or 30 channels. To produce economic PCM systems for longer lines require higher line speeds. A hierarchy of PCM speeds similar to the hierarchies used for FDM has not yet been fully developed. In U.S.A., the primary PCM group of 24 channels, T1 carrier (1·544 Mbit/s) is multiplexed digitally into T2 carrier at 6·312 Mbit/s, which contains four T1 systems or 96 voice channels. Long distance PCM transmission seems to become economic in the region of hundreds of megabits per second, but the economic speed becomes less as terminal costs decrease and as some of the other factors, such as the economy in control signalling, are taken into account.

2.3 DATA ON THE TELEPHONE NETWORK

A distinction must be made between the transmission of digital information over systems designed for digital transmission (as in PCM) and transmission over the, basically analogue, telephone network. The telephone channel is an alien environment for digital data. This will become clearer in the last part of the chapter where the characteristics of the network are described in more detail. Here, the intention is to give an elementary introduction to data transmission over the network.

Where possible, in this chapter and later, we use examples taken from the recommendations of CCITT. This International body, the Comité Consultatif Internationale de Télégraphie et Téléphonie, is part of the International Telecommunications Union which is an organ of the United Nations. The technical agreements reached by CCITT are expressed as recommendations covering the international connection of telephone and telegraph systems and, more recently, of data carrying circuits and networks. National telecommunication authorities such as European PTTs, operating companies such as American Telephone and Telegraph together with representatives of interested International bodies such as ISO and interested companies such as IBM take part in the discussions.

The recommendations for the international connections tend to influence design features of national networks. CCITT also recommends interfaces between data networks and the attached terminals. Such recommendations are welcomed by computer and terminal manufacturers because, if they are widely adopted, the number of variants of equipments to meet different national practices is reduced.

CCITT plenary meetings are held at four-year intervals and they approve the work done by working parties during the years between. The reports of these plenary meetings contain useful experimental data as well as recording the agreements reached. Some of the most useful papers are listed in the reference 11 on page 62.

The telephone channel cannot handle very low frequencies or the DC component of a signal because of the transformers used in the transmission bridge. The presence of carrier systems introduces distortion (of phase, principally) at both extremes of the band, leaving the central frequencies as the most suitable location for data signals. Clearly a typical digital waveform such as the one in Figure 2.7(c) is quite unsuitable for the telephone network.

For this reason, and others that will appear later, a special equipment is needed to transfer digital signals into a form compatible with the network and to interpret the received signal. This is often known in the U.S.A. as a data set and in the U.K. and other countries as a modem. The word *modem* will be used here.

Data can be transmitted, via modems, over connections made by dialling. Alternatively, a circuit can be leased from the network authority and equipped with modems specifically for data transmission. This is called, variously, a leased circuit or a private wire. The term used here will be *leased circuit*. Such a leased circuit will, in general, go through trunks of various kinds and through carrier systems, but the circuit used can be selected and, by various means, it can be given better properties than most switched connections.

Duplex and Simplex Operation of Circuits

It is a familiar property of a telephone circuit that it can pass speech signals in both directions. On the other hand a single channel containing amplifiers can transmit signals in one direction only. When data are sent over telephone circuits there are three possible modes of operation that must be distinguished.

Because of the two-way property of the telephone circuit, it is possible to send data in both directions, if necessary at the same time. This is called *duplex* operation. Effectively, such a duplex circuit behaves like two channels that can be used independently, one in each direction.

Another possibility is to use the circuit only for unidirectional transmission.

A third possibility is to use the circuit in one direction at a time, but to change over from one direction of transmission to the other so that data can flow either way. An example of this mode of operation arises in radio-telephone equipment that can transmit or receive according to the position of a switch, but not do both together. When one party has finished speaking he says 'over' and both parties switch over so that transmission can take place in the other direction.

Unfortunately, the terminology for these three modes of operation is not standardized and in particular the CCITT definitions are not those used by the majority of computer engineers.

Operation of circuit	Computer engineers	CCITT
Both ways together	duplex	duplex circuit
Either way, but not together	half duplex	simplex circuit
One way only	simplex	channel

Table 1.   Terminology for types of circuit

Table 1 shows the terminologies in common use. The term which can cause confusion is 'simplex' and we propose to avoid using it in this book. By using the terms 'full duplex' and 'half duplex', two of the possibilities are described unambiguously. The other case can be described as a unidirectional channel, but data communication rarely uses just one such channel. A return path is usually needed.

'Half duplex' can be used to describe the way in which a circuit is used. Thus a circuit which is capable of full duplex operation is sometimes used half duplex to simplify procedures. But where a circuit is only capable of half duplex operation, some time is taken in switching the circuit round whenever the direction of transmission is reversed.

The Modem

Figure 2.11 shows the situation of the modems, at each end of a telephone connection. Both-way transmission of data is shown, therefore each modem contains equipment to send data over the line (transmitter) and to receive and interpret the signals (receiver). The intention is that digital data presented at A shall emerge at B, and that presented at C shall emerge at D.

Figure 2.11. Use of modems on the telephone network

The modem must operate rather like a modulator to prepare a baseband signal for transmission over a band near the middle of the voice channel. In the receiving section the modem behaves like a demodulator. A combination of the initial letters of modulator and demodulator forms the term *modem.*

The preparation of a digital signal for the telephone network begins with the baseband signal, that is the signal before it has been shifted in frequency. The waveforms which represent the digital values and the transitions between them must be suitably rounded to avoid sending a wider band of frequencies than is strictly necessary. Some fundamental questions about baseband signalling of digital information are dealt with in Chapter 5.

The most familiar modulation method is *amplitude modulation.* Used for digital data in its crudest form it would consist of 'keying' the carrier on and off with the binary signal, but the variation of mean power according to the digital pattern would be unacceptable in a telephone carrier systems. Amplitude modulation is nevertheless used for modems of the highest performance, where 4, 8, or even 16 levels of signal are used to compress 2, 3 or 4 bits, respectively, into each signal element. A scrambler (see page 164) which makes the data 'pseudo-random' can be employed in these elaborate systems, and by this means large excursions of mean power are avoided. It is important to be able to recover the carrier exactly at the receiver, so the unwanted sideband is not completely suppressed. Instead, the method used is *vestigial sideband* or VSB. In this method, the filter which cuts off one sideband has a roll off which is antisymmetrical about the carrier frequency. It allows the vestigial sideband to carry just the signal components needed to replace those attenuated on the other side of the carrier. This is the method also used in television broadcasting where there is the same need to preserve the waveform of the baseband signal.

The theoretical treatment of VSB modulation, demodulation and noise performance has been treated extremely well in a number of books[2,3,4] and will not be repeated here because modem design is not our principal concern.

Frequency modulation using a binary signal is the same thing as frequency shift keying or FSK—the use of two frequencies to represent the 0 and 1 states respectively. This is the modulation method used in the simplest modems, and an example of it will be described in more detail below.

Phase modulation by a digital signal leads to a finite number of phases, and the most-used number is 4, since four phases in quadrature are easily generated. An absolute phase reference is not possible. An accidental shift of phase could occur, and if each phase has a unique digital representation, these digit values would all be transformed after the shift. To prevent this effect, digital values are sent as phase *shifts* rather than phase values. In the 4-phase system, each signal element transmits two bits, and there are also 8-phase systems sending three bits per signal element.

The theoretical treatment of frequency and phase modulation can be found in references 2, 3 and 4.

Although we have kept to the conventional view of modulation in which the baseband digital waveform is suitably shaped and applied to a modulator, it is possible to generate digitally modulated signals directly. This approach, which is indicated in Chapter 5, underlines the essential unity of the three methods of modulation. It is an approach with great potential since it makes use of digital circuits with only the simplest of filters.

An Example of a Modem

It is not the intention to enter fully into the subject of modem design, which is an extensive subject. One particular modem will be decribed in order to give an idea of what is required in this type of equipment. In Chapter 5 some of the techniques that enter into more advanced modems are treated.

We shall describe a modem which complies with the CCITT recommendation V21 for duplex operation up to 200 bit/s. Data transmission over the telephone network at 200 bit/s employs only a small bandwidth, and this allows two channels to be accommodated at once so that modems can be designed for full duplex operation. Such modems are typically used between a simple terminal and a computer centre, and they are being extended to operation at 300 bit/s to serve faster character printers.

The principle of signalling is frequency shift keying in which one frequency is used for sending the 0 state and another the 1 state. The convention is always that 0 is the higher frequency. The two directions of transmission use different pairs of frequencies, as follows:

Channel No.	0 state	1 state
1	1,180 Hz	980 Hz
2	1,850 Hz	1,650 Hz

These are sometimes expressed as $1,080 \pm 100$ Hz and $1,750 \pm 100$ Hz but the centre frequency is not, in fact, used. Where there are no data to send, the lower, or 1 state frequency is sent.

There must be agreement between the two ends on the allocation of channels 1 and 2, and this is decided on the basis that one telephone originates the call, and the data sent by the calling subscriber uses channel 1.

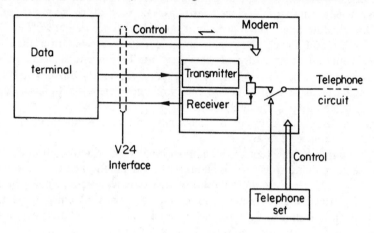

Figure 2.12.   Modem interface

Figure 2.12 shows the situation of the modem in more detail. It has an associated telephone which is connected to the telephone line until a call has been made. Between the modem and the subscribers data terminal an interface is defined at the place shown in the figure. The equipment to the right of the interface is the responsibility of the network authority and that to the left is the subscriber's responsibility. Not only does the transmitted and received data pass across this interface, there are also control circuits to help set up the call. The interface is the subject of an important CCITT recommendation V24 which applies to modems for signalling up to 20 kbit/s. In U.S.A. this is known as the EIA specification RS 232. It has been defined internationally so that subscribers equipment can be designed for use in many countries. For higher speed modems the same scheme of control circuits is used, but the data lines in either direction are balanced twisted pairs as defined in another recommendation, V35.

One particular design of 200 bit/s modem operates in the following way. The transmitter in the modem is a simple oscillating circuit in which values of L or C are changed according to the digit value by switching in extra components. Without special precautions there will be phase discontinuities, but these appear to be acceptable, at least at the 200 bit/s rate. The signal from the oscillator is put through a band-pass filter to remove frequency components outside the band.

The received signal is again band-pass filtered. By amplifying and slicing the signal, a variable frequency square wave is produced, which is applied to two tuned circuits which discriminate the 0 and 1 state. These tuned circuits give signals which are rectified and the two circuits, when resonating, give rectified signals of opposite polarity in a common output channel. Finally, the voice frequency components are filtered out and the signal is squared to become the data output.

The choice of frequencies depends on which end makes the call, and so a single modem may be required to function as caller or called party. The control of such conditions, as well as the setting up of the data path, is the business of electronic and electromechanical logic in the modem, concerned with the control circuits of the V24 interface. For example the band pass filters are transposed between receiving and transmitting channels according to whether the call is originated or not, and this is one function of the control circuits.

Modem Control Circuits

The circuits in the CCITT interfaces that are concerned with controlling the modem are used in setting up and closing down the call. If the calling end is a simple data terminal, like a teleprinter, the call will be established manually at that end, but the called subscriber may be a computer which answers automatically and, by a suitable interplay between computer system and modem over the V24 interface *control circuits*, handles its part of the call procedure automatically.

But the calling terminal can also be computer controlled, and this means that dialling information must pass over the interface. There are further variations if a call is made by an operator who later rings back the *calling* subscriber. All these variants have to be allowed for in the interface. The interface deals with modems of various speeds, some of which have a choice of signalling speed and some of which need time to condition themselves before transmission of data begins.

To deal with this variety of circumstances the recommendation of the interface includes 34 control circuits and defines the use of each. For automatic calling a further 13 are described. The general principles of operation and the procedures for automatic calling and automatic answering are also described in the V24 specification.

For each modem design a choice is made from the available control circuits and the call procedures are adapted to suit the characteristics. But modem designs are made as flexible as possible, and by various internal connections (straps) they can be adapted to different situations. Thus the number of different ways that a modem pair can actually be operated when settting up a call and closing it down is extremely large.

We shall describe the one variant that is mostly commonly met with, the call originated by a simple terminal (with manual control) and answered by a computer centre (with automatic answering).

To the user, it is simple. He lifts the handset of the telephone and dials the computer centre. If the call is successful, after a short pause he hears a tone on the telephone receiver. This is the 1650 Hz signal meaning 1, as sent by the *called* end modem. When he hears the tone he pushes the 'data' button on the telephone and his terminal is connected to the computer. At the end of the call the tidy way of closing down is to let the computer disconnect. This produces a warning sound from the terminal equipment which tells the caller to replace the handset, an action which releases the telephone circuit and the data button.

The signalling between the two ends used for this procedure is carried out entirely by the presence or absence of a modem-generated signal on the line. In the absence of data this is 980 Hz from the calling end and 1650 Hz in the return direction. This is often loosely referred to as the presence of 'carrier', but that is obviously not quite correct—it is the 'ones' signal.

The circuits used in the case of the 200 bit/s modems for the situation we are describing are as follows. They are described by their conventional circuit numbers which are not the same as the pin numbers. In fact, a 25-way connector is used.

Circuit No.	Name	Source	Function
105	request to send	terminal	tells modem to send 'carrier'
106	ready for sending	modem	response of modem to 105
107	data set ready	modem	response of modem to 108
108	connect data set to line	terminal	tells modem to connect to line
109	carrier detector	modem	signal that carrier is received
125	calling indicator	modem	signal that ringing current is received

Each control line can either be in the *on* state at $+6v$ or the *off* state at $-6v$.

The sequence will now be described. It is shown diagrammatically in Figure 2.13. The telephone at the terminal is used to make an ordinary call which goes to the computer's modem and telephone. Although the modem there is 'disconnected', the ringing current is detected in the modem and line 125 goes *on*. At the computer end a special variant of line 108 called 108/2 *data terminal ready* is employed, and this is already on. The effect is that the calling indicator line 125, immediately has the effect of connecting the data set to the line. This is like answering the telephone by raising the handset (going 'off-hook') and it causes the telephone exchange to stop the ringing current. It also puts line 107 to *on*, which tells the computer what has happened. The computer system takes control of the procedure, and what happens next can depend on the requirements of the telephone administration. They may require a silent period on the line, to avoid startling an accidental caller. When the procedure continues, the computer puts line 105 on, which asks the modem to send the 'carrier' or 1 state signal. (It may be necessary

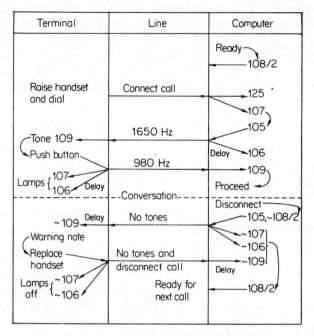

Figure 2.13. Sequence of events in setting up a 200 bit/s call

to send a 2100 Hz tone for the first three to four seconds to disable any echo suppressors.) After a delay which allows things to settle, the modem returns the *on* state on line 106.

At the calling terminal's end, the sign that this has happened is the tone on the line. The user presses the 'data' button. which acts like line 108 and connects the modem across the line in place of the telephone. In this simple kind of terminal the other control lines are not really needed, except for 109 which will cause a warning note to be sounded from the terminal if the 'carrier' is lost after the modem has been connected to the line. Line 107 will go to *on* and line 106 will follow a short time afterwards; these could be used to operate lamps to show the user that the connection is ready.

Back at the computer, the 'carrier' is received and line 109 goes *on*. This indicates to the computer that the connection is ready, and the computer begins its dialogue with the terminal.

The connection can be closed down from either end, by removing the signalling tones. The computer disconnects by setting lines 105 and 108/2 to *off*. When it has verified that the modem is disconnected (lines 107 and 109 *off*) it can restore 108/2 to *on* so that further calls will be answered immediately.

At the terminal end the signal that the call has ended is the warning note due to 109 going *off* when 'carrier' is lost but 107 is still *on*. The user must then replace the handset on the rest, which releases the telephone call. The response of circuit 109 is delayed by 400 ms to avoid accidental disconnection either way.

We have described the procedure over the V24 interfaces for just one type of modem in one situation. It can be more complicated, and the interface is augmented from time to time to meet new circumstances in the use of modems.

Acoustic Coupling and Push-button dialling

We have described a modem which was designed initially to operate at 200 bit/s and provide a full duplex channel. We described the control methods that are used with a manual terminal for calling a computer which has automatic answering.

At the calling terminal's end all the signals used after the call has been dialled are at voice frequencies and thus can be carried by sound waves into the telephone transmitter (microphone) and out of the its receiver. Equipments are made in which the telephone handset is placed in a cradle or box so that each end of the handset is coupled acoustically to a corresponding microphone or speaker. The modem used is not connected electrically to the telephone, so this *acoustic coupler* can easily be applied to a telephone anywhere. Such an acoustic coupler with a data terminal forms a convenient, portable, data terminal that can be used wherever there is a telephone.

Telephone authorities at first discouraged the use of acoustic couplers, but later have tended to recognize that it would be difficult to prevent their use, and have either tolerated them or offered guidance on their correct design. A badly designed coupler could affect other telephone users, because the network is not intended for transmission of pure tones. Crosstalk, overloading of amplifiers and interference with control signalling is possible. The most useful acoustic couplers are those which adopt the standards of the CCITT recommendation V21 for modems or a similar standard adopted by a country's network. Such couplers can use the same telephone connections to computer ports as other, electrically connected, modems.

Unfortunately, acoustic couplers add a new range of design difficulties to data transmission over the telephone network, which is already rather a matter of compromise than of sound engineering. The acoustic performance of the telephone is variable, particularly the telephone's carbon-granule transmitter, or microphone. Nevertheless, acoustic couplers seem to meet a need for a portable terminal. They need to be mechanically matched to a particular design of telephone, usually the one most common in the country. They do not always work well with different designs and shapes of handset.

The push-button telephone dial, after a call has been connected, is able to transmit the pairs of tones (used for dialling) to a receiver at the other end of the line. The receiver must be capable of responding to the shortest pulse of tones normally encountered, and should be reasonably discriminating against the voice. This scheme to transmit data has the merit of using a sending device which, in some countries, is becoming widespread. In the opposite direction, from computer to telephone, voice messages are used, either composed from pieces of recording switched onto the line, synthesis from digital records or synthesis by rule from recorded phonetic descriptions.

The range of usefulness of these systems is difficult to predict. They have a restricted keyboard and voice response is fleeting, but because they use only a telephone they will be applied wherever their limitations allow.

Start-stop Transmission Methods

The modem we described (and the corresponding acoustic coupler) transmits a signal with two states, which can be called 0 and 1. It does not itself transmit binary digits, because there is no built-in timing device to say which states of the line correspond to the digits being sent. The line can change its state at any time, subject to the limitation of pulse length distortion at high rates. Instead of speaking of 200 bit/s it would therefore be more correct to say 'a minimum of 5 milliseconds between changes of state'. The channel offered by such a pair of modems (and also by most telegraph-connections) is called *anisochronous* because it has no associated clock. Figure 2.14(a) depicts such a signal. In the time direction the smallest allowed interval between transitions is specified, but no more.

To carry data, additional structure must be put into the waveform, and the most common format in use today is the 'start-stop' format of which an example is shown in Figure 2.14(b). Here the first transition from 1 to 0 determines the timing for a group of bits that follow—eight in the example. Suppose the rate is nominally 200 bit/s, then at regular 5 ms intervals after

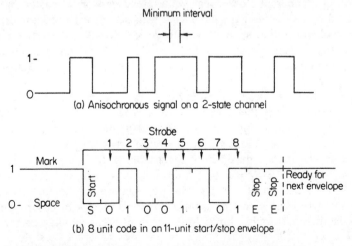

(a) Anisochronous signal on a 2-state channel

(b) 8 unit code in an 11-unit start/stop envelope

Figure 2.14. Anisochronous channel and a start/stop format

the first transition, further transitions can occur. To read the waveform correctly, it must be strobed at times 7·5, 12·5, 17·5... measured in milliseconds after the first transition. After the eight information-carrying intervals, there are two more intervals in the 1 state, shown at E in the figure, then the channel is ready for a new group of eight bits in the same format.

The whole set of 11 units is called an envelope; the first unit is the start bit, the last two are stop bits and the rest carry the data. In telegraph terminology the 1 state is called *mark* and the 0 state is called *space*—a relic of the printing telegraph receiver which 'marked' the tape.

The principle of start-stop transmission was established in the electromechanical era. The start pulse released a clutch to allow a shaft to perform one revolution and stop again during the stop pulse. It is perhaps less appropriate for electronic equipments. Each start bit creates a new clock in order to strobe the following data bits. Systems in which the clock is maintained are generally easier for electronic equipment.

Isochronous Transmission

If a separate clock is provided, each signal element can carry data, and there is no need for start and stop bits or for resynchronization at each envelope. The carrying of data with an uninterrupted clock is called *isochronous* transmission. It requires the clock to be available at both ends of the transmission path, and there are several ways in which this can be achieved.

An isochronous network could have a clock waveform carried all over the network and held in constant phase relationship to all data carrying waveform. From the clock, strobe pulses can be derived wherever they are needed. The provision of a coherent clock over a widespread network is costly, but since it is shared by all of the many channels it can neverless be economic.

A second and commoner method is to carry the clock in the data waveform itself, so that it can be reproduced by a clock extraction method at the receiving terminal. This is the method used for data links set up via the telephone network.

Figure 2.15 illustrates some isochronous waveforms from which a clock can be extracted. In (a), there are relatively narrow pulses in each clock period and their positive and negative polarities carry the data. In (b) each bit is carried by wide pulses and there can be two transitions for each bit. At the alternate clock periods marked by the triangles, transitions always occur and form the clock. Example (b) is a non-return to zero or NRZ waveform, while (a) is an RZ waveform. Example (c) is more difficult because at the 0 symbols there is no clock information. A local clock can be brought into step when there is a pulse, but a long string of zeros would lose the clock phase.

In Chapter 5 the basic principles of data transmission are explored more

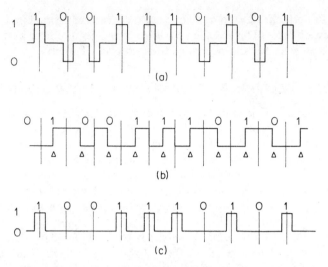

Figure 2.15. Examples of isochronous data-transmission
waveforms

fully, more efficient isochronous waveforms are described and methods are described which overcome the problem of strings of zeros in a waveform like that of Figure 2.15(c).

Isochronous transmission should generally be prefered to anisochronous because it makes better use of the channel. The more advanced modems are basically isochronous because they must carry more than one bit at each clock period. Such a modem, for example, uses phase modulation with four possible phases in each period. It therefore carries two bits in each period and must be supplied a clock and with information bits at a regular rate.

The data transmission needs of a simple terminal are often intermittent and seem to require start-stop transmission. But an isochronous channel can deal with this situation by carrying a special *idle* character when there is no data to transmit.

The start-stop envelope, or something like it, can easily be carried on an isochronous bit stream. The string of ones which is carried during the 'silent' periods is, indeed, very suitable to maintain the clocking in transmission systems like that of Figure 2.15(c). This method could be called 'isochronous start-stop' but it has not yet been widely used. In some circumstances it would be simpler than the 'idle character' method, which depends on the maintenance of a character structure on the channel.

The basic facility provided by an isochronous channel is the transmission of a regular stream of binary digits. Data communication demands more than this because the data has a structure which gives it meaning to the users. At the lowest level this is simply the eight-bit character or byte. A way must then be found to establish at the receiving end the structure of the bit stream as a succession of bytes. This is called *framing*. It is a requirement in many data transmission schemes and we return to it later, in Chapter 7.

2.4 THE TELEPHONE CONNECTION AS A CARRIER OF DATA

A telephone connection through the public switched network provides a channel of approximately 3.5 kHz. Leased circuits can be obtained which employ any of the levels of frequency division multiplexed channels. In practice, groups of 1, 12 or 60 telephone channels have been used, and these correspond to the nominal 4, 48 and 240 kHz bandwidths. But by far the most experience has been obtained with single voice channels, whether switched or leased, and our discussion of the telephone connection as a data carrier will be confined to these.

All the difficulties in using the telephone channel for data arise from the careful and economic design of the network for speech. Features of the channel which do not affect speech quality have not been controlled. Those things which are troublesome to data are not generally defects for telephone transmission.

The performance of the channel will be discussed under three headings, usable bandwidth, distortion of the transmitted signal, and noise. The latter includes extraneous signals and short disconnections.

Usable Bandwith of the Channel

The bandwidth which can be used for data transmission is determined partly by distortion at the extremes of the band but an important additional constraint is the avoidance of certain frequencies used for the telephone network's control signalling system. It is important that data signals should not use the signal frequencies that control the seizure and release of trunks.

The first action of a signal receiver is to break the voice channel at the point where it is located, so that the signal will not go forward into the next section and have a multiple effect. This 'splitting' can take place very quickly so that, even if the connection is not broken, data can be lost. To avoid trouble with the majority of signalling systems it is recommended that signalling frequency components should not last more than 25 ms. Unfortunately, signalling systems were allowed to develop in an uncoordinated way. These are some frequencies that have been used:
600, 750, 1200, 1600, 1900, 2000, 2040, 2100, 2280, 2300, 2400, 2500, 2600, 3000 Hz.
Clearly it would be impossible to find a useful data transmission method that avoids all these frequencies and would be universally and internationally safe against imitating control signals.

It is sufficient in practice to avoid the main systems which are in wide use, and the CCITT recommended frequencies for modems represent a compromise of this kind. Figure 2.16 shows the limits that signalling systems impose on switched connections in the U.K. network, which (when combined with the distortation at the ends of the band) leave only the band from 900 Hz to 2130 Hz conveniently available for data. The figure shows how the chosen frequencies of the 200 bit/s modem and the CCITT recommended 600/1200 bit/s modem (with its 75 bit/s return channel) fit into this limitation. Restrictions similar to those in Figure 2.16 but different in detail, apply in other countries.

Although leased circuits are not switched, some have signalling arrangements on them. Circuits used only for data are usually free of restrictions due to signalling, but some circuits are used to carry voice for part of the time, so they operate in some respects like a switched connection, with ringing from either end. It is these circuits which have the signalling limitations.

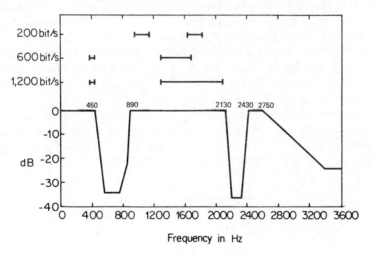

Figure 2.16.   Restrictions of power level on U.K. switched connections and signalling frequencies of common modems

Distortion

Distortion is the term used for unwelcome changes to the transmitted waveform, including any additional signals due to the transmitted signal itself. The forms of distortion which trouble the transmission of data were usually of no serious consequence to speech. They include non-linearity, phase jitter, frequency errors, and echoes, attenuation distortion and group delay distortion. We shall deal briefly with the first four and in more detail with the latter two sources of distortion.

Non-linearity can give rise to harmonics and to sum and difference tones when more than one frequency is transmitted. The frequencies used by the simpler modems and by push button dialling are chosen to be fairly immune to these effects, and it is only at higher speeds such as 4800 bit/s and more that non-linearity matters.

Phase jitter can be due to power supply ripple affecting FDM carrier systems, and there are also sudden phase changes called *phase hits*.

Frequency errors are due to carrier systems which mostly use vestigial sideband with suppressed carrier. The carriers at the two ends are not synchronized, so small frequency shifts are produced, of the order of 10 Hz when several carriers are employed in the connection. The shifts can be cancelled out if the data transmission modulation system transmits its own pilot frequency.

Echoes in a 2-wire system would be due to mismatch at the ends, but the echoes mostly met in practice are caused by the imperfect balance at the transition between 2-wire and 4-wire transmission. The echo paths are shown in Figure 2.17. The hybrid transformers at B and C ideally should prevent any coupling of the go and return paths. In practice, echoes can be produced, either at the end A which is sending (talker echo) or end D which is receiving (listener echo). These echoes can be particularly troublesome in multipoint and polling schemes, and may force the system to wait a short while when it changes from polling out to receiving data.

The attenuation of listener echo relative to the originating signal should be at least 15 db to avoid affecting the receiving modem. In the adverse conditions presented by a good (low attenuation) 4-wire trunk circuit with poor terminations, echoes of this order can be found. In leased circuits it should be

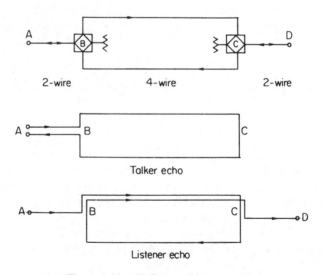

Figure 2.17.   Talker and listener echo

corrected when the circuit is tested and equalized, but the presence of echoes on long, switched connections is an occasional hazard.

On long circuits, typically 1500 miles or more, the echo may be troublesome in the normal use of the telephone circuit for voice conversation. In such circuits, echo suppressors will be fitted. These are inserted in the 4-wire portion at both ends. They operate by sensing the presence of a voice on the pair incoming from the long line, and, when it is sensed, inserting a 60 dB attenuation into the outgoing pair. The attenuator stops the echo returning to the long line, and it holds on for a short time after the signal stops. Unfortunately these echo suppressors will prevent full duplex operation of data channels.

To avoid this it has been agreed internationally that a 2100 Hz tone should be produced when necessary during the setting up of modem connection and that this tone will disable the echo suppressors. After the tone has stopped, frequencies in the 700 Hz to 3000 Hz region will hold the echo suppressors in the disabled condition, so the modem signals will keep them out of action. Calls within countries of the size of U.K. do not need the 2100 Hz disabling tone.

Attenuation Distortion and Phase Distortion

The telephone connection can be thought of as a filter, and the distortion it produces can be described by the attenuation and phase shift as functions of frequency. Attenuation is of interest for voice transmission, but the ear is fairly tolerant of loss at the ends of the spectrum. Phase change is almost irrelevant to the ear and has not been controlled for speech purposes. Not surprisingly, it is the phase characteristic of the channel which is the most serious form of distortion for data.

For a filter, it is natural and convenient to express its characteristic by the attenuation and phase shift at each frequency. For a transmission line, the phase shift would be difficult to measure, and the inevitable delay down the line implies a phase change which is strongly dependent on frequency, even for a perfect line. There is a more convenient measure of the phase characteristics of a line which is called *group delay* or *envelope delay*. The relationship of group delay to the phase characteristic will be explained.

Group Delay and its Relation to Phase Shift

If a signal proportional to $\cos \omega t$ is put into the channel and a signal proportional to $\cos (\omega t - \beta)$ emerges at the far end, the quantity β is the phase shift. To measure β in absolute terms with no ambiguity of 2π, the signal would have to be traced from end to end. Because the channel delays the signal, β is positive and the point of the wave where $\omega t - \beta = 0$ occurs at a later time (t increases) as β increases down the line. The phase shift can be measured also as a time delay rather than a phase change and this quantity is called the 'phase delay' and is given by

$$\Delta t \text{ (phase)} = \frac{\beta}{\omega} \qquad (2\text{-}1)$$

Phase and phase delay are functions of frequency and hence of ω. If a complex waveform like a pulse is transmitted its shape may be altered because the different parts of its spectrum are delayed differently. To show this effect in its simplest form, consider an amplitude modulated signal with a very small modulation frequency so that the signal is confined to a small band. The signal is proportional to

$$S = (1 + A \cos \varepsilon t) \cos \omega t \qquad (2\text{-}2)$$

where ε is small. After passing through the channel, the components of the signal at frequencies $\omega - \varepsilon$, ω and $\omega + \varepsilon$ have been subjected to different phase delays.

$$\left. \begin{array}{ll} \text{at frequency } \omega, & \beta(\omega) \\[2mm] \text{at frequency } \omega - \varepsilon, & \beta(\omega) - \varepsilon \dfrac{\mathrm{d}\beta}{\mathrm{d}\omega}(\omega) \\[4mm] \text{at frequency } \omega + \varepsilon, & \beta(\omega) + \varepsilon \dfrac{\mathrm{d}\beta}{\mathrm{d}\omega}(\omega) \end{array} \right\} \qquad (2\text{-}3)$$

To see how the signal S is affected, expand equation (2-2), giving

$$S = \cos \omega t + \frac{A}{2} \{ \cos (\omega + \varepsilon) t + \cos (\omega - \varepsilon) t \} \qquad (2\text{-}4)$$

After passing through the transmission channel, and being subjected to phase delays given by the expressions (2-3) the output is

$$\begin{aligned} S' &= \cos (\omega t - \beta) + \frac{A}{2} \left\{ \cos \left[(\omega + \varepsilon) t - \beta - \frac{\mathrm{d}\beta}{\mathrm{d}\omega} \varepsilon \right] \right. \\ &\quad \left. + \cos \left[(\omega - \varepsilon) t - \beta + \frac{\mathrm{d}\beta}{\mathrm{d}\omega} \varepsilon \right] \right\} \\ &= \cos (\omega t - \beta) \left[1 + A \cos \varepsilon \left(t - \frac{\mathrm{d}\beta}{\mathrm{d}\omega} \right) \right] \end{aligned} \qquad (2\text{-}5)$$

In these equations, β and $\mathrm{d}\beta/\mathrm{d}\omega$ can be taken as evaluated at ω. The form of equation (2-5) compared with the input signal of equation (2-2) shows that

(a) the carrier is delayed by the phase delay, β/ω
(b) the modulating waveform is delayed by $\mathrm{d}\beta/\mathrm{d}\omega$

This quantity, the slope of the phase characteristic, is the group delay, and Figure 2.18 shows graphically how it is defined and how it differs from phase delay.

The result expressed in equation (2-5) is independent of the amplitude A and frequency deviation ε, if the latter is small, therefore any modulating waveform of sufficiently narrow bandwidth travels through the channel with the group delay, even a broad, modulated pulse, for example. Corresponding concepts of group velocity and phase velocity are used in Physics for describing wave motion in dispersive media. The bunches of waves are the 'groups' after which the *group* velocity and *group* delay are named.

Phase shift is difficult to measure for a transmission channel when the ends are far apart. Even relative phase shift at different frequencies may be difficult to measure because of the small frequency shifts in carrier systems. Therefore the slope of the phase characteristic, which is the group delay, is the most practical measure of phase distortion.

The absolute value of group delay is not important, so the characteristic which is often plotted shows group delay relative to the minimum value which it takes in the voice band.

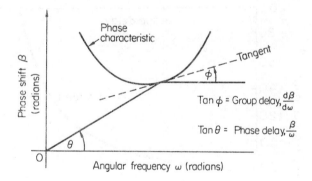

Figure 2.18.   Relationship of phase, phase delay and group delay

The Attenuation and Phase Characteristic of Audio Circuits

The characteristics of a speech channel are obtained by adding together the attenuations of each section of the transmission (measured in decibels) and adding together the group delays of all the sections. The plot of attenuation against frequency, or of group delay against frequency takes a different shape for transmission over pairs of wires (audio circuits) and over FDM carrier systems. Consider audio circuits first.

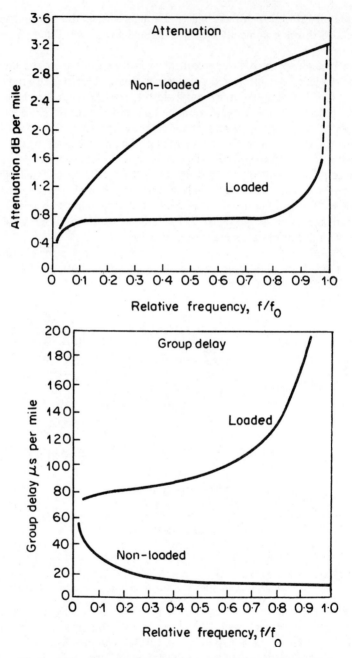

Figure 2.19.   Attenuation and delay characteristics for loaded and non-loaded cables (Reproduced by permission of Bell System Technical Journal)

A pair of wires has an attenuation proportional to the square root of frequency, and a group delay which is small. For speech purposes, the attenuation is corrected by inserting into the circuit, at regular intervals, lumped inductances called loading coils. These, with the intervening line sections function rather like a lumped-component delay line, and exhibit a cut off above a certain frequency. The cut off frequency is placed just above the usable voice band. Unfortunately, the loading coils, while improving the attenuation introduce a group delay which increases with frequency. Figure 2.19 shows attenuation and delay curves for comparable loaded and non-loaded cables used in U.S.A. In this figure the frequency scale is shown relative to the cut off frequency, which is 3520 Hz for the particular loaded cable. The group delay of 10 miles of loaded cable at 2800 Hz is 1·3 ms, a value 0·5 ms greater than at low frequencies. Such a difference of delay would not, by itself, take a circuit beyond the limit for data transmission at medium speeds, but it is one contribution to the total. Very long audio circuits, of the order of 100 miles, introduce group delay differences that are significant in 1200 bit/s transmission.

The curves in Figure 2.19 relate to correctly loaded audio circuits. Some circuits exist with heavy loading and with irregular loading that is adequate for voice but has a very bumpy group delay characteristic.

The Attenuation and Phase Characteristics of FDM Carrier Systems

A well-designed carrier system has a very flat attenuation characteristic with a sharp cut off at each end of the band. The phase characteristic is parabolic in shape. Examples from the U.S. network are plotted in Figure 2.20. Channels 1 and 12 of a primary group may be affected additionally by the filters used to extract the group from the supergroup. These end channels can be avoided in setting up leased circuits, but can appear in any switched circuit.

A careful study of switched circuits in the Bell System in U.S.A. has been reported by Alexander, Gryb and Nast[5,6]. They produced a plot of the extremes of 90% of all group delay characteristics, which is reproduced in Figure 2.21. An equaliser to deal with this variation of group delay must clearly leave residual delay variations of the order of 0.5 ms at 1000 Hz and 2400 Hz. Outside this range, the variations of delay can be larger. The curves were obtained by experimental measurement, and each included a number of carrier systems and possibly some audio cable, as these happened to occur in particular connections. The measured curves were not smooth, but had ripples due to mismatch and the consequent echoes. It is not generally possible to remove the ripples in attenuation and delay curves by equalisation, when they are due to echoes with long delays. The curves were however smoothed before they were combined to produce Figure 2.21.

Equalisation

The attenuation and phase distortion of a telephone channel can, in principle, be compensated by inserting a complementary filter into the circuit, at either end of the line. This process is known as *equalising* or *conditioning*

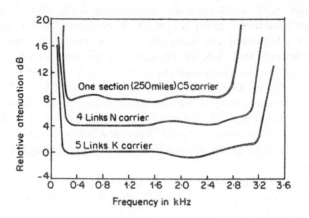

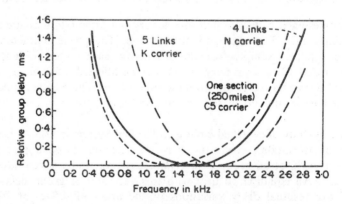

Figure 2.20. Attenuation and group delay for FDM carrier systems (Reproduced by permission of Bell System Technical Journal)

the circuit. For a leased circuit it is possible to insert a filter which is accurately matched to the inverse of the line's characteristic and then, in principle, the line should have little distortion of amplitude or phase. If there are arrange-

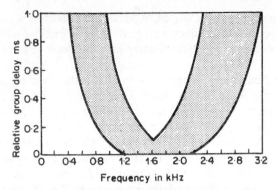

Figure 2.21.   Extremes of group delay curves for 90% of calls
(Reproduced by permission of Bell System Technical Journal)

ments to switch in alternative circuits in the case of failures, these must be equalised separately.

Network authorities will provide leased circuits equalised to meet certain specifications. For example Figure 2.22 shows a typical group delay specification. The group delay curve is plotted relative to the minimum group delay at any frequency in the band. This *relative* group delay cannot be negative, and will touch the frequency axis. The relative group delay curve for a circuit which meets the specification must fall below the hatched region.

It has been found possible to correct the group delay of leased circuits in the U.K. network by the 'prescriptive' method. The delay curve is not measured, but is estimated from a knowledge of the carrier systems and the

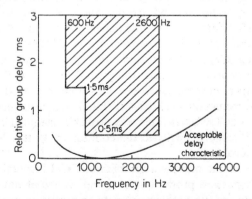

Figure 2.22.   Group delay specification

length of audio cable in the circuit. A set of filter sections is available which can be put together to produce an equaliser. The method allows a characteristic to be obtained with group delay no more than 75% of the limits of Figure 2.22.

For a switched circuit an equalization filter (other than an adaptive filter) must be a compromise derived from a mean among all the characteristics experienced in calls. The study of the U.S. networks shows that residual group delays of the order of 0.5 milliseconds must be expected, and that some circuits will go well outside this limit. National networks differ greatly in the quality and specifications of their equipment. The rates at which data can be handled over switched lines will therefore differ from country to country. Where international recommendations for modems exist, the proportion of connections over which they operate satisfactorily will also differ from country to country.

The subject of adaptive equalisation will be returned to in Chapter 5.

Noise and Interruptions

The noise which is significant for data transmission is that which causes data errors. Impulsive noise due to particular events (such as contact closures in electromechanical equipment or transients in power cables) is the main source of errors. The 'white' noise due to thermal and similar effects is properly called *psophometric noise* and rarely causes trouble.

Impulsive noise arises from specific causes, but the number of sources is so large that they cannot all be identified and eliminated. In older types of telephone exchanges there are plentiful sources of impulsive noise, for example in rotary switches with contacts that can become 'microphonic'. All electromechanical telephone exchanges produce impulsive noise.

The telephone authorities or main network operators of about 10 countries have submitted to CCITT careful studies of the performance of telephone circuits. The most useful surveys are referenced at the end of the chapter. Data for the Bell System are given in the paper by Alexander, Gryb and Nast[5,6] and there is a survey of the U.K. network by M. B. Williams[7].

The Alexander, Gryb and Nast survey in 1959 was followed a decade later by a set of three papers[8,9,10] under the general title of '1969-70 Connection Survey'. The papers covered: analogue measurements, medium speed data (synchronous transmission at 1200-4800 bit/s) and low speed data (start-stop transmission at 150 bit/s). This was probably the most extensive survey ever made, and it sampled switched toll connections of the Bell network but did not include local loops.

The reports[11] of the plenary assemblies of CCITT contain papers which survey data transmission properties for a wide range of national networks. To get a good idea of the problems of data transmission over the telephone network all these sources should be consulted, because there are differences in sampling of connections, methods of measurement and interpretation of results which make it difficult to give a short summary that is authoritative. But we shall try to describe some of the general characteristics of errors due to noise and interruptions.

Errors due to Impulsive Noise

Noise pulses occur with various durations and it is not surprising that the errors due to them occur in bursts. The length distribution of these bursts is important when an error detection system is designed. Unfortunately, it is difficult to define precisely what is meant by a burst. If two noise pulses are close together, an examination of the bits in error may lead to considering them as just one burst. Arbitrary rules are used, such as taking any sequence of 10 correct bits to act as a separator between bursts. In some of the published data, a burst is defined as 'more than n bits in error in a block' and its length is the number of bits between the first and last error. This leads to some very long 'notional' bursts made up from two or more noise pulses with all the intervening bits correct.

In Figure 2.23 the distribution of burst lengths is shown from the results of four surveys. The proportion of bursts which have a length (in bits) greater than a certain number x is plotted against x. Roughly, the length distribution is exponential—the probability of a burst length x falls off exponentially with x. The data for probabilities below 1% is very approximate because the tests typically covered of the order of 1000 bursts. With the exception of the Netherlands test, the average number of bits per burst was small, less than two.

The conclusion to be drawn from Figure 2.23 is that bursts are typically short, and very rarely more than eight bits long. It is doubtful whether longer bursts do happen with the appropriate low probability or whether there is an abrupt limit at eight or so bits. These data were taken with 1200 to 2000 bit/s transmissions.

The data plotted in curve D for the Netherland survey are not strictly comparable with the others because they include the effect of short disconnections. These, as we shall see, are spread over a wider range of times and at least a half of them are longer than the 10 millisecond range of Figure 2.23.

The results of the Bell network surveys also show longer bursts but they seem to have a predominant short burst component, like the one described above added to a long burst component with a longer average, which is also exponentially distributed. It is also reported in reference 9 (page 1381) that 75% of the 'carrier off' indications which would normally be regarded as momentary disconnections (dropouts) were found to be due to 'severe line signal disturbance such as high level additive impulse noise'. It seems extremely difficult to disentangle dropouts from noise.

A careful study of the error statistics reveals that there is another kind of

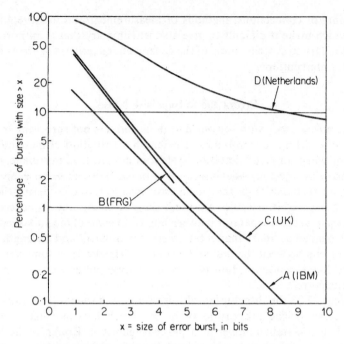

Figure 2.23.   Distribution of size of error bursts

Sources of data

A. IBM experimental 4-wire transmission at 2000 bit/s on a
   leased circuit from London to Rome. Reported in CCITT
   Blue book, supplement No. 37. (For references see page 62.)
B. Federal Republic of Germany tests on many connections at
   1200 bit/s on the switched network. Reported in CCITT
   White book supplement No. 14.
C. U.K. Post Office tests on a 386 mile leased circuit at 1200 bit/s.
   Reported in CCITT White book supplement No. 15.
D. Tests by Netherlands Post Office in conjunction with IBM
   via a number of switched circuits at 1200 bit/s. Reported in
   CCITT Blue book supplement No. 32.

burst. The noise pulses (which cause the short bursts of errors) are themselves
clustered into periods of about 5 seconds. Evidently mechanisms such as
dialling and pulsing between registers occupy that sort of time. Error correction designs should take account of the peak rate that occurs in these 'super-
bursts' rather than the overall mean burst rate.

   The error rate can be expressed as the probability that any bit will be in
error. For example a rate of 10^{-3} would mean that 1 bit in 1000 is in error
(on average). If there were on average, say, 2 bits per burst this would imply
a burst for every 2000 bits, on average once in 1·6 seconds at the 1200 bit/s

rate used in most of the tests. A circuit with this error rate is approaching the point where the error correction schemes which are commonly used become inefficient.

It is meaningless to quote 'average' error rates as a guide to system designers, even for one country's network. A particular connection has a rate which varies greatly during the day, in a way that is correlated with the level of telephone traffic. In one U.K. survey a leased circuit showed an error rate varying over the range 10^{-4} to 10^{-7}. The daily average varied with the day of the week from 2×10^{-5} on Wednesdays to 3×10^{-7} on Thursdays, for no obvious reason. Error rates on switched circuits will vary greatly with the particular circuit that happens to be set up. If a bad circuit is obtained it is worthwile to redial.

By testing the error rate on a large number of connections, long distance and local, in many parts of a country, statistics for the distribution of error rate among switched connections can be built up. Figure 2.24 shows the results of four such surveys, two in the U.S.A. on Bell System connections and two in the U.K. The curves cover the range of error rate from 10^{-3} to 10^{-6}, roughly corresponding to 'rather poor' and 'rather good' respectively.

The ratio of error rates between the worst and best surveys is about 50, and each network has improved considerably. The best 10% of lines are more than 1000 times better than the worst 10%, if the slope of the curves is maintained in the missing parts of the picture.

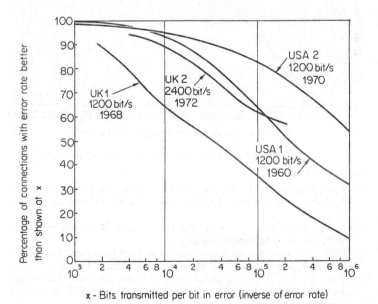

Figure 2.24. Distribution of error rates on switched telephone connections

It is an interesting fact that, although the difference between the networks is great, the difference between the various connections one is likely to dial on either one of the networks is much greater. From the most recent surveys, the best 60% of U.K. connections could be like the best 80% of U.S. connections, that is, all better than 10^{-5} error rate. But any such comparison is subject to all the provisos about differences in the measurements. Perhaps there is a need for a CCITT recommendation on network measurement procedures.

Errors due to Circuit Interruptions

Any telephone circuit, leased or switched, is liable to short interruptions (as well as long ones). These short breaks are due to maintenance work and

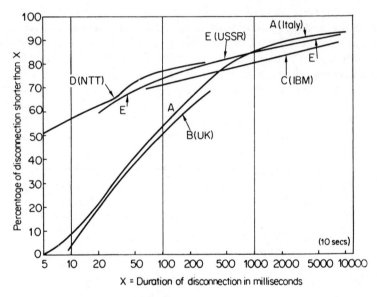

Figure 2.25.   Distribution of duration of disconnections

Sources of data

A. Test by Italian administration on three lines at 2000 bit/s. Only results from line (b) are plotted. Reported in CCITT White book supplement No. 13.

B. United Kingdom tests on a 200 mile circuit. Reported by M. B. Williams. (For references see page 62.)

C. IBM test on a 4-wire leased circuit at 2000 bit/s from London to Rome. Reported in CCITT Blue book supplement No. 37.

D. Tests by N.T.T. on a circuit of 750 miles between Tokyo and Fukuoko using radio relay links. Reported in CCITT Blue book supplement No. 38.

E. Tests in U.S.S.R. on a long distance circuit. Reported in CCITT White book supplement No. 41.

the automatic changeover of equipment in carrier systems. Various parts of the carrier terminals and repeater stations have standby equipment which is switched into circuit when faults occur, or during maintenance work. The units changed over include amplifiers, carrier sources and power supplies.

In Figure 2.25 the distribution of lengths of interruption from a number of measurements on different networks is plotted. In each case the majority of all interruptions were less than 100 ms in duration. These distributions show less similarity in their general shape than was the case for bursts of errors due to noise. They are dependent on the design of the carrier systems used. Now that the effect of these breaks on data is known, future equipment designs and maintenance methods should take account of it, and reduce the incidence of short breaks, but it will be a long time before this has a useful effect on data transmission.

There is no reason to expect noise pulses and disconnection to be correlated, since they arise from different mechanisms. In different networks and different circuits, one or other may predominate as a cause of errors. In the surveys by some network authorities, disconnections are ignored, while in others they are given special treatment. The survey of the Japanese telephone network, in particular, states that most errors were caused by circuit interruptions.

The Development of Data Transmission on Telephone Channels

The most significant feature of telephone networks for data transmissions is their variability. Experience obtained in U.S.A., for example, must not be applied without care to other countries. Even countries which are otherwise technically advanced may not have invested so much capital in their telephone networks that they form a satisfactory, general solution to the problem of providing data transmission. Features which may have seemed unimportant in speech networks, can prove to be an impairment for data purposes. Examples are the placing of signalling frequencies and the frequent changeover of equipment in carrier systems. Changes to the telephone network to accommodate data must necessarily be slow—in line with the obsolescence of telephone equipment—and out of line with the rapid development of data systems.

Information theory gives a limit to the rate of data transmission on telephone channels which is much greater than we presently achieve. Therefore there is no fundamental limitation at the present level. But it is extremely unlikely that practical methods of 'encoding' the signal will be found that get close to what information theory gives as the fundamental limit. Such developments as adaptive equalisation, to correct the phase characteristic, and modulation methods which avoid simulating the control signals will extract more capacity from switched circuits. It would therefore be rash to predict where the practical limit of telephone circuits as digital channels lies.

Probably, the most difficult of the distortions to correct will finally be echoes and non-linearity. In Chapter 5 the question of fitting data signals to an analogue channel is considered in more detail.

The variability of telephone channels is such that it will never be possible to guarantee the operation of a modem system on a switched circuit except at the lower speeds. The adaption of digital data to the speech channels is basically a matter of compromise and probability. This is in sharp contrast to channels which have been designed specifically for digital transmission.

It is very important that in all future technical development of the telephone network the needs of data are taken into account. For example, the development of the local network should not squander bandwidth that might be needed for future digital systems, and PCM equipment should not be allowed to restrict codes or introduce slips in synchronization.

There are good historical reasons for the way the telephone system has developed and there are valuable lessons to be learned from it for the future of data communication networks.

2.5 APPENDIX

Reconstruction of a Waveform from Samples

In PCM transmission, instead of transmitting an analogue waveform, its samples, taken regularly at 8000 per second, are transmitted. The effect of this on the waveform and the method of reconstruction is best seen by looking at the spectrum of a sampled waveform. Figure 2.26(a) gives an example of the power spectrum $P(f)$.

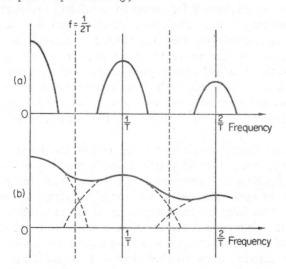

Figure 2.26. Spectra of sampled waveforms

Sampling can be regarded as multiplying the original waveform by a sampling waveform; in our example a fairly narrow square wave was used. This is exactly like modulation by a carrier and it has a similar effect. The spectrum does indeed show the sidebands of a modulated signal at frequency I/T where T is the sampling rate. (Multiplication corresponds to balanced modulation, so there is no carrier component, only sidebands.) However, the sampling pulse is a periodic waveform with spectral components at frequencies 0, 1/T, 2/T, 3/T... and in the spectrum, each of these introduces sidebands. Frequency 0 gives a 'sideband' which is like the spectrum of the original waveform.

There is an interesting duality between the sampled waveform and its spectrum. The sampling period is related to the intervals of the spectral 'bunches'. The spectrum of the sampling pulse appears as the envelope of the whole spectrum. The individual bunches exhibit the spectrum of the original waveform.

In Figure 2.26(a) we have made the picture simpler by assuming that the original waveform's spectrum did not extend beyond a frequency $\frac{1}{2}$T. This ensured that the sidebands of adjacent bunches did not overlap. Figure 2.26(b) shows the waveform's spectrum extending beyond $\frac{1}{2}$T and the sidebands have overlapped.

Now consider the reconstruction of the waveform. If the original waveform was in the band 0 to $\frac{1}{2}$T the first 'sideband' is a separate one and it can be selected by a low pass filter set to cut off at the dotted line, $f = \frac{1}{2}$T. The waveform out of this filter would have precisely the shape of the original waveform, that is, a faithful reconstruction from the samples is possible. But an attempt to reconstruct the waveform in this way from the samples in the case of overlapping sidebands would fail, and the resultant waveform's spectrum would be the correct spectrum 'folded over' at $f = \frac{1}{2}$T.

From this argument the result known as the 'sampling theorem' is obtained. It can be stated thus:

A waveform with its spectrum limited to frequencies below f_0 is completely determined if samples of its amplitudes at intervals $\frac{1}{2}f_0$ are known.

Applied to PCM transmission this means that a speech waveform with frequencies limited to less than 4 kHz can be reconstructed completely from 8000 samples per second. In order to ease the design of the low pass filter which reconstructs the waveform, the bandwidth should in practice be restricted a little more, say to 3.5 kHz.

The sampling theorem makes no mention of the shape of the sampling pulse because samples, in the mathematical sense, are taken at discrete times, and this corresponds to infinitely thin sampling pulses. When the waveform is reconstructed from pulses that have finite width it affects the spectrum slightly.

If the pulse is narrow, the effect is small on the lowest 'sideband', which is the one used for reconstruction. It is easily allowed for in the characteristic of the reconstruction filter by giving a slight lift to the higher frequencies in the passband.

References

1. Cattermole, K. W., *Principles of Pulse Code Modulation*, Iliffe, 1969.
2. Bennett, W. R., and Davey, J. R., *Data Transmission*, McGraw Hill, 1965.
3. Lucky, R. W., Salz, J., and Weldon, J. R., *Principles of Data Communication*, McGraw Hill, 1968.
4. Lathi, B. P., *Communication Systems*, Wiley, 1968.
5. Alexander, A. A., Gryb, R. M., and Nast, D. W., 'Capabilities of the telephone network for data transmission', *Bell Syst. Tech. J.*, **39**, No. 3, 431 (May 1960).
6. Morris, R., 'Further analysis of errors reported in "Capabilities of the telephone network for data transmission"', *Bell Syst. Tech. J.*, **41**, No. 4, 1399 (July 1962).
7. Williams, M. B., 'The characteristics of telephone circuits in relation to data transmission', *P.O. Elect. Engr's. J.*, **59**, Pt 3, 151 (Oct 1966).
8. Duffy, F. P., and Thatcher, T. W., 'Analogue transmission performance on the switched telecommunication network', *Bell Syst. Tech. J.*, **50**, No. 4, 1311 (April 1971).
9. Balkovic, M. D., Klancer, H. W., Klare, S. W. and McGruther, W. G., 'High-speed voiceband data transmission performance on the switched telecommunications network', *Bell Syst. Tech. J.*, **50**, No. 4, 1349 (April 1971).
10. Fleming, H. C., and Hutchinson, R. M., 'Low-speed data transmission performance on the switched telecommunications network', *Bell Syst. Tech. J.*, **50**, No. 4, 1385 (April 1971).
11. Reports of the Plenary meetings of CCITT, published by the International Telecommunications Union, Geneva.
    The reports of the CCITT plenary assemblies, which take place at intervals of four years, contain detailed, and in many cases authoritative accounts of data performance measurements on national telephone networks. The recommendations form a useful record of the progress of data communication, but it should be remembered that national practice may be different.
    3rd Plenary (Blue Book) Volume VIII Data Transmission
    The following papers in the supplement contain comprehensive surveys of data transmission experience using the telephone network:
    No. 26 France p242
    No. 32 Netherlands p321
    No. 34 IBM (WTEC) p328
    No. 36 Japan (NTT) p355
    No. 37 IBM (WTEC) p361
    No. 38 Japan (NTT) p377
    4th Plenary (White Book) Volume VIII Data Transmission
    The following papers in the supplements are recommended (each paper has its own page numbering):
    No. 9   United Kingdom
    No. 13 Italy
    No. 14 Federal Republic of Germany
    No. 15 United Kingdom
    No. 41 USSR

CCITT Recommendations

These are refined at each plenary, and the following are important recommendations concerning data transmission using the telephone network:

V3   – International alphabet No. 5
V15   – Acoustic coupling
V21   – 200 baud modem for use in the switched telephone network
V23   – 600/1200 baud modem for use in the switched telephone network
V24   – Interface between data terminal equipment and data communication equipment
V26   – 2400 bit/s modem for 4-wire leased circuits
V26b – 2400 bit/s modem for use in the switched telephone network
V27   – 4800 bit/s modem for leased circuits
V35   – V48 kbit/s transmission on group band circuits

These recommendations concern the users of future data networks:

X1   – User classes of service and data signalling rates for public data networks
X2   – Recommended user facilities available in public data networks
X20   – Interface between data terminal equipment and data circuit terminating equipment for start-stop services in user classes 1 and 2 on public data networks
X21   – Interface between data terminal equipment and data circuit terminating equipment for synchronous operation on public data networks.

Chapter 3
Computer Interaction

3.1 INTRODUCTION

A computer's interaction with the outside world takes place through the input-output system, sometimes called the I-O system. In the earliest computers there was not always a need for a well-defined I-O system, and the handling of peripherals was done in an ad-hoc way. The I-O task was light and consisted of input from media such as punched cards or paper tape and output to similar media. By using such external storage media, 'data preparation' and output printing could be detached from the machine.

The main historical stages in development of the I-O system have been:

1. The recognition of the system as a separate entity, with buffering and device-control functions.
2. The development of a unified I-O philosophy for all peripherals, with a standard interface and general purpose I-O software.
3. Separation of I-O function in a 'front end' processor.
4. The increasing importance of direct interaction with the computer, both locally and at a distance.

In the course of these developments, which are the subject of this chapter, the meaning of the word 'peripheral' has been extended. To the true peripherals, at which data enters or leaves the system, have been added external stores such as magnetic drum and discs, which effectively extend the machine's storage capacity. Because these devices had the same properties as peripherals, from the computer's viewpoint, it was natural to connect them to it through the I-O system. The way they integrate with the computer's software may be very different from the true peripherals, for they usually are part of a store hierarchy.

Interactive peripherals such as teletypewriters and keyboard/displays pose special I-O problems because of the large numbers of them that are handled at once. The usual approach has been to design a 'multiplexer' which is really a controller for a group of identical devices, and is purpose-built for the type of device it is controlling. The new development in data communication technology with which this book is mainly concerned should lead to a unified I-O philosophy for *distant* terminals of many different types, and this is rather similar to the changes in design method which took place earlier in relation to local terminals. It is only because an apparently foreign communication technology intervenes that the extension of unified design methods beyond the computer room has been delayed. In the absence of unified methods, interaction between distant computers and terminals tends to be specific to particular manufacturer's products. This may seem to be beneficial to the dominant computer manufacturers, but the cost to computer users is significant and this reduces the total market for teleprocessing systems and equipment.

In our study of the communication systems of computers, the point of contact with these computers is, of course, the I-O system. When communication is a minor function, a simple adaptation of the existing I-O system is sufficient to handle it. But those computer systems which predominantly handle data from a communication network (and these increase in number) require a more radical scheme of adaptation. The communication network itself should be adapted to suit computer traffic and this is our principal subject of study.

In an attempt to arrive at better designs for computer-adapted communications, we must include in the study a sufficiently large slice of the total system. The I-O system of a computer comes into this slice. We choose to regard the communication function as beginning when a block of data is ready in the computer's store for transport. It ends when the data are stored in the destination computer or presented at the appropriate terminal and when all the checks and 'administration' are completed.

This is not at present a conventional viewpoint. The traditions of communication technology are based on the telegraph and telephone networks and tend to limit the communicator's job to much less than we have suggested. But the cost of adapting both terminals and computers to a predetermined data network is considerable and, without a study of the whole problem (as defined above) there is no likelihood of minimizing the cost to the end user, who pays, by one route or another, for the service.

The chapter describes the external interaction of computers, with emphasis on the I-O system. There are some aspects of the problem of external interaction which are very general, applying even to a simple push button on the operator's console. We begin with such general considerations and move on to the development of I-O systems.

3.2 INTERACTION WITH EXTERNAL EVENTS

Peripheral devices present special problems to a computer because the events that interact with the computer are outside the computer's control. Within any system of logic, such as a computer, events occur in an orderly

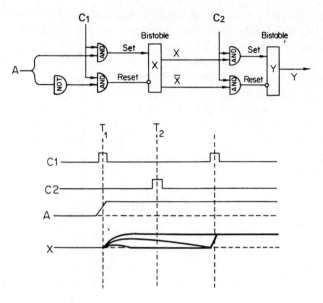

Figure 3.1. A race hazard in synchronizing an external
event

sequence and their times can be controlled. An external event can give rise to a 'race hazard' where the precise outcome depends on small errors in timing, and could lead to a misoperation. The existence of this risk is not always fully understood—yet it is always present[1].

To demonstrate this risk, it is merely necessary to assume that an input defined by a logic level changes state at an arbitrary moment and then analyse the logic needed to synchronize the change with a clock. Figure 3.1 shows a frequently used arrangement. Here A is a logic level derived from outside the system. It could, for example, be derived from a contact on an operator's key, and its timing is arbitrary. The objective is to devise a signal which is timed relative to one of the clocks C1 or C2. The logic diagram shows A used to set or reset a trigger X at clock time C1. The assumption made is that X has settled down before the time of C2 so that trigger Y will be set or reset cleanly.

To see the risk it is necessary to look beyond the logic diagram at the waveforms. According to the timing of A, trigger X will eventually rest in one or other of its stages. The figure shows the waveforms in some near-critical conditions. There is, in principle, a timing of A which results in trigger X hovering indefinitely between its stable states. Even in the presence of noise there is such a timing of A, though to know the exact moment it would be necessary to know the noise waveform. The existence of this hovering state can be proved by a topological argument which maps the timing of A continuously onto the signal level of X at time T_2.

In any condition close to the metastable state the displacement increases exponentially at a rate depending on the bandwidth and loop-gain of the trigger's feedback path. In practice, therefore, the probability of error is extremely small if the interval $T_2 - T_1$ is long enough. For example, the gain bandwidth product of the trigger feedback path will be of the order of 10^9 Hz, so a synchronizer designed to have a delay of 10 ns would have an error probability of the order of 10^{-4}. This is unacceptably high, but a delay of 50 ns, with probability of 10^{-22}, is adequate. The cascading of synchronizing units like those in Figure 3.1 does not affect the relationship of delay and error probability to any large extent.

It is possible, then, to formulate some general guidelines for interaction with external events. Suppose that the external device can be expected to react fast, but will not be operated very often. For example it could be a relay that operates in 1 ms but is changed only to assist in loading a magnetic tape. Then the best plan is to sense the relay after 5 ms, when it certainly should have settled. The sensing can be synchronized with the computer's internal timing, and the chance of finding the relay in an indefinite state is very low. On the other hand, suppose that the external event has a rather indefinite timing. A synchronizer such as that in Figure 3.1 will be needed. But the event, once it starts, may repeat rapidly. For example, a track on a magnetically coded card may reach the reading head after a certain delay, then generate both data and clock pulses rapidly. Instead of synchronizing each event to the computer's timing, it is often better to store the data locally. Then from the computer's point of view the uncontrolled event only happens once—it is the signal that the local data are ready to be transferred. Such relatively rare events are easier and safer to synchronize because they permit longer delays and, as we found earlier, the longer $T_2 - T_1$ can be made, the shorter is the interval of hazard.

The existence of this race hazard is of theoretical interest because it is one of the limits to the reliability of computers, but, properly handled, it can be less than the effects of thermal noise. Because of the delay at any synchronizing event it is better to use a buffer that loads in synchronism with the external source of data. Such buffers are valuable anyway in holding off the need to respond to external events, so the synchronizing requirement is not onerous.

Input-Output by Direct Program Control

The earliest computers could afford to devote the whole processor to the detailed control of one peripheral, because their I-O load was negligible. A typical input peripheral would provide a number of bits in parallel such as from reading a punched card. In order to show the time at which the data was valid, a separate strobe line is provided from the reading mechanism. Figure 3.2 shows these signals, with their timing tolerances, drawn in the form of the shaded areas where the state of the signal is uncertain. There are systematic errors due to the mechanism and random fluctuations, on the strobes as well as the data.

For direct control by program a number of instructions were available to the programmer to 'start tape reader', 'stop tape reader', 'start card reader for one cycle' and so forth. Having started the mechanism, this kind of program was entered:

1. If strobe is *on* then go to 2, else go to 1.
2. Store data from reader.

The program was forced to cycle on instruction 1 until the first time that the strobe arrived, then read and store the data. All that is needed to make it work is a strobe, like Strobe A, lying within the times T_1 and T_2 which defines the safe period for valid data. But the program, though it might desert the peripheral to do a little calculation after instruction 2, would soon return to 1 and would be in danger of reading the same data again. To avoid this an instruction should precede those given above, namely

0. If strobe is *off* then go to 1, else go to 0.

If the program samples the strobe often enough the transition from instruction 1 to instruction 2 always takes place at the leading edge of the strobe, and it becomes possible to employ a longer strobe such as B in the figure, which is sometimes convenient.

The inevitable race hazard occurs because the program cycle of the computer is unrelated to the strobe. Therefore the strobe is being applied to a synchronizer, in effect. But with mechanical devices the testing of the strobe need be repeated only on a millisecond time scale, and with microsecond logic or better the probability of hitting the hazardous condition is vanishingly small.

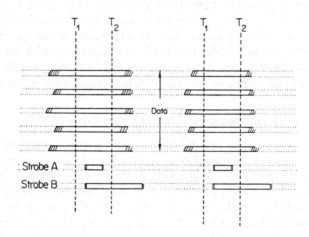

Figure 3.2.   Strobing of data channels

The Use of Storage and a Flag

The direct method employed the processor almost continuously to look at the state of the peripheral. It was possible to employ some of the time between peripheral events, but only by a 'dead reckoning' of the time available to the other processes, which were usually part of an I-O data conversion.

The next step of historical development was to store the data at the periphery so that the time at which the computer picked it up was less critical. The strobing of the input lines is then a local, autonomous function resulting in reliably stored data. The problem for the designer is to organize the transfer from this store.

For this purpose an additional one bit store analogous to the strobe line is provided. This is usually called the *flag*. As soon as the data have been stored reliably and allowing a small timing margin, the flag is *set* (to 1). Then the program has a short while in which it can test the flag. When it finds the flag *set* it reads from the peripheral store and the reading action *clears* the flag to 0. The peripheral store can be cleared at any time until data are again strobed into it from the incoming data lines. A second reading is impossible because the flag is not set.

The race hazard in this system arises when the flag is set because the reading of the flag's condition is timed to the computer's cycle. It is no solution to control the flag setting from the computer because that would merely shift the hazard to the earlier event.

The flag for output is set when the computer transfers its data to the peripheral store. It is cleared when the store is read by the peripheral device at its own timing, to control magnets or recording heads, etc. In this case the early reading of the store is important so that the computer has latitude in rewriting. When the store is empty the flag is cleared to signal to the computer that the output of data is again possible. Therefore the computer's sequence of operation is to test that the flag is *clear* then transfer data to the output store.

The two stages of an input cycle are

1. If flag is *set*, go to 2, else go to 1,
2. Read data (thus clearing flag).

For output

1. If flag is *clear*, go to 2, else go to 1,
2. Output data (thus setting flag).

In some popular systems the output flag is inverted, but this is only a matter of terminology. If we can assume that in both cases, instructions 1 and 2 always occur together, they can be combined into two single instructions for input and output respectively.

3.3   *THE INTERRUPT MECHANISM*

Direct interaction with external devices by interrogation of a strobe or flag is satisfactory when the computer deals with only one external device at a time and can devote much of its time to that device. The weakness of the method is that the conditional transfer of control must be at the correct points in the program to catch the strobe or to catch the flag before the next event overtakes it. For practical purposes the computer must stay in an I-O program during the whole process.

Computers that interleave the I-O processes for several peripherals and do some data handling at the same time must be able to have their 'attention' directed at almost any moment to take account of external events. This is true of most of the computers that use communication systems, and even more so of the computers that *control* the switching of data in a communication network. For this sort of application a different mechanism was devised to enable them to handle external events efficiently—the *interrupt*.

The 'attention' of the computer can be said to be directed to the instruction being obeyed. The part of the computer's logic which determines this is shown schematically in Figure 3.3. A register called the 'instruction pointer' holds the address of the current instruction (ACI). This address is used to fetch from the stored program the current instruction (CI) and place it in the instruction register, in which position it controls what happens next. The figure illustrates also the notion of a *pointer*, which is widely used in describing the operation of computer systems, including, as we shall see in later chapters, data switches. In this case the *contents* of the 'instruction pointer' become the *address* of the current instruction. In the figure, the contents of a register, whether in a main store or a special register, are shown inside the rectangle and the *address* or *name* of the register alongside. The instruction pointer is so called because its contents point to the place where the current instruction is held. The transfer of CI from its place in store to the instruction register is shown dashed, and no pointer is involved here. The convention used is that pointers have full lines and data transfers are shown with dashed lines.

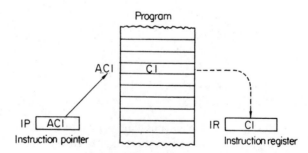

Figure 3.3.   The instruction pointer and register of a simple computer

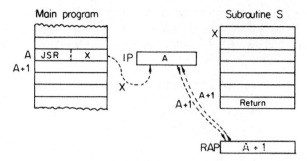

Figure 3.4.   A simple subroutine mechanism

The normal sequence of events is that the instruction CI is fetched, then while it is being used the contents of IP are incremented by 1 so that the next word in the store will be taken for the next instruction. The regular progression from one instruction to the next is sometimes altered by a so-called 'jump' or 'transfer of control' which results when IP is loaded with a new address.

The interrupt mechanism is a different way to cause a jump. An external event causes a number to be placed in IP so that the computer jumps into a different program. The operation which is in progress at the time is allowed to finish before the jump takes place.

The interrupt mechanism we have described leaves behind it a problem, namely what to do with the interrupted program. Since the interrupt can occur at any time, no precaution can be taken by the program itself to ensure its eventual recovery. There are two aspects to the problem:

1. How to ensure that the interrupted program is returned to.
2. How to preserve any partial results of that program, such as the contents of special registers.

But these problems are not unfamiliar to computer designers because they have to be faced when a subroutine is entered. Figure 3.4 shows this situation. At the point A in the main program the service of a subroutine S is needed. The special instruction 'Jump to subroutine' is used; 'JSR' X in mnemonic form. It puts X into the register IP but saves the value of A that was in IP by placing A + 1 into a special register or store called RAP (for return address pointer) and associated with the subroutine. At the end of the subroutine's operation the instruction 'Return' loads A + 1 from RAP into IP and the main program resumes at the instruction after the one where it left off.

The same kind of mechanism is able to deal with interrupts, but in this case, no provision has been made in the main program. Figure 3.4 will still serve, but instruction A is any instruction in a program. Something happens externally while the instruction from A is being executed, such as a number signalled as ready for input. The interrupt has the effect of forcing a control jump to X, i.e. loading X into IP. The 'subroutine' is an interrupt routine intended to take care of the input event. When it is completed, control returns to $A+1$ as though the main program had not been interrupted.

Saving of Register Contents and Return Addresses

We have dealt with only one aspect of the interrupt or subroutine jump, namely the return to the interrupted or main program. The other aspect was the preservation of partial results. These might for example be held in accumulators or registers belonging to the computer's control mechanism which can be used by any program. The subroutine or interrupt routine could be entrusted with the task of storing these data in a safe place and returning them before it returns control. In bigger computers which deal with many interrupts this would be time consuming, so the interrupt and subroutine *hardware* is made to carry out the saving of special registers.

A convenient way to deal with return addresses and the contents of special registers is to use a *stack*. The term 'stack' is used to denote an area of store accessed in a special way. Figure 3.5 shows how it works. A succession of cells in the store is given up to the stack, beginning at the *stack base* SB, which may be marked by a stack base pointer. At any one time, a particular cell ST is denoted the *stack top* and its address ST is stored in the stack pointer. When any new word is to be stored in the stack, ST is incremented by 1 and the word placed there. When a word is to be read from the stack it is taken from the current ST cell and ST is decremented by 1. The effect is that the word read is always the last remaining one to have been written. This is summarized as 'last in - first out'. The arrangement of Figure 3.5 shows the addresses increasing in the downward direction, which is the convention usually employed for storage cells in an addressable store. It would be more like a real stack (such as a stack of plates) if it had been shown the other way up.

The stack is a natural way of storing data that corresponds to unfinished business, because it ensures that the tasks will be resumed in a sensible order.

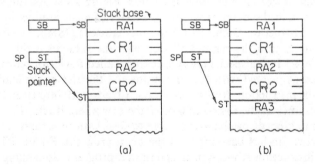

(a)   (b)

Figure 3.5.   Use of a stack to store return addresses and
contents of common registers

Applied to the interrupt or subroutine jump, typical contents of the stack are shown in Figure 3.5(a). The first jump that was made has required the storage of the return address RA1, which was followed immediately by the saving of the contents of common registers (CR1). Then before the new process was completed a second jump was made leading to the storage of RA2 and CR2. Now the stack pointer contains the address of the last component of CR2 that was entered. Suppose now that a further subroutine or interrupt jump occurs. The stack pointer moves to the next cell and RA3 is stored there as shown in Figure 3.5(b), and so forth. As the various tasks are completed, the current register contents will be replaced and the return addresses used to restart unfinished tasks and ST will move back towards the stack base.

Disabling and Enabling of Interrupts

The purpose of an interrupt mechanism is to allow an external event to get the attention of a computer quickly. To ensure this, the mechanism should always be ready to operate, but there are some circumstances when an interrupt would disrupt the system. This situation arises when there are many different external causes of interrupt which need to be handled in different ways.

If there are many sources of interrupts, they can occur at any time and might coincide. Those that are not dealt with immediately must wait, and each interrupt source has its own one-bit store or 'flag' that is set when it is requesting an interrupt. Because interrupts must be handled quickly it is customary to provide hardware to handle priorities and present just one of them to the computer at a time.

The interrupt routine is written as a completely separate routine. It is, in effect, a subroutine which can be called from anywhere in the program. Its first task is to preserve any data that have not been stacked away by hardware and are in the working space it will need. Then it must examine the flags to find the cause of the interrupt and jump to the appropriate part of its program. At the same time, the recognition of the flag must reset it, so that it is ready for further interrupts of the same kind. Up to this stage it would be disruptive for a further interrupt to happen, however urgent. Therefore the hardware *disables* all the interrupts immediately one is recognized by the processor and it is the job of the interrupt routine to *enable* them again at the right point.

In the simplest computers an interrupt always jumps to the same starting point in the interrupt routine and, there being only one level of priority, it is usual to re-enable interrupts only when the interrupt routine is finished. It must be arranged, therefore, that the interrupt mechanism is enabled *after* the return to the program from which the jump was made.

In a more elaborate computer a number of interrupt classes are defined, and each one has a word in the main store containing a pointer to the start of its interrupt routine. This avoids the need to search all the flags to find the cause. Disabling of interrupts can also be selective and it is then determined by an interrupt 'vector' which is a word having a bit to represent the enabling/disabling of each interrupt class. This vector is loaded into a special register where it controls the ability of further interrupts to be effective. This vector is among the data saved if a new interrupt does occur, and by this means the 'interruptability' of a program is restored again when it resumes control.

The Organization of Interrupts

No matter what hardware priority mechanism is provided it is still the job of the system programmer to see that interrupt handling is done efficiently. Chapter 13, which concerns the software of data switching computers, gives examples of how this can be achieved. The assignment of suitable priorities to certain classes of interrupt is only part of the story.

An important principle is to keep as short as possible the pieces of program that cannot be interrupted. If the servicing of an interrupt is a long process the interrupt can be acknowledged and a note made of the requirement. These notes can then be put into queues and the rest of the servicing handled by normal, interruptable programs. Where the servicing of an interrupt is short and simple it can be carried to completion, to avoid adding further 'red tape'. If there is a priority system, high priority should only be given to interrupts that can be dealt with very quickly and need a quick response.

We have described interrupts as coming from the I-O system because this is the subject of the chapter, but in many computers there are also interrupts coming from inside the system. These are caused by unwanted events in the running of a program, such as an attempt to obey a nonsense instruction or to access a part of the store not authorised for a particular program. Like external interrupts they need the attention of special routines which could not be provided by having jumps in the program. Their interrupt service routines should, if possible, observe the same constraints that apply to the servicing of external interrupts, or the response of the system to external events will suffer.

A third class of interrupt is caused by internal clocks and timers. If a process must be carried out at regular intervals it can be initiated by a *clock interrupt*. This is produced by a pulse counter that is designed to generate an output at the required interval. By software counters in the clock interrupt service routine, clock driven processes can be started at still longer intervals. A *timer* is set up by program to give an interrupt after a certain time has elapsed, like an alarm clock. This could be used, for example, where a computer sends a message and expects a reply in one second. The timer is set to two seconds, for example, and if the reply does not come it causes an interrupt and the computer takes the appropriate action, such as trying again. For all practical purposes a clock or timer can be treated as an external device.

Real-time Requirements

The I-O system of a computer comes into contact with the less-controlled outside world. Inside a computer, the designers can control the timing of events. The outside world is 'uncontrolled', in this sense, which produces timing or synchronization problems at the boundary. We have already met one of these problems in the synchronizing of an external event to the fine-scale timing of the computer (e.g. its clock pulse). The problem we shall now discuss is the inter-relation of programs with external events on a longer time scale.

Consider as an example a rotating disc store which has already selected the track it needs and is now waiting for a certain block to come round, in order to read it or overwrite it. Assume that the matching of the block addresses is done by some hardware attached to the disc which gives an interrupt when it recognizes the wanted block. When the block address matches, there is very little time for the computer to respond with an order to read or write. If it misses its chance, the block is lost. The maximum time allowed between an interrupt and the essential response it needs is sometimes called the *crisis time*.

The crisis occurs, of course, when the computer does not quite make the rapid response in time. To avoid such an 'overdue response' the programs which respond to the interrupts must be carefully planned, and priorities must be given to those events with the shortest crisis times. It is not always the highest speed peripherals that need the highest priority, nor do all aspects of the control of one peripheral have the same urgency.

Redesign of the I-O device hardware can completely alter the crisis times. Consider the disc store again. If there is a buffer in the disc store hardware which can store one block, the immediate crisis is removed. For when the addresses match, the store can be read into the buffer (or written from the buffer) without intervention from the computer. Then the crisis time becomes of the same order as the time of passage of one block where, before, it fitted into the small space between the address and the block.

In the design of I-O systems and communications hardware a lot can be done to reduce, or even remove, the more stringent real-time requirements. For example, Chapter 13 describes the software for a main switching centre (or node) of a data network where the rules of interaction have been designed to avoid almost completely the need to consider real-time responses. So although the system gives a rapid response, dealing with about 1000 short messages per second, no individual external event *must* be acted upon within a fixed crisis time. A second example is the NPL experimental local network, referred to in Chapter 7, in which control of the flow of data is extended outwards to all users. Any problem the central control computer has in meeting deadlines will at worst momentarily hold up data input from one of the users, but no data will be lost or corrupted as a result.

Nevertheless, real-time requirements cannot always be avoided, particularly with mechanical devices such as discs, drums or printers that cannot be stopped and started suddenly, given also a limitation on the amount of special buffer storage that is to be associated with these devices. No matter how well the treatment of interrupts has been organized to meet the crisis time considerations, there is always the possibility that the response will be overdue. For this situation there are three recommendations to the system designer:

1. A check should be made that the crisis time response requirement has been met. This can sometimes be determined by hardware (like the flag mentioned earlier) but it may require program intervention, for example to check that the correct block *was* read.
2. The system programmer must face the possibility of an overdue response and devise a strategy to recover from the failure, such as repeating an operation.
3. However effectively the system reacts to overdue responses and corrects their effects the failures should be logged for the operators and maintenance engineers. They may indicate incipient trouble.

The Need for an Interrupt Mechanism

We have described three methods of interaction with external events: direct program control, the use of flags and the interrupt mechanism. These are of increasing complexity and power, and the interrupt mechanism allows the computer to react to many kinds of event, apparently at the same time, if necessary with different response times. For example, to an interactive typewriter it gives an immediate echo of each character, a quick acknowledgment response at the end of each line of type and a slower reply when a complete message is recognized.

But there is another approach to the problem. Rather than complicate the I-O system and its programs by making it respond to all demands, we control the demands made on it. Even in such an onerous real-time situation as a stored-program controlled telephone switch this approach can be adopted. By suitably queuing demands in the periphery, a simple I-O philosophy is possible, using direct control by the program. This approach is indicated where the computer's main job is to respond to events and there is a big load of external events which justifies continual attention from the control program. Communication systems usually have this kind of I-O demand. Chapter 13 illustrates how the interrupt system with which a computer is equipped may be masked (by software) from the programmer, who works in terms of a 'semaphore' mechanism, which is more convenient.

So although the interrupt mechanism is the most common means of interaction with external events, it is not necessarily the best mechanism in all circumstances. Probably it works best with sporadic and unpredictable demands when the computer's main task lies in 'internal' processes.

3.4 BLOCK TRANSFER AND THE I-O CHANNEL

Three ways of arranging the interaction between a peripheral and the computer have been described; direct control by conditional jumps, the use of flags and the interrupt mechanism. Any of these could be used to load 8-bit characters or bytes into store from a paper reader. The reader runs at most at, say, 100 bytes per second so the expenditure of a dozen interactions for each byte that is handled would not be a big load on the computer.

This simple method does not extend to fast peripherals which can handle 100,000 bytes per second or more, such as magnetic tapes, discs and drums. For these peripherals it is necessary to reduce the number of times the computer must attend to them. The data is therefore organized into *blocks* which are written or read as one operation.The process of reading a block from a peripheral is initiated by an instruction from the computer. It then proceeds autonomously, without the computer's intervention, reading the block into a pre-arranged area of store. At the end of the transfer there is perhaps an interrupt to allow the computer to record the completion and act on it if necessary. The block transfer is sometimes called an *autonomous data transfer* or ADT.

The significance of the block transfer is that it requires many accesses to the main store. The process of accessing a block of store is frequently used in all computer systems, including communication switching machines, so it will be explained in more detail. Figure 3.6 shows one arrangement. The

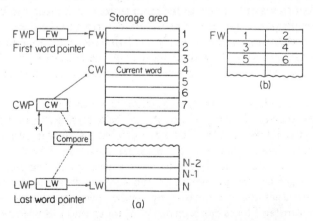

Figure 3.6. A block transfer mechanism for N words

storage area is shown as divided into words, but the length of the word is not important. If, for example, the input process uses 8-bit bytes while the main store is organized in 16-bit words then the store would actually be laid out as shown in Figure 3.6(b), and at each access, only one byte of the accessed word would be used, the other byte being kept intact. In Figure 3.6(a) the block transfer is assumed to store (or read from store) one word at a time. There are three important store addresses to be remembered, the addresses of the *first* and *last* words of the block and the address of the *current* word. These are held in three special registers called FWP, CWP and LWP, meaning first word pointer, current word pointer and last word pointer. Initially CW = FW. Then as each word is stored (or read from store) CW is increased by 1 so that the next word will be stored (or read from store) at the next address. Before the incrementing, a test is made in the unit named 'compare' and if CW = LW the block is full, an interrupt or other suitable signal is sent and no more transfers attempted until the mechanism has been reset.

Consider the storage of data coming from an input device. There are three reasons why the input process might be terminated:

1. The input device has determined that the block is complete.
2. The word read from the input has had a special form which signals the end of a block—an end of block marker.
3. The available store is full, CW = LW.

In each case the usual outcome is an interrupt, allowing the programmer to decide what should happen, which is more flexible than building the response into hardware.

The need for CW and LW to be stored is clear, the former to keep a note of the current position and the latter to detect that the available store has been used up. It is less certain that FW need be kept, once the process has begun. We have treated the transfer as though it had full use of the store in question, but this is only a part of the main store, which must also be used for many other purposes. The transfers we are describing take their turn to use the store mechanism and are interspersed with the other kinds of transfer. This gives rise to a need for protecting the storage area from interference by other processes which may have gone wild because of program or hardware errors.

Consider data input. It may be required that words FW, FW + 1, ... CW − 1 which have received their input data should be accessible. In that event only the region from CW to LW need be protected. A similar situation could obtain during data output, where the earlier part from FW to CW − 1 has been dealt with and could begin to receive new data. Therefore in some situations it is only the pointers CW and LW which are relevant. But the block transfer does not necessarily complete the operation. It may be necessary to repeat a transfer if there has been an error, for example. Sometimes all three pointers are needed, and the whole block from FW to CW remains protected.

It has been assumed that the pointers are held in special registers, but in many practical situations there could be scores of block transfers in progress at a time. Then it is more economical to hold the pointers in the store. The operation of storing or reading one word of the block then requires more than one store cycle. Since CW can be read, incremented and stored again in one cycle, the process could be carried out by three cycles using store addresses CWP, LWP and CW respectively. In some computers where the store holds long words, CW and LW can be accessed in one cycle, allowing one step of the block transfer to be completed in two store cycles.

The I-O Channel

Input and output operations carried out with entire blocks at a time can relieve the central processor of work. The main store is involved, but only to the extent of accessing the data, and the necessary store cycles are interleaved with those of the processor. If the whole processor was involved in the transfer there would be several more store cycles per word, to fetch instructions and do such 'red tape' as counting and address modification. The block transfer is more economic but it entails a separate piece of equipment to carry out and control the block transfer. This is called an I-O channel. Big computers may employ several channels.

The channel must have a connection to all the peripherals it handles. This is the I-O interface and is described later. The connection to the peripheral does not carry data alone because all peripherals need control signals as well.

Consider a simple terminal such as a paper tape reader. It could very well employ these control signals from the computer:

Read one character, then stop
Start reading continuously
Stop reading

The tape reader is also the source of outgoing control signals, which in computers are generally referred to as *status* information. Examples are:

Tape loop tight (reading stopped for safety)
Tape run out
Reader switched off, inoperable
Gate open for loading tape, temporarily inoperable

The precise choice of the control and status repertoire is very dependent on the application, and it is possible to manage with fewer than the signals mentioned. More complex peripherals have a bigger repertoire. A magnetic tape deck has controls for rewinding and loading it and status signals for the conditions of rewinding and loading.

Looking in the other direction the I-O channel connects with the computer where there is a program which sets it into operation and receives its status signals for completion and various other conditions. The gradual development of computers and operating systems has led to a very indirect link between the programmer and the peripherals he uses. To describe it in detail would be difficult and tedious. Instead, a simplified description will be given of a channel based on the IBM System 360 range, so that the principles are explained.

The programmer usually has little knowledge of the I-O system and states his intentions in a high level language. The systems programmer who wrote the I-O program had to concern himself with the details, which is just as well, for there are many of them. Indeed one cannot avoid the impression that too many specialists have left their mark on the I-O systems of large computers and that some useful simplification would be possible.

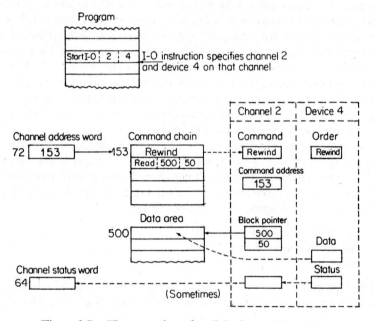

Figure 3.7.   The operation of an I-O channel (simplified)

The channel is set in motion by an instruction in the program, but not a very informative one in the case of the 360. It simply says something like 'Start I-O in channel 2, device 4'. Figure 3.7 shows the parts of the system involved in the process. Before executing the instruction the program must put a pointer into the 'channel address word' which is contained in absolute address 72. This pointer tells the channel where to find its first command, and in our particular example this is in address 153. *Commands* are the 'instructions' which control the I-O channel, and they have a format which is quite distinct from the instruction set of the computer. They can call for peripheral operations like 'rewind' which are set in motion by control signals and they can call for block transfer, specifying the area of store which is to receive or provide the data. A peripheral operation will usually require several commands and these make up a simple 'program' or *chain* of commands. It is also possible to jump to a new address for the next command, in fact the chain of commands is in every way like a set of instructions to a computer but the 'computer' in question is just the I-O channel.

Having initiated a chain of commands the program proper continues its work. The completion of the task reaches it as an interrupt, and it can then find the cause of the interrupt by examining the 'channel status word' at absolute address 64, which has been loaded by the I-O channel.

To do its work the I-O channel must hold the current command, the command address, pointers and counters for block transfer, and status information which is *en route* between the device and the program. These are shown in Figure 3.7. The dialogue between the channel and the device is elaborate, and much of the status information is dealt with directly. Only those events, such as completions or failures, that need the program's attention give rise to interrupts. The systems programmer writes the instructions and the command chains, but even he is unaware of the dialogue between channel and device.

A second command in the chain might specify a block transfer to read data into an area of the store, using block pointers to control it. In the figure this is illustrated by the reading of data from device 4 into a block of size 50, starting at address 500. Remember that pointers are shown by full lines and data transfers by dashed lines.

Figure 3.7 also shows a third kind of 'instruction' which is more primitive than a command, and is called an *order*. This is the result of the simple command, like 'rewind' which is passed as a control signal to the peripheral device for action.

Unfortunately the terminology such as 'command' and 'order' differ for different machines. The example that has been described comes from a rather complex I-O system and much of the detail has been removed for ease of explanation.

The I-O Interface

In early computers the attachment of peripherals was treated as a separate problem for each peripheral, but when the variety of different peripherals began to increase indefinitely, and each computer configuration could be chosen from any among this variety, it was necessary to define a *standard interface* between the computer and all its peripherals. This I-O interface is a point of physical attachment. The interface is not a piece of equipment but a conceptual boundary across which signals and procedures are rigorously defined. On one side of the interface is the channel, already described, and on the other the peripheral device, adapted as necessary to the demands of the interface.

The interface definition begins with a description of the connector and the electrical signals it carries. It goes on to define the meaning of the signals and the 'protocol' or procedure that must be used on each side of the interface. The precise definition is lengthy and complex, but the principles can be explained in an informal way if they are simplified, as they will be here. To give an idea of the precision needed in interface definition, an interface is described in detail in the Appendix on p. 531.

It is important that the interface definition should not completely define the meaning of the signals that pass through. It obviously should not concern itself with the data that goes between peripherals and computer and might be regarded as 'transparent' in a certain sense to this data. Similarly, though it recognizes the separate existence of 'control information' travelling outwards to peripherals and 'status information' returning from them, the interface definition must be transparent to its actual content. The repertoire of control and status messages is separately defined for each peripheral, though with uniform conventions for those functions that are common to most of them.

Figure 3.8 shows the location of an I-O interface as it is provided in most data processing computers. Each channel has its 'highway' or 'bus' to which the peripherals are attached by controllers. Since each peripheral has its own special demands for local control, timing and buffering, the controller is special to each kind of device. Some controllers can have many devices attached to them, particularly when these are simple devices like teletypes. In channel 2 of the figure the controller handles a communication line via a modem. It treats the line like a peripheral, receiving data by a read command, and transmitting it by a write command and it uses interrupts to report special conditions (like 'end of text') to the computer.

Figure 3.9 shows one form of the interface in more detail. The transfer of information is carried out in parallel over the outward bus or inward bus.

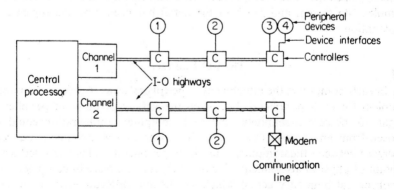

Figure 3.8.   The I-O highway interface

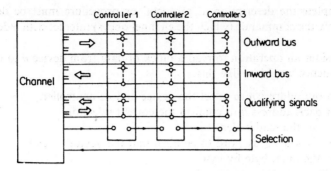

Figure 3.9.   The interface lines – an example

The number of lines is a feature of the system but a common case would have eight bits plus parity (nine lines) in each group. The information in question can be a byte of data, of course, but it can also be:

1. an address on the outward bus to identify the device being selected.
2. an address on the inward bus to confirm the selection, or identify a device requesting attention.
3. a control signal or 'order' to the device.
4. a status report from the device.

The group of lines denoted 'qualifying signals' determine which of the six categories of information (three inwards, three outwards) is on the lines and deal with the timing or sequencing of the transfers. This is where the complexity of the interface definitions begins.

The selection line is a special one and not a parallel connection to all the controllers. Such an arrangement is logically necessary in any highway interface, though this exception makes it cease to be strictly a highway or bus. The selection line or its equivalent is needed to deal with *contention*, which is the term used when a number of devices on a highway can make demands at any time and *contend* for the attention of the central device, in this case the channel. Demands for attention come from the controllers whenever they complete an autonomous action, like rewinding a tape, an action which takes a sufficient time that the highway is employed, meanwhile, on other tasks. This is a sort of 'interrupt' function. If two such demands are present at the moment the channel becomes free it must be made to choose one of them unambiguously. This it does via the selection line where a signal is diverted into the first controller it reaches which has a demand to make. The effect of this organization in a loop is to give priority to the controller connected first on the loop. The selection line of the highway can sometimes be connected up to exploit this priority usefully.

The interface, as we have described it so far, is a means for transferring qualified information (data, address, control/status) to and from a controller.

To complete the description a 'protocol' or procedure must be defined to show how the commands (which the channel obeys) interact with a designated device.

Consider an operation to read a block of data from device n to the store. The sequence would be like this:

1. Send out address n to select the device and its controller.
2. Send back address n to confirm the correct selection.
3. Send out the read order.
4. Read back a status word to confirm that the device is ready.
5. Read the data, byte by byte.
6. Finally, cancel the device selection.

This sequence is carried out entirely by hardware in many computer systems, and is an interplay between the channel and the controller of device n. The channel and the I-O interface has to be devoted to the one device for the whole time, and if the transfer is rapid enough this is valid. The term often used for such transfers is the *burst mode* of operation. But slow devices could not be allowed to hold up the channel so, once the read order has been given and confirmed, they must relinquish it, then request and obtain selection again for each byte transferred or a few bytes if they have a buffer. In this mode the data transfer phase becomes more complex, like this.

1. Request attention, using a line in the 'qualifying' group of signals.
2. Obtain selection on the selection line.
3. Read back address n to describe the source of the data.
4. Confirmation from channel.
5. Read data (one byte or a few bytes in quick succession).
6. Cancel the device selection.

This mode allows several devices to share the channel, with their commands all in operation at the same time. It has been called the *multiplexing* mode of operation. The choice between burst and multiplexing mode is usually fixed by the nature of the device as a source or acceptor of data and some devices can use either mode, selecting the mode under program or manual control.

The brief description does not do justice to the complexity of the I-O highway's procedure, which is the heart of the interface definition. The complexity comes from meeting in one system the requirements of a great diversity of peripheral devices.

The control of the interface rests mainly with the channel, and derives from the interpretation of commands, but at the other end, it requires some logic in each controller. For very simple terminals, such as teletypes, paper tape readers and punches, or incremental magnetic tape cassettes, the full complexity of channel and interface is not appropriate. Small or specialized computers, according to their range of intended application, use various

simpler arrangements in which the channel or highway is either simplified
or replaced by a more primitive function.

The value of the comprehensive I-O highway interface lies in its universal-
ity. In particular it can be adapted to any kind of communication channel and
to peripherals of any complexity. But the I-O channel which uses 'hard-wired'
logic is not flexible enough for all circumstances, as we shall see.

The I-O Processor

The channel operates on commands in the way that a processor operates
on instructions, and an I-O command can put into operation an elaborate
procedure over the I-O interface. A system of this complexity is an obvious
candidate for microprogramming[2], in which microinstructions from a fixed
store control the sequence of elementary steps needed to execute an I-O
function. One can go further and replace the channel by a small computer
which handles the I-O operations on behalf of the main processor. Such an
arrangement is adopted in many large computer systems and in some process
control computers. Figure 3.10 shows a possible arrangement in which the
main store can be accessed by the central processor, which does the data
processing, and by two I-O processors. Each I-O processor has its own I-O
highway to which controllers are attached, and it effectively takes the place
of a channel.

The advantage over 'hard wired' channels is the flexibility of the I-O
processor. It becomes possible, for example, to specialize their functions so
that one I-O processor handles external storage, with its block transfers of
moderate size, and another handles the true input and output peripherals.

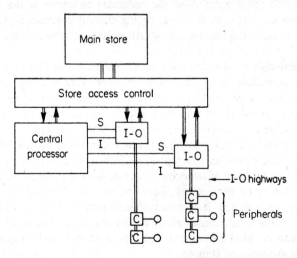

Figure 3.10.   A computer system with I-O processors

Communication between the I-O processors and the central processor is mainly done by using areas of main store to exchange messages. Interrupts can go in either direction, through lines shown in the figure as S and I, so that I-O processing can be initiated and completion or exceptions of various kinds signalled back. A bigger repertoire of I-O functions can be provided by a stored-program I-O system, and these functions can be augmented when new and more complex peripherals are attached. The various I-O processors can use different programs to suit their particular set of peripherals. Whereas, with an inflexible channel, quite complex control requirements for a device must be done locally by fixed logic, it now becomes possible to exercise more detailed control from the I-O processor, and simplify the local logic.

But there are dangers in loading more and more functions onto the I-O processor, not because of its cost or performance, but because the split of functions between the various parts of the system becomes obscure. Modifications, or adaption to different configurations, may not be straightforward. This, perhaps, is the reason that I-O processors have not been used by some of the biggest computer manufacturers. The trend is towards I-O processors, and it is probable that even more specialization of function by separate processors will be developed.

3.5 THE ATTACHMENT OF COMMUNICATION LINES

When the need for on-line communication with computers at a distance was first realized, the object was simply to move some of the peripherals to a distant point and connect them by communication links to the existing I-O system.

According to this simple view, the necessary function of the I-O system must be extended, through the line, to the distant peripheral. One of two methods was used, depending on whether the peripheral was simple or complex.

Simple terminals such as teleprinters were already familiar as communication devices operating in a start-stop manner over a telegraph or telex (switched telegraph) network. At somewhat higher speeds a similar anisochronous signal could be carried by a telephone line using modems. It was therefore possible to communicate with distant teleprinters almost as easily as with local ones. All that was needed was a controller on the I-O interface designed to handle a number of teleprinters. When the controller was designed to handle a large number of teleprinters at one time it came to be known as a *multiplexer*, but since the use of the word in two different senses can be confusing we have called it a *terminal multiplexer*. Figure 3.11 shows a multiplexer of this kind connected to a number of teleprinters. A terminal multiplexer can be used to control a group of similar and simple terminals whether they are local or remote.

The success of this simple plan, and its cheapness when the communication

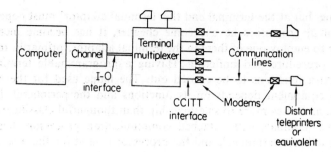

Figure 3.11. The 'multiplexer' for simple terminals

lines were short, led to its adoption for new kinds of terminals such as the character displays. Some of these displays are designed as teletype equivalents in all respects except for displaying text instead of printing it. Even the clearing of the screen, which has no counterpart on the teleprinter, can be avoided by rolling the text upwards in the way that a sheet of paper shifts upwards at the line feed operation. The next stage was to increase the speed of simple terminals to 600 bit/s, then 1200 bit/s, still retaining the start-stop format. Both leased and switched telephone lines were employed.

Any terminals that can be driven on a character-by-character basis and for which the control signalling requirements can be handled by the CCITT interface could be substituted for the teleprinter in Figure 3.11, given a multiplexer able to deal with the data rate. More details of such multiplexers will follow later.

Now let us examine the connection of remote peripherals with greater demands such as a line printer, or a dynamic display, which draws complex figures described by a 'display file'. The peripherals need a buffer store attached to them because the device itself uses data at a high and variable rate. They are also very vulnerable to data errors.

Communication over the line is organized into blocks with error checking by redundancy and the block is sent again if an error is found. Now we are concerned with a communication system designed for data, and the detailed consideration of it is postponed until Chapter 6. Since the transmission is organized into blocks, it is possible to have a format which allows, and distinguishes, data and control signals. Figure 3.12 shows the arrangement in a schematic form. The communication adapter is in two parts, one for handling the procedure of the I-O interface and the other to deal with the line. The error control procedure can be handled by program at the computer end

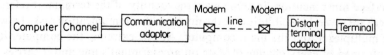

Figure 3.12. Communication systems for a complex terminal

of the line, but at the terminal end the 'terminal adaptor' must cope with it.

As small processors have become cheaper, it has become increasingly common to employ one of them in the terminal adaptor, primarily to handle the line procedure and buffering. Having a programmable terminal then allows extra functions to be carried out. The name used for the complete terminal equipment depends on its functions and the peripheral devices it contains, and owes more to salesmanship than thoughtful classification.

Simple terminals with attached communication processors tend to be called 'intelligent terminals', and the processor is used for the first stages of data validation, or to produce a check balance in the case of accounting transactions. When a small group of mixed terminals is looked after by such a processor it is frequently connected to a batch processing computer with a fairly quick turn-round of jobs. Then it is called a 'remote batch' or 'remote job entry' terminal and the processor deals only with communication and buffering. If the remote processor carries out a more complex function, such as modifying a 'display file' for a dynamic display it is recognized as a 'satellite processor'. If it handles messages for a cluster of simple terminals it is called a 'message concentrator'.

The communication techniques used in all these systems will be described later, because they are used in different ways in a variety of networks. The techniques used in the terminal multiplexer are, however, more specialized, and merit a brief description here.

The Terminal Multiplexer

'Time-sharing' is a name which, correctly used, means the rapid sharing of a central processor's time among many computing processes. It has come to be associated with the kind of 'scientific' or 'problem-solving' computer service that interacts with many users at the same time, giving each of them a rapid response. When these time-sharing systems came into use, their terminals were mainly teletypes (teletypewriters) communicating in start-stop mode at 110 bit/s or thereabouts. A method was needed for connecting a few dozens of these terminals to the computer. Figure 3.11 shows the kind of arrangement, where the new piece of hardware is, of course, the terminal multiplexer. Some of the terminals are local and some are remote, joined to the multiplexer through modems and switched or leased lines. In later developments there has been a mix of terminals at different speeds but all using the same start-stop envelope.

Because many terminals are involved, the information sent over the I-O interface must mention, in some way, the identity of the terminal it refers to. There are several possibilities for the division of communication tasks between the multiplexer and the main computer. At one extreme, the computer itself is informed of every change of state on any terminal's line and it carries out the reconstruction of the binary data from the start-stop waveform. This is not unreasonable if the only task of the computer is to assemble and disassemble the data, but it puts a load on the computer. So the method often used is to assemble the 8-bit bytes or characters in the multiplexer and pass each complete one, with its line identifier, to the computer. In the outgoing direction the multiplexer is supplied with a byte and its line identifier and then spells it out as a start-stop waveform on the appropriate line. (The ways into the multiplexer are often called the *ports* of the computer system, and since their connection to physical lines or modems can be altered, the identifier which accompanies a byte on the I-O interface refers to a *port*.)

There are two ways to design the multiplexer. Each port can be provided with a converter between the serial, start-stop and the 8-bit parallel forms and with a store to hold the byte of data. Then the common equipment does no more for input than collect the completed input bytes and add their port-identifiers. With low cost logic this scheme becomes feasible. The alternative approach uses the common equipment to sense each change of state on all lines and to accumulate bytes in a common store.

Conversion from Start-stop to Stored Byte

Taking the first of these alternatives, the equipment associated with each port must be capable of making the conversion (both ways). It is the *input*

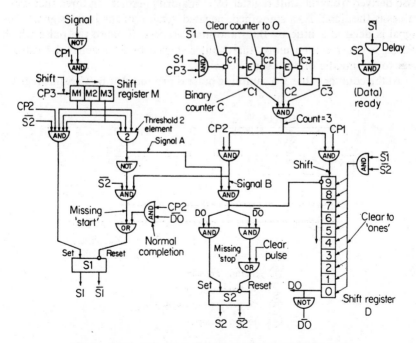

Figure 3.13.   Start-stop signal receiver – logic diagram

which presents most problems because the timing of the signal must be re-established at the start of each envelope. Only the input logic is described here.

Figure 3.13 shows a possible system of logic, which takes the signal input shown at the top left and produces the byte output in shift register D. Figure 3.14 shows the timing of the operation, but not in the finest detail.

The timing of the whole operation must be taken from the first signal transition from 1 to 0. But noise on the line might start the device operating, and cause a bogus character to be received. To obtain some degree of noise immunity the system demands three successive 0 values before it recognizes the initial transition. Then after the system has started, it examines the waveform at the sampling points which are designed to be in the middle of the signalling elements D0, D1 ... D9. The sampling times are derived from the 3-bit counter labelled C which is incremented at the clock pulse rate which is eight times the bit rate of the start-stop signal. Each time the counter value reaches 3, a sample of the input waveform is taken.

The system is driven by three phases of clock pulse CP1, CP2 and CP3, so that shift registers can be set, tested and shifted at different times. The incoming signal is sampled at the clock rate and the three most recent samples are held in negated form in the shift register M, which is strobed by CP2. The starting transition is detected by the 'threshold 2' gate and sets trigger S1. Also derived from the shift register by a 'majority verdict' on three successive values is the signal A, a smoothed, negated version of the input signal. This signal is delayed a little by the smoothing process. Because the pulse which sets S1 is delayed even more, the counter started by S1 reaches the value 3 near to the middle of each signal element.

At the counter value 3, a sampling pulse is produced at B. The shift register

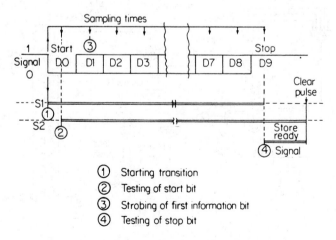

① Starting transition
② Testing of start bit
③ Strobing of first information bit
④ Testing of stop bit

Figure 3.14.   Start-stop signal receiver-timing diagram

D is initially set to contain all 1s and the D9 bit is cleared to 0 at the sampling time, if the signal at A is 1. Just before each sample is stored the shift register is advanced by one place.

The testing of the first signal element is used to verify that there is, indeed, a correct start digit. This is a further guard against the triggering of the system by noise. If the start digit is found to be absent S1 is cleared, while in the normal event S2 is set and the process continues. From this point onwards at each sample time the D9 position of the register is made to take the current bit value from the line. The process continues until the start bit reaches D0, its final position. Then because the zero has reached this stage, at the sampling time, S1 is cleared. The stop digit is also tested and if it is absent S2 is cleared and the process aborted. Some systems may require this abnormal condition to be reported to the computer because it shows 'loss of synchronism' which could invalidate subsequent characters. The counter is cleared when S1 is cleared and the process is then complete with the data in D. A signal is generated to indicate that the store has been filled. The common equipment of the multiplexer detects this and reads the byte from D, using lines not shown in the figure. It then restores the system by the 'clear' signal, which simply resets S2.

A Terminal Multiplexer with Common Logic

In this alternative approach a common system of logic works on behalf of many ports, using a core store, or semiconductor store of a similar type, to store the intermediate results from all the channels. Figure 3.15 shows the arrangement.

Suppose that all the channels work at 200 bit/s and are strobed at 8 times the line bit rate or 1600 times per second. If each strobe employed one store cycle then 600 channels would use 960,000 store cycles per second—a practical figure. So the common set of logic could serve a big collection of lines, or ports. The line bit rate for the channels described above totals 120,000 bit/s and the system's capacity might be dispersed over a collection of lines of

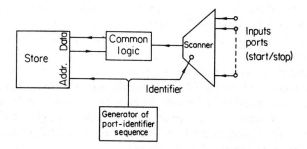

Figure 3.15.   Schematic of input multiplexer with common logic

higher rates or mixed rates, totalling this figure, say 300×200 bit/s plus $25 \times 2,400$ bit/s.

The ports must be strobed by the scanner in such a sequence so that each one is strobed at the correct rate. At the same time the current port identifier is used to extract from store the intermediate state of the system for that port. The logic of Figure 3.13 could be almost literally followed, when the stored data would consist of the states of all the triggers and registers in the figure, namely

M1 M2 M3 S1 S2 C1 C2 C3 D0 D1 D2 D3 D4 D5 D6 D7 D8 D9

Using these data and the value given for the input signal (from the scanner) the state of the logic can be advanced by one step, corresponding to one clock pulse in the original logic, then the data sent back to store. In practice, the logic might be altered to suit the new situation, but the principle is the same.

Completion of a byte starts a new process to prepare the input data for the I-O interface. For example, the data (already in D1 to D8 of the common logic) could be sent to a new area of store where they are queued for output. This part of the process requires extra store cycles interpolated between the regular store cycles carried out on behalf of the ports. The speed of the store chosen takes account of this and of possible demands for store cycles for output. But the handling of these complete bytes is a relatively rare event, and in most cases input and output do not occur at the same time for a given port.

An advantage of common logic is that many extra facilities can be added at little extra cost. For example certain control characters can be made to cause interrupts or to alter the effect of succeeding characters on the line, and input bytes can be echoed back to the terminal as soon as they are received. The stored word can contain extra bits which are not changed and cause different ports to be treated differently.

The Link between Terminal Multiplexer and Computer

The terminal multiplexer, whichever scheme is used for its internal logic, is likely to be connected to the computer through the I-O interface and a channel. Figure 3.11 shows such a method of connection.

The operation of the channel and the interface allows a large number of separate peripherals to be accessed through one connection, using the multiplexing method of operation. I-O operations must be initiated for all the active terminals, and many I-O commands are nominally being obeyed, though each one becomes active only when a byte is ready to be transferred. For very large numbers of terminals this method, though very general in application, is inefficient, and a front end processor or FEP is used to relieve the computer of its communication chores.

There is a different reason why the straightforward use of the channel is sometimes avoided. When the terminal multiplexer uses the common logic method, and employs a store for all the intermediate states, there can be a saving of cost by using the computer's main store for the purpose. The multiplexer must then have a means of direct access to the store, and it becomes a special kind of I-O processor, fitted in the situation shown in Figure 3.10. This arrangement is often used in small computers, which themselves are sometimes acting as front end processors to a large machine, see Figure 3.16(b).

3.6 THE FRONT END PROCESSOR

The front end processor or FEP is a rather flexible concept so that, like many other computer terms, this one has no precise meaning.

The FEP can be distinguished from the I-O processor because it lies outside the peripheral interface. It has become quite common for an FEP to

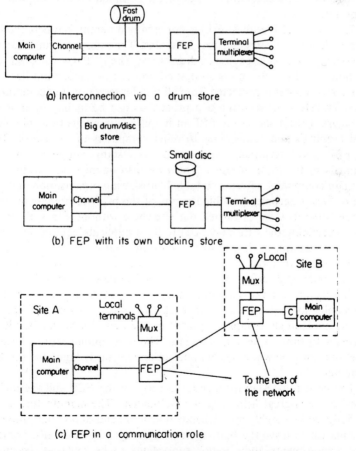

(a) Interconnection via a drum store

(b) FEP with its own backing store

(c) FEP in a communication role

Figure 3.16.   Various configurations of front and processor

be a small computer not supplied or supported by the main computer's manufacturer. Nevertheless is must be carefully designed to suit the main computer's hardware and software standards.

Our main concern is with the FEP which undertakes communication tasks, but first let us look at FEPs of other kinds. Figure 3.16 shows some configurations that have been used.

In Figure 3.16(a) the main link between FEP and the main computer is a magnetic drum. This arrangement is used in a very successful time-sharing system. The FEP handles all the communication tasks and assembles complete messages on the drum for attention by the main computer. Only when it recognizes a command from the user that needs the service of the main computer does it set that machine a task, which is does by a message on a special region of the drum. Thus, all the rapid interaction needed by terminals is handled in the FEP and the main computer uses a longer time-scale, appropriate to its substantial tasks of the compilation and running of user programs.

The system of Figure 3.16(b) is not greatly different, but here the backing store is divided to carry out two functions. The main computer handles the file system, using its large disc or drum store. The FEP has a small disc which can hold files for a few users so that editing can be carried out here. Again, the main computer is protected from all rapid interaction and communication tasks. Transfers between the two processors can be mainly in large blocks.

Figure 3.16(c) shows the FEP in its pure communication role, handling local terminals and connections to other computers in a network. Through the FEP, local terminals can connect to distant computers and distant terminals to the local machine. The FEP also handles data traffic between the main computers. Given a suitable load-sharing organization and duplication of files it becomes possible for one of the main computers to be out of service while its work is carried out elsewhere without a loss of service. To function reliably the FEP may need to have duplicate equipment, because it is an essential link in the network's 'fail-safe' feature.

It is likely that the use of FEPs will increase, for several reasons. The channel and I-O interface has been designed to be very general and becomes inefficient for a large communication task. Manufacturers' systems of communication software are remarkable for their generality of application, but are exceedingly complex, difficult to use and almost impossible for the customer to tune to his requirements. The telecommunications hardware is expensive, and the whole system puts an unnecessarily high load on the main computer.

The need for design independence between the FEP and the main computer can be a great help in later development. The manufacturers' systems are designed in a highly interdependent fashion, and allow only those enhancements which leave the basic system unchanged in all details. Some of the FEP arrangements allow major subsystems to be replaced, because their interfaces are simple and well defined. For example, it is possible that a system of the kind pictured in Figure 3.16(b) will allow the view of the system from a user's terminal to be conditioned almost entirely by the FEP. Then a main computer from a different manufacturer could replace the current one with a minimum of disturbance. Systems of the kind of Figure 3.16(c) can use a variety of main computers in one network.

Software Interfaces for the FEP

The complexity of communication software in the main computer is a consequence of its striving after generality of application. The writing of FEP software for a specific application is, by comparison, much easier, though all the tasks it carries out are similar. It must handle the communication interfaces, polling (if this is used), error control, diagnosis and so forth.

Although the FEP software may be purpose-built, the software in the main computer which deals with the FEP needs careful attention, and as far as possible it should be standard software. There is more than one way to achieve this.

The standard communication software could be used, in spite of its complexity, and particularly if the communication load is not heavy. Then the FEP is joined to the I-O channel and behaves exactly like one of the normal communications adaptors. Such an FEP is sometimes called *transparent* because it gives to the main computer a 'familiar' picture of the terminals. Actually the trick is one of mimicry rather than transparency. The advantage of such an FEP can be its cheapness compared with the standard equipment, but it has the special advantage that it can be made to accept 'foreign' terminals, not from the main computer's manufacturer, and adapt their image to the familiar one.

A second possibility is to use the standard software associated with different peripherals, such as disc drives. The FEP then protects the main computer from all the communication tasks, and leaves it with only those that are common to all peripherals. This could be described as 'impersonation'. It is a possible approach in configurations (b) and (c) of Figure 3.16. Where the connection is made, not directly to a channel but through a drum store as in configuration (a), the standard software for that drum could be used.

Only if mimicry or impersonation is not possible should the more drastic solution be employed of writing special software in the main computer. This would be justified only for a big system which has a heavy communication load.

References

1. Catt, I., 'Time loss through gating of asynchronous logic signal pulses', *IEEE Trans. Electronic Computers*, **EC-15**, 108 (Feb 1966).
2. Ahearn, G. R., Dishon, Y., and Snively, R. N., 'Design innovations of the IBM 3830 and 2835 storage control units', *IBM J. of Res. and Dev.*, **16**, No. 1, 11 (Jan. 1972).

Chapter 4

Private Data Networks

4.1 INTRODUCTION

There are many types of private communications network in operation today. They may be broadly classified into those which employ lines leased from public telecommunications authorities and those which do not. These latter include railway signalling systems using trackside cables; the monitoring and control of electricity grids and natural gas and oil pipelines using microwave links; the telemetry of environmental data for estimation of water resources using both cables and radio links; the collection of shop floor data, information distribution and many similar applications. For private networks of these kinds which do not use public lines, the type of signalling method most appropriate for each requirement may be employed, for there are no restrictions other than the physical ones set by the communications media used. But when public circuits are leased to form private networks there are certain extra restrictions which must be taken into account when designing the network. This chapter is mainly concerned with the use of leased lines, their advantages compared with the use of the switched network, and their remaining limitations when used for transmitting data. The private networks of the banks and airlines are given as illustrative examples.

4.2 THE USE OF THE PUBLIC TELEPHONE NETWORK

When public telephone circuits are leased for incorporation in private networks the switches at local telephone exchanges (central offices in the USA) are by-passed by jumper circuits which make permanent connections between the subscribers local lines and the appropriate junctions at intermediate exchanges. When long distances separate the ends of a circuit it may pass through a variety of intermediate transmission plants. Each type of transmission plant is, of course, designed to be compatible with other types, allowing them to be freely connected in tandem without affecting the speech signals being carried. Equally important for the telephone network, is that the speech signals generated by any subscriber must not upset the functioning of the network, and very careful attention is given to this point by the designers of telephone signalling system.

The transmission of data through an analogue speech circuit is achieved by converting the data to resemble speech signals for passage through the circuit, and restoring it to its original form at the far end. This poses two kinds of problem: there may be characteristics of a telephone circuit which change with time, or type of transmission path, in a way unimportant for speech, but troublesome for data traffic, while the characteristics of data traffic may differ from speech sufficiently to upset the operation of the telephone network. The latter problem is of great concern to the communications authority who provides safeguards to ensure that the well being of the network and its other users is not prejudiced by any one class of user. These safeguards are sometimes physical; for example, the modems used for transforming data to and from a speech-like signals contain filters, which prevent interference with the control signalling systems used in some parts of the telephone network (see Chapter 2, page 45). In addition, regulations may be framed, or tariffs designed, to ensure or encourage an acceptable pattern of usage of the network. These safeguards are very likely to restrict in some measure the free use of telephone circuits for purposes other than carrying speech.

The Advantages of Leased Lines

The use of leased circuits rather than switched brings a number of advantages.

1. The chance of misconnection is greatly reduced, with a potential increase in privacy.
2. The circuits are always ready for use, because delays due to dialling and connection are avoided.
3. The parameters of each circuit are much more constant, because the transmission path is always the same.
4. The impulsive noise associated with switching is greatly reduced, and noise arising from sliding contacts is eliminated.

The increase in privacy arising from the elimination of switches is an obvious benefit, but the user must not forget that failure of equipment can still cause a complete loss of data, or perhaps, worse, its misdirection; while an increase in crosstalk could result in the 'overhearing' of data by someone else, although the chance of it being intelligible to them is, in general, remote.

The removal of delays due to dialling and waiting for a connection is particularly important where computers are concerned; delays in completing transactions make it necessary to keep storage space in the computer occupied and this increases costs and limits the number of transactions that may be handled simultaneously.

With the more constant parameters of a leased circuit, better equalisation or conditioning is possible, than is the case with a switched circuit, where the route taken and the type of plant involved may vary with each call. The better equalisation of a leased line allows data to be transmitted at higher rates; typically twice that obtained through the switched network.

Further increase in effective transmission speed is obtained by the reduction in noise when switches are eliminated from the circuit; with less impulsive noise, the probability of corruption of a message is lower and the need for retransmission of messages is reduced, while a general lowering of circuit noise improves the signal to noise ratio and raises the theoretical limit on the speed of transmission.

Problems with Leased Lines

The advantages accruing from the removal of switches are offset, to some extent, by the restrictions remaining due to the sharing of common transmission paths by both leased and switched circuits. For example, if the leased circuit passes through a frequency-division multiplexed link, such as a twelve-channel carrier circuit or a coaxial cable circuit, small frequency shifts may occur. These arise from the successive modulation and demodulation processes that take place as a channel is modulated up and down the frequency spectrum. Pilot tones are used to synchronize oscillators in the modulators and demodulators, to give a frequency control which is more than adequate for speech circuits, even when several links are in tandem. However, the frequency changes remaining may make it impossible to transfer data in the form of a variable frequency as is common in some telemetry schemes. On the other hand, if the transmission path includes a time-division multiplexed digital link, precautions must be taken to avoid long strings of certain patterns in the data, otherwise the regenerators used to restore the quality of the signal as it passes through the transmission system may lose synchronism. These unfortunate patterns do not occur in the speech signals for which the system was originally designed, and it is necessary to introduce special measures which ensure any undesirable sequences in data are broken up before transmission takes place. It is clearly important for the designer of communications networks incorporating leased lines to be fully aware of their characteristics, and there have been cases where considerable difficulties have subsequently arisen, when some minor characteristic has been overlooked during the design stage of a data network.

The Cost of Private Networks

Some large organizations operate private telephone networks using transmission facilities leased from the telecommunications authorities. These networks ensure vital communications services are retained at an acceptable level regardless of the loading on the public telephone network. Though often heavily employed during the daytime, the leased lines are seldom used at night, and with the addition of modems may be adapted to carry data traffic at only marginal cost. A data network formed in this way is, clearly, not suitable for real-time data processing, but can be very attractive for batch processing or the updating of data banks outside normal working hours, because the cost of data transmission is relatively insignificant.

When the immediate and guaranteed availability of data communications facilities is required, there is no alternative to the use of circuits leased especially for the purpose. Where a network has to be geographically widespread the cost may be considerable, but will be less than that obtained by taking the switched circuit costs over a twenty-four hour period, because in the calculation of tariffs some allowance is made for savings in switching plant that is not required when circuits are permanently wired, or 'jumpered', at the exchanges.

The actual cost of a private network depends upon particular tariffs and circuit lengths, but where a leased line can be actively utilized for a sufficiently long period each day it will be more economical than a switched connection; this period is, typically, about five or six hours. However, the possibility of failure of circuits must be considered, and it will generally be necessary to provide some stand-by facilities for use in an emergency. These may take the form of an ability to change to the switched network (where dialling may continue until a usable line is found) or the provision of additional leased lines. Generally the former solution is adopted and when 'fall-back' to switched lines occurs, the signalling speed has to be reduced to suit the characteristics of the available circuits. Where extra leased circuits are employed, they will normally be used to form a non-critical part of the communications network so, again, failure will bring a reduction of overall operating capacity. The question of reliability must be carefully considered during the design of private networks, and the continuing cost of stand-by facilities must be weighed against the likely losses arising from total or partial failure of the network for various periods of time. Only then will the true cost of the network be determined.

The Reduction of Costs

In a large distributed data processing network the expenditure on leased lines may be an appreciable proportion of the overall cost, so it is not surprising that much effort has been devoted to its reduction. Most of the measures adopted improve the efficiency of utilization of the lines, but some are necessary only because the tariffs charged by the public telecommunications authorities do not properly reflect the resources actually employed.

The distribution of cost in the switched telephone network varies in different countries but, generally, the cost of local loop lines to subscribers exceeds that of switching plant, while long distance circuits are relatively cheap. The tariffs to subscribers do not generally take account of variations in length of local loops, and there is usually a fixed standing charge common to most users, while the tariff for long distance calls is much greater than for local ones, even though the trunk circuits are far more efficiently used, and so are proportionately cheaper, than local loops. In addition, there are various schemes designed to encourage the increased use of the telephone network outside peak hours, with reduced tariffs for certain times, or under certain circumstances. This is particularly true in the U.S.A. where many different options are offered to subscribers. Naturally, much ingenuity is devoted to the selection of options to minimize the overall cost of data networks, but this may be undesirable if it distorts their natural form. It is one thing to design data networks to overcome the physical limitations of speech circuits, but quite another to meet the constraints of artificially chosen tariffs which, conceivably, might be changed at some future date.

Private Exchanges

An example of how costs may be reduced in a network by exploiting tariffs is the use of private telephone exchanges by geographically polarized organizations. By siting exchanges near their main centres advantage may be taken of the tariff differential between local and trunk calls. This is illustrated in Figure 4.1 which shows how the local grouping of subscribers concentrates traffic onto leased trunk lines using them more efficiently and reducing costs.

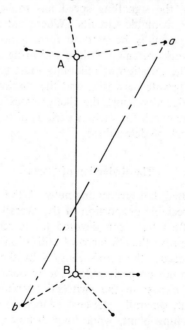

Figure 4.1. The private exchange

This is, of course, precisely what happens in the public telephone network with public exchanges. The use of private exchanges to reduce costs would not be.possible if the tariff charged by the telephone authority reflected the resources actually employed. It is worthwhile only because the organization that leases the trunk circuits is able to capitalize on the artificially high cost charged by telephone authorities for them when they form part of a long-distance public telephone call. An organization large enough to have a private telephone network with its own exchanges has a good basis for a data network. Although, of course, the carrying of data on this network may disrupt its use for telephony, in the same way that the carriage of data may disrupt the public telephone network.

Using Lines Efficiently—Network Topology

A desirable aim in designing a private network of leased lines should be to reduce costs by making more efficient use of the individual lines, so as to reduce the length or number of lines required. Clearly, this means that as

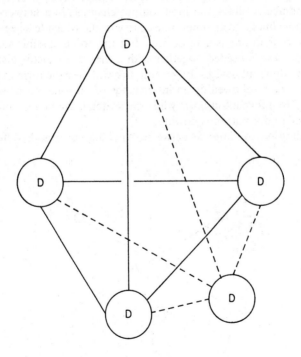

N Devices ; (N-1) channels per device
$\frac{N(N-1)}{2}$ links required

Figure 4.2.   Fully connected network

much traffic as possible must be carried by each line in the network, but it also means that the failure of any line carrying a high traffic load is likely to be more serious for the network as a whole. So, a compromise solution between efficiency, and the tolerance of the network to faults, has to be found.

The simplest method of joining together a number of distributed devices would be to use a line between each pair of devices to form the fully-connected network illustrated in Figure 4.2. Each line carries only the traffic between the two devices which it joins and each device communicates with another by selecting the appropriate output channel.

This is an impracticable solution for a large network because, with N devices, there are $N(N-1)/2$ lines, while each device has $(N-1)$ input-output channels. And, as the figure shows, the addition of an extra device needs many more lines (shown dotted) and a modification to each existing device, while the addition of duplicate lines to increase tolerance line failure would be expensive. A conceptually similar situation arises when discussing the idea of a standard interface in Chapter 6, page 180.

If the number of lines and input-output channels in a network are to be reduced, some lines and channels must carry traffic which has been generated between more than one pair of devices. For this to be possible some kind of switching process is needed, together with a means for distinguishing traffic belonging to different devices. In general, this will take the form of an instruction to the switch followed by an interchange of information between a pair of devices. No information flows while the switch is changing, and no switch changes while information is flowing.

Depending on the interval between switching commands different types

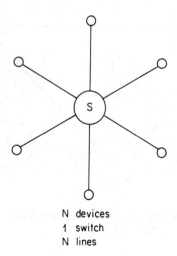

N devices
1 switch
N lines

Figure 4.3.   Star network

of network may be identified, and there are examples of networks where switching takes place between bits, characters, packets, blocks, messages, or complete calls. The latter, of course, is the way the public switched telephone network appears to its subscribers.

When switching is introduced into a network, the simplest arrangement is the star network where a single switching centre is provided to which each device is joined as illustrated by Figure 4.3. With this scheme only one line is needed for each device and each device needs only one channel, although the switch needs a channel for each device. While spare channels remain at the switch, it needs only the addition of one other line to include an extra device, but the cost of duplicating all lines to increase reliability would be quite high.

Well known examples of a single central switch are the local telephone exchange and a computer with an individual leased line to each of its remote terminals. With a telephone exchange, subscribers first communicate instructions to the switch, then communicate with each other through it. With the central computer, terminals usually communicate only with the computer — such as with a bureau service. Sometimes, however, they may exchange information through it also, in which use, of course, the computer acts as a message switch.

The reliability of a star network is critically dependent on the central switch or computer. The failure of this suspends all activity in the network, whereas an individual line failure affects only one device. Where high reliability is required, a duplication of facilities at the switch will be essential,

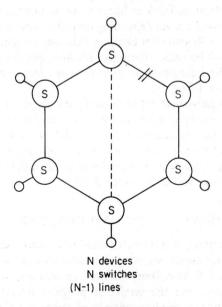

N devices
N switches
(N-1) lines

Figure 4.4. Mesh network

with some method of automatically changing over to stand-by equipment. This can add very considerably to the cost of the switch.

In contrast with the single central switch case, the association of a switch with each device yields a network of the form shown in Figure 4.4. This is usually called a reticular or mesh network. With N devices and N switches, (N−1) lines are required, but with one extra line a duplicate path becomes available between each pair of devices.

In such a network further lines may be added and each one further increases the number of alternative routes available; eventually every switch would be joined to every other switch to give a network similar in form to Figure 4.2 but with every junction point or node occupied by a switch.

The reliability of a mesh network can obviously be made as high as desired. To connect a given number of devices in a simple ring needs no more lines than to connect them as a star, and each extra line enhances the whole network to some degree. The major expense lies in the number of switches that are required, but it will be apparent that these are much simpler than the central switch of a star network. They merely have to pass through traffic for all devices except the local one, and they may all be identical. The failure of a single switch affects only one device and, if this should be an important one, it is possible to duplicate the appropriate switch relatively cheaply in comparison to the total cost of switches in the network. These topics are considered in more detail in Chapters 8 and 10 in relation to shared private networks and packet switching networks.

Any given practical network is likely to lie somewhere between the two extreme cases discussed above, depending on tasks to be done and the reliability required. There will generally be more than one switch, but less than one per device; there will be some alternative routing, but not every path will be duplicated; while there may even be sub-networks identifiable which appear to be of star or mesh form.

The choice of a particular network configuration must reflect the pattern of traffic flow between devices and this will also determine the type of switch that is required. It may be necessary for a switch to make, at any one time, a single connection between any two of a number of lines, or to simultaneously make several such connections. The nature of some of the switching functions performed in networks will be considered below.

4.3   MULTIPLEXING AND CONCENTRATION

In a practical system of terminals joined to a central computer it is very unlikely that all terminals would be simultaneously active. Indeed, the computer software will have been designed to support an expected average number of terminals, and the service it provides would be unacceptably degraded if all terminals tried to operate at once. Equally, the service will

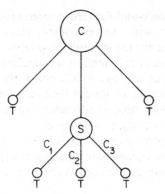

Figure 4.5. Multiplexing
and concentration

be under-utilized if only one or two terminals are in use. The average terminal activity will depend to some extent on the type of system, but typically, some 10 to 20 per cent of available terminals might be considered a normal working load for a central service. The pattern of usage of particular terminals may vary also, and on lines to some of them there may be long periods with little or no information flowing between the terminal and the computer. If the active periods on several lines never coincide it is clearly possible to switch a single line to replace them in turn. This is shown in Figure 4.5 where three of the terminals have been joined through a switch to a single line from the centre. Note the topological similarity between the main system and the sub-system connected to it; both are, of course, star networks. With such an arrangement, the single line between the switch and the computer carries the aggregate traffic of all the lines it replaces, but it may still be of the same type because the information transfer rate required never exceeds that formerly demanded from any one line. The shared line is therefore used more efficiently and the cost saving may easily exceed the cost of the switch that is required. A switch used in this manner is called a multiplexer.

It may not be possible always to ensure that only one input line to a multiplexer is active at any one time, and if no restriction is to be placed on the behaviour of terminals connected to it, there will be a need to provide an outgoing line from the multiplexer having a capacity greater than that of any input line. If the capacity of the output line exceeds the sum of the capacities of all the input lines, the switch still performs the function of a multiplexer.

Obviously, the average capacity of the output line from a switch must at least equal the total average input rate otherwise information has to accumulate at the switch, or be lost. However, there is no reason why the potential capacity of the input lines should not exceed that of the output line, and in this case the switch is known as a concentrator. One method of concentration, called store-and-forward concentration, is to provide some storage capacity at the switch to temporarily store the excess information which accumulates whenever the instantaneous input information rate exceeds the output rate: the excess information accumulating is transferred to the computer when the input rate again falls below the capacity of the output line (see Chapter 6 on the use of storage with data links page 187). The other method of concentration, hold-and-forward concentration, requires some control of the input line activity, to hold up terminals so that the instantaneous input rate to the concentrator cannot exceed the output rate. This control is usually done by a process called polling (see page 108). Sometimes a combination of storage and polling may be used to effect the concentration of information onto a single line.

Another application of multiplexers is illustrated in Figure 4.6. This shows how a multiplexer at each end of a link may be used to derive a number of low speed channels from a single high-speed channel. An example is the Dataplex service offered by the British Post Office. This uses the frequency division multiplexing method (see Chapter 2, page 21) to derive 12 separate 110 bit/s channels from a single telephone channel. Sometimes time-division multiplexing is used to achieve a similar result as is described in Chapter 7, page 237.

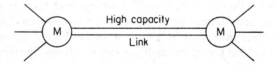

Figure 4.6.   Another   use   for   multiplexing

Multipoint Circuits

An important method of increasing the efficiency with which lines are used is to connect them together to form a multipoint or multidrop circuit. This connects a number of geographically separated devices by a single circuit that

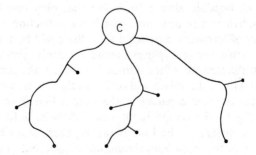

Figure 4.7.   Multipoint lines with terminals

passes from device to device. A number of multipoint circuits may be joined to a central computer as shown in Figure 4.7. In the U.S.A. a multipoint circuit is sometimes called a way-wire.

A multipoint circuit scheme is only possible when the times of use of each terminal can be staggered, and the total average rate of data transmission does not exceed the capacity of the circuit. However, there are many applications where these criteria are satisfied. In addition to the saving in line costs, the multipoint circuit needs only one modem for each terminal and one for the computer, instead of two for each connection when point-to-point circuits are used.

It is clear that two terminals on a multipoint circuit may not simultaneously converse with the computer, so it is customary for the computer to interrogate each terminal in turn, holding a short dialogue where necessary before passing on to the next terminal. The intermittent nature of the dialogue between a terminal and the computer may be disguised from the user by using buffer storage at each terminal. The buffer store exchanges data with the computer

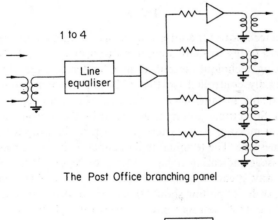

The Post Office branching panel

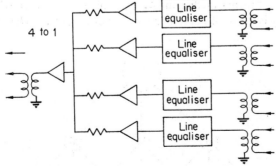

Figure 4.8. Multipoint circuit connections

at the maximum speed permitted by the modems and intermediate circuit, but it communicates with the terminal itself at the speed set by the user. If the circuit speed is high enough, the user is unaware of the intermittent nature of the data flow between the terminal and the computer. The process of interrogating terminals from the computer is known as polling and is described later.

The advantage of multipoint circuits is offset in practice by a reduced reliability and increased difficulty of maintenance compared with schemes which use point-to-point circuits. This arises because one modem failure may render the whole circuit unusable, while a fault is often much more difficult to locate. Nevertheless, multipoint schemes have been used very successfully, particularily in British bank networks, where adequate provision can be made to overcome the effect of line or modem failure, by overlapping the areas served by different lines. A typical bank network is described on page 122.

The method by which several modems may be joined to a common line is shown in Figure 4.8.

Polling

Polling is a technique for controlling the use of lines by an agreed protocol between devices trying to share a common transmission path. It is similar to the handshaking technique described in Chapter 6, page 178 because the devices are rigidly controlled (so that only one of them sends information along a line at any instant) by an exchange of control signals or messages between them. Sometimes polling is governed by the central computer which sends a control message to each terminal in turn, inviting it to transmit an information message. The terminal replies either with such a message, or with a control message indicating it has nothing to report. When the polling is done in this way great flexibility is obtained, because the computer may reorganize the order of polling should this become necessary, but rather a high proportion of control messages have to pass through the network and this tends to make it rather inefficient. An example of a network where polling is done centrally is the multipoint arrangement of Figure 4.7. Here it is óbviously

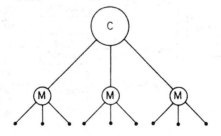

Figure 4.9. Multiplexers with terminals

vital to control the activity of the terminals so that only one can send information at a time.

Another technique of polling possible when multiplexers are used, is to allow each remote multiplexer to poll the terminals connected to it. This is more efficient than polling from the central computer because each multiplexer is operating in parallel, and there are fewer control messages involving the computer itself. In the arrangement shown in Figure 4.9 the computer polls the multiplexers, and these connect the computer to the terminal that happens to be next on their own local polling list. Although this method

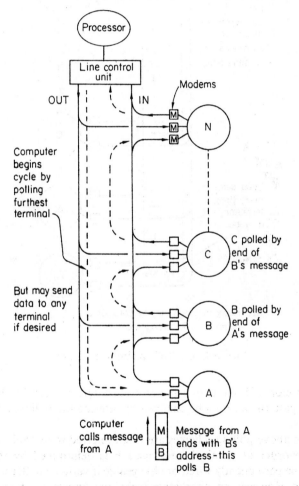

N.B: Reply message may be data or a
negative acknowledgement.

Figure 4.10.   Hub polling scheme

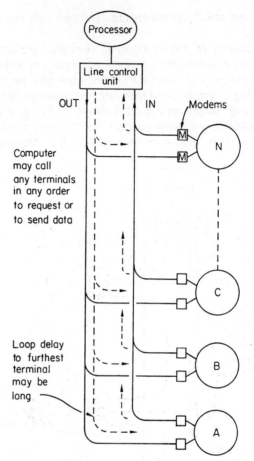

NB.: Reply message may be data or a
negative acknowledgement

Figure 4.11.   Roll call polling scheme

of polling is more efficient than using central control, it is less flexible because
the polling pattern can only be changed by altering the polling tables in the
multiplexers.

Both the above polling schemes are often referred to as 'roll-call' polling
because the order of terminal interrogation is determined by stored lists,
which may be permanently wired or changeable if variable patterns of polling
are required. However, an alternative technique known as 'hub go-ahead'
or more simply 'hub-polling' is used on some multipoint circuits. With
hub-polling, the computer invites the first terminal to send a message, if none
is ready the first terminal passes the request to the second terminal and so on.

This is particularly efficient when terminals are generally inactive and lines are very long. Whenever a terminal replies with an information message the computer deals with it, and then resumes the polling sequence by inviting the next terminal to proceed. In this way an active terminal near the beginning of the circuit is prevented from monopolizing the attention of the computer. This type of polling is commonly used in telemetry systems, for example, where a long circuit is used to collect data from measuring instruments distributed along the length of a pipeline.

The disadvantage of hub-polling compared with roll-call polling is the additional modem and equipment required to give the necessary extra intelligence at each terminal; the two schemes are contrasted in Figures 4.10 and 4.11.

Contention

An entirely different technique for controlling the flow of information in a network is that of allowing each device to indicate when it is ready to transmit information, rather than waiting to be polled and asked if it is ready.

This is not easily possible with the multipoint configuration because the 'ready' signals would interfere with each other, but with a star arrangement the use of contention for flow control can have important benefits. In the simple star configuration of a central computer having an individual line to each terminal, each active terminal may send a signal to the central computer to indicate readiness to communicate a message. This signal may be arranged to cause a program interrupt and in this way all terminals equally contend for the attention of the computer. The situation is a little more complex when multiplexers are employed, because the terminals have to contend for the attention of the multiplexers, which in turn have to send a signal to attract the attention of the computer.

A particular terminal may experience some delay before it receives the computers attention. This delay may well be less than with the polling method, because there is no need for the network to carry control messages to enquire if inactive terminals have information messages for the computer. However, the polling control messages enable the computer to keep track of the state of the network through the polling tables; with contention, messages may arrive from terminals in any order, and for this reason they must carry an address indicating the point at which they originate. These addresses detract from the efficiency of the network.

The choice between the use of polling and contention depends on the network configuration, on the relative activity of terminals, and on the proportion of time individual terminals are active. Indeed, some designs of network may include both polling and contention where each technique happens to be more appropriate.

The Use of Small Processors

In the network configurations discussed in previous sections the central computers have been shown with a number of input-output channels and it has been assumed that programs in the computer would be used to carry out polling, sort messages from different terminals and so on. Many of the tasks performed in handling communications circuits are relatively simple, but highly repetitive, and can make considerable demands on the time of the computer. It often proves more economic to perform these functions by a small separate computer called a front end processor (FEP). The main advantages of this approach are:

1. The cost of hardware to attach lines is often less with a small computer, possibly because different constructional methods are used.
2. The processing load removed from the main computer will considerably increase the power available for computational purposes.
3. It becomes possible to separate the complete system cleanly into two parts: the main processor and the communications network. This gives increased flexibility and may allow one part to be enhanced or replaced without affecting the other.

The introduction of small computers in addition to the front end processor

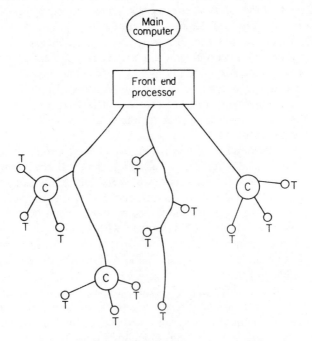

Figure 4.12. Multipoint lines with terminals and concentrators

is well worth consideration, particularly in a big private network where considerable benefit may be gained from the use of small computers distributed at suitable points throughout the network. For example, by using small processors as the concentrators, the dialogue between these and the front end processor may be more complex. This can improve the efficiency of the network by permitting more sophisticated line control procedures, which may also facilitate recovery from failure situations. Again, some of the functions previously performed by the main computer, or the FEP, may be delegated to the concentrator giving a more immediate response to the terminal. The polling of local lines, or resolution of contending terminals, the checking and formatting of messages, the correction of errors, guidance to operators and similar tasks, are typical of those conveniently performed by a concentrator with a reasonable degree of processing power. The concentrator may be connected by individual lines to the front end processor; by multipoint lines, or by a mixture of both as shown in Figure 4.12.

Multiple Computer Centres

Very large organizations may, with advantage, employ more than one data processing centre, each of which may have its own network of terminal devices serving a group of subscribers. Sometimes the centres perform different functions; perhaps one may deal with clerical tasks like pay roll and stock control, while another is used for scientific computation or to provide a bureau service. There will be data banks associated with the centres, and there may be good reason to exchange information between them. This leads to the idea of connecting the centres by a network.

Various configurations are possible with a large network of this kind; they may be generally similar to those already discussed for networks of terminals connected to a single processor, when the overall system will simply comprise two or more such networks linked as is shown in Figure 4.13. Here three identical centres are joined.

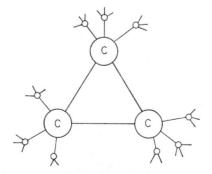

Figure 4.13. Multiple computer network

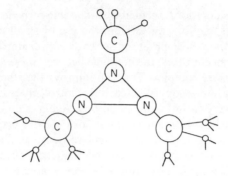

Figure 4.14.   Use of communications
network

The main processor centres may alternatively be joined to a high-level or trunk network using separate processors as switching points as in Figure 4.14. A third possibility (shown in Figure 4.15) is to provide each main processor with a front end processor which handles the local terminals and the trunk links to other centres. This latter arrangement has the advantage that terminals may still communicate with remote centres when the local main processor is out of action. On the other hand, if one of the front end processors fails, its terminals get no service at all. The arguments concerning the choice of a configuration of interconnected centres are similar in principle to those already considered for the connection of devices in general, and need not be repeated here.

The economic factors in chosing the number of centres in a private network are very complex. The capital cost of each centre is usually easy to estimate and will include the buildings themselves, with special services like air conditioning, the main computers and their backing stores, any peripheral processors or special devices such as microfilm printers, and the distributed communications network itself.

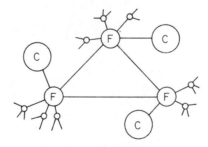

Figure 4.15.   Use of front end processors

The continuing cost of operation is less easy to estimate for it includes site rental, staff salaries, operating and maintenance costs of equipment, rental of lines, and the loss which would be incurred when part or, indeed, the whole of a centre or its network happened to be out of action. This last cost has to be related to the extra capital equipment and other items necessary to provide enough redundancy to ensure a minimum acceptable service.

The Use of Data Banks

One other factor of importance is the number and location of data banks. Some organizations need a single common data bank covering all their activities. This allows all operations to be carried out using identical data, and all updating of information is done centrally. A basic problem with any data bank is that of how to update an item of information while it is being frequently interrogated. This problem is easier to cope with when there is one common data bank. However, if all of the information concerning a large organization has to flow into and out of one bank there is likely to be severe congestion during periods of maximum activity, and there will also be a physical security risk.

It is easy for an organization to change its method of working when computers are introduced and, without the management's full appreciation of the danger, to gradually become so dependent on data stored in a central bank that its loss would mean the collapse of the organization. For this reason alone it is worth considering the use of more than one data bank so that vital information may be duplicated. This will be more costly than a unified system because the unit cost of storage falls with an increase in the amount of information stored, and the problem of updating becomes more difficult. However, once it has been decided to have more than one data bank, it is worth considering if banks should be sited near the point where information most naturally accumulates, or is interrogated.

The updating problem with multiple banks is essentially one of exchanging messages between the data banks; so the time taken to do this represents the extent to which data at a particular bank will be out-of-date. The type of network employed to link the data banks will clearly affect this time, and if it is possible to determine the cost of having relatively out-of-date information (and this must cost something) a case may be made for a better, and faster, communications network than might otherwise seem to be necessary.

It is likely that data banks would be associated with the computing centres of an organization, and the choice of the number of centres, the processing power and information storage capacity at each centre, the type of network joining together the centres, and the type of network connecting terminals to each centre will depend on what the organization has to do. The choices made by particular organizations are discussed in the following sections.

4.4 BANKING SYSTEMS

Every day millions of business transactions take place in the world and the majority of these involve the transfer of financial information in one form or another. It is not surprising therefore that computers are being used by banks everywhere for a variety of purposes, and that data transmission is playing an increasingly vital part in their daily business. In most countries there are a large number of banks with relatively few branches, but in Britain there are now four major banking groups: Barclays, National Westminster, Midland, and Lloyds. The first two each have over 3,500 branches, the third over 2,500, while Lloyds has over 2,000. The total of more than 12,000 represents about 90% of all British branch banks.[1]

The general pattern of activity in banking falls into four main areas: the

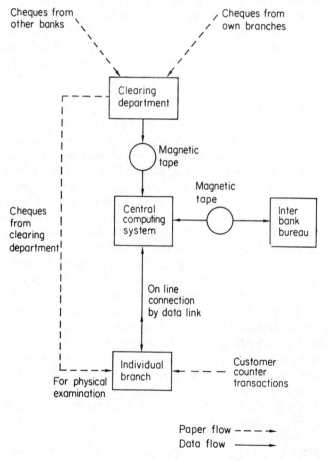

Figure 4.16. Banking activities

clearing operation; the Interbank Computer Bureau (now the Bankers Automated Clearing Services Ltd.); the central accounting services; and the branch functions, as shown in Figure 4.16.

The clearing operation is necessary to redistribute balances between the branches of each bank and between the banks themselves, as a result of cheques paid in each day. The clearing department of a bank receives all the cheques drawn on current accounts held by its own customers. The amounts have to be checked and the cheques sorted so they can be sent to the branch on which they are drawn. Also, the information printed on them in magnetic ink characters is read and is transferred to magnetic tapes for later input into the central accounting system.

The Interbank Computer Bureau handles other transactions between banks involving the movement of funds between them, such as standing orders which call for regular transfers from an account in one bank to an account in another. These are handled by exchanging magnetic tapes, and in this area the banks—through force of circumstances—played a major role in getting agreements on standards for format of blocks etc. It is quite possible that —again through a need to reach agreement so that business may be done— the banks will set standards for exchange of information through data networks also. Here, the recently formed Inter-Banks Research Organization (IBRO) is likely to be an important factor.

The data networks and central computer systems of the banks are generally intended to handle the accounting work of all their branches, and the change to decimalization on February 15th 1971 was a considerable spur to the early development of these centralized accounting systems. Now they are operational a number of new services to customers may well begin to appear.

Between them the big groups have spent some £150 m. on computers, and computer networks and there is, no doubt, still a great number of possibilities open to them to expand their use of computer techniques in the next few years. Because almost every type of transaction eventually involves a transfer of funds, the form of the data networks used by the banks may well set a pattern for networks intended primarily for other purposes, and it is worth examining in some detail the structure of a typical bank network. Also, because the structure of such a complex thing as a large network reflects the nature and operation of the organization it serves, it will be fruitful to look at the historical background that governed the evolution of the present network of one particular bank—Lloyds.

Lloyds Bank—Background

The Pall Mall branch of Lloyds is a large one situated in Central London; it handles many of the pay accounts for the Armed Services. By considerable foresight, punched card equipment was installed just prior to the 1939-1945 World War, so the branch had early experience in mechanization. When this type of equipment came to be replaced towards the end of the 1950s, a careful analysis was made of the branch's operations to determine just what kind of system was needed. The branch comprised five sections—almost branches in themselves—and the overall branch account balancing operation often continued well into the evening. A random access central accounting system with enquiry terminals in every section was planned around an IBM 305 RAMAC system. (This was in 1960 when magnetic tape schemes were generally in vogue.) Accounting would be progressive and no paperwork would be required with on-line terminals, as balances would be available on request. Eventually, when the Pall Mall system came into operation, it met all expectations, but was now based on two IBM 1401s which had meanwhile superseded the 305, and had an excess capacity for about 20,000 more accounts than were held at Pall Mall.

The successfull demonstration of computer accounting in one branch led to a decision to extend the system to take over the accounts at five nearby branches in London's West End. No basic system changes were made and input information was sent from branches and punched on cards at Pall Mall. Enquiry stations could not be used remotely (there were no data links then) so a print-out of account balances had to be made during each night and delivered to branches ready for use the next day. To do this, the file of accounts had to be accessed twice, and an embarrassing rush of information for punching tended to arrive at the end of each afternoon. This kept staff working late, and delayed the preparation of account balances.

At about this stage, IBM introduced the 1050 teleprocessing terminal capable of transmitting paper tape at 135 bit/s and fitted with a receiving printer. Lloyds realized that if the branch accounting centre could be joined by data links to remote branches provided with the 1050 it would be possible both to enlarge the scope of their system and to reduce the last minute rush of input information. This would be accomplished by arranging for the branches to prepare punched tapes of batches of entries to be periodically transmitted to the centre, and acknowledged by the return, for local print-out of the batch responses and associated rejections. This concept of paper tape input was so successfull that punching equipment was also installed in branches near the centre so that ready punched tapes could be physically delivered for direct input to the computer. In this way the load on the central preparation section was much reduced.

Having proved the feasibility of this scheme, Lloyds decided in 1964 to enlarge their computing facilities. Pall Mall became the West End Centre and a new City Centrè was planned. Both were to be equipped with IBM 1410s, again with random access disc stores, giving a capacity of 250,000 accounts at each centre. This increased capacity made it possible to handle much more input information than was produced by branches near London and it became necessary to extend the data collection facilities in order fully to load the centres.

By installing the 1050 at several key branches such as Cambridge, Portsmouth and Southampton, where input information could be gathered from groups of nearby branches, it became possible to organize the collection of sufficient extra input information. Small branches could deliver or telephone their entries to branches with tape equipment; these, in turn, could punch and deliver tape to the nearest branch having a transmitting terminal. In principle, all input data could now be collected but the problem of the output of results still remained. The totals of batches of entries could be transmitted back to each 1050 for comparison with locally produced totals, so that incorrectly received tapes could be retransmitted, but the complete print-out of the balances of customer accounts for each branch was not feasible, and these had to be available by 9.0 a.m. the next day. Central printing had to continue, with delivery to branches during the night. However, by the carefully coordinated use of rail and van about 60% of branches could be served.

When IBM introduced System 360 in 1966, Lloyds decided to replace their existing computers. The considerable upheaval involved gave them the welcome opportunity to reappraise their continuous on-line accounting technique, whereby files were updated as transactions occurred. As explained earlier, this method of current account processing had originally been devised for use only within the Pall Mall branch but expediency had subsequently led to its extension to remote branch accounting. However, the method had several disadvantages when used in this context, particularly when a rapid feedback of information to branches was introduced. The overall work of a branch must balance at the close of business each day, but at times during the day the various debit and credit entries arising obviously cause the transient balances at individual accounts to fluctuate, sometimes significantly. This can lead to needless concern and even unwarranted activity to try and find non-existent errors or to correct positions which could well rectify themselves later in the day. Also the accounts files at the centres had to be accessed continually for updating, during the day, and again for print-out of updated accounts after close of business, ready for delivery by the morning. This was more tiresome with big files. Accordingly it was decided to keep, instead, an accumulation of the entries arising during the day, and to defer updating and the preparation and printing out of account records until daily close of business.

The introduction of System 360 was a watershed in the development of the Bank's current accounting sytem, and continued extension of the network was planned, using the new 3940 teleprocessing terminals, which used 600 baud lines to increase the speed of data input and print out. A Birmingham centre was opened with two 360/40s and the 1410s at the City centre were replaced by three 360/40s. Each machine could handle about 250,000 current accounts, so the gross processing capability was now some 1·25 million such accounts, or about half the total number held by Lloyds. By 1967 all these accounts were on the computers but input was still by tapes and output by physical delivery. This was a severe problem with the more remote branches and, with Decimalization looming nearer, a review of operations was undertaken in the light of the remote printing terminals that had just become available.

There were two approaches to remote printing to choose between. The first was the Burroughs TC500 system.[2] This was a terminal designed specially for banking, capable of handling general calculations locally, and (by connection to multipoint lines) able to communicate directly with a data processing centre. The second was the IBM 3980 system, comprising a terminal, again designed specifically for banking, used with a concentrator incorporating software for handling local computations. A number of the concentrators could be connected to multipoint lines to the main centres. After some calculations of the number of terminals, multipoint lines and modems necessary, and a consideration of line maintenance problems, Lloyds decided on the IBM approach.

With the introduction of the 3980 system, the computing power at the Centres was further increased. The 360/40 computers at the City Centre were replaced by 360/65s—two being used to give reliability of service. But the subsequent replacement of the two model 360/40s at the Birmingham centre by twin 360/65s gave an overall capacity markedly in excess of that needed to handle the whole of Lloyds' current accounts, and it became possible to consider taking on other types of processing tasks also.

Meanwhile Decimalization day had arrived and, as planned, Lloyds had every customer's current account on the central files. Input was in four forms: physical delivery direct to centres; paper tape from earlier 3940 terminals; paper tape physically delivered to the nearest network access point; and direct entry from the 3980 network terminals. But regardless of the type of input the centre treated it as coming from on-line terminals, using a standard record format for storing the data on the disc files. A mixture of methods was used for output, too. Branches near the centres still received physical delivery of print-outs; but print-outs for remote areas were done first thing every morning on the 3982 printing terminals, while for the rest of the day these were used for entry and enquiry work.

The advent on on-line keyboard terminals made possible a new method of checking transmission errors. Previously, paper tapes with batches of entries and their totals were transmitted. (In fact, the tape was sent backwards so the total—needed for account balancing—arrived first.) The immediate return of the total gave a check to the sender that it had been correctly received. In contrast, with the keyboard entry of batches, the local 3981 concentrator checks formats and acknowledges receipt (at its store) of batches, which are numbered by the branch however it likes, provided numbers do not repeat during any one day. At any time, an operator may call for a list of batches that have reached the centre, and may make any desired amendments.

The success of the 3980 system has encouraged a progressive changeover

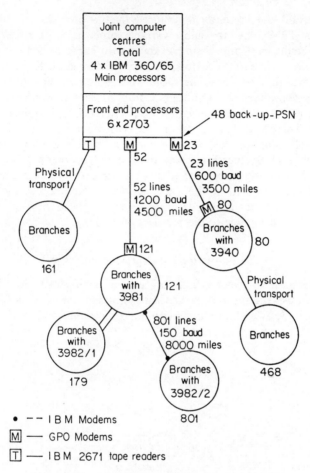

Figure 4.17. Lloyds Bank teleprocessing network
October 1971

of earlier equipment, and the state of the Bank's network in October 1971 is illustrated by Figure 4.17.

At the present time, Lloyds prepare each day for every branch a print-out showing the state of each of its accounts as at the close of business the previous day. In addition, any branch with a terminal (those without one may telephone a branch that has) may request details of the individual underlying transactions from the date of the last printed ledger sheet available to them, up to the previous day's close of business.

The service given to customers is clearly first-rate because of the modern data processing methods that have been adopted by Lloyds bank, and the availability of their widespread data network opens up many possibilities.

An important one, recently announced, is the provision of on-line cash dispensers, IBM 2984, to enable variable sums to be obtained by using a personal credit card and a simple keyboard. These dispensers in selected branches are on-line to the centres and may check credit before releasing cash. Not only will they help customers, but will relieve counter staff of one of the more common duties. Another application based on twin IBM 360/40s is the share registration service valuable to a smaller, but important, class of customer. There is also an Executor and Trustee service, while the Bank also does payroll computations, both for itself and as a service to others.

It is very clear, therefore, that there could be many other interesting developments taking place in the banking world in the next few years, not least of these may well be the introduction into the banks, themselves, of improved management methods based on the application of modern operational analysis technique to the business of banking.

The Lloyds Bank Teleprocessing Network

The centralized branch accounting system now operated by Lloyds Bank is based on two centres: one in the City of London, the other in Birmingham. Each centre deals with a roughly similar processing load using twin IBM

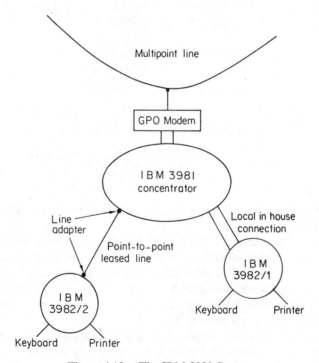

Figure 4.18.   The IBM 3980 System

360/65 computers, which support a data handling network allowing communication with all branches. The networks employ various means of communication: some physical transportation of data occurs; some data is punched on paper tape and transmitted over data links; there is some direct input and output of information using the IBM 3980 system. The present state of the networks is summarized by Figure 4.17 but they are evolving towards a more complete use of on-line terminals as more 3980 equipment is introduced and the earlier methods of handling data are superseded.

The IBM 3980 system is shown in Figure 4.18. It comprises the 3981 concentrator, and the 3982 keyboard-printer terminal. The 3981 is based on a small computer—the IBM 1130—which contains enough core storage to hold programs to handle small routine computations, to look after transmission line control procedures, and to provide buffers necessary for data storage during the polling of terminals. The terminals contain no storage, and two versions are available. The 3982-1 which is used locally to the concentrator, and the 3982-2 which contains line adaptors—private modems—enabling it to be used over leased lines; in other respects the two versions are identical.

A number of concentrators may be connected by Post Office modems to a multipoint line, and groups of such lines are handled at each centre by three 2703 transmission control units. These exchange messages of up to 256 bytes with the concentrators to govern the polling of terminals and to carry out other basic line and network control functions. Depending on the storage provided, each 3981 concentrator may handle a number of local and remote terminals. With the assistance of the Post Office, the physical configuration of the network has been chosen, where possible, to enhance reliability by connecting nearby branches to concentrators on different lines. In an emergency due to equipment or line failure, work could be transported between these branches to maintain a basic level of service.

In Lloyds' network, there may be up to four concentrators per line, and there is at present a maximum of ten terminals per concentrator. A typical branch will make 400 entries every day in batches of 30 entries at a time; each entry comprising between 7 and 49 characters as shown in Figure 4.19. Each branch will, therefore, produce about 10,000 characters yielding up to about 0·5 million characters on a multipoint line. These are transferred mainly between 11·00 and 12·00, and between 14·00 and 15·30. Overlaid upon traffic due to entries, there is that due to branch enquiries; these may originate from within the branch, or at the request of a customer, and can happen at any time—though a peak in such traffic seems to occur, perhaps understandably, at around 11·00.

All network terminals are polled by the 2703 transmission control units, so the frequency of interrogation of each terminal depends upon the total activity on the particular multipoint line to which it is connected. Each batch comprises about 750 characters, and at a maximum keying rate of 5 per second

```
                    INPUT MESSAGES FROM A 3982 KEYBOARD


KEY  -  ( FIELD TYPE : LENGTH IN BYTES )
TOT - TOTAL KEY ; SEL - SELECTIVE TRANSMIT KEY ; ENQ - ENQUIRY KEY
EOE - END OF ENTRY KEY

1)  JOB HEADER       1+7+1 BYTES

    ( SEL )( INDICATOR : 1 )( BRANCH : 4 )( SPACE )( JOB : 1 )( EOE ).

2)  BATCH HEADER    2+7+1 BYTES

    ( TOT )( EOE )( INDICATOR : 1 )( BATCH : 4 )( SPACE )( CREDIT,

    or DEBIT : 1 )( EOE ).

3)  CREDIT ENTRY    UP TO 48+1 BYTES

    ( CREDIT : 1 )( ACCOUNT NUMBER : 3--7 )( SPACE )( DESCRIPTION : 0--7 )

    ( AUTHORISATION : 1 )( SPACE )( AMOUNT : 0--11 )( SPACE )

    ( CLEARED : 0--8 )( SPACE )( ONE DAY UNCLEARED : 0--8 )( EOE ).

4)  DEBIT ENTRY     UP TO 30+1 BYTES

    ( DEBIT : 1 )( ACCOUNT NUMBER : 3--7 )( SPACE )( DESCRIPTION : 0--7 )

    ( AUTOMATIC or NOTICE GIVEN : 0--2 )( SPACE )( AMOUNT : 0--11 )( EOE ).

5)  ENQUIRIES       1+14+1 BYTES

    ( ENQ )( BRANCH : 4 )( SPACE )( ACCOUNT NUMBER : 3--7 )( SPACE )

    ( TYPE OF PRINT-OUT : 1 )( EOE ).
```

Figure 4.19.   Input messages from a 3982 keyboard

would take about 3 minutes to enter. To read this out at 1200 baud, i.e 120 characters per second, takes about 6 seconds. The ratio of the time to key in data, to the read-out time is about 30:1; so if all terminals were simultaneously in use only 30 could share a single port into the 2703. However, the diversity in terminal usage means that they are never all active at once, and the use for four concentrators with up to ten terminals each is quite acceptable.

Each of the active local lines into a 3981 concentrator is assigned a short buffer of about 50 characters, sufficient to hold an entry; when full the contents of these short buffers are transferred to a single buffer with a capacity of 256 characters. Whenever this buffer is either full, or contains a message with a priority flag, a positive acknowledgment is returned by the 3981 when it is next polled by the 2703 line controller. The average block length depends on the frequency of messages with priority flags, and is, typically, about 116 characters. Each block contains messages from all the terminals that have been active since the previous block was delivered. The actual frequency of polling of each concentrator depends on the number per line, and the number and activity of the terminals associated with each concentrator.

A minor problem arises with the introduction of the IBM 2984 automatic cash dispenser, as it is essential to poll this device at least once every 20 seconds. It is necessary, therefore, to use a priority flag for their messages and this results in a reduction in the previous average message length of about 116 characters. It is anticipated that the cash dispenser polling interval will be not more than 12 seconds. This more frequent polling and the need to handle the cash dispensers on a higher priority requires changes to be made to the software in the central computers. These not only have to cope with a larger number of shorter messages, but also have to scan the input messages to select those originating from dispensers for immediate attention.

The introduction of the cash dispenser has also meant some changes in the way the keyboard terminals communicate with the concentrators. The dispensers must have priority over the entry keyboard, because they serve customers directly. Two dispensers may be associated with one 3982 terminal and one of the dispensers is fitted with three buffers. These store, temporarily, the outputs from both dispensers and the keyboard, while waiting for the polling signal from the 2703 at the centre.

One of the most vital areas in the design of any real-time system is the mechanism for recovery after a failure. Obviously, the service must be restored as rapidly as possible, without loss or duplication of information if this can be managed. At the centres, in Lloyds' network, all the accounting input is constructed into the format required for the account posting sequence of operations and is written on to two separate disc files. If an error is detected or a data network failure occurs a reconstruction program is used to read these files and create two new files which contain all the batches of accounting entries wholly and correctly received up to the time the error occurred. A separate index is maintained to record the commencement and completion of each batch of accounting input originated by each terminal. So, in the event of the reconstruction program being run, the branch can make a terminal enquiry to obtain a list of those batches that have been correctly received by the central system. The branch may then cancel and re-enter information that has not been processed correctly. All the discs finally produced at the end of the day are sorted and merged with other sources of data to enable the account posting sequence of operations to commence.

4.5   AIRLINE NETWORKS

One of the first commercial applications of remote access computing was in the automation of airline reservation system. This is not surprising because the requirements for such systems are, basically, a centralized file of transient information about flights, seats and people, and a method of accessing and manipulating the file simultaneously from many geographically separate places.[3] Even the first examples of remote access real-time computer systems seemed to offer, very readily, these features; so most airlines embarked upon real-time seat reservation schemes at an early stage. Their systems varied widely in scope, function and complexity and some have been more successful and have cost less than others. To a large extent this reflects the general ignorance of the problems of real-time computing when these schemes where conceived; but equally, considered as 'guinea-pigs', the airline systems have both highlighted and helped to solve many of the problems. The larger airlines have now moved on to include other aspects of their operations within their computer systems.

The seat reservation problem is simply that of controlling the sale of seats on each flight to maximize the utilization of the aircraft while avoiding overbooking and annoyance to passengers. This must be done in the light of the parallel selling of tickets by many agencies, and possible subsequent changes of plans by passengers. In such a situation the rapid feedback of information is obviously advantageous and explains the attractivness of the real-time system.

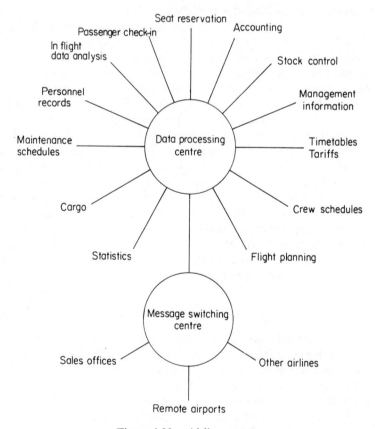

Figure 4.20. Airline systems

By extending the system to cover the check-in of passengers at the airport, their arrival may be confirmed against the reservation lists. This allows any last-minute changes to be taken into account, and any seats not taken up may be sold to anyone on a stand-by waiting list. This is important because a typical aircraft has between 100 and 200 seats, so a single seat on a partly-filled plane may represent a few percent of the income for that flight.

A further extension of the real-time system to the calculation of loading factors for each aircraft brings another advantage: the actual weights of checked-in baggage and estimated weights of passengers can be used to determine how much cargo may be carried and, if cargo reservation also forms part of the computer system, each flight load may be optimized just before take-off for maximum profitability.

Not every sales office will be connected to the reservation system by on-line terminals and many bookings have to be made by telephone or telegram Also, quite often, journeys involve a series of flights on services operated by different airlines, so that several reservation systems may have to be interrogated by the ticket issuing authority to determine the availability of seats. For these reasons, message switching is an important feature of the airlines operations, some having their own private communications networks, others subscribing to networks shared with other airlines.

The types of operation that may be performed by an airline system are illustrated by Figure 4.20. This shows that, apart from the tasks that merit the use of a real-time system, there are other applications for computer systems that are of a less urgent nature. These include accounting and the collection of statistics, the production of maintenance schedules and the control of stocks of spares, the calculation of crew schedules, and the determination of new timetables and tariff structures as well as handling the more usual types of management and company control information common to any large organization.

The development of computer systems to meet this wide variety of requirements has been done in various ways by different airlines and to a large extent their systems have evolved as new types of terminals and computers have become available. The British European Airways BEACON network is a typical airline system, and is particularly interesting because it is beginning to make use of the SITA network (see Chapter 8) for the extension of its facilities further into Europe.

The BEA BEACON Network

The BEA automatic seat reservation system was based originally on two UNIVAC 490 computers located at the West London air terminal. This project has had several stages of development. Operation of the seat reservation system in BEA's London sales office began in 1965 with the introduction at the West London site of the UNIVAC uniset terminal, which is based on a special keyset and an adapted Teletype 35 page printer adapted specially for airline use. Some 250 of these terminals have been installed in London and are supported by nine UNIVAC 49 buffer processors. These have 8K stores with words of seven bits and can concentrate up to 32 Unisets into the central computers.[4]

By 1967, the seat reservation system was being extended to other offices in the United Kingdom and in 1968 Paris, Amsterdam and Dublin were also joined to the West London computer centre. Leased lines operated at 1200 baud were used, with the type 49 buffer processors at each office, and where possible the communication network was chosen with duplicated connections to ensure a reliable service. The form of the network is shown in Figure 4.21. Each of the U.K. offices (with the exception of the Glasgow

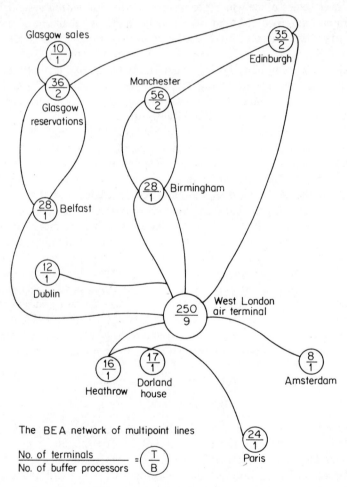

Figure 4.21.   BEA Reservation Office network

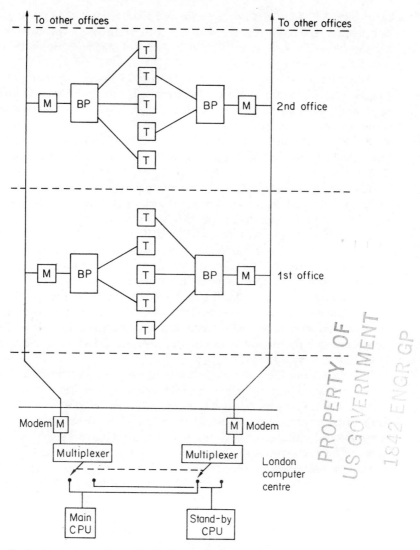

T-Terminal; M-Modem; BP- Buffer processor

Figure 4.22.   Duplicated connections in the BEACON network

sales office) has more than one link with the London Centre. In the larger offices with two buffer processors one is joined to each line, and the terminals are arranged so that alternate ones are connected to a different processor as shown in Figure 4.22.

A decision to enlarge the scope of the BEACON network of BEA was made in 1967 when three new projects were planned: passenger acceptance and load control PALC; cargo acceptance and load control CALC; and flight information and control of operations FICO. In 1968 the two original Univac 490 processors were replaced by two 494 machines, and a third was added the following year.

The passenger acceptance and load control system operates at West London Air Terminal and Heathrow Airport. It was the first to use cathode-ray tube displays because it was essential to have a small quiet instrument that would fit into the check-in desks. The screen size of these displays made by Bunker Ramo is $3\frac{1}{2}$ inches square, sufficient for only four lines of 16 characters, but quite adequate for the task of passenger acceptance. As a back-up for the PALC system there are three large UNIVAC uniscope 300 self-contained displays on direct lines to the central computers. These displays store and present the next 30 flights due out of the airport up to about 5 hours ahead, and if the central computers goes out of action, or the lines fail, the stored information is frozen and used as the basis for a manual fall-back scheme.

The cargo acceptance and load control system serves exclusively the BEA cargo centre at Heathrow and also employs cathode-ray tube terminals. But a much larger screen size is required to present, efficiently, the necessary information and Ferranti displays are used, together with Ferranti Argus 400 processors as display controllers and Olivetti printers operating at 40 characters per second. The larger screens require an exchange of fairly long messages with the remote computing centre and 4800 bit/s lines are used to give an acceptably rapid response.

For the flight information and control of operations system, which serves BEA's operations control centre an even bigger screen size is required and Cossor 425 2000-character displays were chosen together with the ICL Termiprinter for hard copy output. With 4,800 bits/s lines nearly 4 seconds is required to fill the screen, and this is bordering on the acceptable limit for an operator interacting with the computer. It is possible, therefore, that the line rate will be increased, eventually, to 9,600 bits/s.

While the PALC, CALC and FICO schemes were being developed consideration was being given to extending the automatic seat reservation scheme using the SITA network described in Chapter 8, page 295. SITA provide and maintain this network which is growing rapidly and offers economic, long distance communications, because the costs are shared among many users. Also, because it is a shared network it greatly eases the problem of inter-communication with other airlines.

In London, only two medium speed lines are required to connect the BEACON computer centre to the SITA message switching centre instead of several expensive multipoint lines to the continent. The remote terminals, in this case, the UNIVAC uniscope 100 display with a 1000 character screen and its own core store and control logic, will be sited in more than twenty European cities; in these cities BEA only has to provide local multiplexing equipment to connect a group of displays at its local reservation office to the nearest satellite processor of the SITA network. The Rome and Milan offices of BEA were connected to the SITA network in late 1971. The initial success has encouraged BEA to go ahead rapidly with connecting other offices, to make the service they can offer to passengers in these cities comparable with that already provided at their U.K. offices through the original automatic seat reservation network.

One problem that may arise is the delay introduced by the SITA network, which was designed to handle 95% of peak hour transactions, i.e. a forward message and return reply, in under six seconds. This delay is negligible for ordinary message traffic, and ordinary teleprinter messages are now handled very rapidly indeed, but for conversational use of display terminals the occurance of such a delay may be more serious, particularly if a number of small errors have to be corrected by the central processors in London. The increase in speed of the SITA network communication links to 4,800 bit/s will improve the present response time and the queuing delay in its node computers will be reduced, where necessary, by replacing existing equipment by enhanced versions with greater throughput capacity.

The reason for concern about response time is, of course, that there is no local processing of information at the terminals, and all editing has to be done by the London centre. However, it would be costly to provide local editing facilities of any consequence, and as the data banks must be stored at the BEACON centre, the system adopted is the only sensible one for long-term development because the cost of extension is minimized by simplifying, as far as possible, the terminal equipment at the reservation offices.

The decision to use the SITA network made it necessary to change from the polling of terminals used for the U.K. multipoint line network, to a free-wheeling i.e. interrupt-driven, central system. With the conventional polling method the satellite processors or terminal controllers wait for a request from the centre before sending information; but terminals connected by the SITA network are polled by their local SITA satellite processors. These send transaction messages over the high-level network to the BEACON computers which must be ready to accept them as they arrive. This has required a number of changes to be made in the software for these computers.

Comparison of Private Networks

Both the examples that have been discussed to illustrate the development of private networks have demonstrated an important point: the extent of their growth and evolution is extremely difficult to anticipate, and prepare for during the initial design stage. Furthermore, changes in design philosophy may have to be made to take account of circumstances brought about by the very existence of the network itself, and by the development of new kinds of terminal device. It is most important, therefore, to retain a high degree of flexibility both in the hardware and software aspects of any network. It is often said, with some truth, that flexibility costs money. But the lack of it may eventually prove even more costly to a large organization, if it becomes unable to adapt to changes in its environment.

In the case of the bank network, the introduction of on-line cash dispensers was only feasible because the network and central file of customer accounts already existed, but an extra load has been placed on the network due to the need for rapid polling of these new terminals. In turn, this has brought about the need to modify the software in the central computers.

The airline network, too, has had similar problems. The central file of seat reservations has promoted the efficient use of aircraft and has justified the extension of the network to offer on-line service to many reservation offices, but the use of the SITA network has entailed a change from polling terminals under the control of the central computers, to waiting for interrupts as terminals become active. This has entailed the extensive modification of software at the centre also.

Perhaps it is not surprising that the two networks have many similarities. For example, each uses multipoint lines connecting concentrators, or buffer processors, to the computer centres, with the concentrators handling several terminals—in the Lloyds' case connected by Post Office leased lines and situated in individual branches, in BEA's case, clustered in reservation offices.

Lloyds' network has about four times as many terminals as the U.K. portion of the BEACON automatic seat reservation service. However, the extension of the latter to the continent will bring many more terminals into operation, while the variety of terminals handled by the BEACON centre is greater by virtue of the visual displays used for the passenger and cargo check-in systems.

Both networks handle information as quite short messages of a few tens of characters, and have had to adapt their central software to handle terminals more rapidly as the network has evolved. Finally, though there are many similarities, the networks are fundamentally incompatible and could not share equipment should this ever be desirable. Whereas this is an unlikely requirement, it is not so unlikely that, one day, people might wish to book an airline journey and have their bank transfer funds automatically to cover its cost.

The lack of standards now for exchanging information between systems may be merely an inconvenience; in the long term the facilities available to the public may be severely restricted, or far more costly than necessary, if such standards cannot be agreed. It is to be hoped that the use of shared networks will help create conditions conducive to the acceptance of standards which will benefit all users of data networks in the long run. However, a much more certain way to achieve compatibility, at least in respect of the communications aspects, would be the introduction of a public data network. This would set standards in the same way that the Modem Interface Specification V24 recommended by CCITT has done for communications using the telephone network.

References

1. Sayers, R. S., 'Computers in banking', *Data Processing* (July-August 1969).
2. 'The Burroughs TC 500 terminal', *Data Processing* (May-June 1969).
3. Plugge, W. R. and Perry, M. N., 'American airlines' SABRE electronic reservation system', *Western Joint Computer Conference*, 593-601 (May 1961).
4. Fowling, J. R., 'Developing an international, dedicated computer network', in *Computer Networks–International Computer State of the Art Reports*, Infotech Ltd. (1971).

Chapter 5

Data Transmission

5.1 INTRODUCTION

The communication system carries out the entire task of moving data from one subscriber to another, including the interfacing, switching and multiplexing. One part of the whole system is the transmission equipment, and it is this part which is more specialized in its functions. The rest of the system is like the equipment that might be found in any digital system. Communication through the telephone network was the subject of Chapter 2, and in the present chapter some more basic ideas are introduced.

It is almost true to say that every transmission path, whether it is an optical path, a wave-guide, transmission line or radio link, carries an analogue signal. But there is an important exception in the animal world in nerve fibres which continuously regenerate their pulses, at least in amplitude. There have been attempts to copy the nerve's properties in the *neuristor*, but these have no present-day application to telecommunications. In practice we deal with analogue paths and sometimes they stretch from a modem at one extreme end of the line to a modem at the other extreme end, sometimes just between a pair of regenerators where the digital signal is restored.

The relationship between the analogue path and the digital information it carries[1,2] is the chief theme of this chapter. The digital channel is characterized by the statistics of the bit stream and the coding that may be applied to it. The analogue path is characterized by pulse waveforms and their spectra. Therefore an important topic is the effect of digital methods of encoding the data on the power spectrum of the signal. The calculation of these effects is not simple but it gives a useful insight into the relationship between the analogue and digital aspects of the channel.

A second topic is the preservation of the digital channel's transparency to binary patterns in spite of limitations of the analogue path.

When a basically analogue system such as the present telephone network is used to carry data by placing a modem at each end, there are many problems because the information-carrying waveform must survive in one leap all the

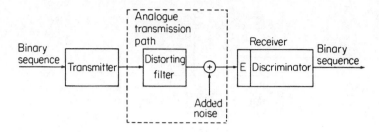

(a) Data transmission system

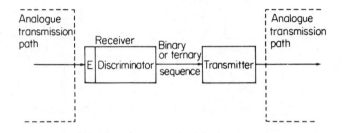

(b) Essentials of a regenerator

Figure 5.1. The components of a data transmission system

noise and distortion introduced over the link. On the other hand, transmission equipment intended for digital information can be designed with extra freedom because of the regenerators.

Transmission systems can be separated into *baseband* systems and those which employ a band of frequency separated from zero frequency. In the former, the design usually begins with a simple digital waveform, whereas the latter, traditionally, employs modulation to shift a baseband signal to higher frequencies. Later, we shall find that this distinction is not fundamental and that there is a method for generating the transmission signals which makes no distinction between the two kinds. But in most of the chapter the attention will be on baseband transmission.

The elements of a data transmission system are shown in Figure 5.1(a). The binary sequence is converted by the transmitter into a waveform that is adapted to the transmission path. At the other end the waveform has a distorted form where it enters the receiver. The task of the receiver is to reproduce exactly the incoming bit sequence.

The transmission path can be regarded as a filter, specified by its attenuation and phase characteristics with noise also added. To compensate for the distortion, an equalising filter, shown at E in the figure, precedes the part of

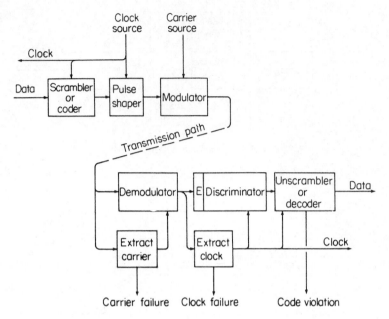

Figure 5.2. A data transmission system in more detail

of the receiver which discriminates on the signal and produces the binary decisions. Such a combination of filter and discriminator is typical of many pattern-recognition systems.

Figure 5.1(b) shows the essentials of a regenerator, which can be placed at any point in the transmission path to divide it into sections, over which the distortion and noise problems can be treated separately. But although the middle of the regenerator could be carrying a binary sequence, it is often in a pseudo-ternary representation, because of digital coding methods employed at the transmitter.

The data transmission system of Figure 5.1(a) is shown in more detail in Figure 5.2, which assumes a synchronous channel and includes optional features such as digital precoding and analogue modulation/demodulation. The channel carries, in addition to the digital data, the clock and the carrier used for modulation, but since these are periodic signals they can in principle be carried by a very small extra channel capacity. The carrier is only the concern of the transmission system, but the clock is used at both ends to interpret the data signal. We shall find that there is sometimes an advantage in having the clock and carrier in a definite phase-relationship, i.e. coherent. The receiver of the data can often make use of the three signals which indicate failures in the carrier, clock or code, to deal with fault conditions.

5.2 TRANSMISSION WAVEFORMS

The most obvious waveform for representing a string of binary digits is the square wave in which each bit that is a 1 corresponds to a suitably timed square pulse. The whole waveform can be regarded as the sum of the set of rectangular pulses shown in Figure 5.3. If we know the way that one such pulse passes through the system the rest will follow by the superposition of similar pulses at different times. Right through to the discriminator the system is *linear* in its response, so that superposition is valid.

This waveform is not quite practical because of its sharp edges, which imply a broad spectrum. A simple, isolated pulse like the one in Figure 5.4 has a continuous spectrum, which is its Fourier transform. In this case the transform is given by

$$\frac{A(f)}{A(o)} = \frac{\sin \pi f/f_0}{\pi f/f_0} \text{ where } f_0 = \frac{1}{T} \tag{5-1}$$

The shape is worth studying and it will reappear several times in different contexts. The function $\sin \pi x / \pi x$ has zeros at $x = 1, 2, 3$, etc. and also at $x = -1, -2, -3$, etc. but *not* at $x = 0$, where it takes the value $+1$. Thus, of all the integer points along the x axis it selects one special one, $x = 0$, to be non zero. In equation (5-1) the amplitude of the spectrum has been normalized to equal 1 at $f = 0$.

Truncation of the higher frequencies in the transmission path will alter the waveform and it seems better to start off with a more rounded waveform, one which gives a Fourier transform converging more rapidly to zero. The

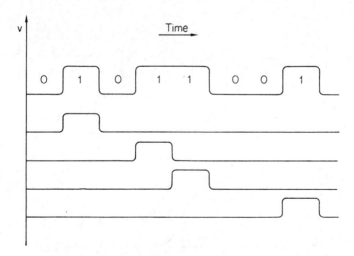

Figure 5.3. A binary waveform shown as the superposition
of pulses

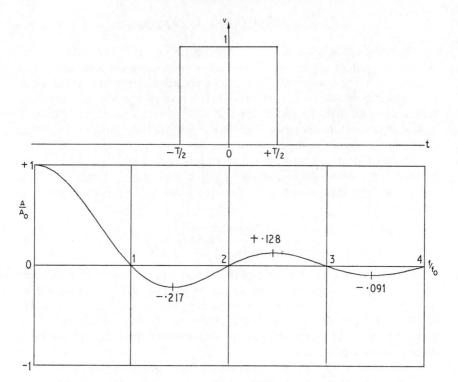

Figure 5.4. Isolated square pulse and its Fourier transform

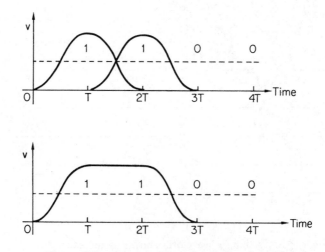

Figure 5.5. Superposition of raised-cosine pulses

most satisfactory, simple waveform is the raised cosine or sine squared pulse curve.

This is a segment of the curve:

$$v = \tfrac{1}{2}\left(1 + \cos\frac{\pi t}{T}\right) \qquad (5\text{-}2)$$

This waveform is shown in Figure 5.5 together with its superposition effect. The period T is half of the total width of the raised curve. When adjacent pulses spaced by time T are superposed their rising and falling edges compensate exactly, and a string of ones is represented by a flat-topped waveform. The pulses have another fortunate property, that if they are sliced at half the peak amplitude the transitions occur at regular intervals. This is shown by the dotted line in Figure 5.5.

The Fourier transform of the raised cosine pulse is given by

$$\frac{A(f)}{A(o)} = \frac{\sin 2\pi f/f_0}{2\pi f/f_0\left(1 - \dfrac{4f^2}{f_0^2}\right)} \qquad (5\text{-}3)$$

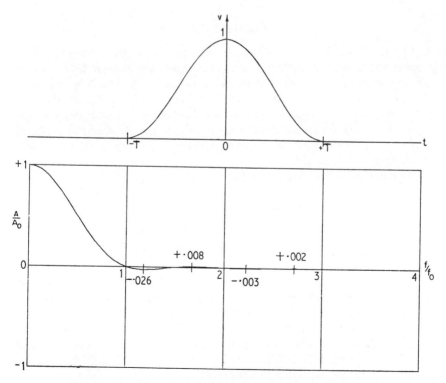

Figure 5.6.   Raised cosine pulse and its Fourier transform

which decreases along the frequency axis as $1/f^3$, a much more satisfactory spectrum than that of the square pulse. This spectrum is shown in Figure 5.6, and its first minimum has a value of only -0.026. The spectrum has zeros at all the frequencies that had zeros in Figure 5.4, and others at the intermediate, halfway points.

The two waveforms, square and raised cosine, have been constructed to have good superposition properties. If the waveforms are faithully reproduced at the receiver, by sampling them at the centre of the pulses, the binary sequence can be reconstructed without interference from neighbouring pulses. An important question is suggested, whether better waveforms can be devised which have these two desirable features:

1. A limitation in their spectrum to a finite bandwidth, which means that the Fourier spectrum is zero above a certain frequency.
2. The waveform at certain sampling points accurately represents the state of only one bit of the binary sequence.

The answer is that such waveforms do exist and, as if by chance, they have the shapes we have already met as Fourier transforms in Figures 5.4 and 5.6.

Band-limited Pulse Forms

Figure 5.4 shows a square-wave pulse and its Fourier transform. (The Fourier transform has cosine and sine components, but the sine component is zero for a waveform which is symmetrical about $t = 0$.) The relationship of waveform and Fourier transform has a duality, which implies that the spectrum and pulse shapes can be interchanged. The result is shown in Figure 5.7. The waveform has the shape $\sin \pi x / \pi x$, and the spectrum is cut off sharply at f_0. The width of the main part of the pulse, from zero to zero, is T, which equals $1/f_0$, as before.

The duality can be summarized as

$$\text{square pulse} \; - \; \frac{\sin \pi x}{\pi x} \; \text{spectrum}$$

$$\frac{\sin \pi x}{\pi x} \; \text{pulse} \; - \; \text{sharp spectrum cut off}$$

The desirable property of a band limitation has been achieved, and so has the pulse sampling property we required, because there are zeros at $\pm\frac{1}{2}T$, $\pm T$, $\pm\frac{3}{2}T$, etc. and a maximum, $v = 1$, at $t = 0$.

We can now return to the question of sampling a band-limited waveform and reconstructing it from its sample, a matter which arose first in Chapter 2 in connection with PCM. With the aid of the ideal band-limited waveform $\sin \pi x / \pi x$ it can be explained in a different way.

Suppose we had a waveform w of which we knew only that it was band-

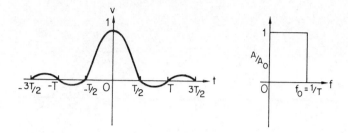

Figure 5.7. Symmetrical pulse shape with sharply band-
limited spectrum

limited, and had no spectral components above $f = f_0$. Now let us sample the
waveform at intervals $\frac{1}{2}T$ where $T = 1/f_0$ and let their values be $a_0, a_1, a_2 \ldots$
as shown in Figure 5.8. For each of these samples we construct a band-
limited waveform of the shape $\sin \pi x/\pi x$ with its maximum at the sample
point and zero at all other sample times, like $F_1(t)$ in the figure which has
its maximum a_1 at sample time $\frac{1}{2}T$. Adding all these waveforms together gives
a band limited waveform that clearly passes through all the sample points.

This method of reconstruction is the equivalent in the time domain of the
method described in Chapter 2. (See Appendix to Chapter 2, p. 60 for reconstructing a waveform from the sample pulses by a low pass filter.) It is a
further illustration of the sampling theorem which states that a waveform
limited to frequencies below f_0 is completely determined if its sample amplitudes at intervals of $1/2f_0$ are known. For a given bandwidth or frequency
limitation f_0, the sampling interval needed to determine the waveform
$(1/2f_0)$ is known as the Nyquist interval. It gives two samples for each cycle
of the cut-off frequency, f_0.

The pure band-limited waveform is not practical for data transmission
because of its slow convergence to zero. If there was a small error in the
timing of the sampling points the errors due to successive bit positions would

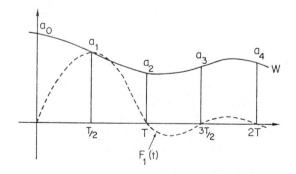

Figure 5.8. A band-limited waveform and part of
its reconstruction

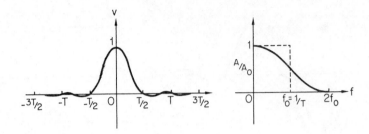

Figure 5.9.   Pulse shape with a spectrum of raised cosine cut-off form

decrease with time as $1/t$. It is well known that infinite series of the form $\Sigma(1/n)$ do not converge, so the slightest timing error would have increasingly large effects.

If the dual of the square pulse system is not satisfactory, it seems more likely that the dual of the raised cosine system will be, and this is illustrated in Figure 5.9. With this waveform any error due to mistiming will decrease with time as $1/t^3$, and this gives no problem of convergence. The improved pulse shape is paid for by an increased bandwidth having frequencies up to $2f_0$. The corresponding sharp cut-off is shown dotted in the figure for comparison. Nyquist proved that any symmetrical roll-off of the spectrum about f_0 would preserve the zeros at the sample points. The waveform is a practical one because the overshoots are very small and can be approximated, or ignored beyond the first one or two. But the spectrum does not make full use of the band 0 to $2f_0$ and this results in a lower rate of data transmission than the band up to $2f_0$ could theoretically allow. Pulses are sent at intervals $T/2$ which is twice the Nyquist interval for a bandwidth of $2f_0$.

The maximum data rate of a band-limited analogue channel depends on the Nyquist interval and the number of different levels of signal that can be sent. If four levels can be used, as in Figure 5.10, then each pulse carries two bits; for eight levels it is three bits and so forth. In this situation we must

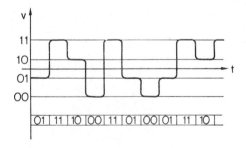

Figure 5.10.   Four-level waveform carrying 2 bits per symbol

distinguish the rate of sending binary digits from the rate at which analogue samples are transmitted. Successive signal levels are sometimes called *symbols*, and the symbol rate, measured in symbols per second, is sometimes expressed in the unit called *baud* after Baudot. For example, a system with four levels (two bits per symbol) could operate at 1200 baud and have a channel capacity of 2400 bits per second.

Telephone channels are designed for speech, with its wide range of signal levels, so they would be expected to handle many levels of data signal satisfactorily. Good quality channels have been used in practice with 16 levels. The rate at which independent samples can be sent is limited by the Nyquist interval because samples taken at closer intervals are not independent. So if W is the bandwidth, the Nyquist interval is $1/2W$ and the maximum sampling rate is 2W. If there are 2^n signal levels which can successfully be discriminated the maximum channel capacity is $2nW$. This is the form taken by Shannon's famous formula when it is applied to data transmission. But when the spectrum of the pulse is not sharply cut off, as in Figure 5.9, the actually sampling rate is less than 2W. For a variety of reasons the theoretical capacity of a channel is not usually achieved.

The Duobinary Signalling Method

The 'ideal' band-limited waveform had the $\sin \pi x/\pi x$ shape and gave samples at intervals $\frac{1}{2}T$ which were zero at each sampling point except at the centre of the pulse. The subsequent discussion has been concerned with practical waveforms which meet the same criterion of zero *intersymbol interference*. The spectrum of the waveform must certainly contain components up to a frequency $f_0 = 1/T$, and the practical waveforms went beyond this theoretical minimum.

It is possible, nevertheless, to design methods of transmitting and receiving signals in which there is deliberate intersymbol interference. One of these methods, called duobinary, has been used in practice and will be described. The pulse spreads over two sample periods, but elsewhere it gives zero samples, so the samples, taken at intervals $T/2$ are

$$... 0, 0, 0, 1, 1, 0, 0, 0, ...$$

A waveform with this property is

$$v = \frac{\frac{4}{\pi} \cos 2\pi t/T}{1 - 16t^2/T^2} \tag{5-4}$$

The pulse and its spectrum are shown in Figure 5.11. The spectrum is part of the function $\cos \frac{\pi}{2} fT$. The sampling points are at $\frac{1}{2}(n+\frac{1}{2})T$ and only the two at $\pm\frac{1}{4}T$ are non zero.

The result of the intersymbol interference is to produce a three-valued

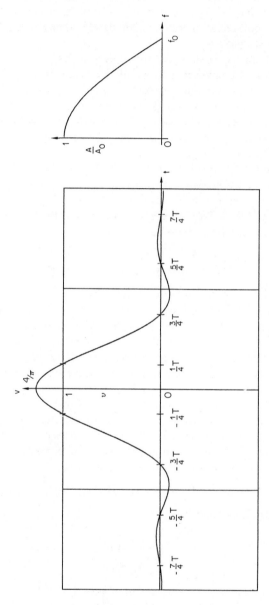

Figure 5.11. The duobinary waveform and its Fourier transform

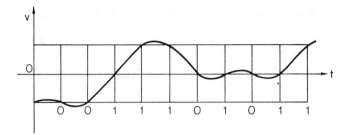

Figure 5.12.   A waveform with intersymbol interference

signal. Starting with a 4-level signal in the same way would produce a 7-level signal but we shall keep to the simplest case.

An example of the waveform for a particular binary sequence is shown in Figure 5.12. Note that transitions from one extreme to the other do not happen within a single sample period T. This property is associated with the restricted spectrum, which is entirely inside the band 0 to $1/2T$.

This technique is related to an old trick in telegraphy called 'doubling the dotting speed', or 'double dotting' for short. The mechanical receivers would run in the normal way at the 'dotting speed'. The operators found that at twice this speed the signal could still be interpreted, but in a new way. Two pulses in succession were sufficient to move the armature over, but a reversal left it in the middle of its travels, rather as Figure 5.12 shows.

The interpretation of the samples at the receiver is simple enough, if the binary output corresponding to the previous symbol is used to convert the present one. The interpretation of the $+$ and $-$ levels is unambiguous, but a sequence of 0 levels corresponds to alternate binary values and for these the phase depends on the past values. This small difficulty can be overcome by a device due to Lender[3], who gave the resultant code the name 'duobinary'.

In Lender's system, the complement of the input binary sequence b_n is applied to a binary counter to produce a modified sequence c_n, which is then encoded to form the ternary waveform. A *one* in the input b_n causes *no change* in the modified sequence c_n and this corresponds to either $+$ or $-$ in the waveform. A *zero* input causes a *transition* in the modified sequence c_n and 0 in the waveform. Here is an example

input sequence b_n	1	1	1	0	0	0	1	1	0	1	0	0	1
modified sequence c_n	0	0	0	1	0	1	1	1	0	0	1	0	0
coded value a_n	$-$	$-$	$-$	0	0	0	$+$	$+$	0	$-$	0	0	$-$

Using this precoding makes the interpretation at the receiver very simple, because both $+$ and $-$ levels correspond to binary 1, and level 0 to binary 0. The waveform can be rectified and then discriminated at one signal level.

Relationship between the Band-Limited Waveforms

Our discussion of signalling waveforms began with the square and the raised cosine pulses, both of which had Fourier transforms of indefinite extent. We then moved on to band-limited waveforms, starting with a 'classical' waveform which is the transform of the square pulse. It can be described by the function

$$f_1(x) = \frac{\sin \pi x}{\pi x} \tag{5-5}$$

This waveform produces no intersymbol interference, because, of all the samples at integer values of x, only $f_1(0) = 1$ is non-zero.

In addition to $f_1(x)$, two other band-limited waveforms have been used in this chapter. One (shown in Figure 5.9) has a raised cosine spectrum and the other is the waveform used in 'duobinary' signalling. In spite of their different properties and uses, these three waveforms are closely related, in a way that will now be described, using Figure 5.13.

Suppose that two $f_1(x)$ waveforms are added together at adjacent pulse intervals, as though an isolated pair of 1s was to be signalled. Using the displacements $x = -\frac{1}{2}, +\frac{1}{2}$ respectively, this produces the new waveform given by the function

$$f_2(x) = f_1(x + \tfrac{1}{2}) + f_1(x - \tfrac{1}{2}) = \frac{\cos \pi x}{\pi(\tfrac{1}{4} - x^2)} \tag{5-6}$$

This is the duobinary signalling waveform of equation (5-4) normalized to have a 'period' of unity by setting $x = 2t/T$. Indeed, the way it was formed ensures that it has the sampling properties required for duobinary.

Consider the effect of the transformation given in equation (5-6) on the spectrum of the function; $f_2(x)$ is the convolution of $f_1(x)$ with a function that has two very narrow pulses at $x = -\frac{1}{2}$ and $x = +\frac{1}{2}$, and that particular function has a Fourier transform $\cos \pi y$. So the transform of $f_1(x)$ is multiplied by $\cos \pi y$, giving the spectrum of the duobinary signal, which is also shown in the figure. The functions $f_1(x)$ and $f_2(x)$ are plotted in the main part of Figure 5.13 with their spectra inset.

Now apply the transformation once more, giving:

$$f_3(x) = f_2(x + \tfrac{1}{2}) + f_2(x - \tfrac{1}{2}) = \frac{2 \sin \pi x}{\pi x(1 - x^2)} \tag{5-7}$$

The function $f_3(x)$ clearly has a transform proportional to $\cos^2 \pi y$ in the pass-band $|y| < \frac{1}{2}$. and this is precisely the property of the waveform with a symmetrical spectrum roll off which we plotted in Figure 5.9. It is indeed the same waveform. All three functions and their spectra are compared in Figure 5.13.

It is sometimes thought that the duobinary signalling method, by virtue

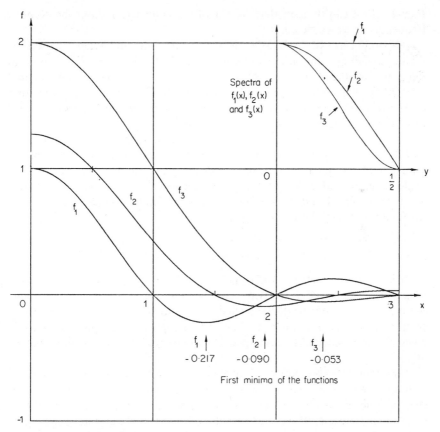

Figure 5.13. Band-limited waveforms f_1 f_2 and f_3 with their spectra (inset)

of its toleration of some intersymbol interference, allows more samples per second than the sampling theorem would predict, but this is not so. The band limit, in our notation, is at $y' = \frac{1}{2}$ and there is one sample per time interval $1/2y'$, which equals 1. What is gained by duobinary is that the theoretical maximum binary signalling rate for a given bandwidth is achieved using a waveform which is practical.

Turning now to $f_3(x)$, we have a waveform which is normally used *without* intersymbol interference, though the values it takes at the integer values of x are $f_3(0) = 2$, $f_3(1) = 1$, $f_3(2) = 0$, and zeros at all the higher integer values. Of course it is the zeros at the *even* integers (with the exception of $x = 0$) that are employed. In other words the pulse repetition period is 2. This is one way of explaining why the 'symmetrical roll off' waveform has extra zeros between most sample points; they are the zeros at 3, 5, 7, etc. The Nyquist frequency in the scale adopted is $\frac{1}{4}$, and by reference to the spectra in

Figure 5.13 it can be seen that the roll off is symmetrical about the Nyquist frequency, as we expected.

To summarize the properties of waveforms $f_2(x)$ and $f_3(x)$, as used for digital signalling: duobinary obtains a practical waveform which uses no more bandwidth than does $f_1(x)$, at the cost of (tractable) intersymbol interference while the symmetrical spectrum roll off obtains a waveform that is even more convergent to zero, with no intersymbol interference, but with twice the bandwidth for a given signalling rate.

The method of using $f_3(x)$ that we have described above employs only half the binary signalling rate that is theoretically possible. At the expense of intersymbol interference, the full rate (a pulse repetition period equal to 1) could be employed. If 0 and 1 are represented by signal levels symmetrical about zero volts, the effect of the binary sequence on the signals sent at sample times can be shown by this example:

binary	0	0	0	0	1	0	0	0	0	0	1	1	1	1	1	1
signal	-2	-2	-2	-1	0	-1	-2	-2	-2	-1	$+1$	$+2$	$+2$	$+2$	$+2$	$+2$

It is a curious fact that the signal can still be interpreted at the receiver after it has been sliced at the two levels $+\frac{1}{2}$ and $-\frac{1}{2}$. Thus the positive states $+1$ and $+2$ need not be distinguished, nor the two negative states. Negative sample values are interpreted as binary 0 and positive sample values as 1, while a sample value of 0 is interpreted as a change from the previous binary digit.

Using the $f_3(x)$ waveform in this manner, possibly with Lender's modification, achieves the same speed as duobinary signalling with a more rapid spectral roll-off. What must be paid for these advantages is that the slicing levels are at a quarter of the peak signal level, so the noise immunity is poorer.

5.3 TAILORING THE SPECTRUM OF THE TRANSMITTED SIGNAL

There are two factors that affect the spectrum of the transmitted signal. One is the pulse waveform, and this must be carefully shaped if the spectrum is important. The other is the sequence of digits[4]. We shall consider what can be done by precoding the bit sequence, and then how to generate accurately shaped waveforms.

The Effect of Bit Sequence on the Spectrum

The Fourier transforms in Figures 5.4, 5.6, 5.7, 5.9 and 5.11 are the spectra of single pulses, and single pulses have continuous spectra, whereas periodic waveforms have discrete spectra. Data transmission waveforms consist of strings of such pulses with a 'random' element depending on the bit pattern actually being sent. A mathematical analysis of the spectra of these waveforms shows that they can have both continuous and discrete spectra at the same time. The spectrum will depend on the statistics of the bit stream being transmitted, and by recoding the data it is possible to change the spectrum.

A data communication system does not handle isolated pulses or periodic waveforms, but pulse trains constructed from the bit pattern being carried. To understand the transmission requirements and crosstalk effects the spectra of these pulse trains must be known. In the calculations which follow it is assumed that the bit pattern is random; the bit values are independent and take 0 or 1 with equal probability. To complete the investigation it would be necessary to know the spectrum for all possible bit patterns, but there is no easy way to characterise the whole collection of possible spectra, so we shall keep to the case of random bit patterns. The mathematical treatment which follows is not essential to the argument and can be skipped over, but its meaning can be understood intuitively if not in a formal way. The results are important in understanding how coding methods affect the spectra of transmitted waveforms.[5]

To begin with it is necessary to represent the transmitted waveforms. The pulse $v(t)$ which we have already studied had a spectral amplitude $A(f)$ at frequency f. Such pulses can be centred around times 0, T, 2T, 3T ... where T is the interval between samples. To allow for different levels we shall introduce the amplitudes $a_0, a_1, a_2, a_3 ...$ for the pulses centred around $t = 0, 2T, 3T ...$ and the resultant signal waveform is given by summing over all the relevant pulses:

$$S(t) = \sum_n a_n v(t - nT) \tag{5-8}$$

The term in a_1, for example, is $a_1 v(t-T)$ which is a pulse of amplitude proportional to a_1, and centred around $t = T$.

If the waveform in equation (5-8) is averaged over a large number of specimens of the waveform, carefully aligned relative to the clock but ignoring any 'framing' due to the method of coding, a new 'average' waveform is obtained.

$$av\{S(t)\} = av\{a_n\} \sum_n v(t - nT) \tag{5-9}$$

It is easily seen that this is periodic in t with period T, but it may be zero if the average of a_n is zero. Some waveforms $v(t)$ make the function in equation (5-9) a constant, for example the square pulse or the raised cosine pulse. If it is not zero or constant, then the signal average of equation (5-9), because it is periodic, has a discrete spectrum at $f_0 (= 1/T)$, $2f_0$, $3f_0$ etc. and this is the discrete part of the spectrum of $S(t)$.

Practical systems normally make this term (5-9) equal to zero, either by using a suitable waveform $v(t)$ or by having a zero average for a_n. For example PCM systems use three levels for a_n; $+a$, 0 and $-a$ and contrive that alternate ones are represented by $+a$ and $-a$, so the average amplitude is zero.

If the average waveform is subtracted, the remaining component is $S(t) - av\{S(t)\}$ and this is best treated by calculating its power spectrum, which is normally continuous. The spectrum is expressed as

$$P(f) = \frac{1}{T} |A(f)|^2 \left\{ R(0) - m^2 + 2 \sum_{K=1}^{\infty} [R(k) - m^2] \cos 2\pi k f\, T \right\} \qquad (5\text{-}10)$$

In this equation $A(f)$ is the spectrum of the individual pulse, and the expression in curly brackets which multiplies it shows the effect of the bit pattern, represented by the sequence of amplitude a_n. The meaning of the terms is that m is the average of a_n and $R(k)$ is the autocovariance of the time series a_n. This means that $R(k)$ measures the covariance of the sequence of amplitudes with the same sequence shifted in time by k periods. Thus $R(0)$ is the mean square amplitude. Equation (5-10) gives the spectrum which remains when the discrete spectrum derived from equation (5-9) has been removed.

Some Examples of Coding

In order to illustrate the use of equation (5-10) let us apply it to a method of coding in which each group of four adjacent bits has just two ones and two zeros. The zeros and ones are represented by $a_n = -1$ and $+1$ respectively and the waveform like the one shown in Figure 5.14. For clarity $v(t)$ has been represented by non-overlapping pulses, but this is not essential. Since the mean of a_n is zero, the power spectrum is given by equation (5-10) and this can be written as

$$P(f) = \frac{1}{T} |A(f)|^2\, C_1(f) \qquad (5\text{-}11)$$

so that the factor $C_1(f)$ can express the way in which the spectrum is affected by the coding. The factor $C_1(f)$ is proportional to the power spectrum of the waveform that would be obtained if $v(t)$ happened to be a very narrow pulse centred at $t = 0$. If this was applied to a suitable filter the power spectrum would be multiplied by the factor $|A(f)|^2$ and the pulse expanded to $v(t)$.

For the coding of Figure 5.14 in which '2 out of 4' code is used it is easy to calculate the covariances, and we obtain $R(0) = 1$, $R(1) = -\frac{1}{4}$, $R(2) = -\frac{1}{6}$, $R(3) = -\frac{1}{12}$ and all the higher autocovariances are zero.

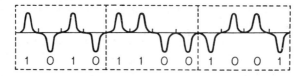

Figure 5.14.   A waveform representing a '2 out of 4' code

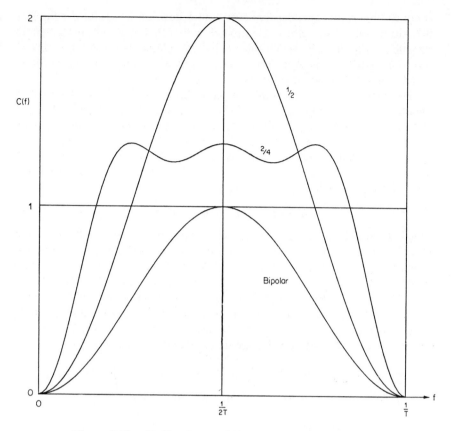

Figure 5.15. Coding factors for examples given in the text

The result is

$$C_1(f) = \tfrac{2}{3}(1 - \cos 2\pi f \, T)(2 + 2\cos 2\pi f \, T + \cos^2 2\pi f \, T) \qquad (5\text{-}12)$$

This is plotted in Figure 5.15. The '2 out of 4' coding leads to a notch in the spectrum at $f = 0, f = 1/T$ and multiples of this frequency. This coding method could be a useful way to tailor a spectrum to a finite frequency band. By using larger groups of digits, such as '3 out of 6' or '4 out of 8' a sharper notch can be produced in the spectrum. The '1 out of 2' code gives a coding factor

$$C_2(f) = 1 - \cos 2\pi f \, T \qquad (5\text{-}13)$$

This is shown in Figure 5.15 for comparison. With this coding, each bit is represented by two successive pulses of opposite polarity, the two binary values having the representations $+ -$ and $- +$. The bit rate is half that of unrestricted binary pulses, and this method of coding is used where bit rate is not so important. The fact that every pulse position is occupied simplifies the extraction of the clock. Compared with other methods of baseband signalling without a DC signal this one is very simple. It is used in magnetic recording where it is sometimes called 'phase modulation' but a more descriptive form is 'twinned binary'.

The most widely used method of coding for baseband signals is called 'bipolar', and this, like our earlier examples, uses three signal levels, zero and equal positive and negative. Binary 0 in the input is represented by $a_n = 0$, and binary 1 is represented by either of the other two levels. Each successive 1 that occurs is coded with opposite polarity, as Figure 5.16 illustrates. The autocovariances are $R(0) = \frac{1}{2}$, $R(1) = -\frac{1}{4}$, all others being zero, and this leads to a coding function

$$C_3(f) = \tfrac{1}{2}(1 - \cos 2\pi f\, T) \qquad (5\text{-}14)$$

This is plotted in Figure 5.15. The coding factor is similar in shape to that of twinned binary but it carries one bit of data with every pulse interval (double the rate of twinned binary) and has half the average power because only half of the pulses are non zero. This makes it a good choice for digital signalling. But the missing pulses could be a problem if there are too many of them and the clock timing is lost. Because a data stream could certainly have a long string of zeros something must be done to modify the bipolar coding method. Ways to do this are described later.

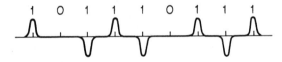

Figure 5.16.   The bipolar method of coding

Generation of Shaped Pulses by Digital Methods

We turn now to the generation of pulse waveforms. The shape of a pulse can be characterized either by its amplitude as a function of time or by its spectrum. If the spectrum is known a filter can be constructed, in principle, to generate the pulse shape. For the pulses we have described, the phase characteristic of the filter must correspond to a constant group delay, and this can be difficult to achieve. A better method may be to generate the waveform directly, but the mechanism must generate not just one pulse but a signal composed of many, possibly overlapping, pulses that are superposed.

The device to be used is called the binary transversal filter[6,7] and is shown in its simplest form in Figure 5.17. The waveform to be produced is sampled at equal intervals of time Δt and the amplitudes measured are denoted $b_{-4}, b_{-3}, b_{-2}, b_{-1}, b_0, b_1, b_2, b_3$ and b_4. It is assumed that outside these limits the amplitude is small enough to be ignored.

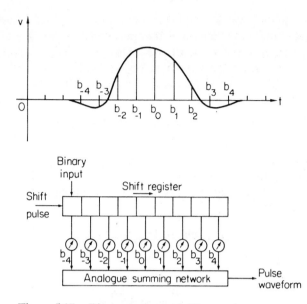

Figure 5.17.   Binary transversal filter used to generate
a waveform

The pulse-shaping device for this waveform consists of a nine-unit shift register, the output of which is nine signals each having the possible voltage levels V_0 and 0. These are fed to nine attenuators with outputs proportional to the sample amplitudes b_{-4} to b_{+4}. These amplitudes are both positive and negative, so it is convenient to insert amplifiers with a gain of -1 or take signals of both polarities from the shift register. The voltage levels produced by the shift register must be as accurate as the waveform requires. A single 'one' bit inserted into the shift register is shifted at the waveform sampling speed and the output of the summing network will be a staircase waveform approximating the desired shape. Now a succession of 'one' bits can follow one another through the shift register, being inserted whenever a pulse is to be generated. The sampling rate is a multiple of the repetition rate. The output waveforms due to successive paths can overlap, and the superposition will be correctly done in the summing network.

If the signalling method demands shaped pulses of more than one amplitude to be added into the stream, additional shift registers and sets of attenuators are needed, and the summing network or networks must add all the outputs together. For example, in the case of three levels $(+1, 0, -1)$ two shift registers will be needed.

The error due to approximating the waveform by a staircase is a waveform with zeros at each waveform sampling point and this has a spectrum which is centred around the waveform sampling frequency and its harmonics. By making the sampling rate a suitably large multiple of the pulse repetition rate the spectrum of the 'noise' caused by the approximation can be well separated from the spectrum of the wanted pulses. Then a simple, low pass filter will remove the noise or, looked at another way, will smooth out the waveform. For further details see the Appendix to Chapter 2, page 60.

Direct Generation of Modulated Signals

The binary transversal filter can be used to generate not only baseband waveforms but also any kind of waveform which a transmitter might produce. The type of waveform which normally comes from a modulator and uses a band above zero frequency can also be generated in this way. For example, the waveform

$$V = \frac{\sin \pi t/T}{\pi t/T} \cos 3\pi t/T \tag{5-15}$$

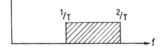

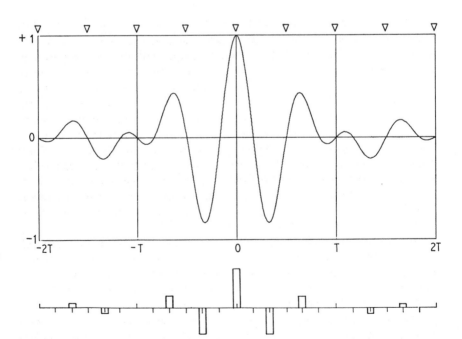

Figure 5.18. Digitally produced modulated waveform, $k = 3$

would normally be obtained by using the band-limited signal represented by its first factor to modulate a carrier of frequency 3/2T. The band-limited signal has a spectrum from 0 to 1/2T so the waveform of equation (5-15) should be contained in the band $3/2T \pm 1/2T$ that is to say 1/T to 2/T. Figure 5.18 shows the waveform and its passband. The special feature of this waveform is the large number of zeros. If it is sampled at regular intervals 0, T/6, 2T/6 etc., only two out of the six samples per Nyquist interval T are non-zero in addition to the central maximum. The lower part of the figure shows the waveform represented by samples at these points, and this kind of waveform can easily be produced by a binary transversal filter. The 'noise' due to the approximation can be cut off by a low pass filter cutting at about 3/T because the band-limited waveform thus produced is fully defined by samples taken at a Nyquist interval of T/6, which is the sampling interval we have actually used.

This method of generating 'modulated' signals is called *digital echo modulation*[8,9,10], the word echo referring to the small pulses which accompany each main pulse. The repetition rate used in data transmission is shown by the

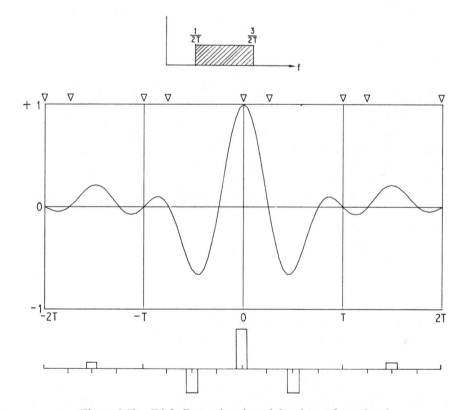

Figure 5.19.   Digitally produced modulated waveform, k = 2

triangular markers at the top of Figure 5.18, which all correspond to waveform zeros except the central one. If the waveform made up from such pulses carrying binary data is sampled at these points there is no interference between different pulses, but timing errors would be cumulative, as with the classical $\sin \pi x/\pi x$ waveform. A practical system must taper the waveform more sharply and thus round off the sharp band-pass spectrum. Because only a finite number of samples in the waveform generator is possible, the rounded off spectrum is inevitable. The amplitudes of the echos, which are four parameters in our example, can be adjusted to minimize the signal outside the band.

There is a collection of useful waveforms like that of equation (5-15) which can be produced by a binary transverse filter. One kind described by Croissier and Pierret used a waveform

$$V = \frac{\sin \pi t/T}{\pi t/T} \cos k\pi t/T \qquad (5\text{-}16)$$

The example we described in equation (5-15) was the case $k = 3$. Odd values of k all behave in the same general way except that $k = 1$ is a baseband system. The nominal waveband in each case is

$$\frac{k+1}{2T} > f > \frac{k-1}{2T} \qquad (5\text{-}17)$$

The even values of k also give useful waveforms that can be generated by 'echo modulation' but their zeros do not form an evenly spaced sequence. The example $k = 2$ is shown in Figure 5.19, and above the waveform, pointers show where the centres of the other pulses should be, to send binary digits without intersymbol interference at the Nyquist rate of 2 per period T. They are not evenly spaced but form two regular series separated by a time interval T/4. The condition of 'zero intersymbol interference' observed for these waveforms is more usually associated with baseband signals that are sampled at regular intervals to produce the binary output. It is interesting to find the condition holding for 'modulated' waveforms. If they are to be treated at the receiver by demodulation in a conventional way lack of intersymbol interference is not a necessary condition.

The use of these modulators over the telephone network raises a further problem due to the small frequency shifts that can happen when voice channels pass through some FDM carrier systems. To avoid this the waveform from the digital modulator is passed through a conventional modulator and the resultant signal is sent over the voice channel together with a pilot at carrier frequency. The difference of the signal and the pilot is preserved when both are subjected to a small shift.

The significance of the integral factor k in equation (5-16) is that each time a waveform is to be generated for a new signal element the carrier phase is the same so the shape of the waveform is the same. The method was extended by Choquet and Nussbaumer[10] so that the waveform obtained from a number of different modulation methods such as phase modulation and VSB amplitude modulation could be produced by digital methods. The waveforms could all be constructed from components of the form of equation (5-16) together with similar components with cos $(\pi t/T)$ replacing sin $(\pi t/T)$. Their achievement was an excellent demonstration of the essential similarity of the various methods of modulation that are used.

5.4 EQUALISATION

We now turn our attention from the transmitter, and the methods by which signals are constructed, to the receiver, and in particular to the correcting filter shown in Figure 5.1 which compensates for the (linear) distortion of the transmission path. Examples of the distortion were given in Chapter 2 when the properties of the telephone network were discussed. The process of correcting the line-distortion is called *equalisation*.

In a purpose-designed digital transmission system the choice of regenerator spacing, along with all the other design parameters, is made to reduce the equalisation problem, and all that may be needed is a simple filter. The more complex equalisation methods to be described here are needed when the distortion is severe or when it varies so much that a filter would not cope unless it could be adjusted automatically.

It might seem that the equalising filter must have the exact inverse of the line characteristics in the frequency band employed, if it is to correct the signal, but unlike voice or video signals, digital signals are constrained to have certain pulse shapes. This fact allows the design of the filter to be simplified. We shall discuss the *transversal filter* as an equaliser, and have already met its close relative, the binary transversal filter, as a pulse generator.

The Transversal Filter as Equaliser

The transversal filter is shown in Figure 5.20. In place of the shift register there is now a delay line so that the input waveform can be reproduced at the various equally spaced taps with successive delays. Each tap is later than the

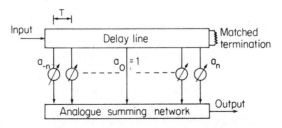

Figure 5.20. Transversal filter with adjustable taps

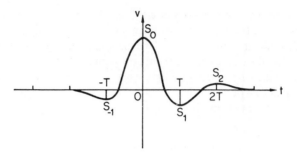

Figure 5.21.   Example of a received waveform with its
samples

previous one by the sampling interval T. These several waveforms are
multiplied by factors a_{-n}, a_{-n+1} ... a_0 ... a_{n-1}, a_n and added. The multiplying factors are adjustable, except a_0, the main waveform for which the
other components are corrections. The multiplying factors can be negative as
well as positive and this can be arranged by having two summing arrangements, one for each polarity, and combining their outputs with an amplifier
of gain -1 in the negative channel.

The key observation to be made is that T should exactly equal the interval
between the received pulses. Suppose now that Figure 5.21 represents the
pulse received when a single pulse is transmitted. The samples at intervals T
are S_{-1}, S_0, S_{+1}, S_{+2}, all others being small, but when the correcting filter
is properly adjusted its output should have zeros at all these sample points
except S_0, to avoid intersymbol interference. We shall describe how the
transversal filter could be adjusted to achieve these zeros. Suppose as an
example that S_1 was the largest sample next to S_0 and let r denote the ratio
S_1/S_0. Take initially the setting a_{-n} ... a_{-1}, a_1 ... $a_n = 0$.

The delayed waveform from the tapping of the delay line controlled by a_1
produces the maximum (S_0) at the time of S_1 in the main signal. If it is
multiplied by $-r$, by setting $a_1 = -r$ then the new output will have a
zero at S_1 time and the other samples will also be changed, but at most by
$r^2 S_0$. If we now suppose that the biggest sample in the new output waveform
is at S_{-1}, a_{-1} should next be adjusted, and so forth. It is fairly clear that this
procedure will converge if r is small, though it will probably be necessary at
some stage to return to a_1 and correct it again. This method of setting up the
transversal filter will give, for a single input pulse, an output which is zero
at all the sampling points except the central one. Having set up the filter
for a sampling interval T, any sequence of pulses at intervals T having the
given shape can be received and sampled correctly, without interference from
one pulse to the next. The system may be used for multi-level signals but it is
adjusted with isolated, full amplitude pulses.

The Eye Diagram

Correction at precisely the sampling points is theoretically correct, but takes no account of tolerances. Alignment of an equaliser requires a more complex measure of its accuracy and tolerance and this is provided by the eye diagram.

The waveform that leaves the equalising filter will be sampled at the appropriate times (usually at equal intervals) and the results of the samples should be unambiguous. This must still be true in the presence of any inaccuracies in timing and amplitude, whether in the waveform generator at the sending end, the equalising filter or the discriminator. It must be true for all possible sequences of neighbouring pulses which could contribute to inter-symbol effects.

Waveforms as received at the discrimination point can be recorded with all the sources of error included. Because of the different values of each digit and its neighbouring digits there will be many possible signal waveforms. When all these are recorded in overlaid form the *eye diagram* is obtained.

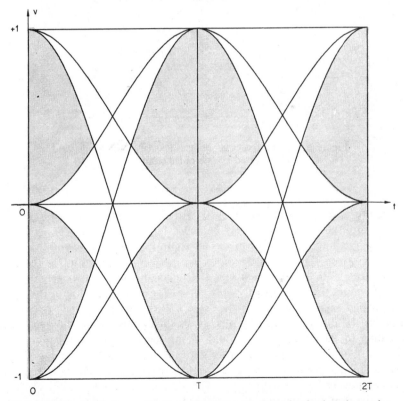

Figure 5.22. Perfect eye diagram with three levels and raised cosine pulse shape

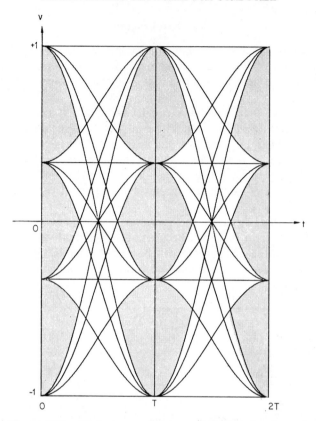

Figure 5.23.   Perfect eye diagram with four levels and
raised cosine pulse shape

Figure 5.22 was made in this way with the following assumptions. The signal amplitudes were accurately balanced ternary ($+1$, 0, -1), as used in bipolar signalling, the waveform was an accurate raised cosine and there were no other errors. The figure therefore is a perfect eye diagram for these circumstances, and because each curve is affected only by two neighbouring ternary values there are exactly nine curves for each transition in the figure. The shaded regions are called the 'eyes'. With this figure it is possible to visualize the discrimination by placing small regions inside the eyes corresponding to the sampling times and slicing levels with their tolerances. The freedom from discrimination errors depends on all the waveforms skirting round the discrimination regions so that the decision taken is indicated unambiguously by the path taken. The signal undertakes a kind of slalom round the sampling regions. If the eye is big enough to include these regions completely the system should operate without error. Figure 5.23 shows an

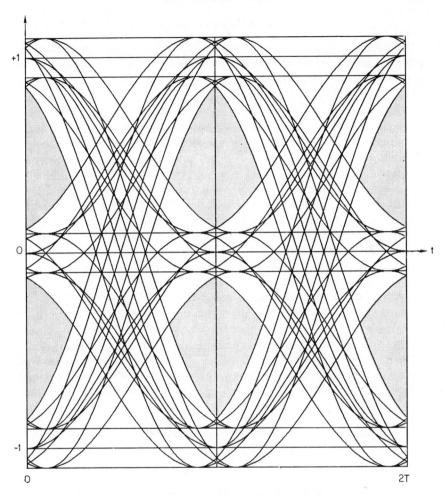

Figure 5.24.   Eye diagram with amplitude and phase errors

eye diagram for a signal with four levels. The signal is discriminated at three levels, corresponding to the three eyes at each sampling time.

The real eye diagram of a data transmission system can be seen by using an oscilloscope to show the waveforms at the point where discrimination takes place. A random pattern of bits is sent, so that all the different cases of intersymbol interference actually happen. Either the persistence of the oscilloscope screen or the use of a recording camera allows very many traces to be seen together, forming the eye diagram. Figure 5.24 was constructed for a three level signal with variations of $\pm 10\%$ in level and $\pm \pi/10$ in phase to give an imperfect eye diagram. The eyes are therefore smaller.

Automatic and Adaptive Equalisation

An automatic system to set up the gains in the transversal filter could work in one of two ways. Either it could use a special sequence of pulses to set up the system, like a training session before the transmission begins, or it could adjust continuously during transmission. The former is called *automatic* and the latter *adaptive*. In practice both methods are used[11] and an adaptive system often relies on a training session before transmission to get nearly into adjustment. The adaptive device is used on higher performance modems which may have 8 or 16 levels, to make good use of a telephone circuit. Adjustment on all the levels at once would be difficult. Training is therefore carried out with first a binary signal, then four levels, eight levels and so on until the working number of levels is reached. Data are then applied and the adaptive phase of operation started. Some automatic designs are confined to learning with special patterns such as single isolated pulses, but a fully adaptive version will be described. For best operation it needs a randomized train of bits (achieved in a way described later). If there happened to be a big change in line characteristics which closed the 'eyes' the modem would restart the training sequence and be out of action for several seconds.

Figure 5.25 shows the principle of the adaptive equaliser in the form which it takes for binary waveforms. The transversal filter has $2N+1$ stages, N before and N after the centre point. In this device the centre tapping is also adjusted and this is equivalent to adaption of the slicing level, or gain control. The sampling gate is shown, also the slicing stage, out of which comes a decision. This decision is used to generate the precise signal which should

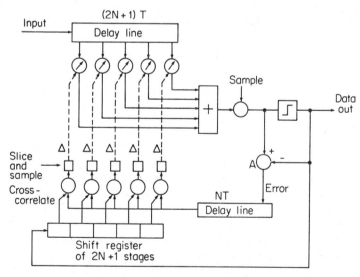

Figure 5.25. Adaptive equaliser for random binary signal

come from the equaliser. The comparison unit A produces a measure of the error in the signal at the sampling point. Of course, the error found is only valid if the decision itself was correct, and the success of the device depends on a large proportion of correct decisions from the start.

The analogue input signal and the (digital) output signal are delayed, one by a delay line and the other by a shift register, the latter being driven at a rate to keep it in step. The other delay line delays the error sequence by NT (T is the sampling interval) while the shift register has $2N+1$ outputs corresponding to the binary output of the discriminator delayed $0, 1 \ldots 2N+1$ steps. Each of these delayed outputs, which has possible signal levels $+1$ or -1, is correlated with the error signal in one of the correlators shown. For the middle one of the $2N+1$ correlators the error is correlated with its own binary digit, while for the others it is correlated with the earlier or later binary digits. The correlation is done by multiplying the signals, taking account of sign, and integrating the product. When the integral exceeds a certain threshold either positively or negatively, it is reset and the gain of the corresponding tap on the transversal filter is adjusted by one increment in the opposite sense. Thus a positive correlation, when reset to zero, causes the tap gain to move in the negative direction. The increments are small, typically less than 1% of full scale so more than 100 steps are needed to reach adjustment. This feature makes the system resilient to occasional noise bursts.

Intuitively it can be seen that the adjustment is being made to the most appropriate tap for each correlation output. For example if positive errors are typically associated with positive decisions made two intervals earlier this will give a positive correlation at the unit which is two stages downstream of centre. The corresponding tap will be made more negative, and the chief effect of this is to reduce the errors in question. The theory of its operation is given by Lucky.[11]

This adaptive equaliser can be simplified even further if the error measure

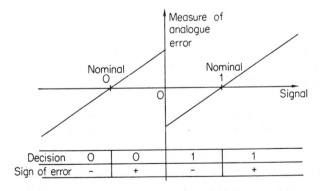

Figure 5.26. Discrimination of 2-level signal to produce error sign

in its analogue form is replaced by a binary signal which is the *sign* of the error. Then the correlators are replaced by modulo 2 adders feeding two-way counters. If the input digits are correlated the counter begins to move steadily up or down until it overflows. The overflow resets the counter to zero and shifts the gain of the tap by one increment. In this simplified system both the sign of the error and binary output are obtained by discrimination on the analogue sample. Figure 5.26 shows the situation when there is one bit per sample. The central slicing level decides which binary digit goes to the output. The two additional slicing levels placed at the nominal signal levels distinguish positive and negative errors. The discrimination device is exactly like one used for four level (two bit) signals but the least significant bit becomes the 'sign of the error'. To modify Figure 5.25 in order to accommodate 4, 8 or more levels in the received signal waveform, the discriminator has one more bit than usual (twice the number of levels), the least significant bit becomes the sign of the error and the most significant bit goes into the shift register.

5.5   BIT SEQUENCE TRANSPARENCY

The term *transparency* is widely used, and often in an ambiguous way. To ensure that its intention is clear, the word should always be qualified, and in the present context it is *bit sequence transparency* that concerns us. Bit-sequence transparency is the ability to convey *any* sequence of bits.

The task of a binary transmission channel is to convey a sequence of bits from the sender to the receiver. It therefore has an interface at each end, capable of transferring binary digits in sequence. If there are certain sequences of bits which are not conveyed correctly by the channel, it is not bit sequence transparent. An example of non-transparency would be the inability to recover the clock if a long series of 1s is sent.

Several measures to preserve transparency will be described, and clock recovery is mentioned because it is often linked to transparency.

The Scrambler

The Fourier spectrum of a data signal depends on the binary sequence it represents. Periodic or repeated sequences can give rise to peaks in the spectrum. These are undesirable when the telephone network is used for transmission and, at the worst, they might cause breakthrough to neighbouring channels. It would be better to have a binary sequence which appeared to be random. But repeated sequences do happen in data, particularly strings of zeros.

The adaptive equaliser works best with a random data sequence, and a random bit sequence sometimes helps the recovery of the clock at the receiving end. For these reasons, in some modems, a *scrambler* is employed which encodes the input binary sequence so that it is unlikely to have repeated sequences. It is not possible to prevent repeated sequences with absolute certainty, but at least the common repetitions in incoming data can be removed. The scrambler at the sending end is, of course, matched by an unscrambler at the receiving end. Figure 5.27 shows the principle of a type of scrambler based on the 'feedback shift register'. The logical elements in the figure carry out modulo 2 addition, otherwise known as 'exclusive OR'. Modulo 2 addition for binary digits is simply addition ignoring the carry digit.

In this scrambler (and the unscrambler) the output of several stages of the shift register are added together, modulo 2, and then added, modulo 2, to the data stream. In the scrambler, the feedback configuration is used, and the shift register is shifted at the bit rate of the channel. It is well known that this feedback shift register can generate a pseudorandom sequence, given zeros as data input, assuming it starts in a non-zero state. With a fortunate choice of the taps on the n element delay line a sequence of $2^n - 1$ states can be produced before it repeats. The data input is obviously scrambled by such a device.

The unscrambler takes the same general form in the feedforward configuration. If the two shift registers contain the same bit sequence (which they should, ignoring delays, if there are no errors on the line), then the two bit patterns added into the channel at gates A and B are identical. Since the second addition cancels out the first it follows that the original sequence S is restored.

The operation of these 'feedback' and 'feedforward' shift registers is analysed in the appendix to this chapter on page 173. These devices are widely used in communication systems, as generators of pseudorandom numbers, scramblers (as above) and for the generation of cyclic sum checks (a subject to which we return in Chapter 6).

Introduction of scramblers alters the error performance. Consider a single, isolated error bit. It can be thought of as passing through the unscrambler to cause an immediate output error, then it goes into the shift register and re-emerges at each tap. In the example of Figure 5.27, each isolated bit-error would thus be turned into four bit-errors in the received stream. But

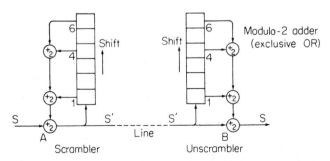

Figure 5.27.   A scrambler and its corresponding unscrambler

at least there is no permanent 'loss of synchronism' between the two devices causing errors to continue.

Sequences with repeated patterns could well occur but with low probability. If the data S was all zeros and the shift register empty, S′ would be all zeros too. An extra device can be added, as shown in Figure 5.28, to prevent some harmful sequences. This is a scrambler recommended by CCITT and it guards against sending long strings of zeros or ones which could give difficulties with clock recovery in certain kinds of modem. If the outputs from stages 1 and 9 of the shift register remain equal for 32 steps, the counter overflows and an extra 1 is injected into the loop. The same logic is repeated at the receiving end and it restores the original sequence, for the same reason as before.

The CCITT recommended scrambler, shown in Figure 5.28, has the unusual feature of a negator which is inserted into its loop. This has no significant effect on the operation except that the 'exceptional' state of the scrambler, which in the previous example had zeros everywhere, now has the shift register full of ones, and the data input of all zeros preserves this state. In any shift register with an even number of taps the effect of the negator in the loop can be regarded as one of negating the sequence on the line itself.

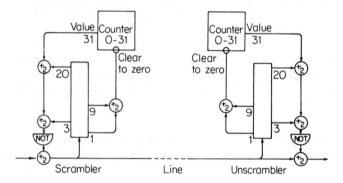

Figure 5.28.   Scrambler which guards against repetitions

Clock Recovery

In synchronous transmission a clock signal must be recovered at the receiving end to gate the received waveform and reform the digital sequence. The clock information must somehow be carried in the transmitted signal but clearly a very small part of the channel's information capacity need be given over to the clock. The methods of carrying the clock information and recovering it vary with the coding method used and with the modulation method if one is used. Two examples will be given, one suitable for a modem used on the telephone network, the other suitable for a baseband system.

The first example is derived from the U.K. Post Office modem number 7A

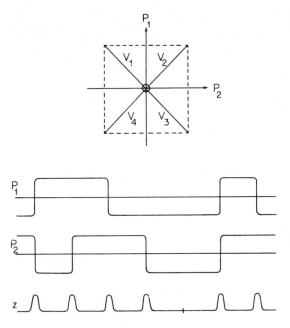

Figure 5.29. Derivation of a zero-crossing signal
from two signals

which employs phase modulation. There are four phases, carrying two bits per symbol, and the normal digit rate of 2400 bit/s is achieved by modulating the 1800 Hz carrier at 1200 baud.

Figure 5.29 shows the four phases used by means of the vectors $V_1 - V_4$. Demodulation employs two phases at carrier frequency in quadrature, so that the components of the signal vector in two directions are obtained, and these components have been called P_1 and P_2. In the lower part of the figure the two recovered baseband signals are shown and their combined zero crossings are obtained as the signal Z. This is the signal which will be used to time the clock. A clock waveform must be produced in which the pulses would come neatly between the Z pulses, and it must not be affected by absent Z pulses.

A crystal controlled oscillator is used which can hold the frequency constant enough so that only relatively slow adjustments of clock phase are needed. Figure 5.30 shows how pulse counters are used to produce the 1200 bit/s clock. The clock is compared for phase with the zero crossing signal Z, and a decision made whether it is early or late. Accordingly, a pulse is subtracted from, or added to, one of the counters. For rapid resynchronizing, a change of 4% in phase is made, but when the phase is close enough the system changes to a fine control of $\frac{1}{2}$% steps. The fact that some of the Z pulses are missing (where there were no transitions) does not affect the

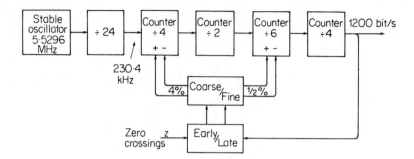

Figure 5.30.   Automatic clock-phase adjustment

operation, but very long sequences with no phase transitions would allow the phase of the clock to wander.

A much simpler method of clock recovery can be used for the bipolar signal. It is merely necessary to rectify the signal as shown in Figure 5.31 to produce a waveform with a strong component at the clock frequency where the bipolar waveform, as we found earlier, has no frequency component. The rectified signal is used to lock an oscillator which is tuned to the clock frequency, and from this oscillator the clock is derived. This simple system has a 'fly-wheel' effect of much shorter duration than the set of counters. Because it is sensitive to the pulse pattern a small timing-jitter is introduced.

In PCM transmission this method is used to recover the clock at each of the regenerators. The jitter introduced by successive regenerators adds up, because it is linked to the bit pattern, and after a certain number of regenerators it is necessary to insert a regenerator with a more elaborate clock recovery system.

Because the regenerators must be simple, there cannot be more than a few consecutive zeros together in the pattern of bits. When the first PCM systems were designed this was achieved by coding the speech sample in a particular way. This unfortunately leaves the system unable to handle data, which can have strings of zeros. In later designs, including the 2.048 Mbit/s PCM system recommended by CCITT, the binary stream has been coded in a special way

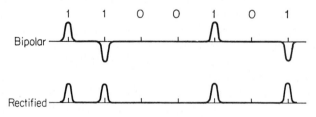

Figure 5.31.   Rectification of bipolar signal for
clock recovery

that allows any sequence of bits to be transmitted without an excessive string of zeros on the line.

Two of these coding methods which ensure bit sequence transparency will be described. They are called 'pair-selected ternary' and 'high density bipolar' respectively. Croisier[12] has reviewed pseudoternary codes very well.

Pair-Selected Ternary Coding

In this code, the binary sequence to be transmitted is treated as a sequence of pairs of bits.[13] The bipolar signal has three possible levels which we shall write as +, 0 and −. The correspondence of the bit-pairs to the signals is as follows:

$$
\begin{array}{lll}
00 & \text{becomes} & -+ \\
11 & \text{becomes} & +- \\
10 & \text{becomes} & +\,0 \ \text{ or } \ -0 \\
01 & \text{becomes} & 0+ \ \text{ or } \ 0-
\end{array}
$$

Where there is a choice, it is made so that the + forms and the − forms are used alternately.

Here is an example of PST coding:

$$
\begin{array}{llllllll}
\text{binary} & 10 & 00 & 10 & 01 & 11 & 00 & 10 \\
\text{PST} & +0 & -+ & -0 & 0+ & -+ & -+ & -0 \\
 & \uparrow & & \uparrow & \uparrow & & & \uparrow \\
 & + & & - & + & & & -
\end{array}
$$

The arrows point to the pulses where the table gives a choice and, according to the rule, they are alternately positive and negative.

The PST coding ensures that no more than two adjacent 0 symbols occur in the PST coded output. This is excellent for the maintenance of regenerator clock timing. In other respects the PST code is not so good. A possible output from PST coding is $-+, 0+, +-$ where three positive pulses occur without a negative between them. This so-called 'disparity' presents a slight problem at the regenerator's input stage.

Where the pulse combinations 00, $++$ or $--$ occur they must straddle the 2-bit frame, so their presence in the signal enables it to be framed correctly. But a string of zeros in the binary input gives a PST signal $-+-+-+$ which, if framing is lost due to noise, could equally well be interpreted as a string of ones.

The coding factor $C(f)$ which we introduced in equation (5-11) to show the effect of coding on the Fourier spectrum can be calculated for PST. By counting cases the autocovariances can be determined, and are $R(0) = \frac{3}{4}$, $R(1) = -\frac{9}{32}$, $R(2) = -\frac{1}{16}$ and $R(3) = -\frac{1}{32}$. The correlation that does occur is due to the alternation of + and − in the choice. A pair is equally likely to change this 'parity' or leave it unchanged, so there is no correlation beyond adjacent pairs, just as there is no correlation beyond adjacent bits in bipolar.

The coding factor thus calculated is given in equation (5-18) and plotted in Figure 5.32. The mean power and the spectral maximum are increased, compared with bipolar by factors $\frac{3}{2}$, $\frac{5}{4}$, respectively. The coding factor is

$$C_4(f) = \tfrac{1}{8}(1 - \cos^3 2\pi fT)\,(7 + 4\cos 2\pi fT + 2\cos^2 2\pi fT) \quad (5\text{-}18)$$

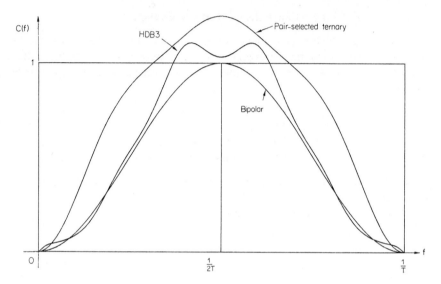

Figure 5.32.   Coding factors for bipolar, HDB3 and PST

High Density Bipolar Coding

In the ordinary bipolar code, successive pulses are of opposite signs. This is not so in PST where the 'bipolar rule' is violated frequently. In the high density bipolar code, bipolar violations are used, but sparingly and only to carry the extra information needed to replace strings of zeros.

There is a series of high-density bipolar codes[14] which are known as HDB1, HDB2, HDB3, etc. Code HDBn avoids the occurrence of more than n pulses of level 0. The most important of them is HDB3 because of its adoption by CCITT, and this will be described.

HDB3, like the other codes of the series, uses the bipolar rule wherever possible. But whenever the string 0000 happens in the binary sequence, it must use something other than the signal 0000 on the line. It is replaced by a special sequence which is distinguished by including in it a bipolar violation. Expressed as though it was part of the binary input, the special sequence is one of these:

$$0\ 0\ 0\ V \quad \text{and} \quad 1\ 0\ 0\ V$$

Here, the 1 is represented in the signal, following the bipolar rule, by levels

+1 or −1, the 0 by level 0 and V by +1 or −1 violating the bipolar rule. An example of HDB3 coding follows, in which the special sequences are in boxes.

The choice of 000V or 100V is made in such a way that the violation pulses themselves take the levels +1 and −1 alternately.

binary	1 1 0 1	0 0 0 0	0 0 1	0 0 0 0	0 0 0 0	1 0 1 1
rule	1 1 0 1	1 0 0 V	0 0 1	0 0 0 V	1 0 0 V	1 0 1 1
signal	− + 0 −	+ 0 0 +	0 0 −	0 0 0 −	+ 0 0 +	− 0 + −

Note that 100V is used when there has been an *even* number of ones since the last special sequence. Also, that the special sequences can follow one another if the string of zeros continues.

The Spectrum of HDB3

The power spectrum of an HDB3 signal can be expected not to differ much from that of a bipolar signal. Calculation of the spectrum (for random binary data) uses, as before, the autocovariance of the signal. In all the examples given before in the chapter, the span of the covariance has been strictly limited and the values of R(0), R(1), R(2) etc. could be obtained by simple methods amounting to no more than counting cases. The calculation for HDB codes is more difficult, and illustrates how a more general rule can be treated.

To simplify the illustration, HDB1 will be used to demonstrate the method. A state diagram is shown in Figure 5.33 which represents a generator of HDB1 signals. The arrows show the possible transitions among the twelve states of the system and each is labelled with the transition probability. At each clock pulse, one transition is made and the label in the new box denotes the pulse level generated.

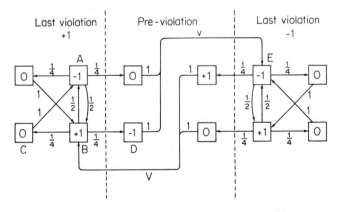

Figure 5.33. State diagram for a generator of HDB1 signals

For example, state A could be entered to represent a binary 1 by generating a pulse with level -1. The next bit can be 1 (with probability $\frac{1}{2}$) and it generates $+1$ by transition to state B. The other possibility, binary 0, splits into two cases 00 or 01 which have different effects because the first one leads into a violation sequence. The other case, 01, gives rise to the state transitions $B \rightarrow C \rightarrow A$ and generates 0, -1. The violation sequence for binary input 00 is given by transitions $B \rightarrow D \rightarrow E$ and generates -1, -1.

The two halves of the diagram cope with the rule of alternation of violation polarities. Violations occur at the transitions by way of the paths marked V to states B or E and the shape of the diagram assures the alternation of polarities.

From Figure 5.33 a matrix of transition probabilities can be constructed, and it is called $\|P\|$ where each element p_{ij} is the probability of transition from state i to state j.

Starting from any state i, suppose one clock pulse leads to state j and the next to state k. The probability of this occurrence is $p_{ij}p_{jk}$. If all the possible intermediate values are taken into account the probability of transition from i to k by any allowed route is given by

$$p_{ik}^{(2)} = \sum_{j=1}^{12} p_{ij}p_{jk} \tag{5-19}$$

The right hand side of the equation is the (i, k) element of the product of $\|P\|$ with itself. So the transition probabilities for two successive transitions are given by a new matrix.

$$\|P^{(2)}\| = \|P\|^2 \tag{5-20}$$

In a similar way it can be shown that the transition probabilities for the result of n transitions occurring at n successive clock pulses are given by the elements of the matrix.

$$\|P^{(n)}\| = \|P\|^n \tag{5-21}$$

Now suppose that the generator runs and let q_i denote the unconditional probability that the system is in state i. We also denote by X_i the signal level ($+1$, 0 or -1) generated at the state i. It is then possible to write down an expression for the autocovariance.

Consider this sequence of events. The state of the system begins at i. After n clock pulses it arrives at j. The probability of the occurrence, for a given value of n is given by multiplying q_i, the unconditional probability of being in state i, by $p_{ij}^{(n)}$ the probability of the transition, starting in i. So the event has probability $q_i p_{ij}^{(n)}$. The first state is associated with a signal level X_i and n pulses later the final signal level is X_j. The contribution of this sequence of events to the autocovariance $R(n)$ is

$$X_i X_j q_i p_{ij}^{(n)}$$

and by adding over all possible starting and finishing states

$$R(n) = \sum_{ij=1}^{12} X_i X_j \, q_i p_{ij}^{(n)} \qquad (5\text{-}22)$$

There is a special case with no transition, namely

$$R(o) = \sum_{i=1}^{12} X_i^2 q_i \qquad (5\text{-}23)$$

The X_i values can be read from the state diagram of Figure 5.33 and it is not difficult to calculate q_i. In principle they can be obtained by the limit of $\|P^{(n)}\|$ for large n, but the simple form of the state diagram allows all the q_i to be expressed in forms of the probability of state B. For example, all entry to state A is from B, and this occurs with probability $\frac{3}{4}$. Then, adding together all the q_i, since the sum is 1, the values are obtained. B (and E) have an unconditional probability of $\frac{4}{21}$, the highest value reached.

Proceeding in this way the autocovariances for HDB1 were calculated, and were

$$R(0) = \frac{16}{21}; \qquad R(1) = -\frac{1}{3}; \qquad R(2) = \frac{5}{84}; \text{ etc.}$$

The state diagram for HDB3 has 24 states. To produce a satisfactory power spectrum curve near the origin it was found necessary to calculate at least as far as $R(63)$ which is -0.0001. The long-term autocovariance with this code is negative, and $R(n)$ decreases exponentially with n, but it takes 28 terms to fall by a factor of 10. The power spectrum of HDB3 is plotted in Figure 5.32. It lies close to the bipolar curve, and improves on PST code except near the origin. The mean power is increased, compared with bipolar, by the factor $512/465$, close to 10%.

The long-term autocovariance and the bump in the spectrum near the origin are due to the bipolar rule applying to violations, which are comparatively well-spaced events. There are some codes of a similar kind without this feature, but they generally have larger disparity. In the application to PCM, which CCITT has recommended, the effect of the spectral bump on the power in the audio band must be checked because PCM channels share cables with audio pairs. Although the power at low frequencies is about 20 times the bipolar value it is low enough to avoid audible crosstalk.

5.6 *APPENDIX*

Feedback and Feedforward Shift Registers

Figures 5.27 and 5.28 showed feedback and feedforward shift registers used in a scrambler and unscrambler respectively. These devices are also used to generate pseudorandom binary sequences (which can be used for

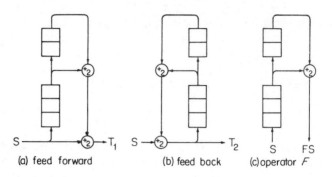

Figure 5.34.   Illustrative shift register devices

testing and adjusting equipment) and to construct sum-check characters and test for errors. Their use in error checking is described in Chapter 6.

To describe their operation we shall use a simple example of a five-bit shift register which is shown in Figure 5.34 in the feedforward and feedback arrangements. Each operates on an input sequence of bits S and produces an output sequence T.

Let us introduce the operator E which represents the effect of delaying the sequence by one bit. $E^3 S$ is the sequence obtained by delaying S by three bits. The feedforward device can easily be expressed in these terms because S is added (modulo 2) to $E^3 S$ and $E^5 S$ which come from the shift register. Consequently, with addition always *modulo 2*,

$$T_1 = (1 + E^3 + E^5)S$$
$$= (1 + F)S \text{ where } F = E^3 + E^5 \tag{5A-1}$$

The expression F has been introduced to describe the effect of the shift register part of the system irrespective of its feedback or feedforward connection, as shown in part (c) of the figure.

Operators of this kind, made up from the E operation and addition have the linear superposition property which is used in the analysis of linear filters, except that addition being carried out *modulo 2* means that the coefficients take only the values 0 and 1.

There are two alternative ways to analyse the feedback device. Consider a sequence S entering it and being returned as FS via the feedback path. It circulates again as $F^2 S$, then again as $F^3 S$ and so forth. The resultant output is

$$T_2 = (1 + F + F^2 + F^3 + F^4 + \ldots)S \tag{5A-2}$$

Another approach is to note that if T_2 is the output of the feedback device, FT_2 returns through the feedback path and $S + FT_2$ leaves the adder to become the output T_2.

Therefore $\qquad T_2 = S + FT_2$

from which $\qquad T_2 = \left(\dfrac{1}{1+F}\right) S \qquad\qquad$ (5A-3)

An operator such as $1/1+F$ requires some mathematical justification, but a simple idea is to expand it as a power series. Remembering that subtraction modulo 2 is the same as addition this gives the series $1 + F + F^2 + F^3 + \ldots$, agreeing with equation (5A-2).

The feedforward and feedback devices can be regarded as filters, and because their operators are $1 + F$ and $(1 + F)^{-1}$ respectively they are complementary. Put in tandem they can reproduce the input sequence exactly.

To understand them as 'filters', since they have the superposition property it is sufficient to know their response to the unit impulse. For the examples given in Figure 5.34 and showing the sequences one above the other to keep the time relationship the result would be

```
S     01000
T₁    0100101000 ...
T₂    01001011001111100011011101010000 | 1001 ...
```

The output from the feedforward device is finite in extent, but the feedback device produces a sequence of 31 bits, which then repeats indefinitely.

With an input of zeros, the feedback device has two types of behaviour, it can be full of zeros, or producing the sequence of 31 bits. Since its shift register of five stages has 32 possible states, the 31 states of the 'active' device and the single state of the empty device exhaust all the possibilities.

(In other shift registers with different size and different tapping points this may not be true, for example a 6 bit register can have one empty state and three different 'active' states each with sequences of length 21.) If the expression $1 + F + F^2 + F^3 + \ldots$ is expanded in terms of the elementary operator E, where $F = E^3 + E^5$, the power series has as coefficients the binary sequence which is the response to the unit impulse, thus

$$\frac{1}{1+F} = 1 + E^3 + E^5 + E^6 + E^9 + E^{10} + E^{11} + \ldots \qquad (5A-4)$$

This shows the feedback device as though it was an infinite shift register feedforward device.

In the scrambler/unscrambler pair the feedback device is the scrambler, and the simpler feedforward device is the unscrambler. As a result, any bit errors added to the sequence on the transmission channel have only a finite error effect in the unscrambler. In the example of $F = 1 + E^3 + E^5$ each isolated error bit would produce three error bits in the final output. This is sometimes expressed by saying that the system is 'self-synchronizing', by contrast with systems where errors are perpetuated.

The feedforward device is a kind of *multiplier* by $1 + F$, and the feedback device a *divider*. The result of the division sum can be a recurring binary number, and this is a way of explaining the repeated sequence. Remember, however, that the multiplication and division algorithms use modulo 2 addition.

The theoretical treatment of these devices in the literature often treats the sequences as coefficients of polynomials which are multiplied or divided by other polynomials, the coefficients being added modulo 2. The treatment given here using operators is easier to understand if the mathematical method is accepted without formal proof.

References

1. Nyquist, H., 'Certain topics in telegraph transmission theory', *Am. Inst. Elect. Engrs. Trans.*, **47**, No. 2, 617, (April 1928).
2. Sunde, E. D., 'Theoretical fundamentals of pulse transmission' (in 2 parts), *Bell Syst. Tech. J.*, **33**, No. 3, 721 (May 1954), 987 (July 1954).
3. Lender, A., 'The duobinary technique for high-speed data transmission', *Trans. Am. Inst. Elect. Engrs. (Communication and Electronics)*, **82**, 214 (May 1963).
4. Gorog, E., 'Redundant alphabets with desirable frequency spectrum properties', *IBM J. of Res. and Dev.*, **12**, No. 3, 234 (May 1968).
5. Bennett, W. R., 'Spectra of quantized signals', *Bell Syst. Tech. J.*, **27**, No. 3, 446 (1948).
6. Kallman, H. E., 'Transversal filters', *Proc. IRE*, **28**, 302 (July 1940).
7. Voelcker, Herbert B., 'Generation of digital signalling waveforms', *IEEE Trans. Communication Tech.*, **COM-16**, No. 1, (February 1968).
8. Croisier, A., and Pierret, J. M., 'High efficiency data transmission through digital echo modulation', *IEEE Int. Conf. on Communications*, 29/9, (June 1969).
9. van Gerwen, P. J. The use of digital circuits in data transmission, *Philips Tech. Rev.*, **30**, No. 3, 71 (1969).
10. Choquet, M. F., and Nussbaumer, H. J., 'Generation of synchronous data transmission signals by echo modulation', *IBM J. of Res. and Dev.*, **15**, No. 5, 364 (Sept. 1971).
11. Lucky, R. W., and Rudin, H. R., 'Generalized automatic equalisation for communication channels', *Digest Tech. Papers IEEE Int. Communications Conf.*, 22 (1966).
12. Croisier, A., 'Introduction to pseudoternary transmission codes', *IBM J. of Res. and Dev.*, **14**, No. 4, 354 (July 1970).
13. Sipress, J. M., 'A new class of selected ternary pulse transmission plans for digital transmission lines', *IEEE Trans. Communication Tech.*, **COM-13**, 366, (1965).
14. Falcoz, A., and Croisier, A., 'The high density bipolar code—a method of baseband transmission', *Colloque Int. sur la Teleinformatique*, Paris, 54 (March 1969). (In French.)

Chapter 6

Information Flow Control, Storage and Coding

6.1 INTRODUCTION

In this chapter, the control of information flow in systems is discussed with reference to simple computing systems. The concept of handshaking that arises leads on to the idea of an interface between parts of systems and the benefits of a standard interface. The use of an interface to link two autonomous systems shows the need for storage in the link between them.

The advantages of associating storage with data links are considered and examples are given of various techniques for overcoming difficulties arising when links are used with computer systems. A discussion of error control methods with particular reference to data links is given, and the consideration of coding for error control leads on to the use of coding for information exchange.

6.2 INFORMATION FLOW CONTROL

When information is passed from one system to another it is rare for the flow of information to occur solely in one direction. Generally some kind of interaction occurs between the two systems in order to control the way in which one system transmits and the other receives the information. It is necessary for each system to know that the other is ready to cooperate in the transfer of information; sometimes the rate of transfer has to be governed, and if errors can occur a means for their elimination is needed. Usually, this control of information transfer between two systems requires the interchange of additional information which is often not regarded, or even identified, as part of the overall communication process, but which must not be overlooked in the design of a communications channel or network intended to link the systems together.

The problem of information flow control arises in all systems, even those comprising organizations of human beings. Indeed, some qualitative feel for the problem may be gained by considering how people communicate with each other, both individually and in groups. Great use is made of feedback; though this may take many forms, and only rarely is information broadcast without some regard for how it is being received and the effect is it having. For example, a manufacturer embarking upon an advertising campaign expects an increase in his sales figures, and will modify his campaign if this does not happen. The feedback here is remote, but none-the-less real, and effective.

A measure of the effectiveness of a communications channel can be gained by considering how it constrains the behaviour of systems which it inter-connects. For example, when two people converse with each other face-to-face, their interaction includes gestures and facial expressions that are often more eloquent than words, and which play an important role in controlling and enhancing the exchange of information. But when a telephone channel is interposed between two people the way they interact and communicate is radically changed. No longer is the presence of the other party visually apparent, so their conversation must include additional information to allow for this fact. For instance, the slightest interfering noise is likely to evoke expressions like 'are you still there?'. The value of the telephone has made it worth-while for people to evolve procedures for using it effectively and most users are unaware in any direct sense of these procedures, as they are largely unaware of the procedures governing face-to-face communication that they learnt during childhood.

To appreciate the factors which must be considered in designing a communications channel to link computer systems it is relevant to consider how two such systems communicate when joined directly together, and what constraints they will experience when using the channel.

Control by Handshaking

The idea of using a series of interlocks which ensure that a sequence of events occurs in a correct manner appears in many forms. It is fundamental to the control of asynchronous systems and, as described in Chapter 3, is exemplified in computer systems by the use of flags and semaphores. The same concept is also encountered outside the computer in the control of peripheral devices and communications links. In these areas the concept of a *standard interface* has emerged in which a defined set of connections is used for a range of peripheral devices, or links. The flow of information across an interface must be controlled as rigidly as that within the computer. The term *hand-shaking* was coined to describe the controlled transfer of data across an interface where one side 'shakes hands' with the other to effect the transfer of one unit of information.

The word 'handshake' has become widely used to refer generally to con-trolled transfers of information of all kinds. For example, in the familiar telephone network there is one handshake between the user and the network for each telephone call. This handshake comprises the subscriber's request for a particular connection, the granting of the connection by the network, the request to clear by the subscribers, and disconnection by the network. The subscriber is not normally conscious of the completion of the disconnection; this is implicit in his ability to make another call.

The simple handshake described above can be decomposed into a number of detailed 'lower-level' handshakes, such as 'lifting the receiver', and getting 'dialling tone' in reply. Each handshake is an inter-system interlock, e.g. if anyone dials without waiting for dialling tone, things go wrong. This interlock could be really positive, in the sense that the telephone system could have been designed so that the dial could not be moved unless dialling tone was present. But with intelligent human subscribers, and the fact that

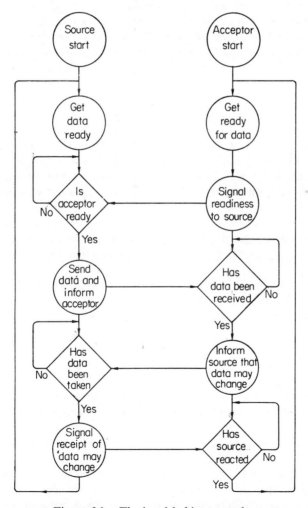

Figure 6.1.   The handshaking procedure

dialling tone usually appears very quickly, a positive interlock is not required. This is not the case with less intelligent, automatic terminals, where a positively interlocked series of handshakes is essential to govern interactions between them.

Handshaking, and hierarchies of handshake procedures, are absolutely fundamental and must be a prime factor considered in the initial design of any interactive system. It is not possible to partition a system effectively at a point where handshaking cannot occur.

The essential features of a handshaking procedure are shown in Figure 6.1 where simplified state diagrams for a source and an acceptor are given on the left and right respectively. The crosslinking signals are those necessary to interlock the source and acceptor operations in order that only one item of data is transferred between them for each cycle of the complete diagram. Beginning at the top of the diagram, the two 'start' conditions cover any necessary initialization; thereafter, the individual source and acceptor cycles are traced, pausing where indicated for the appropriate crosslinking signal.

The Standard Interface

The concept of an interface needs careful definition because it has come to have two different meanings: it may be a 'black box' joining two devices; or it may be a defined set of signals and wires for connecting devices together. In the former case, the idea of a 'standard' interface is not very practicable, but a standard interface which is a common set of signals used for joining several different devices is a most valuable concept. The use of a standard interface provides a flexibility that can drastically reduce system development time and maintenance effort, and allows adaptation and evolution as requirements change.

Suppose N different kinds of information source have to communicate with M types of information acceptor. Without a standard interface, $N \times M$ connecting units are required, if all possible kinds of connection are to be possible; this is illustrated in Figure 6.2. The interfaces here meet the first definition of the term and are purpose-designed to join together two different devices or sometimes a limited range of similar devices. With the wide variety of devices and systems, there is always plenty of interface designing to be done, because the introduction of a new source device requires a new interface for each existing acceptor device, with which it must communicate—and vice versa.

The other definition of an interface is illustrated by Figure 6.3. Here, the idea of a standard interface is introduced. This is a defined set of signals that flow between two devices or systems across an identifiable boundary between them. It may be necessary to design a matching unit to convert the standard interface signals into others suitable for operating a particular source or

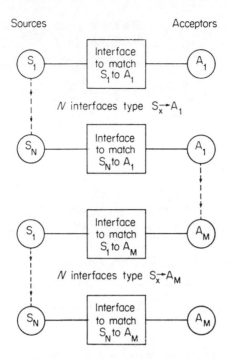

With N sources and M acceptors
all possible types of interconnection would
require the use of $N \times M$ interfaces

Figure 6.2. Purpose-built interface

acceptor, but only a single matching unit is required for each device. Further-more, the introduction of one new device requires only one new matching unit regardless of the number of devices already in existence. The total number of matching units required for N sources and M acceptors is $N + M$ which, for more than three devices, compares well with the $N \times M$ interfaces needed without the standard interface concept.

So useful is the idea of a standard interface that manufacturers of large computers all have standard interfaces which allow a particular peripheral device to operate with a whole range of their computers; a feature of consid-erable convenience both for themselves and their customers. The manu-facturers of small computers also have their own interface standards; these are usually published in detail and permit customers to incorporate the computers into their own data processing systems.

Unfortunately, the interfaces defined by the various manufacturers are incompatible with each other, although they are broadly designed to perform

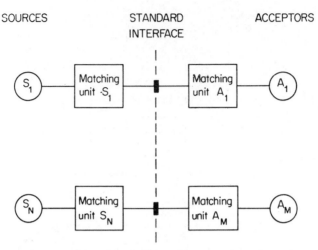

A matching unit each of N sources and a matching unit
for each of M acceptors giving a total of $N+M$ units

Figure 6.3.   The Standard Interface concept

similar functions. This is inconvenient for independent manufacturers of
peripheral devices, and for designers of systems using computers from
different manufacturers. There is a clear need for an interface standard which
is independent of particular manufacturers. The value of such a standard
would be greatly enhanced if it received international recognition.

At present, the only interface standard accepted internationally is that
recommended by the CCITT (Comité Consultatif International de Télé-
graphique et Téléphonique) for connections between modems—supplied or
authorized by telephone and telegraph administrations—and customers data
terminal equipment. This interface already discussed in Chapter 2, page 37,
is concerned solely with the serial transmission of information on a pair of
wires; even so, each type of modem may have several wires carrying control
signals selected from a list of some 34 given in the V.24 recommendations of
the CCITT.[1] (Electrical Industries Association Specification EIA RS232
in the USA.)

The use of the modem interface is mandatory in many countries for
equipment connected to the public telephone network; so, when two systems
made by different manufacturers are linked by data transmission circuits
(as is increasingly the case) they may be considered as joined by CCITT
interfaces. In such circumstances, it is essential to agree upon a procedure for
the exchange of information between the two systems. Information exchange
procedures do not form part of the interface specification, which is concerned
merely with the passage of signals across the boundary between devices.

In principle, the CCITT interface could be used as a general purpose interface for interconnecting data processing equipment. But devices which handle information as parallel words or characters would require serial-to-parallel or parallel-to-serial convertors. This would be expensive, and might unduly limit the rate at which information could be transferred.

As there are many devices which operate fundamentally by handling information in a parallei form, there is an economic case for an interface with the wide acceptance of the CCITT interface, but which permits the exchange of information as parallel words or characters. The interface detailed in British Standard Specification 4421[2] is intended for this purpose; and, because it is the only company-independent standard interface and has also been used for joining together computers made by different manufacturers, it is worth discussing in some detail to illustrate the considerations important in the specification of an interface. A description of British Standard Specification 4421 is given as an appendix, see page 531. There is no standard of this kind recognised in the U.S.A., but work on the definition of such a 'device' standard interface is under consideration by the International Standards Organization.

Linked Autonomous Systems

In the examples of the control of information flow already considered the problems of coupling two devices or processes have been discussed, and the handshake principle and its application to the standard interface has been examined. Similar principles apply to the interconnection of two autonomous systems, and will be described in relation to the behaviour of two linked multi-access systems each of which is assumed to have a single controller. Both systems are dealing with several channels while attempting to communicate with the other. A multi-access computer handles many channels by servicing them sequentially, but at a high rate compared with the activity of individual channels. Each channel seems, therefore, to have the full attention of the central processor. The success of any multi-access system depends on the way its operating system schedules the servicing of the various channels and this, in turn, depends on the effective use of storage and interlocks. Usually, flags are employed to indicate the state of each channel, and the operating system or executive deals with channels according to some scheduling algorithm chosen by the system designers. No matter what any channel may do, the overall system cannot be held up because the executive has complete control. But the situation is different when two such systems are connected by a common channel which contains no storage. Such a channel cannot be commanded by both systems, and the executive of one system cannot behave freely if the other executive commands the common channel.

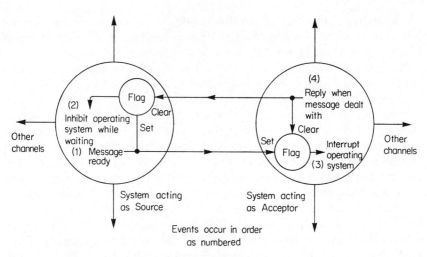

Figure 6.4.   Systems linked without storage

The problem is illustrated by Figure 6.4 which shows two multi-access systems: one is acting as a source of a message to be received by the other acting as an acceptor. When the message is ready, the source system will set a flag to prevent further internal activity while the channel is passing the message to the acceptor system. But if this is busy dealing with its other channels, the source will be held up until the common channel is serviced. The problem arises essentially because the two systems are operating asynchronously and it is unlikely that the source will attempt to send a message just when the acceptor is ready to receive one. In fact, the source has to commit itself to an interaction with the acceptor and, once committed, can make no further action until the acceptor has responded. An alternative arrangement would be to make the acceptor signal when it was ready for a message. In this case the acceptor would be held up waiting for the source. Without the use of intermediate storage it is impossible to avoid one of the systems being held up by the other.

An example from everyday life occurs when one asks a telephone operator to get a number, and is told she will ring back. One is then virtually chained to the telephone until she does so.

Systems Decoupled by Storage

The use of storage between systems is shown in Figure 6.5. Assume the store is empty and the source system wishes to send a message to the acceptor system. The executive detects that the store is empty and may schedule a transfer of a message when it is convenient. The 'message ready' signal can

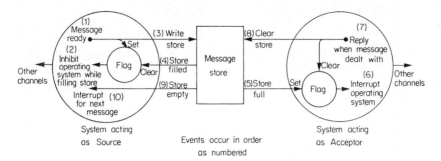

Figure 6.5.   Systems linked with storage

be used to start the filling of the store and the flag which inhibits further source activity is set only while the store is being filled. Thereafter, the source is free to deal with other channels. The acceptor need only pay heed to the store when it contains a message. There is no requirement for rapid attention to the store, so the executive in the acceptor may schedule the reading and clearing of the store when it is convenient.

The effect of the store between the two systems is to decouple them; but, of course, the store must be large enough to hold the longest message that can pass between the systems in a single transaction.

It is possible to define two fundamentally different interfaces: one at the input and the other at the output of the store, as evident in Figure 6.5. At the input, the store indicates when it is empty and is committed to accepting a message, however long the source takes to respond. At the output, the store indicates to the acceptor when it is full and is committed to wait until the acceptor responds by reading the message. It is not possible to define a single standard interface to serve both as an input and as an output interface for a store, because the functions it has to perform differ in the two positions. If a single standard is required it must be defined either to hold up a source, or to hold up an acceptor. The interface to British Standard 4421 corresponds to the store-input type of interface which holds up the acceptor.

In practice, it is usually inconvenient to have a store between two systems linked by a parallel interface; so instead, a store must be included inside one of the systems. Because the 4421 standard contains no guide on where the store should be placed, it is common for device designers to include a store in both source and acceptor to ensure that at least one is present when any two devices are coupled, whatever other designers may do.

When the two systems are far apart it becomes necessary to join them by a data link. It is then very convenient to include storage in the data link, where it can perform other functions in addition to decoupling the two systems from each other.

The Simple Buffer Store

The value of a store as a simple buffer was discussed in the previous section which described the interaction between two autonomous data processing systems and showed the need for storage in the link connecting them together. Whether this storage is in the link itself, or within one of the systems, it may be regarded as having an input and an output interface. The flow of information into and out of the store is controlled by logic forming part of the interfaces on each side, so that the store temporarily delays the passage of information from one interface to the other, acting as a buffer between the systems which it joins.

A simple buffer is illustrated in Figure 6.6. Simplified logic is given to show how the store operates. When the 'data has been accepted' signal has been received from the acceptor and a 'new data is ready' signal from the source, both bistable circuits S and A will be set and the resulting AND gate output will read new data into the store; at the same time, R is set to remove

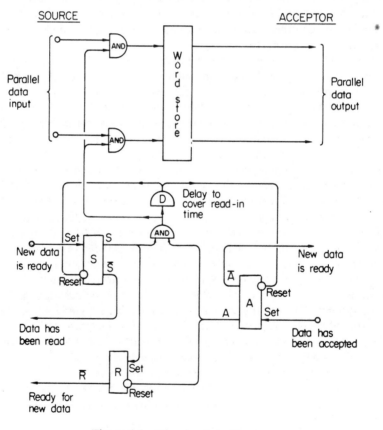

Figure 6.6.   The simple buffer store

the 'ready for new data' signal. After a short delay D to cover store read-in time, bistable circuits S and A will be reset; the output from S indicates the 'data has been accepted' by the store, while the output from A indicates the 'new data is ready' for the acceptor. When the data has been read by the acceptor, the 'data has been accepted' signal sets A, and the resulting output resets R to indicate the store is 'ready for new data'. It should be noted that the delay D must be long enough to prevent a possible race condition in the resetting of S and A.

The interaction between the source and the store involves three signals: the 'ready for new data' indicates when the store contents may be changed, the 'new data is ready' initiates the reading-in of new data, while the 'data has been read' informs the source when it may turn its attention elsewhere.

The interaction between the store and the acceptor requires only two signals: the 'data has been accepted' which indicates the store contents may change, and the 'new data ready' which shows when this has occurred.

In Figure 6.6, both in the case of input and of output, the information is transferred through parallel interfaces; so the time taken for the transfers will be short and may be ignored. But, in general, it is necessary to make a distinction between the desired delay, which is introduced by loading and unloading the store at convenient times, and the undesired additional delay due to the time taken for information to pass in and out of the store. This is especially the case when the quantity of information is large and when the information flow takes place serially. These conditions apply when storage is used to convert parallel words from a computer or a peripheral device into a serial form suitable for transmission along a data link which joins them together.

6.3 DATA LINKS WITH STORAGE

Data links used in conjunction with storage and associated logic form a basic building block of data communications networks. The use of stores brings a number of important benefits depending on their size and location and it is possible to overcome many of the disadvantages inherent in the use of data links as part of data processing systems. The functions made possible by stores are the buffering of one system from another; the conversion of data between serial and parallel forms; the correction of errors by retransmission, and the concentration of data to increase the utilization of data links. Often a single store fulfils more than one of these functions. The following sections consider these various functions of storage in greater detail.

Parallel-Serial-Parallel-Conversion

The speeds of data input and output are usually different when a store is used for parallel-serial conversion. For example, a computer may transfer a word through a parallel interface into a store in less than a microsecond. This store can pass the data into an attached data link to a remote peripheral device of terminal at a much lower speed. Sometimes this speed is determined by the characteristics of the terminal and sometimes by the line; but in both cases the computer is freed for other activities while the transfer to the terminal takes place, and advantage may be taken of the otherwise undesirable delay caused by a slow data link to allow the computer to deal with other links or peripheral devices.

The procedure for converting data from a parallel word to an equivalent serial form is illustrated in Figure 6.7 which is similar to the previous figure in its parallel input. The serial output is achieved by using a shift register for the store with an associated clock to shift out the data. The signal from the delay D following the completion of input sets bistable O and this causes the clock to shift out the data; the clock is counted and, when the correct number

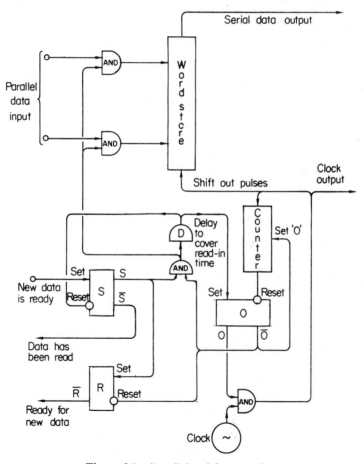

Figure 6.7. Parallel-serial conversion

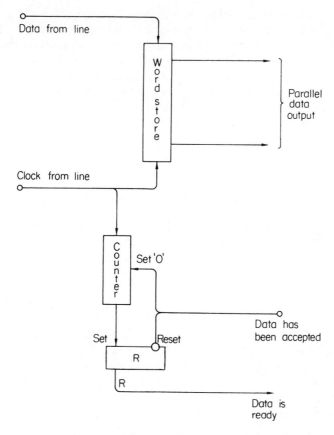

Figure 6.8.   Simple serial-parallel convertor

is reached, bistable O is reset. The resulting output signal indicates that the store is 'ready for new data' and resets the counter to zero. When new data has been stored, bistable O is set and the cycle begins again.

The reverse procedure, serial-to-parallel conversion, will be required at the input to a computer and the simple scheme shown in Figure 6.8 could be used if the interval between successive data words was always greater than the time taken by the computer to accept each word. For it will be appreciated that the handshaking feature necessary to ensure no data is lost is not provided by the arrangement of Figure 6.8 or, indeed, by the arrangement of Figure 6.7 that was used to generate the serial data words.

There are some applications where the lack of close control by hand-shaking is acceptable, because the sytem design ensures satisfactory operation in some other way. For example, there is no need for a start-stop telex machine to signal receipt of each character because its characteristics are known and may be taken account of by the device at the transmitting terminal. (This, of course, can occur only after handshaking has been used in order to initiate and confirm the call.) Other examples where handshaking is not employed are found in synchronous systems, where the information transfers occur at times determined by a clock, common to both the source and the acceptor. In the cases where a common clock is not available, or where the source and acceptor are constrained to operate asynchronously by their method of internal operation, handshaking is needed to give a close control of information transfer. The next section considers how this may be achieved through a data link.

Handshaking through a Data Link

The control of information transfer by a handshaking procedure comprising an exchange of signals between a source and acceptor of data is fundamental to data processing systems. It is necessary, therefore, to examine how the handshaking procedure may be extended over a data link. Clearly, the source must be prevented from sending each data word until the acceptor is ready to receive it; so, a return channel is needed between acceptor and source to carry an acknowledgement of receipt. The parallel-serial-parallel convertors of Figures 6.7 and 6.8 may be adapted as shown in Figure 6.9 where the acknowledgement signal from the acceptor is used to reset R. (The local signal produced by bistable O when the serial word is despatched is not needed. But a switch could be used at point X to select either the local, or remote reset signal for R to cater for synchronous or asynchronous (handshaking) operation as required.)

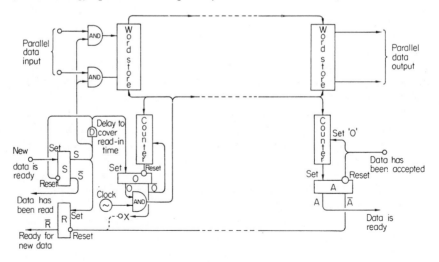

Figure 6.9.   Handshaking over a serial link

The need to wait for the acknowledgement introduces additional delay and this reduces the rate at which information may flow in the forward path. It is interesting to compare the effective transfer rate with the actual line rate to determine the penalty caused by the end-to-end handshaking procedure.

Speed Limitation due to Handshaking

The effective rate of flow of information through a data link when regulated by end-to-end handshaking is less than the transmission rate along the link. This is due to the delay after each word transmitted while the acknowledgement is returned by the receiver to release the next word. The forward transmission path is, therefore, active only intermittently.

A simple illustration is given in Figure 6.10. The effective rate R_E is the number of bits per word N divided by the time interval between successive fillings of the transmitting buffer store.

The time interval is the propagation delay round the loop 2T, typically 20 μS./mile, plus the time to transfer a word out of the store, i.e.

N/R, where R is the line rate.

$$\text{Thus, } R_E = \frac{N}{N/R + 2T}$$

$$= R \cdot \frac{N}{N + 2TR} \tag{6-1}$$

In equation (6-1) the term 2TR represents twice the number of digits that could be stored in the forward transmission path of the link. So, to maximize the effective transfer rate, it is necessary to make the length of the word transmitted large compared with the number of bits stored in transit along the line. The graph of Figure 6.11 shows how the effective transmission rate varies with the ratio of word length to the number of bits stored in the line.

As the number of bits stored in the buffers associated with a given link is increased, the time for one bit to pass through the buffers and the line also increases, so the delay introduced by the whole transmission path is increased and the source and acceptor at the ends of the link are less well coupled.

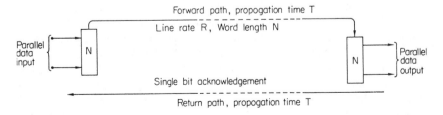

Figure 6.10. The handshake delay

However, this may be remedied to some extent by employing a different configuration of buffers in conjunction with a full-duplex link, by which further information may be transmitted on the forward path while an acknowledgement of previous information is simultaneously received on the return path. This is discussed in later sections.

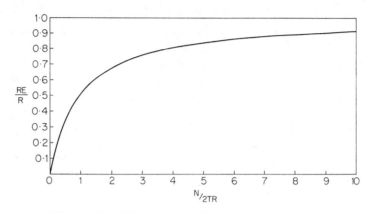

Figure 6.11.   Effective throughput with handshaking

Double Buffering

In the examples so far considered the stores associated with data links have been sited at the ends of the link, and have been loaded and unloaded through parallel interfaces. Furthermore, the sources and acceptors connected to the stores have been assumed to be so fast in operation that the time to load and unload stores, other than through the line, may be neglected. When this is not the case, advantage may be gained from using additional storage to decouple the source and acceptor from the stores forming the parallel-to-serial and serial-to-parallel convertors used in the transmitters and receivers. While these are sending and receiving data serially, the source and acceptor may be communicating with the extra buffer stores which will be ready to exchange data rapidly with the serial stores when appropriate. In fact, extra buffering is rarely needed at the transmitter, because the data may be read rapidly into the parallel-serial store, whatever the speed of the source. But, the receiver may have to communicate with acceptors of any speed. If an acceptor is slow to take the data from the serial-parallel store, the acknowledgement will be delayed and the link throughput reduced.

A convenient way of providing double buffering is to associate the parallel-to-parallel buffer shown in Figure 6.6, with the serial-to-parallel convertor shown in Figure 6.9, to form the buffered line receiver illustrated in Figure 6.12. The action of this device is as follows: as soon as a serial word has filled the serial store a transfer takes place into the parallel store, and an acknowledgement is returned to the transmitter to release the next word. At the same time, the acceptor is informed by a 'new data is ready' signal and begins to read it out of the parallel store. The acceptor operation now overlaps the transmission of the next word and the time of one complete transfer is that of the slower process, rather than the sum of both of them. This is like the decoupling of the two multi-access systems discussed earlier.

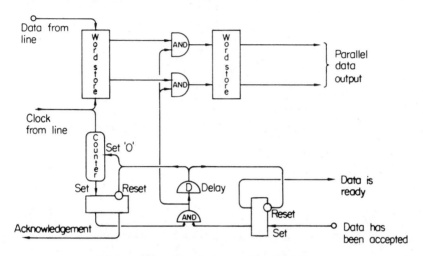

Figure 6.12.   The double-buffered receiver

Data Links with Intermediate Storage

The advantages of using storage at the ends of data links have been discussed in the previous sections. A large data communications network may have several data links in tandem and, while it is possible to decompose the network into individual links for analysis, the behaviour of tandem links with intermediate storage is worthy of special consideration, particularly when the links differ in bandwidth.

A single buffer between two links is illustrated in Figure 6.13. Data and clock pulses from the input source link, and the output acceptor link, are applied to the shift register store for alternate periods determined by the clock pulse counter. The counter output operates the bistable B which switches the input and output gates of the register. The inhibition signals prevent the source link from sending new data while the acceptor link is reading the previous word and vice-versa, providing the handshake interlock necessary to prevent loss or repetition of information. The flow of information is shown at the bottom of the figure where the source link is assumed faster than the acceptor. At a speed R_S the source takes time T_S to fill the store; then, after a changeover delay T_D, the acceptor empties the store at a speed R_A, taking a time T_A.

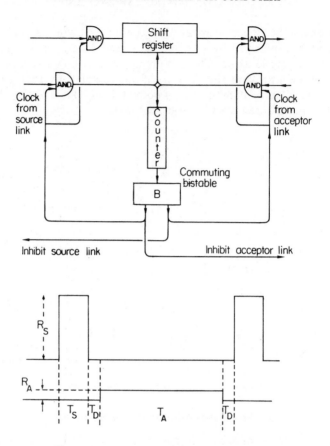

Figure 6.13.   Use of intermediate storage

Clearly, the data transfer rate for the tandem links with a single serial store between them is less than either link alone, because each is active for only part of the time. An improvement, allowing the slower link to run at nearly full capacity, is the addition of a second store. This is another example of double buffering, and permits one of the stores to be filled by the source link, while the other is emptied by the acceptor link. Two arrangements are possible, as shown in Figure 6.14. A store assigned to each link, with parallel data transfer between stores, or the switching of stores alternately between links. The two schemes are equivalent and their effect is shown at the bottom of the figure; again the source link is assumed to be faster than the acceptor. Note the rapid filling of both stores at speed R_S, and the slower emptying at speed R_A. The acceptor link now transfers information almost continuously with its activity broken only by the delay needed to switch stores or make parallel transfers. But, of course, the source link must be controlled to regulate the flow of data, so that none is lost when both stores are full.

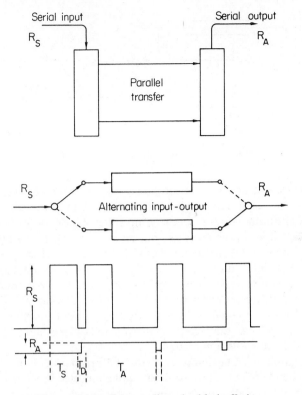

Figure. 6.14.   Intermediate double buffering

The Use of Long Blocks

In the earlier sections we have shown how storage has been used in data links both to carry out the necessary parallel-to-serial and serial-to-parallel conversions, and to decouple the source and acceptor attached to the link, from the stores used for conversion. In each case handshaking has occured over the same size of word throughout the complete chain of stores from the source to the acceptor. It has been shown that handshaking over a long distance reduces the transfer rate unless long words are used, and this leads to

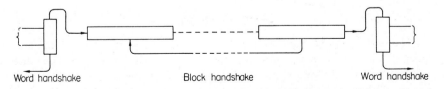

Figure 6.15.   Two types of handshake

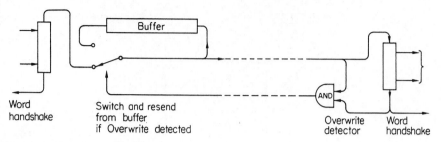

Word handshake   Switch and resend from buffer if Overwrite detected   Overwrite detector   Word handshake

Figure 6.16.   High-speed transfer method

the idea of *block* transfer over the link where a block of several words is transmitted for each handshake acknowledgement received. Words are transferred from the source to the transmitter block store and from the receiver block store to the acceptor, but blocks are transferred over the data link. It is possible to identify two forms of handshake: that between the block stores over the link, and that between the block stores and the devices to which they connect. This is shown in Figure 6.15. The interaction between the acceptor and source is now less tightly controlled because, if the acceptor ceases operation for some reason, the source will still continue filling the next block; only when the receipt of the previous block fails to be acknowledged will the source be inhibited.

The situation may be improved with the arrangement of Figure 6.16, where the block buffer at the transmitter is not connected in series with the line. Instead, the line signals also pass into this buffer which is made just longer than the number of bits stored in the line. The assumption is made that the acceptor will be able to receive the data and the transmitter operates continuously. A detector in the receiver monitors the handshake with the acceptor and, if new data arrives before the previous word has been accepted, the transmitter is informed. The source is inhibited and the contents of the block buffer are transmitted continuously until the acceptor catches up.

It should be noted, that this scheme requires the simultaneous transmission of signals in both directions between the ends of the data link, whereas the previously described schemes have sent signals alternately in the forward and return directions. It is necessary for this scheme, therefore, to use a full duplex data link.

Elastic Buffering

The use of long blocks to overcome the effect of delays through long data links, as described in the previous section, has a disadvantage when the acceptor at the receiving end is slightly slower than the source at the transmitter. Although no data are lost, there is a frequent need to retransmit blocks which arrive before a previous one has been accepted. This is avoided if

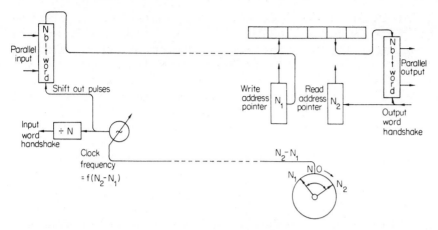

Figure 6.17.   Elastic buffering

the source is slightly slower than the acceptor. It becomes necessary to distinguish between the need to retransmit a block due to the detection of an error (this is discussed later) and the retransmission necessary if data are sent too rapidly. The former cannot be avoided but the latter can be reduced considerably (if the instantaneous speed of the acceptor does not vary markedly from its average speed) by the use of an elastic buffer at the receiver. In principle the scheme is similar to that used in PCM Telephony described in Chapter 7, page 246. A full duplex link is required because control signals indicating the amount of information stored in buffers at the receiver is continuously returned to the transmitter to adjust the speed of information transfer in the forward direction. In this way, the buffer is prevented from becoming full, so no information is transmitted that cannot be accepted by the receiver and there is no need to retransmit information other than for error control purposes. A practical realization is given in Figure 6.17.

At the receiving end of the link, the write address of the circular buffer is incremented as bits are written into it from the incoming line, while the read address is incremented as bits are read from the circular buffer into the output word buffer. The two counters N_1 and N_2 are modulo N adders where N is the size of the circular buffer; logic, not shown in the figure, has to be provided to prevent the value stored in either counter overtaking the value stored in the other. The scheme is like a clock face going from 0 to N, with the contents of the two counters behaving like two hands following each other around the face. The difference between the two hand positions is fed back to control the transmitter clock speed. This adjusts the transmission rate to keep the receiver circular buffer half full. The clock pulse train is divided by the parallel word length N, and used to control the speed of the data source; only when the previous word has been sent into the line may a new word be requested by a return handshake across the input interface.

An extension of the elastic buffer technique may be valuable when two computers communicate together. Each computer will be concerned with managing the allocation of its store most efficiently: one of these allocation tasks is the assignment of store blocks to prepare or receive messages concerned with the other computer. When the link is long, the lengthy delay in receiving replies to requests for storage space in the remote computer will make the task more difficult. It is likely that, to optimize the use of the data link, a computer may need to acknowledge a request for store by indicating space when none exists, but is expected to be available by the time the messages arrive. This topic is discussed in more detail in Chapter 11, page 387.

The Effect of Noise

The discussions so far have assumed that the transmitted information passes through a data link without corruption and that the control of information transfer is needed only to ensure the source and acceptor that communicate through the link remain in step so that no information is repeated or lost. However, the possibility of errors being introduced during transmission introduces the problem of the control of flow in the presence of noise. The most common solution is to provide a means of error detection and to arrange for information in error to be retransmitted. This reduces the effective throughput of a link due to the time required for retransmission. The reduction is greater when longer blocks are used because the taken time to repeat them is greater, and the probability of corruption of a block is increased with block length; on the other hand, the detection of errors may be done more efficiently in long blocks. The pattern of the noise, whether uniformly distributed, or occuring in bursts, makes the exact behaviour of a particular design of system difficult to determine. Obviously, there is an optimum block length for any given noisy line to give the maximum throughput, although its determination may not be easy. The problem has been studied by Chu.[3]

To improve the throughput of data on a long distance circuit there is the possibility of using intermediate stores to obtain a high data rate in the presence of noise. The blocks of information handled may be smaller because of the

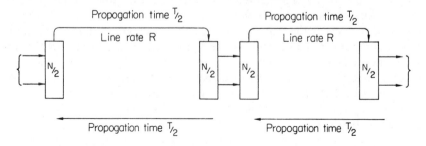

Figure 6.18.   Reduction of delay by storage

reduced loop delay on each short link, while the probability of error is reduced due to the shorter distance between stores, and the time for retransmission of a corrupted block is reduced due to the smaller block size.

Figure 6.18 shows the link of Figure 6.10 split into two halves. The propagation time is, of course, half that of the original link so, from equation (6-1) the word length may be halved for the same effective transfer rate. Once the flow of information has settled down the two tandem links operate in some respects in parallel because each link simultaneously passes on a word. However, the words are half length so the data rate is the same as for the single link. But when an error occurs the repetition will happen on one of the links only, and take only half as long to complete.

Automatic Retransmission Schemes

The idea of looking for errors in received information and asking for it to be repeated is an obvious way of correcting errors and has been used in many different systems. A familiar use is in radio telegraphy where high rates of error occur and the technique is called ARQ for automatic repeat request.

A data link using automatic retransmission of faulty blocks for error correction may be regarded as a reliable link of variable transmission characteristics having an equivalent bandwidth which is a function of the noise on the link. The source and acceptor control the information flow by separately handshaking 'independently' with the link; this also has an internal end-to-end handshake procedure governing block retransmission, as shown in Figure 6.15.

The simplest type of retransmission scheme uses a single buffer, or its equivalent, at each end of the link, and the handshaking between the ends of the link is similar to that described on page 190.

The equivalent bandwidth follows from equation (6-1). It is

$$R_E = F \times R \left(\frac{N}{N+2TR} \right)$$

where F is a reduction factor dependant on the noise. If the probability of an error occurring in a block is p, the effective number of blocks is reduced by the factor $(1-p)$, so $F = (1-p)$. The effective rate with simple buffers is therefore:

$$R_E = (1 - p) R \left(\frac{N}{N+2TR} \right) \tag{6-2}$$

A second scheme is illustrated by Figure 6.16 where information is transmitted continuously until an error is detected when the transmitter returns to the last correctly acknowledged data block and repeats it, together with all succeeding data blocks.

If B blocks are transmitted and the probability of a block being in error is p, the number of effective blocks is $B(1-p)$. If the transmission rate is

S block/s, the time to transmit all the blocks will be B/S seconds. However, for each incorrect block the retransmission causes an extra delay depending on the propagation time for the loop, 2T. The probability of incurring this delay is p, so the total time to transmit B blocks is $B/S + 2pT$. The effective rate is therefore

$$S_E = S \left(\frac{B(1 - p)}{B + 2pTS} \right) \qquad (6\text{-}3)$$

This equation is similar in form to that for the single buffer case except for the term $2pTS$ in the denominator. Thus for a given probability of error an equivalent distance may be derived in terms of the single buffer case. When p is zero, of course, the data rate is equal to line rate R bit/s or S block/s.

Block Numbering Procedures

On very long data links, particularly those using a circuit through a satellite relay, the delays may be several hundred milliseconds and will demand extremely long block lengths if a reasonably effective data transfer rate is to be obtained using end-to-end handshaking procedures for error control. The necessary length may be much greater than is needed for a typical message, and, indeed, several short messages might well be stored along the transmission path through a satellite link. The usual solution is to allow several short blocks, each of single message length with error detection information, to pass into the link before an acknowledgement is expected for the first block. In principle, this is precisely the same as the scheme discussed on page 196 and likewise requires a full duplex communication channel. However, it is usual to make full use of the channel by arranging for the transmission of information blocks to take place in both directions simultaneously; the necessary acknowledgements for blocks in one direction are returned either between, or included within, information blocks in the other direction.

A running account of blocks sent is maintained at each transmitter, and copies of blocks are stored until a positive acknowledgement has been returned to indicate correct receipt, allowing the store to be released for a new block. At first sight, the advantage of this scheme over the use of one long block lies only in the convenience of having each message occupying its own block. However, when noise corrupts the link one or two messages only may be affected and retransmission may begin with the first wrongly received message, whereas if a long block were employed the whole block would have to be resent whenever an error occured.

When noise corrupts a message on the forward link, the receiver will return a negative acknowledgement requesting the retransmission of that message. However, the delay through the link will allow several other messages to follow before the transmitter can be stopped, and these must be resent as

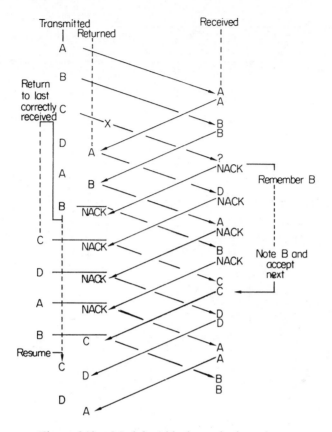

Figure 6.19.   Modulo-4 block numbering scheme

well. It is also possible for noise on the return channel to corrupt an acknowledgement which will falsely request the repetition of a correctly received message.

The account of messages sent and received is kept by numbering messages modulo n, so the message numbers repeat after a count of n. The value of n must be chosen with regard to the loop delay to permit sufficient messages to enter the link before the transmitter must stop to wait for an acknowledgement of the first message. A typical sequence that might occur on a link with modulo-four numbering is illustrated in Figure 6.19. When an error is detected, the transmitter returns to the last message known to have been received correctly and repeats from that point. Meanwhile the receiver replies with negative acknowledgements until it recognizes the repeated message previously received in error.

An indication of the logic required to implement a modulo 8 scheme is given by the simplified diagram of Figure 6.20. In the middle of the figure,

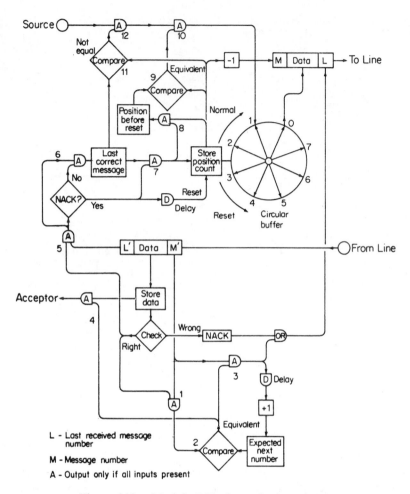

Figure 6.20.   Modulo-8 block numbering scheme

the received message is stored and checked for validity. If it is wrong, a negative acknowledgement is sent by the next return word. If it is right, the message number is passed through gate 1 and compared at 2 with the expected next message number. If these are equivalent, gate 3 allows the received message number to pass to the next returned word and also (after a delay and the addition of one) to the expected next message number store. At the same time, the stored data is released by gate 4 because the expected message has been received. A correct check also permits gate 5 to pass the last received message number from the received word to be checked for a negative acknowledgement. If it is not a negative acknowledgement, its number is passed by gate 6 into the last correct message store. If it is a negative acknowledgement, gate 7 allows the last correct message number to be used to reset the counter of the circular buffer. At the same time, gate 8 passes the position of the buffer to a memory which is compared at 9 to determine when the buffer has completed the retransmission of corrupted messages. Gate 10 is closed while retransmission takes place to prevent overwriting of the buffer. The outgoing message number is derived from the circular buffer counter, while it is necessary to compare at 11, the last correct message number, with the buffer position to prevent overwriting when no acknowledgement is received.

The Modulo-Two Scheme

The simplest block numbering arrangement is the use of alternate blocks numbered modulo-two. An example is the scheme used in the serial links developed at the National Physical Laboratory for the data network at its Teddington Laboratory.[4] The NPL serial link is a basic building block of the network and comprises two line terminals fitted with parallel interfaces similar to British Standard Specification 4421. Each of the terminals transfers information received through its parallel interface to the other terminal,

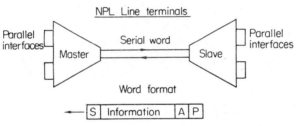

Start bit, S; Alternation bit, A; Parity bit, P

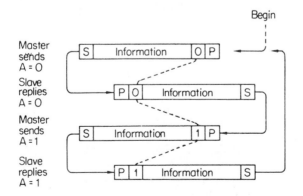

Word exchange sequence without errors

Figure 6.21.   The NPL line terminals

where it is presented at the local parallel interface. So, in effect, each interface is recreated at the remote terminal. The line terminals are joined by a full duplex serial link which is used in a half duplex manner with the terminals exchanging alternate serial words. Apart from the information bits these words have a start and a stop bit, a parity bit, and a modulo-two counter bit called the alternation bit. One of the terminals is designated the master and changes the state of alternation bit of the next word it transmits following the receipt of a correct input word. But if a corrupted input is received the alternation bit state is kept unchanged. The slave terminal is arranged to behave in a complementary way: changing the alternation bit to indicate errors, and keeping it the same when a correct input is detected. The NPL line terminals are shown in Figure 6.21 with, below, the alternation bit sequence when a correct cycle occurs.

The operation when errors occur is illustrated by Figure 6.22. Normally, the cycle round the largest loop is traversed as each exchange of words is completed correctly. But if an error is detected by a line terminal (whether master or slave) it breaks the expected sequence of change in alternation bit state. This causes one of the smaller loops to be taken until the error is corrected.

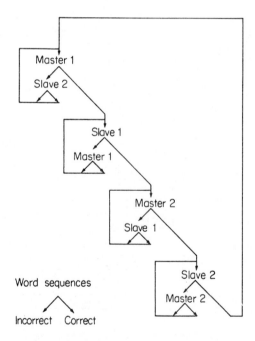

Figure 6.22.   NPL network : line-terminal
error sequences

Individual Message Correction

The techniques already described for correcting errors by returning to a message known to have been correctly received and repeating all messages from that point is inefficient when long links are used with short messages because many messages are included in the error control handshake time. For example, if a satellite link of 48 kbit/s had a forward transfer delay of 250 milliseconds there would be 24,000 bits stored in the link for each handshake. With messages of 1 Kbit, twenty three might have to be unnecessarily repeated for a single corrupted message. Clearly, the maximum efficiency would be obtained if only those messages actually corrupted were retransmitted. To do this, requires a more detailed running account of the state of each message to be kept at the ends of the link, together with a more elaborate procedure to ensure recovery is possible when errors occur. The complexity of the control logic to achieve this makes the idea of using a computer an attractive one, when it becomes possible to use the type of procedure used to control message exchanges in message switching networks, where the repeat of an individual message may be requested if it is found to be in error.

6.4   ERROR CONTROL

The purpose of error control is to ensure that the information received by an acceptor is as intended by the source. There must be some means for the acceptor to deduce when received information contains errors, and a mechanism for removing them. Two types of error control may be identified: forward error control where sufficient redundant material is included with the information to allow the acceptor to detect an error and to infer the correct message, and feedback error control, where some redundancy is needed to reveal errors, but correction is made by retransmission. A variation of the latter scheme is the repeated transmission of a non-redundant message until the acceptor signals an acknowledgement; here the redundancy lies in the repetition of the same message. The acknowledgement may take two forms: a signal indicating the receiver has detected more than one identical message, or the correct return of the received message: in either case the transmitter moves on to the next message.

In all the above schemes the introduction of redundancy decreases the capacity of the channel for carrying information. The choice of which scheme to employ for a particular application depends upon the ease of introducing the redundancy, the kinds of error possible with a given type of link and the performance criteria to be met.

Shannon's Theorems

It is intuitively acceptable that the inclusion of redundancy in a message enables error detection and correction to be achieved; the redundancy in natural language that allows spelling and other mistakes to be rectified is apparent to everyone. But it was not until Shannon's work was published in 1948[5] that the use of redundancy to achieve reliable communication in the presence of noise was put onto a sound mathematical basis. His second theorem states that a coding method exists by which information may be transmitted over a noisy channel with an arbitrarily small frequency of occurence of errors provided the rate of transmission is less than a uniquely defined quantity called the channel capacity.

Unfortunately, to achieve error-free transmission at a rate comparable with the channel capacity requires very long codewords and, in practice, much shorter words must be used. The problem remains of selecting coding methods for best performance for no optimum choice of coding method has yet been demonstrated.

Even before his work was published studies had been made of ad-hoc encoding methods to allow errors to be detected and corrected, and since that time much effort has been devoted to devising techniques for doing this as efficiently as possible using the minimum redundancy to obtain a desired performance. Some of the principles employed are discussed in the next sections.

The Use of Parity

Perhaps the most common method of detecting errors is the use of parity. With this method, the digits of a binary word are inspected and an extra digit is added. This digit is chosen to be 'zero' or 'one', as necessary to keep the total number of digits in the 'one' state either odd or even according to prior agreement. For example, if even parity is declared, each transmitted word will be made to have an even number of digits set to 'one'; so, if the word is corrupted by the change of any one digit during transit, the received word will be of odd parity and may be rejected.

A convenient method of generating a parity digit is by successive modulo-two addition of the digits of the word as shown in Figure 6.23. A similar arrangement serves to detect parity at the receiver. In effect, an equation connecting all the digits by modulo-two arithmetic is formed at the transmitter, and is checked at the receiver. If the original word comprises W digits, the transmitted word will have $W+1$ digits. There are twice as many states or combinations available with $W+1$ digits, but only half are used for the data. So the use of parity involves the surrender of half the possible information states. In return, any odd number of digit corruptions will be detected. Unfortunately if even numbers of digits change their value the parity remains the same and the errors are undetectable. This may not seem too good a bargain, but there are applications where the use of a single parity digit is very convenient, particularly to check the transfer of data as parallel words. For example, the ISO code for Information Interchange, page 224, contains seven data bits which may be used with an eighth parity bit to fit nicely onto

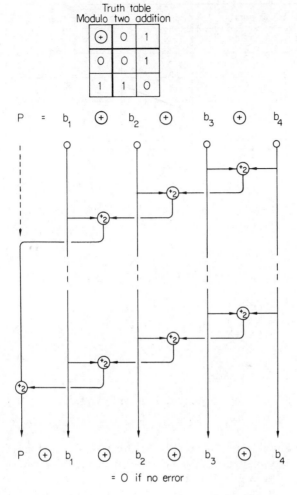

Figure 6.23. Parity generation and checking

eight-track paper tape. The single parity bit allows the detection of any one faulty track in a paper tape reader or punch. Another example is nine-track magnetic tape with eight data bits and one parity bit, while a single parity bit is often used internally in computers to check the validity of transfers between the store and central processor. The single parity bit is acceptable for error detection of systematic errors in parallel transfers because, although a given faulty transfer may not be detected, the changing patterns of data will increase the chance of failures with at least some transfers. This will eventually throw doubt on the performance of the transfer mechanism employed.

Weight	No error			code	Error in digit								
	2^1	2^0	P		2^1	code	2^0	code	P	code			
0	0	0	0	a	1 0 0	g	0 1 0	f	0 0 1	e			
1	0	1	1	b	1 1 1	h	0 0 1	e	0 1 0	f			
2	1	0	1	c	0 0 1	e	1 1 1	h	1 1 0	g			
3	1	1	0	d	0 1 0	f	1 0 0	g	1 1 1	h			

(a) 2-bit code – Even parity

0	0	0	(a)	0	0	0	(a)
0	0	1	e	0	0	1	e
0	1	0	f	0	1	1	(b)
0	1	1	(b)	0	1	0	f
1	0	0	g	1	1	0	(d)
1	0	1	(c)	1	1	1	h
1	1	0	(d)	1	0	1	(c)
1	1	1	h	1	0	0	g

(b) Straight binary   (c) Gray code

Figure 6.24.   A parity code

The use of parity is illustrated by Figure 6.24(a). The four states possible with two binary digits are shown at the left of the table with a parity digit chosen to give even parity. Listed beside each code value are the three error patterns obtained by a corruption of one digit of the original pattern; these error patterns are labelled in lower case letters and it is clear that of the eight possible combinations of the three bits (two data bits plus a parity bit) half are used for true information and the others indicate errors. A particular error state may be reached by changing a single digit in three of the four chosen true states.

It is interesting to arrange the eight possible states in ascending value as in Figure 6.24(b), where the relative positions of the true and error states are shown. An alternative arrangement in Figure 6.24(c) is known as the Gray code; it has the property that only one digit changes value in progressing from one state to an adjacent state; this makes it valuable for coded plates used to translate mechanical movement into a digital equivalent. With the Gray Code, uncertainty at a code changeover position can only give the state on one or other side of that position, whereas the ascending value arrangement, with more than one digit difference between adjacent states, can give large errors if one digit is misread. By arranging the eight states in the Gray Code, the odd and even parity states are made to alternate and it is easy to see that an error in one digit unambiguously results in an error state. This is shown in another way by Figure 6.25. The corners of the cube represent the code states and movement along an edge corresponds to a change of one digit. The states chosen as true are at opposite corners of a face and are separated by a corner representing an error state.

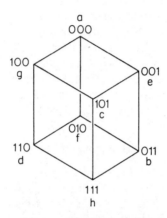

Figure 6.25.   Hamming
distance

M out of N Codes

The simple parity digit has been shown to separate the possible states of a word of $N+1$ bits into two equal groups; one of these is used for data and the other indicates errors. The error detection ability is increased by using less of the possible states of a word for data; this may be achieved by an M out of N code.

One version, used by IBM, is the 4 out of 8 code. In this code eight bit characters are used which must have four bits at 'one' and four at 'zero' for each valid state.

The number of ways of chosing M from N is

$$N!/M!(N-M)!$$

so for the IBM code there are 70 valid states out of a possible 256. If all errors were uniformly distributed this code would be about 1·8 times as effective as the seven bit plus parity code which has 128 valid states out of 256.

Another important use of the M out of N code is described by the CCITT for parallel data transmission modems in Recommendation V.30[6]. A three times one out of four code is employed using three groups of four frequencies. One tone from each group of four is transmitted simultaneously so there are 64 possible states. Also recommended is a more robust variation using the two times one out of four code with the upper and lower groups of frequencies. This gives a $4 \times 4 = 16$ state code. (See Chapter 2, page 21.)

Another recommendation allows 256 combinations or an eight bit code to be transmitted as two sequential groups of four bits using the two times one out of four code.

All these schemes are envisaged for low-cost data transmission over telephone channels at speeds up to 20 characters per second.

A third application for M out of N codes is the error detection scheme devised by Van Duren for use with radio telegraphy. The 32 states of the five unit code used for line telegraphy are represented by 32 of the 35 states of the three out of seven code; two remaining states represent all mark and all space and the last is not used. An automatic request for retransmission (ARQ) scheme is used to correct the errors that are detected. The three out of seven code is illustrated in Figure 6.29, page 218.

Hamming Distance

The cube representation of Figure 6.25 was used by R.W. Hamming[7] to illustrate the concept of 'Hamming distance' which is useful in considering the properties of codes. The Hamming distance is defined as the number of digit positions by which two states differ from each other, and for the case considered above is two, both for the set of even and for the set of odd parity states.

The detection of errors is obviously more certain when only a few of the possible states are used to represent true values of data. There is less chance of the corruption of a digit leading to another true value instead of an error state, because the true values may be separated by a greater Hamming distance. In the three bit cube of Figure 6.25 the choice of two values, at opposite corners of the cube for data (for example, $a - 000$ and $h - 111$) leaves six states for error indication, and the true states are separated by two corners giving a Hamming distance of three.

Besides allowing the detection of any two digits in error the correction of a single error is possible if maximum likelihood decoding is employed. This assumes one error is more likely than two, two more likely than three and so on. If this is true, a particular single digit error will be corrected by changing an error state to the nearest true state: in the cube of Figure 6.25 the change will be to an adjacent true corner. However, if this is done, an error in two digits will indicate a state which is adjacent to the other true state and will be incorrectly decoded. The code may be used for single-error correction or for single and double error detection, but not for both purposes at the same time.

In order to be able to correct single-bit errors, all states that differ by a single bit from a given true state must be identified as its equivalent. For an N bit code there will be N single-error states for each true state so the total number of states needed to indicate one true unit of information is $N+1$. However there are 2^N possible states, so the number of true states that may be uniquely indicated is $2^N/(N+1)$.

In general, an error-correcting code of N bits will comprise a number of information bits M and a number of checking bits C; so $N = M+C$. The number of information states will be 2^M and we have seen that for single-error correction there must be $2^N/(N+1)$ states for each information state: thus $2^N/(N+1) = 2^M$, therefore

$$\frac{2^{M+C}}{M+C+1} = 2^M \text{ or } 2^C = M + C + 1 \tag{6-4}$$

In the three-bit code of Figure 6.24(a) any pair of opposite corners may be defined as two true states of a single bit code, i.e. $M = 1$. The other bits may be regarded as check digits, so, $C = 2$. This just satisfied the equation (6-4)

A next possibility is to use three check bits, when the maximum value of M is four, giving $N = 7$ bits. This is particularly useful because it fits into an eight-bit byte, and may be arranged as a Hamming code.

Hamming Codes

An important class of single error-correcting codes was devised by R.W. Hamming[7]. In these codes the parity check digits are assigned to particular positions where their weights indicate which digits of the whole code are in error.

The Hamming code with four information digits and three check digits is shown in Figure 6.26. An error such as (a) where the second data bit M_2 is changed from one to zero will be decoded as code value 0 instead of 2. If the data bits are assumed valid, the check bits C_1 and C_3 will appear erroneously as ones. The weights of these are 1 and 4 making 5 so the 5th digit, i.e. M_2 is in error. A similar situation arises for case (b) where data bit M_3 in code value 11 is changed from zero to one, and is detected as value 15 but apparently with check bits C_2 and C_3 wrong; C_2 and C_3 indicate bit number 6, i.e. data bit M_3 is incorrect. When a check digit is corrupted as at (c), the erroneous digit is still indicated by the check digit weight; in this case, bit 2 equals C_2. The parity check bits may, of course, be generated and detected by modulo two addition as for the single parity bit case shown in Figure 6.23, page 207.

The Use of Sum Checks

In discussing the detection of errors in a mechanism which transfers in parallel a number of digits, it was pointed out that the changing patterns of data would eventually reveal systematic errors even if particular transfers

Digit position	7	6	5	4	3	2	1
Information digit	M_4	M_3	M_2	M_1			
Weight	8	4	2	1			
Check digit					C_3	C_2	C_1
Weight					4	2	1

Formed by modulo-2 addition of message bits:

$$M_4 \oplus M_2 \oplus M_1 = C_1$$
$$M_4 \oplus M_3 \oplus M_1 = C_2$$
$$M_4 \oplus M_3 \oplus M_2 = C_3$$

	7	6	5	4	3	2	1	
0	0	0	0	0	0	0	0	⎫
1	0	0	0	0	1	1	1	⎬ a
2	0	0	[1]	1	0	0	1	⎭
3	0	0	1	1	1	1	0	
4	0	1	0	1	0	1	0	
5	0	1	0	1	1	0	1	
6	0	1	1	0	0	1	1	
7	0	1	1	0	1	0	0	
8	1	0	0	1	0	[1]	1	⎤ c
9	1	0	0	1	1	0	0	
10	1	0	1	0	0	1	0	
11	1	[0]	1	0	1	0	1	⎫
12	1	1	0	0	0	0	1	⎪
13	1	1	0	0	1	1	0	⎬ b
14	1	1	1	1	0	0	0	⎪
15	1	1	1	1	1	1	1	⎭

Figure 6.26.   A Hamming code

were not well protected. The detection may be made more certain by using a sum check following a succession of parallel transfers; this shows up some of the errors that are missed by the parity digit. Figure 6.27 shows a typical sequence of parallel words with parity digits, and below, a corresponding sum check. The sum check may be the arithmetic sum of the foregoing words, or the modulo-two sum which is easier to engineer, or it may be the parity along the block of corresponding digits in each word. In this case, it is usual to talk of longitudinal or column parity, while word parity is called transverse or row parity. Even parity has been chosen for both longitudinal and transverse parity in the example shown and, clearly, the additional information allows certain errors to be deduced. Any single bit error, as at (a) and (e), would violate both row and column parity and the position of such an error is indicated by the rows and columns affected. Various other types of error

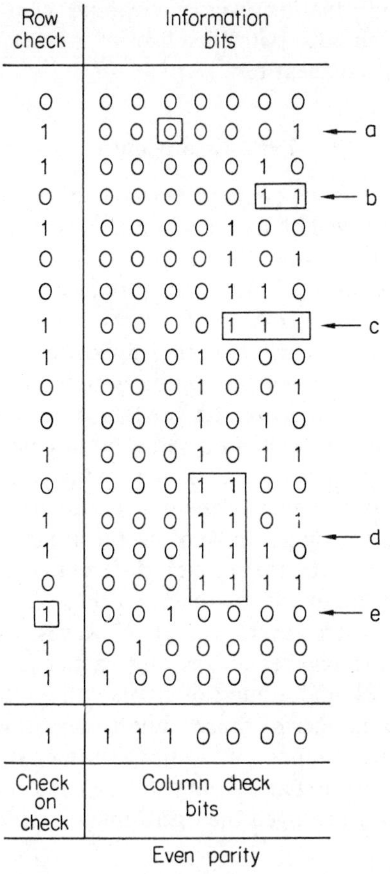

Row check	Information bits	
0	0 0 0 0 0 0 0	
1	0 0 [0] 0 0 0 1	← a
1	0 0 0 0 0 1 0	
0	0 0 0 0 0 [1 1]	← b
1	0 0 0 0 1 0 0	
0	0 0 0 0 1 0 1	
0	0 0 0 0 1 1 0	
1	0 0 0 0 [1 1 1]	← c
1	0 0 0 1 0 0 0	
0	0 0 0 1 0 0 1	
0	0 0 0 1 0 1 0	
1	0 0 0 1 0 1 1	
0	0 0 0 [1 1] 0 0	
1	0 0 0 [1 1] 0 1	← d
1	0 0 0 [1 1] 1 0	
0	0 0 0 [1 1] 1 1	
[1]	0 0 1 0 0 0 0	← e
1	0 1 0 0 0 0 0	
1	1 0 0 0 0 0 0	
1	1 1 1 0 0 0 0	

Check on check	Column check bits	

Even parity

Figure 6.27. The block sum check

may occur depending on the medium used to carry the information. For example, with magnetic tape, a faulty oxide coating may affect a group of adjacent digits; a pair of digits as at (b) would be undetected by transverse parity, but would violate the longitudinal parity; the error would be detected, but not located. At (c) three errors in one row would be detected and located, whereas a patch at (d) would be undetectable.

The ability of any error detection scheme to reveal errors depends on the types of error that can occur and it is difficult to determine the ability in a practical case, although theoretical calculations may be made based on various assumptions. For instance, if uniform probability of a digit error is assumed the chance of patterns occuring that would be undetected may be calculated. But the value of such calculations is doubtful considering the kinds of error that may occur in practice. In particular, the errors encountered when transmitting information over a telephone channel require a special type of code which can cope with the effect of a burst of interference which corrupts a number of adjacent bits.

Burst Error Control

When information is transmitted through data links using the public telephone network the type of error encountered is different from that considered in the previous sections. The impulsive noise commonly found (see Chapter 2, page 55) causes a burst of disturbance which, because the digits of the message are transmitted serially, affects a sequence of adjacent digits.

In discussing the use of parity and the application to Hamming codes, the idea of using sets of equations connecting groups of digits by modulo two addition was described; these equations enabled deductions about errors to be made. When the digits occur in a serial bit stream, one possible way of formulating similar sets of equations is to pass the bit stream through a shift register so that a short sequence of the digits is available at any instant. The shift register contains a sliding sample of the bit stream and by taking outputs from selected positions along the register, the bits may be related by modulo-two arithmetic to form equations similar to those already described in the case of parallel words. However, with serial words, the progression of the bit stream through the register allows any particular bit to appear in the equations several times, and a burst of errors will be 'scanned' by the equations and analysed a number of times while passing through the register.

It is useful to regard the function of such a shift register as a linear operator applied to the sequence of bits flowing through the register. Depending on how the shift register is arranged the operations of multiplication or division may be performed.

In principle, shift registers could be used for error detection by arranging for the sequence of information digits at a transmitter to be multiplied by an operator before transmission and divided by the same operator after reception. If there were no errors introduced, the result of the division would be the original information sequence without a remainder; but if errors had occured, there would be a remainder, unless the error sequence was also exactly divisible by the operator. The art of divising a good practical code lies in chosing an operator that will not divide exactly into the kind of errors that are to be detected.

The use of shift registers in this way was discussed in Chapter 5 in connection with the scrambling and unscrambling of data before and after transmission through a telephone channel. This is done to avoid undesirable bit patterns which have an unwanted power spectrum. An explanation of the technique appears in the appendix to Chapter 5, page 173, where the feedback shift registers of Figure 6.28 are described in terms of multiplication and division by an operator $1 + F$.

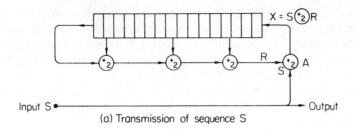

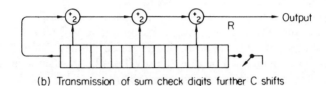

(a) Transmission of sequence S

(b) Transmission of sum check digits further C shifts

Figure 6.28.   The cyclic sum check

In a practical data link using shift registers for error control a slightly modified technique is adopted to avoid the multiplication process before transmission. Otherwise, any marker characters in the bit stream such as Data Link Escape (DLE), Start of Text (STX) etc. will be obscured. Instead of multiplication, a finite length of the original sequence is divided by an operator to produce a remainder, and the actual transmission comprises the original sequence followed by the remainder. At the receiver, a similar division process produces a locally generated remainder for comparison with that sent by the transmitter. Any differences result from the introduction of error sequences which cannot be divided exactly by the chosen operator.

The remainder generated by the division process at the transmitter may be regarded as a sum check, resulting from the process of modulo two addition used in its preparation; it will be of length equal to the number of bits in the shift register. This register is taken through several cycles to form the sum check which is called a cyclic sum check, and will, of course, be a function of the whole of the sequence used in its preparation. The operator used for division is called the generating function or generating polynominal.

The process for generating the required sum check is illustrated by Figure 6.28 (a) which shows an input sequence S fed simultaneously to a data link and to an encoder formed by a shift register divider having C stages. The result of the division process is the sequence $X = (1 \oplus F)^{-1} S$ where F is a function of the particular stages connected to the modulo-two adders and $\oplus$ indicates the modulo 2 addition operation. At the end of the sequence, a bit pattern is left in the shift register which would generate the remainder of the division operation, if it were shifted a further C places with the register input at X held at zero. While this is done, the data link is switched from the input sequence to the remainder line R, so the remainder is transmitted down the link immediately following the sequence S, as shown in Figure 6.28(b).

At the receiving end of the link the divider arrangement of Figure 6.28(a) is repeated. In the absence of transmission errors, the sequence will be generated at X as it was generated by the sending end's divider, during the period while the sequence S is being received. At the end of this period a further C shifts will generate the remainder R but, at the same time, the transmitter will have switched to sending the remainder it has also generated, and this will appear directly following the input sequence. If no errors have occured, the modulo-two adder A will have two identical inputs R, one through the link, the other formed locally, and its output X will be a succession of C zero's. At the end of the sum check cycle these will have been shifted into the register, so all stages will be zero. This will not be so when a detectable error has occured during transmission over the link.

Error Detecting Capability

To assess the ability of any decoder to detect errors it is necessary to consider what happens when a particular pattern of errors is divided by the function of a selected number of bits positions chosen to reveal the errors. Only those patterns that do not divide exactly will be found.

Some general observations may be made about detectable error patterns. For example, in the previous section the dividing function was $(1 \oplus_2 F)$ where F is the modulo-two sum of selected bits. If there is an odd number of bits in error the modulo-two sum F will be unity so the dividing function $(1 \oplus_2 F) = 0$. In this case, division without a remainder will be impossible. Any odd number of bits in error will, therefore, be detected.

When a burst of errors is shorter than the length of the sum check, division without a remainder is again not possible, so all such errors are found. However, when the burst length is equal to the sum check one of the possible error patterns may match the sum check and will be undetectable. When the burst is one digit longer than the check, two matching patterns are possible i.e. the extra bit may be one or zero. This reasoning may, of course, be extended to longer bursts.

The probability of various long patterns occuring may be calculated, or perhaps simulated, if particular distributions of errors are assumed and, generally, the protection provided is remarkably good with only a few check bits.

As an example, if the information bits are uniformly likely to be in error, the number of possible patterns in a burst of length equal to the sum check length C bits is 2^C; typically, this may be sixteen bits, so the probability of the undetected burst is one out of 2^{16} patterns or about one in sixty thousand.

CCITT Recommendation V41

This recommendation given in the White Book[8] describes a practical error detection scheme using a sixteen-bit cyclic sum check for information blocks of 260, 500 and 980 bits. The 5th, 12th and 16th stages of the shift register are used to form the dividing function, and a computer simulation of performance using an error distribution measured from actual links indicates an error rate improvement factor of about 50,000 for a block size of 260.

Also included in the recommendation are techniques for obtaining synchronism between the encoder and decoder and a procedure for numbering blocks to ensure blocks are not lost or duplicated if detected errors cause the retransmission of certain blocks.

6.5   INFORMATION EXCHANGE CODES

Codes have been used to convey information for a very long time, because natural language may be regarded as a code for passing ideas between people. Generally, however, the concept of coding is used in a more restricted sense and natural language itself is usually the information which has to be encoded in some way for transmission or storage; subsequently, the reverse process of decoding is required to restore the intelligence to its original form. Obviously, the recipient and originator of the information must agree in the coding and decoding procedure, and this naturally leads to the possibility of encryption by employing coding methods, hopefully unique, to conceal information from third parties.

Consideration of written language shows that a basic set of unique symbols or patterns—letters, figures, brush strokes, etc.—is fundamental to coding, and that these basic patterns are associated in sequences or strings to convey more information than would be possible with the primitive set alone. Often, the same basic alphabet set is used for several human languages and, clearly, the groupings of patterns must be agreed as well as the basic set. The proliferation of human languages based on substantially the same alphabet indicates that agreement on this alphabet is much easier than agreement on how it should be used; the same situation arises with computers and their languages.

The most basic of all information indicators is the presence or absence of a mark, symbol or signal giving a two state or binary indication, i.e. yes-no, on-off, go-stop, space-mark, zero-one, etc. Obviously, a sequence or a group of such indications is required to convey more than two conditions, and the term 'code' is used to describe an agreed set of meanings assigned to the different patterns or combinations possible with a group of digits of a given size. The term 'code' is sometimes used to describe a particular combination of the digits also, and one may talk of the code representing a given symbol. If there are n binary digits in a code, there will be 2^n possible combinations,

No. of alphabet No. 2 signal	Letter and figure case	5-unit international code No. 2	7-unit international code No. 3
1	A —	Z Z A A A	A A Z Z A Z A
2	B ?	Z A A Z Z	A A Z Z A A Z
3	C :	A Z Z Z A	Z A A Z Z A A
4	D (1)	Z A A Z A	A A Z Z Z A A
5	E 3	Z A A A A	A Z Z Z A A A
6	F (1)	Z A Z Z A	A A Z A A Z Z
7	G (1)	A Z A Z Z	Z Z A A A A Z
8	H (1)	A A Z A Z	Z A Z A A Z A
9	I 8	A Z Z A A	Z Z Z A A A A
10	J (1)	Z Z A Z A	A Z A A A Z Z
11	K (	Z Z Z Z A	A A A Z A Z Z
12	L)	A Z A A Z	Z Z A A A Z A
13	M	A A Z Z Z	Z A Z A A A Z
14	N ,	A A Z Z A	Z A Z A Z A A
15	O 9	A A A Z Z	Z A A A Z Z A
16	P 0	A Z Z A Z	Z A A Z A Z A
17	Q 1	Z Z Z A Z	A A A Z A A Z
18	R 4	A Z A Z A	Z Z A A Z A A
19	S '	Z A Z A A	A Z A Z A Z A
20	T 5	A A A A Z	Z A A A Z A Z
21	U 7	Z Z Z A A	A Z Z A A Z A
22	V =	A Z Z Z Z	Z A A Z A A Z·
23	W 2	Z Z A A Z	A Z A A Z A Z
24	X /	Z A Z Z Z	A A Z A Z Z A
25	Y 6	Z A Z A Z	A A Z A Z A Z
26	Z +	Z A A A Z	A Z Z A A A Z
27	carriage return	A A A Z A	Z A A A A Z Z
28	line feed	A Z A A A	Z A Z Z A A A
29	letters	Z Z Z Z Z	A A A Z Z Z A
30	figures	Z Z A Z Z	A Z A A Z Z A
31	space	A A Z A A	Z Z A Z A A A
32	(not used)	A A A A A	A A A A Z Z Z
	signal repetition	—	A Z Z A Z A A
	signal α	(permanent A polarity)	A Z A Z A A Z
	signal β	(permanent Z polarity)	A Z A Z Z A A
	[1] See Recommendation S.4		

Figure 6.29.   CCITT Alphabet No. 2 and codes No. 2 and 3 (Reproduced by permission of the International Telecommunications Union)

patterns or codes that may be represented, and the problem arises of agreeing on the meaning to be conveyed by each pattern. There have been a number of codes devised for different purposes and the more important of these will be discussed below.

The early five-digit Murray code used for telegraphy was the basis of the CCITT international code number 2 still used today for telex machines operating at 50 baud. Figure 6.29 shows the symbols of the international alphabet No. 2, their representation in the five-unit code, and also in the seven-unit international code No. 3 used for error control in radio telegraphy (see page 210). The first twenty-six combinations are assigned two meanings, determined by the case shift combinations, 29-letters, and 30-figures. This idea of shifting from one case to another allows more symbols to be represented than would be possible with a one-to-one correspondance between symbols and code patterns.

In general, if M combinations of an N-unit code are used as shift commands, M cases each of $2^n - M$ combinations are available. The total will be $M(2^n - M)$ which is a maximum when $M = 2^{n-1}$. This gives $2^{2(n-1)}$ possibilities compared with 2^n without shifting commands; an improvement of 2^{n-2} times. However, the efficiency of shifting codes depends on the sequence of symbols in the information being handled. When case changes are rare, the gain is considerable; but with frequent case changes the large number of shift commands is a disadvantage. Also, it is impossible to know the meaning of an isolated pattern without knowing to which shift case it belongs.

The use of the two-case code for telegraphy made a useful saving by reducing the average length of messages, because the relatively infrequent case changes with natural language messages makes the average number of units for each symbol only slightly greater than five. If a six-unit code had been used without shifts the average length would, of course, be six units. And, because the messages were interpreted by people, it was usually obvious when the wrong case was assumed by the receiver and rectification was easy.

Internal Computer Codes

In the early days of computers, various arbitrary codes were devised by designers to represent information within the computer. Computers had words of various lengths and the words were divided into fields. One field might represent one operand, another a second operand while a third would be an operation to be performed. Programming was tedious because these arbitrary machine code patterns had to be memorized and manipulated. Later, programming was made easier by using mnemonic instructions based on alphanumeric symbols, and in the U.K. teleprinters were often used in program preparation and for the output of results. This was possible because the mnemonic symbols were translated into the arbitrary code patterns by special programs, called compilers which compiled a list of machine code patterns from the symbols which were more acceptable to human users. The shift feature of the teleprinter code proved to be an inconvenience and it became customary to use six-bit codes within the later computers; some computer designs handing six-bit characters internally are still in existance.

The growth in the range of commands, instructions and symbols needed within a computer, led to the introduction of internal six-bit, three shift codes by some designers, while others went to an eight-bit internal code. The former gives 183 combinations, the latter 256, with the added advantage that shifting is obviated. The eight-bit code is called the extended binary-coded-decimal information code or EBCDIC code, because it was derived originally from the use of two four-bit characters packed together in what became known as an eight-bit byte. The use of the sixteen combinations possible with four binary digits to represent the ten decimal digits is commonly known as the binary-coded decimal BCD code, an example of a six-bit inter-

Zone and Shift / Numeric	00			01	
	α or β	δ		α or β	
0000	0	TC_7	Data Link Escape		space
0001	1	DC_1	Device Control	!	(exclamation)
0010	2	DC_2		"	(quotes)
0011	3	DC_3		#	(number)
0100	4	DC_4	Stop	£	(pound)
0101	5	TC_8	Negative Acknowledge	%	(percent)
0110	6	TC_9	Synchronous Idle	&	(ampersand)
0111	7	TC_{10}	End of Trans. Block	'	(apostrophe)
1000	8	CNCL	Cancel	(	(left parenthesis)
1001	9	EM	End of Medium	)	(right parenthesis)
1010	: (colon)	SB	Substitute	*	(asterisk)
1011	; (semi-colon)	ESC	Escape	+	(plus)
1100	< (less than)	IS_4	File Separator	,	(comma)
1101	= (equals)	IS_3	Group Separator	-	(hyphen/minus)
1110	> (greater than)	IS_2	Record Separator	.	(stop)
1111	? (question)	IS_1	Unit Separator	/	(solidus)

Figure 6.30.   Six-bit internal machine code

nal computer code is the ICL 1900 code shown in Figure 6.30, while the EBCDIC code used in IBM System 360 machines is given in Figure 6.31.

International Codes

The need to extend the control of the computer to external peripheral devices, and to improve the communication between programmer and computer, required a greater range of symbols than was possible with the 5-unit telegraph code, and work began in the United Kingdom on a seven unit code. This was taken up by the International Standards Organization and many countries were involved in agreeing upon an international seven-bit code for information interchange. Eventually, agreement was reached on the code shown in Figure 6.33 as given in ISO/R646: 6 and 7-bit character sets for information processing interchange. Most of the code combinations represent unique symbols, but some alternatives are allowed to suit national requirements.

01 continued	10			11		
δ	α	β	δ	α	β	δ
TC_0 Null	@	_		P	p	
TC_1 Start of heading	A	a		Q	q	
TC_2 Start of text	B	b		R	r	
TC_3 End of text	C	c		S	s	
TC_4 End of Transmission	D	d		T	t	$ (dollar)
TC_5 Enquiry	E	e		U	u	](r.h. bracket)
TC_6 Acknowledge	F	f		V	v	↑
BEL Bell, Alarm	G	g		W	w	←
FE_0 Back Space	H	h		X	x	N_2
FE_1 Horizontal Tabulation	I	i		Y	y	N_3
FE_2 Newline	J	j		Z	z	N_4
FE_3 Line Feed	K	k		[(l.h. brkt)	N_1	\\\ (delete)
FE_4 Form Feed	L	l		α	α	α
FE_5 Carriage Return	M	m		β	β	β
SO Shift Out	N	n		δ	δ	δ
SI Shift In	O	o				

Figure 6.30.   Six-bit internal machine code (continued)

In the United States work on the national version of the ISO code was largely completed at an early date and this was published by the Americ an National Standard Institution ANSI as the United States of America Standard Code for Information Interchange, or USASCII code; commonly called the ASCII (pronounced askey) code.

In parallel with the work in the International Standards Organization, the same proposals were studied by the CCITT with particular regard to the aspects of the code relating to the control of communications facilities and, eventually, the same code was published as the CCITT recommended international telegraph alphabet No. 5.

There is sometimes confusion between these various international codes and they are occasionally regarded as different codes. The true situation is that the ISO code, which has been accepted by a number of countries, specifies a set of unique relationships between codes and the symbols they represent, these symbols may safely be used for international exchanges of information. The CCITT alphabet No. 5 is exactly the same as the ISO code except for a

EBCDIC	Bit Configuration	EBCDIC	Bit Configuration	EBCDIC	Bit Configuration	EBCDIC	Bit Configuration
NUL	0000 0000	SP	0100 0000		1000 0000	PZ 7/11	1100 0000
SOH	0000 0001		0100 0001	a	1000 0001	A	1100 0001
STX	0000 0010		0100 0010	b	1000 0010	B	1100 0010
ETX	0000 0011		0100 0011	c	1000 0011	C	1100 0011
PF	0000 0100		0100 0100	d	1000 0100	D	1100 0100
HT	0000 0101		0100 0101	e	1000 0101	E	1100 0101
LC	0000 0110		0100 0110	f	1000 0110	F	1100 0110
DEL	0000 0111		0100 0111	g	1000 0111	G	1100 0111
	0000 1000		0100 1000	h	1000 1000	H	1100 1000
RLF	0000 1001	.	0100 1001	i	1000 1001	I	1100 1001
SMM	0000 1010	¢ [	0100 1010		1000 1010		1100 1010
VT	0000 1011	.	0100 1011		1000 1011		1100 1011
FF	0000 1100	<	0100 1100		1000 1100	⌐	1100 1100
CR	0000 1101	(	0100 1101		1000 1101		1100 1101
SO	0000 1110	+	0100 1110		1000 1110	⌐	1100 1110
SI	0000 1111	|	0100 1111		1000 1111		1100 1111
DLE	0001 0000	&	0101 0000		1001 0000	MZ 7/13	1101 0000
DC1	0001 0001		0101 0001	j	1001 0001	J	1101 0001
DC2	0001 0010		0101 0010	k	1001 0010	K	1101 0010
TM	0001 0011		0101 0011	l	1001 0011	L	1101 0011
RES	0001 0100		0101 0100	m	1001 0100	M	1101 0100
NL	0001 0101		0101 0101	n	1001 0101	N	1101 0101
BS	0001 0110		0101 0110	o	1001 0110	O	1101 0110
IL	0001 0111		0101 0111	p	1001 0111	P	1101 0111
CAN	0001 1000		0101 1000	q	1001 1000	Q	1101 1000
EM	0001 1001		0101 1001	r	1001 1001	R	1101 1001
CC	0001 1010	!]	0101 1010		1001 1010		1101 1010
CU1	0001 1011	$	0101 1011		1001 1011		1101 1011
IFS	0001 1100	*	0101 1100		1001 1100		1101 1100
IGS	0001 1101	)	0101 1101		1001 1101		1101 1101
IRS	0001 1110	;	0101 1110		1001 1110		1101 1110
IUS	0001 1111	¬	0101 1111		1001 1111		1101 1111
DS	0010 0000	—	0110 0000		1010 0000	RM 5/12	1110 0000
SOS	0010 0001	/	0110 0001	—	1010 0001		1110 0001
FS	0010 0010		0110 0010	s	1010 0010	S	1110 0010
	0010 0011		0110 0011	t	1010 0011	T	1110 0011
BYP	0010 0100		0110 0100	u	1010 0100	U	1110 0100
LF	0010 0101		0110 0101	v	1010 0101	V	1110 0101
ETB	0010 0110		0110 0110	w	1010 0110	W	1110 0110
ESC	0010 0111		0110 0111	x	1010 0111	X	1110 0111
	0010 1000		0110 1000	y	1010 1000	Y	1110 1000
	0010 1001		0110 1001	z	1010 1001	Z	1110 1001
SM	0010 1010	7/12	0110 1010		1010 1010		1110 1010
CU2	0010 1011	,	0110 1011		1010 1011		1110 1011
	0010 1100	%	0110 1100		1010 1100		1110 1100
ENQ	0010 1101	_	0110 1101		1010 1101		1110 1101
ACK	0010 1110	>	0110 1110		1010 1110		1110 1110
BEL	0010 1111	?	0110 1111		1010 1111		1110 1111
	0011 0000		0111 0000		1011 0000	0	1111 0000
	0011 0001		0111 0001		1011 0001	1	1111 0001
SYN	0011 0010		0111 0010		1011 0010	2	1111 0010
	0011 0011		0111 0011		1011 0011	3	1111 0011
PN	0011 0100		0111 0100		1011 0100	4	1111 0100
RS	0011 0101		0111 0101		1011 0101	5	1111 0101
UC	0011 0110		0111 0110		1011 0110	6	1111 0110
EOT	0011 0111		0111 0111		1011 0111	7	1111 0111
	0011 1000		0111 1000		1011 1000	8	1111 1000
	0011 1001	6/0	0111 1001		1011 1001	9	1111 1001
	0011 1010	:	0111 1010		1011 1010		1111 1010
CU3	0011 1011	#	0111 1011		1011 1011		1111 1011
DC4	0011 1100	@	0111 1100		1011 1100		1111 1100
NAK	0011 1101	'	0111 1101		1011 1101		1111 1101
	0011 1110	=	0111 1110		1011 1110		1111 1110
SUB	0011 1111	"	0111 1111		1011 1111	EO	1111 1111

Figure 6.31. EBCDIC code

minor option concerning two currency symbols. About half a dozen symbols of the ISO code may be varied to suit national needs, otherwise all implementations are identical.

The ASCII code is merely the American national version of the ISO code, although it is often regarded as different. As an example of the closeness of national versions the only differences between the United Kingdom and the United States versions are shown in Figure 6.32.

UK	USA	ISO Position
£	#	2/3
↑	^	5/14
		¦	7/12
–	~	7/14
\ or $_{10}$ or $\frac{1}{2}$	\	5/12

Figure 6.32. Comparison of U.K. and
U.S.A. codes

Information Control Codes

A problem that arises frequently, is that of keeping separated a number of functions that may be performed through essentially the same channel or medium. For example, in the telephone network it is common to use frequencies within the speech channel to carry signalling and control information. This is called in-band signalling and has the advantage that the control information is closely associated with the speech information it is controlling. On the other hand, under unusual circumstances it is conceivable that the speech information might be mistaken for a control signal, and this is one of the problems encountered when data are carried as analogue signals over a telephone circuit. Another example arises in the design of a computer where there are advantages to be gained by making the programs and the information they operate upon share a common store, because it may be more efficiently shared between them. However, the possibility of mutual interference, perhaps under fault conditions, makes it necessary sometimes to keep the two in separate stores.

Essentially, the problem is to balance the potential inefficiency arising when functions are rigidly separated, against the possibility of malfunction through confusion when the barriers between functions are vague. This problem is encountered in the design of information exchange codes, where some of the characters will be information carrying symbols and others may control the way information is handled.

One method of including control functions in a code is to allocate certain

THE CODE TABLE OF THE ISO 7-BIT CODED CHARACTER SET

Bits					b7	0	0	0	0	1	1	1	1
					b6	0	0	1	1	0	0	1	1
					b5	0	1	0	1	0	1	0	1
b4	b3	b2	b1	Row / Column		0	1	2	3	4	5	6	7
0	0	0	0	0		NUL	(TC₇) DLE	SP	0	(@)	P	`	p
0	0	0	1	1		(TC₁) SOH	DC₁	!	1	A	Q	a	q
0	0	1	0	2		(TC₂) STX	DC₂	"	2	B	R	b	r
0	0	1	1	3		(TC₃) ETX	DC₃	£	3	C	S	c	s
0	1	0	0	4		(TC₄) EOT	DC₄	$	4	D	T	d	t
0	1	0	1	5		(TC₅) ENQ	(TC₈) NAK	%	5	E	U	e	u
0	1	1	0	6		(TC₆) ACK	(TC₉) SYN	&	6	F	V	f	v
0	1	1	1	7		BEL	(TC₁₀) ETB	'	7	G	W	g	w
1	0	0	0	8		FE₀ (BS)	CAN	(	8	H	X	h	x
1	0	0	1	9		FE₁ (HT)	EM	)	9	I	Y	i	y
1	0	1	0	10		FE₂ (LF)	SUB	*	:	J	Z	j	z
1	0	1	1	11		FE₃ (VT)	ESC	+	;	K	([)	k	(⦸)
1	1	0	0	12		FE₄ (FF)	IS₄ (FS)	,	<	L	(⦸)	l	(⦸)
1	1	0	1	13		FE₅ (CR)	IS₃ (GS)	-	=	M	(])	m	(⦸)
1	1	1	0	14		SO	IS₂ (RS)	.	>	N	(^)	n	(⦸)
1	1	1	1	15		SI	IS₁ (US)	/	?	O	—	o	DEL

NOTES ABOUT THE 7-BIT SET TABLE

① The controls CR and LF are intended for printer equipment which requires separate combinations to return the carriage and to feed a line.

For equipment which uses a single control for a combined carriage return and line feed operation, the function FE_2 will have the meaning of 'New Line' (NL).

This substitution requires agreement between the sender and the recipient of the data.

The use of this function 'NL' is not allowed for international transmission on general telecommunication networks (Telex and Telephone networks).

② For international information interchange, $ and £ symbols do not designate the currency of a given country. The use of these symbols combined with other graphic symbols to designate national currencies may be the subject of other Recommendations.

③ Reserved for National Use. These positions are primarily intended for alphabetic extensions. If they are not required for that purpose, they may be used for symbols and a recommended choice is shown in parentheses in some cases.

Some restrictions are placed on the use of these characters on the general telecommunication networks for international transmission.

④ Positions 5/14, 6/0 and 7/14 of the 7-bit set table are normally provided for the diacritical signs 'circumflex', 'grave accent' and 'overline'. However, these positions may be used for other graphical symbols when it is necessary to have 8, 9 or 10 positions for national use.

⑤ For international information interchange, position 7/14 of the 7-bit set table is used for the graphical symbol (overline), the graphical representation of which may vary according to national use to represent ~ (tilde) or another diacritical sign provided that there is no risk of confusion with another graphical symbol included in the table.

⑥ The graphics in positions 2/2, 2/7, 5/14 of the 7-bit set table have respectively the significance of 'quotation mark', 'apostrophe' and 'upwards arrow'; however, these characters take on the significance of the diacritical signs 'diaeresis', 'acute accent' and 'circumflex accent' when they precede or follow the 'backspace' character.

⑦ For international information interchange position 2/3 of the 7-bit set table has the significance of the symbol #. Within a country where there is no requirement for the symbol £, the symbol # may be used in that position.

⑧ If 10 and 11 as single characters are needed (for example, for Sterling currency subdivision), they should take the place of 'colon' (:) and 'semicolon' (;) respectively. These substitutions require agreement between the sender and the recipient of the data.

On the general telecommunication networks, the characters 'colon' and 'semicolon' are the only ones authorized for international transmission.

Figure 6.33. ISO 7-bit code (Reproduced by permission of the British Standards Institution)

combinations as control characters. This was done in the case of the ISO code which has, in addition to the 95 printing symbols and 'space', a further 32 control characters of various kinds. Some of these govern the behaviour of devices such as printers, others control the format of messages and the operation of data links. The complete standard is a great tribute to very many people who met on committees throughout the world, and managed to reconcile conflicting requirements in various areas of computer and communications applications. However, because of the problems that can arise when codes for fundamentally different purposes are intermingled, it is sometimes better to keep them separated more clearly than is the case with the ISO code. With the 7-bit ISO code, bits 6 and 7 are both zero when indicating a control character. Thus one quarter of the total possible 128 combinations of 7 bits are control characters. Unfortunately, the corruption of a bit in another character could lead to the false indication of a control character, and this cannot be avoided when all code combinations are available to all users. A parallel may be drawn with the telephone channel case, because the use of control characters mingled with data characters is similar to the use of in-band signalling.

An alternative, is to divide the information and control characters into two groups placed in separate fields. If the two are distinguished by an extra bit, for example by subsequently adding another digit to an information character, it is impossible for a corrupted information code to be mistaken for a control code. This is the scheme adopted in the local area data network developed at NPL (see Chapter 7, page 261) where a ninth bit is added to eight-bit data characters. The ninth bit is set to one when accompanying a data character, and to zero when associated with the network internal control characters, which are also of eight bits. Because the ninth bit is not accessible to the users, it is impossible for them to simulate a control character and cause the network to malfunction. It is, of course, possible for a network control character to be corrupted to a data character, but the loss of the control character itself would normally be detected and an alarm action would be taken.

What essentially happens when an extra bit is included is that the control and data characters are separated into a two-level hierarchy; the data characters at the lower level may be affected by, but cannot affect, the control characters in the level above. The penalty paid for this decoupling, into two levels, depends on the number of control codes required. This is because the total possible combinations available are divided equally between control and data, and any in the control field that are not need for control purposes are wasted. However, the possibility of introducing redundantly coded control codes must not be overlooked.

A third possibility mentioned in regard to the CCITT code No. 2 on page 218 is the use of a shift code to move between a control code set and a data code set. The danger is that the shift codes may be corrupted causing a string of control characters and data to be mistaken for each other. Also, it is difficult to arrange a two-level hierachy, because once the control level has handed over to the data level, it cannot regain control unless the data field contains a shift code. A modification to overcome this problem leads to a fourth possible scheme for separation. This only permits a change between levels to occur at particular times such as the end of a block or packet. In effect, the organization into a two-level hierachy is achieved by inserting at predetermined, preferably regular, intervals in an information stream a gap where a shift code may occur. The control level of the hierachy has the option of taking control at that instant, or leaving the channel or information space to the data level. With this scheme the probability of corruption by noise is lower, because the corruption must occur at a definite time.

The four possibilities discussed above are illustrated by Figure 6.34

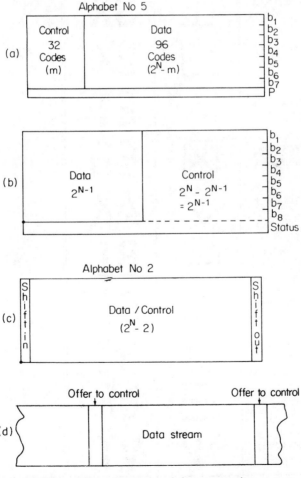

Figure 6.34.   Control and data separation

Code table position (Column/Row)	Character	Pictorial representation	2-character alphanumeric representation	Code table position (Column/Row)	Character
0/0	NUL		NU	0/12	FE4 (FF)
0/1	(TC1) SOH		SH	0/13	FE5 (CR)
0/2	(TC2) STX		SX	0/14	SO
0/3	(TC3) ETX		EX	0/15	SI
0/4	(TC4) EOT		ET	1/0	(TC7) DLE
0/5	(TC5) ENQ see Note 1		EQ	1/1	DC1
0/6	(TC6) ACK		AK	1/2	DC2
0/7	BEL		BL	1/3	DC3
0/8	FE0 (BS)		BS	1/4	DC4
0/9	FE1 (HT)		HT	1/5	(TC8) NAK
0/10	FE2 (LF)		LF	1/6	(TC9) SYN
0/11	FE3 (VT)		VT		

NOTE 1. The following symbol is an alternative pictorial representation of the enquiry

Figure 6.35.   Graphic representation of non-printing characters
(Reproduced by permission of the British Standards Institution)

Pictorial representation	2-character alphanumeric representation	Code table position (Column/Row)	Character	Pictorial representation	2-character alphanumeric representation
⤋	FF	1/7	(TC10) ETB	⊤	EB
⬱	CR	1/8	CAN	⧖	CN
⊗	SO	1/9	EM		EM
⊙	SI	1/10	SUB		SB
	DL	1/11	ESC	⊖	EC
	D1	1/12	IS4 (FS)		FS
	D2	1/13	IS3 (GS)		GS
	D3	1/14	IS2 (RS)		RS
	D4	1/15	IS1 (US)		US
✓	NK	2/0	SP see Note 2	△	SP
⎍	SY	7/15	DEL	⁄⁄⁄	DT

character: NOTE 2. The space character is normally a non-printing graphic.

Figure 6.35.   (continued)

which shows at the top the use of a group of control codes contained within the body of a code, as with the ISO code. The upper middle diagram shows how one bit is used to separate a code into two fields; this reduces the available codes to half, while keeping them quite clear from the control codes. In the lower middle diagram a shift code with two shifts is shown to give almost double the available code combinations at the expense of keeping account of which shift is in use. The bottom diagram shows the regular times at which a shift is allowed to take place.

In fact, the ISO code is provided with shift-out and shift-in codes to make it possible to escape to other codes such as EBCDIC. Indeed, there is more than one way of escaping from the ISO code, although procedures for doing so have yet to be agreed in some cases.

To conclude this discussion of the control aspects of information exchange codes it is worthwhile pointing out that a difficulty arises when non-printing control characters are included in a code, because they are not visible when the code is printed out. Suppose there is a printer intended to produce textual output. It will be necessary to have format control characters like 'form-feed' and command characters to start and stop various operations. Also, the printer will produce reply characters indicating status conditions such as 'out-of-paper'. Normally, of course, none of these would be printed.

Now if a programmer wishes to list a program he has prepared to control the printer, a dilemma arises. Ideally, all possible code combinations should produce a visible indication in his listing, and characters that do not print should do so. What is really needed is the ability to operate at another level during program development and arrange for the printer to print as well as obey the complete character set. A special character is then required to shift into and out of this level of operation. Internationally agreed representations for non-printing symbols are shown in Figure 6.35.

In practice, printers to print all characters do not yet exist, but the problem of controlling ordinary printers remains, and is solved in one of two ways. Either, the printer is driven entirely by coded characters (often the ISO code is employed and a selection of the non-printing characters is used for control purposes) or an extra signal line is provided in the printer interface. A signal on this line indicates that the character being presented to the printer is a control code and not a symbol to be printed. These two methods are analogous to the use of control codes mixed with data codes, and the use of a separate bit to distinguish data and control fields.

When a data link is employed to a remote printer extra lines in the interface are not available and all control must be done through the data field. In this case, the alternatives are to mingle together the control and data codes, or to shift between control and data phases of operation. The latter procedure is to be preferred because it may be extended if necessary to give further features at a later stage, whereas once all the code combinations have been allocated further expansion is impossible.

Once the idea of shifting between phases of operation, or levels in a hierarchy, is accepted it can be elaborated to the use of more than one character to indicate shifts; eventually this idea leads to that of an exchange of short messages and finally to that of a command and control language.

Information Control Procedures

It is relatively easy to select an arbitrary set of control characters or messages to govern the flow of information in a private data network and Chapter 4 covers the techniques that may be used for this purpose in a network using leased lines. But it is much more difficult to devise methods which will be sufficiently unambiguously defined to enable them to be implemented independently by separate designers. However, it is absolutely essential to achieve such a definition if two different computer systems are to be able to converse over a public data network, or indeed if a data terminal is to be able to communicate with a number of computer services.

In the early manual message switching systems the problem was easily solved by plain language message headings, for the later semi-automatic systems stylized headings were devised using groups of characters that were very unlikely to occur within a normal message and, this technique is, of course, still used in telegraph systems today; the types of character group used for control purposes are illustrated by Figure 6.36. This shows some of the Alphabet No. 2 character strings covered by CCITT recommendation S4.

The present day conventional computer-based message-switching systems evolved from the earlier automated telegraph switching centres, so, perhaps naturally enough, they tend to use strings of characters as message delimiters in much the same manner. Usually, all the characters in a message are examined by a program in the computer, which looks for a match between the message and various control character strings held in the computer memory. Though very flexible, and easily changed, this kind of operation is most wasteful of computer power. Unless special hardware is used, it can be so time-consuming that the rate of transit of messages is but a fraction of that obtainable with the packet switching technique. This is because a packet switching network uses a well defined packet structure in which the position of control characters is fixed precisely; therefore, the message need be inspected only at appropriate points where these characters are known to occur. Furthermore, it becomes feasible to use hardware for some control operations with a further increase in the speed of message handling; these possibilities are discussed in Chapter 10.

ISO Control Procedures

Unfortunately, until recently, all of the considerable amount of work done in national and international committees on standards for controlling infor-

Sequences of combinations from international alphabet No. 2 which are devoted to special purposes and should not be used for other purpose when the equipment on such networks introduces special facilities for which these sequences are reserved.

a) ZCZC start-of-message signal in retransmission systems using perforated tape or equivalent devices;
b) ++++ end-of-telegram signal in retransmission systems using perforated tape or equivalent devices;
c) NNNN end-of-message signal, a switching signal in switching systems using perforated tape or equivalent devices for retransmission; also used for restoring the waiting signal device in accordance with Recommendation U.22;
d) CCCC for switching into circuit, by remote control, a reperforator (or equivalent device);
e) SSSS for switching into circuit data transmission equipment, in accordance with Recommendation V.10;
f) FFFF for switching out of circuit, by remote control, a reperforator (or equivalent device);
   NOTE: The shifted codes or secondaries of these combinations—although they are not be used for the purposes devoted to these sequences—are subject to the same restrictions in use, the equipment having to recognize only the sequence of combinations.

In international services these sequences are:

+:+: = corresponding to ZCZC
ZZZZ = corresponding to ++++
,,,, = corresponding to NNNN
:::: = corresponding to CCCC
,,,, = correspond.ng to SSSS

g) the signal "line feed" (combination No. 28) followed by 4 signals "carriage return" (combination No. 27) for the signal of operator recall on a telex connection made over a radio-telegraph circuit (see Recommendation U.21).

Figure 6.36.   Control code sequences from Alphabet No. 2 (Reproduced by permission of the International Telecommunications Union)

mation flow, was based on extending the ISO code. This led to rather complex standards that are very difficult to implement with cheap hardware, and a new approach is now becoming more widely favoured.

The ISO code has ten communications control characters which were thought by the code designers to be adequate for their intended purpose, although the precise way they were to be used was left for later definition. These characters were used subsequently to develop procedures for data link control based on five phases of data transfer as shown in Figure 6.37, namely: circuit connection; link establishment; message transfer; link termination; and circuit disconnection. These phases were associated with single and multiple data link systems using simplex, half duplex and duplex operation; this resulted in the definition of about a dozen different categories of control procedure. At the same time, it was found necessary to introduce additional control functions such as 'mandatory disconnect': achieved by using a two character sequence obtained by preceding certain control characters by a DLE character, e.g. DLE EOT = mandatory disconnect.

A particular use of the DLE character, known as the double DLE technique was defined to permit transparent transfer of non-ISO code messages which contained in the body of their text codes representing ISO control characters. (This could occur if the message was produced, for example, by sampling an analogue signal.) In the transparent mode, any intended control characters are prefaced by DLE, so control characters without DLE in front are ignored. However, the DLE character may occur within the message itself, and in this case an extra DLE character is inserted next to it. At the receiver, one of the DLE characters is suppressed and the other passed through as data. This solution has a serious drawback when a long string of DLE characters occurs in the message. Each is doubled, so the string becomes twice as long. To be truly transparent, therefore, a transmission channel would normally have to be operated at half its maximum rate, so that the double

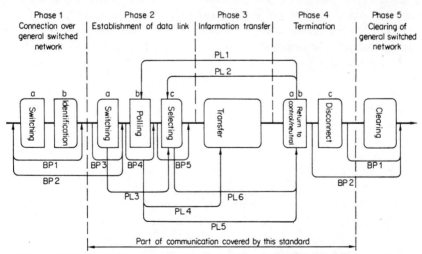

Figure 6.37.   Five phases of data transfer (Reproduced by permission of the British Standards Institution)

length strings of DLE characters could be sent at twice the normal speed over the link to maintain the normal message transmission rate. Of course, the probability of long strings of DLE characters in normal messages is low, so the scheme is workable. But it is not very elegant and is another manifestation of the problem of separating control and data functions discussed earlier (see page 223). This same problem also arises with the more recently proposed standard for data link control procedures discussed in the next section.

High-Level Data Link Control Procedures

The difficulties of implementing, simply, the ISO control procedures have led to renewed activity in standards organizations resulting in a new approach to defining control procedures in an attempt to separate data link control from other control functions. Essentially, this has to be done by defining the structure of the message itself, rather than procedures which allow messages to be structured by users of data links.

The basic concept used is a frame, this, as shown in Figure 6.38, is a block which is delimited, in front and behind, by a bit sequence (0111 1110) called a flag. The front flag serves the purposes of synchronization, and indicates the start of control information; while the rear flag identifies the cyclic check sum which occurs just before it. The flag may be used as an idle character between frames, and bit stuffing is used to mask any appearance of the flag sequence that occurs within the frame itself.

The bit stuffing is done at the transmitter by inserting a zero after a run of five successive ones, while the receiver always removes a zero detected after a sequence of five ones. This prevents the false representation of the flag (zero; six ones; zero) by a string of six ones in the message itself.

As in the previously described method using double DLE for separating control and data the insertion of extra bits into a message stream takes some of the channel capacity. In this case, a long string of ones would be increased by factor 6/5 because each group of six ones would be stuffed by a zero, making seven bits total. The transmitted message stream must either be longer by this factor; or, if the message is to occupy the same length of time on the line as it does passing to and from the users equipment, it must be transmitted at a line rate higher by this factor than the rate allowed to the user. The only way this difficulty can be avoided is by the use of a block length indicator as discussed in Chapter 10, page 375.

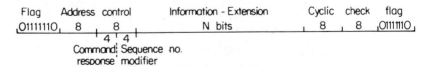

Figure 6.38.   High-level data link block format

bit 1   Sequence / modifier
           bit 1 = 0 ;   Modifier in bits 5 - 8
           bit 1 = 1 ;   Sequence No. in bits 5 - 8
bit 2   Command / Response class
           bit 2 = 0 ;   Information
           bit 2 = 1 ;   Supervisory
bit 3   Respond
           bit 3 = 0 ;   do not initiate response
           bit 3 = 1 ;   initiate response
bit 4   Block length
           bit 4 = 0 ;   Short   Flag, address, control, cyclic check, flag
           bit 4 = 1 ;   Long   Flag, address, control, information, cyclic check, flag

Figure 6.39.   Control field format

The present international work on message format standardization is directed towards the definition of the contents of a frame appearing between two flags. At the moment, the first eight bits following the first flag are allocated for link addressing: of the next eight bits, the first four are for command and response information, and the second four are a sequence number or command modifier. If necessary some further bits as yet undefined, would serve as control extensions; while the remainder of the frame is dedicated to users information followed by a sixteen-bit cyclic sum check and the closing flag.

The structure of the command-and-response field is shown in Figure 6.39 and is related to the idea of primary and secondary stations on a link. Only one primary station is allowed, and the eight bit field is designated as follows: bit 1 indicates whether a sequence number, or a modifier is present in bits 5-8; bit 2 indicates the class of information; bit 3 is used by the primary station to call for a response; bit 4 indicates the presence or absence of an information field. Bits 5 to 8 contain either a sequence number relevant to one of the secondary stations, or a modifier. Modifiers have, so far, only been defined for 'disconnect', 'status request' and 'initialize'.

From the foregoing brief resumé of current work on the standardization of control procedures it can be seen how complex the subject has become. This is, primarily, because a proper division has not been made between control and other information. This division can be made in systems that are structured in a hierarchical fashion, such as the ARPA network (see page 300). A hierarchical system does not, in general, appear complex within each level of the hierarchy. However, when viewed as a whole, the complexity will be inescapably governed by the tasks that have to be performed. So the overall appearance of a well designed system is likely to be much the same, regardless of the way it is designed. But the problem of design and comprehension of each sub-system is much less when the hierarchical approach is used. This approach in relation to communications system design is discussed further in Chapter 10, page 350.

References

1. Recommendation V24, *CCITT III Plenary Assembly Blue Book*, *Vol. VIII* (1964).
2. *British Standard 4421*, British Standards Institution, British Standard House, 2 Park Street, London W1.
3. Chu, W. W., 'Optimal fixed block size for computer communications', IFIP Congress 71, Ljubljana.
4. Bartlett, K. A., 'Transmission control in a local data network', IFIP Congress 68, Edinburgh. North Holland Publishing Company (1969).
5. Shannon, C. E., and Weaver, W., *The Mathematical Theory of Communication*, Urbana, University of Illinois Press (1949).
6. Recommendation V30, *CCITT IV Plenary Assembly White Book*, Vol. VIII (1968).
7. Hamming, R. W., 'Error detecting and correcting codes', *Bell Syst. Tech. J.*, **26**, 147 (April 1950).
8. Recommendation V41, *CCITT IV Plenary Assembly White Book*, Vol. VIII (1969).

Chapter 7

Digital Multiplexing

7.1   INTRODUCTION

Multiplexing is the method by which several channels of communication are combined into one. The combined channel must carry all the information, so it is usually of higher bandwidth (or channel capacity) than the individual channels from which it is composed. We have already met (in Chapter 2) frequency division multiplexing where telephone channels are translated to higher frequencies by modulation so that many of them can be carried in one channel of higher bandwidth such as 48 kHz. This is similar to the way in which audio and television channels are multiplexed in the radio wave spectrum.

In this chapter methods of multiplexing digital channels will be described. The capacity of a digital channel is measured by the number of binary digits per second it can carry, and this will be called its *digit rate*. The multiplexed channel generally has a higher digit rate than each of its constituent channels. There are many schemes for the multiplexing of digital channels. In each case the binary digits of the constituent channels fall into place in the combined channel according to some rule. The combined channel therefore divides its time between the constituent channels. In a very general sense this is time-division multiplexing, but the use of that expression for all the varieties of digital multiplexing would be misleading. We shall use it only for the simplest variety of digital multiplexing which will now be described.

7.2   TIME-DIVISION MULTIPLEXING

For analogue signals such as a speech waveform it is possible to multiplex channels by time-division instead of frequency division. The principle is shown in Figure 7.1, where the four channels C1, C2, C3 and C4 are combined into one channel CC. The horizontal boxes at the top of the figure represent shift registers. Each of the squares is a two-state device or trigger and at each clock pulse the pattern of bits in the register shifts one place to the

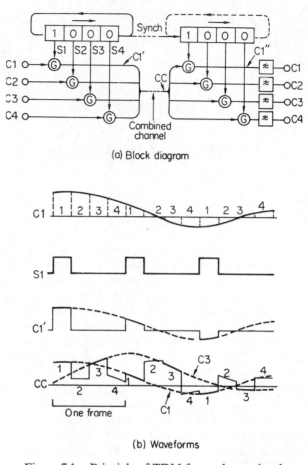

(a) Block diagram

(b) Waveforms

Figure 7.1. Principle of TDM for analogue signals

right. The output from the right side can be shifted around into the input at the left side so that the pattern of bits recirculates. A single 1 circulating in the shift register is shown as the method for producing the selection signals S1, S2, S3 and S4 which, each in turn, take the 1 state at successive steps of the register. These signals are applied to gates which allow the analogue signal to pass through with unit gain when the digital signal is 1. At other times the gate attenuates completely. The four signals are shown combined in the figure, in what is effectively an analogue adder.

The sampled signal at C1′ is shown, and below it in the figure is the combined signal, CC, in which there are interleaved, pieces from each of the constituent channels. At the receiving end similar gates G driven from a similar set of selection signals select the separate channels which reappear as before, C1″ copying C1′ and so forth. Finally the sampled waveforms are put through low-pass filters and, if the conditions of the sampling theorem are met, the output signal of each channel is a reproduction of the input.

As a transmission method this has little attraction, for in order to reproduce the amplitudes of the samples correctly the channel would have to be carefully equalised to prevent intersymbol interference. The method is used inside small telephone exchanges where the bandwidth considerations are not a problem. Our interest in it is chiefly as an introduction to time-division multiplexing or TDM, its abbreviated name. Before leaving the analogue system, note that extremely accurate timing would be needed to avoid 'sneak' pulses in waveform C1″ from the neighbouring channels C2 and C4. This can be avoided by having the gating pulses at the receiver somewhat narrowed, indeed the transmission of the CC waveform might be easier if the waveform returned to zero between samples.

The two sampling switches must 'rotate' in step. In the figure we took the arbitrary precaution to connect them by the 'synch' channel. But supposing the two ends were correctly synchronized at the start, they should stay synchronized. The information carried by a synch channel is therefore zero, or only as much as is needed to correct slippage due to noise. There is an incentive to incorporate this small amount of information with the signal instead of providing a separate channel.

A familiar example of TDM for transmitting an analogue signal is the television picture and its scan. Our eye/brain sensory apparatus provides the low-pass filter which enables us to see a collection of consecutively scanned lines as though each was presented continuously. In the television signal the synchronizing is done by line and frame pulses that can be separated from the video signal itself and are fitted into the TDM scheme.

The method by which the scanning mechanisms at each end of a TDM channel is kept in step is called *framing*, by analogy with the way the picture 'frame' is held in a television signal. The *frame* is a complete cycle of operation; in our simple example the set of four samples for C1, C2, C3 and C4 comprise one frame.

Digital Time-Division Multiplexing

To apply the TDM method to a number of digital channels it is hardly necessary to alter the scheme shown in Figure 7.1. The figure becomes a logic diagram in which the gates G are AND gates. The low pass filters are replaced by triggers which are set and reset to regenerate the constituent channels with correct timing. But the ease with which digital data can be stored allows us to use a different mechanism for digital TDM, which has almost the same result. This is shown in Figure 7.2. The channels C1 to C4 carry binary digits which are presented in phase with Clock 1 so that the clock applied to the four AND gates transfers the bits at the same time into the shift register. Then

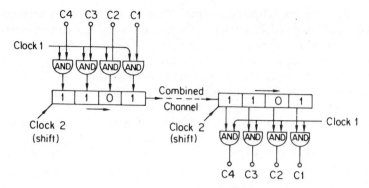

Figure 7.2. Digital TDM system using shift registers

Clock 2 which runs at four times the rate of Clock 1 sends the data serially onto the transmission path, in the sequence C1, C2, C3, C4. The bits are received in a similar shift register shifted by the Clock 2 which must be sent over the transmission path as part of the data transmission system. By 'division by 4' the Clock 1 can be recovered at the receiver, and this transfers the pattern stored in the shift register into the four separate channels. At this point they are narrow pulses and will probably be reshaped to a form suitable for Clock 1, the slower clock.

Suppose the four channels C1 to C4 have the binary sequences:

$$a_1b_1c_1d_1 \ldots, a_2b_2c_2d_2 \ldots, a_3b_3c_3d_3 \ldots, a_4b_4c_4d_4 \ldots,$$

then the combined channel carries the bit pattern:

$$a_1a_2a_3a_4b_1b_2b_3b_4c_1c_2c_3c_4d_1d_2d_3d_4 \ldots$$

A signal produced by TDM is itself a binary sequence, which can be carried by the same basic mechanism that would carry the constituent channels, but operating at a higher rate. This contrasts with TDM applied to analogue signals, for the signal CC in Figure 7.1 has special transmission requirements not present in the simple voice channel. It can therefore be said the TDM is a natural method for combining digital signals, in the same way that FDM is a natural method for analogue signals.

The digital channel which carries the combined signal must carry the clock information, and all the constituent channels must be synchronized to the common clock. This clock is needed at both ends of the multiplexed channel for stepping on the scanners or shift registers.

There are two basic problems in digital TDM, how to ensure that the frames are identified correctly at the receiver end and how to deal with an incoming signal if its clock is not exactly correct for the multiplexed channel.

In the television signal, framing was carried by a type of signal not found in the video part of the waveform. The multiplexed digital signal cannot afford to use such a method because it must be carried as a binary sequence over a normal digital channel, with no provision for 'out of band' information. The multiplexed channel must be a simple binary sequence because this channel itself may need to be multiplexed at a higher level in the communication network. Therefore, framing information must be carried by some kind of coding in the binary sequence.

Multiplexing of PCM channels

In Chapter 2 the method of representing a voice signal by 'pulse code modulation' was described. Voice waveforms are sampled at 8000 per second and each sample is represented by a 7 or 8-bit binary number. The near-logarithmic relationship of the transmitted number to the measured sample was described.

PCM systems are used to carry a group of channels, 24 or 30 at a time, using time-division multiplexing. The multiplexing methods used in PCM will serve to explain methods of framing and adaption to a 'foreign' clock.

The coder, which takes an analogue sample and produces the digital representation, and the decoder, which reverses the process at the receiving end, are relatively expensive equipments, and therefore are shared between the channels of one PCM system, what might be called a PCM 'primary group'. So the process at the sending end is *not* to code the individual channels and multiplex them digitally. The multiplexing is done *first*, on the analogue signals, after which the common coder handles each sample in turn. This is shown schematically in Figure 7.3. The scanner and distributor are the devices shown in Figure 7.1 and carry out the TDM process. At points A and B the signal has successive analogue samples from one channel after another. Operating on these, the coder produces, on the line, a pattern of binary digits in which the digital representation of one channel is followed by that of the next channel, and so forth.

The PCM system described in Chapter 2 was the one recommended by CCITT and this system will be used to illustrate multiplexing and framing in the present chapter. Each sample is coded into eight bits (one of them a sign bit). Because the time division is done *before* coding, these eight bits appear consecutively on the line. There are 30 channels in the group, but the framing method allows space for 32, allowing the extra two channel positions to carry

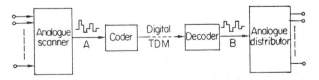

Figure 7.3. Schematic of PCM

framing and signalling information in a way that will be described. The complete frame therefore contains 8×32 or 256 bits. These fall into 32 *slots* of 8 bits each.

The samples are taken at 8000 per second for each channel and each fills a slot. For each sample interval of 125 µs a whole frame is filled, and the digit rate is therefore 8000×256 or 2048 kbit/s. (Earlier systems are typified by 'T1 carrier' which is widely used in U.S.A., carries 24 channels and operates at a rate of 1544 kbit/s.)

Framing and Control Signalling

The 30 channel system employs 32 slots numbered from 0 to 31 as shown in the top part of Figure 7.4. Each of the squares represents the 8-bits sample in the respective channel, except that the channels in slots 0 and 16 are replaced by special bit patterns for framing and signalling. We have called them F for framing and S for signalling, respectively.

The framing pattern is in bits 2 to 8 of slot F, and consists of the digits 0011011, but is sent only in alternate frames F1. In the other frames, F2, bit 2 has the value 1 so that, assuming the framing is correct the phase of F1/F2 is easily detected. The bit labelled FA in the figure carriers the framing alarm. In the squares which are unlabelled, the use of the bits has not been decided, but they are held at value 1 while they remain spare.

The framing pattern can arise by chance in any of the slots, as a voice sample, but it would not persist. The probability of persistent framing simulation rapidly becomes vanishingly small as the length of simulation increases. The frame defined by the F slot is actually 512 bits long (2 ordinary frames) because of the alternating patterns F1 and F2. Such a frame can be derived from the clock associated with the incoming signal, but when the equipment is started up it will generally be out of phase. At the time when F1 is expected the bit pattern in positions 2 to 8 is examined. If it is not the framing signal,

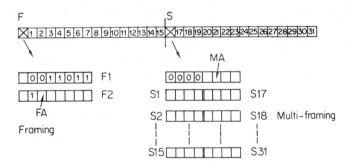

Figure 7.4.   Framing scheme for 30-channel PCM, with control signals

the divider which derives the frame is given an increment to make it try a new position. This continues until the correct F1 pattern is found and possibly as many as 256 tries will be needed. Then having found F1 the system looks for F2 at the appropriate time. If it fails, the search for F1 is resumed again, but if F2 is found the system looks again for F1. Only when the sequence F1-F2-F1 has been found is it assumed that the frame alignment has been correctly identified.

During the search for frame alignment the audio channels are disconnected to avoid the sending of noise from the misaligned bit patterns. The bit FA on the return channel is made 1 to tell the sending end of trouble, because it might be due to a fault in the make-up of the digital signal. When the alignment has been found these conditions are restored to normal, and at each slot F1 the framing pattern is checked. When an error is observed three times in succession it is assumed that the alignment is wrong, the audio channels are disconnected, FA put on and the search is stated again. The search process takes many frames, but because the error rate on digital channels is so low it will not be used very often. The intervals between framing errors would be measured in hours or days because slippage requires not just errors on the line but a loss of clock pulses during the disturbance. The exact strategy for detecting loss of framing and searching for framing is a matter of choice, and is not a critical design feature.

The framing signal F uses a sequence of two frames. Control signalling is carried out with a 16-frame cycle which makes up a 'multiframe'. The framing device which establishes the multiframe has an easier task than the framing of the 256 bit frames. The pattern it uses consists of four 0 bits in the first occurrence of S in the multiframe. In each of the remaining occurrences of S there are two 4-bit fields used for signalling. Each of the 30 signalling fields contained in the S positions of the multiframe carries the control signals for one of the voice channels, as shown in Figure 7.4 where S1 to S15 and S17 to S31 match the numbers in the slots. It is arranged that the pattern used in signalling never allows the 4-bit fields to take the value 0000, so the multiframing pattern 0000 is unique. Loss of multiframing is signalled to the sending end by using the bit MA in the return channel.

Each voice channel is allocated one 8-bit slot per frame. The frames come at 8000/s so that it has 64 kbit/s available for speech transmission. Multiframes occur at 500/s and contain four bits of signalling information per channel, therefore each channel has 2000 bit/s of signalling capacity.

The control signalling scheme we have described has a control channel associated with each speech channel. If a common signalling channel is used slot S provides a digit rate of 64 kbit/s (like any other slot) which is also very adequate. An important factor in the economy of PCM transmission is the simplicity of its signalling methods, which avoid the need for generating and detecting tones, with the attendant problems of voice or data simulation.

T1 Carrier

In our description of the principles of PCM the system used as the example has been the 2·048 Mbit/s system recommended by CCITT. This system has incorporated the lessons of almost a decade of development since the first PCM systems went into operation.

The first PCM system to go into wide use was the T1 Carrier system in the Bell network in U.S.A. After this was introduced, literally dozens of variations of the basic ideas were adopted or proposed by national authorities before CCITT achieved a measure of agreement. It now seems likely that two standards will continue to be used widely, the T1 Carrier[1] and the CCITT 2·048 Mbit/s systems.

T1 Carrier samples the speech waveform at 8000/s and codes each sample in a seven-bit word, to which an 8th bit is added for signalling. (The CCITT scheme, it will be remembered, has its signalling fields occupying two 'speech' channels.) Twenty-four channels are assembled into a frame of 192 bits with just one bit added for framing. So the frame is 193 bits long and the digit rate in consequence is 193×8000/s or 1·544 Mbit/s.

The framing signal must be distinguished from other bits, although it contains only one bit, and this is done by making the framing bit alternate from one frame to the next. This alternation is unlikely to happen to any bit in a speech sample because it would imply a 4 kHz component in the speech, and this is beyond the spectrum allowed through. Signalling bits change only rarely. The framing device at the receiving end enters a search phase if the frame alternation shows errors coming too fast, and in the search phase it moves on one digit whenever it finds an error until the alternation rule has not been broken for eight frames, then it locks on.

The problem of maintaining regenerator clocks in the presence of strings of zeros was dealt with in T1 in a way that was peculiar to PCM. The speech sample, after companding, is digitized into a binary number in the range 1 to 127. In fact, 1 represents the extreme positive voltage and 127 the extreme negative, and a zero voltage is represented by 64. Since the value 0 is not used, all 7-bit samples have at least one bit which is non-zero. The extreme (and unlikely) case is 1000000 followed by signalling bit 0 then by 0000001, which has 15 successive zeros. The regenerator was designed to operate up to this limit.

This method of dealing with the zeros problem is not helpful for data transmission, and it is fortunate that later PCM systems have used coding by *violations* to signal strings of zeros, a method which is helpful for all users of the digital transmission path. Data systems using T1 Carrier (and similar early PCM designs) are obliged to insert 1s at regular intervals for the benefit of the regenerators.

Higher Level Multiplexing of PCM Channels

The multiplexing of 24 or 30 voice channels is carried out at the point of conversion to a digital representation. The carrying of speech at these digit rates of 1·5 to 2 Mbit/s is economic where it employs existing pairs over distances from 5 to 50 miles, approximately. In the U.S.A. a second level of the hierarchy is provided by T2 Carrier which combines four channels of T1 Carrier using time-division multiplexing of the digital signal. It operates over digital transmission channels at 6.312 Mbit/s and extends the length of line over which PCM is economic. But PCM cannot compete over long distances with FDM except at higher speeds where more voice channels are carried on each bit stream. The details of digital multiplexing hierarchies have yet to be worked out.

In the PCM primary group, such as T1 Carrier or the CCITT 30 channel scheme, the group of bits which represents one sample is sent in one slot in the frame. When a number of these primary groups is further combined by TDM, the bits of a particular sample are separated. This would make it difficult to return from PCM to audio channels other than by separating out the primary groups. This is like the frequency multiplexing hierarchy, where lines are always handled in primary groups of 12 channels, and individual characters cannot easily be separated from higher order multiplexed groups.

PCM has been introduced into telephone networks first as a *carrier* system, that is a means of combining channels for transmission. But time-division is also a powerful method for switching because contacts or switches of the 'space division' kind can be replaced by logic gates, and delay or storage can be used to move a sample from time-slot to time-slot. In Chapter 9 we return to the subject of switching in the time domain. Such switches require that all the time-division channels reaching the switch shall have synchronized clocks and synchronized frames.

There are therefore two situations in which several PCM carriers must be adapted to a common clock; where they meet at a time-division switch and where they meet in a higher order multiplexer. For switching the problem is complicated by the need for frame synchronism as well. For multiplexing it is possible to adapt the stream of digits by *bit stuffing* to the rate of the multiplexer. The process is sometimes called *pulse stuffing*. We use the term 'bit stuffing' because it can be related to *byte stuffing* which also occurs in certain data systems.

Speech presents a more difficult problem than data when the clock rate has to be adapted to a 'foreign' channel because of its fundamentally iso-chronous nature. Whatever happens on the way, the bit stream and its original clock rate must be restored at the far end, and the clock must be at a uniform rate.

The Elastic Store

The bit stuffing method employs *elastic stores*, and these stores have several applications in data transmission and PCM (see page 196). Figure 7.5 shows diagrammatically an elastic store with a capacity of 16 bits. Each square represents a bistable device or trigger which is a storage cell for one bit. At any given moment one cell is selected for storing the next bit to arrive and a different cell is selected for reading out. Their addresses are denoted as S and R. From the R cell and to its right the cells marked by crosses hold bits that have been stored and await reading. The storage region carries over if necessary from cell 15 to cell 1 and always ends at the S cell.

Input to the elastic store consists of storing a bit in the S cell then adding 1 to the value of S, so that the 'store' pointer moves to the right as bits are stored. Following it up is the 'read' pointer which moves to the right after a cell has been read. The bits that have been stored and read remain until their cells are overwritten. The R and S cells can be selected by gates controlled by 4-bit counters which overflow from 15 to 0. Assuming that the R and S pointers remain apart, the pattern which is read out will be the input pattern, delayed. The delay can vary within limits and the clock which controls input can differ from the output clock, though averaged over a period there must be as many 'reads' as 'writes', or the store will become empty or full.

A measure of the fullness of the store is needed, and this is given by O, the occupancy. $S-R$ measures the occupancy, except than when $S < R$ the measure is $S-R+16$. These two cases are shown in the figure. If O decreases it signifies that the store is more empty, until at $O = 1$ there is danger that reading will overtake storing. At the other extreme $O = 15$ implies that storing may overtake reading.

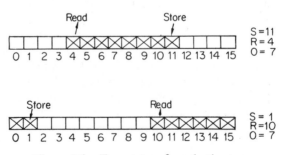

Figure 7.5.   Two states of an elastic store

Bit Stuffing

Elastic stores are used in the bit-stuffing system[2,3] illustrated in Figure 7.6. The object of the system is to provide a data link for the data presented with Clock 1 and to reproduce these data, with a clock, at the output. It must carry

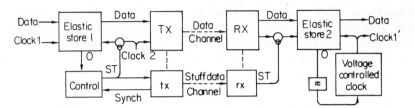

Figure 7.6.   The principle of bit stuffing

this data over a multiplexed channel which uses a clock (Clock 2) with a slightly different rate. The reason for the difference is that Clock 2 belongs to the multiplexer and must be common to all the channels yet each constituent channel has its own clock. In order to carry the data, Clock 2 must have a higher rate than Clock 1, so the multiplexer is designed with its clock rate higher, by a small safety margin, than is needed even for the extreme case of a fast 'Clock 1'. Let us denote by d the rate difference of the two clocks measured in bit/s.

The method used is to pop extra bits into the incoming data stream at predetermined points so that the rate is increased to that of Clock 2. These are the 'stuffed' bits. In order that the system adjusts to the rate difference d, bits are stuffed or not in a controlled manner. The occurrence of a stuffed bit must be signalled to the receiving end so that it may be removed. This requires an extra data channel built into the multiplexer. The figure shows only one channel of the several that share the multiplexer, and for simplicity the channel for the stuff data is shown separately.

The process begins at elastic store 1 which receives data at the rate of Clock 1 but, in the absence of stuffing, reads it out again at the rate of Clock 2. As a result the occupancy of the store will gradually reduce. At some level of occupancy the box marked 'control' decides it is time to stuff a bit. To do this it sends a pulse on the line 'ST'. This has two effects: it inhibits the Clock 2 input which reads elastic store 1 and it signals the event over the stuff-data channel to the receiving end. The Clock 2 pulse into the transmitter TX sends the stuffed bit down the data channel, but it was never read from the elastic store and is therefore meaningless.

At the receiving end the ST pulse inhibits the Clock 2 train so that the stuffed bit is not stored in the elastic store 2. The bit sequence in that store is therefore correct but there is still the problem of recovering Clock 1. The clock coming into the storing side of elastic store 2 has on average the same number of bits per second as Clock 1, but occasional bits are missing. This is what is known as a stuttering clock. To smooth the clock (and the output of the store which it controls) a servo system is used. The occupancy of the store is transformed into an analogue signal and is subjected to a low pass filter which removes or least greatly attenuates the transients due to the missing clock pulses. This signal is used to control the rate of a new clock, Clock 1′, which becomes the reconstructed Clock 1 and controls store output. The servo system maintains a constant average store occupancy by adjusting the rate of Clock 1′. Only a small jitter remains in the reconstructed clock.

Stuffing pulses need only be rare events. With clocks in the megahertz range it is relatively easy to maintain the oscillator frequency constant to a few hertz over long periods, using crystal oscillators in small temperature-controlled enclosures. So the stuffing data for a whole group of channels can be accommodated in a very low-speed part of the multiplex structure. Typically this would share a slot with the framing information. At higher levels of the multiplexing scheme there is no need for further control signalling channels because these are already packed in at the primary group level.

It is also possible to code the stuffing data very redundantly, by repetition or other methods, so that errors in these data are very unlikely. These precautions are taken because a stuffing error destroys framing in the multiplexed channel and consequently in all the constituent channels.

Stuffing data for any one channel may have to wait a short time for its slot to arrive in the low-speed channel. The elastic stores can afford to wait if their capacity is sufficient. Then the stuff-data system, which is *tx* in Figure 7.6, signals to the 'control' unit that the time to stuff has arrived. The stuffed bit can have a predetermined place in the framing structure so that it is easy for the receiving end to remove the correct bit.

7.3 SYNCHRONOUS NETWORKS

Bit stuffing is a complex mechanism, and must be applied to each channel of a multiplexer, allowing little common equipment. It cannot easily solve the problem of synchronization at a time-division switch because of the need for the frames of each incoming multiplexed channel to coincide. In the long run, it is likely that synchronization of the whole network[4] will prove a better method when the amount of digital transmission and time-division switching has increased.

Suppose that each switching centre in a network had a clock and frame which coincided in time. Because of the delay in transmission it would be necessary to delay the signals further on their arrival on a switch until their frames coincided, and the total delay in transmission would need to be a multiple of 125 microseconds, which is the assumed time for each frame. But this is unnecessarily restrictive because frames need not coincide at each switch; it is merely necessary that the 'round trip' delay between a pair of switches would be a multiple of 125 microseconds. The round trip delay for switches A and B is the sum of the padded out delays from A to B and B to A. With this condition, if we take switch A as datum the frames which arrive at B determine its framing and the frames returned to A will synchronize with A because the round trip is an integral number of frames.

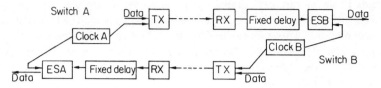

Figure 7.7.   Synchronization of two switching centres

Synchronism of this kind, once set up, will persist only if the various clocks have exactly the same frequency and the transmission delays are constant. To accommodate phase shifts between the clocks and delay changes, the channels are provided with elastic stores in addition to the fixed, padding-out delay. In Figure 7.7, the output of elastic store B (ESB) is taken at the rate of Clock B, while its input is locked to Clock A. If the frequency of B is greater than A, the store ESB will gradually empty. Similarly, store ESA will fill. The effect of temperature changing the transmission delay of the channel is that both stores fill or both empty.

The effect of transmission delay changes can be accommodated by having sufficiently large elastic stores, but frequency changes have a cumulative effect. To counter this the frequencies of the clocks must be adjusted according to the measured store occupancies O_A and O_B, and it is $O_A - O_B$ that should control the changes. For this purpose the value of O_A is coded digitally and sent in some of the spare bits of the multiplexer's frame to B and the value of O_B is sent likewise to A.

To preserve the symmetry of the situation each end can decide, from the value of $O_A - O_B$, what clock adjustment is needed. The adjustment can be made at each end from each controller. The clock at B, for example, will receive commands to change speed from its own controller and, via the data in the channel, from the controller at A. It will receive similar pairs of signals from all the links coming into the switching centre. For reliability, it acts on a concensus of these many commands. If there is too much disagreement it does nothing.

For a complex network it is by no mean certain that such a control system, which alters all the clocks together, will be stable. Theoretical studies have shown that stable situations can be set up, but there are also undesirable situations when the stores have been pushed to their limits, but no clock receives unequivocal signals. The full design of the system therefore has a number of complexities not described here.

The stability problem can be simplified by not regarding all the links as part of the control network. It is possible that the network switching hierarchy will be reflected in the hierarchy for clock control. The top level, which has the fully-connected transit centres, will be fully connected for clock control and this will produce the clock rates on which the remainder of the network depends in an hierarchical manner. At each level, there are sufficient links between the switching centres of the level to guard against the loss of control over any one link. Those links which do not take part in the frequency control will have fixed delays and elastic stores, the occupancy of which will be controlled by the other, indirect paths, which need never be more than two links in tandem.

Byte Multiplexing

The preceding sections relate mainly to PCM. Now we shall look at multiplexing methods likely to be used for data.

The eight-bit byte is an important unit of data in computer systems. Its importance comes in the first place from the eight-bit codes for information exchange which have been adopted by the International Standards Organization and the CCITT. Secondly the input/output systems of many computers are based on the eight-bit byte, which is reflected in the data width of 8 in their I/O interface bus. Finally, many computers organize their stores in eight-bit bytes or have their word length a multiple of eight bits.

It therefore seems reasonable that a data communication system should recognize the eight-bit structure and provide a means of preserving this unit throughout the network. We take the eight-bit byte as the normal unit of data and refer to it simply as a byte.

When the data channel is regarded as a stream of bits without internal structure the natural method of time-division multiplexing would be to interleave a bit at a time. The four channels C1 to C4 in Figure 7.2 (page 240) were interleaved in this way. But for data structured in bytes it would be possible, even natural, to preserve the bytes of the constituent channels as bytes in the multiplexed stream, i.e. to interleave bytes. The arrangement shown in Figure 7.8 will achieve this. The two channels C1 and C2 are assumed to arrive with coincident byte timing. Each input is loaded, a byte at a time, into one of the two shift registers. At the moment when both registers are full, the 16 transfer gates are operated to transfer the data in parallel to the 16-bit shift register. This is shifted out to make the combined channel CC by means

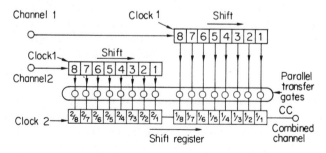

Figure 7.8.   Byte interleaving of two channels

of Clock 2, which runs at twice the rate of Clock 1. On the combined channel, a byte from channel 1 is followed by a byte from channel 2. The figure shows only 2 channels for simplicity and can be extended to make up a frame with any number of bytes.

A byte-interleaved stream will be used when the subsequent handling of the data requires bytes to be presented as a whole. If the bytes come from many different terminals, for example, they may need to be stored in different parts of a main store, for switching purposes. It is more efficient to use such a store with the byte as the unit of storage, rather than the bit. Switches of this kind, using storage, will be met in Chapter 9.

The mechanism of Figure 7.8 can be used to change the data on a channel from bit interleaved to byte interleaved, by adding a switch at the input which directs the bits to their correct shift registers. This process is shown in Figure 7.9 for the case of four channels, where, for simplicity, the parallel byte transfers have been drawn in a schematic way. The single 1 circulating in shift register S moves on for each bit received from the input. The crosses in the input registers show the data bits already loaded when the top register has just increased from three bits to four. When all the shift registers are loaded the parallel transfer of 32 bits takes place. The output shift register is unloaded at the same speed as the input stream. The net effect of the transformation is that each set of 32 received bits is sent out, in a different sequence, during the frame following the one when they were received.

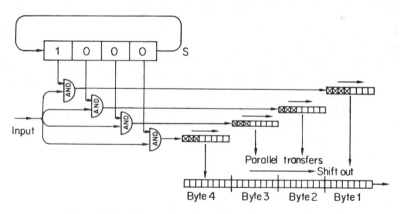

Figure 7.9.   Conversion from bit to byte interleaving

Digital Multiplexing in Local Data Networks

A public data communication network, or any network operating on a large scale, will be organized as a hierarchy, like the telephone network. At the lowest level of this hierarchy is the local network which has traditionally been arranged as a 'star' of multicore cables spreading out from the local switching centre. The local network makes up the largest component of capital cost of the whole system and it seems that for public data networks the dominance of the cost of the local area is even greater than it is in the telephone network. On the other hand it is much more difficult to achieve economies in the local network and it tends to have under-used equipment because traffic is sporadic in nature.

Multiplexing may be used in the local network because quite simple digital transmission systems can carry digit rates of the order of megabits per second. The data rates of terminal users are typically in the range of 100 bit/s to 10,000 bit/s. The degree of complexity that is possible in the multiplexing scheme depends on how many subscribers are grouped together and therefore available for multiplexing. In the years 1975 to 1980 this number is likely to be relatively small, except in city centres, but the wider use of teleprocessing systems will in due course lead to multiplexing in more than one stage.

In addition to the saving of local line cost, multiplexing in the local network can prepare the channels for a time division switch. A multiplexed primary group of 24 or 30 PCM voice channels can be handled directly by a TDM switch without the need for demultiplexing and thus save most of the cost of multiplexing. Although data may well be handled differently from PCM speech the same economies can be obtained if the multiplexing, at least up to a certain level, prepares for the switching process.

Local Area Signalling

In the telephone network 'signalling' is the term used for the exchange of digital information between switching centres. These 'control signals' seize and release trunks and carry the routing information forward through successive switches. On the other hand, signalling is not always recognized in the local area, where it consists of all the information passing between telephone instrument and the switching centre other than the customers voice. The principal telephone local area signals are off/on hook, dialling (by impulses or tones), and ringing current. For a data network there are similar requirements for digital information other than subscriber's data to pass between the data terminal and the switching centre to which it is connected.

The exact arrangement depends on the kind of terminal. On the one hand there are simple terminals like the teletypewriter which can use only the codes corresponding to printed characters and a few other operations. These terminals cannot be expected to engage in special protocols or procedures. They require the network to handle the call in a way the terminal user can understand, and for these terminals all the control signals must have a simple effect at the terminal, such as lighting a signal lamp. On the other hand there are 'intelligent terminals' and computers which can be made to treat the control signal as a separate data channel over which call set-up and clear-down procedures take place according to a well-defined protocol.

The simple terminals do not have to generate or receive control signals directly, because their interface is not directly with the transmission path. The equipment which terminates the network is called the *network terminating unit* or NTU, and this unit, which belongs to the network authority, handles the control signals. It also provides the lamps and buttons which are all that the subscriber need understand. The design of this unit and its protocol are described later in more detail.

Table 7.1 gives a list of the signals which might pass between a simple

---

A. Signals from terminal to switching centre

1.	Hello	Initiates a call, corresponds to 'off-hook'.
2.	End of block	Signifies the end of a block of data.
3.	Interrupt	When the terminal is receiving data, this stops the flow and allows the terminal to send (half duplex operation).
4.	Goodbye	Closes down a call, corresponds to 'on-hook'.
5.	State	24 control signals expressed in 5 bits of the control signal to signify one of the 6 states of the system and the operable/inoperable state of the terminals as source and acceptor of data. A response to 'enquire'.
6.	Ready for byte	When the NTU is in the 'receive' state this signal is sent to the data switch whenever the terminal is ready to receive an envelope.
7.	Nack	An error indication sent if a received control signal is invalid or data is received at the wrong time.

B. Signals from switching centre to terminal

1.	Idle	Sets the NTU in the idle state, as for example when a call is closed down.
2.	Proceed to select	Sets the NTU in the state in which dialling or selection data is sent to the switch.
3.	Reject	Indicates that the attempted call has not been completed.
4.	Call	Signifies that a call is in progress, but without allowing the sending or receiving of data.
5.	Send	Sets the NTU in a state to allow data to be sent from the terminal.
6.	Receive	Sets the NTU in a state to request (by signal A6) data from the switch.
7.	Enquire	Stimulates the NTU to report its state (by one of the signals A5) to the switch and also the state of the peripheral.

Table 7.1. Control signals for a simple terminal

terminal and its nearest switching exchange. These have been shown as 'messages' which are sent momentarily, rather than as persistent conditions. An example of a persistent condition is the telephone off/on hook which is signalled by the presence of a DC path across the line. We have shown a similar condition in the table by the pairs of signals A1 and A4. These signals are the ones used in an experimental network at the U.K. National Physical Laboratory, and their use is described later in the chapter.

The 'dialling' which tells the switching centre the destination of a call is not shown as a signalling function because it is proposed to handle this via the normal data path. The correct word to use here is *selection* because the dial is a telephone device only. The signal 'proceed to select' sets up the terminal for the selection phase. Keyboard terminals use their keyboard for selection data.

Control Signalling by 'Qualifier Bit'

Local control signals require a small capacity channel of their own, between the terminal and the switching centre, and one that does not interfere with the transparency of the customers' data channel. The full extent of the 'vocabulary' of local control signals is not known, and may always be subject to local variations to meet special needs, so it would be prudent to have a generous provision of alternative control signals.

One way in which this can be achieved, at the cost of an extra bit for each byte of customers' data, is shown in Figure 7.10. Each byte of data is fitted into a nine-bit *envelope*. The extra bit is the *qualifier bit* and when it has the value 1, the eight-bit byte which it accompanies is treated as customers' data. The network is 'transparent' to this data and passes it through from one subscriber to another except for the selection phase. If the qualifier bit has the value 0, the eight bits carry the control signals such as those given in Table 7.1.

When we considered the communication requirements of computer peripherals we met the same need for an additional channel for information other than the data itself, and in this case, the outgoing information (to the

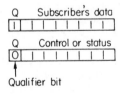

Figure 7.10. Control signalling in the local network with envelope of 9 bits

peripheral) was called 'control' and the ingoing was called 'status'. This, of course, is quite distinct from the control signalling considered here, which concerns the communication network alone. Nevertheless, there is a possibility that a small part of the network's control signalling capacity could be offered to the subscriber to help him format his data. Such a proposal would have implications for the network as a whole, because it would carry these particular signals from subscriber to subscriber.

The eight-bit field for control signalling is generous, but with good reason. Whatever size of envelope was used, it would only be possible to dedicate an unrestricted set of binary digits to the customers' data, in the interests of transparency. One bit must be added to this field to allow for signalling. The larger the field, the smaller is the loss of channel capacity due to the extra bit. But on the other hand, when the resultant 'envelopes' are multiplexed they must eventually be presented at the switch 'envelope interleaved' and a large envelope adds to the cost of the shift registers used for interleaving. Since the eight-bit byte is an accepted unit for computers and terminals, the nine-bit envelope is a good choice for local data systems. It raises the problem of incompatability with the eight-bit unit of PCM systems, but these do not yet extend to the local area. We have to consider the future integration of data and digital speech in the local area. Digital speech, when it enters into multiplexing schemes with time-division local exchanges, will not be able to sustain paths for ringing currents and DC or tone signalling. It therefore seems likely that the $8+1$ envelope proposed for data will be just as suitable for speech.

Table 7.1 listed some of the signals that will be carried over this local signalling channel. Allowing for many new functions that will be added, it is unlikely that all the combinations allowed by the 8-bit field will be needed. The spare capacity can be used in two ways. A simple error detecting and error correcting code could be used, for example a Hamming code, to provide a robust and error-free signalling channel. But since the signals are not sent very often, repetition of signals could be used to provide immunity to errors rather more simply.

An additional possibility is to use part of the capacity of the signalling

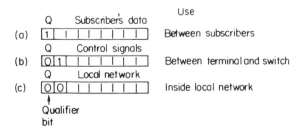

Figure 7.11. Division of signalling channel between two uses

channel for other purposes in the local network and some of these other uses are described later in connection with particular network designs. They are connected with byte stuffing and the acknowledgment of bytes over a local link. If the use of the signalling channel is to be divided up logically, a single bit can be used as an indicator, in the way shown in Figure 7.11. The format of subscribers' data in Figure 7.11(a) is unchanged, but when the qualifier bit is 0, the second bit determines the use of the remaining six-bit field. The pair 0, 1 is used as in Figure 7.11(b) for control signals between the terminal and the switch, while the pair 0, 0 in Figure 7.11(c) indicates that the signal relates to one of the other functions in the local network itself.

A Synchronous Network

In order to illustrate the way that multiplexing principles can be employed, a particular design of local network will be described. The design was the result of studies by the U.K. Post Office.[5]

It employs an envelope containing an eight-bit byte and a qualifier bit which designates the contents of the byte as customers data or a control signal. In addition, the envelope has a single bit used for framing, making the envelope size up to ten bits. The local network has two levels of multiplexing, as shown in Figure 7.12. Its operation is synchronous, with the clock supplied by the data switch, on which the local network is dependent.

Subscribers connect to the network at network terminating units, which allow four different (maximum) digit rates; 600, 2400, 9600 and 48000 bit/s. In each case rates lower than this maximum value are possible. To accommodate a lower rate, the NTU inserts 'dummy' bytes wherever the terminal has no data to send. This procedure can be called *byte stuffing*. If the terminal wishes to use the full speed of the system it can accept a clock from the network, together with the byte framing. When the stream of bytes arrives at

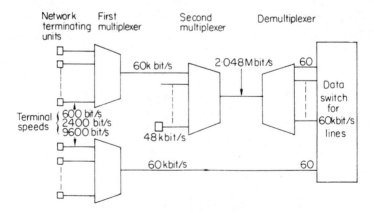

Figure 7.12. Schematic of a local network

the destination terminal the dummy bytes can be discarded and the clock to the terminal stopped for the duration of the missing data. This has been called a *stuttering clock* and the method of presenting data is referred to as *burst isochronous* because, when the clock output is present (for an integral number of bytes) the data is isochronous, but the clock appears in bursts.

The method of handling stuffed bytes is quite different from the method we described earlier for bit stuffing, and much simpler. The dummy byte is actually a control signal, and this can be handled through the switch exactly like a data byte. Thus the synchronism of the network is preserved, though it can provide a data channel of any speed. Both parties to a call must use the same speed option and they must be prepared to receive data at the actual rate that it is sent. So they may need to agree on a peak data rate as well as a network speed option.

Most sources or acceptors of data will in due course be adapted to use the network clock and take account of the stuffing mechanism at the sender's end and the stuttering clock at the receiver. For those needing a steady clock at a rate not offered by the network, buffers could be provided in the network terminating units. The restoration of the user's clock at the destination could in principle be handled by an elastic buffer and a clock source controlled by the buffer's occupancy, in the way that is used in bit stuffing. But this complication is unlikely to be needed. Most users who cannot accept eight-bit bursts of data will probably chose to run at a full network rate and avoid the complication of restoring the non-standard clock.

Because there is a ten-bit envelope to carry eight data bits, the digit rates offered at the network's terminals are carried on its tranmission paths by rates which are increased by a factor 10/8, that is, at 750, 3000, 12000 and 60000 bit/s.

The first multiplexer handles a combination of the three lower speeds and multiplexes then by time division onto a 60 kbit/s channel. It uses bit interleaving, for simplicity. To make the allocation of time slots easier, the multiplexer is divided into five sections and any section can be adapted to one of the speeds. A section includes one channel of 9600 bit/s, four of 2400 bit/s or 16 of 600 bit/s.

The second multiplexer shown in Figure 7.13 is the heart of the local network. At this point the bit-interleaved streams from the terminals are rearranged into byte-interleaved streams for the switch. We return in Chapter 9 to the subject of switching time-division multiplexed data, and it is shown that there are economic methods, using storage, that can be applied with byte interleaving. It is for this reason that the multiplexing scheme converts to byte interleaving at the second multiplexer.

The incoming 60 kbit/s streams contain mixed speed groups, but each 12 kbit/s section is homogeneous. By demultiplexing, cross-patching and remultiplexing, speed homogeneous groups of subscriber's channels, bit interleaved at 60 kbit/s are produced. Three of these are shown in the figure,

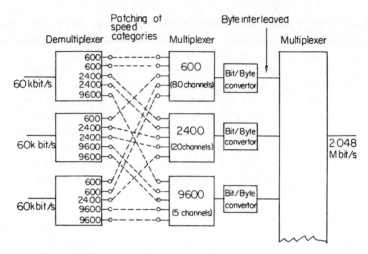

Figure 7.13.   Internal structure of the second multiplexer

one for each speed. In practice the mix will be determined by the population of terminals. Each of these homogeneous groups is converted to byte interleaving. Finally, the 60 kbit/s streams are multiplexed for carriage on the 2·048 Mbit/s link to the switch.

Referring to Figure 7.12, it can be seen that the last stage of multiplexing acts simply as a carrier for 60 kbit/s channels, and that these are the basic units on which the switch operates. The multiplexer-demultiplexer pair can therefore use any scheme that is convenient, for example bit interleaving. The emerging 60 kbit/s channels are, of course, byte interleaved and made up from speed-homogeneous groups of subscribers.

Figure 7.13 shows the functions of the second multiplexer schematically and the unit could indeed be built in roughly the form that is shown. The function of the equipment shown in the figure is simply to rearrange bits in time-slots, and there are other ways in which this could be done, allowing for the fact that the cross-patching must be adaptable as the population of terminals changes. The use of an addressable store (such as a core store) to switch data is the subject of Chapter 9 and the methods used could be adapted to this multiplexer.

In Figure 7.12 a first multiplexer is shown sending a 60 kbit/s stream directly to the data switch. Where terminals are connected to multiplexers in the immediate neighbourhood of the switch, there will not be enough of them to justify a second multiplexer. For these terminals the bit-byte conversion is carried out at the data switch, which must incorporate part of the second multiplexer's functions to serve all the 'odd' data channels it collects locally.

The switching methods that are applied to byte-interleaved streams are dealt with in Chapter 9. At the input to the switch, control signals are separated from subscribers' data bytes. But the dummy bytes (which take the external form of control signals) must be sent through the switch to the destination. Therefore the switch must, in effect, be able to pass nine bits of the envelope through to the output.

7.4   MULTIPLEXING WITH ADDRESSED BLOCKS

The digital multiplexing methods described so far employ a fixed cycle of operation. The multiplexing frame is repeated regularly, and each bit in the frame has its particular function. For each of the channels which make up the multiplexing structure the various bits that arrive fall into predetermined positions in the frame.

It is possible to multiplex digital data without assigning any fixed places in the frame to the constituent channels.[6] The use of the multiplexed channel is then assigned dynamically to the various channels. In order to identify the data on the multiplexed channel it must have added to it an address, and since it would be wasteful to add an address to just one or two bits, in practice 'dynamic multiplexing' is carried out with blocks at at least one byte in length.

Figure 7.14 illustrates the principle. The blocks of data are all of the same length, and the multiplexed channel carries a regular pattern of address-block. Each incoming channel is provided with a buffer able to take at least one block. The control device searches for a full buffer, then sends out its address over the line, followed by the block itself. In the example given there are four channels and therefore a 2-bit address. The use made of the multiplexed channel depends on the demands of the constituent channels. In the example shown in the figure, it appears from the picture of the data stream that channel 3 is most heavily used. Multiplexing of this kind can be used to transmit a number of channels over one transmission path. The

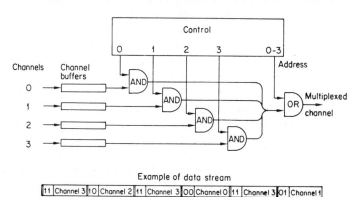

Figure 7.14.   Dynamic multiplexing with fixed blocks

demultiplexer at the receiving end has a similar form with the data flows reversed. The control unit examines the address and opens one of several gates to direct the data to a channel buffer. From this buffer the data is transmitted over its channel at the appropriate rate.

Dynamic multiplexing can handle an arbitrary mix of channel capacities and is not restricted to certain specific digit rates in the way that is typical of fixed-cycle multiplexing. More important still, the portion of its capacity given up to each channel can vary. If the channels are used sporadically, the capacity of the multiplexed channel need only be sufficient for the actual peak demand.

Suppose now that a multiplexed channel is serving a number of data terminals. At any one time, only a small number of these will be making calls, and those making calls may only be sporadically active. If fixed-cycle multiplexing is used, the only way to reduce the channel capacity is to provide a switch. Such a switch is called a concentrator, and it can be remotely controlled from the nearest data switching centre. Then each channel on the multiplexer is allocated to a particular terminal for the duration of a call. They are, in effect, 'addressed' but over the time scale of a call, a longer period than in the case of dynamic multiplexing.

Concentration by means of a circuit switch takes no notice of the activity, or lack of activity, in a line that is currently making a call. Dynamic multiplexing takes account of variations in activity over the time-scale of a single block.

Dynamic multiplexing carries with it the possibility that the available line capacity will be exceeded, and blocks will then have to be discarded when they try to enter buffers that are still full. This is an example of *congestion*. A circuit concentrator that responds to *calls* instead of data blocks also has the possibility of congestion. Indeed the only way to avoid congestion entirely is to provide for all channels as though they could be handling data at one and the same time. This is the fixed-cycle multiplexer with no concentration.

For large groups of terminals, concentration is possible with a very low probability of congestion. Similarly, the averaging of data traffic by dynamic multiplexing can be made to have a very low congestion probability.

There are several details of the system of Figure 7.14 which need further study. In the multiplexed data stream there is a succession of addressed blocks but the sporadic nature of the traffic might find none of the buffers full at the moment that a block was due to be sent. This could be handled by means of an empty block, for example by dedicating one of the address values to the empty state. But it would be inefficient to wait a full block interval if, in the meantime, a buffer became full. To allow variable gaps between transmitted blocks it is necessary to begin each one with a starting sequence that can be distinguished from the inter-block gap. In the simplest form the gap consists of zeros and the first bit of a block is always 1. This structure is shown in Figure 7.15. The 1 which starts a block is the *start bit*, and is like the start bit of a start/stop code, except that here we have an isochronous channel. There is no need for a stop bit because the blocks have a fixed length. In the extreme case, blocks can be juxtaposed, as the second and third ones are in the figure, with only the start bit between them. If the 'framing' is lost there is a danger, when the blocks are closely packed, that it will be some time before it is restored again, and there may then be a need for a longer start pattern, one which is not too frequently picked up accidentally in the middle of a block.

The buffers in Figure 7.14 hold only one block, and if the data on the incoming channels are arriving at a steady pace without interblock gaps, there is a good chance that they will not be taken away by the multiplexer before the next block starts to arrive, at least when the load on the channel is not light. Double buffers deal with this problem.

In the following sections two embodiments of addressed block multiplexing are described.

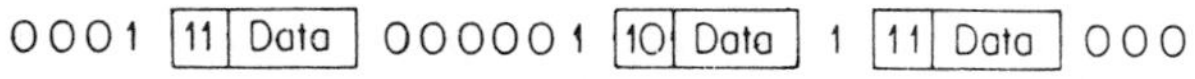

0 0 0 1 |11| Data | 0 0 0 0 0 1 |10| Data | 1 |11| Data | 0 0 0

Figure 7.15.   Interblock gaps and start bits

A Local Network Employing Addressed Bytes

A local data communication network[7] was put into operation at the National Physical Laboratory of the U.K. in the summer of 1971. It is used to interconnect a variety of terminals, computers and information services over the site of the laboratory. The switching centre of the network employs packet switching, (which is the subject of later chapters) but our present interest in the network lies in its multiplexing method. A prime requirement was to interconnect subscribers employing any digit rate within the network's total capacity. Because it connected experimental equipment that was constantly being changed, all outlets of the network needed, potentially, a high channel capacity although few would use it at any one time. It was clearly a case for addressed block or 'dynamic' multiplexing.

The data block chosen was the byte because data input and output at the periphery of the network was handled by the British Standard Interface, which controls the flow in units of a byte (see page 531).

The unit which the network handles is therefore the addressed byte, which is contained in an envelope with one of the four formats shown in Figure 7.16. At different levels of the multiplexing structure the address has 0, 3, 6 or 9 bits. In the formats there are additional bits concerned with the transmission of the envelope. These are S, the start bit which allows the envelope to begin at any time; Q the qualifier bit which allows it to carry control characters; Ab the alternation bit which is used in the procedure for error correction over the transmission link and P, the parity bit.

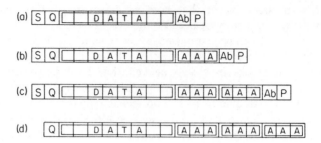

Figure 7.16.   Envelope structures used in the NPL local network

Part (a) of the figure shows the byte as it leaves the terminal, in the form which it takes in transmission to the first level multiplexer. The eight-way dynamic multiplexer adds three bits of address information to indicate the line on which it was received and in transmission to the next level of multiplexer the format shown at (b) is used. The bits Ab and P do not pass through the multiplexer, but take on new values appropriate to each link. The next two multiplexers each add three bits of address so that the envelope leaving the top level multiplexer has a 9-bit address. This envelope is not transmitted over a link because the top level multiplexer is adjacent to the switch, and for this reason the bits S, Ab and P are not shown in Figure 7.16(d).

The three levels of multiplexing give the switch access to 512 lines if all the outlets are used, and incoming bytes are presented to the switch with a full address identifying the line of origin. Outgoing bytes start with a nine-bit destination address, and as each three-bit section of address is used to direct the envelope to the correct multiplexer output, the section is stripped off, reducing the format as shown in the figure until the bare byte arrives, with its qualifier bit Q, at the terminal.

Figure 7.17 shows the arrangement of multiplexers and the modular construction of the network, all of which operates as a multiplexing scheme to deliver addressed bytes to the switch. Each module in the system is a two-way or full-duplex device, so the multiplexers act also as demultiplexers for the outgoing data. The multiplexers are placed at convenient points anywhere on the laboratory site and connected by a pair of 'line terminals' joined by two coaxial cables, one for each direction of transmission. The transmission rate on all lines is 1 Mbit/s, approximately. Buffers in each line terminal enable them to offer a 'handshake' type of interface at each end, similar to British Standard 4421. They therefore only accept data if they have space in the buffer.

The various constructional units of Figure 7.17 can be assembled in many ways connected by the 'network interface'[8] which transfers the addressed bytes. Where two constructional units are close together they can be joined directly, but for longer distances the line terminals and connecting cables can be inserted. In the example shown in the figure, M1 is connected

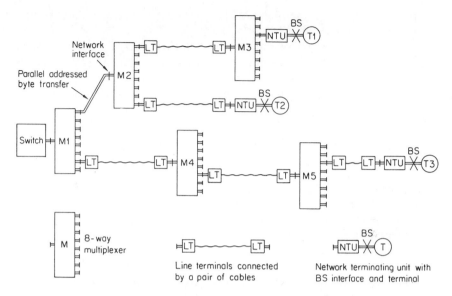

Figure 7.17. Schematic of the NPL network, showing a possible configuration and the constructional units

directly to M2 but M2 is distant from M3, so a transmission system is interposed. Terminals are connected to the network by the British Standard 4421 interface which is byte-parallel. The network terminating unit handles the control signalling functions mentioned earlier. It can either be connected directly to a multiplexer or through a transmission system. The subscribers of the network comprise a wide variety of computers and all kinds of peripherals from line printers to simple keyboards. Those attached computers which offer a service to many users via the network may be connected to the second rank of multiplexers, in the way that T2 is connected via M2 in the figure, but most subscribers come in at the lowest level. The purpose of higher-level connection is to increase priority in the use of network capacity.

Flow Control

Because each path or multiplexer in the network handles data at a variable rate there is a possibility of congestion, of a kind which would not prevent a call being set up but could slow down or stop the flow of data. In any network with variable flow rates it is necessary to have some method of *flow control*. This is like the need for control of road and air traffic, but whereas roads and the air space provides a very large buffer to hold frustrated traffic, in a data network the buffer storage is a matter for separate and economical provisioning. This gives flow control in data network great importance, and we shall return to the subject in later chapters.

Handshaking over the interfaces is a very local control of flow control which contributes to the overall system.

Consider first the flow of data envelopes in Figure 7.17 from the terminals to the centre. Each transmission system is able to stop the input of a further envelope if its output is blocked. Each input of the multiplexer is informed, by the network interface whether an envelope is ready for collection. The multiplexer finds the next envelope for transmission inwards by a rapid scan over these interfacers. Having found it, the multiplexer transfers the byte inwards to a buffer where it is ready for transfer by the network interface to the next level inwards. Terminals operating at various speeds present data envelopes to the network and if the rate exceeds the capacity at any point, the buffers will fill on incoming paths. The network interface with its handshaking, ensures that no data is lost. As space becomes available, envelopes move inwards in an orderly fashion.

Next consider the flow outward from the switch to the terminals. If any congestion occurs due to one terminal not being able to receive data fast enough it will fill up buffers towards the centre until a multiplexer is blocked. At this stage data would be prevented from arriving at other terminals. The switch does not have the means of knowing the precise rate at which a terminal can accept data and some terminals have a variable rate depending on the content of the data itself, as for example an incremental plotter which may draw short or long vectors from similar data patterns. Furthermore, a terminal can cease to accept data for several reasons. Therefore the output flow needs an extra scheme of control.

The method used is to send a request from the network terminating unit for each byte of data that can be accepted. The terminal signals its readiness over the British Standard Interface, and this causes the network terminating unit to send a control signal 'ready for next byte'. The address of the envelope in which this signal arrives tells the switch from where in the store to extract the requested byte. In this way, only one byte of data can be in transit from the switch for each destination, and congestion at the multiplexers is avoided. The cost of the scheme is the extra traffic in 'ready' signals and the time of transit, which reduces the data rate available to distant terminals.

The handshaking of output bytes across the whole network is additional to the acknowledgment procedure that takes place over each link. When the links are long, their overall data rate can be kept high by allowing more than one byte to be in flight on a link, but the outgoing data rate for any terminal connection is still limited by the need to request each byte from the periphery.

In the NPL network there is no priority scheme at the multiplexer. The eight input channels are examined for incoming data on a 'round-robin' basis, whether or not they are heavily loaded. It is interesting to see the effect of this simple rule when there is congestion at the switch. In the extreme case, buffers dealing with input are almost always full and the multiplexer simply takes an envelope from each in turn, never having to miss a channel for the lack of data. It is then operating like a fixed-cycle multiplexer and the available capacity is allocated equally among the terminals at a given level. Since ingoing data envelopes contend for channel capacity with 'ready' signals, the output rate of a terminal must be added to its input rate for congestion purposes. Such heavy congestion is, of course, a misuse of this type of network, but it shows us that the effect of congestion is to cut down the rates of the fastest channels.

The digit rates of various terminals vary between, say, 50 bit/s and 50,000 bit/s. By sacrificing some of the rate of the high speed terminals the performance of all the slow ones can be preserved, so the effect of 'round robin' multiplexing is generally beneficial. But computers which serve a large number of terminals have been connected, like T2 in Figure 7.17, to an intermediate level multiplexer so that they do not react too soon to congestion. The sporadic nature of the data traffic makes a theoretical analysis or simulation of this type of network very difficult. An experimental approach is possible. In practice, conflict between real traffic has not been observed, even where very fast terminals such as storage tube displays share a multiplexer with slow terminals. An unlimited demand for traffic capacity can be simulated at the British Standard Interface, and calls can be set up between such unlimited terminals. Such 'fast' calls are found to share the unused capacity of the network equally between them, but the performance of the network for slow terminals is not impaired. The simple 'round-robin' rule at the multiplexer has therefore proved very satisfactory in practice.

Local Control Signals in the NPL Network

Having described the method of flow control it is possible to return in more detail to the question of local control signalling mentioned earlier. The NPL network offers a worked-out example of local control signals and their use in setting up and closing down a call.

Figure 7.18 shows schematically the operation of the network terminating unit employed for simple terminals. The subscriber's side of the NTU consists of the two British Standard Interfaces (used to connect the terminal) and the small control panel with its four lamps and four buttons. The network user who has a simple terminal, must learn the use of this control panel. For computers and intelligent terminals, different arrangements are made, allowing the terminal itself to undertake the protocol, at the level of the control signals if necessary.

The network terminating unit has seven states, numbered 0 to 6 in the diagram. The first of these is shown by no lamps being lit, and signifies that the network is out of action. This state is not set up by a control signal, but by the 'inoperable' line in the network standard interface. When the network is operational but the terminal is not using it, the 'idle' state is indicated by just the left hand lamp, and it is the button which is illuminated (labelled

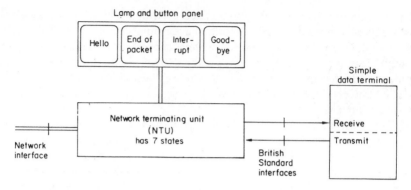

(a) Equipment for a simple data terminal under manual control

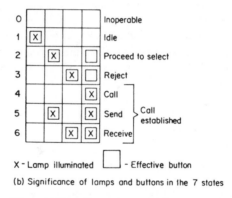

(b) Significance of lamps and buttons in the 7 states

Figure 7.18. Operation of the network
terminating unit of the NPL network

Hello) which initiates a call. The 'proceed to select' phase is shown by the lighting of the next lamp, coloured green, which generally invites the subscriber to *send* data, in this case selection data. If the call is selected correctly and the called subscriber is not busy and is reported as operable, the *call* light will go on (state 4), and very soon afterwards the green *send* light to show that data may be sent.

A call that is rejected, whether because of errors in selection data or a busy or inoperable called terminal, is shown by the red *receive* lamp without the call lamp (state 3). The receive state is appropriate because the network may need to send a qualifying message to terminals suitably equipped to display it.

When a call is received, the call state (state 4) is entered at once, then when data are ready for reception the red *receive* lamp goes on.

The control signals used for interaction between the NTU and the switch are those listed in Table 7.1. From the terminal to the switching centre there are seven types of signal of which the first four simply report that one of the four buttons has been pressed. Buttons 1 and 4 initiate and close down a call. Button 2 lets the switch know that a data block is complete and ready for forwarding; it is a consequence of the store and forward method of operation by the switch. Actually the end of a block is usually signalled by a designated key on the keyboard of a terminal, and the button is provided for exceptional use. Button 3 is operative only in the state where data can be received. It enables the user to halt a stream of data coming from the switch, to break in for sending a message. Typically this could hold up output from a computer (the other subscriber) so that a 'stop' or similar message could be given on the keyboard.

The signals from the switch to the NTU allow it to set up any one of the states 1 to 6. The seventh signal is 'enquire' which tells the NTU to report its state to the switch. This is done by the 'state' signals (A5) which have 3 bits corresponding to the lamps which indicate the states 1 to 6 and 2 bits to report the state of the subscriber's terminal, as shown by the 'operable' lines of the British Standard Interfaces.

Note, therefore, that user-network interaction takes place via the switch. For example, the completion of the selection data is signalled by 'end of block' from the keyboard or button 2. The NTU immediately enters the *idle* state, but after a fraction of a second in response to signals it goes to *call* or *reject*, and then from *call* to *send* when the switch is ready for data. In the *send* state, when 'end of block' is signalled the NTU goes into the *call* state, but usually a new buffer is ready immediately and the state returns to *send* as a result of a signal received.

Dynamic Multiplexing in Loops

The advantage of dynamic multiplexing is its instantaneous response to changes in the load of the individual channels. The NPL network formed an example of a *tree* connected structure employing this method. An alternative

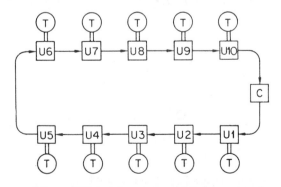

Figure 7.19.   A loop-connected data network

structure that has been used is the loop[9,10] shown in Figure 7.19. The units U1 to U10 are connected by one (simplex) transmission path which forms a loop and includes a special unit C. In general, data on the loop travel round from one unit to the next. The time available on this data path is divided into addressed blocks, with end-of-block markers and two special bits in each block. One of these bits determines whether the block is empty or full, the other serves to discard data that cannot be delivered. At each of the units, the blocks arriving are examined to see if their address corresponds to the terminal served by that unit. If one does, the block is marked as 'empty' and the data are extracted into a buffer for the terminal. When the terminal has data to send this is held in a buffer. The unit searches for an empty block and inserts the data there, with the destination address.

A block may pass once through the special unit C. At this point the 'discarding' bit is set (having been cleared when the data were loaded onto the loop). If a block arrives at C with this discarding bit set, it has failed to find its destination and is discarded, leaving an empty block.

A further function of the unit C is to maintain the block format. Each unit in the loop must contain some delay, at least the delay necessary to hold the address. Unit C provides the extra delay that will be needed to make up an integral number of blocks.

The simple structure of the loop lends itself to theoretical treatment and simulation, in order to find out its behaviour with different traffic levels. It is sometimes called a *Pierce Loop* after one of the investigators who have written about it. Topologically it has some attractions because it tends to use less transmission path length than star-connected multiplexing schemes. It is a weakness of the scheme in its simple form that a break anywhere in the loop, due to a faulty unit or transmission path, disconnects all the terminals in the loop. To avoid this, the paths can be made bi-directional and a break healed by folding the loop back on itself. In Figure 7.20 the break between U5 and U6 is healed by rearranging the loop, turning the transmission blocks back at U5 and U6 so that they visit each unit twice in the cycle.

In order to extend flow control through the loop, each block delivered must

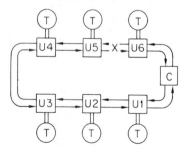

Figure 7.20   Redundant loop
system with a fault

be acknowledged to the source when the output buffer is empty. This avoids the possibility of a unit not being able to accept a block because its buffer is full. An acknowledgment scheme of this kind will be essential where loops are connected together in an extensive network.

Two loops can be connected together by a special 'transfer unit', common to both of them. This unit extracts blocks from one loop into a buffer and places them in the next empty block on the other loop. The buffer must be big enough to avoid losing blocks or, better still, a scheme of network flow control must be devised. There is a close analogy between a tree structure and a hierarchy of loops. Multiplexers correspond to loops and links between multiplexers correspond to 'transfer units'. This is shown in Figure 7.21.

In the tree system, the multiplexer's choice of the next block is made by a rapid search, but in the loop system empty blocks are presented in turn to particular terminals or transfer units. In consequence, a terminal may gain an advantage from its position in the loop. For example, in Figure 7.19, if the terminal on U2 receives a lot of data it will leave many empty blocks on the loop. The terminal on U3 has the best chance of using these spaces for its input to the loop, but the terminal on U1 derives little benefit. But if every block transferred is acknowledged round the loop, a terminal relinquishes as many blocks as it takes up, and there is no advantage or disadvantage due to position on the loop.

The analogy between the tree and loop structures allows the flow control and handshaking arrangements, that have been studied in relation to trees, to be extended to loops. The analogy is not restricted to trees, because loops can be connected together to form an analogue of any layout consisting of nodes connected by links. In this way, the routing and flow control methods described later for 'nodal' networks can be applied to interconnected loops.

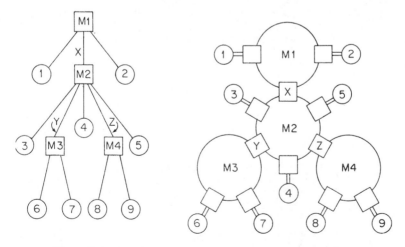

Figure 7.21.   The analogy between loop and tree structures

Fixed-Cycle and Dynamic Multiplexing Compared

Fixed-cycle multiplexing provides channels with definite digit rates, suitable for carrying isochronous streams of bits. Dynamic multiplexing deals with channels of variable data rate, and requires flow control if there is a possibility of congestion.

In dynamic multiplexing a block structure is imposed on the data. At the lowest practical level the block is one byte, and in the examples of this present chapter the blocks used in any one system have been of constant length, though this is not essential.

Multiplexing by addressed bytes becomes inefficient if the address is much bigger than the data block. It can therefore be used only among a group of a few hundred or so terminals and is suitable only for a small local network or a small part of a local network. By using bigger blocks, it is economic to multiplex bigger groups of terminals, but if acknowledgment or handshaking is needed, the use of blocks of constant size is inefficient for the acknowledgment signals. In the following chapters the use of blocks of variable length is introduced, and this takes us beyond what is normally described as time division multiplexing.

References

1. Fultz, K. E., and Penick, D. B., 'The TI carrier system', *Bell Syst. Tech. J.*, **44**, No. 7, 1405 (Sept. 1965).
2. Bruce, R. A., 'A 1.5 to 6 megabit digital multiplex employing pulse stuffing', *IEEE Int. Conf. on Communication*, 34/1 (1969).
3. Witt, F. J., 'An experimental 224 Mb/s digital multiplexer-demultiplexer using pulse stuffing synchronization', *Bell Syst. Tech. J.*, **44**, No. 9, 1843 (November 1965).
4. Thomson, D., 'Synchronisation of an integrated digital transmission and switching network', *P.O. Elect. Engr's. J.*, **64**, No. 3, 190 (1971).
5. Williams, M. B., 'Developments in data communications', *P.O. Elect. Engr's. J.*, **64**, No. 2, 70 (July 1971).
6. Hasegawa, T., Tezuka, Y., and Kasahara, Y., 'Digital data dynamic transmission systems', *IEEE Trans. Communication Tech.* **12**, No. 3, 58 (Sept. 1964).
7. Scantlebury, R. A., 'A model for the local area of a data communication network—objectives and hardware organization', *Proc. A.C.M. Symposium*, Pine Mountain, Ga. (October 1969).
8. Barber, D. L. A., 'Experience with use of the B.S. Interface with computer networks and peripherals', *Proc. A.C.M. Symposium*, Pine Mountain, Ga. (October 1969).
9. Farmer, W. D., and Newhall, E. E., 'An experimental distributed switching system to handle bursty computer traffic', *Proc. A.C.M. Symposium*, Pine Mountain, Ga. (October 1969).
10. Pierce, J. R., 'Network for block switching of data', *Bell Syst. Tech. J.*, **51**, No. 6, 1133 (July 1972).

Chapter 8

Message Switching Systems

8.1. INTRODUCTION

The topics discussed so far have mainly concerned communications systems that provide a real, or apparent, direct connection between one subscriber and another. This kind of connection is important because it permits the immediate interchange of information between subscribers, allowing them to interact together until they are satisfied that the information exchanged is as each intends it to be. In this way, errors introduced by the network, and by the subscribers themselves, can be corrected as soon as they occur. The public switched telephone network is the outstanding example of such a network; it operates, of course, by setting up between subscribers a connection in the form of a sequence of point-to-point circuits, joined together by switches at the junctions between them. The disadvantage of needing a connection between subscribers before they can communicate is that all the communication links and switches necessary to make the connection must be available for the duration of their conversation, and both subscribers must be free to interact at the same time.

An entirely different communication technique is for the subscribers to exchange information by sending each other messages. The advantage of doing this is that the subscribers need not be simultaneously involved with each other, and the message transfer may take place when it is most convenient. This is particularly attractive when direct interaction is difficult, for example, when the people communicating with each other are in different continents with different local times.

The exchange of messages between people requires an intermediary prepared to accept the responsibility for faithfully conveying the information with which it is entrusted. This intermediary must store the messages until the recipient is ready to accept them and, in the case of a mechanized message handling system, it is usual for a copy of each message to be held so that a failure of the communication circuits can be overcome by retransmission of any corrupted portions of a message. If a number of separate connections have to be set up in sequence between subscribers, it becomes feasible to associate message storage facilities with the junction between connections, so that messages are transferred from store to store. Because a direct connection from subscriber to subscriber is not required, it is possible to wait until circuits become free between one store and the next, before messages are forwarded through them. For this reason, the method is known as store-and-forward message switching.

In this chapter, the techniques used in message switching are discussed with particular reference to their use in conjunction with computer systems.

8.2   TELEGRAPH MESSAGE SWITCHING

The store-and-forward method first arose in telegraphy when the speed of operators using mechanical keying became a limiting factor on costly long-distance circuits, which were intrinsically capable of much higher transmission speeds.[1] Keyboards were devised to produce a paper tape, punched to indicate the dots and dashes of the morse code, then used for encoding information. The paper tape could be transmitted at high speed by an automatic sender, and several operators working in parallel could supply enough tapes to keep a circuit operating at maximum speed, because these tapes were stored and forwarded as the circuit became free. Although this increased the efficiency of line utilization, the operators at the two ends of the line were decoupled from each other and could no longer converse together as they had done previously, due to the delay introduced by storing messages on tape and queuing tapes while waiting for transmission over the line.

An alternative method of improving line utilization is to use some form of multiplexer to time share the line between several operators. This has the advantage that each operator appears to have a line to himself, so the ability of operators to interact with each other is retained. A practical method of multiplexing, which allowed up to six operators to use a single line, was introduced by Baudot in 1874. His scheme, shown in Figure 8.1, used a mechanical scanner which sampled six keyboards in turn, accepting one symbol from each at every revolution. The keyboards comprised five keys, and a five unit code was devised with all symbols represented by constant length combinations of the five units. This departure from the earlier variable length coding, used by Morse to match the shorter codes to the frequently used symbols, was necessary to facilitate the interleaving of symbols from the various keyboards. The output from Baudot's multiplexer was a serial digital binary signal of six channels with five bits per channel; a marker introduced once per revolution of the scanner, completed the frame of this early time-division system.

A similar mechanical arrangement at the receiving end of the line was used to demultiplex or distribute the signals from each channel to particular

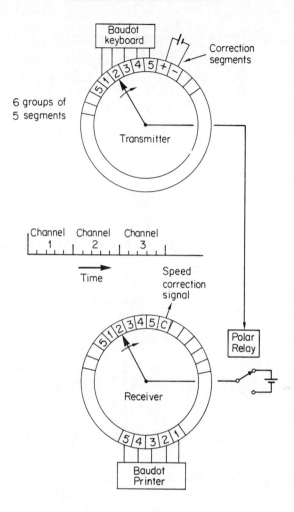

Figure 8.1. Baudot's multiplexed channel scheme

receiving devices. These were designed to decode the incoming five unit codes into individual symbols and print them onto paper.

It is interesting that, in Baudot's system, the printer made use of mechanical decoding to uniquely determine each symbol, but the encoding was done by the operators. Today, the use of five keys seems cumbersome and difficult and, in the later scheme devised by Murray, this feature was replaced by the use of tape punches with typewriter-like keyboards which prepared tape just prior to transmission. This is shown in Figure 8.2. A five unit code was also used by Murray and this became the basis of the International Alphabet No. 2 which is still used today (see Chapter 6, page 218).

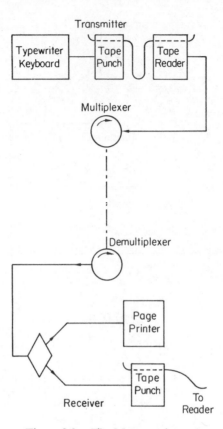

Figure 8.2.   The Murray telegraph

The use of paper tape punches at the receiving terminals of the Murray telegraph system allowed messages to be stored easily in a machine readable form, and this possibility led to the introduction of manual store-and-forward switching centres (described later) where messages could be relayed to various destinations after tearing off and sorting incoming tapes ready for transmission to the appropriate destination, rather as letters are sorted in the mail service.

The idea of circuit switching, too, was considered in some of the first telegraph systems; as early as 1850, Dumont devised an exchange with plug boards and wiper switches which in many respects foreshadowed the later step-by-step switching exchanges used for telephony.[2] But when the telephone was introduced in 1876 there was, naturally enough, an extremely rapid development of circuit switching techniques during which the earlier telegraphy schemes were soon overtaken. No doubt this was due to the simplicity of use and cheapness of the telephone instrument which could be used, and afforded, by members of the public at large; whereas the skill needed to use the early telegraph keyboard and the cost of the output printers prohibited the use of telegraphy on a wide scale. However, in the early 1930's the invention of the start-stop teleprinter, made the public switched telegraph (Telex) service possible and it has grown steadily in size ever since. The use of frequency-division multiplexing to carry several telegraph channels on a single voice channel has helped by providing economic transmission facilities, and the present growth rate for business use is now quite large.

The earlier developments in telegraph switching were, therefore, mostly concerned with store-and-forward techniques, particularly in the United States where lines were longer and more expensive than in Europe. These techniques developed independently of line switching ideas and progressed through manual, semi-automatic and fully-automatic systems to the modern message switching systems. But it seems increasingly likely that in Europe there will be a gradual integration of both telegraph message and circuit switching into the data networks of the future. For although (as will be shown later) the traffic characteristics of messages between people differ from those between computers, the volume of traffic between computers may well become increasingly large compared with that between people. It is quite likely, therefore, that all digital information that is not time dependent, will be combined, one day, and handled by the packet-switching types of network treated in Chapter 10.

Early Switching Centres

The early store-and-forward telegraph message switching centres were known as torn-tape centres because operators, literally, tore tape from punches on incoming circuits, and placed them in the appropriate transmitters after examining the destination address in the message header. Some torn-tape centres still exist, and the same principles, of course, are found in the later mechanized switching centres.

In torn-tape centres, the torn-off tapes are stored or queued in baskets while waiting to be placed in the appropriate paper tape reader. Queues may also form at the incoming tape punches during peak loading times, when several messages may arrive before an operator can get round to inspecting them and sorting them to the right tape reader. A typical torn-tape centre is shown in Figure 8.3.

The first mechanized telegraph message switching centres were, naturally enough, based on torn-tapes centres; they were organized in the same way, and paper tape was still used for storing messages. An arrangement typical of that time is shown in Figure 8.4. A set of busbars was arranged to make it possible to connect any of several incoming lines with the various outgoing lines to other switching centres. Each incoming line had a tape punch which reproduced the messages arriving at the centre. The tape from the punch was automatically fed to a tape reader which read it out into the appropriate

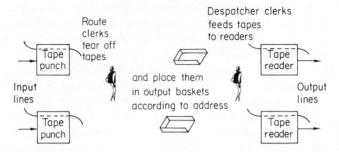

Figure 8.3.   Manual message switching

outgoing line as selected by an operator. The operator would make a note of the destination address and serial number of each input message and connect the reader output through a plug and jack arrangement to the busbars. As soon as the busbar became free it was seized by the next waiting tape reader, a message number generator was activated to transmit the next outgoing message serial number which was followed by the output from the tape reader. A group of symbols indicating the end of the message was recognized by suitable decoding circuits and arranged to stop the reader and release the busbar as soon as the message had been sent.

In these semi-automatic message switching centres the operators kept track of the serial numbers of incoming messages and could request repetitions if any were lost, they also set-up the routing connections inside the centre according to the destination address accompanying each message. A certain degree of variation was tolerable in the format of the messages while human operators were involved at the switching centres, but when the remaining

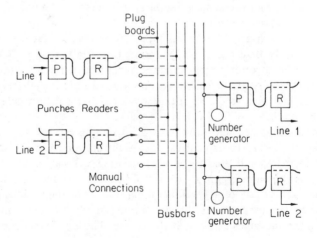

Figure 8.4.   Partially automated scheme

functions of checking serial numbers and routing were mechanized, more standardization became necessary; this process of agreeing on standards to permit the introduction of increased mechanization is, of course, still a major problem.

Modern Message Switching Systems

The advent of the digital computer and the rapid development of new storage techniques made possible radical improvements in message switching systems; it is now common for computers to be used for switching messages, and for the messages to be stored on magnetic discs or drums while waiting to be processed or to be transmitted onward to their destination. As these improved systems were made by modelling their structure on the earlier manual ones, computer programs had to be developed to perform the functions originally done by people; in big systems these programs can become extremely complex. However, the speed and flexibility of the computer-based systems allows a wide variety of services to be offered to the users of modern message switching systems.

A typical present day system is the IBM 5910 which is shown in Figure 8.5. It comprises the 5974 modem adaptor and multiplexer; dual 5978

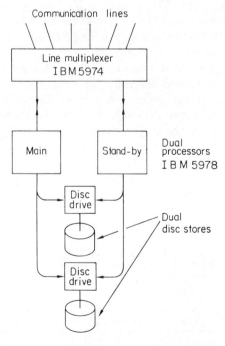

Figure 8.5.   The IBM 5910 message switching system

processors, and duplicated disc backing stores. The replication of equipment gives a very high reliability, and this may be readily extended to the subscriber by the use of separate lines from the multiplexer. Each channel in the multiplexer can carry out low-level processing tasks such as character assembly, and code conversion, and can also handle transfers directly to and from the main stores of the two processors. Extensive use is made of microprogramming techniques which may be changed easily, thus giving a highly flexible input/output system.

At any one time, one processor is on-line, and the other is in the stand-by state. The active processor updates the standby, which has a time-out of about one second. If no information is received within this time the stand-by processor takes over control.

The capacity of the system is 480 telegraph channels or the equivalent in the range 50 to 9600 bit/s. Sixty lines are handled by a modular block in the multiplexer; each of these lines can have a variety of modems. With an average message length of 300 characters, and an average multiple address of 1.3 destinations, the switch can handle, typically, five messages per second with a transit delay of around 300 milliseconds. This is when a fast store, which can handle a byte in about 0.6 microseconds, is employed. There is a useful 'break-in' facility for interrupting very long messages to allow the processing of urgent short ones.

The connection of the 5910 system to a computer may be done in two ways; it may be made identical to a remote terminal of the computer, or an IBM standard selector channel may be used to link the Central Processor Unit of the 5910 to that of the computer.

The organization of the software is shown in Figure 8.6. Only the portions shown shaded are purpose-designed; the remainder is common to most applications. The message reception and assembly and any necessary code translation functions, are mostly microprogrammed, and after these processes have operated on the message it is stored ready for analysis and routing. At this stage special application dependent tables are consulted. The processed message is then placed on backing store to await delivery. The queue and de-queue processes are responsible for writing and reading discs, and, when a message is read, it is passed to the disassembler for breakdown into characters which are handed to the transmission processes for despatch to line.

The extensive use of modularity in the 5910 hardware makes for high

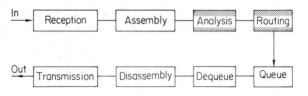

Figure 8.6. The software organization

reliability and flexibility. The use of modular software allows a variety of standard programs to be married together, with a minimum of new software, when a new application is required.

The services offered or planned by the Western Union Company in the United States are typical of what has been made possible by the digital computer. Western Union is, of course, traditionally a message carrying organization and, because the long distances between cities in the U.S.A. have always encouraged the use of store-and-forward techniques to maximize line utilization, this same technique has, naturally enough, been the basis of their new computer-based services. These are:

1. INFOCOM, which will be described in detail below.
2. SICOM—the Securities Industries Communication System which gives information on the state of the stock market to its subscribers.
3. Bank Wire Service—the need for this service arises from the fact that there are 14,000 separate banks in the U.S.A. which need to exchange credit information rapidly. The banking situation in the U.K. is quite different (see Chapter 4, page 116).
4. Legal Citation Service—this is a data bank of Case Law accessible to subscribers to the service.

INFOCOM is a general-purpose communications service offering a range of data or telegraph private switched services through a common shared network connecting mainly low-speed keyboard machines. All subscribers are physically joined to this common network but, by establishing closed sub-networks using restricted addressing, INFOCOM provides each subscriber with what seems to him to be a private network. This appears to have limited outlets and is accessible only to authorized members of the group to which he belongs.

The INFOCOM service handles Telex to Telex messages, and Telex to TWX (the A.T. & T. version of Telex which has now been sold to Western Union). A third possibility is that Telex messages may be translated into telegrams which are delivered manually. These messages may be sent 'paid' or 'collect'. It is also possible for customer's computers to be linked directly into the INFOCOM system by using an agreed fixed format message from the customer.

The following types of terminal and service may be connected to the INFOCOM network:

1. A private wire to a teletype machine operating at 150 baud using 8-bit ASCII code.
2. A party line to a group of teletype machines (up to six terminals can share a single access to the network).
3. A Telex service at 50 baud using CCITT alphabet No. 2, each terminal having access to the network through a Telex exchange. Subscribers

connected to the network can have access to other similar subscribers, to the public telegraph system, to the Telex system, to TWX, an international carrier, or the Canadian network.

4. The final possibility is a 2400-baud link to connect INFOCOM to a subscribing computer. This last service will enable the INFOCOM system to act as a communications processor for computer service bureaux.

The facilities offered by the INFOCOM service are:

1. Simplified message format compared with earlier systems.
2. Code and speed conversion between five-level code, 50 baud, Telex stations, and the eight-level code, 150 baud, Telex machines.
3. Complete privacy between any nominated group of stations.
4. Two levels of message priority.
5. Multiple address, whereby a message may be sent to a group of addresses.
6. Alphanumeric addresses.
7. Message storage and retrieval—messages are held on drum storage for four hours and on tape for ninety days.
8. Itemized billing for individual stations—there is no objection to stations in a private group being rented by different companies, or one company renting stations to another.
9. One station in a group may be nominated as the control station. It can obtain status reports and can direct the system to pass the message for a station that is out of order onto any other station.
10. The delivery time for a 50-character message is less than two minutes.

Computer Centres are located in Chicago, New York, San Francisco and Atlanta, with concentrators in other cities. All four message switching Centres are joined by 4,800 bit/s data links to form a fully connected mesh network.

The Computer Centres are based on the use of two UNIVAC 416 machines with 65,000 word core stores and 16 input/output channels. One of the machines is a processing computer, the other a communications controller. These two machines are joined by a 66,000 word/second data link, and there is a third, standby, machine which can be rapidly switched in to replace either of the other machines. For back-up storage there is a small Sperry-Rand type 330 drum of 165 K characters. This contains the operating system programs, which may be reloaded if it becomes necessary to restart the system. It also contains special subroutines used in collecting statistics and similar tasks.

There is a large 44 million word Sperry-Rand drum on which incoming messages are stored and a number of back-up tape decks on which messages are also stored, so that the integrity of the system may be maintained in case of equipment failure.

There are various diagnostic facilities for compiling error statistics for checking on customers' complaints and tracing whether messages came into and left the system, and a pair of printers which print out logging and fault messages to the operating staff.

8.3 THE CHARACTERISTICS OF NETWORKS AND USERS

The discussion of telegraph message switching in the earlier sections contrasted the techniques of circuit-switching and store-and-forward switching. It is worthwhile now to examine the properties of the two techniques from the point of view of the user, to see how they influence the way he may operate; equally important, and more usually considered, are the characteristics of the users behaviour and their impact on the design of a communications system.

The way two people communicate and interact depends almost entirely upon the delay inherent in the communication channel between them. A useful way to think about human behaviour is to liken it to a multi-access system handling multiple interrupts. The degree of conscious attention given to any task is dependent on the priority assigned to it. Normally, face-to-face interaction with another person is a high-level activity, often involving exchange of concepts with very high information content, which is usually efficiently coded. A high proportion of available attention is given to this kind of interaction.

When a telephone call is made, the channel characteristics do not unduly restrict the ability to communicate. The call set-up procedure and time taken are acceptable, and the direct connection with no apparent delay permits immediate interaction; so both parties in communication give their full attention and cooperate together in the exchange of information. Only when delays approaching one second are introduced is any effect observed, probably caused by the lack of immediate feedback of the sort usually given by one party when the other is speaking, i.e. grunts etc. The introduction of much more delay, as when a telephone answering machine, is employed, turns the channel into a kind of message switched system, and it is very unlikely that people would communicate verbally to any extent through such a system.

A Telex call, being a direct connection, is sometimes used by operators to hold conversations, but the delay due to typing makes it rare for ordinary subscribers to do so. Usually, the Telex network is used as a high-speed telegram exchange service which is very convenient for business because of the rapid interchange of messages possible. However, the immediacy of the communication process is lost, so the subscribers do not interact together; instead, each message is treated by them as an interruption of their other activities and is dealt with as soon as convenient after it arrives. There are definite advantages in this mode of co-operation because neither subscriber is committed at a particular instant and may divide his time between the 'conversation' and other activities. This permits the transaction to proceed at a reasonable pace, and subscribers are not held up unduly while waiting for a response to their last message.

When a subscriber is engaged in transactions with several other subscribers during the same period, telephone and Telex calls may be difficult to make due to the high probability that one or other of the terminals will be busy when an attempt is made to call it. Some private circuit-switched systems offer the possibility of queuing callers for a busy terminal, called 'camping on busy', but generally a subscriber who finds another engaged has no alternative but to start all over again later.

A message switching system using store-and-forward switching obviates the need for repeated attempts at establishing a call, by accepting the message and undertaking to deliver it when this becomes possible. Sometimes different grades of service are available and an express message will be guaranteed an attempt at delivery at the earliest possible moment. Often, in a large organization, the Telex service can appear as a store-and-forward system because a single terminal and operator is made to serve the whole organization through the internal mail. In this case, the behaviour to the user is indistinguishable from a message store-and-forward service, to which he has a direct connection. Finally, whenever more delay is tolerable the ordinary public mail service may be used; this is, of course, also a store-and-forward system.

In addition to the possibility that the called subscriber may be unavailable or engaged, there is a chance that the communication service itself may be congested. With a circuit-switched network the result of congestion is the

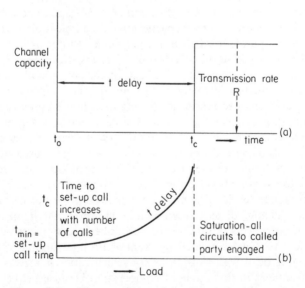

Figure 8.7.   Characteristics of circuit-switched networks

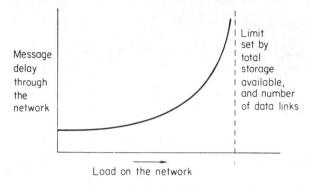

Figure 8.8. Characteristics of message-switched networks

inability of one subscriber to make a call to another, even though that subscriber would be quite able to accept a call.

The bottleneck may be in the switches or, more often, in the junction or long-distance trunk circuits; but either way, the appearance to the user is as shown in Figure 8.7. There is a connection delay which increases with the total load on the network as given at (b). But, as is shown at (a), once a connection is established the information exchange may take place at a rate R governed only by the physical properties of the particular circuit, and the subscribers themselves, or their equipment.

With a store-and-forward system an increase in the overall load naturally results in congestion, but the appearance to the user may not be immediately apparent, for the system continues to accept messages, at least for a while. The local switching centre usually can take and store further information, but may not be able to forward if for some time, although eventually, of course, no further messages will be accepted until some relaxation of the congestion allows those taken earlier to be despatched. With the mail service, the normal outward sign of congestion is the increase in delay. For example at Christmas, letters take longer to arrive; but the peripheral stores, in the form of public post boxes, are so large that they never, under usual circumstances, refuse to accept messages. However, during the strike of British Post Office workers in 1971, the boxes had to be sealed to prevent any input occuring into the system, while it was not operational. The appearance to the user of a store-and-forward system is illustrated by Figure 8.8. There is a minimum time necessary to transfer a message through the network. This comprises the time to travel between switches at the transmission speeds of the intervening links and a minimum message handling time at each switching point, including the time taken to read a message into and out of the stores associated with the switches. As the load on the network increases, queues develop at switches while messages wait to be processed, or for links to become free. This causes

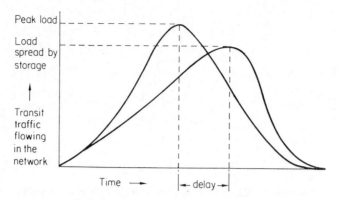

Figure 8.9.   Effect of storage in message switch

an increase in the time for messages to pass through the network as shown in the diagram.

Another way of looking at the store-and-forward network is to regard it as a large distributed set of stores which gradually fill as the load on the network increases. The peak load is therefore shifted in time by an amount depending on the available storage. Figure 8.9 illustrates this point by showing how a peak load is reduced, but at the expense of being delayed. The area under each of the two curves represents the total number of messages handled and is, of course, the same for both curves. But, in a practical network, there will be some upper limit to the instantaneous capacity of the network; perhaps due to limited transmission speeds, or switching capability. Clearly, the peak demand on the network is less with the increased use of storage which spreads the load over a longer time period. However, the delay increases as the load is spread and the time taken for messages to pass through the network also increases, as was shown in Figure 8.8.

If the load on almost any public service is plotted over a twenty-four hour period a demand curve similar to Figure 8.10 is obtained. The capital cost of providing the service is governed by the peak amplitude of the demand curve and it is obviously an advantage if the curve can be made more uniform in amplitude by shifting some of the peak load to other times. The use of differential tariffs with reduced rates outside peak hours is a means of encouraging a shift of peak traffic to less busy periods.

If the demand curve is examined more closely in a reduced time interval, it is seen to combine the sum of very many individual demands with an average value which fluctuates rapidly. It is the upper limit of this fluctuation which represents the peak demand, and there is an advantage to be gained by smoothing these rapid fluctuations to reduce the peak.

With the telephone network, the smoothing occurs because subscribers obtain a busy tone when they dial a call, and try later: this is the way a circuit switched system appears to users at peak load times. With a store-and-forward network, the messages will be accepted (if the store at the first switch is large enough) but delivery will be delayed. In the latter case, the originator of the message is spared the task of repeatedly trying to begin an interaction with another subscriber, but the interaction will proceed more slowly as the network load increases. With the circuit switch, the start of an interaction will be delayed as the load increases, but once begun it may proceed at a speed unaffected by loading on the network.

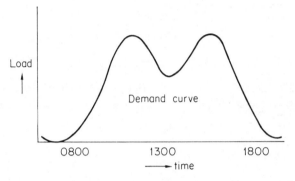

Figure 8.10.   Load on a public service

The Behaviour of Data Systems

In discussing the characteristics of networks, an analogy was made between a human being and a multi-access computer to describe the way people communicate with each other. But, the computer works much more rapidly, so, although the problem of meeting the communication needs of computers is essentially very similar to that of suiting people, the time scale is much shorter. In fact, three conditions may be identified: that of interaction between a person and a computer; that of interaction between two, or more, computers; and that of interaction between a computer and a remote sensor or peripheral device.

To a large extent, the interaction between a person and a computer is governed by the characteristics of human beings. The average rate of input and output obviously are determined entirely by the person (unless the whole system of communication links and remote computer is so ill-designed as to hamper his performance) and, the nature of his interactions will depend on the job he is doing. The present level of sophistication reached in the design of interactive systems makes it necessary to have a frequent interchange of messages between the user and the computer. The kind of interaction that can occur during a transaction with an information service is shown in Figure 8.11.

Notice that quite short commands—underlined—from the user can result in long replies from the computer, and that these may require some thought on the users part before he again instructs the computer. In essence, therefore,

HONEYWELL

ON AT 10:10 G265 A 27/04/72 TTY 7

USER NUMBER - -
SYSTEM - - <u>BASIC</u>
NEW OR OLD - - <u>NEW</u>
NEW FILE NAME - - <u>DLAB</u>
READY.

<u>10 PRINT "X" , "X↑2"</u>
<u>20 LET X=1</u>
<u>30 LET Y = X↑2</u>   Note   User's input is underlined
<u>40 PRINT X ,Y</u>
<u>50 LET X=X+1</u>
<u>60 IF X>10 THEN 80</u>
<u>70 GO TO 30</u>
<u>80 END</u>

<u>RUN</u>

DLAB   10:15   G265 A 27/04/72

X	X↑2
1	1
2	4
3	9
4	16
5	25
6	36
7	49
8	64
9	81
10	100

Figure 8.11. An interaction with a computer bureau

the interactions are sporadic, and characterized by a variability of length with a tendency towards short messages. This has been observed experimentally by workers at the Bell Telephone Laboratory.[3]

    The interactions that take place between one computer and another are somewhat different from those between two people, or those between a person and a computer. To some extent, the form of interchange depends on the tasks performed by the computers, and indeed, on the way the exchanges are constrained by the intervening data links. If both computers are multi-access computers engaged in handling transactions, and a particular trans-action demands that one system communicates with the other, the interchange is likely to in the form of short messages to transfer data from one system to the other. On the other hand, one computer may require to transfer a com-plete file to another machine, perhaps to up-date information about a com-pany's operations. In this case, it is often assumed that much longer messages would pass between them. Even so, it is likely that the messages would be broken-up into shorter blocks with intermediate validity checks carried out to make sure all was well, as it is generally unsafe to rely on the links' ability to provide error-free data transfers.

When a validity check is to be made, the use of short blocks has two advantages. Firstly, it can economize on high-speed storage in the two com-puters, for it reduces the amount of store occupied by a data block at the sending computer, while a copy is transferred to the other machine and checked for correct arrival. Secondly, a short block has less chance of being corrupted by a line disturbance than a long block, so the likelihood of having to retransmit it is lower. For these reasons, the shortest possible block size is to be preferred. However, when the computers are far apart, the long signal propagation time between them makes it desirable to use long blocks to maximize the quantity of information transferred for each handshake acknowledgement. A compromise block length therefore has to be accepted.

Apart from the advantages attached to the transfer of long data files by relatively short messages, the need for long transactions between computers is likely to be reduced as more on-line usage is introduced. At present, much updating of files occurs in a batch processing manner after business hours are ended. This calls for the transfer of long files. However, if the records were amended on a transaction basis as the business was carried out, there would be no need for the subsequent updating of files. As there is, potentially, an economic advantage in keeping up-to-date files the trend towards on-line operation with short transactions may be expected to continue.

The interactions possible between a computer and remote peripheral devices other than those used by human operators could be of many kinds. There are a growing number of private networks for telemetry and control of oil and gas pipelines, electricity grids and so on, and there are already a few cases where the public telephone network is used; for example, river level measuring devices are available that can dial-up a flood-warning centre when a critical water level is reached. The interactions occuring between such devices are also generally likely to be of short duration; but in any case, the total volume of traffic arising from such sources is unlikely to be great, though the reliability and accuracy required are high.

It was the appreciation of the likely characteristics of the data traffic that would arise with remote access computer systems, and the probable rapid growth in the volume of such traffic that led to proposals for packet-switching data networks. But before examining these proposals it is desirable to consider in more detail the basic characteristics of data traffic.

The Characteristics of Data Traffic

It is necessary to understand the nature of data traffic to enable the appropriate choice to be made between possible alternative methods of carrying it, and to examine whether new techniques need to be developed to handle it more effectively.

The behaviour of computer-based systems was discussed in the previous section and shown to depend on three factors; the computer itself, the remote peripheral devices it serves, and people making use of the services it provides.

A computer is characterized by the handling of information internally at very high rates, typically tens of Megabits per second. The operation of the various peripheral devices is scheduled to keep them as active as possible and this leads to the transfer of information in relatively short blocks of up to a few thousand bits. When a computer is connected by telephone lines to remote terminals, the disparity between the internal speed of the computer and the lines makes it necessary to introduce storage and, sometimes, auxiliary communications processors. The communication between the main computer and the storage or auxiliary computers may then be of the same form as other internal traffic i.e. relatively short blocks. This is illustrated by Figure 8.12, which shows information flow between the central processing unit and the other parts of the computer.

The behaviour of peripheral devices depends on their principle of operation. Mechanical devices like printers and paper tape punches and readers are constrained by strength of materials to operate up to a few-thousand bit/s.

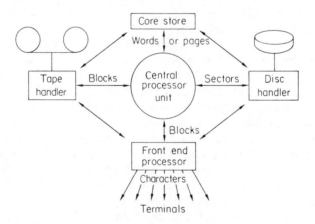

Figure 8.12.   Internal message paths

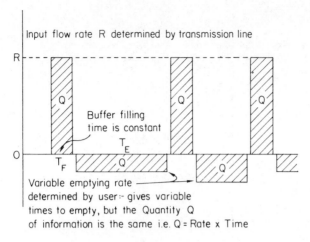

Figure 8.13.   The use of a line buffer

Magnetic tapes and discs can range from a few tens of kbit/s to a few mbit/s, while electronic devices, like cathode-ray-tube terminals, may be operated at speeds approaching that of the computer itself. Very often peripheral devices contain buffers which decouple them from the data link. With slow mechanical peripherals the buffers fill rapidly through the link, which is then idle while the device reads the data from the store. Where the link is dedicated to such a peripheral device little advantage is gained from the use of buffer storage; but when several such devices are grouped, the use of storage allows the link to be shared by them. The flow of data to a terminal fitted with a buffer is illustrated by Figure 8.13.

The third factor affecting data traffic is the way people behave, when using data terminals. If they are using keyboards the rate will be only a few tens of bit/s, and it is often the case that buffers are added to collect a block of data rather than allow the sending of characters as they are typed. Again, this is only useful if one data link, or computer input-output channel, can be shared between several keyboards, by interleaving the blocks which each produces. The rate of receipt of information by people depends on how it is presented. Pages of text, if read carefully, would require an average rate of transmission of about two hundred bits/s. However, sometimes people scan pages quite quickly, and it is preferable to have them produced rapidly; there is then a pause before the next is required. Much the same happens when graphical information is presented; it is usually better for a picture to appear at once, and then be held while the user examines it at leisure.

From the above considerations it is apparent that data traffic, although covering a range of characteristics depending on its source, is broadly characterized by a tendancy to fairly short messages, often exchanged at quite

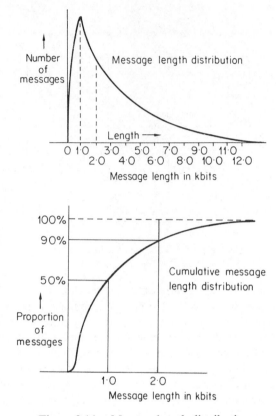

Figure 8.14.   Message length distribution

high speeds. This is illustrated in Figure 8.14. This figure shows qualitatively how the number of messages varies with the length of message averaged over all types of system involving data transmission; both the message length distribution and the cumulative distribution are shown, and it is clear that the majority of messages are less than about 2,000 bits in length.[3]

The time taken to transmit messages of various lengths is shown in Figure 8.15 where the time is plotted against message length for different speeds of transmission. The loop delays for 10, 100, 1000, and 10,000 mile circuits are also shown. It is worth noting that, for a message length of 1,000 bits and a transmission speed of 48 kbits/s, the message length is equal to the number of bits that could be stored in a 1,000 mile circuit loop.

Because the message transmission times are so short, the use of circuit switching is really inappropriate, for the time to set-up and clear circuits is much longer than the message transfer time. Indeed, the end of a message may well have left the transmitting device before the beginning reaches the receiver. The message switching principle is more appropriate for data traffic, particularly the high-speed, fixed-format message technique known as packet switching.

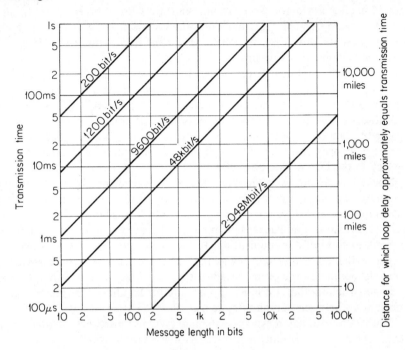

Figure 8.15.   Message transmission speeds

The Packet Switching Principle

The principle of packet switching was first put forward in the early 1960's by Paul Baran while working at the RAND Corporation on military voice communications networks.[4] Baran proposed a mesh network of computers joined by communications circuits that handled digitized speech in short bursts. The mesh form of network gave many alternative paths between any two subscribers trying to communicate with each other, and an adaptive routing method called the hot potato technique was proposed to give reliable communication; even if parts of the network were destroyed by enemy attack while calls were in progress. Only when no possible path remained were two subscribers prevented from conversing.

Each burst of speech was preceded by a destination address and was directed by each node in the general direction of the destination. The nodes handled the bursts like hot potatoes, getting rid of them as soon as possible. This gave a rapid progress of information through the network, which behaved as a very high speed store-and-forward information switching network. The speed of processing required to handle speech in this way is very high and the delays in mesh networks using store-and-forward techniques are generally rather long for satisfactory speech communication. So, although the feasibility has been demonstrated experimentally, the cost is too high for commercial use at present. But it seems very likely that improving technology will eventually change this situation.

The idea of a mesh network which handles information in short bursts seems very well suited to the communication needs of remote access computer systems and, since 1966, the concept has been developed both theoretically and practically at the U.K. National Physical Laboratory, in the context of a possible National Data Network.[5] The technique has also been used in private networks, notably that built by the Advanced Research Projects Agency in the U.S.A., see page 300.

Packet switching is often regarded as a particular form of message switching especially suited for handling data traffic. Superficially, this is indeed the case, but there are very important differences between conventional message switching, and packet switching and the latter is, in reality, an entirely separate method of communication. In fact, there are resemblances between packet switching and circuit switching also, because the packet switching principle combines those major advantages of both circuit switching and message switching that are most appropriate for handling the interchange of information between computer systems.

With conventional message switching systems, messages of any length are accepted in their entirety and stored as such at each switching point during their passage from switch to switch towards their destination. The network takes full responsibility for maintaining the integrity of the message, and elaborate procedures are employed to ensure that this is achieved. The accent is on reliability, rather than speed, in the information transfer between subscribers, and the messages are held by the network until the recipient is ready to accept them, however long this may take. It is not intended that subscribers should interact rapidly with each other through a message switching network, so the type of interaction common between telephone users to overcome errors introduced by the network, or indeed their own mistakes, is not possible. This is why the accuracy of information transfer through a message switching network is so important.

With packet switching systems, information is exchanged in the form of short packets, and the time of transit of these messages through the network is kept low; the subscribers are expected to interact with each other by exchanging packets, in much the same way as they would interact by exchanging information through a circuit-switched connection. Because the subscribers interact together, they may take part in the validation of the information exchange procedure; this can cope with their own errors, as well as any introduced by the network. However, this does not imply that a packet switching network is

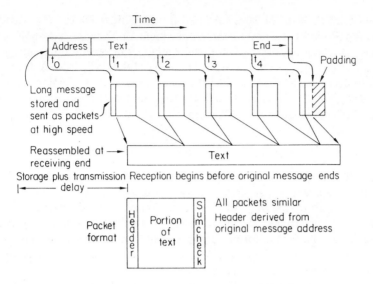

Figure 8.16.   The packet switching principle

unreliable; indeed, because information is not retained in it for long periods the chance of information being corrupted while it is static is reduced, while the probability of corruption during transmission can be the same as for a conventional message switching network.

The design of packet switching networks is dealt with in Chapter 10, but it is worthwhile pointing out here that long messages are readily handled by a packet switching network if they are broken up into short packets for transmission and reassembled again at the destination. This method of operation is often called *cut-through* and is shown in Figure 8.16. The use of cut-through has important advantages: the fixed packet structure permits efficient handling, and the absence of indefinitely long messages prevents the blocking of transmission links and keeps the queues at switching points small. Storage at switches is made sufficient only for a few packets and the total amount of information stored in the network is low. The result is that the delay through a packet switching network is much smaller than through a normal message-switching network and the rate of throughput of information can be much higher. Where message storage is required as a service to subscribers it must be provided externally to the network, rather than as an integral part of the switches in the manner usual in a conventional message-switching network. This separation of the storage in the network into two parts; that used primarily for scheduling the efficient use of communication lines, and that used for providing services and storing messages, clearly confers some very important benefits for handing data traffic and a considerable amount of attention has been given to the design of packet switching networks in the United Kingdom and in the United States. The Advanced Research Projects Agency of the Department of Defense has sponsored a packet switching network which links computers of several different types at many research centres distributed across the U.S.A. The ARPA network is an important example of a shared private data communications network, and is described in this context later. It is also used to illustrate practical aspects of network design in Chapters 10, 11 and 12.

A Comparison of Message and Packet Switching

The difference between packet switching and message switching begins with the messages and packets themselves. Messages are the units of information recognized by the users of networks. Consequently their length must be moderately unrestricted. To make them suitable for formatting by people, messages usually have a format depending on certain markers or codes.

Packets are designed for handling by computer, and so have a fixed format. To keep their transit time low, a maximum length is set, and if messages longer than this maximum have to be carried, they are split into packets for transmission. Their format is not suitable for use by people.

Message switching emphasizes the responsibility of the network for the message, because no response or feedback is expected—the delivery of one message is a complete transaction. Because message systems were not associated with computers, but with big organizations, the need to replicate messages, sending identical copies to many locations, has been met. Computers would distribute information selectively, not using replication. Packet switching serves interactive systems where a response is expected, so the loss of a packet is generally less troublesome than a data error introduced in transmission.

Packet switched networks aim to deliver packets with minimum delay, and do not hold them for delayed delivery. If the called terminal (or computer) is busy, the conversation will probably not even begin, but when it does begin it is likely that many packets will be exchanged before it ends.

The kind of transit delay expected in a packet switched system can be estimated roughly by noting that a 2048 bit packet can be sent over a 2·048 Mbit/s link in one millisecond. The transit delay for one node will be a small multiple of this service time, determined by the queue length plus the processing time for each packet. Because of the fixed packet size, service time is constant, and it can be shown that even for 80% saturation the mean queue length is two (not including service position) so the mean queuing component of the transit time is 2 milliseconds. The processing component is likely to be comparable with this time also. In practice a much lower occupancy is used, less than say 25%, to provide a margin for error in traffic estimation. The contribution of queuing to mean transit time for a U.K. national network with such links is less than 5 milliseconds, and 10 milliseconds is rarely exceeded. This is in marked contrast with message switching, where transit delays of minutes are normal.

So, although the store-and-forward principle is employed in both kinds of systems, their objectives are different, and the performance expected is very different.

8.4. SHARED PRIVATE NETWORKS

In Chapter 4 the use of private data communications networks with lines leased from common carriers was discussed. Essentially, such networks use store-and-forward message switching techniques and, being entirely the concern of a single organization, may use any message format and other standards most suited to the particular needs of the organization. The Western Union INFOCOM service, described on page 279 of this chapter, is typical of several other message switching networks which attempt to serve the needs of more than one organization. This task is complicated by the problem of agreeing standards for a wide range of users and this is made even more difficult if the basic problem of transferring messages between subscribers is combined with that of offering services which are provided as an integral part of the network.

However, because a group of organizations with similar requirements is more readily able to devise common standards, there are a number of shared private networks in use or planned. There will undoubtedly be many such similar, but incompatible, data networks in a few years time. This situation is likely to worsen unless the PTTs manage to agree on really comprehensive, advanced, standards and begin to implement public data communications networks. The kinds of standards and the forms of network required are discussed in Chapter 10.

Of the many shared networks now in existence, two have been chosen for closer study; one is the airline network established in Europe by the Société Internationale de Télécommunications Aéronautique, the other is the Advanced Research Projects Agency network in the U.S.A.

The SITA Network

The Société Internationale de Télécommunications Aéronautique (SITA) was originally established in 1949 by a group of airlines, as a non-profit making organization which would provide them with a cheaper means of exchanging messages. This was needed to facilitate the sale of seats on their aeroplanes, to exchange operational information and for the location of baggage that had gone astray. For these purposes SITA organized a common service in the form of a worldwide low-speed message switching network handling teleprinter traffic; this was well established by the time computer-based airline seat reservation systems began to be implemented, as already discussed in Chapter 4, page 125. Because of these new systems, a review of the SITA network was undertaken. In 1964, the decision was made to adapt its design, to keep pace with the new patterns of traffic that were expected to arise during the next ten years.

The anticipated traffic to be handled by the modified SITA network was of three kinds:

1. Type A: data traffic between computer systems requiring a rapid response; this would comprise single address messages using various types of 5, 6 or 7 unit information codes.
2. Type B: conventional teleprinter traffic using either CCITT alphabets No. 2, or No. 5, with messages having single or multiple addresses and of lengths up to 4000 characters.
3. Type C: single address data traffic requiring a response time similar to type B, and using CCITT alphabets No. 2 and No. 5.

The transit times through the network for type A traffic was to be of the order of 3 seconds, while the other two categories would have three levels of priority indicated by a label—QU, 2 minutes; QN or no label, 30 minutes; QD, 12 hours. All messages handled by the network were to be protected from loss or mutilation, and facilities were required for the repetition of type B and C messages that had already been delivered, and for holding them if the destination was unable to accept them.

The computer-based seat reservation systems already in use controlled their remote terminals by polling through networks of leased lines. The redesigned SITA network was required to provide for handling this kind of terminal. In addition, the new network would have to match into the existing telex systems operated by PTTs and into other shared networks such as its American counterpart ARINC (Aeronautical Radio Incorporated) which serves some 90 U.S. airlines, and any private networks operated by companies such as BOAC, PANAM, KLM to name just a few.

When the SITA network was being reappraised in 1964, it was already connected to over 100 centres and about 100 million conventional telegrams per year were being handled. This number was increasing at a rate which would double it in less than four years. To cater for this growth in existing traffic and to satisfy the anticipated new requirements a high-level or trunk network was planned; this would provide an improved service and new facilities to a large part of Europe, and also North America, and would join together areas of smaller message concentration using the existing communications methods. High-level network centres were chosen in New York, London, Paris, Amsterdam, Brussels, Rome, Frankfurt, and Madrid, each having a defined area for message collection and delivery. These main centres were to be joined by data links, which needed to operate at, at least, 2400 bit/s to achieve the short response time specified for type A traffic. This response time criterion led to a decision to use store-and-forward block

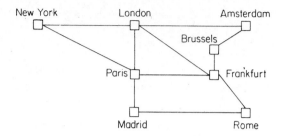

Figure 8.17.   The SITA high-level network, 1970

transmission in the high-level network, with blocks of variable length up to a maximum determined by the response time, and transmission efficiency. Each block would have a header giving addresses and control information to guide it through the switching centres, and the overall efficiency would, clearly, be increased by using longer blocks for a given header size. On the other hand, the shorter the block, the less likely would be the chance of its corruption by noise, with the consequent need for its retransmission. Also, shorter blocks would allow a more rapid response for high priority messages, because the waiting time for a lower priority block to end would be shorter. However, an overriding factor that influenced the choice was the average message length of the existing telegraph traffic, which was less than 200 characters. Indeed, 95% of all messages had less than 250 characters. It was, therefore, decided to use a 256 character block, with a 250 character information field available for carrying message. A long message would be transmitted as a sequence of two or more blocks.

The requirements to cater for codes of up to seven units led to the adoption of an eight-bit character as standard with seven information bits and an eighth bit giving overall odd character parity. An alphabet similar to CCITT No. 5 was chosen for control purposes, and all other characters in the information field were to be padded up to seven bits where necessary. For example, with the existing telegraph messages in alphabet No. 2, the start and stop bits would be removed from each character and the remaining five information bits would be augmented by a sixth bit indicating the shift case, and a seventh bit which was always 'one'. This would prevent an alphabet No. 5 control character being falsely simulated by a message character.

Following feasibility studies,[6] a system was designed and a specification was prepared for the computer centres. This allowed them to be introduced into the existing network of low-speed circuits in such a way that modification to form the high-level network was readily possible later. Univac 418 II systems were chosen for New York, Frankfurt, Brussels, Rome and Madrid, while Phillips DS714 Mk II systems were installed in the larger London and Paris centres, and at Amsterdam. The high-level network shown in Figure 8.17 was completed in 1970 and has been in service ever since.

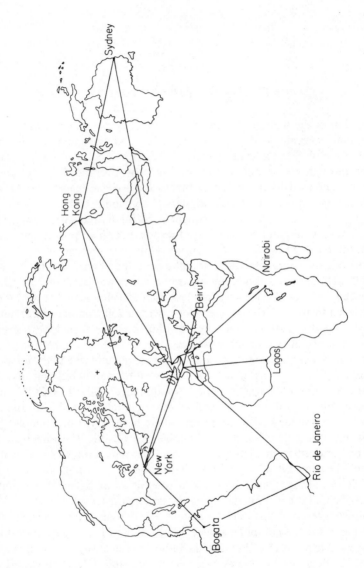

Figure 8.18.   Some planned SITA developments

In parallel with the development of the main network, the existing networks were progressively modernized, a process that is still continuing. At first, the manual message switching centres were replaced by multiplexers capable of handling several low-speed devices such as teleprinters, and later satellite processors were introduced. These are able to cope with a wide variety of traffic, and can control the input-output terminals designed specifically for airline automatic systems. Figure 8.18 shows some possible extensions of the SITA network likely to be made in the next few years.

The High-level Network

The SITA high-level network was designed with three aims in view. Firstly, to improve the service for conventional traffic; this has been done and transit times have been reduced from hours to minutes. Secondly, to provide a service for handling short data messages; this, too, has been done and has enabled British European Airways to extend its data transmission network into Europe. Thirdly, to offset rising cost of conventional communications facilities; this has more than been achieved, for the efficient use of circuits and the reduced number of operating staff has brought about a fall in the cost per message.

Because the SITA network has proved so successful, it is worthwhile examining the procedures devised for ensuring the integrity of the messages it handles. This is done on two levels: the individual blocks passing along each link are protected against mutilation, loss or duplication, while complete messages are similarly protected between their points of entry to, and exit from, the network.

The protection of blocks in transit between centres is achieved by adding to each block an even parity check character; this augments the odd parity bit used with each character and much improves the chance of detecting errors (see Chapter 6, page 213). As long as blocks are available, they are sent continuously and are checked for correct parity at the receiving end of a link. (If no blocks are available the transmitter sends a link check message every three seconds.) An acknowledgment is generated for every received block indicating whether it was correct (ACK) or incorrect (NAK); these acknowledgments are interleaved between blocks being received on the return channel. If a full length block were being received on the return channel, the acknowledgment for several short blocks sent on the forward channel would be delayed. A block numbering scheme is, therefore, employed and the acknowledgment signals carry the number of the last block correctly received.

The loss or duplication of blocks is prevented by arranging for each transmitting centre receiving a correct acknowledgment (ACK) to erase the associated information blocks, while if an incorrect acknowledgment (NAK) is received the centre repeats all blocks with numbers following that carried by the (NAK) signal. At the receiving end of a link the detection of a faulty block inhibits reception and all further blocks are rejected until the block previously found to be faulty has been correctly received.

If after retransmission a series of blocks is not correctly acknowledged, it is repeated a further three times. If a correct acknowledgment still fails to appear, the communications circuit is assumed to be faulty and traffic is diverted to another route. Meanwhile, a print-out is produced advising operators of the situation, and check messages are sent continuously into the faulty circuit until it is found to be operating correctly again.

When a link between centres becomes faulty, or is restored following a fault, a status message is sent automatically to all other centres. This message causes all routing tables in the network to be modified accordingly. Should all the links to a centre, or indeed the centre itself, fail, the low priority messages for the centre are stored at entry points until the centre becomes operational again. However, the high priority messages must be dropped, and the polling of all remote terminals belonging to computers served by the out-of-action centre has to cease.

The automatic rerouting of blocks during fault conditions makes it possible for some blocks of a long message to arrive out of sequence, and to overcome this problem an entry-exit block numbering scheme is used. This operates in a similar manner to that used on individual links, but a separate series of numbers is used for each type of traffic and for each pair of network centres. The entry centre holds all blocks until they have been correctly acknowledged as received by the exit centre. Individual blocks are not acknowledged, but there is at least one acknowledgment provided for every 16 blocks. The entry-exit block numbering arrangement enables the blocks of a multi block message to be reassembled correctly, and ensures none are lost or duplicated.

It is interesting to contrast the SITA network which has evolved from the needs of a specific group of users—the airlines—with the ARPA network, designed as a research project, which is discussed in the following section.

The ARPA Network

The Advanced Research Projects Agency is operated by the Department of Defence of the United States. It was formed to promote advanced projects of all kinds, following the early and unexpected success of the U.S.S.R. in launching the first man-made earth satellite. Computer science was an obvious field where new projects could readily be conceived; the renowned Project MAC at the Massachusetts Institute of Technology was one, ILLIAC IV at the University of Illinois another, while several other computer projects were also begun at universities all over the U.S.A. Of these, some twenty continue to be supported. In 1966, at MIT, experiments were conducted with two computers joined by a data link; this work led to the proposal for a network of data links connecting several of the centres where ARPA funded projects were in progress. This ARPA network, begun in 1967, is possibly the most important computer project in the world today, because it links together, and is beginning to coordinate, the work of advanced research establishments spread all over the U.S.A. Its role as a cohesive force associating, otherwise, separate groups of research workers is a most important aspect of the project.

When initially conceived by L. G. Roberts[7] in 1966, the ARPA network was based on the use of 2·4 kbits/s data links, but further consideration, encouraged by the theoretical studies that had been carried out independently in the U.K. by the National Physical Laboratory, led to the adoption of high-speed group-band links. These now connect small computers in a mesh network forming a packet switching communications system shared by the sites which it joins. All the sites are funded by ARPA, and the network is, therefore, a private shared network. However, it is, at present, unique in the use of high-speed lines, which give a coast-to-coast transit time in the region of 100 ms. This is much less than is achieved in other high-level networks—such as the SITA network—and allows new concepts in interactive computer-to-computer communications to be developed. In fact, most other data networks have been designed for connecting distributed terminals to central computer systems, whereas the ARPA network was intended from the beginning to link a relatively large number of advanced data processing systems, many of which already supported their own networks of terminals.

Initially the ARPA network comprised two parts: a network of data processing systems which were called HOSTs, and a communications sub-

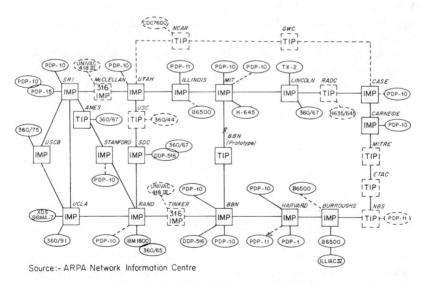

Source:- ARPA Network Information Centre

Figure 8.19. The ARPA network, 1972

network of packet switching node computers known as IMPs (Interface Message Processors). In August 1971, a new type of node computer for handling terminals was introduced for sites which had no HOST system. This TIP (Terminal Interface Processor) makes the powerful new services, which are being developed on some of the HOST systems, readily accessible at sites which could not otherwise afford such facilities.

Because the ARPA network is itself a research project, it is developing continually, but a typical example of its structure (in mid-1972) is given in Figure 8.19. This shows the large number of IMPs and TIPs already installed and indicates the variety of computer systems which can now be joined together. The communication sub-network has undergone some changes since it was originally designed (these are discussed in Chapter 11), but essentially it has proved very effective in coordinating research at the centres it connects. These centres are developing techniques for using the network effectively, and several projects are being conducted aimed at providing new services and facilities that would not be feasible without the sub-network. The design of the ARPA communications network and the way it is being used are discussed in the next sections.

The Communications Sub-network

The contract for the design and implementation of the communications network was awarded to Bolt, Beranek and Newman of Boston, Mass. They designed the IMP shown in Figure 8.20 around an augmented, ruggedized, version of the Honeywell DDP 516 computer using 12K words of store with 16 multiplexed channels, and 16 levels of priority interrupt.[8] Special hardware to control interfaces to HOSTs and data links, and to monitor the IMP's internal behaviour was designed by B.B. & N.

An IMP can serve up to four HOSTs, provided the total number of HOSTs and data links does not exceed seven. An identical operating system, occupying some 6K store words, is used for all IMPs leaving 6K words for message storage; but a protected 512 word block contains programs which allow an IMP detecting an internal software corruption to reload a copy of the operating system from another IMP.

The messages passing between a HOST and an IMP are controlled by a HOST to IMP protocol, and may vary between 1 and 8095 bits in length. These messages are partitioned into packets with a maximum size of about 1000 bits, each having a cyclic sum check added by hardware during transmission into a data link. The packet format is shown in Figure 8.21. The particular link used for each packet is selected by the IMP according to its estimation of the transit time to the packet's destination using each available link. The transit time estimates are recomputed every half second and are based on an interchange of estimates and past records with neighbouring IMPs. The dynamic re-estimation of transit delays allows links to be selected

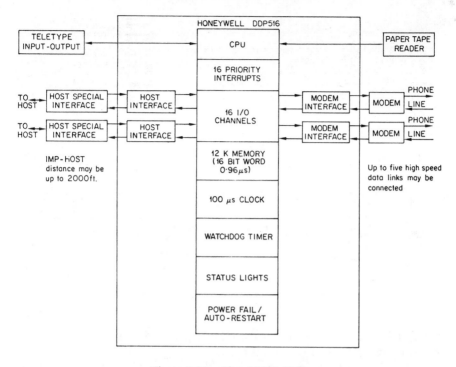

Figure 8.20. The ARPA IMP

to minimize the transmission delay, and to maximize the total throughput of the network; but, of course, the successive packets of one message may follow different paths. This is discussed in detail in Chapter 12, page 442.

When an IMP receives a packet from another IMP an error check is performed. If the packet is error free it is stored and a positive acknowledgment is returned to the sending IMP allowing it to release the storage area occupied by its copy of the packet. However, if the received packet is in error, or if the receiving IMP is unable to accept it, the packet is ignored. The sending IMP waits a preset time for a positive acknowledgment; if one does not arrive, the packet must be assumed lost and a copy is retransmitted possibly by another route.

Once a packet has been stored and acknowledged, a receiving IMP must determine, by examining the destination address, whether the packet is to be delivered to a local HOST or forwarded to another IMP. In this latter case, the packet is placed in the queue for transmission in common with any outgoing messages from local HOSTs. But if the packet is for local delivery, the IMP checks to see whether all associated packets have arrived; if so, it reassembles them into the proper order and delivers the complete message to

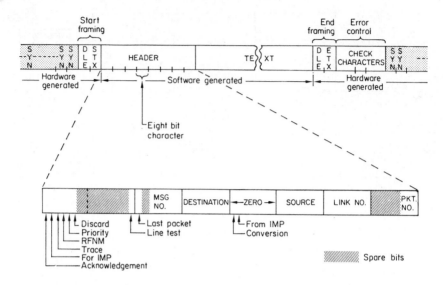

Figure 8.21.　The ARPA packet format

the HOST. The HOSTs control the interchange of message between themselves using a HOST to HOST protocol.

As well as handling messages, an IMP is arranged to detect and report data link failures and also gather performance statistics. In the absence of normal traffic, each IMP transmits idle packets on unused lines at half-second intervals. The lack of a return packet or incoming traffic on any line for more than a preset time indicates a faulty line and allows routing tables to be updated accordingly. The return to normal of the line is indicated by the resumption of idle packet traffic. Internal performance statistics are also collected by each IMP and are automatically transmitted to a specified HOST for analysis. This HOST is, thereby, able to formulate a picture of the overall state of the whole network. A useful feature novel to the ARPA network is the trace message. Any HOST message may have a trace bit set; when each IMP processes any packet of such a message it records the packet arrival time, the queues on which it resides, the time spent in these queues and the departure time. These records are also sent to a specified HOST for evaluation; they allow a very detailed picture to be formed of how the network handles messages.

The Terminal IMP (TIP)

The Terminal IMP is a lower power version of an IMP based on the Honeywell DDP316 computer, fitted with a multi-line controller (MLC) designed and built by B.B. & N. to handle up to 64 channels for asynchronous

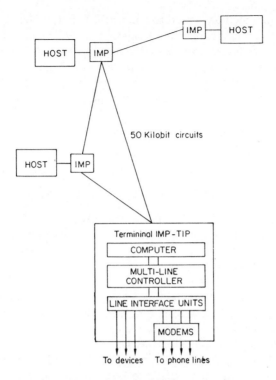

Figure 8.22.   Terminal IMP connections

terminals; these may be connected directly, or through telephone circuits, see Figure 8.22.

The MLC has a cycling buffer store which samples each channel every 50 μs, giving a maximum rate for output or synchronous input of 19.2 kbit/s. However, the aggregate rate must not exceed about 100 kbit/s, although a wide variety of terminals of differing speeds may be mixed together within this overall limit. The asynchronous format uses start and stop bits and, because each character is sampled eight times, the maximum rate is 2,400 bit/s for this type of terminal.

The TIP is designed to appear to the main network as a HOST, so the TIP program must implement the HOST to IMP protocol internally between its terminal handling, and trunk-line handling partitions. In addition, it has to satisfy the HOST to HOST message exchange protocol and the TELNET protocol designed to convert the messages from terminals—which of course, use their own codes and procedures—into a common network form called the Network Virtual Terminal (NVT) (see Chapter 11, page 416). This allows terminals to use services with which they could not communicate directly because of hardware incompatabilities.

An interesting method is used to handle the variety of terminals that may call a TIP. As soon as a connection has been made to a channel of the MLC, the user enters a character specific to that type of terminal. The MLC samples this at a high speed, generating a bit pattern which identifies the terminal uniquely. The TIP software then sets the correct sampling rate for the channel and selects the code-conversion tables appropriate for the terminal type.

Applications of the ARPA Network

Once the communications sub-network was in operation it encouraged people to think positively about ways in which it could be used. It had always been intended to gather information about the behaviour of the sub-network and this is being done by the Network Measurement Centre at the University of California, Los Angeles (UCLA), which is responsible for system modeling, and the Network Control Centre operated by B.B. & N. in Boston, where the states of the IMPs, the lines and HOSTs are monitored. As a result, changes in the way the sub-network operates are being made, these are discussed in Chapter 11, page 399.

The construction of the communications sub-network and its assessment by performance monitoring were, naturally enough, the major initial activities; although some early use was made of the network as a facility by the RAND corporation in conjunction with the Universities of California at Santa Barbara and Los Angeles, and by Stanford Research Institute. However, many other applications soon began to be developed and this will continue for a number of years, particularly when the ILLIAC IV (which is a very powerful parallel-processing computer system) and the 10^{12} bit direct-access store being developed for use with it, are available on the network. To a large extent the more advanced uses depend on the agreement of high-level procedures for exchanging information and controlling interactions through the network, and it is interesting to see how this is being achieved with such a large group of users, operating many different types of computer.

The Network Working Group (NWG) with members from each HOST site is responsible for technical coordination and management and has several sub-groups working on various protocols. These are discussed below. The vital dissemination of technical information throughout the growing network community is achieved by a three-level documentation scheme. The most formal papers are known as 'Documents' which are issued as a statement of network policy by the chairman of the NWG. A 'Request for Comments' (RFC) may be issued by any member of the NWG as a means of proposing new technical standards and promoting the exchange of ideas between members of the group. A guide to RFCs is published monthly by the MITRE Corporation of Boston. Finally, a complete collection of all Documents, RFCs, memoranda, etc. is deposited at the Network Information Centre (NIC) operated by Stanford Research Institute (SRI) which publishes a comprehensive index, and has a computer-based network information system which is accessible from remote terminals through the network. The excellence of these arrangements for information dissemination and document control plays an important role in the success of the project, by coordinating research at the ARPA sites. These sites are given in Table 8.1.

ARPA site identifier	ARPA network organization
ABERDEEN	Aberdeen research and development center
AFETR	Air Force Eastern Test Range
ALOHA	Aloaha network, University of Hawaii
AMES	NASA Ames Research Center
ARPA	Advanced Research Projects Agency
BBN	Rolt Beranek and Newman
BELVOIR	USAMERDC, Fort Belvoir
BURR	Burroughs Corporation, Paoli
CASE	Case Western Reserve University
CCA	Computer Corporation of America
CMU	Carnegie-Mellon University
DCAO	Defense Communications Agency Operations
DOCB	Department of Commerce, Boulder
ETAC	USAF-ETAC
FNWC	Fleet Numerical Weather Center
GWC	Air Force Global Weather Center
HARV	Harvard University
ILL	University of Illinois
ILLIAC	NASA Ames Research Center
LBL	Lawrence Berkley Laboratory
LLL	Lawrence Livermore Laboratory
LL	M.I.T. Lincoln Laboratory
MCCL	McLellan Air Force Base
MIT	M.I.T.
MITRE	Mitre Corporation
NBS	National Bureau of Standards
NYU	New York University
RADC	Rome Air Development Center
RAND	Rand Corporation
SAAC	Seismic Analysis Array Center
SDC	System Development Corporation
SU	Stanford University
TINK	Tinker Air Force Base
UCLA	University of California Los Angeles
UCSB	University of California Santa Barbara
UCSD	University of California San Diego
UCS	University of Southern California
UTAH	University of Utah

Table 8.1   Organizations in the ARPA network

High-Level Protocols

When the network was designed the interface between the IMPs and the HOSTs was defined by B.B. & N. and procedures or protocols were worked out for controlling the flow of packets between IMPs (the IMP to IMP protocol), and the flow of messages between HOSTs (the HOST to HOST, or network control protocol). But the way in which the heterogenous HOST systems were to communicate could not, initially, be determined. However, under the Network Working Group a 'layered' approach to the specification of protocol has been adopted. The inner layers are the original HOST to IMP and HOST to HOST protocols, and several higher-level protocols have since been defined by the community of HOST sites. These form a hierarchy of protocols covering various kinds of interaction between HOSTs.
These protocols are:

1. The Initial Connection Protocol (ICP), providing a standard method for processes in different HOSTs to establish a connection.
2. The Telecommunication Network (TELNET) protocol, used to provide communication between a keyboard terminal and a terminal-serving HOST. This uses the Network Virtual Terminal to overcome terminal hardware differences.
3. The Data Transfer Protocol (DTP), specifying standard methods of formatting data for passage through the network, allowing it to be used to implement higher level protocols.
4. The File Transfer Protocol (FTP) defines standard methods for reading writing and updating files stored at a remote HOST in an endeavour to shield users from the differences between filing systems at various sites.
5. The Data Reconfiguration Service (DRS) attempts to deal with the problem of reconciling the different input-output data formats that are used by various applications programs. It uses an interactive procedure between user processes and an interpreter called the Form Machine (analogous to filling out a form by hand).
6. The Mail Box Protocol (MBP) provides a service for passing messages between people, and is widely used to facilitate the work of protocol development by members of study groups.
7. The Graphics Protocol (GP) is being considered by a group thinking about the difficult area of specifying standard ways of handling graphical information.

It is clear that the development of computer usage in the U.S.A. is bound to profit markedly from the coordinated efforts of so many people in developing these advanced concepts, it is also clear that without the ARPA network project to act as a catalyst, the coordinated approach would have been difficult, if not impossible, to organize. As the project develops other people will undoubtedly wish to join and it is not easy to see, at this stage, how far-reaching it will eventually become. The ARPA network is considered again in Chapters 10, 11 and 12.

References

1. Freebody J. W., *Telegraphy*, Pitman, London (1958).
2. Barton, R. W., *Telex*, Pitman, London (1958).
3. Jackson, P. E., and Stubbs, C. D., 'A study of multi-access computer communications', *AFIPS Conference Proceedings Spring Joint Computer Conference*, **34**, 491 (1969).
4. Baran, P., 'On distributed communication networks', *IEEE Trans. Communication Systems*, *CS*-**12**, 1-9 (March 1969).
5. Davies, D. W., 'Communication networks to serve rapid response computers', *Proc. IFIP Congress, Invited Papers*, 72 (1968).
6. Silk, D. J., 'Routing doctrines and their implementation in message switching networks', *Proc. Inst. Elect. Engrs.*, **116**, No. 10, 1631 (October 1969).
7. Roberts, L. G., 'Computer network development to achieve resource sharing', *AFIPS Conference Proceedings Spring Joint Computer Conference*, **36**, 543 (1970).
8. Heart, F., 'The interface message processor for the ARPA computer network', *AFIPS Conference Proceedings Spring Joint Computer Conference*, **36**, 551 (1970).

Chapter 9

Data Switching Principles

9.1 INTRODUCTION

A switched data communication network gives each subscriber the possibility of connecting to any other. For reasons of security a group of subscribers (such as a bank and its branch offices) may wish to be functionally separate from the remainder, but they can achieve this separation while forming part of a larger, switched network, if the switching is properly controlled. Even leased lines may be routed through switches if data switching is cheap and reliable. So it is probable that nearly all public data networks, and some private ones, will be switched networks.

Telecommunication switching has been developed intensively for the telephone network, and it is to be expected that many of the principles used in the telephone system will be applied to data switching. An analogue telephone signal is switched by connecting circuits together. Multiplexing is used for the purpose of transmission between switching centres but the circuits are fully demultiplexed at the receiving end so that separate telephone circuits enter the switch.

The telephone switch usually operates at the present time by means of metallic contacts, and in modern systems these switching points are in matrix-like arrays, in crossbar switches or in reed relay arrays[1] that have a similar function.

A new phase of development of telephone switching is now under way and uses the digitally-represented speech information produced by pulse code modulation. The digital speech channel can be handled by techniques of logic and storage, and this opens up new switching possibilities which have potential for compatibility with data.

The PCM channels are time-division multiplexed for transmission, and the new developments in telephone switching are aimed at operating directly on the multiplexed channels. In this way the same kind of economy that comes with TDM transmission can be gained in switching TDM signals. Less switching equipment is needed, but it operates at a higher speed, sharing each path and switch between many speech channels. But the rate usefully employable in switching is limited by store speeds and is lower than the rate which is economic for transmission. Furthermore, there are many different multiplexing schemes such as were described in Chapter 7, and the schemes chosen for transmission are not necessarily those which lend themselves best to switching. At present, the 'primary' PCM groups of 24 or 30 channels are the units employed in time-division switches. In order to switch channels in hundreds or thousands, a combination of time and space division switching is needed. The elementary principles of such switches are described below.

Speech, whether represented in analogue form or digitally, is switched by extending a *circuit* from one subscriber to another. The circuit, in digital terms, is a synchronous channel at 56 kbit/s or 64 kbit/s. Data, on the other hand, can use channels of many different capacities, and usually a lower capacity than speech such as 600 bit/s, 2,400 bit/s and 9,600 bit/s. In consequence a TDM switch for data can carry very many channels using a basic mechanism which would only handle 24 or 30 speech channels.

The switching requirements of data differ from those of speech in the following respects:

1. Widely different data rates must be handled economically.
2. Fast set up and clear down of connections is needed to allow very short calls.
3. A variety of multiplexing arrangements can be used with advantage.
4. Sporadic data (short bursts with silent periods) should be treated economically.
5. Some data can be stored, as in packet switching.
6. Anisochronous channels must also be handled.

Because of the many special features, it is unlikely that data switching will ever be entirely 'compatible' with speech and join with it in a universal switch. The need at the present time is to understand the special requirements of data and the most economical switching methods.

The chapter begins with a simple treatment of space-division switching. At a later stage, this is combined with time-division in a composite form of switch.

9.2 SPACE-DIVISION SWITCHING

The switching of physically separate circuits is called space-division switching. Modern methods employ arrays of switching devices. These devices can be logic gates but more often they are metallic contacts, contained in an array of relays or a crossbar switch.

At the top left of Figure 9.1 a simple 4 × 4 switch of this kind is shown as part of the whole figure. In it the four vertical circuits have access to the four horizontal ones through 16 crosspoints which are shown conventionally by

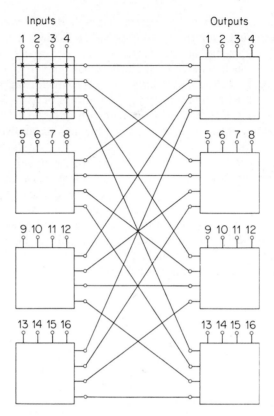

Figure 9.1.   Interconnection of crosspoint
matrices

the crosses. In general, one crosspoint in each row and column can be
operated to connect a circuit through the switch. Such switches have been in
use for a long time, in arrays such as 10×20. The crossbar switch has an
ingenious mechanism to latch the switch contacts mechanically into position
by using magnets associated with each row and column of the array. To save
power, the magnets can be released, leaving the contact mechanically held.
The switch matrix is *non-blocking* in the sense that any free input can reach
any free output, regardless of the other connections that have been made.
The 4×4 switch, for example, can be fully occupied in any one of 4! or 24 ways.

The crossbar mechanism is perhaps the most widely used telephone switch
today, but its control magnets are not ideal for electronic control, so crossbar
switches are giving way in electronically-controlled exchanges to arrays of
reed relays. The 'modular' construction of these arrays allows the size of the
matrix to be varied more, but the principles of switching are unchanged.

Figure 9.1 shows how arrays of 4×4 matrices can be interconnected so that each switch gives access to all the switches in the next column. Consider any of the inputs 1 to 4 on the top left switch. They can be found a link to any switch in the second column, and hence to any outlet. So the combined switch provides *full accessibility* for each input to any output.

But the switch of Figure 9.1 does not have the non-blocking property; in fact it severely restricts the pattern of connections. Suppose for example that input 2 is connected to output 8. Between the corresponding 4×4 switches there is only one connection. So inputs 1, 3, 4 are blocked from outputs 5, 6, 7.

In Figure 9.2 the connection scheme of Figure 9.1 is shown repeated. For convenience the symbol for a switch has been altered to a 'straight through' form and only a skeleton of connections is shown. It can be shown that with this arrangement any one of the 16! fully occupied states of the switch can be achieved so in that sense it is non-blocking. Networks of this general kind can be constructed with the minimum number of crosspoints that are known to give full availability. To specify all $n!$ permutations of n circuits requires $\log_2 (n!)$ bits. For large n this approximates to $n \log_2 (n)$. It is interesting that this is also the number of elementary steps needed to sort n items. In fact, arrays of rather less than $n \log_2 (n)$ switches of the 2×2 size can be constructed which allow all the $n!$ connection patterns to be achieved. So with just $4n$ $\log_2 (n)$ crosspoints an unrestricted switch for n lines can be constructed.[2] It can, incidentally, be constructed instead out of 4×4 switches as in Figure

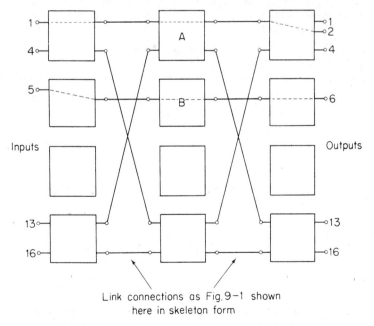

Link connections as Fig. 9-1 shown here in skeleton form

Figure 9.2. Switching network (full availability, by rearrangement)

9.2, with a small saving of crosspoints, but this fact is today of little more than theoretical interest. One reason is that non-blocking is not a firm requirement of most telephone switches; even in the central part of the switch, which is the most heavily used part, a given circuit is in use less than half of the time. A second reason that the full theoretical performance of the switch in Figure 9.2 cannot be used is that the switch may often need to be rearranged to accommodate a new connection. This is expressed by saying that it is a *rearrangable* network or that it exhibits *transient blocking*.[3]

To show this, imagine that the switch is fully used and there are 16 connections filling it. In particular, connections shown in the figure go from input 1 via switch A to output 2 and from input 5 via switch B to output 6. Now try to transpose these connections, requiring the switch to connect input 1 to 6 and input 5 to 2, leaving the rest unchanged. Since these connections nowhere meet in a common switch the change cannot be made without rearranging some existing connections.

There are, of course, even bigger switch arrays that are non-blocking without the need for rearrangement, but there would be a big saving of crosspoints when switching thousands of lines if rearrangement were allowed. Possibly, with electronic control, it may become practical.

Figures 9.1 and 9.2 serve merely to illustrate some general ideas in switching by means of crosspoint arrays. It must also be remembered that in practice the switch has more than one electrical connection to complete for each call. At the very least it has the two wires that make up a telephone connection or the four wire connection in a trunk exchange, while in electro-mechanically-controlled exchanges there will usually be an additional wire for control.

The switching network of a telephone central office (or exchange) employs a complex array of switches, interconnected in several stages rather like Figure 9.2. The trend is away from the 10×20 switches towards smaller units of 4×4 or 8×8, because these smaller switches, although they need more stages of switching to get full accessibility, economize in total cross-points. Figure 2.1 (page 17) showed how the call could be routed from the line through the switch to a 'junctor' or link and back through the switch to the line. This trick doubles the effective number of switching stages. Counting all the switching stages, there and back, the usual number is 6 or 8. A description of a typical network can be found in reference 1.

9.3 SWITCHING OF ANISOCHRONOUS SIGNALS

The methods used for the switching of anisochronous signals depend, to some extent, on the nature of the signals, and their 'meaning'. For example, a network that handles start-stop envelopes in well known formats is able to regenerate these envelopes with correct signal levels and timing whenever their distortion has become excessive. It is also able to extract the binary data from each envelope and to store it in the switch. Such a switch is described later in the chapter. A network could be designed to handle a variety of start-stop formats and speeds if the format and speed was indicated when a call was set up, or could be identified at the start of the call.

But 'anisochronous' can be taken more stringently to mean that a transition from 0 to 1 or vice versa can take place at any time. We shall describe first a switch designed for anisochronous signals of this kind.

The Principle of the Basic EDS Switch

EDS (meaning Electronic Data Switch), developed by Siemens, is a system for switching telegraphic and data circuits which are presented individually to the switch rather than multiplexed. The switch is described here in its earliest and basic form.[4] The EDS system as a whole allows many additional

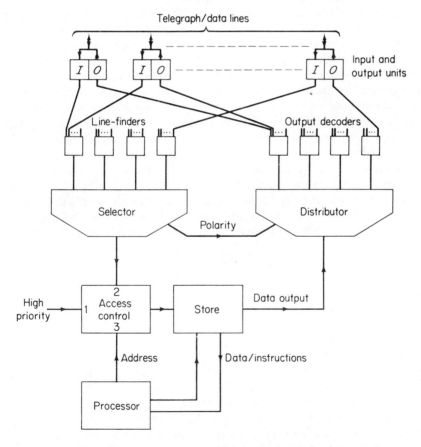

Figure 9.3. Principle of the EDS switch

units to be added for special purposes. The basic switch to be described is for anisochronous signals. To be more precise, the signals have two states, which we can call 0 and 1, and transitions between the states can occur at any time, subject to such restrictions as a minimum interval between transitions. There is no network clock and no easy way to multiplex these signals. Signals in a start-stop format will probably be the most numerous signals in the EDS network, but data signals and facsimile will also be switched. This type of signal is not quantised in the time coordinate, though it has only two signal states. The switch has to be able to transmit each transition as it occurs, with a minimum (or constant) delay. The switch need not concern itself with the way in which the signal represents binary data, telegraph characters or facsimile pictures. It has been called 'transparent' and to make that term more definite it should be called *time-analogue transparent*. Of course it can carry signals which are isochronous from the subscribers' point of view, provided that the subscriber organizes his own clock.

Figure 9.3 shows the principle of the EDS switch. The incoming signal is· applied to an input unit of which one is provided per line. A group of input units is connected to a line finder. When a transition occurs in any incoming signal, the occurrence is stored on a trigger in the input unit and reported to the line finder. The line finder, when any transition is reported, rapidly scans its lines to find the one responsible. It then clears the trigger in the input unit and reports the transition, with its line address, to the selector then it waits for the acknowledgment of the report by the selector.

The selector's function is similar to that of the line finder. It scans rapidly to find a reported transition with its address, acknowledges it and passes the full address (by adding the line finder's identity) to the access control.

Thus a transition may queue at the input unit, in the line finder and in the selector, but will eventually be reported at the centre, with its full line-address. At this point, we have, in effect, an addressed *bit* rather than the addressed *byte* encountered in dynamic multiplexing. The value of the 'bit' is actually the sign of the transition, i.e. $1 \to 0$ or $0 \to 1$ and this passes down the chain where it emerges at the centre on the line marked 'polarity'.

The switch is the store shown near the bottom of the figure. If a transition occurs on line *a* and this line is connected to line *b* the operation is as follows. The selector reports 'line *a*' and this transforms simply into the address for *a* in the store. At this address the value *b* of the output line is found and delivered to the distributor.

Now the operation moves outwards again to the periphery. The distributor reports a transition on *b* to the appropriate output decoder which reports the transition to the output unit. Here, there is a trigger which changes state and thus records the new state of the outgoing line. The polarity could be deduced from the sequence of previous changes, but a single error would cause the output to be negated, so the polarity is carried right through the system, bypassing the store.

Most data and telegraph connections are duplex or half duplex, therefore if transitions go from *a* to *b* they must also go from *b* to *a*. A second entry is made in the store to handle this connection. The whole switch can be regarded as a '4-wire' arrangement in which each direction of a connection is handled separately, and the transition to '2-wire' form is made in the combined 'input/output' unit.

Many of the details of the actual EDS switch have been omitted from Figure 9.3 for clarity. Between the I-O units and the line finders/output decoders there are additional 16-way multiplexers, each connecting to 16 I-O units. The capacity of a line finder or output decoder is 4096 lines. High speed lines which have priority are in a special section of the switch with its own multiplexers, line finders and decoders. These signals reach the store by a different route, but the ordinary distributor is used to drive their decoders. To get good reliability, all equipments except the I-O units are duplicated. Below the selector/distributor level, the duplicate equipments are connectable in any combination so that while there is one servicable store, processor, etc. the system will not degrade.

Contention for the Store

The passage of a transition through the switch has been described. These transitions arrive anisochronously from all the lines and several may arrive together. When this happens, some have to wait for access to the store. They will not be lost (unless the next transition on the same line happened to catch up with them and this would be a gross overloading of the switch).

Figure 9.4 shows the sequence of events when three lines A, B and C

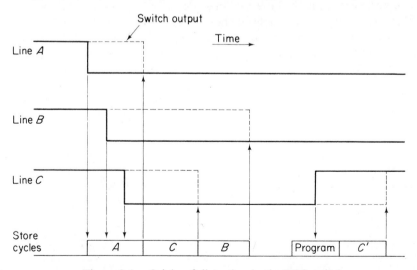

Figure 9.4.   Origin of distortion in the EDS switch

present transitions close together in time. Line A starts off the store cycle marked A, and at the end of it the output transition occurs, which is shown by a broken line following signal A itself. Line B has to wait and the output is considerably delayed. The figure shows two further features of the system. One is the priority which is accorded, in the example, to line C. Certain lines, the faster ones only, reach the store through the access control by a special priority route. There is also a programmed processor which is using the store and this has the lowest access priority, but when a cycle is in operation for the program it must be completed before even high priority channel C can use the store (see C′).

The system works satisfactorily because the store cycle is short enough to ensure that the variable queuing delays are small. The variability introduces distortion into the timing of the signals. The very 'transparency' of the switch which allows it to ignore the significance of the signals makes it also unable to restore any timing errors it has produced. Distortion in the timing of transitions has long been known in telegraphy and is called *telegraph distortion*. In passing through a number of switches in tandem the distortion will increase, and for this reason it must be controlled to a low level at each switch. For data in start-stop form there is a temporary clock implied for each envelope. For example, in 50 baud telegraphy, transitions can occur at no smaller interval than 20 ms. Telegraph distortion can be expressed as a fraction of this unit interval and typically must be held to less than 2% in any switch. But the nature of the queuing problem is that the delay cannot be specified with certainty. Only the probability of not exceeding 2% distortion can be given.

The load on the store can be measured by the number of transitions that occur per second, summed over all lines. For a start-stop signal of 8 bits in a 10 unit envelope, for example, there will on average be $5\frac{1}{2}$ transitions per envelope. The effect of the distortion caused by the load is felt by all lines as a certain variability of output timing, and a time shift affects the high speed lines most. It is for this reason that the priority is given to the highest speed of line.

The magnitude of the effects can best be illustrated by an example, given in Table 9.1. Here a mix of connections is assumed which is strongly weighted

Transmission speed baud	Number of connections made	Percentage of store cycles	Rate of occurrence of 2% distortion
50	4275	13	years
200	375	5	years
2400	275	39	~1 hour
9600	75	43	~10 seconds

Table 9.1

towards slow lines, but the 9600 baud lines contribute 43% of the store cycles, not counting those due to the program. Transitions are assumed to happen at half the baud rate, and they total 800,000 per second. A store with 0·5 microsecond cycle time was assumed, which allows plenty of capacity for the program.

The example shows the importance of the priority given to the 9600 baud lines, which nevertheless have the worst distortion. To achieve this performance depends on having only a small proportion of these high speed lines. An increase in the load on the store would have a considerable effect on the distortion. For this reason the principle used in this switch will, in practice, be supplemented by space division switching at the higher speeds.

The Significance of the Basic EDS Switch

The interest in this switching principle lies in the way in which it uses a single store to replace all the complexity of space-division switching, yet achieves almost the same result. The distortion problem is caused by the uncorrelated nature of the incoming demands, and will not apply in synchronous networks.

We have not yet described the setting up of a call. When a call is first made, the store address is found to contain a marker which signifies that the called line has been idle. The transitions which represent dialling are reported to the processor which assembles the number, then tests the called line and, if the connection can be made, puts the appropriate line addresses into the two relevant cells of the store. In this way the processor controls the state of the 'switching matrix' simply by having access to the common store.

The weakness of the system lies in its basic principle of handling each line without reference to the form of the signal. The way in which the distortions add through a network of basic EDS switches is foreign to the whole scheme of digital data handling. In fact, the switching principle provides a channel which retains its analogue character in the time dimension and is hardly a digital channel in the true sense.

In the realm of telegraphy and start-stop data switching at low speeds the distortion probability is low and the basic EDS switch becomes highly economic, especially where the number of lines to be switched is large.

Digital Encoding of Anisochronous Signals

Anisochronous signals like those handled by EDS are subject to telegraph distortion which can accumulate not only in switching but also in transmission. In a Telex (switched telegraph) network which has a standard speed and start-stop format it is possible to fit regenerators at strategic points, such as tandem switches, to restore the timing. The proliferation of speeds and formats introduced by early data equipment will probably prevent such regeneration in the network. Certainly the EDS principle of 'time-analogue transparency' forbids regeneration.

Although synchronous transmission, allied to time-division multiplexing and switching, is likely to be the method used in newer equipments and systems, including public data networks, there will still be some start-stop and other transmissions which will be treated as essentially anisochronous. This will probably apply to data and telegraph messages carried at 200 bit/s, or less. To accommodate these signals in a modern, synchronous network they must be encoded as a stream of bits. Telegraph distortion will not affect the bit stream, but the encoding and decoding adds an extra source of distortion that must be minimized.

The simplest method, which has been called '*bulk redundancy*', uses the binary values, 0 and 1, to encode the anisochronous signal's level, by sampling at the bit rate. Clearly a signal element of the anisochronous channel must be encoded as a rather long string of ones or zeros if distortion due to the time-quantisation is to be kept small, hence there is considerable redundancy. The method is illustrated in Figure 9.5.

In order to guarantee less than a certain level of distortion the number of bits per minimum signal element (i.e. the interval between transitions) must be kept above a certain minimum number. Some of the redundant bits can then be better employed by encoding the time of the transition more accurately. Figure 9.6 illustrates this for the case where the bit interval is divided into 4, and two bits are used to encode the time of each transition.

Whenever a transition occurs, the next bit in the encoded sequence records the new signal level (as in bulk redundancy). The two bits which follow contain the more precise timing. In all, three bits are thus given over to specifying a transition and any bits that remain before the next transition simply continue to indicate the signal level. Since the time quantum is 1/4 of the bit interval and the minimum signal element is three bits long, the maximum distortion is 1/12 of the signal element. Instead of 2 bit encoding, one could use 1 bit or 3 bits, for example. Transition encoding with 3 bits gives a maximum distortion of 1/32.

There could be transmission difficulties in the long strings of 1s and 0s

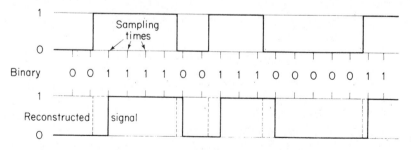

Figure 9.5. Encoding by bulk redundancy

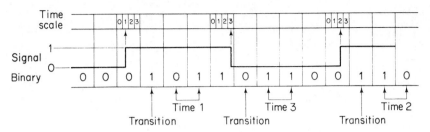

Figure 9.6.   Transition encoding with 2-bit time field

which this method of coding produces. In the form in which it was proposed by the Japan Telephone and Telegraph Public Corporation it used sequences 1010 ... and 0101 ... to represent 0 and 1. This is practical if there is a fixed reference point for odd and even pulses, as there would be in PCM transmission equipment with its eight-bit samples. But a network designed for unrestricted data should be able to accept the strings of repeated symbols with no trouble.

Start-stop Signals Switched by Byte Storage

In the basic EDS switch each signal change at the periphery was reported to the centre, in due course, by two items of information: the polarity of the change and its address of origin. This is similar to the 'addressed byte' which was described in Chapter 7, page 261, under the general heading of dynamic multiplexing. It would normally be thought that a single bit was too small a unit of information to merit incorporation with an address, but the basic EDS switch does this for a special purpose. It is not primarily concerned with multiplexing but with transmitting a signal change very quickly.

If the same general method is now extended to the switching of addressed bytes, the use of the central store is much better because each store cycle now transfers a whole byte instead of just one transition of the start-stop signal. Such a method has been used in a number of designs of Telex switch. Figure 9.7 shows the principle. At their entry to the switch the start-stop envelopes are received and converted to 8-bit parallel form, in which form the data are carried through the switch. At the exit, the parallel bytes are converted back to the serial start-stop form. In contrast with the basic EDS switch, the speed and envelope format of each line must be known, though it need not be the same for each line if a suitable range of 'receivers' and 'transmitters' is available. The receivers and transmitters of a given line, shown at opposite ends of the figure, actually can be mounted together to serve the line and may use common equipment, particularly if the line is used half duplex.

At the input end a dynamic multiplexer is used. It can be built in several stages of multiplexing, each unit of which stores a byte and its partially-

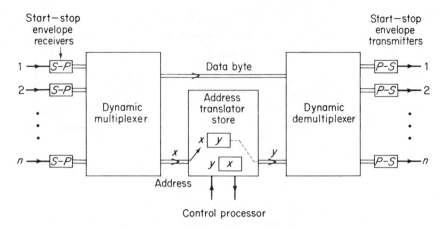

Figure 9.7. Switching of start-stop signals by byte storage

formed address until the byte has been received and acknowledged by a 'handshake' from the next higher multiplexer. This process produces addressed bytes in a controlled manner on a single channel at the centre.

Now suppose that lines x and y are connected together. The central *address translator* has merely to convert address x, when it arrives, to the value y and vice versa. This is done by using a conventional store and storing value y at address x and value x at address y. In the example shown in the figure a byte has arrived at the centre from line x. The data byte passes straight through to the demultiplexer but the address x is used to extract from the store the contents of cell x and the 'translated' address y is passed to the demultiplexer, so the byte is delivered to the transmitter on line y. There is no need here for flow control in the demultiplexer, which we encountered in the NPL network (on page 263) because the outgoing line has presumably been selected to have the same bit rate as the incoming one that feeds it. The switch introduces little delay and delivers each byte as it arrives, acting like a circuit switch.

The most important difference from the basic EDS switch is that this switch is completely unaffected by the variability of delay due to contention for the store. There is no telegraph distortion, and the transmitted bytes are sent out regenerated. The receiver/transmitter pair is of course more complex than the I-O unit of the EDS switch but the progressive reduction of the cost of logic will reduce the importance of this factor. The method of setting up calls is similar to EDS, and is achieved by giving the control processor access to the translator store, where it picks up the selection (i.e. dialling) sequence, tests the destination address for a free line and completes the connecting by placing the values x and y in the pair of addresses concerned with the call. The data handling capacity is potentially at least eight times that of a basic EDS switch with a similar store. The byte-handling switch could carry, with one store, more than 1000 simultaneous calls at the 10,000 bit/s rate which is the upper limit of the form of EDS switch we described.

Supposing that a network was built with dynamically multiplexed trunk circuits carrying addressed bytes, then these could be brought into the multiplexer of the switch at the appropriate point, and the addressed byte output taken from a corresponding place in the demultiplexer. The byte switch has all the advantage of dynamic multiplexing: it need be built with only the capacity of the data traffic. It does not have to provide for the total channel capacity of the lines, which is typically much higher.

9.4 SWITCHING IN A SYNCHRONOUS NETWORK

In a synchronous network, time-division multiplexing is used to carry many circuits on one physical channel. The method used to obtain synchronism of the whole network to a common clock was described in Chapter 7. When the multiplexed channels arrive at a switch, their frames must also be made to coincide, which can be done by using an elastic buffer with a maximum capacity of a least one frame. The entire scheme of network synchronism is complex, but it can be justified by the economy of TDM transmission and the relative simplicity of time-division switching.

In the general case, many TDM channels arrive at the switch, requiring a combination of time and space-division switching. In the first place, let us treat time-division alone, so that its principles can be seen more clearly. Used for data, a switch of the purely time-division kind can be quite powerful, and there might be a case for time-multiplexing all the channels into a switch so that time-division switching alone could be used.

Time-division Switching of one Multiplexed Channel

Figure 9.8 shows the principle of a switch which is based on time-division alone, and employs an addressable store to hold data which is 'in transit' between one time slot and another. The multiplexed input and output channels are assumed to be byte interleaved.

As each byte of the input stream is received, it is converted to parallel form ready for storage in the data store. At the same time, the channel counter produces x, the number of its channel. With x as its address (or a number derived from x by addition) the byte is stored in cell x of the data store. We call the stored byte $B(x)$ to show its origin.

The channel value x is also applied to the address translator, where it selects the address y, which determines the input channel from which output x derives its data. So address y is used in the data store to extract $B(y)$, the data byte stored there earlier from input channel y. Similarly, $B(x)$ will later be extracted when channel time y comes around and x, taken from the cell y of the address store, is used to address the data store. At the output, the data

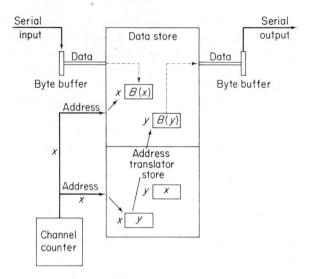

Figure 9.8.   Switching of single TDM channel

byte is reconverted to serial form, and the bytes are correctly interleaved again.

There are several important differences here from the asynchronous, dynamically multiplexed switch of Figure 9.7. A byte comes in with one channel and cannot be put out until the right channel number comes up in the frame cycle, so it must be stored. Since each channel is represented by a time-slot in the frame, whether the channel is in use or not, the time must be provided, and also the space in the data and address stores. The size of switch is chosen for the channel capacity rather than the actual data carried. Suppose now that the bytes are accompanied by a qualifier bit which distinguishes between data and control signals. Even if the control signals do not pass through the switch, the qualifier bit should, because it indicates whether the byte slot is being used at the time and distinguishes actual data (which could be all zeros) from the idle byte used when no data were carried. So the store will be nine bits wide.

Each channel slot in the TDM frame is the occasion for three store cycles, two in the data store and one in the address store. These two stores can be separate or combined in one store, where all three cycles occur in succession. The coming of semiconductor stores which are economic in small sizes makes separate stores the probable choice. The control processor must be able to access both stores. From the data store it receives control signals, including the selection data from the subscriber. It puts control signals back into this store for onward transmission. From the address translation store it can determine whether a line is free and must place the pointers x and y which constitute the state of the switch connections. Since the address store has spare

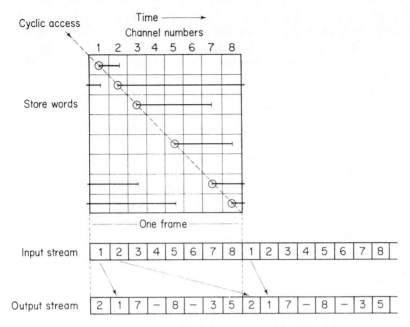

Figure 9.9.   Use of the data store in Fig. 9.8.

capacity it can be used also for other switch control purposes even though the data store may be fully employed.

Let us look more carefully at the operation of the data store, and for this purpose assume that only eight channels are being multiplexed. Figure 9.9 is drawn with connections made between 3 line-pairs:

$$1\text{-}2, \qquad 3\text{-}7, \qquad \text{and} \qquad 5\text{-}8$$

At the top of the figure the use made of the eight words of the store is shown. Input to the store is controlled by the direct line from the channel counter, so word x receives data at time x in the frame. Input to the store is thus said to be *cyclic*. On the other hand, it is the *acyclic* nature of the output from the store which gives it the switching property. At the bottom of the figure two frames are shown as they appear on the input and output lines, with each square representing a byte of data. The numbering shows how the data are transposed in the output. Since this is done by delay, in half of the cases data bytes move into the following frame. The arrows show how this works for the duplex connection 1-2.

In this data store, the read and write cycles must take place alternately In each channel slot, a cyclic *write* and an acyclic *read* takes place. (A cyclic *read* and an acyclic *write* would be just as effective.) Looking at the connection 1-2, or at any other single connection, one can see that when one word of the pair is in use, the other is empty, so an economy would be possible by using a single word for both purposes. There are two ways to do this.

The first method is to employ data stores only for the connections actually made, not for each line served by the switch. This uses at most only half the number of words. When a connection from x to y is set up, a free data store z must be found and allocated. Then in the address translator store both words x and y contain the pointer to z. At each channel time-slot the channel counter accesses the address translator and twice in the frame, at times x and y the address z is found. Using address z, the data store is read and the contents sent to the line and then the incoming data is stored in word z. This has the same effect as Figure 9.8, but only one address selection is needed in the data store for both the read and the write, which would perhaps make it faster in operation than with two full store cycles. But the control processor has been given the extra task of allocating a free z value to each new connection, which adds to the per-call overheads.

The second method depends on restricting the kinds of connection which the time switch can make (so that it no longer provides full access) while restoring the full access feature elsewhere in the total switching system. In the time-division switch there are two kinds of lines, equal in number. One of them writes into the store and reads from it at an address determined only by the time that its channel slot comes up, that is *cyclicly*. The other kind of line reads and writes by reference to the address translator store, that is *acyclicly*. Call the two classes of line 'cyclic' and 'acyclic' respectively. Then it is always possible to connect a cyclic line to an acyclic one, with both directions of transmission handled by the same storage word. The word in question is permanently associated with the cyclic line, while the acyclic line makes the address adjustment which constitutes the switching action. The space-division part of the switch is used to allow the incoming lines to appear at the time-division switch in either a cyclic or acyclic guise, so the apparent restriction of connections is removed.

Suppose that a store can carry out its read/write operation in $\frac{1}{2}$ microsecond, then its capacity, when all its connection potential is used, is 16 Mbit/s because it handles eight-bit words of data. This would enable about eight groups of 2·048 Mbit/s (30 channel) PCM to be switched, which is 240 telephone channels. Used for 9,600 bit/s data channels, it could handle about 1600 of them, or corresponding numbers of slower channels, provided that they are all time-division multiplexed by byte interleaving.

A Group of Time-division Multiplexed Channels

A purely time-division switch is limited to a few hundred PCM telephone lines per store, at the store speeds which are easily obtained with today's technology. No doubt there will be improvements in store technology, but there will still be a need, at least for telephone switches, to combine space and time-division switching. The way this can be done is suggested by the switching network of Figure 9.2 (page 313). It will be recalled that this switch gave full access to each line and was non-blocking if the existing calls could be rearranged to accommodate any new one. By adding extra switch units to the middle column, and using *rectangular* switching matrices elsewhere to give full access to the extra units, the arrangement can be made non-blocking without rearrangement. These properties of switching networks will not be explained further because they form part of an extensive theory, developed for telephone networks, which would take us too far from our main subject. The switching network of Figure 9.2 can be drawn in a way which clarifies the pattern of linking between the three stages, and this is sketched in Figure 9.10 using, for simplicity, the same 4 × 4 scheme as in Figure 9.1. But remember that here we are switching the 8-bit bytes in parallel form, so each line of the figure represents eight lines or, if a qualifier bit is included, nine lines. In part (a) of the figure there is shown the three-stage array redrawn in a three dimensional form. It can easily be verified that this diagram is not different from Figure 9.2 but the links between the three stages of switching are easier to understand. The dimensions of the separate switches, and the numbers of

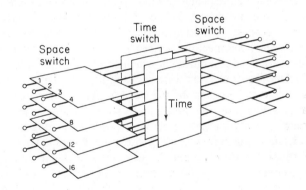

(a) Space—time view of the switch

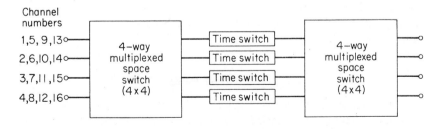

(b) Physical form of the switch

Figure 9.10. A space-time-space switching network

them in each stage, can be varied to suit the switching requirements, and they need not all be 'square' arrays.

Now let us look again at part (a) as a figure in space and time, with time in the vertical direction. Then the four space-switches at each end are actually the *same* switch used four times over during the TDM frame. Each time it is used, the connection pattern will be different, so that it takes on, in turn, the role of all four space-switches shown in the figure. The middle section consists of four separate time switches, which permute the bytes between the four time slots in the TDM frame. The physical arrangement is shown in part (b) of the figure which is actually just a plan view ignoring the time dimension. Each of the lines in part (b) of the figure represents eight or nine lines each carrying four channels by means of synchronous TDM.

Now consider the control of such a space-time-space switch. When one of the space switches is set up to carry a full complement of connections, at each time slot, four of the 'crosspoints' are connected, to connect four input channels to their corresponding outputs. For each line, two bits are needed to specify the connection, making eight in all. At each time slot a different connection pattern is specified, making four sets of eight bits in total. The connection pattern repeats in each frame, assuming that no call has disconnected in the meantime. To control the crosspoints (each of which has eight or nine gates, to switch a parallel byte) a store is needed which extracts the eight-bit connection pattern in synchronism with the channel counter. Referring now to Figure 9.8 which shows the time switch, it can be seen that the 'address translator store' of each time switch is accessed in just such a cyclic manner. By extending the word size of this store, all the information needed to switch the time-multiplexed space switches can be obtained, thus economizing in store access circuits. A word of warning is needed when trying to understand the more complex switching networks of actual telephone offices. The space division data may be stored in one of the time switches, to economize in equipment, but the relationship of the space switches to those time switches that store their data can be quite arbitrary. In principle, they are separate mechanisms.

The switch just described was a space-time-space array. Equally well a time-space-time or even a space-time-space-time-space array could be designed. Today's economics seem to favour the space-time-space arrangement.

Mixed Data Rates

Time-division switches have been described in the two preceding sections and these switches have handled channels which all had the same data rate. This is more appropriate to the switching of PCM speech than to data, where different speeds must be handled. The choice of speeds could, for example, be 600, 2,400, 9,600 and 48,000 bits, and it would be possible to provide four

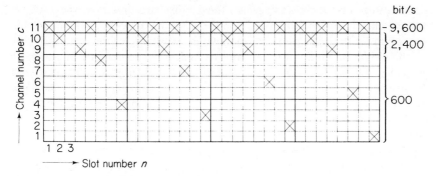

Figure 9.11.   Interleaving of bytes for 3 data rates in a 19,200 bit/s channel

switches, one for each speed, because lines of different speeds cannot be usefully connected in a circuit switch. Nevertheless, channels of different speeds are multiplexed for transmission, and there would be a saving of cost if one switch could cope with the whole set of speeds.

By way of example, Figure 9.11 shows 11 channels time-multiplexed together. There are eight channels of 600 bit/s, 2 of 2,400 bit/s and one of 9,600 bit/s in the example. The whole lot is carried by a channel of 19,200 bit/s. The diagram shows the interleaving of *bytes*, and the whole frame occupies 1/75 second, since the lowest speed is 75 byte/s.

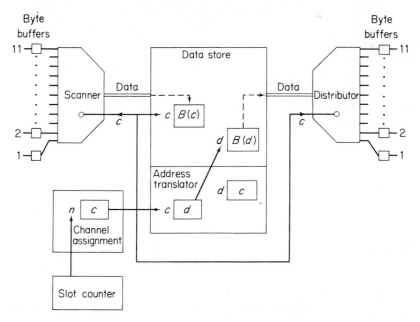

Figure 9.12.   Time-division switch for mixed rates

Consider first the case in which the 11 lines are presented separately to the switch, without multiplexing. Figure 9.12 shows how they can be switched by means of a single time-division switch, working on the same principle as the switch of Figure 9.8. In order to multiplex the channels a scanner is provided which does not scan regularly but according to the pattern of Figure 9.11. To provide some flexibility in re-aligning channels when new subscribers are connected or old ones leave or change their data rate, the multiplexing pattern comes from a table in a store (named 'channel assignment') which gives c, the channel or line number, as a function of n, the time slot number. The table is a representation of the functional relationship shown in Figure 9.11. The channel number is used for selection in the scanner, and in the distributor at the output which distributes the TDM channel to the 11 separate lines. The scanner and distributor and the data store operate on complete bytes, with the qualifier bit added if necessary. Each channel has a byte buffer at input and output.

The channel number c is used to control the cyclic writing into the data store. The acyclic reading is at store position d, which is derived from c using the address translation. In this way the connection pattern $c-d$ of the channels is determined. The data store contains only as many storage locations as there are channels.

An alternative would have been to treat the switch as a switch of time slots, and represent the connection $c-d$ separately in each time slot in which it occurs. This would work, but the signal delay through the switch could be almost a whole frame, much more than is necessary or desirable in the case of high speed channels. The data store and address translator would be larger to allow entries for each time slot. So the method shown is better in every respect.

Multiplexed Channels with Mixed Data Rates

The example used in Figures 9.11 and 9.12 is, of course, unrealistic because the number of channels shown is very small. When a data switch handles large numbers of subscribers it may still be possible to employ a single time-division switch, but it is unlikely that the channels will all arrive individually. They will usually be time-division multiplexed. In Chapter 7 a multiplexing scheme was described which was designed for this situation. It delivered its data streams at 60 kbit/s to the data switch, a rate which allows one 48 kbit/s, $5 \times 9{,}600$ bit/s, $20 \times 2{,}400$ bit/s or 80×600 bit/s streams to be carried, and each 60 kbit/s stream carried only one of these data rates. Furthermore the unit of data which was interleaved was the ten-bit envelope containing the eight-bit byte of data. These multiplexing arrangements were made specifically to ease the design of the switch.

Figure 9.12 can serve as a picture of the switch, with only small modifications. The scanner now multiplexes groups of 60 kbit/s, interleaving envelopes.

Each incoming line is provided with a double buffer for one envelope, to enable the envelope to be taken by the scanner as a single unit of data. The scanner must operate cyclicly, so it is driven by the slot counter. At the output end, the distributor runs in synchronism with the scanner, and double byte buffers synchronize the outputs. With these arrangements, the data stream on which the switch operates is similar to the one described in Figure 9.11, and the switch itself can be like the one shown in Figure 9.12.

A single time-division switch could handle, perhaps, 2·4 Mbyte/s, which corresponds to 400 lines of the 60 kbit/s (or 6 kbyte/s) variety. Judged by the levels of data traffic now experienced or predicted the switch has a good capacity. Evidently, many data switching exchanges could be based on a single data store. Improvements in store technology should allow for future increases in data traffic.

The arrangement shown in Figure 9.12 can be compared with the space-time-space switch. The scanner and distributor are the space-division switches, but take a simplified form because their connection pattern is not a part of the switching function and it does not change as new connections are made. If extra time-division switches must be added, the more general form of switch in Figure 9.10 is used. In effect, this can be achieved by replicating the equipment of Figure 9.12 and giving all the scanners and distributors access to all the byte buffers. In any one time slot a byte buffer communicates with only one scanner or distributor, so the arrangement of scanners behaves like a time-multiplexed crossbar switch (and the distributors likewise). In practice it is a very 'rectangular' switch because not many scanner/distributors will be needed.

Comparing this with the space-time-space division switch of Figure 9.10, the main difference is that it handles a set of mixed data rates. A longer frame is used so that the low rate channels can be carried. Correspondingly, each switch carries more channels. The amount of control data is greater, and so is the data store. There is an additional constraint for the switching of the higher speed channels which is that each slot which they occupy in the frame must be carried by the same space path and use the same storage word in the data store, to reduce delay. Fortunately data circuit switches of this complex variety will not be required for a long while.

9.5   BLOCKS LARGER THAN THE BYTE

The idea of packet switching was introduced in Chapter 8. Time-division switching can employ mechanisms which store just one bit or signal transition, as in EDS, or one byte as in the switches we have described above. Packet switching goes further and requires the switch to store a block of many bytes before it sends the block forward. The basic motivation for packet switching has been described. In the chapters which follow there will be more details of the operation of a packet switching network. Here, we are concerned only with the handling of blocks of data in the switch.

It would be possible to handle the data entirely under program control with very little special hardware, but this would greatly reduce the packet handling capability of the switch because the store would be used for many other things than access to data. As with circuit switching, it is better to devote a store (or several stores) to the handling of the data. This is how the process is described below, but where data rate is not paramount the store would be shared with the control computer.

Figure 9.13 shows the input part of the process. It assumes that several data input lines are to be served and that each one carries several data channels, time-division multiplexed. If the multiplexing is byte interleaved, a double byte buffer on each line allows all channels to be byte interleaved by the scanner on an eight or nine bit path. Thus far, the system is the one proposed for circuit switching. Inside the main part of the switch, things are different. The input to this equipment consists of the channel identifier A together with the byte of data B(A) associated with that channel.

The storage of a block of data can be controlled by two stored words. One, labelled CW(A), is the address of the current word for storing B(A). The other, labelled LW(A), is the address of the last word of the packet buffer. These two pointers and the corresponding packet area are shown in the figure. After B(A) has been stored at address CW, the values of CW and LW are compared. If they are equal an interrupt tells the control processor that the packet store is full. If not, CW is incremented by 1.

Output is not shown in the figure but is exactly analogous. At any one time, the packet switch may be engaged in input and output for several different packets, and the next input byte will probably go to a different packet. A given packet store is being used either for input or output or is spare. After packet input, the control processor will set up the CW and LW words to initiate output, and after output the packet will remain in the store a little while until its correct receipt is assured, then the space will be used again.

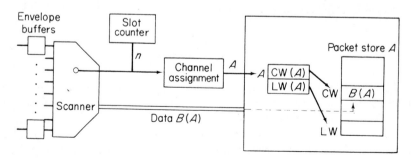

Figure 9.13.   Packet input, showing one channel only

In Figure 9.13 the input lines carry channels which are time-division multiplexed in a fixed frame and byte interleaved. This is the multiplexing method which is also most suitable for circuit switching. One version of it, described in Chapter 7, was the scheme studied by the U.K. Post Office which presents 60 kbit/s streams to the switch.

A channel carrying dynamically multiplexed bytes has each byte accompanied by the address of the sub-channel it represents. This method of multiplexing is also very suitable for use in the switch, because the items A and B(A) which the switch employs are simply the address and the byte. The synchronous property, or the absence of it, is immaterial to the packet switch.

A packet switch will usually handle data channels of two kinds. The first of these is typified by the simple terminal which sends and receives a string of bytes and the second is typified by the links to other switches of the network. A large number of simple terminals are multiplexed on one line into the switch, as in the figure, but links of the network itself carry complete packets, that is, they are *packet interleaved*. This particular distinction is lost when the data reach the store, because all the channels must share the use of the store. Therefore, each byte that is stored will usually go into a different packet from that of its predecessor, and similarly for output. In other respects, however, the treatment of the simple terminals and network links is different. These are matters for the later chapters.

Combination of Circuit and Packet Switching

A comparison of Figure 9.12 and 9.13 shows that circuit switching and packet switching have a lot in common (the difference in the way that the scanner is controlled in the figures is due merely to a different scheme of multiplexing). In each case, the given address is translated by a store reference, then the new address is used to access the stored data. The equipment outside the store would be identical, assuming that the input channels were made up in the same way. This is of some practical importance because the local network is an expensive part of the whole communication system, and it seems that this part can be shared between circuit and packet switching. It would be possible for a subscriber to chose either service on a single connection.

The main difference in the two switching principles lies in the allocation of space in the data store. For the circuit switch, each of the channels entering the switch has a single word of store associated with it. The store may perhaps be wastefully used, but there is no problem of allocation. For the packet switch, each packet must be granted an allocation of store before it starts to arrive and, after the packet has left and correct receipt has been assured, the store allocation must be returned to the pool. The size of the storage area needed depends on the amount of activity, and cannot easily be compared with the circuit case. It will generally be small in a transit switch (one which does not handle subscribers' lines) and large in a local switch (one which has many active subscribers).

It is quite possible to use one store for both kinds of switching, and this would be very advantageous if the choice between the two switching methods is likely to alter as data users gain experience. The 'address translator' store has a fixed allocation of space for each subscriber's channel, and it could contain, also, the pointers CW and LW used in packet switching. For the data store proper, there would be a region given over to the fixed addresses used for circuit switching and an additional region for dynamic allocation to packets.

Now consider the control signals that are used in the circuit switching function, and in particular the selection data from subscribers and the route signalling that passes between successive switches. These data must be assembled into messages of several bytes before the switch can act upon them or pass them on to the next switch, and this is a packet switching function. A combined switching system can handle these control packets using the same hardware and much of the software provided for handling subscribers' packets.

Allocation of Storage to Packets

The allocation of storage to packets and the retrieval of that storage into the pool is a familiar problem in computer software. The use of a *free list* is well known, but will be described here for completeness since it is an essential part of the way that packets are handled in switching centres.

Store allocation is greatly simplified if all packets are given the same amount of space. It is true that ready-formatted packets in transit can have their size specified in the heading, but these do not take up much space. The packet stores being used for input from terminals and output to terminals are the most numerous. When a packet is being assembled at input its size is unknown so the space of the maximum packet must be allocated. Store allocation schemes for blocks of several sizes have been devised, but the extra processing time has not been worthwhile. We therefore assume, in what follows, a constant store size for all packets. The packets themselves can vary in size and will not always use all the space allocated to them.

The store region that is to be used for packets is already divided up into

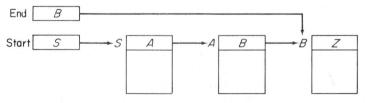

Figure 9.14.   A list of free packet stores (store envelopes)

packet-sized areas ready for allocation. Each of the packet areas has space for the packet and in addition some space for additional data needed in handling the packet. The whole thing could be called a 'store envelope' since it has a 'heading' as well as the space for a packet to rest. The store heading is additional to the packet's own heading. In the simplest case the heading is just one computer word. Several envelopes of this kind are shown in Figure 9.14.

When store envelopes are not in use they are held in a 'pool' ready for allocation. This is organized in the structure shown in the figure, which is called the *free list*, and is a list of free spaces. A fixed location contains the starting address, S, and at address S the first store envelope begins. In the first word the address of the next envelope is held and so on. Thus each envelope contains in its first word a *pointer* to the next envelope in the list. The final envelope, in this case labelled B, can contain a special heading which indicates that it is the last envelope. At the same time, there can be provided centrally an *end* pointer giving the address (B) of the last envelope, though this feature is not always needed.

The figure is misleading in one respect because it gives the impression that the members of the list are linked together in the sequence that they occupy in the store. Even if this were true at the start, after many envelopes have been allocated for use by packets and returned to the list, their linkage connections would go quite randomly over all the envelopes in the store. The normal condition has free envelopes linked in an arbitrary sequence.

Figure 9.15 shows a packet store being used to store a packet from channel X. The packet store must be traceable from X, in order that the packet can be found again for output. Word X is therefore made to point to word B which is the starting address of the store. In the following words, X + 1 and X + 2, the pointers CW and LW can be stored, so that successive inputs go to CW and its successors, stopping if LW is reached in the usual way. In practice, the store location shown as X will be *derived* from the channel number X not identical with it. As an additional refinement, the heading of the store envelope is used to point to X, the channel which at present 'owns' it. This will be useful if something goes wrong, for example if the channel

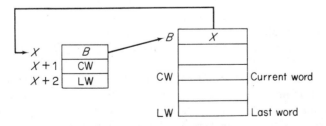

Figure 9.15. A packet store labelled B and used on channel X

information has been corrupted. A scan through all the store envelopes will shown which ones are in use, and where they are being used.

When 'envelope B' has been loaded with the packet it must be reallocated, to a different channel, for output. The packet remains stored in the same place, only the word X and the pair of pointers between X and B need be changed.

To see how the allocation of a store envelope is made, we must go back to Figure 9.14. The easiest store envelope to get is at S, the first one, so let us allocate that one. When it is removed from the free list, the START pointer should point to A. This is all that is strictly necessary to remove envelope S from the list, but there may be a need for a count to be kept of the quantity of remaining free envelopes, since this information is otherwise obtainable only by scanning the whole list.

To return a packet labelled Y to the list, it is easiest to insert it at the start and to do this START is given the value Y and the heading of Y is given the value S that START formerly held. The counter, if there is one, is increased by 1.

There may be a reason for returning envelopes to the end of the list. It might be desired to circulate the use of the envelopes and not favour those at the start. In that case, to return envelope Y the value Y is given to END and the heading of envelope B is made to point to Y, while the heading of Y is made to be Z, the 'end of list' marker.

Simple subroutines will carry out these standard operations on the pointers. If all goes well, no envelopes will ever be lost. They will either be in use or on the free list. In practice there could be an error such as a fault causing the process of allocating an envelope to be halted in mid-stream. Such errors could put certain envelopes or strings of envelopes out of use. To guard against this the envelopes should be examined one by one as a background task to see if any are in an abnormal state. Probably the best action to take is to record the abnormality for later analysis and return the envelope to the free list.

The Queueing of Packets

When packets are handled at switching centres it may be necessary to place them on queues, for example to await a free link to another centre. In general these queues should be rather short but a mechanism must be set up for handling queues of any length. There will usually be a queue for each outgoing link.

Figure 9.14 can be taken to be a picture of a queue organization, using the same structure as the free store. We have described how a store envelope can be taken from the start of the list and returned to the end of the list. If envelopes containing packets are linked together with the kind of list shown in the figure they can be operated as a queue. A packet is added to the queue, let us say, at the end, using the END pointer. The routine which *services* the queue operates on the first packet, indicated by the START pointer.

In the design of such a queue mechanism, there are two things needing careful attention. Firstly it must be possible to represent an empty queue, for example by storing a special indicator in the pointers. Secondly, the queue mechanism must not be allowed to slow down the servicing of a packet when it is added to the empty queue. For this purpose, the head of the queue can be made into the 'service position'. Suppose, for example, that the queue contains packets waiting for output, then the output will take place directly from the store envelope designated in START. In this way it becomes a simple matter to attach a packet to the empty queue and begin the output process. Under light traffic conditions this will be the most frequent use of the queue.

The queue for output on a network link needs a further requirement, because after a packet has been sent it has to be kept until there is some assurance of correct receipt. To deal with this, three pointers to the queue can be held, one for the *tail* at which they are attached, one for the point at which *output* occurs and one for the true *head* of the queue where the packet will be discarded.

There is a different method of organizing an output queue, which is shown in Figure 9.16 and is sometimes found to be more efficient. The packets in the queue in the figure are labelled A, B, C ... H and are referenced by the words held in the *circular buffer*. The head, output and tail positions of the queue are indicated by three pointers to certain items in the buffer.

To add a new packet to the queue, the tail pointer is incremented by 1 and the new value (6) indicates the word of the circular buffer in which the pointer

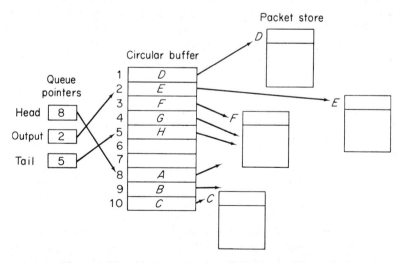

Figure 9.16.   Output queue employing a circular buffer

to the packet must be put. To discard a packet the head pointer is referred to. In the figure it points to word 8 which contains A. The store envelope at A is returned to the free list, after which the head pointer is incremented by 1. These operations are rather simpler than processing the queue as a list. The size of the queue is easily calculated from the queue pointers. The buffer is referred to as 'circular' because word 1 is regarded as following after the last word (word 10). Incrementing a value 10 in any of the queue pointers produces the value 1. A queue organized by a circular buffer has a finite size, which may be a difficulty, but it can also be useful. Little space is wasted because the packet store uses only the space necessary for the actual size of queue. The available store envelopes are dynamically allocated to the various queues.

These two forms of queue illustrate the fact that a data structure and its representation in a computer store are two different things. The good software designer choses a representation that is not only correct in its structure, but also efficient to use.

The Match between Multiplexing and Switching

Figures 9.8, 9.12 and 9.13 show time-division switching schemes employing the storage of bytes or packets. The switch is very simple in each case and has a capacity of several megabytes per second. To make a reliable system more than one switch would be needed and an element of space-division would be added to give the lines access to several switches.

The three figures each deal with a different multiplexing scheme in their input/output channels. Figure 9.8 has one TDM channel containing a number of constituent channels which are byte interleaved and all have the same rate. Figure 9.12 has a number of separate, unmultiplexed channels of different rates. In Figure 9.13 data channels of various rates have been byte multiplexed, outside the switch, into a number of streams which are presented to the switch, synchronized, and at the same total rates.

A common feature of all three methods is that the central part of the switch, the part between the scanner and the distributor, receives and sends out information as bytes (or envelopes) of data with associated channel addresses. If convenience of switching was the main consideration, we would therefore favour a multiplexing method which used an 'addressed byte' or 'addressed packet', in other words a dynamic multiplexing method. The addressed byte seems best adapted to a local area, where transmission economy is less significant and the address overhead can be tolerated. The addressed packet is better adapted to long distance traffic.

The real importance of these schemes of multiplexing and switching is the difference they make in the service offered to the network user. Dynamic multiplexing is well adapted to variable data rates and the sporadic transmission of data. It uses transmission and switching resources in proportion to the data actually sent, not the peak channel capacity requirement. Packet switching allows convenient blocks of data to be interleaved and presented to a computer at the rate which best suits it.

The switching methods for time-divided channels which have been described in this chapter can be matched to fixed-cycle TDM, dynamically multiplexed bytes or packets. What we have described above are the data switches. The control of these switches—the setting up and clearing down of connections and the handling of packets through a network—has not been described. In the following chapters the control aspects of the packet switched network are described because this is the less familiar kind of network and it is specifically designed for data communication with computers.

References

1. Feiner, A., and Hayward, W. S., 'No. 1 ESS switching network plan', *Bell Syst. Tech. J.*, **43**, 2193 (Sept. 1964).
2. Clos, C., 'A study of non-blocking switching networks', *Bell Syst. Tech. J.*, **32**, 406 (1953).
3. Goldstein, L. J., and Leibholz, S. W., 'On the synthesis of signal switching networks with transient blocking', *IEEE Trans. Electronic Computers EC*-**16**, No. 5, 637 (Oct. 1967).
4. Kammerl, A., 'The electronic data switching system EDS', *Colloque Int. sur la Téléinformatique*, Paris, 305 (March 1969).

Chapter 10

Network Structure for Packet Switching

10.1 INTRODUCTION

In comparison with the concepts of message switching and circuit switching, that of packet switching is very new. In 1964, while working at the RAND corporation in the U.S.A., Paul Baran[1] introduced the principle in proposals for reliable military communications systems; soon afterwards, at the U.K. National Physical Laboratory, Donald Davies argued the virtues of this technique for a public data communications network. The basic concept of packet switching was introduced in Chapter 8, page 291; in this chapter the concept is developed further, and the structure of a packet switching network is examined in detail. Methods of using the network are considered, and the optimum structure for a packet is discussed.

10.2 A PUBLIC DATA NETWORK

The studies begun at the National Physical Laboratory[2] in 1966 were aimed at the design of a public data network. At that time multi-access computing had been proved sucessful, and private data networks of many kinds were being implemented or planned. Also a few groups of organizations were considering the design of shared networks. Looking ahead, it seemed that a proliferation of data networks would be bound to appear; they would, perforce, be similar in principle and use similar techniques, but differences of detail due to designers whims would make them incompatible. This has since proved to be the case, and mergers between organizations with their own networks have usually meant the virtual scrapping of the majority of the existing equipment.

The existence of a public data network would go a long way towards overcoming some of the problems of incompatability between different ways of communicating information between people and computers, and between computers and other computers, because it would set standards common to all. This would have an effect similar to that of the CCITT modem interface standards which are used on a world wide scale. Although the point-to-point data link using the telephone network is a relatively simple part of any data system, the modem interface standards have been most helpful to users in bringing some commonality in networks at this level.

A properly conceived public network performing multiplexing, concentration and other standard functions common to most networks would, seemingly, be even more valuable to users in the future by bringing standardization at a higher, procedural, level. Ideally, such a network should be available on a world wide scale; but the problems of reaching agreement on complex technical standards, between nations at different stages of economic and technological development, and often with considerable investment in existing systems, make this difficult to achieve.

In the absence of a world wide network there seem clear advantages in having, at least, a national network to reduce incompatibility between future private and shared computer systems and to bring the benefits of computer usage to small organizations and companies. This kind of consideration, coupled with an appreciation of the shortcomings of the telephone network when used to carry digital data traffic, led to the program of research at NPL into techniques suitable for building a public data network.

From the beginning, the packet switching principle was advocated by NPL, and this has, indeed, been adopted for some private and shared networks, although the packet sizes and formats usually differ in arbitrary ways. Nevertheless, the principle may now be considered well proved and national public networks now being planned may be expected to be in operation in a few countries from about 1975 onwards. There will also be an experimental network linking research establishments in various European countries coming into use at about the same time.

The early work at NPL attempted to design a national network—in the light of techniques then available—with an optimum blend of hardware for routine tasks such as packet error checking, and software for complex operations like routing and flow control. The resulting design appeared capable of response times measured in tens of milliseconds for a nationwide link. Such a performance would bring marked changes in the way computer systems could be operated, for a group of computers situated many miles apart could converse as if they were close together.

It will be several years before this kind of performance can be made available on a wide scale through a public network, although the rapid advancement in hardware and software techniques since the original theoretical designs of NPL would undoubtedly allow the predicted performance to be achieved in any practical network. Indeed, the performance may be so much improved in practice that it could be seriously worth considering whether the majority of communications traffic could not be handled efficiently by the packet switching method in the more distant future.

The Packet Switching Concept

The concept of packet switching was introduced in Chapter 8 as a special form of message switching; however, whereas message switching systems are intended to meet the needs of human users, the packet switching network is designed primarily for computer to computer communications. It has a much more rapid response which matches the internal behaviour of computers, and handles information in much the same way as does a computer.[3] At the same time it can readily match the speed of attached computers to that of the terminal users, by virtue of its internal storage.

A time-shared computer system is able to serve many users apparently simultaneously because it is inherently much faster in operation than any one user and, by switching rapidly between them, is able to share its resources among them, serving each one at a rate convenient to him. This is achieved by using storage to smooth out the traffic flow: the users are allowed to fill and empty buffer stores at rates suitable for them, while the computer communicates with the same stores at very much higher speeds. The use of storage in this way provides a match between the users and the much faster computer.

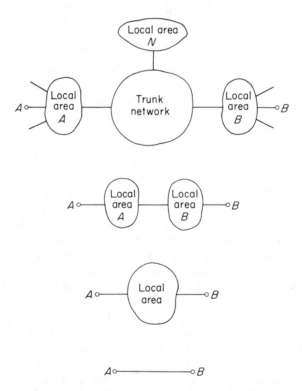

Figure 10.1.   The connection of two subscribers

The storage in this case is located within the computer and each user has a separate connection with it. But a very great advantage is gained by distributing some of the storage within the communications network that connects users with a computer, because it can be used to share high-speed communications links between users in much the same way as the computer itself is shared. This can make better use of the links; but far more important to the user is the rapid response he gets by sharing a high-speed channel rather than having sole use of a lower speed one.

The prime purpose of store-and-forward packet switching is to enable communications resources to be used efficiently and in such a way that they may be shared by many users operating in an intermittent fashion giving each user a rapid response from the communications network just at the instant when this is required. The rapid response is obtained by the use of short, fixed-format packets which allow the maximum degree of mechanisation of handling and switching within the network, but if the chosen packet is not also used for handling information outside the network there will be a need for conversion to and from the packet format at its boundaries.

As conceived at NPL, the national network would consist of a country-wide high-level or trunk network handling fixed-format packets, with a number of local areas where packets would be assembled and disassembled, and a translation would be made between the trunk network and a wide variety of subscribers equipment. This concept is shown in Figure 10.1. The task of the trunk network shown at the top, is to annihilate distance by providing such a rapid transit of information passing through it, that for all practical purposes any pair of local areas can be considered as joined directly together, as indicated in the middle of the diagram. If this is the case, they may be regarded as a single local area through which two subscriber A and B may communicate as if they, too, were joined directly, as shown at the bottom of the figure.

Of course, two subscribers linked by a network cannot possibly have the full freedom to communicate that would be possible if they were, indeed, side-by-side and joined by a piece of wire, but the aim of the whole network is to offer an acceptable degree of performance for the majority of users. It can do this only by having characteristics and resources superior to anything required by an individual user, and sharing these resources between active users on demand.

However, it is almost always true that high performance communications and computing resources are proportionately cheaper than low performance ones, which is, of course, the reason why techniques for sharing them between many simultaneously active users have been developed. It is also the reason why the major cost of any system resides in the portions unique to an individual user, for the cost of these cannot be shared. Thus, the local area cost will be predominant and special care is needed in its design. This will be considered in a later section; the next section deals with the basic trunk network.

The Basic Trunk Network

The trunk network shown in Figure 10.2 was proposed by NPL as a model of the kind of network suitable for the U.K. It comprises a mesh network of nodes joined by data links. Such a network has more than one path between each switching node and this redundancy provides the reliability essential in a network that serves very many subscribers.

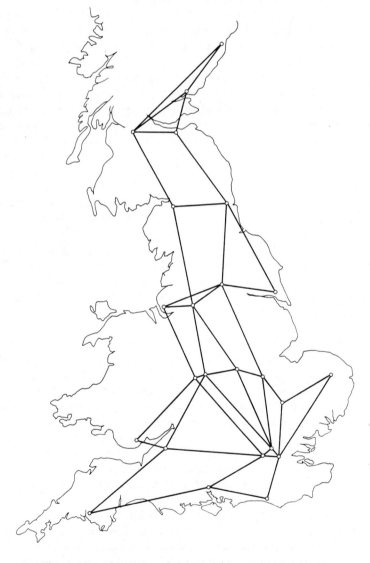

Figure 10.2 Structure of the model U.K. trunk network

The local areas prepare packets of data which are well defined in structure and size so that, as far as possible, hardware may be used instead of software for handling them at the nodes. Each packet has a destination address in a fixed position; this minimizes the software needed for inspection at nodes in order to decide which routes it must follow in progressing through the network, from the local area of entry to the local area of exit.

Apart from the reliability afforded by multiple paths between the points of entry and exit, another advantage of a mesh network with packet switches at its nodes may be appreciated by considering the situation when only two local areas are using the trunk network. In this event, they may exchange information at a rate determined by the effective number of parallel paths between them. If they are capable of so doing, they can share the whole resources of the trunk network to obtain a very superior performance indeed.

As more local areas attempt to use the network, the performance obtained by each one of them falls, and the ultimate design criterion for chosing the mesh network's resources is the minimum acceptable response time between any two local areas when the maximum traffic load is being carried during peak periods; if necessary, taking into account the probability that some links will be out of action. At all other times, the performance actually obtained will be superior to this design minimum.

The useful load sharing property of the mesh network of packet switches derives from the use of dynamic multiplexing (see Chapter 7). This is briefly illustrated by considering the example of a single communication link which is required to handle several channels. With time- and frequency-division multiplexing, used for telephony, the available bandwidth is divided into a fixed number of channels, where the channel capacity is the same irrespective of how many of the channels are in use, as shown in Figure 10.3 and Figure 10.4. When only a few channels are active great wastage occurs, but this does not matter with speech for little would be gained by giving the channels a greater capacity at off-peak times. But with computers the situation is quite different; the vital requirement is for a high-speed transfer of each item of information and this is best done by arranging for the link to carry packets

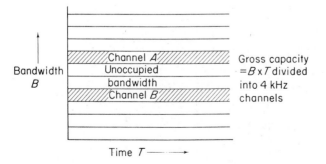

Figure 10.3. Frequency-division multiplexing

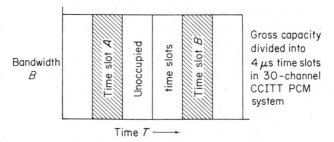

Figure 10.4. Time-division multiplexing

from each subscriber at its maximum speed, together with an address so that packets may be interleaved for transmission and sorted out again at the receiving end. This arrangement is illustrated by Figure 10.5, showing how the quantity of information that may be exchanged in a given time by individual subscribers is much higher when few of them are active. This, quite clearly, is most valuable in the case of computers as it can be used to enhance their performance at off-peak times. Perhaps equally important is that, however many happen to become active, some information can still be exchanged by every computer, although the quantity passing in a given time is much reduced because the intervals between sending a packet get longer and longer as the number of active subscribers is increased, as is illustrated by Figure 10.6. This shows how the information transmission capacity between two local areas falls as the total network traffic increases. The result of this reduction in capacity is an increase in the delay experienced by each packet as shown in Figure 10.7.

The use of packet switching with fixed-format packets accords conveniently with the transmission of information along data links in the form of blocks, with error detection and retransmission for error correction as discussed in Chapter 6, while well known techniques for handling blocks of information within a computer, by manipulating the addresses of the blocks rather than the blocks themselves, make it possible to design high-capacity packet

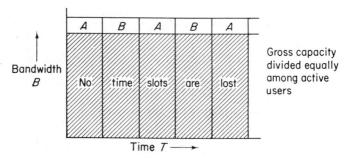

Figure 10.5. Dynamic-addressed multiplexing–packet switching

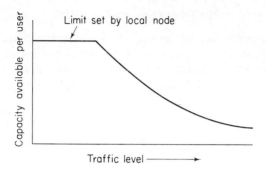

Figure 10.6. Load sharing ability of mesh
networks

switches using inexpensive small computers (see Chapter 13). Early
theoretical studies at NPL indicated an equivalent bandwidth of about
one megabit per second would be readily obtained for a node computer; later,
this was confirmed in practice by the performance of the IMP computers of
the ARPA network (see Chapter 8, page 300), which is a good example of a
packet switching mesh network realized on a national scale, even though it is
not a public network.[4]

With the ARPA network, the local areas are represented by the HOST
computers which may communicate with an adjacent node using messages of
any length up to 8080 binary digits. These are stored in the node and transmitted as a succession of packets of 1024 bits through the network to the node
nearest to the destination HOST computer, where they are reassembled ready
for passing to the HOST. The ARPA IMP is, therefore, not quite the same
as the NPL proposed node because as well as switching packets, it also carries
out part of the process of assembly and disassembly of messages into packets.
In the NPL proposal this was entirely done by the local area leaving the nodes
to handle already formatted packets. The relative merits of the two schemes
will be discussed later in connection with the optimum structure for a complete network.

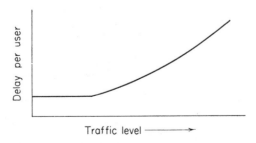

Figure 10.7. Increase of delay with load

The Basic Node Packet Switch

A further appreciation of the operation of the trunk network may be gained by briefly considering the various activities performed by the nodal switch when handling through traffic destined for other nodes.[5] A full treatment of the software involved in such a switch is given in Chapter 13,

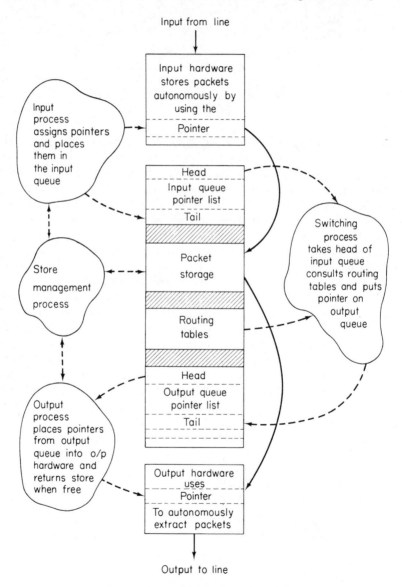

Figure 10.8.   The basic node switch

and this simplified present discussion will merely refer to processes which carry out defined tasks. These processes could be software programs, or they could be purpose-designed hardware. At this stage the form they take is immaterial to an understanding of the functions they perform as shown in Figure 10.8.

The trunk circuits between the switches are assumed to operate in a full duplex manner so that each node can simultaneously send and receive packets on all its links to other nodes. Associated with each incoming link is an input process which takes each packet and stores it in an input queue located in an area of store assigned by a storage allocation process. The address pointer which indicates where each packet is stored is placed on a queue ready to be dealt with by a switching process.

The switching process takes the input queue pointers in turn and locates the address of the next packet. It then consults a routing table which lists the order of preference of use of outgoing links for each of the possible packet destination addresses, and places the packet pointers onto the appropriate output queues associated with the outgoing links.

Each of the outgoing links has a process which takes the packet pointers in turn from the output queue and locates the packets in the store prior to despatching them along the link to the next node switch.

The routing table is the key to the behaviour of the node and therefore the whole network; its entries may be fixed so that packets between any two local areas attached to the network always take the same route, or they may be varied to alter the routes taken by packets at different times in order to overcome link failure or congestion. This variation may be made within the timescale of a typical exchange between local areas, so that successive packets of a given message take different routes, or a route may be selected and held for the duration of a single 'conversation' between local areas.

Network Topology and Routing

To take advantage of the redundancy given by the multiple paths that are available between any two nodes of a mesh network it is necessary to have a means for changing the route followed by packets so that failed portions of the network may be by-passed. It may also be worthwhile using a similar scheme to by-pass temporarily congested parts of the network, and this kind of dynamic routing of packets may increase the gross capacity of the network, by spreading traffic uniformily amongst all the nodes and links that are operational at any instant. Another factor affecting the capacity of the trunk network is the match between its topology and the pattern of traffic it has to carry. For example, if the traffic flowed mainly from north to south, there would be little purpose in having most links in the east-west direction. Nevertheless, one of the advantages of a mesh network is its ability to adapt itself in some degree to changing traffic patterns, given suitable dynamic routing capabilities at each switching point. However, it is obviously better to try and match the network to the traffic pattern expected when it is a full load, and methods of deciding the optimum network topology are discussed in Chapter 12.

The simplest form of nodal switch merely requires a routing table showing which of the links between itself and adjacent switches should be used for packets destined for each of the attached local areas. Adaptive routing of various kinds is achieved by modifying these routing tables while the network is in operation. A technique for doing this is discussed more fully in Chapter 12.

Whatever routing method is adopted, it is necessary for the packets to contain an unambiguous address indicating the output port to the local area for which they are destined; this allows the network to behave as a large distributed switch which eventually delivers to the appropriate output port, the packets inserted at any input port. An equivalent star arrangement of a single central switch with storage having direct connection with each local area is, of course, possible. It is sometimes convenient to regard the trunk network in this way when considering how local areas communicate with each other, for it may be regarded as a 'black box' with a variable packet transmission delay depending upon the instantaneous traffic load being carried on behalf of all the active local areas.

Two fundamental and related problems now arise: that of controlling the flow of packets between the local areas and the trunk network; and that of controlling packet flow between two local areas through the trunk network. In both cases some form of handshake control is required; in the first case, the control is necessary to prevent the trunk network becoming overloaded by too much traffic, while in the second, end-to-end flow control avoids the loss or duplication of packets by preventing one local area sending packets at a rate inconvenient for another. For this to be possible the local area receiving a packet will need to know its origin; it can then acknowledge its arrival by sending a reply. An additional address of origin must necessarily be associated with each packet; this address may be added by the sending local area, or possibly by the node to which it is attached.

The best method to use for the control of traffic flow within and through the network depends on the way the network is structured; we therefore discuss the structure of packet switching networks before considering in more detail how traffic flow can be controlled.

10.3 DATA NETWORK STRUCTURE

In common with all complex systems a data network must be organized properly so that it may be designed, constructed and maintained efficiently, and can be extended and adapted to meet changing requirements as these arise. A hierarchical structure with well defined interfaces between the levels of the hierarchy provides the necessary properties and allows the various levels to be developed almost independently, and concurrently. Both the original NPL proposed national network and the ARPA network are basically hierarchical in form, although they depart from an ideal structure in important ways, as will be discussed later.

The NPL proposals envisaged a mesh trunk network, with packet switching nodes, which joined together a number of local areas each comprising an interface computer with a star network of links to terminals and computers belonging to the network's subscribers.

The ARPA network, as initially conceived, also employed a mesh network with packet switching nodes called IMPs, but the local areas were represented by existing HOST computers, which already supported their own network of terminals. Later, the introduction of the terminal IMP allowed sites without

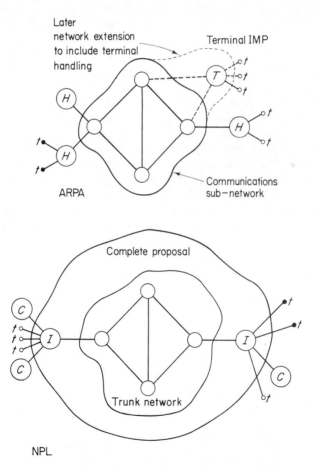

Figure 10.9. Comparison of ARPA and NPL schemes

a HOST to be joined into the network. The similarity of the ARPA and NPL schemes is illustrated by Figure 10.9.

The NPL proposed trunk network and the ARPA network both leave the problem of terminal addressing to the local area, and HOST respectively; these are allowed to use the message space freely for the purpose of inter-communication. There is nothing wrong with this approach; indeed, it is necessary to allow the overall size of the packet to be fixed. But it is also an undesirably vague approach, because no standards are set in the difficult area of terminal-to-terminal and terminal-to-computer communication. The use of the ARPA network was, at first, restricted for lack of such standards, and intensive discussions on HOST-to-HOST 'protocol' took place before the network could be freely employed, while discussions on higher level pro-cedures and standards are likely to continue for a long time.

The higher level interactions between subscribers are of no concern to the network and they take place by an exchange of information that may occupy any number of packets. However, as successive levels of hierarchy are built up, there is a tendency on the part of the designer of each level to take a portion of the packet for address or control information so that the residual size remaining for other levels is uncertain. In practice there may well be a number of levels of structural hierarchy which will need to have an associated address structure; some levels will be within the network and properly considered as belonging to the communications authority, others will be outside the network and within equipment belonging to the subscribers. It follows, therefore, that there is a level which forms a boundary between subscribers and the network. At this level, and indeed at the others also, interface parameters must be defined to enable communication between the adjacent levels. However, whereas the boundary between the telephone network and its subscribers is an obvious one—the telephone handset, it is much more difficult to identify the proper position to define an interface between a public data network and its subscribers.

This difficulty is partly due to the way present private data net-works have evolved; with many of the fundamental communications functions like multiplexing being done by equipment belonging to the sub-scriber, rather than to the communications authority. This makes it difficult to introduce new schemes where basic communications equipment can be standardized, so it may be shared by several subscribers and maintained on their behalf by the authority. The other serious problem is the way the majority of the operating systems of existing large computers have, tradi-tionally, been designed. Peripheral devices are strictly controlled by the computer which behaves in a god-like fashion. This makes it virtually in-capable of communicating with another computer on equal terms.

The earliest designs for systems based on a single computer were—perhaps naturally—organized so that the computer governed, rigidly, the operation of all its peripheral devices. Later, when these peripheral devices had to be situated remotely and operated through data links, the polling technique was devised so that the computer still remained in control of the whole network (see Chapter 4).

The inefficiency associated with polling in a large network of mainly inactive terminals led to the development of interrupt-driven systems where the computer is less autocratic; while in some real-time interactive situations such as process control the computer has to respond rapidly to the environment by reacting within certain time limits.

The trend towards making the computer subservient to its environment is continuing with the connection of computers into shared networks. Here, the traditional view of the computer as the arbiter of all activity gives way to that of the network as the central agency facilitating communication between several computers. These, in some respects, appear as peripheral devices to the network, and their internal organization has to reflect this fact.

Basic ideas are beginning to crystalize on methods whereby groups of computers may mutually interact, while individually engaged in different activities. The problems of achieving worthwhile interaction between computers are being identified in a practical way in the ARPA network and in the NPL local network[6] and it is becoming clear that a hierarchical structure is required in which the basic trunk network has successive layers built upon it; some of these layers may be in different computers or within a single computer.

As outlined above, the design of computer systems has evolved from the original ideas of a computer-centred structure to the present, and still evolving, concept of a network-centred structure. This concept will be examined in the next section to illustrate the basic requirements and structure of a complete system of distributed computers and terminals, and to identify positions where it might be feasible to identify interfaces and draw partitions between parts of the system. In order to do this it is necessary to look briefly at how computer operating systems are structured, at the way terminal to terminal interactions occur, and how terminals communicate with a computer.

Operating System Structure

Current thinking about the way to structure the software, and particularly the operating system, of a computer revolves round the concept of a process. A process is capable of carrying out a defined task and has a defined interface through which communication with other processes can take place. Processes may be either active or dormant and it is customary to talk of 'waking' processes to make them active, and 'putting to sleep' processes that are to be made dormant. Communication between processes takes place in terms of messages and a process becoming active will examine a queue of input messages to determine what its next job must be.

There may be many kinds of process, for example, input processes, output processes, file handling processes etc. An operating system will be based on a collection of such processes and will contain other processes such as store allocation and resource scheduling processes. The concept of co-operating processes will be further developed in Chapter 13, and it is sufficient to note here that the modern concept of a software system is a hierarchy of processes which are able to communicate by messages according to defined rules. Such rules have become known as a procedural interface, or a protocol for interprocess communication.

This concept of a modular software system is clearly a powerful and flexible one, and it is one of the aims of an efficient computer network to try to provide for interprocess communication between processes which are situated in a number of different, geographically-separated computers.

Terminal-to-terminal Communication

A consideration of the way a group of people may use a terminal to communicate with another group of people will illustrate two fundamental, and related, ideas that are encountered over and over again in connection with hierarchical systems.

Figure 10.10 shows two terminals joined by a direct connection, and two groups of subscribers, denoted as *calling* subscribers and *called* subscribers. For convenience the calling subscribers are assumed to use one terminal and the called subscribers the other; although in practice subscribers of either terminal could be calling subscribers attempting to communicate with called subscribers at the other terminal. It will also be assumed that no two sub-scribers attempt to call each other simultaneously. At any instant only one conversation can take place between the two terminals; but, of course, an indefinite number of subscribers may use the terminals over a period of time, so the link may be considered to permit the mapping of the set of calling subscribers on to the set of called subscribers.

The first fundamental consideration that emerges is that of communication between the sets of subscribers and the terminals. There are two aspects to this; the interaction between the calling subscriber and the terminal when initiating a connection, and the interaction between the terminal and the called sub-

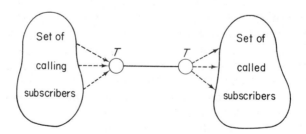

Figure 10.10   Mapping of subscribers

scriber when accepting a connection. The idea is very familiar in the case of the telephone network where people readily learn the procedure and protocol necessary to make telephone calls, and to receive telephone calls.

The second fundamental idea is that of communication between the calling and called subscribers, through the medium of the terminals and interconnecting link; but in a manner which is independent of these, and does not affect them. In order for this to be possible, a separate set of procedures has to be established for end-to-end communication, and these procedures must be independent of those used for subscriber-to-terminal communication. Again, by analogy with the telephone system, once a connection is made, the people using it must speak the same language, and must agree on conventions as to who speaks when.

The relationship between the two sets of procedure described above is that of two adjacent levels in a hierarchy of procedures. The subscribers are at one level, and the link at another, and it is necessary for the subscribers first to interact with the link level in order to establish the connection which enables them to interact with each other at their own level.

The interaction between adjacent levels in a hierarchy occurs in many guises in all kinds of systems. For example, Figure 10.11 shows the two

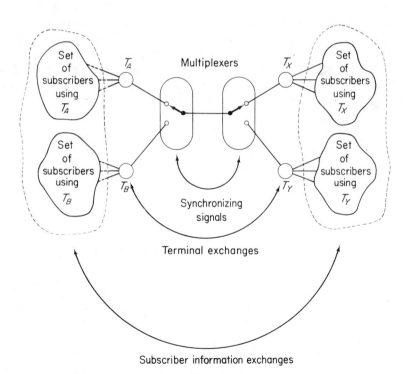

Figure 10.11.   Levels in a hierarchy

terminals connected by a multiplexing link. If this link operates at a high speed, many pairs of terminals may communicate without the subscribers being aware that there is no direct connection. But there is now an extra level of hierarchy introduced between them and it is essential for the multiplexers to remain in step. Some kind of multiplexer-to-line and multiplexer-to-multiplexer communication therefore has to take place, unknown to the subscribers. Obviously, this kind of thing can happen at any level but the two types of communication always occur, namely: communication between equivalent levels in a hierarchy, and communication between adjacent levels in a hierarchy. Many examples of this will be encountered later when considering the structure of a complete system.

Terminal-to-computer Communication

A convenient way of handling terminals joined to a computer is to provide a 'terminal process' within the computer. Such a process represents, or models, terminals within the computer software and is responsible for the interactions necessary to deal with them, including any vagaries peculiar to a particular type of terminal. Figure 10.12 shows that, within the computer, the terminal process may communicate with several other processes in an analogous fashion to the way that a number of different users outside the computer may make use of the same terminal. There is, therefore, a one-to-one mapping of terminals and active terminal processes, but there may be a many-to-one mapping of users on to higher level 'server' processes. It is common for different users at different times to employ the same terminal to call a computer and to make a selection from a range of services. There are

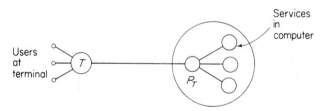

Figure 10.12. Mapping of users and services

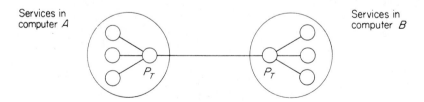

Figure 10.13. Mapping of server processes

clear similarities between the mechanism of terminal-to-terminal communication and that of terminal-to-computer communication, while it is obvious that the same principles will apply to computer-to-computer communication also. This is illustrated by Figure 10.13. The analogy between the interaction of different processes situated in two computers, with that of different subscribers sharing two terminals is clearly seen by comparing Figure 10.12 and Figure 10.13.

The Call Concept

The concept of a call is very familiar to everyone who is accustomed to using the telephone network to make a telephone call, but because it seems such an obvious idea, it is worthwhile examining it critically to ensure we have a really clear understanding. Two aspects will be considered: the subscriber's requirements and view of the network; and the network properties required to meet the subscriber's needs. It will be necessary to use terms commonly understood in relation to the telephone network, but the intention is to bring out principles underlying the call concept, in a way that can be applied to a data communications network.

As far as two subscribers are concerned, a call exists between them when they can exchange information as if they were joined by a direct physical connection. That is, everything sent into the network by either subscriber is received by the other. An initial dialogue, or interaction must take place between the subscribers and the network to establish the call; but thereafter the network plays no part—other than to faithfully transfer information between the subscribers—until a second dialogue with the subscribers causes the call to be discontinued. Each subscriber's view of a call will, therefore, be a continuing, though possibly discontinuous, interaction with another subscriber lasting from the call establishment dialogue to the call disconnection dialogue.

If two telephone subscribers were to set up a call, and then each were to hand his telephone to another person, the call would exist between two new people, but the network would have no knowledge of this new situation, because the 'switching' had occured externally to the network. It is doubtful whether the two new people concerned would think of this as a new call either; although, strictly speaking, it is so, because they have become connected by a link, which previously did not exist between them. This is an example of two levels of hierarchy, where the lower level (the network) is unaware of what happens at the subscriber level above. To further underline this point, it is usual to talk of telephoning a person. In fact, of course, the telephone network only allows calls to be made from one telephone instrument to another one, so a further confirmation dialogue, or sometimes a 'switching' procedure, is required before a calling subscriber can be sure he is connected to the person with whom he actually wishes to communicate.

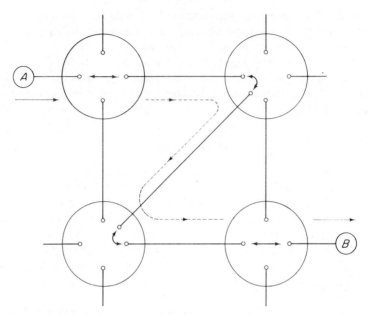

NB: switch setting instructions must pass through network
to set switches before data can flow

Figure 10.14.   A circuit-switched connection

Within the network it is more difficult to define a call, for it is not necessarily the case that subscribers are joined by a physical connection, although
they expect the network to behave as if this were so. To make this possible,
the initial dialogue between subscribers and the network to establish a call
must cause the network to store a record of that call for as long as it exists;
this record may be kept in different ways resulting in networks that internally
are organized differently, although the external appearance to subscribers
may be made identical.

The first possibility is shown in Figure 10.14. Here the intervening switches
between subscribers are set for the duration of the call, which is 'remembered'
by each switch. This is the conventional circuit-switched type of connection
where the knowledge of each call is distributed and stored throughout its
length by virtue of the set positions of switches and the dedicated circuits
that they connect.

To establish a circuit-switched call, the network control signalling information, generated from the subscribers initial calling dialogue, has to flow
from switch to switch, setting each in turn until the called terminal is reached.
If this is not free, an engaged signal is returned and, unless the calling subscriber releases the call, this state continues indefinitely, with switches set and
circuits occupied. If the called terminal is free, the connection to it is made and

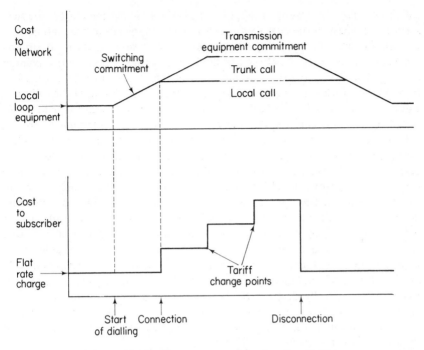

Figure 10.15. Resources used in circuit switching

ringing tone is returned to the caller; though further activity outside the network's control, i.e. the answer by a called subscriber, has to take place to complete the connection dialogue and join the calling subscriber to the person who has answered the call. Until a called subscriber accepts the call, network resources at all levels are occupied without payment from the subscribers. (Networks could be designed differently, e.g. a charge could be made for attempts to set up calls even though they proved unsuccessful.) But, of course, once someone answers, any further dialogue occurring to get hold of the right subscriber is, generally, paid for by the caller. From the network's point of view, its resources are occupied though, for the calling subscriber, the desired 'call' may not yet have properly commenced.

To summarize, the way resources are occupied during a call in a circuit switched network is illustrated qualitatively by Figure 10.15. This shows the rising cost of setting up a call, the constant cost of holding it regardless of whether information is flowing, and the fall in cost as resources are released at disconnection time. These characteristics arise because the switches and circuits, between calling and called subscribers, are held for the duration of each call. However, the information flowing between subscribers is not stored by switches (other than for slot changing in a TDM system) and the resource occupancy is unaffected by the quantity of information passing through the calls that have been set up. Figure 10.15 also shows how the cost to the subscriber is related to the cost to the network by a typical tariff structure.

Another way of arranging a call between two subscribers is to employ a packet switching trunk network of the kind described earlier in this chapter on page 344. The network as a whole has no knowledge of calls except in a transient form while a packet is actually passing through one of the switches. But if, as shown in Figure 10.16, the information about a call is held at the periphery of the network within a local area, a stream of information from a subscriber may be partitioned into packets in the local area and despatched into the trunk network, preceded by a header containing routing information derived from the stored knowledge of the call. As the successive packets of a call are passed from switch to switch the header is used by each switch to select a circuit to the next. A switch, therefore, has no need to remember details of each call; but it must store information about routes to all possible destinations, and may have to store the subscriber's packets temporarily while waiting for a circuit to the next switch to become available. With packet switching, then, a switch has no knowledge of a particular call, except while it is handling a packet associated with that call. Once this packet has been successfully despatched, the switch need retain no memory of it. However, the network must have room to store at its periphery the details of all the current calls, if it is to maintain for subscribers the illusion that they are joined together.

With a packet-switched network it would be possible to allow subscribers to provide the necessary routing instructions for each packet, instead of doing this in the local area. In this case, the concept of a call no longer holds for the

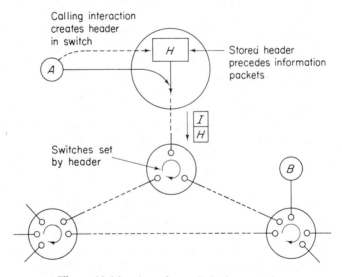

Figure 10.16. A packet-switched connection

network other than while it is handling a packet passing between two subscribers. It might be argued that the despatch by a subscriber of a packet preceded by a header is logically equivalent to making a call, because it comprises the input to the network of routing instructions followed by the transfer of information. However, although the 'called' subscriber may be able to reply by returning a packet to the 'calling' subscriber, any continuing interaction between them would have to be prefaced by further headers. The similarity with the concept of a call therefore only exists for an interaction involving the exchange of a single packet in each direction.

Because a packet switching network has no knowledge of calls, it may handle an indefinitely large number of them, although the rate at which it transfers successive packets of each individual call decreases as the number of calls increases, assuming they are dealt with in strict rotation. The limit on the number of calls will be set only by the ability to store, outside it, the details relating to each of the calls. As stated above, this may be done by the local area network, or by the subscriber, depending on the structure of the network. The topic of network structure is treated in detail later (see page 365). At this stage, however, it is worth noting that if the local area stores details of the calls, each line to a subscriber carries, during any one call, information exchanged with only one other subscriber. But, if the subscriber stores details of the calls, his line to the trunk network may carry interleaved packets exchanged with a number of other subscribers. In fact, of course, this is how the local area network itself manages to carry many 'simultaneous' calls, when it provides a call-maintaining facility for subscribers.

An interesting variation of the call concept is the use of an abbreviated address. Here, the initial information passed to the local area by a calling subscriber contains the full routing instructions necessary to establish a call to another subscriber. These instructions are stored in the local area for the duration of the call, as before, but a short address identifying these instructions is returned to the calling subscriber who prefaces subsequent information packets with that address. It then becomes possible for the line between

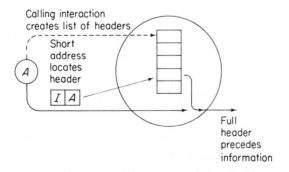

Figure 10.17.   Abbrieviated headers

subscribers and the network to carry information from several calls inter-leaved on the line, by using the shorter, abbreviated, address to locate the full instructions. These are then used by the local area to provide the header which guides each packet to its destination. This scheme is illustrated in Figure 10.17, and is intermediate between the packet and circuit switched cases, in that each subscriber may have a number of 'simultaneous' calls using interleaved packets up to a limit set by the addresses returned to him by the local area.

The way in which the resources of a packet switching network are occupied during a call is difficult to decide, because it depends on the physical structure of the network. A qualitative indication is given in Figure 10.18. This may be compared with the circuit switched case already given in Figure 10.15. The appropiate tariff structure is still a matter of debate.

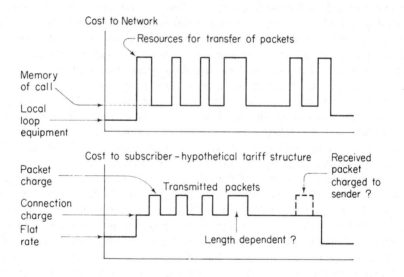

Figure 10.18.   Resources used in packet switching

Types of Connection Required

It is now necessary to identify the kinds of interconnection that must be provided by a general purpose data communications network in order to serve the needs of subscribers who may have a variety of terminals and/or computers.

Suppose there are a number of local areas containing people who wish to make use of services provided by computers. The people will use terminals to communicate with programs in the computers; these terminals and com-puters may be in the same, or different, local areas. Two local areas are shown

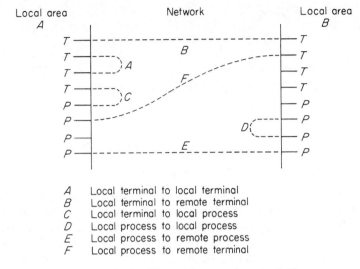

A	Local terminal to local terminal
B	Local terminal to remote terminal
C	Local terminal to local process
D	Local process to local process
E	Local process to remote process
F	Local process to remote terminal

Figure 10.19.   Types of connection required

in Figure 10.19, which illustrates the six simple kinds of call that may be established with a one-to-one connection between ports into, and out of, the network.

Apart from these simple calls there are two other forms of interconnection that may be required.

The first form involves multiple connections between network ports so that one terminal may simultaneously send the same information to several others (i.e. the multiple address message typical of message switched systems) or the converse situation where several terminals wish simultaneously to send information to a single destination. If this were a terminal, the information would be jumbled on its printed page. This is obviously unacceptable, and provision has to be made to prevent this happening, and also to avoid network congestion arising from any attempts at such multiple calls to a single destination. But in the special case of a fast computer that can simultaneously handle interleaved information from many slow terminals, multiple connections will be allowed, provided the total information reception rate required does not exceed the computers processing capability. Otherwise, again, the network would become congested.

If a conventional circuit switched network is employed the multiple connection calls have to be established as a number of individual calls linked outside the network, as exemplified by Figure 10.20. But the use of a packet switching network allows such calls to be handled differently, because packets from several sources to a single destination, and vice versa, can be interleaved through a single network port.

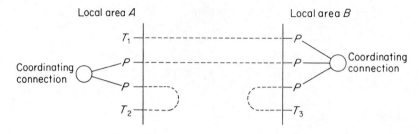

Terminals T_1 T_2 and T_3 joined by processes

Figure 10.20.   Multiple connection calls

The second form of connection that may be needed is a sequence of links between several network ports. These would be required if a call from a user at a terminal to a service made it necessary for other services to be consulted, before the interaction could be completed. This might happen if several data banks had to be interrogated, as shown in Figure 10.21. Again, with a conventional circuit switched network separate calls must be made, but with a packet switched network interleaved packets may be used; this is particularly important if the information exchanges are of short duration.

To provide the various kinds of facility discussed above requires a well structured data network; such a structure is discussed in the next section.

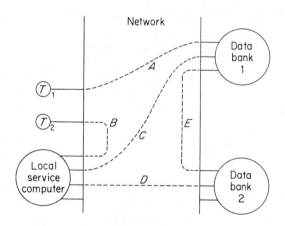

A   Terminal 1 calls data bank 1
B   Terminal 2 calls local computer
C   Computer calls data bank 1
D   Computer calls data bank 2
E   Data bank 1 calls data bank 2
NB: *B* could give rise to *C D* and *E*

Figure 10.21.   Sequential types of calls

The Ideal Hierarchical Network

It is now possible to examine a hierarchy of logical levels that might be identified in a data communications system, based upon the use of a packet switching trunk network, and intended to provide the kinds of connection discussed in the previous section. The discussion will take into account the principles of computer, and network, organization developed earlier in this chapter.

As previously explained, the reason for using the packet switching trunk network is to provide subscribers with a very small share of a wide-band, long-distance communication system, so that the response time they experience is very short. It may be regarded as a single high speed switch, which does not contain a knowledge of calls. This implies that packets of information must be preceded by a header containing full routing instructions for that packet, as far as the trunk network is concerned. That is to say there must be sufficient space in the header for a unique address identifying every input and output port of the trunk network.

The trunk network will be regarded as the first level in our network hierarchy, upon which all the others are built. The next level is the local

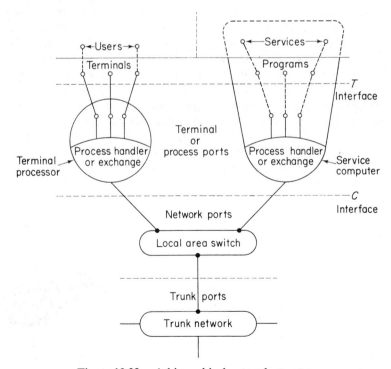

Figure 10.22.   A hierarchical network structure

area switch as shown in Figure 10.22. The local area switch has a number of connections from the area it serves, and a single connection to the trunk switch. In practice there could be more than one physical connection from the local area into the trunk network, but these will appear as a single port when we are regarding the trunk network as merely a simple switch. The local switch is responsible for knowing about calls through the trunk network; each oi the lines radiating from it into the local area are network ports, and it has a directory of all network ports in its own, and other, local areas. The information it passes to the trunk network must carry a header identifying the destination local area, but the destination network port may be either contained within the packet in full, or as an abbreviated address. The latter indicates that a particular packet is part of a call that has already been set up by an exchange of information between the two local area switches, which have stored the full details of the call now identified by the abbreviated address.

We now have a network where information can be exchanged between any network port and any other network port on a call basis. Indeed, the only difference between trunk ports and network ports is that trunk ports can have no knowledge of calls, whereas network ports may.

Each of the network ports of a local area will be, in general, connected to a process handler or 'exchange' which is similar in many respects to the local area switch but has many more ports. It has to have a knowledge of all other process ports in the network, with which it is entitled to communicate. The process exchange controls calls between processes, these may be local calls within the process exchange or may be calls to processes in other process exchanges through the medium of the local area switch if they are to other local process exchanges, or through the medium of the local area switches and intermediate trunk network in the case of a remote process.

It is now possible to see how terminals should be connected to the trunk network. A special type of process 'exchange' with connections to a group of terminals is used; this has a sub-process corresponding to each terminal. Terminals and processes are, therefore, at the same level in the network hierarchy. This is a most important concept because it enables the network to be regarded as connecting together processes. As we have already seen some of these processes will be identified with terminals, and will enable a communication to take place between any terminals connected to the network. The other processes will, in general, give access to services which are available through the network. These services will be defined as any facility with which the user may wish to interact. Sometimes a process will be uniquely identified with a service, in the same way that a terminal might be uniquely identified with a user. But in the general case the assumption will be made that an indefinite number of users may use a terminal, and that an indefinite number of services may be available through the medium of a process. This means that users and services will be considered as equivalent levels in the hierarchy.

Furthermore the boundary between users and terminals, and between services and processes, will be regarded as the boundary of the overall communication network, which must be able to make calls between users and services. Both of these are outside the control of the designers of the network.

The physical structure of the network implies an address structure, and this in turn, implies a packet structure and protocol for establishing, maintaining and clearing calls. There may also be a need for interaction between the various levels in order to control the flow of information between them, and to take care of failure situations of various kinds. Before discussing these topics however, it is worth looking at the ways the terminals would communicate in practice with the terminal processes, because it would be too expensive to provides individual physical connections as shown in Figure 10.22. Instead, the upper left portion of that figure can be expanded to become a terminal processor with an associated terminal access network. An example of this is the NPL local area network which has been described elsewhere (see Chapter 6, page 203, and Chapter 7, page 261).

10.4   THE TERMINAL ACCESS NETWORK

The concept of the terminal access network is illustrated by Figure 10.23. It is assumed that a number of terminals are distributed geographically and connected by one or more levels of multiplexing or concentration to a computer which acts as the terminal processor. It is likely that the information in this network of terminals would be handled in very short units, possibly as characters, or even as single bits, which may be interleaved in order to keep the response time between individual terminals and terminal processes short. An address must be associated with each unit of information exchanged between the terminal processor and the terminal, but the smallness of the unit handled will make it uneconomic to include the complete routing information and it will always be necessary to use the concept of a call between the terminal and the terminal processor. Each call will be, therefore, preceded by a call establishment procedure, though this may be implicit in the case of a permanent heading of the kind available in the NPL network.[6]

When a terminal becomes active and establishes a call the terminal processor creates a process. This may either represent the terminal or it may represent the call that is being established by that terminal (the distinction between these is discussed in detail in Chapter 11). Once the process has been established, subsequent information is exchanged between the terminal and this process through the medium of an input/output process, which is common to all communication with terminals and which interacts with the hardware concentrators distributed about the terminal access network.

The main purpose of the terminal access network is to reduce the cost of connecting terminals into the local area switch, and a variety of methods

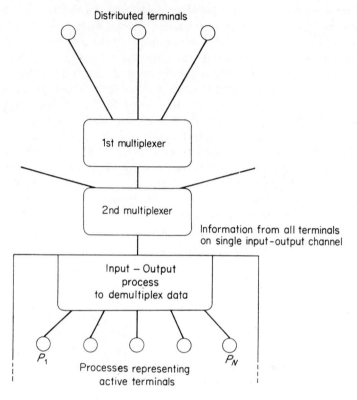

Figure 10.23.   A terminal access network

could be adopted to achieve this end. The NPL uses a great deal of distributed hardware for this purpose, whereas with the ARPA terminal interface message processor (TIP) dial-up lines are used join the terminals to the TIP, which is connected directly into the nodal network. There are, clearly, various other methods of achieving the desired end of cheapening the cost of terminal connection. One of the most promising is that of using a ring network as discussed in Chapter 7, page 267.

It is worth noting in reference to Figure 10.23 that a connection between terminal processes may be made within the terminal processor, so that a call may be easily made between any two terminals connected to that terminal processor. The hardware multiplexers need have no knowledge of calls and behave as simple switches which always transfer units of information along predetermined paths; only in the terminal processor may the process of call establishment result in a variable path for information between terminals at different times. The terminal processor is the first level in the network at which the concept of a call is realized and is the first point at which units of information from terminals can be assembled into packets. For the case when a complete call could be contained within a packet, the header attached by the terminal processor would be sufficient to transmit it through the remainder of the network to its destination. In such a case, the concept of the call would not apply for that particular transaction anywhere else in the network. Because the terminal processor is the first point where information units are assembled in packets, it is the appropriate place to implement special facilities to deal with peculiarities of terminals, and in particular, it is the most appropriate place to provide echoplex operation if this is required (i.e. to return a copy of each character to the terminal, see Chapter 11, page 412).

Network Interfaces and Address Structure

It is now possible to examine the interfaces and address structure required for the idealized network that was shown in Figure 10.22. But whereas the structure of the network was described working from the trunk network outwards towards the users, it is more convenient to describe the interfaces and address structure by working in from the users towards the trunk network.

At the users and services level, considered to be outside the network, any degree of complexity in addressing may be devised by subscribers in order to allow users and groups of users to cooperate and services to interact with one another if this is necessary. There will be no further discussion here about this level because it is not relevant to the design of the network; but it is clearly desirable for network parameters at lower levels to be defined so that subscribers may develop their own interactions (and the protocols governing these interactions) on a sound basis.

It is clear that the logical structure of the network can be implemented in a variety of ways. It would be possible to combine the node, the local area switch and the terminal processor into one computer, or it would be possible to separate them into different computers that were also separated geographically. The way in which particular networks have been realized will be discussed later, but an immediate problem that becomes apparent is that of defining the interface between the network and the outside world.

The concept introduced earlier, of a boundary between services and users on the one hand and the network on the other, seems not to be feasible in practice, because the subscribers are of two kinds. There are those with computers capable of supporting several processes and communicating interleaved packets belonging to several calls on a single connection. This corresponds to the interface C between the process exchange and the local area switch shown in Figure 10.24. On the other hand, there are the subscribers with terminals, which are able to engage in only a single call at any one time. These need to be connected to the network through an interface as shown at position T.

There is no reason why a network should not have interfaces at two

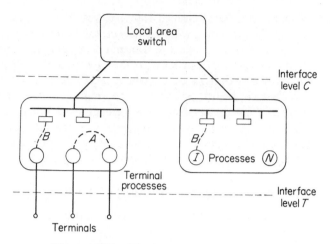

Figure 10.24.   The terminal and process level

levels, but to avoid the necessity of two kinds of connection between subscriber's equipment and the network, a physical and procedural interface must be designed, capable of being used at either of these two levels. The simpler interface to define is that between manually operated terminals and the network. There will generally be a one-to-one connection between such terminals, so each terminal will have to be uniquely identifiable by the network. However, there would be difficulty if a multi-access computer were connected to the network through this terminal interface. Physically only a single line is needed to connect such a computer to the network because the information flowing on the line will be interleaved messages or packets relating to the several simultaneous conversations being carried on by the computer, and it will be possible to identify, within it, an interface corresponding with that between the network and a simple terminal. This occurs at the point where interleaved packets are sorted into individual channels matching the appropriate processes. If the network boundary were to be defined at the terminal interface level, the multi-access computer would have part of its software within the network, and the subscriber owning and operating the computer would have to cooperate closely with the network designers in producing suitable software. This would have to be rigidly defined by the network authority and tests would have to be devised to ensure a particular implementation could not damage the network through malfunction. For this reason, it seems better to define the network interface at the interleaved packet level, but to include facilities for handling an individual terminal at this level. There is, fortunately, a close resemblance between a multi-access computer and a terminal processor, which can conveniently serve as a model for the designer of any special software packages necessary to match the multi-access computer to the network.

The Interleaved Packet Interface

The interfaces at the output of a terminal processor and of a multi-access computer are similar and occur at the junction marked C in Figure 10.24. Each line crossing this interface carries interleaved packets with an address indicating the terminal or process of origin and destination. The number of processes that can be allowed will be determined either by the size of the address field allocated in the packet, or by the storage resources that have to be allocated within the terminal processor or multi-access computer for each call that has to be maintained at any particular instant. Also there may be a further limitation in the resources available in the local area switch on the other side of the interface, for, when a call is established through the network, there is information stored in various parts of the network to allow a path to be found by each packet belonging to that call as it passes through the network. The space required to store this information represents an allocation of network resources required to maintain the call. To this must be added the additional resources required to actually transfer the packet through the network.

Inside the terminal processor there may be connections representing calls between the terminals that it serves; each of these connections (shown dotted

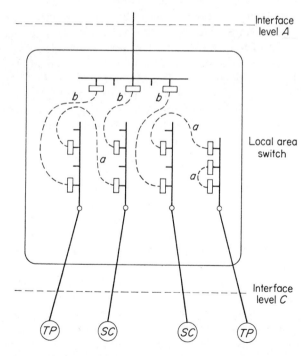

Figure 10.25.   The local area switch level

at A in Figure 10.24) will require a process and a pair of buffers assigned to it when a call is set up. There may also be connections to other terminals on other terminal processors, or between terminals and processes in various multi-access computers connected to the same local area switch. For these connections, processes and buffers, too, have to be assigned and are indicated by a dotted line at B within the terminal processor of Figure 10.24. The small rectangles represent these resources that are allocated to 'remembering' calls that have been established.

The next level up from the terminal processor and the subscribers computers is the local area switch (see Figure 10.25). In this processor, 'local' calls are established between the various connected lines from Terminal Processors and Subscriber Computers, while there may be a link to the high-level trunk network which acts as a switch connecting the local area with other similar local areas. All lines attached to the local area switch carry interleaved packets with a level C address, except those to other local area switches (whether through the trunk net or not); these have a level A address corresponding to the local area switch. Within such switches, the 'connections' are made in terms of a 'mapping' of a pair of addresses on each other; there will therefore seem to be a many-to-one mapping of lines, but a one-to-one mapping of packet addresses. 'Calls' may be made between two input lines, as exemplified by dotted lines 'a', or between input and output lines, as shown by dotted lines 'b'. It is clear that the number of active output packet connections will be some fraction of the total active input connections, with the remainder of the input connections representing local calls.

There are close similarities between the local area switch and the terminal processor in that a 'mapping' of addresses constitutes a 'call'. Resources to remember the mappings must be provided, together with buffers for in-transit packets. There are several input lines corresponding to one address level, and one output line corresponding to the next higher address level. Also, looped calls can occur between lines at the lower level, or cross-connections may be made to the higher level. But, whereas the input lines to the local area switch have addresses needing inspection, those to the terminal processor do not, because, as far as the terminal processor is concerned, the lines connect to only one terminal, which is, therefore, uniquely identified. Looped calls illustrate the general principle that there may be activity at one level that does not involve the next above; for example, subscribers may converse with each other outside the network, and services inside any one subscriber computer may interact without occupying ports to the network.

In the levels considered so far, extra addresses are added as the packet moves up through the hierachy to keep a record of its point of origin. But this does not happen in the mesh networks of a national (or international) trunk system. In a mesh network all links are at the same level and the whole network can be regarded as a distributed switch. No addresses can be added by the nodes—other than for transient routing or some other internal purposes—as they have no complete knowledge of the packet destination. This knowledge is held at the local area switches and the terminal processors as a result of the initial dialogue between network and subscribers when a call is set-up. It is necessary therefore for addresses used in the mesh networks to be added by the local area switch.

It might be possible to connect several local area switches to one node computer which would make use of the level A address to distinguish between them. But if this were done the node computer would be assuming some of the functions of the local area, and the demarcation line between local area and trunk network would pass through the node computer. Instead it will be assumed that the nodes are simple and have only one local area switch attached. It is now necessary to examine how the addresses are produced.

The Dial-Up Procedure

It is, of course, vital to have a unique absolute address for each terminal and process port in the network, but the packet addresses used at any instant need only represent the calls actually in progress. This could considerably reduce the size of the packet address fields needed in a fully developed network. When a call is set-up there will have to be a translation from the absolute address to a 'call' adress which will accompany each packet belonging to that call. The 'call' addresses must be taken from a pool of 'vacant' links and returned after the call is over. The size of the address pool must exceed the expected highest number of simultaneous active calls, unless, of course, an

1) Port A requests a call to Port B sending full address of B to LAS-A

2) LAS-A sends packet to LAS-B signalling that Port A requires connection to Port B and giving true addresses of A and B and a call address for direction A to B, say, X

3) LAS-B checks B is free and sends an acknowledgement signalling packet to LAS-A accepting call and giving true addresses of A and B and a call address for packets for direction B to A, say, Y

4) All packets addressed to LAS-B-X go to Terminal or Port B; all packets addressed LAS-A-Y go to Port A; until

5) The call is disconnected by an exchange of disconnect packets

Figure 10.26.   The dial-up procedure

upper limit is set to prevent congestion occuring. The dial-up procedure is illustrated in Figure 10.26, which shows how shortened addresses are agreed between two local area switches LAS A and LAS B for the duration of a call. It is clear that these shortened addresses are equivalent to the abbreviated addresses discussed earlier, but are used within the network rather than by the subscribers. It is worthwhile looking at the size of address fields required. This will depend on the ratio of terminals and process ports to local area switches. The absolute address of the local area switches must accompany every packet, but the terminal address may be assigned for the 'call' duration, so there is merit in having many terminals associated with each local area switch.

The Composite Interface Computer

Up until now, the terminal processor and local area switch have been considered as two separate entities, each dealing with a different level in the network hierarchy. But there may be a disadvantage in using separate computers for these two functions because the information has to pass through both computers before reaching the trunk network, and with this arrangement the lines to subscribers are of two types; those to terminals, and those to subscriber computers. This reduces flexibility in the local area, and it would be better if any line could be used for a subscriber's terminal or computer without having to make hardware changes to the network. On the other hand, the traffic from a subscriber's computer may be much greater than from a terminal and there may be operational advantages in keeping traffic separated into two categories. The difference between the two types of line is that computer lines carry interleaved packets, while terminal lines do not.

The result of combining the local area switch and terminal processor in one machine is shown in Figure 10.27. It is, of course, assumed that this machine, which is equivalent to the original 'interface computer' proposed by NPL, is capable of carrying the total traffic. In Figure 10.27, information from all the local area lines is combined by a distributed local access network and arrives at the single input-output channel of the interface computer regardless of whether it originated from terminals or from computers. The local area is assumed to handle interleaved characters but these are sorted out by the hardware and the autonomous store-access mechanism so that for each input line there is a pair of buffers which collect characters for that line. If the line comes from a terminal only one pair of buffers is required, but if it is from a computer several may be needed; there must be a pair for each active call, otherwise calls cannot proceed independently. There is an immediate problem that the interface computer must have enough resources to assign all the required buffers, so it would be unreasonable to expect it to accept a change from mostly terminals to mostly subscriber computers without a radical increase in its capacity. Nevertheless, if the mixing of lines is considered desirable, it would probably be better to treat all lines as packet-interleaved lines, with terminal lines as a special case. The packets from terminals differ from those from computers because they lack the process identification address and there may be a case for adding a dummy or null address to packets at the terminals. This would make the structure of the packet uniform, regardless of its origin, when it arrives at the interface computer. This is the technique adopted by the British Post Office for their experimental packet switched service.

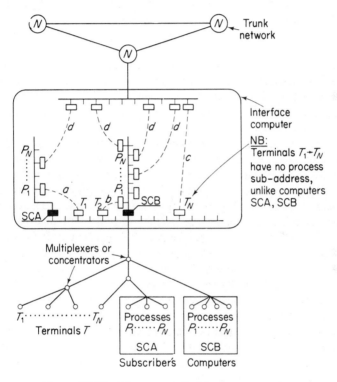

Figure 10.27.   The composite interface computer

Packet Structure

There are several factors that influence the choice of parameters and structure of the packets used in a network. Major factors are the physical structure of the network, the way traffic is handled by the network, and the nature of the traffic itself. These factors cannot be fully determined when a network is designed, and they may well change with time in an indefinite manner. The choice of the packet is, therefore, somewhat arbitrary. This means that independently designed networks are likely to differ in packet structure, but equally, that a standard packet should be acceptable for most applications.

Arising from existing private networks using block transfers of data, there have been two formal attempts to standardise on packet formats; one is based on the ISO code, using the double DLE escape method; the other is the high-level control procedure method which uses a flag (0 111 111 0) to delimit the block. Both of these methods, which are described in Chapter 6, page 233, can suffer from an increase in packet length due to the 'stuffing' technique used to provide a transparent message space. In the former case the length is doubled if a string of DLE characters occurs in the message; in the latter case, the length increases by at least a factor of 6/5 when a string of ones is encountered.

There seems to be only two methods of avoiding the undesirable increase in length of a message when particular kinds of information appear within it. One uses an idle/sync character together with a packet length indicator; the other uses an idle/sync character with a fixed packet length. The former scheme is potentially more flexible.

In either case, the idle character normally indicates the absence of meaningful information between packets; but the occurrence of idle characters within a packet causes no difficulty because they are known to be part of the message. The effect of noise causing corruption of idle characters and consequent false packet 'starts' must be well guarded against by a cyclic sum check—this can be located relative to the start of the packet—together with an error recovery procedure, which ensures the packet will be repeated if it is incorrectly received. It is also worthwhile chosing a special packet start character which is as different as possible from the idle character, rather than using the packet length character itself. The use of a packet start character obviously gives a more robust system and does not preclude a packet length equal to the binary value of the idle character, as would otherwise be the case.

The indication of the start of a packet, therefore, requires a sequence of three characters—idle, start, length. Thereafter, the information space is completely transparent, i.e. any codes may be used. The idle character could be the ISO SYN, or the 0 111 111 0 flag. Or, perhaps, the idle and non-idle (start) codes should be chosen for the maximum robustness of synchronisation and packet detection, i.e. the Hamming distance between them should be a maximum. A basic packet format incorporating these features is shown in Figure 10.28.

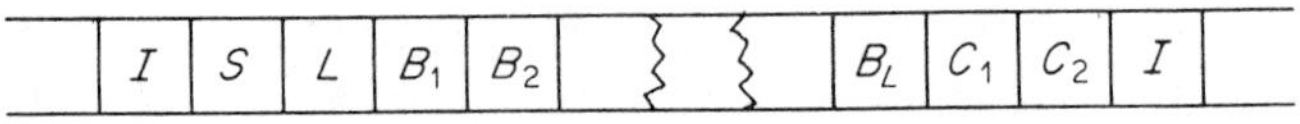

I = Idle byte; S = Start byte; L = Length byte; B_i = Data byte i; C = Check byte

Figure 10.28.   The basic transmitted packet

$$I, S\left[T, L, N\ (B_1, B_2\dots\dots B_L) C_1, C_2\right] I$$

T = Type byte; L = Length byte; N = Packet number byte.

Figure 10.29. The basic packet structure

In processing a packet two possibilities must be taken into account; the first is dynamic processing as it arrives from a data link, the second is static processing after it has been passed into a store. In either case, it may be necessary to vary the processing depending upon the type of packet, e.g. network control packets, subscriber's information packets, acknowledgements etc., so a type indication T should be associated with each packet. In addition, a packet number N is required so that acknowledgements may be related to the appropriate packet, and to allow the correct order of a sequence of packets to be determined statically. However, the idle-start sequence discussed above is only necessary in dynamic processing to locate the beginning of the packet, and will be removed when a packet is stored. The basic structure of a packet may, therefore, be regarded as shown in Figure 10.29.

This basic structure contains all the features necessary for communication between two equivalent levels in a hierarchy, and could, in principle at least, be employed in a 'nested' fashion at a number of levels. However, it is necessary to add a further feature to facilitate communication between two adjacent levels in a hierarchy. This must allow the packets belonging to a call, previously established through a network, to be uniquely identified from those of other calls. The technique to be recommended here is like the use of abbreviated addressing (see page 361). It demands the inclusion of Destination and Origin addresses with the packet header. However, as far as the handling of the packets is concerned, these addresses are complementary to the packet number, and must be concatenated with it to uniquely identify the packet. This same general format can apply at any level, and an example is given in Figure 10.30 of the form of the packets passing along a serial link between computers at adjacent levels in a network hierarchy.

It may be of interest and useful to express the nested packet structure in the form of a tree as in Figure 10.31. This illustrates the levels of hierarchy in the idealized network of Figure 10.22, set out as a nested packet below which appears an equivalent tree structure.

$$I, S\left\{T, L, N\left[T', L', \frac{N'}{DON}\ (B_1\dots\dots B_{L'})\ CC\right]CC\right\}I$$

T' = Type; L' = Length; N' = Destination + origin + number

NB: N' Uniquely identifies $(B_1\dots\dots B_{L'})$

Figure 10.30. Example of nested packets

... I, S (NODE (LAS (TP/SC (Process (Terminal))))) C, C, I ...

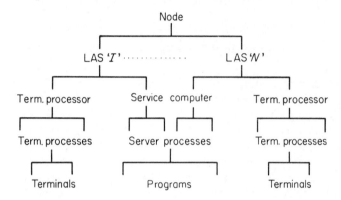

Figure 10.31. Packet format and equivalent tree structure

Packet Length

If a hierarchical packet structure is employed, each level has a length character which indicates the size of the information nested within that level, this permits changes to be made in the size of information fields at one level without seriously affecting other levels. There now arises the problem of chosing the packet length. This has been considered earlier in relation to response time and error control in Chapter 6, page 191. Here we will examine if from another viewpoint.

Although there is not a universal acceptance of the eight-bit byte for information exchange, it is essential to have a basic building block for use in information handling systems. An eight-bit byte seems about the right size for the purpose, and will have the same kind of relationship with data base structures that the Roman alphabet has with natural language. This view is supported by the existence of the ISO code (see Chapter 6, page 224). It seems reasonable, therefore, to base the packet on units of eight bits, and a length character of this size would allow a maximum length of 255 characters. It is likely that system designers will chose this as the maximum length at whatever level in the hierarchy they are working. For example, the SITA network and some bank networks handle packets of around 250 characters —usually a few are arbitrarily used for a header. This length of packet would, therefore, conveniently carry both SITA and Bank packets; it would encompass the 192-character block used by the World Meteorological Network, and would take two of the ARPA network packets.

If the hierarchical scheme of Figure 10.30 is used, each length character should refer to the total length as seen at that level in the hierarchy. As the block is built up from the inner level, the appropriate length is determined by

$$IS\left|\, T_1\, N_1\, L_1\, \{T_2\, N_2\, L_2\, [T_3\, N_3\, L_3\, \text{(DATA)}\, CC\,]\, CC\,\}\, CC\, \right|\, I$$

Figure 10.32. The extended hierarchy

adding the known new header and check bits to the existing length character to form the new one, though the existing one is retained unchanged also.

Unfortunately, a problem arises if the *inner* level length is allowed to be 255 because more than eight bits are needed for the overall length character. There is a parallel situation in the choice of an eight-bit byte by both computer system designers and PCM telephony system designers, because it is a convenient and 'natural' size. Unfortunately, the result has been that it is impossible to add an extra status or qualifying bit to an eight-bit data byte and pass the whole through a PCM channel.

The choice of a maximum overall length of 255 characters has an attraction from the point of view of using hardware at the trunk link level, because it is easy to load the length character into a store and count it down to find the packet end. However, if only a few fixed-length headers were used (indicated by the 'type' code) the appropriate length could also be added by the hardware. An even better arrangement is to make one of the 'type' code bits an additional length bit to give a $1+8=9$ bit length code.

It could be argued this is inelegant because we are effectively looking only at one point in a hierarchy, which could, in principle, be extended as in Figure 10.32. Here we would have to decide how big L_1 should be and so on. It is also possible that the data field might be used by the subscriber's computer to handle logical links, i.e. to sub-comutate the packets. So, within a 'private' network using the public one as a carrier, a format such as in Figure 10.33 could be employed within the network data field.

At the subscriber's level there will be some concern about the size of the information field finally remaining after such schemes have been implemented. However, we can set broad limits on the minimum and maximum lengths to be expected in the overall system including the network and the portions within the subscriber's systems.

Both the NPL and ARPA networks use 128 character packets; this will be the minimum size of data space likely to be expected by the new subscribers.

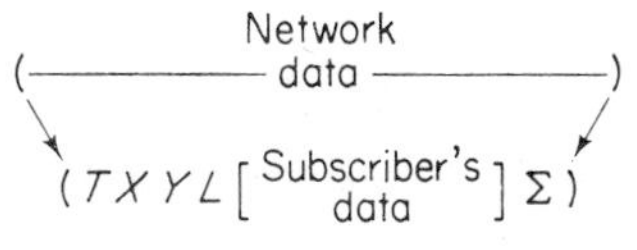

Where T = type, X and Y are link or store addresses, L is the length and Σ a sum check; all generated by the subscriber's computer

Figure 10.33. Use of standard format by subscriber

But as the SITA and Bank networks already use 255 character packets, this seems overwhelmingly the right choice for the data space, for a future public network that may have to carry packets from existing networks.

The maximum overall packet size will be data, plus all headers added at higher network levels, but if the headers become too large compared with the packet length the inefficiency will be intolerable. The proposal made above for nine length bits gives a total of 511 characters with 255 for data, and 256 for headers. This is obviously adequate, so the proposed format would seem the right choice for any public network.

The possibility was mentioned earlier of using fixed length packets. This has much to commend it because the handling problems would be reduced to some extent; for example storage allocation within switches would be easier, and the sum check would be in a known position. In fact, the original packet proposed by NPL in 1967 and shown in Figure 10.34 made use of segmentation to improve the efficiency of handling very short messages, and packets were variable in length from one to eight segments. The 'more' bit indicated whether another segment followed, while the 'hand-over' field was incremented each time a packet passed through a node. This gave an indication of how long the packet had spent in the network. It now seems that the use of a more finely variable length packet offers the greater flexibility necessary for coping with unpredictable future needs. Later, by common agreement, one or more fixed length standard packet formats could be introduced if this proved desirable.

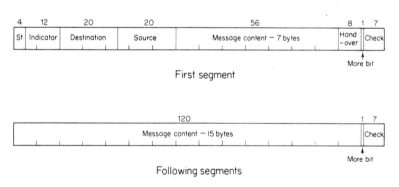

Figure 10.34. NPL proposed packet format, 1967

References

1. Baran, P., 'On Distributed Communication Networks', *IEEE Trans Communication Systems*, *CS-12*, 1-9 (March 1969).
2. Davies, D. W., Bartlett, K. A., Scantlebury, R. A., and Wilkinson, P. T., 'A digital communications network for computers giving rapid response at remote terminals', *Proc. ACM Symposium on Operating System Principles*, Gatlinburg (1967).

3. Roberts, L. G., 'Multiple computer networks and intercomputer communication', *Proc ACM Symposium on Operating System Principles*, Gatlinburg (1967).
4. Roberts, L. G., and Wessler, B. D., 'Computer network development to achieve resource sharing'., *AFIPS Conference Proceedings Spring Joint Computer Conference*, **36**, 543 (1970).
5. Scantlebury, R. A., Wilkinson, P. T., and Bartlett, K. A., 'The design of a message switching centre for a digital communication network', *Proc. IFIP Congress*, Hardware D 26 (1968).
6. Barber, D. L. A., and Davies, D. W., 'The NPL Data Network', *USSR All-Union Symposium 'The Automation of Scientific Research on the Computer base'*, Novosibirsk (Oct. 1970).

Chapter 11

Protocols, Terminals and Network Monitoring

11.1 INTRODUCTION

We saw in Chapter 10 that in a data communication network, communication takes place between processes located in computers. These computers fall broadly into two classes; firstly, service computers, where the communicating processes give access to one or more services such as information retrieval, remote job entry, interactive computation, editing etc., and secondly terminal processors, where the communicating processes represent terminals which permit users to make use of some, or all, of the available services. Generally the two classes will be separate, but there is no reason why a single computer should not act in both a service and user role; for example, when a service computer needs to make use of a back-up service (perhaps a data bank) in order to satisfy some demand from a user, or when two terminal processors need to intercommunicate so that users at terminals can converse with each other.

To cater for the various kinds of communication between processes possible in a network, it is essential to have sets of rules governing interactions to ensure they proceed in an orderly fashion. These sets of rules have become known as *protocols*, and the design and wide agreement of protocols is really the key to the effective exploitation of computers on a large scale.

This chapter is concerned with the difficulties of devising protocols, with the related problem of how terminals should be handled through a network, and with the monitoring and control features that must be associated with a network, to measure and maintain its performance once it is in operation.

11.2 PROTOCOLS

In all communication situations, rules of procedure called protocols are needed to enable things to go smoothly, without errors or hang-ups. We need a protocol to establish 'links' or 'calls' between processes and for clearing down these links and, during the communication phase, we need protocols for

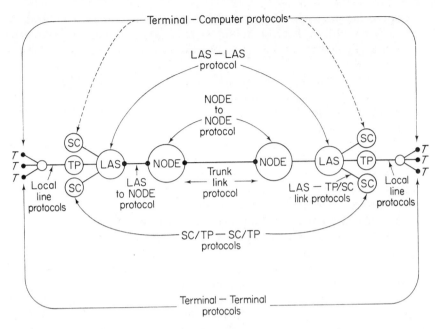

Figure 11.1.   Variety of protocols in a network

ensuring that there are adequate buffers and for interrupting from either end, when the course of the interaction has to be changed.

Arbitrary rules could be devised for particular pairs of processes, but there are clear advantages in trying to define standard protocols for use throughout the network. It is obviously convenient to devise a hierarchical set of protocols for the same sort of reason that it is desirable to define a hierarchical structure for the network itself. There will be low level protocols concerned with establishing and maintaining connections, higher level protocols concerned with the transfer of messages once connections have been made, and still higher level protocols concerned with the transfer of programs, files etc. in terms of the succession of messages. These are illustrated in Figure 11.1, which shows their logical relationships. We have already met some of these protocols in Chapter 6, in connection with information flow control and interfaces, while a further example appears in Chapter 13, where the software needed to operate certain protocols is discussed. In this chapter, the basic principles of protocols are examined and illustrated by references to practical networks.

In general there are three desirable features that should be possessed by each level of protocol: firstly it should be transparent to levels above it, so that nothing sent by a higher level can be affected by lower levels; secondly it should be self–limiting so that it is impossible under normal circumstances to require the provision of potentially infinite storage, or to spend infinite time in a programme loop or waiting state; finally it should be possible to make changes to one level of protocol without requiring extensive changes at other levels.

The concept of a *call*, discussed in Chapter 10, can be used in the definition of a protocol. We are used to the idea of a call between distant terminals or computers, but are less likely to regard it as relevant to links between processes in one and the same computer. Actually, distance is not the important factor, and the logical features of a protocol can be made the same whether the processes being interconnected are in distant computers or co–located. In both cases, too, a call may, or may not, be the relevant concept. If no resources (such as addresses or allocated buffers) are provided for the link between two processes it is rather odd to speak of a call between them. For example the sending of a single addressed packet from process A to process B does not commit them in any way, though it might be the start of the protocol for setting up a call which *will* occupy resources.

The use of a hierarchical network structure leads to two basic kinds of protocol; one governs communication between equivalent levels in the hierarchy, the other controls the interaction between different levels. For example, in Figure 11.1, the node-to-node, the LAS-to-LAS (Local Area Switch), the TP-to-TP (Terminal Processor) and the terminal-to-terminal protocols are between equivalent levels; whereas the node-to-LAS, the LAS-to-TP and the TP-to-terminal protocols cross the boundary between adjacent levels. In a properly designed system, boundary-crossing protocols should be confined to interaction between neighbouring levels; there should be no question, for example, of a terminal communicating directly with a node.

Later, we shall deal in more detail with the design of protocols, but first we introduce the idea of a network control program.

The Network Control Program

The operating system in a multiprogrammed computer is responsible for scheduling the allocation of resources among the processes which are competing for them. It also controls the exchange of messages between the processes and is generally in charge of what is going on. It seems desirable to have something similar in each computer connected to a network, in order to monitor and control the way processes use the resources of the network when they communicate through it. This is the Network Control Program (NCP) shown in Figure 11.2.

The NCP in each computer communicates with those in other computers in order to establish calls, allocate storage and control the flow of information between the computer and the network. A group of NCPs forms a kind of distributed operating system which governs the intercommunication of the processes for which they are collectively responsible.

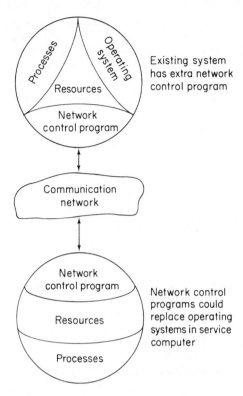

Figure 11.2. The network control program

Within any one computer, there will be a problem of reconciling the NCP with the normal operating system, because both of these will be competing for the computer's resources. The relative weighting given to the requests from the operating system and from the NCP determines the split between the local activity and the activity taking place through the network.

When the computing system is an existing service, such as an ARPA HOST, the relative activity through the network will be low; but as the technology of networks develops we will see the emergence of service computers whose activity is entirely devoted to communications through the network. In this case, the NCP could replace the operating system.

To create an environment in which processes can freely communicate, the Network Control Programs need to exchange messages with each other. There will be one protocol governing such message exchanges, another governing the communication between processes themselves, and yet another governing the interaction between an NCP and its associated processes.

The process-to-process and NCP-to-NCP protocols are examples of communication between equivalent levels in a hierarchy, while the process-to-NCP protocol will, of course, cross the boundary between two adjacent levels.

Protocol Functions

In a well conceived network there will be several levels of protocol reflecting its basic hierarchical structure. There will, obviously, be differences between the protocols at each level, depending upon the particular tasks they have to perform. However, there will be certain fundamental features found in most, if not all, protocols. For example, the control of data flow is a common problem, whether it is characters between terminals, packets between nodes, messages between service computers, or commands between processes within computers.

To ease the development problems of a complex network it may well prove convenient to draw a distinction between protocols that are internal to the network, and those that govern external activities, but the essential similarities between all protocols should be kept in mind to avoid undue duplication of function.

In this section we discuss, in the context of the NCP and its processes, the fundamental tasks that must be performed by protocols, and make some general comments on the ways they can be implemented. Particular types of protocol adopted in the ARPA network, and others (suggested as a result of theoretical work at NPL) are described later.

The protocols covering interaction between the NCPs must permit the following functions to be performed:

1. The opening, maintenance and closing of connections.
2. Flow control.
3. Process initiation.
4. Process interruption.
5. Development and maintenance.
6. Recovery from failure.

The most basic of these tasks is that of opening, maintaining and closing a call. In principle only two commands are required: one to request that the call connection be made and the other to disconnect a call or refuse a connection. The positive acceptance of a request to open a call may be a reply of the same command. A disconnect command may be used in two ways: as a negative response to refuse a call, and as a positive acknowledgement of a request to disconnect a call received from the other network control program.

To cater for failure situations there should be some time limit on the delay that is allowable between sending a connect or disconnect command and receiving a response. This time must be long compared with the normal message transit time. The problem of failure must also be considered in relation to the maintenance of a connection once it is established. If there are long gaps between the admission of messages through an established call there may be some doubt as to whether everything is still operational. A simple way to check this is for the network control program to exchange, at regular intervals, a null message with each of the other network control programs to which it is connected.

The control of the flow of data through a connection has to be regulated so that congestion of the network, or of the subscriber's computers, cannot occur. The simplest method of controlling flow is to ensure that a message may not be transmitted until an acknowledgement has been received in response to the previous message. There is a danger that an NCP could fail and repeatedly send messages, without waiting for a response; it is essential to provide means for each of the other NCPs to ignore these false messages.

The simple method of waiting for an acknowledgment of each packet would allow only one process connected to the network control program to be active at a time. To overcome this restriction it is necessary to distinguish messages from the network control program by a process address; the size of this address determines how many simultaneously active processes may be in communication with each other.

A more complex flow control method was mentioned in Chapter 6 page 196, in relation to elastic buffers. It was suggested that a computer—or, as we now see, its NCP—could dynamically assess the volume of traffic it was handling, and could allocate storage accordingly. It could then commit itself to accepting a number of messages and could indicate this fact to NCPs in other computers. There would need to be an exchange of control messages between all cooperating NCPs, but it is very likely that a scheme such as this would speed up the flow of information in the network.

Generally, communication in a network will be taking place between active processes, but there may sometimes arise the situation where one process wishes to call a process in another computer which is not active, and it may take some time to awaken the process. A network control program endeavouring to open a call with such a process may have to wait an indefinite time and it might be desirable to extend the call opening protocol to take account of this possibility.

Another necessary facility is that of process interruption. This may be required when a process has been initiated, but circumstances have changed and require the process to change its activity in some way. An example is that of a terminal process (controlling a user's terminal) communicating with another process carrying out a computation for the user. The user may wish to stop the computation, because he has changed his mind about what is required. To achieve process interruption there needs to be some kind of 'out-band' signalling so that the NCPs associated with the processes can communicate rapidly outside the channel allocated to these two processes, and break into this channel to alter the course of events.

It is particularly important in any network to be able to develop new programs and equipment without disrupting the normal service of the network, and without incurring the risk that errors in the untested equipment will cause failures of the whole network. A useful tool for testing the network is the ability to echo a message from any level in the network hierarchy. A message is sent from one computer to another, which returns the message, essentially unchanged, to the first. This can be done either by invoking special test processes in each computer or by arranging for the network control program to have special facilities for echoing. A more general facility would be to use an echo command which could precede any message and would cause this message to be returned by any process that decoded the command. This would be particularly useful in the development of new programs, because an echoing process could be made to insert its address, and this would enable misdirected or mishandled messages to be traced.

The final problem is that of recovery after a failure. If a computer or part of the network fails there must be a reliable way of getting back into normal operation afterwards. When the failed portion recovers, a command is required to indicate that any outstanding calls will have been corrupted and should be abandoned. A reply to this command is required to indicate that it has been received, that all calls have been disconnected and that the other NCPs are again ready to cooperate with the recovered portion of the network. An alternative method can be adopted if the network contains an acceptably coherent clock. Each process can have a time-out covering a reasonable delay in the response to any of its messages. If this delay is exceeded, the associated NCP assumes that the remote NCP has gone out of action, and sends an interrogation signal to it at regular intervals. Only when one of these interrogations is answered does it assume that the other NCP has recovered.

In the following sections, protocols are described which are based on practical experience with the ARPA network and the NPL local network experiment.[1,2]

It is usually found that a protocol devised 'from cold' shows up some problems when it is put into real operation. The modifications found necessary in the ARPA network are described, together with some new proposals for an ARPA protocol. The protocol first proposed by the NPL group[3] was found by simulation to be inefficient and it has been completely revised in a more strictly heirarchical fashion, which is also described below.

The ARPA Original Protocols

The ARPA Network interconnects a set of computers known as HOSTs. One or more of these HOSTs can be connected to an IMP and the IMPs are connected together to form a communications sub-network. Information is exchanged between the HOSTs in the form of messages; these are split into packets by the associated IMP and sent from IMP to IMP until they reach the one adjacent to the destination HOST where they are reassembled into the message before being sent to the HOST. The three main reasons for using packets are: firstly, the transmission of a message can begin as soon as the first packet is assembled; secondly, the corruption of information by noise requires the retransmission of a packet rather than a whole message; thirdly, long messages do not block transmission links, because packets can be inter- leaved.

Although the ARPA Network is intended to handle messages and packets, the HOST-HOST protocol is based on the idea of connections which must be established before processes can send messages. Connections are established between sockets through which data may be sent in one direction only. The sockets are identified by a 32-bit HOST number, with 24 bits specifying a user identification while seven bits are freely assignable, the last bit indicating if the socket is to be used for sending or receiving data. When a connection is set up, the receiving HOST allocates a link number which is used together with the HOST number to identify the connection. The link number occupies an eight-bit field, and is an example of the use of an abbreviated, or 'call' address, described earlier in connection with network structure (see Chapter 10, page 361).

Figure 11.3 shows diagrammatically the way that processes are linked via the HOST-HOST protocol. There are potentially 2^{31} receive and 2^{31} send sockets at each HOST, corresponding to the 32 bit socket numbers. The correspondence between these sockets is set up by the HOST-HOST protocol. Each connection from a send to a receive socket is identified by a link number.

The correspondence between processes in the HOST and sockets is maintained by the HOST's 'network control program' (NCP). A process, as shown, may have several send or receive 'ports' each identified with a particular socket. In this way, the correspondence of a sending port at one HOST with a receiving port at another HOST is established. The connections shown are functionally like circuit connections, but really they take the form of entries in tables, used to handle messages from one process to another.

The NCPs in the HOSTs control the communication between different

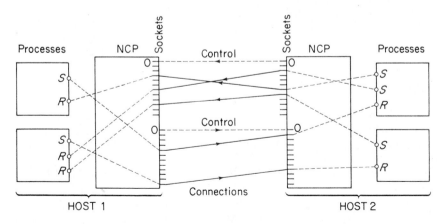

Figure 11.3.   Connections and sockets in the ARPA HOST-HOST protocol

HOSTs through the medium of the intervening network. Each NCP is able to receive messages from other NCPs using its own 'link zero'. This use of the 'link zero' channel allows the NCPs to communicate with each other rather than with processes. However, as far as the network is concerned, these communications appear to be standard messages. The messages exchanged between NCPs can carry one or more control commands. These control commands are used for a variety of purposes in addition to exchanging requests to open and close connections. This means that the exchange of messages between NCPs is used for both HOST to HOST protocol and Initial Connection protocol. This use of the same mechanism in two levels of hierarchy may be regarded as a weakness in the original design of the ARPA Network.

A connection between two processes in different machines is established by arranging for their NCPs to exchange requests for a connection over the link zero channel. The sender specifies the length of the bytes to be used in the communication, while the receiver specifies the link number.

The control commands used to establish and break connections are shown in the first part of Table 11.1, together with the parameters that each command uses. To establish one connection, matching requests must be exchanged by the sender and receiver HOSTs; the socket numbers given in the commands must match.

The receiver specifies the link number, and this number is used in subsequent flow control commands, such as those shown in the table. Link 0 is assumed to be always open for exchange of control commands between HOSTs, and therefore does not need socket numbers, because after a connection is set up the socket numbers are needed only for breaking it.

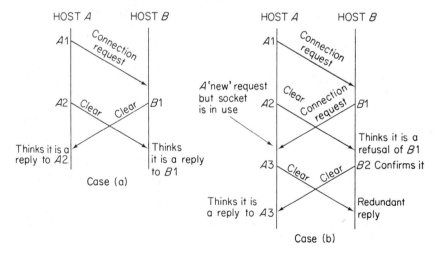

Figure 11.4.   Crossover of control commands in the ARPA HOST-HOST protocol

Command code	Origin of command	Name of Command	Parameters Link number	Byte size	Sender socket	Receiver socket	Message socket	Bit space
STR	S	Sender's connection request		×	×	×		
RTS	R	Receiver's connection request	×		×	×		
CLS	S/R	Clear connection			×	×		
ALL	R	Allocate buffer	×				×	×
GVB	R	Request to give back allocation*	×				M/128	B/128
RET	S	Return of allocation	×				×	×
INR	R	Interupt by receiver	×					
INS	S	Interupt by sender	×					

* The fraction of remaining allocation in 1/128 ths is specified.
Note[1] Echo, reset and error commands have different sets of parameters.

Table 11.1 Commands used in the ARPA HOST-HOST protocol to control a link

Breaking connections is done by an exchange of disconnect requests. Only when this exchange is completed can the connection be forgotten. The exchange of disconnect requests is also used to refuse a connection. This technique avoids any possibility of a 'race' situation which might otherwise occur if one NCP sent a request for connection, but withdrew it just as another NCP was either refusing, or accepting it.

Figure 11.4 shows two such situations. In part (a) a request for connection

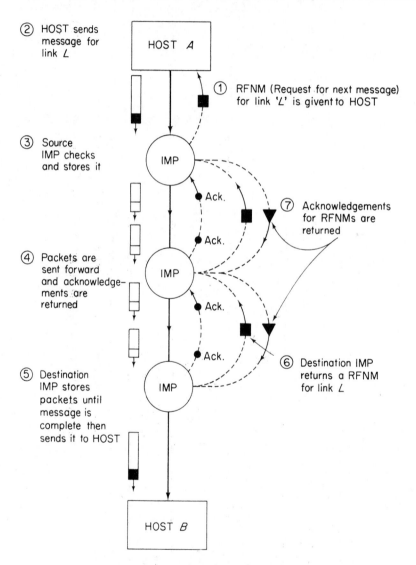

Figure 11.5.   Flow control at network level

is sent, but the originator has decided to abort the request by the clear request (A2). The other party refused the request and this message (B1) crosses with A2. No problem arises because each party thinks the clear request it receives is a reply to its own clear request, and the connection is never set up.

In part (b) a different case is shown in which the HOST B accepts a connection but A has meanwhile decided to abort. In this case, B thinks the clear request A2 is a refusal of his connection request, and he acknowledges it by B2. The other HOST treats the message B1 as a new call request, but the sockets it shows are those shown in A1, and have not been returned in a clear request so they are still in use. A is forced to refuse the request, with A3. Now the commands A3 and B2 cross and each party regards the received command as a reply to its own clear request. Again the connection is correctly terminated.

Thus by having one kind of command for refusing a connection request, aborting a request and clearing a connection, the crossing of commands becomes innocuous.

Flow control in the ARPA Network is managed at two levels. At the network level, shown in Figure 11.5, the limitation is imposed of having only one message in transit through a particular link connection at any one time. This requires the network (in particular the local IMP) to recognize the link numbers in the messages. When the message has been received by the HOST computer a response is sent to the source HOST. This response is recognized by the source IMP, which removes the inhibition of a further message.

The second level of flow control, shown in Figure 11.6, involves the HOST computers. The destination NCP allocates the buffer space for a particular

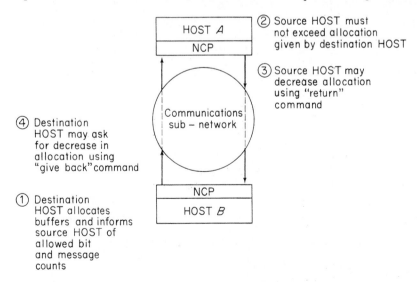

Figure 11.6. Flow control at HOST level

Origin of command	Command name	Parameters	Allocation messages	bit
S	Sender connection request	byte size = 8, sockets (120, 150)		
R	Receiver connection request	link = 5, sockets (150, 120)		
R	Allocate buffer	link = 5, messages 5, bits 5000	5	5000
S	Sends message of 1000 bits		4	4000
S	Sends message of 1500 bits		3	2500
R	Request to give back allocation	link = 5, messages 40/128, bits 50/128		
S	Return of allocation	link = 5, messages 1, bits 1000	2	1500
S	Sends message of 1000 bits		1	500
R	Allocate buffer	link 5, messages 5, bits 1000	6	5500
S	Clear connection	sockets (120, 150)		
R	Clear connection	sockets (150, 120)		

Table 11.2   Example of the use of the ARPA HOST-HOST Protocol

connection within the HOST and informs the source NCP by means of an allocate control command. The allocation is in terms of both a count of bits available for storage and a count of messages. The sending HOST should not exceed either of these allocations. Once the allocation has been exhausted, the sending HOST must wait for a further allocate control command before further messages are sent. The sending HOST can decrease this allocation by using the return command or a decrease may be requested by the receiving HOST by sending a give back by command. This specifies fractions of the allocation to avoid problems that might arise if a return command happened to be in transit.

The second part of Table 11.1 shows the three commands associated with flow control, and their parameters, together with two interrupt commands, Table 11.2 shows an example of their use. The right hand columns show the state of the buffer allocation counts at the sender's HOST after each command has been sent.

After the exchange of requests, link 5 has been established. Then the receiver allocates five messages and 5000 bits of storage space. Two messages are sent, leaving the counters at three messages and 2500 bits. At this stage the receiver requests the giving back of fractions 40/128 of messages and 50/128 of bits. The sender rounds the requested amounts up to one message and 1000 bits, which are the values specified in the 'return of allocation' command. After one more message is sent, and extra buffer is allocated, and the connection is cleared.

The connection established between two NCPs provides a way for one of their processes to interrupt another, even if these are joined only by a simple connection. Either process may interrupt the other. The interrupt requests are transmitted as control commands (interrupt by receiver, and interrupt by sender, see third part of Table 11.1) and are expected to be sent with high priority over the connection between the NCPs rather than waiting for the particular connection between the processes to become free. It is interesting that this facility was incorporated from the beginning, but the use of it only appeared during the development of terminal handling, in particular of the terminal IMP or TIP. The remaining control commands used in the ARPA network, as originally planned, are shown in Table 11.3.

For testing purposes, any NCP can send some text to another, and request it to be returned. For this purpose there are two control commands; echo request and echo reply. The command is followed by the length of the text which is to be returned. If an NCP receives a control command with the echo code it must return the command to the originating NCP with the echo code changed to echo reply. An NCP should only receive an echo reply control command in response to its own echo command.

For errors concerning a single message, such as an incorrect control code, the HOST that discovers the error should send an error command back to the originating HOST. The error command contains an indication of the kind of

Command Code	Name of Command	Message Content		
ECO	Echo Request	8 bits to be returned		
ERP	Echo Reply	8 bits returned as received		
ERR	Error Detected	8 bit Qualifier		Data
	Undefined	0		—
	Illegal	1		Illegal op. code
	Short Parameter	2		Command in error
	Erroneous Parameters	3		Command in error
	Non-existent socket	4		Command in error
	Link not connected	5		Command in error
RST	Reset	—		
RRP	Reset reply	—		
NOP	No operation	—		

Table 11.3   Further ARPA HOST-HOST Protocol Commands

error, and in some cases may have part of the control command found to be in error. For more serious errors, the reset command is provided. This should be used by one HOST to indicate to other HOSTs that it has failed and that any connections to it should be abandoned. Each HOST that receives such a message should reply with a reset reply command. This is the only reply apart from the 'HOST DEAD' error message from the network, that an NCP should expect after a reset message.

The final command shown in Table 11.3, no operation, is a dummy command that should be discarded by the receiver. It is included for possible use in the formatting of control messages, when several control commands are included in one message.

The NPL High Level Network Proposals

As a result of experience with the local area network built at NPL further theoretical studies were made of a high level network.[4] As shown in Figure 11.7, each User Machine (HOST) has a number of active processes. These processes can communicate with the network by calling on the services of an interprocess communication module (network control program) and a link control module which performs some of the functions carried out by the IMP

Procedural levels of a network

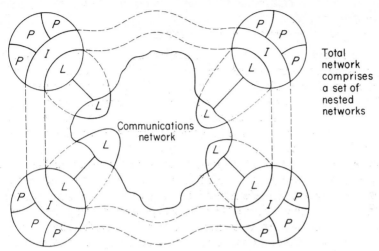

P–Processes; L–Link control module; I–Inter process communication module

Figure 11.7.   Revised NPL proposed network

in the ARPA network. Messages are transmitted across the network by packet switching and the messages are of a similar size to those of the ARPA network. However, it is intended that the messages should be an integral number of bytes rather than of bits.

When two processes wish to communicate they must set up a call. Unlike the ARPA network the calls in the NPL network are duplex and are established between channels in the user machines. In contrast to the 32-bit socket which is used by the ARPA network during the setting up of connections, NPL calls are between two channels each of which is specified within a user machine by an eight-bit field. A handshake procedure like the ARPA procedure is used in the control of calls.

The setting up of calls in the NPL scheme is done by using special message types, rather than by having a special channel in the NCP, as with the ARPA network. There is provision made for up to 16 different message types but only seven have so far been defined. The message types are as follows:

1. DATA, one of the two ways of getting information from one process to another.
2. NEXT, allows the receiver of this to send one data or one D/NEXT message.
3. D/NEXT, a combination of data and next; this is especially suitable for dialogues.
4. CALL, the request to set up a call.

5. END, the request to terminate a call.
6. REQUEST STATUS, request the status counts to be sent to the originator of such a message.
7. STATUS, the response to the request status.

The proposed interprocess control modules are much more involved in error checking than the ARPA network control programs. Each NPL message contains a modulo-16 sequence count of messages on that particular call. This allows the loss of a small number of messages to be detected. In addition to this, modulo-four counts are held of the numbers of DATA and NEXT messages sent and received. It is these modulo 4 counts that are transmitted in the status message.

Flow control in the NPL proposal is achieved by requiring that data messages may only be sent if a NEXT (or D/NEXT) message has been received. In contrast with the ARPA restriction that only one message may be in transit across a connection, the NEXT message permits, in principle, seven messages in transit if the sender has accumulated NEXTs. In practice a fairly low limit would probably be imposed by the interprocess communication modules.

A Packet Switching Protocol

The HOST-to-HOST protocol of the ARPA network operates by establishing and clearing connections, giving the network the appearance to the users of a circuit switched system. A different kind of protocol was proposed by D.C. Walden[5] to accord more with the message switching nature of the network. In this protocol each message exchange is a separate transaction. It seems that the software needed is simplified, but the overheads are greater for heavily used 'connections' because each message must be preceded by the exchange of control packets.

Figure 11.8 shows the principle of the scheme. A process prepares for message exchange by requesting a 'send' or 'receive' operation of its local

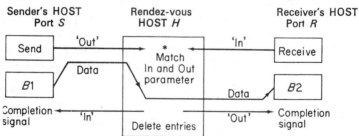

Send/Receive commands specify S, R, H, $B1$ or $B2$ and restart of process
NB: H is usually the sender or receiver

Figure 11.8.   An experimental protocol using messages

NCP. To do this it specifies the buffer which either contains the message or has been allocated to receive it and each party also specifies a 'rendez-vous' HOST. In practice, there is usually prior agreement that the rendez-vous is the sender or receiver, but we take the general case of HOST H in the figure.

The receiver's host executes the 'receive' command by sending the IN message to the rendez-vous. The sender's HOST executes the 'send' command by sending to the same rendez-vous an OUT message together with the data message derived from the specified buffer.

The NCP of the rendez-vous HOST has the job of matching up the IN and OUT messages. When they match, it can delete them from its records and send them out to the corresponding parties. Here the IN and OUT messages act as confirmation of the transfer, while the data message reaches the buffer in the receiver.

Earlier forms of the protocol had fixed the rendez-vous at one or other of the active HOSTs, but neither case is completely satisfactory. A rendez-vous at the receiver is convenient for 'listening' for messages from any sender, but once the need for communication is established, a rendez-vous at the sender is more convenient—so both will be used, but probably not the use of a third party.

ARPA Network Experience

A number of changes have been made in the ARPA network as a result operating experience.[6] The main changes have been made in flow control algorithms and routing algorithms, which are internal to the communications sub-network, i.e. those illustrated by Figure 11.5. The fact that these changes may be made without affecting the external protocols at the HOST-to-HOST level shows the wisdom of using a hierarchical network and protocol structure.

If, in any network, traffic is sent to a destination in excess of the average rate at which it can accept traffic, the stores near that destination will gradually fill up and congestion will spread back into the network from the overloaded destination. By deliberately arranging such an overload condition in the original ARPA network, two kinds of logical deadlock were made to occur. These are called reassembly lock up and store-and-forward lock up.

Reassembly lock up arises when a number of partially reassembled messages have occupied the available free space in a destination IMP. The space cannot be released to accept new packets until a message is completed and sent to the HOST. But this completion is not possible because the packets required are held up in the network waiting for reassembly space to become free.

Reassembly lock up is shown in Figure 11.9. The IMP is shown as having started the assembly of three messages A, B and C, and we suppose that this is all the message assembly space that is available. Packets E1, F1 and G1 are due to arrive on the link from three neighbouring IMPs, and since they

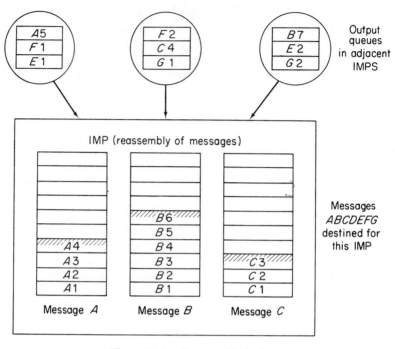

Figure 11.9.   Reassembly lock up

are at the head (with G2) of the output queues no other packets can be sent before them. But there is no room to start assembly of new packets so the system is locked up. If the source to destination IMP protocol for packet exchange allowed for many packets to be discarded and sent again, the problem could be averted—up to a point, but there is a limit to this process because it uses up storage at the sending IMPs.

This is a good example of the deadly embrace situation described by Dijkstra, for example, in relation to the storage allocation lock up occurring in multi-process systems.[7] The difficulty arises primarily because the HOSTs are allowed to set up a number of links each of which has a single message in transit through the network, but this message will be distributed through the network in terms of a number of packets. It is the interference between the packets of the different messages destined for reassembly at a single IMP that causes message reassembly lock up when all the buffer space at the IMP has been allocated. Fundamentally the fault arises through a weakness in the design, whereby storage is allocated on a packet basis, but requested on a message basis; this confusion beween two levels in the hierarchy of a network is primarily the cause of the reassembly lock up problem. Reassembly lock up can occur, of course, whether all the packets arrive along a single link or whether they come to the destination from a number of different links.

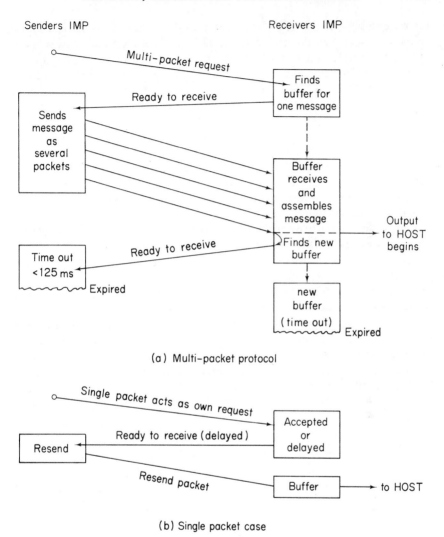

(a) Multi-packet protocol

(b) Single packet case

Figure 11.10.   Revised ARPA IMP-IMP protocol

To avoid reassembly lock up a change in the source to destination IMP protocol is proposed. It is illustrated in Figure 11.10. Essentially the scheme is for each message to reserve the buffer space needed for reassembly before its transmission is started. Part (a) of the figure shows the general case. The sender's IMP makes a request for space—a single packet message to the destination IMP. When a one message buffer has been allocated a 'ready to receive' message is returned, and this initiates the packet by packet transmission of the message to the destination. There it will find adequate space for reassembly. At the end of the process the message is assembled and it starts to be sent over the link to the HOST. At the same time a new message buffer is allocated and a new 'ready to receive' is sent back to the sender.

If the sender has a heavy traffic load, it will probably reply at once with a new packet and the process can continue, so in effect a high bandwidth link has been established between the IMPs. But if no messages are waiting, after a time-out the sending IMP will block the further use of the link and require a 'multi-packet request' to be send. Shortly afterwards the receiver will time-out and release the buffer it has allocated. Note that the high bandwidth link is set-up between IMPs, not HOSTs, and if there are several HOSTs at the sending end any one of them can keep the link open.

But this protocol would be wasteful for just single packet messages which have no reassembly problem, so they have their own simplified procedure, shown in part (b) of the figure. The single packet can be accepted at once, or sent again when the 'ready to receive' is returned.

Store-and-forward lock up takes two forms, direct and indirect. Direct store-and-forward lock up is shown in Figure 11.11. A pair of IMPs has many packets which are due to be routed to each other. The respective output queues have taken up all the packet buffers available, shown as N, so no buffers are available to take up the packets sent. The resolution of this problem is not difficult. No one output queue should be allowed to collect all the packet buffers. If one is reserved for input as in part (b) then one packet can move. If each output queue has one buffer reserved for it, the packets exchanged can get away to other IMPs.

Indirect store-and-forward lock up is shown in Figure 11.12 in the form in

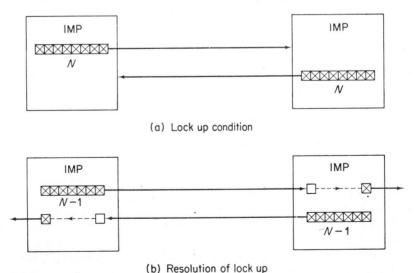

(a) Lock up condition

(b) Resolution of lock up

Figure 11.11.   Direct store-and-forward lock up

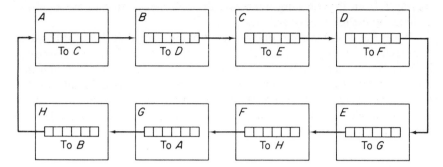

Figure 11.12.   Indirect store-and-forward lock up

which it was observed in simulations of the ARPA network. Here it is necessary to get at least eight IMPs in a ring loaded with packets routed round the
ring, one way. They are shown as destined for the IMP which is two links
away from their present position. This is a contrivance to make it unlikely
that they would be routed the other way, but impossible to dispose of them
quickly as in the direct lock up situation. This form of lock up is not likely
to happen in practice, but it is difficult to devise simple rules to avoid it
completely.

In the original ARPA network design the idea of the software link
RFNM (Request for Next Message) gave protection against congestion due
to a single link or a small number of links. This strategy did not give protection against lock up, but the method was acceptable for the low levels of
traffic encountered in the early days of the network. Further flow control
algorithms have been added to the original IMP design to prevent congestion
and lock up occurring with heavier traffic load. Essentially these allow a
destination IMP to discard packets at the onset of congestion, so that they
have to be retransmitted a short time later by the originating IMP. In this
way traffic is queued at the fringe of the network so that the transit time delay
inside the network continues to remain small. This kind of behaviour is also
obtained with techniques that have been proposed by NPL. Further discussion
of these, and related, ideas is given in the next section, but it is worth noting
here that the dual requirements of minimizing the delay for interactive
traffic, and providing a high band width for the fast transfer of files between
HOSTs, have to be reconciled. To allow a high bandwidth between a pair of
HOSTs the network must be able to carry a steady flow of packets from one to
the other and at the same time must be able to quench rapidly the flow at the
entrance to the source link in the event of imminent congestion occuring at the
destination link. To do this implies that the handshaking should occur over
a large number of packets, i.e. maximum length messages must be used. But
if this is done, a separate provision has to be made to protect short interactive

messages from experiencing unnecessarily high delays, due to the blocking of links by the long messages.

While the flow control problem is that of ensuring that the total traffic in the network does not exceed its capability, the problem of routing is to carry information in such a way that the best use is made of the network, and that the traffic actually in it is transferred as rapidly as possible. To do this it is necessary to distribute the traffic through the network in an optimum manner, and this implies the need for some form of adaptive routing, a subject we return to in the next chapter.

11.3 CONGESTION IN DATA NETWORKS

Congestion can show itself in different ways. In a circuit switched network, further calls may become impossible. In a packet switched network, the transit delay may increase, and this is self-limiting because it reduces the rate at which the network can carry data. Faults, or even dead terminals can cause local congestion which may isolate a section of the network.

A more subtle cause of congestion is a logical error in design causing a 'lock up' of the kind often known as a 'deadly embrace'. It is difficult to predict in advance all the possibilities for such lock ups, but fortunately there are methods of congestion control which make them unlikely.

Congestion control must inevitably mean that some traffic offered to the network is rejected, but in the case of packet switching it is often possible to ration the available network capacity so that the majority of users, who do not need high data rates, are unaware of problems.

Quite small errors of design can give rise to lock ups, so it is worthwhile to test any new network under stringent conditions in an attempt to find any tendency towards lock up. If there is, the nature of the design error is not usually difficult to trace and remove. Examples mentioned above are the reassembly lock up found in the ARPA network, the direct store and forward lock up which was easily cured, and the indirect form which was a rather contrived and unlikely event.

Congestion Control Methods

Control methods can be classified as 'local', 'end-to-end' or 'global'.

Local control is like the use of local rules for routing packets. It can help to reroute traffic round a point of local congestion but because the information is local, control only begins after congestion has built up.

End-to-end control is exemplified by the 'RFNM' used in the ARPA network, and it can reduce the number of packets present in the network but not, as we shall see later, sufficiently to have an effect on global congestion.

Nevertheless, end-to-end control is important because, as in HOST-HOST protocol, it prevents local congestion due to a breakdown. Of course, the chosen protocol may, because of failure, be disobeyed, so there may be a need in practice to set up sentinels which recognise erroneous packets and remove them.

Global control attempts to prevent the general overloading which can cause a slowing down of traffic or eventually a complete seizure. But a central controller is not generally favoured (a) because its control data adds to the load on the system, and (b) because it is vulnerable to failure. A distributed method of control is preferred. There seems to be a need for both end-to-end control (which in any case is part of the mechanism of end-to-end protocol) and global control.

The Effects of Global Congestion

There are two attitudes to global congestion. It can be regarded as the effect of design errors. If each logical possibility for 'lock up' is removed, the network must then be able to move packets and overcome any congestion situation. But, in practice, if the queues are mostly full the freedom to move packets is so restricted that the traffic movement is small.

In order to study congestion, the model must include an entire data network of moderate size and all the details of queuing in nodes, of routing and the control of links between nodes should be accurately represented. The complexity of such a model prevents the use of the analytic methods of queuing theory. Perhaps the model could be simplified sufficiently to apply queuing theory, but in the first place a detailed simulation is necessary in order to validate the approximate model. Congestion was studied using a model network for part of the UK. The topology chosen was the one shown in Figure 10.2 but for practical reasons the number of nodes was cut down to 18 by removing the northernmost six nodes in the figure. The model was very detailed, including all the queues in the nodes, but not the details of the operating system. In all the simulation work to be described, the traffic matrix was based on the populations of the main towns in which the nodes were placed. The traffic between any two towns was taken to be proportional to the product of their populations and this rule makes the total originating traffic at a town proportional to its population. In order to vary the traffic level, so that congestion effects could be produced, the constant of proportionality was altered, keeping the relative traffic levels the same.

The first simulation used a method of routing and link control which had been devised in the early work at NPL. This network showed a bad tendency to lock up, so two small changes in the operating rules of the network were made. The first modification was to inhibit all originating traffic at a node when any of its output queues became full. The second modification was made

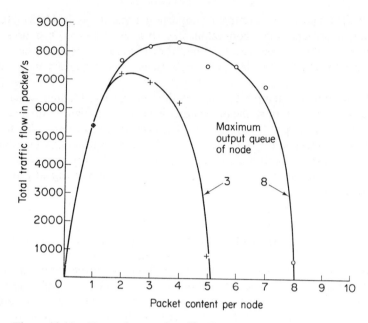

Figure 11.13. Dependence of traffic flow on total packet content

to the routing algorithm and prevented a packet which had only one more link to traverse to reach its ultimate destination from being sent to any other intermediate node. These changes greatly improved the performance.

Using the new model, the effect of global congestion was studied and the characteristics shown in Figure 11.13 were produced. The total number of packets in the system was held constant in an unusual and perhaps artificial manner. Because the simulation had knowledge of the condition of the entire network, it could allow a packet to enter only when one was delivered to its destination. The entering packets were distributed among the nodes and with destinations such that the (proportionate) traffic matrix of the model was preserved. It was thus possible to plot this characteristic of the total flow through the network in packets per second against the number of packets in transit—the total packet content. The packet content was expressed as 'packets per node', in other words the total was divided by 18 to normalize for the size of the network.

Near the origin, the flow is proportional to packet content, because packets spend, on average, a time in the network which is not affected by flow. At the other extreme, as the number of packets in the network increases, the flow falls because the space for manoeuvring the packets between queues has been reduced.

The total amount of storage in the network obviously affects the number of packets it can usefully hold, so the characteristic is plotted for two sizes of maximum output queue. It depends on queue length in an obvious manner.

The aim of network design should be to handle the greatest number of packets per second of which the network is capable, assuming there is a demand from the users for this level of traffic. So we should not allow the number of packets in the system to go beyond the point which produces the maximum traffic in Figure 11.13. A method of control was therefore proposed which would achieve this control of packet content.

Isarithmic Congestion Control

To hold constant the total number of packets in the system implies a global control method and therefore some control messages between nodes to operate this control system. But the extra traffic must be minimized. The system proposed has a certain constant number of *permits* circulating in the system. No packet is allowed to enter until it has acquired one of these permits. The packet can then travel through the network, accompanied by its permit, and it releases the permit when it reaches its destination.

In order to make permits available where they are needed they are sent round the network in a random manner when they are not actually in use.

This mechanism keeps constant the total number of packets in transit plus the unused permits so we called it the *isarithmic* method.[8] This is derived from the words iso (constant) and arithmos (number).

The extra traffic due to those permits which are not attached to packets but are cruising in the network will reduce the traffic carrying capacity slightly. But between two busy nodes they need not be sent as special messages and can take the form of a small field in the header of normal, data-carrying packets. It is also possible for one such field in a header to carry a number representing a small batch of permits, if this proves more economic. Where there is no data traffic, permits must still be distributed, and are put into special messages which take the form of normal packets but carry no user's data. When the traffic is heavy, there will not be a large proportion of unattached permits in transit, so the reduction in carrying capacity will not be serious.

The average transit delay, the traffic capacity and the number of packets in the system are obviously related and one effect of isarithmic control is to put an upper limit on the transit delay experienced for a given source-destination pair. There could, by chance, be longer delays due to local accumulations of packets but the upper end of the transit-time distribution is curtailed.

The isarithmic mechanism, like any other congestion control, operates by excluding excess traffic from the network. It does this by refusing a packet when there is no permit and making these packets queue outside the communication network. To avoid congestion at the local level, or in the interface computers, this flow control must be signalled outward to the user.

The Permit Pool

It is important to minimize the new source of delay which is experienced by packets because of the need to pick up a permit. This delay we call the *admission delay*. Under conditions of light load it is not desirable to have all the unattached permits in movement and make the newly entering packet wait for one to arrive. Instead, we hold at each node a small *permit pool*. In practice this is no more than a number representing the quantity of available permits. A new packet entering the system at a node with a non-empty pool does so without delay and simply reduces the pool by one. Using an analogy in which the permits are thought of as 'taxis' cruising round looking for packets to carry, then the permit pool behaves like a taxi rank. Although taxi ranks are valuable it is clear that not all taxis should be in ranks at any one time and we find in the isarithmic network that the size of the permit pools should be such that some permits are in movement even under light load conditions.

A simulation was made[9] using the same model as before and with the same degree of detail and including the isarithmic mechanism, offering to this model amounts of traffic derived from the traffic matrix mentioned before. The object was to find the magnitude of the admission delay and how it varied with the size of permit pool. In this simulation, since unattached permits can travel in the heading of *any* packet they can go to the front of the output queue and thus receive priority.

Figure 11.14 shows some of the results of the simulation. Each curve is

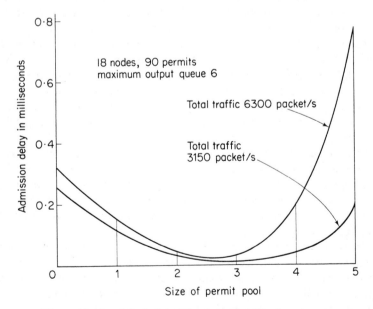

Figure 11.14. Admission delay in an isarithmic network

plotted from six simulation runs, one for each of the permit pool sizes 0 to 5. The smooth curve is added to make the results clearer, but only the integer values matter.

This is the same 18-node model as before with a maximum output queue size of six and five permits per node (90 in all). These settings were designed to keep the packet content at or below the value which gives the maximum throughput. The curves are for two values of total throughput, 3150 and 6300 packets per second. In other runs on the same model it was found that congestion begins at a throughput lying between 8000 and 9000 packets per second. At the higher figure some of the queues of packets waiting for permits, or in the interface computer were steadily increasing because the offered traffic was not controlled. At the throughput of 8000 packets per second, which is very close to saturation, the busiest node—one of the three in London—handles about 850 originating, 850 terminating and 1,100 transit packets per second.

The extreme values of the permit pool size are 0, where there are no pools, and 5, where there is room in the pools for all the permits. The curves show a distinct optimum near the mid-point between these extremes, corresponding to a permit pool size of 2 or 3. At the optimum, the admission delay is completely negligible, even when the flow is as close to the ultimate carrying capacity as 6,300 packets per second, perhaps 80% of saturation. The value of both the isarithmic method and the permit pool is demonstrated.

In this simulation, free permits were directed to any neighbouring node at random except that they did not return over the link by which they arrived. An alternative plan is to associate a new destination with the unattached permit and send more of the permits towards busy nodes. This 'biased redistribution' plan was simulated in a rather simpler model to save computer time and it produced a reduction in admission delay. But the complication of having identifiable, addressed permits would reduce the total traffic capacity and the improvement in admission delay of at most 30% was not thought to be worthwhile, because the delay is so small in any case.

Isarithmic control (with permit pools sufficient to hold one half of the available permits) prevents congestion in the trunk network arising from an excessive total number of packets in transit. The preferred method of redistributing permits, when they become free at a node with a full pool, is to send them at random to neighbouring nodes. They can then be used to admit waiting packets or, if none are waiting, to fill any space in the local pool. If the pool is full they move on to a neighbouring node but not back to the node they arrived from.

A control method of this kind seems to be needed, because the traffic demands of computers can vary so much. There are, however, other sources of congestion which need additional control mechanisms, mostly *local* congestion. The ARPA protocol demonstrates, for example, how the failure of a HOST computer or its node (IMP) can be made to stop traffic which is destined for them from entering the network. Experience will teach us the kinds of congestion situations that must be guarded against. Fortunately, networks in their early years of operation tend to be underloaded; this allows time for gaining experience in congestion control, by simulation and by experiments with artificial traffic.

11.4   TERMINAL CONNECTION PROBLEMS

In discussing the ARPA network, we saw how the communications sub-network uses its internal protocols to support a network of HOSTs, and how the HOST-to-HOST protocols govern the basic interactions between the HOSTs. Within the HOST computers, further levels of protocol hierarchy may be devised to cover more sophisticated kinds of interaction. Some of these higher level protocols are described in Chapter 8, page 308.

Particular problems, of special importance in the context of a public data network, are the connection of terminals and the design of protocols which allow them to be used effectively. Ideally, the connection must be done in such a way that a given terminal may communicate with any HOST or service computer, and vice versa. But this is very difficult to achieve.

In this section we consider the problems of joining terminals to a packet switching network, and, for this purpose, a terminal will be regarded as any device used by people. It can, therefore, take many forms, ranging from a simple pushbutton, through teletypewriters and alphanumeric displays, to complex graphic displays with light pens etc. The network should be able to connect with any of these existing devices, and should be flexible enough to cope with new terminal types that may be developed in the future.

The terminal connection problems may be considered as falling into three areas: the basic physical connection, the procedural interface for controlling the terminal, and the interfaces between the user and remote computing services, and with other users. The physical connection problem involves the hardware interface between the terminal and the network termination unit; the procedural interface covers the special signals and status or control information that has to be interchanged between the terminal and the network; the user interface—perhaps the most difficult area to quantify—involves network command languages, service command languages, user languages, and a variety of man-machine interaction considerations.

The various problems have been solved in different ways in the existing networks that have been discussed in Chapters 4, 6 and 8. Here, the solutions will be considered in the context of a public network.

The Terminal Process

The idealized structure for a packet switching network has already been discussed (page 365) and it was suggested that terminals would be handled by a terminal processor which would contain a process corresponding to each

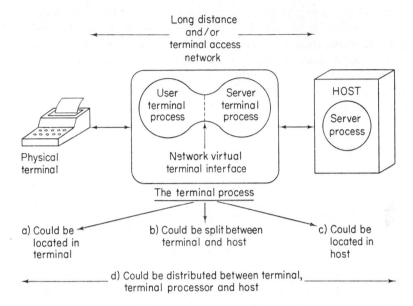

Figure 11.15.   Subdivision of the terminal process

active terminal, and a high level network control program to connect these processes with others elsewhere in the network. In this way, the terminal processor is made to seem like a HOST or User Machine to the packet switching trunk network, through which it communicates with other HOSTs using packets. These other HOSTs may provide services or may be other terminal processors. It is not necessarily the case that the terminal itself communicates with the terminal processor in terms of packets; indeed, in the practical examples of local area networks—the ARPA TIP, and the NPL network—information is exchanged using eight-bit bytes. In both of these networks, therefore, the task of packet assembly and disassembly is performed within the terminal processor.

The physical connection methods used for the ARPA and NPL local networks have already been described and so has the Pierce loop type of connection (see Chapter 7, page 267). It is likely that a practical public network would use some mixture of these and other methods, the choice depending on existing facilities, and on the desired degree of integration with future telephone systems. For the purpose of this discussion, the precise methods used are immaterial and it will be assumed the terminal is connected to, and communicates with, a terminal process, as shown in Figure 11.15. It is convenient, as will be shown later, to assume this has two parts; a user terminal handler, peculiar to the type of terminal, and a server terminal handler, which is similar for most types of terminal. The problem arises of where to locate the terminal process.

Instead of using a terminal processor, as in the ARPA and NPL cases, it would be possible to associate the terminal process directly with terminal; e.g. in the same cabinet, when packets only would be exchanged over the communication links to other portions of the network. So far, a practical economic realization of this scheme has not appeared although large scale integrated logic may change this situation soon. Alternatively, the terminal process could be sited in the remote HOST computer as is commonly the case with present-day computer bureau services.

The advantage of splitting the terminal process into two parts is that these can be physically separated; it may prove very convenient to locate the user terminal handler in or near the terminal and the server terminal handler section elsewhere. Unfortunately, unless a consistent approach is followed a number of difficulties can arise, and the most important are those of echoing and interrupt handling.

The Echoing Problem

It is quite common in present systems to provide feedback to a person at a terminal to indicate the character he has just fed into the system; this is called *echoplex* or *echoing*. There are two possibilities with teletypewriters: they may have a local connection between the keyboard and printer, or they may have separate connections to the remote computer, which performs the required echoing function. Often a switch is provided to select the required mode of operation. If a locally-connected teletype is used with a remote echoing computer, a double printing of each character can occur.

The computer-generated echo is useful because it confirms that the characters have been received correctly, but it involves the transmission of a single character in each direction. No character may be typed until the previous echo has been received. Furthermore, if a data communications network is interposed between the terminal and the computer, echoing may take place at other places, e.g. at the terminal processor, so that multiple printing occurs.

The most satisfactory simple arrangement is for echoing to be performed at the first place where a character is accepted and stored. This will normally be the terminal processor in a public network. But there are occasions where echoing from the remote server process is desirable; for example, during a 'log-in' procedure passwords may be echoed in an encoded form for security, or perhaps suppressed altogether. Again, with a graphics terminal having a touch-wire keyboard, the response will be different at different stages in an interaction, and only the remote server process will be able to determine the correct one. It is desirable, therefore, for each level at which echoing may occur, to provide a command which can be used to suppress it and allow the next higher level of echoing to take place instead. Normally, local echoing is preferable for it avoids complications due to code conversion and delay through the network. In addition, a packet switching network would have to carry each character as a packet which would be rather inefficient, though the volume of such traffic would not be great if it was produced only by terminals operated by people.

Viewed as an error control procedure between users and the network, echoing is logically similar to the exchange of checking messages between remote processes, the main difference is that process-to-process error control is likely to occur using sum or context checks over one or more messages, rather than by returning a copy of each character.

The Interruption Problem

It is necessary in any interactive system to allow the user the privilege of interrupting the computer in order to change the course of the interaction. This kind of interruption is not the same as an interruption of the operating system, such as occurs when handling data transfers from peripheral devices. Such interrupts have to take place in a few microseconds, and this is certainly not possible over any great distance, and even less so through a network.

Fortunately, in the case of a terminal, the interruption facility is merely required to indicate such things as an operator's wish to start an interaction, or to stop the output of information to the local printer. For these purposes a response of a few hundred milliseconds is quite acceptable.

The communications network between a terminal and the service computer must allow the possibility of this kind of interruption. But because it is the server process in the service computer that is to be interrupted, rather than the operating system, the techniques for interprocess communication discussed below may be employed.

Apart from the extra difficulties that are introduced by the insertion of a network between terminal and the serving process in a remote HOST, there are others that exist independently of the use of networks, but which are brought into prominence by the flexibility of interconnection made possible by a network. These are due to the arbitrary differences usually found between terminals of a basically similar nature. The topic of terminal incompatibility is discussed later.

Satellite Links

The problems of echoing and interruption are made more difficult if the delay in the path between the terminal and the remote service computer is increased. A particularly difficult case, likely to become increasingly important, arises if a geo-stationary communications satellite is to be used, where the path length of about 45,000 miles gives a delay approaching one half second. It could be argued that this kind of link is unsuitable for data communications, and it would, indeed, be a considerable hindrance to rapid

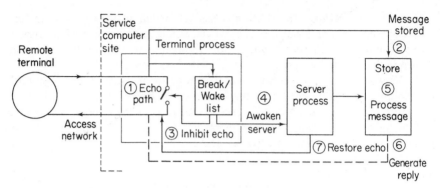

Figure 11.16. A typical echoing scheme

interaction between two computers. However, it should be possible to operate in the presence of such delays where terminals are concerned, without the user being conscious of them—at least for most of the time—by properly locating the user and server portions of the terminal process.

An arrangement common in systems using terrestrial links is shown in Figure 11.16. The terminal process simply echoes each character from the keyboard back to the printer, and also passes it into a store—either in a front-end-processor or in the service computer itself. When a command or character is detected that requires action from the service computer, it causes the server process in the computer to be awakened. The server process then deals with data accumulated since its last period of activity. Meanwhile, the echoing is suppressed in case some output is generated by the server process. Any output is handed to the terminal process for delivery to the printer before the normal echoing procedure recommences. Thus, the terminal process handles character collection, delivery and echoing, while the *wake* commands bring the server process into action.

Figure 11.17 shows a possible arrangement with a satellite link. Echoing is done near the terminal, and any inhibition of printing has to be decided by inspecting the input data stream. Certain commands or characters must inhibit further echoing by breaking the automatic return of further typed characters to the local printer. Such *break* characters will normally be wake characters also, although in some applications the wake characters need not be break characters. For example, a text editor process may take action on an input data stream as a result of normal punctuation marks that have been defined as wake characters, but the input of data need not be inhibited when they occur. On the other hand, a special control character might be chosen to request the output of the edited text; this would be both a wake and break character, but would probably not, itself, be echoed to the printer. In general, some wake and break characters, like carriage return, need to be returned to the printer; others do not.

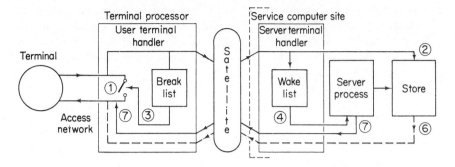

Figure 11.17.   Possible location of terminal handlers

In any given system, it must be possible for the server processes to instruct the terminal processes about which characters are to be used for special purposes. When the terminal process is split, the user terminal handler needs to know about break characters, while the server terminal process is concerned with wake characters; the user terminal handler also needs to know which of the special characters are to be echoed to the printer. These conditions must be established by a dialogue between the server and terminal processes when a connection between them is first set up. In the context of a general purpose, or public, data network it is clearly important to minimize the variety of characters used for special purposes, to reduce the complexity of the terminal processes.

By adopting the techniques outlined above, it is possible for most of the delays in the communication path between terminal and service computer to be lumped with the processing delays, and thereby hidden from the user. For, in most cases when a wake character is typed, the user expects (and will happily tolerate) a processing delay before a response is returned.

Terminal Incompatibility

It is a sad fact that there is little standardization of terminals. This is due to a failure by manufacturers (and their customers) to appreciate the cost of not having standards. Indeed, some manufacturers offer a wide range of alternative features as a selling point, so that even terminals from the same manufacturer differ because users select different options. Only later, when software in a server host has to handle each type of terminal, do the consequences of the small, arbitrary, differences begin to appear.

Apart from the potentially avoidable problems, there are more difficult ones involving the inability of a server process to keep track of what is happening at a remote terminal. It is essential for the server process to 'model' the terminal behaviour; to do so it must have knowledge of all that happens at the terminal. But, with many terminals, such operations as turning on the paper in the printer, and the insertion of tabulation stops, are done by hand. As there is no feedback of information about these events, it is quite impossible for the terminal process to follow them. To overcome these problems the users must be disciplined in such a way that the server process is kept informed of the terminal state. This will be discussed later in relation to Network User Languages.

The arbitrary differences between terminals have been somewhat reduced by the introduction of the ISO code, insofar as the symbols that are available and the codes used to represent them are fixed (see Chapter 6, page 224). But the scope remaining for differences in use of format characters can lead to endless trouble, and when alphanumeric displays are taken into account the situation is even worse. For example, the use of 'backspace' to underline symbols, or to add accents, is not possible with existing visual displays, because only one character code may occupy a time slot in the local store holding the refresh information for the screen. Again, some terminals require 'carriage return' followed by 'line feed', others combine these in 'newline' —as allowed in the ISO code. But if commands for the former are sent to the latter, double line spacing occurs.

At another level, problems arise because some terminals expect to be polled, i.e. they have built in address decoding and their address must preceed each communication to them; others do not, and will print out such an address as if it were data. Again, some terminals have an 'answer-back' feature and can respond with a preset response to a 'who are you' command, others ignore such a command.

The above examples are indicative of a chaotic state of affairs, and the solution seems to lie in splitting the terminal process into a *user terminal handler* portion tailored to a particular terminal device, and a *server terminal handler* of a more general nature, as suggested earlier. This leads to the concept of the *network virtual terminal*, which provides a method of intercommunication between them.

The Network Virtual Terminal

By introducing the concept of a virtual terminal (also called a terminal image) that is assumed to exist between the user terminal handler and the server terminal handler portions of the terminal process, it is possible to make the latter behave in a uniform manner. The network virtual terminal will comprise a standard terminal code for all printing and non-printing symbols, together with a complete definition of the action the sequences of control characters would have on the imaginary terminal. The user terminal handler then has the responsibility of translating between the behaviour of the virtual terminal, and that of the actual one which it is controlling.

Sometimes the translation process will be trivial, at other times it will be impossible. The great advantage to the user is that the difficulty can be quantified and taken into account when selecting terminals for use with the network. A cheap terminal requiring extensive translation may be less desirable than a more expensive one that is easy to handle by software. It may even be possible, through the use of large scale integration, to produce, eventually, a practical realization of the virtual terminal.

A major problem with the concept of a virtual terminal is the definition of how it appears to a user at a practical terminal. For example, it would be possible to arrange conventions for conversion using character strings so that a practical terminal could invoke the facilities of the virtual terminal. In this way two users could communicate as if they each had a virtual terminal. Another possibility is the restriction of intercommunication facilities to that of the least able of the two terminals involved. This would require a selection to be made from the facilities possessed by the virtual terminal. Implicit in these ideas is the concept of the virtual terminal possessing all possible facilities that anyone will require. An alternative idea is to give the virtual terminal a subset of facilities which are possessed by the lowliest of terminals, and allow a kind of basic communication facility to be provided. The former may be too difficult to achieve, while the latter seems unduly restrictive. It is likely, therefore, that the realistic form of the virtual terminal will lie somewhere between these extremes.

The idea of the virtual terminal is being developed in the ARPA network where it is used in conjunction with the TELNET protocol which defines the behaviour of certain control characters.

It will be interesting to see how successful the concept of the network virtual terminal can be in resolving the kinds of incompatability that have been discussed in this section. It must be remembered that all these difficulties have been overcome in private networks in one way or another, it is only the attempt to have a shared network that reveals the differences which, while trivial, make intercommunication very difficult.

The Network User Language

The appearance presented by the network to a user at a terminal will be an important factor determining the utility of the system. If users find that it seems inconvenient, confusing or annoying the system will fall into disrepute.

The more obvious characteristics of the network's appearance are the physical ones such as keyboard layout, choice of font for character display, etc., and the terminal behaviour with respect to echoing, speed of response to interrupts and similar parameters. Although these features are vitally important in the acceptance, or otherwise, of a system they involve psychological factors that are difficult to quantify. Some computer systems are well accepted by the users, others are not, and often the reasons are not at all clear.

The other factors of importance to the user concern the information he has to exchange with the network in order to make use of the facilities it provides.

This leads to the idea of a *network user language* which determines the form of the communication between the terminal user and the network software.

It is important to distinguish between the network user language and the languages which are used for communication with a service through the network. The network user language may be a simple one involving the use of push-buttons and lamps—as in the present NPL local network—or it may be extended to become an interactive language. This is probably necessary if a wide range of facilities is to be made available to a network, and a wide range of users is to be accomodated, ranging from highly skilled programmers, to occasional or naive users.

The kind of commands needed for a network user language already exist in many present day systems, and one of the advantages of a network language would be the unification it might bring in the long run to command languages in general.

Two pitfalls need to be avoided in implementing a network user language of the more elaborate kind; it should not contain nested commands, and should not use backward reference instructions. The first pitfall arises because it would be attractive to allow a sequence of commands to be stored and called by a simple abbreviated name. However, if the simple names could also be called by a single command it would be possible to tie up a considerable part of the network's resources. It is for this reason that PTTs do not permit mechanical redialling of telephone numbers to be employed, because they rely on the subscriber's unwillingness to keep dialling to prevent the network becoming congested.

The use of backward references would make it possible for a network user to write strings of commands which included loops. Again, this could occupy a large portion of the network's resources, and should be avoided.

11.5 NETWORK MONITORING AND MEASUREMENT

In any complex system it is necessary to monitor the behaviour and to make measurements of performance. A computer network is no exception. Some of the measurements are concerned with long-term activities such as network evaluation, accounting, planning for network expansion and the identification of trends in network uses. In these applications the analysis of the data may take place in a leisurely fashion and the data collection will be largely independent of the type of analysis to be performed.

Other types of information are required in a much shorter time scale for such things as traffic control, fault diagnosis, the detection of local malfunctioning, and for general system monitoring and testing. For these applications rapid reports are required about changes of status or abnormal conditions. It is possible that detailed information may be needed occasionally and might be obtained by an operator working in a conversational mode with a network 'operating system'. Such an operating system might be distributed through the network, or might be contained at a network control centre.

It will be necessary to interrelate the measurements made by recording the time at which events occur. This implies that a network timing scheme is required and such a scheme can be used to control regular reporting and time outs as well as to synchronize functions throughout the network. It may be necessary to have both relative timing to coordinate events locally and absolute timing so that activities anywhere in the network may be related. The purpose of a network control centre is to form a focus for the maintenance measurement development of the network. Although it is not essential for the centre to be a unique location it may be desirable to provide special hardware for monitoring services, and so there may be advantages in designating a special centre; however, this could be associated with one or more of the local areas, and would be readily moved later if necessary. An idea of the kinds of monitoring of statistics measurements that might be made can be gained by considering how this is done in the ARPA network.[10]

Monitoring in the ARPA Network

Because the ARPA network is a research tool as well as a communications facility it is provided with particularly extensive monitoring and reporting facilities which are intended to provide information to aid in understanding the nature of computer networks.

There are three basic components to the ARPA measurement system: the IMP monitoring and reporting software, the network control centre and the network timing system. The IMP software allows the monitoring of its own throughput and the status of its connections both to HOSTs and to adjacent IMPs. Some of the monitoring and reporting between IMPs is for the purpose of maintaining their routing tables, while the remainder is transmitted to the network control centre. Reporting is initiated in three ways: by an interrupt, on demand, or at regular intervals.

Interrupt reporting to the network control centre is initiated in an IMP by the following events:

1. Whenever a packet with the trace bits set has been processed (see Chapter 8, page 304).
2. When the setting of one of the sense switches is changed.
3. If the operating system is reloaded through the network.
4. When a transmission error is detected.
5. When the memory protect setting is changed.
6. When the status of one of its statistics programs changes.

The use of interrupt reporting clearly enables the network control centre to keep a very good picture of the important changes that are occurring throughout the network.

Demand reporting is used to activate various programs in the IMPs by a command from the network control centre to make measurements under special conditions. The activation of these programs continuously would place an unacceptable load on the IMP, and would reduce its information handling capability. The kind of thing that can be activated on demand is a analysis program which resides in each IMP, and allows the contents of the core store to be remotely inspected while the IMP is in use.

Regular reporting is used by each IMP to send information to its neighbours as well as to the network control centre. Each IMP sends to its neighbours 'hello' packets on idle links, its clock reading, and information for use in calculating routing tables.

The network control centre receives a report every 52 seconds from each IMP giving the status of each line to adjacents IMPs, each HOST connected to the IMPs, the state of the four sense switches and the memory protect switch, together with throughput counts for lines and hosts. In addition the statistics program in each IMP can send to nominated HOSTs the following:

1. Snapshots every 820 milliseconds. These contain information on the state of true lengths, buffers in use and routing tables.
2. Cumulative statistics every 13 seconds. These give detailed throughput totals including histograms of message and packets lengths, and details about the routing tables.
3. Arrival statistics every 1·6 seconds. Up to 60 arrival times of packet, in units of 100 microseconds, are reported. This is intended to give information for simulation of the network by the network measurement centre at the University of California, Los Angeles.

Clearly, the regular reporting of this amount of information from all the IMPs places a load on the network itself and on the network control centre. In fact the statistics programs are run as a background job so that heavy traffic will cause reports to be delayed. To some extent therefore the network is self regulating and the volume of reporting traffic decreases at peak traffic times.

The network control centre comprises a computer which receives and analyses the reports from each of the IMPs, and reports to the staff at the centre in various ways.

Interrupt reporting at the control centre is done by blinking messages, flashing lights and if necessary, sounding buzzers. A demand report may be requested at any time. It is given in an abbreviated form which draws attention to anomalies and recent changes. Finally, regular reports are made on an hourly basis concerning line and HOST throughput statistics, and on an eight hourly basis concerning line and HOST accumulative statistics and network status history since the previous report.

Timing in the ARPA network is done by a hardware clock which gives an interrupt every 25.6 milliseconds. This is used to update the internal software clock, and it is also possible for the hardware clock to be interrogated to measure time intervals in units of 100 microseconds.

The software clocks in the IMPs are kept in approximate synchronisation by frequent and regular transmissions of their readings to adjacent IMPs. Each IMP uses the reading from the neighbouring IMP to adjust its own clock, and in this way a network absolute timing function is performed.

References

1. Carr, C. S., 'Host-Host communications protocol in the ARPA network', *AFIPS Conference Proceedings. Spring Joint Computer Conference* **36**, 589, (1970).
2. Barber, D. L. A., and Davies, D. W., 'The NPL Data Network', *Proc. All Union Conference 'The Automation of Research on the computer base'*, Novosibirsk (Oct. 1970).
3. Wilkinson, P. T., and Scantlebury, R. A., 'The control functions in a local data network', *Proc. IFIP Congress*, Edinburgh, D.16 (1968).
4. Scantlebury, R. A., and Wilkinson, P. T., 'The design of a switching system to allow remote access to computer services by other computers and terminal devices', *Proc. ACM/IEEE Conf.*, Palo Alto (Oct. 1971).
5. Walden, D. C., 'A system for Interprocess Communication in a resource sharing network', *Comm. ACM*, **15**, 221 (April 1972).
6. Kahn, R. E., and Crowther, W. R., 'Flow control in a resource sharing computer network', *Proc. ACM/IEEE Conf.*, Palo Alto (Oct. 1971).
7. Dijkstra, E. W., *Co-operating Sequential Processes*, Programming Languages Academic Press (1968).
8. Davies, D. W., 'The control of congestion in packet switching networks', *Proc. ACM/IEEE Conf.*, Palo Alto (Oct. 1971).
9. Price, W. L., 'Survey of NPL simulation studies of data networks 1968-72', *Computer Science Division Report No. 60*, National Physical Laboratory, Teddington, UK.
10. Frank, H., Kahn, R. E., and Kleinrock, L., 'Computer communications network design: experience with theory and practice', *AFIPS Conference Proceedings. Spring Joint Computer Conference*, **40** (1972).

Chapter 12

Network Geography, Reliability and Routing

12.1 INTRODUCTION

The design of a communication network can usefully be divided into two phases. The first phase produces designs for transmission links, switching nodes, interfaces and procedures. These things are the components from which many networks of different shapes and sizes could be produced. But an actual communication requirement is quantified by the location of terminals, density of traffic and so forth. In the second phase of design the choice of components is made and their location decided. The switches and links are sized for economy consistent with the desired grade of service. We describe the network characteristics which are designed at the second phase as the *geography* of the network, including within this term the sizing of the components. The second phase is sometimes called network 'planning', but it is really an integral part of the engineering design, and is a large factor in the eventual economics. The word *topology* is also used but strictly has a different meaning since it refers to properties of the network which are independent of its size and shape, such as the connection pattern of links and nodes. Topology in this sense is important, but distances, which affect the cost of links and delays in transmission, are part of the network geography.

The design problem can be given mathematical expression by stating the performance required from the network in terms of traffic flows, allowable delays and reliability and then demanding the lowest cost network to meet these requirements. But although it is easily stated, a straightforward solution of the problem is very unlikely. Looked at as a combinatorial problem, the number of cases to be examined is astronomical. Rapid progress in the study of networks of all kinds has produced a large body of theory[1,2,3], and this has been applied successfully, but rarely in such a way that truly optimal solutions can be demonstrated. In the case of data networks, computer simulation of actual layouts has given some insights, and a number of approximate or heuristic methods have been devised which serve to select layouts that are certainly good but not demonstrably the best.

Within the scope of this book only a small part of this recent work can be covered, and the emphasis will be on explaining the concepts and giving some of the theoretical foundation.

The difficulty of the problem can be judged from the fact that most of the theory is aimed at calculating the performance of networks with *known* geography. The choice of network geography and its optimization is still essentially a matter of trial and error, though for convenience carried out systematically by computer. The various aspects of performance will be considered in this order:

1. Traffic capacity of networks.
2. Reliability (the ability to function after a failure).
3. The routing of packets in a packet switching network.
4. Optimization of network layout.

In a packet switched network the delay experienced by a packet in transit is an important indicator of the state of the network. The approach to congestion in some part of the system can be monitored by the increased delay. Therefore delay is used to compare different routing strategies and minimization of the mean delay time is one of the tools of optimization methods. The most intensive recent work on the subject of network geography has been applied to packet switched systems, first the SITA network[4] then the ARPA network.[5]

12.2 THE DESCRIPTION OF NETWORK TOPOLOGY

The familar picture of a network is a diagram of switching centres and their connections, such as Figure 12.1 (a). We have shown six centres and nine connections between them in the example. The mathematical name for such a structure is a *graph* and there has been developed an extensive *graph theory*, with many applications. The general term for the 'centre' in graph theory is *node* and for the connection the term *link* is used. These are the words we

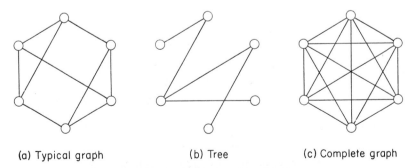

(a) Typical graph   (b) Tree   (c) Complete graph

Figure 12.1.   Examples of networks or graphs

shall use, but the words 'vertex', 'edge' and 'branch' are alternatives that will be found in the literature.

The six nodes with nine links in Figure 12.1(a) are typical of communication networks in that the number of links is neither the least that would connect the nodes (five links) nor the most that could be provided, without paralleling the link (15 links). The extreme cases are, respectively, the *tree* and the *fully connected* network shown in Figure 12.1(b) and (c). Both examples occur in certain sections of actual communication networks. The tree has no loops, and the loss of any link disconnects some part of the network. We have met it chiefly in local networks where the cost of lines is paramount and in some private networks for the same reason. The fully connected network gives the greatest resilience to link failure and so is found in the highest level of network hierarchies, the transit networks. The graph shown in Figure 12.1(c) is called the 'complete graph' with six nodes.

The connection pattern of a network can be specified by numbering the nodes and stating for each node pair whether a direct link exists between them. Supposing that the links vary, then a number can be attached to each link giving its 'traffic capacity'. What this means depends on the network. For a circuit network it would specify the number of circuits carried, while for a packet network it would specify the packets that the link could carry per second. In principle, the link capacity could be different for the two directions of traffic in the link; for example it could be a unidirectional link.

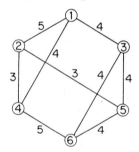

	1	2	3	4	5	6
1	0	5	4	4	0	0
2	5	0	0	3	3	0
3	4	0	0	0	4	4
4	4	3	0	0	0	5
5	0	3	4	0	0	4
6	0	0	4	5	4	0

Figure 12.2. A labelled graph
with the link-capacity matrix

But this is not found in networks in general, except possibly in ring structures, so we shall assume in what follows that a link's capacity is the same for both directions. It could be objected that a link with a fault affecting one direction only breaks this rule, but such faulty links are usually out of action in both directions because acknowledgements are needed for setting up circuits and transferring packets.

In Figure 12.2 the six node example is repeated with link capacities added. It is then described as a *labelled graph*. To describe the same structure numerically, the 6×6 matrix shown in the figure is used. For each node pair there is a zero in the corresponding element of the matrix if no link exists, and if there is a link this element of the matrix gives its capacity. The assumption that link capacity is equal in the two directions gives us a symmetric matrix.

Suppose now that all link capacities were 1, then the matrix would be a binary matrix, and its elements would show the presence or absence of a link. This is called a *connectivity matrix* and it describes the unlabelled graph. The device of replacing all capacities by 1 is a method of describing the network's topology and will be used later to derive a result concerning the reliability of networks.

The labels which we have identified with link capacities would equally well describe other properties of the links such as length, cost, probability of failure or delay in packet transit. In the most general optimization problem any of these parameters could be associated with each link, but here we consider only one at a time, for simplicity. Note also that nodes could be labelled, such as with their capacity to handle calls or packets, the probability of failure or their delay in packet handling.

Cut Sets

In applying graph theory to networks we shall use an important concept known as the *cut set*, which is illustrated in Figure 12.3. Parts (a) and (b) of the figure show *link cut sets*.

A link cut set is a set of links which, when removed, breaks the network into more than one part. It is said to *disconnect* the network. We also require that the link cut set be *minimal* in the sense that any proper subset of the cut set is not a cut set. Expressed another way, any one of the links in the cut set, if replaced, would be able to reconnect the network. Some authors specifically call these sets *minimal cut sets* but, since all the cut sets we use are of this kind, the word 'minimal' will not be used every time. Minimal is not the same as 'smallest' and we shall find minimal cut sets of various sizes in one network.

The link cut set of Figure 12.3(a) contains the three links shown by broken lines. If all three are removed from the network nodes 1, 2 and 4 becomes disconnected from 3, 5 and 6. But if only two of the links in the set are removed there is no disconnection. The cut set is therefore minimal, as we require.

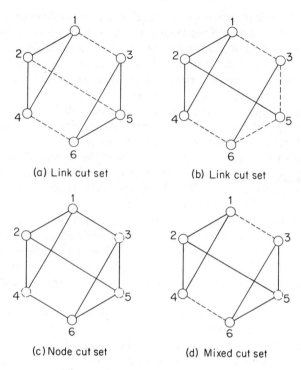

(a) Link cut set   (b) Link cut set

(c) Node cut set   (d) Mixed cut set

Figure 12.3.   Examples of cut sets

The topology is not always as clear as in this example, particularly for large graphs. Figure 12.3(b) shows a cut set comprising four links 1-3, 3-5, 5-6 and 6-4. This is also minimal because any of the four links would reconnect the nodes.

Cut sets can also be formed from nodes, and these are useful for analysing failures due to node unreliability or saturation due to overloaded nodes. In part (c) of the figure a *node cut set* consisting of nodes 3, 4 and 5 is shown. It is a cut set because, of the remaining nodes, set (1, 2) is disconnected from node 6 but restoring any of the nodes would reconnect these nodes. Extending the idea of a cut set further we can define a *mixed cut set* which is a minimal set of nodes and links that, when removed, disconnects the remaining nodes. Figure 12.3(d) is an example.

Often, we are analysing the network from the viewpoint of just one source node S and one terminal node T and then it is the minimal cut sets which disconnect these particular nodes which concern us. These are called *S-T cut sets*. Suppose that S is node 1 and T is node 6 in Figure 12.3. All the cut sets shown in the figure are S-T cut sets for this particular choice of source and terminal.

12.3 FLOW IN NETWORKS

Given a network such as the one shown in Figure 12.2 with its link capacities, we need to know what kinds of flow pattern it can support. If the flow is of one commodity, such as oil, then flows from node 1 to node 6 and from node 6 to node 1, if both are required, will partly cancel. For telephone calls or data packets, on the other hand, they add. The best way to think about this is to regard communication traffic as the flow of many different commodities. Each destination node can be taken to define one 'commodity', namely the calls or packets destined for that node. To check whether a link X-Y has been overloaded, all the commodity flows from X to Y are added, and compared with the X-Y capacity, and all the flows Y to X are added and compared with the Y-X capacity.

We intend to treat here only the simplest case, to find what is the flow limit for one commodity with a single source and a single destination. For our example we shall use Figure 12.2 with the source S at node 1 and the terminal T at node 6. The method of calculation used is called the Ford-Fulkerson algorithm. It leads us to an important theorem which has a central place in network theory. It can later be used to study network reliability, as we shall see.

The Ford-Fulkerson Algorithm

The aim is to find the maximum flow possible from node S to node T. The method is to take any flow (zero, for example) and augment it successively until no more flow is possible from S to T.

Instead of a formal statement of the algorithm we shall describe what happens by means of an example. A more exact statement can be found in the specialist texts[2,3]. Figure 12.4(a) is a graph of the network we are dealing with, showing its link capacities and the numbering of its nodes. In part (b) a simple flow pattern is shown, one which clearly does not exceed the capacity of any link and carries 7 units of flow from S to T. The augmentation of this flow is shown in part (d) in which a simple path from S to T has been chosen and an extra flow of 2 units added along that path. The result is a new flow pattern in (e) which has nine units passing from S to T. The crux of the algorithm is the finding of the path along which the extra flow can be inserted. This part of the algorithm is based on labelling the nodes, and is shown in part (c) of the figure.

The labelling process can be likened to finding a path through a maze. Starting at S, each direction is tried in turn. Direction 1-2 would allow 2 more units of flow out of S so it is a possible start for the path. To remind us of this, a label (1, 2) is attached at node 2 with two items of information: the node 1 from which the flow from S might be received and the extra flow 2. The next direction to be tried is 1-4, where an extra flow of four units out of

S is possible and this is shown on the label (1, 4). The third direction towards node 3 allows no extra flow and no label is attached to node 3 at this stage. We have now lost interest in node 1, which is marked as 'scanned' so that the labelling algorithm will not come back to it.

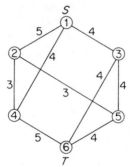

(a) Network and its link capacities

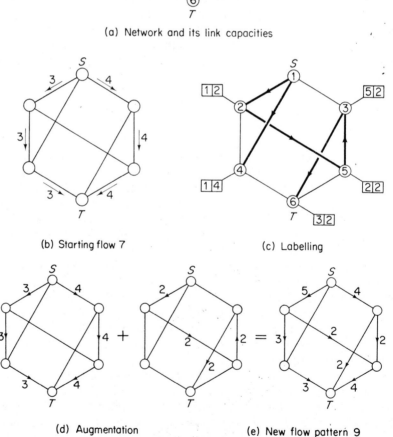

(b) Starting flow 7

(c) Labelling

(d) Augmentation

(e) New flow pattern 9

Figure 12.4.   The Ford-Fulkerson labelling algorithm

To proceed with labelling, labelled node 2 is examined and the two directions of exit from it explored. The direction of node 4 is of no interest because that node is already labelled. A flow of three units towards node 5 is possible, which results in labelling node 5 with (2, 2) to denote the flow of two which could be received via node 2 from S. At this stage, node 2 has been 'scanned' and is out of the running. At the next stage we chose to examine node 5. It is important to realize that if we had chosen node 4 a different result would have been obtained. But the aim is merely to find one path from S to T for the augmenting flow and where there are alternatives either one will do. The next node to be labelled is 3, then finally 6, which is the terminal. If there is a path for a flow to the terminal it will be found, though it may not be the most direct path.

To complete the path-finding exercise the path is retraced from T backwards. The possible flow, which started out as 2, might have been reduced at any stage by capacity limitations of the links. The final flow value, 2, is shown in the label (3, 2) on T and is the amount of flow augmentation that will be possible on this time around. The node references in the labels allow us to

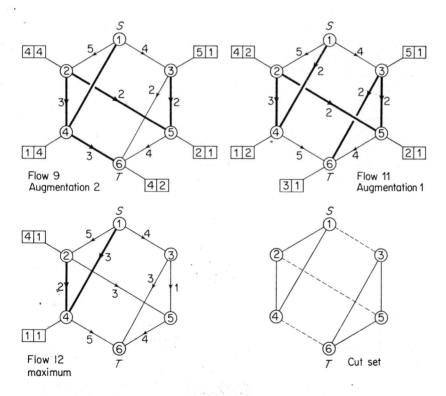

Figure 12.5.   The maximum S-T flow and corresponding cut set

trace backwards so that the whole path T-3-5-2-S is found. Then the flow is augmented as shown at (d) and (e) and the new flow is 9.

Now the whole labelling and augmentation process is repeated, and in the worked example shown in Figure 12.5 we next found a flow 11 then a flow 12. The approach to the maximum would be different if different augmentation paths were used, but the resultant maximum flow would be the same. At the final stage the process could not continue because in the labelling process the tree extending from S did not reach T. The state then reached is shown in the figure.

Two nodes have been labelled. Together with node 1 they form the only part of the network accessible to an augmenting flow. From this set of nodes 1, 2 and 4 all the outgoing links 1-3, 2-5 and 4-6 are saturated. It follows that these three links form a link cut set, and this is shown in the figure. The cut set in question divides the nodes accessible to extra flow from the rest, and the augmentation process stops here because S and T are separated by a cut set of saturated links.

The Ford-Fulkerson algorithm determines the maximum flow that is possible between S and T and shows one pattern of flow which achieves this maximum. It is not always a unique pattern. In our example the loop of nodes 6, 5, 3 could allow an anticlockwise flow of 1 to be superimposed on the flow shown in Figure 12.5 without exceeding any link capacities. But no such changes are possible which would affect the flows in the saturated cut set. The algorithm therefore determines an S-T cut set which carries the full flow capacity in all links of the cut when the S-T flow is at the maximum.

The description of the Ford-Fulkerson labelling algorithm given above does not amount to a proof, it is merely a plausible demonstation of the method. We have also simplified it by using an undirected graph, representing as it does a network in which the capacity of a link is the same for both directions of flow, but this is representative of most communication networks. The algorithm can be developed in a formal manner for directed graphs and the result proved to be the maximum S-T flow.

The Max-flow Min-cut Theorem

This curiously named theorem is a basic theorem in the study of flows in networks and it can be illustrated as a consequence of the algorithm just described.

The termination of the algorithm, illustrated by the example of Figure 12.5, showed a maximum S-T flow and also an S-T cut set for which each link in the cut set carried a flow equal to its capacity. If we define the capacity of a cut set as the sum of the capacities of its links we can express the result of the algorithm by saying that:

'there exists an S-T cut set with its capacity equal to the maximum S-T flow'.

Now suppose that there was some other S-T cut set with its capacity less than the maximum S-T flow. It would not be possible for that flow to pass from S to T because all the flow must pass through the cut set in question. So all other cut sets have a capacity not less than the maximum S-T flow. The result can be summarized in the following statement of the max-flow min-cut theorem:

'the maximum S-T flow equals the minimum capacity of the S-T cut sets'.

This apparently simple result is not in fact trivial to prove, and one of the many proofs is based on a formal statement and proof of the labelling algorithm. The same theorem has been proved for two-commodity flows but is not true for three commodities.

The theorem and the algorithm will be found later to be valuable as a practical method of calculating the probability of disconnection of S and T by link failures.

Flows in a Practical Communication Network

In a practical network calls or messages originate in nearly all nodes and terminate just as widely, and all these flows take place simultaneously. To specify this traffic pattern a *traffic matrix* is used, in which the term T_{ij} is the traffic from node i to node j. This matrix is not usually symmetric because traffic patterns have no such constraint.

Computers tend to send out more data than they receive from terminals, therefore a location with many computers will generate a net outward flow of data. Traffic in packet switched networks is measured by the flow of data. On the other hand circuit switched calls are generally made inwards to the computer, giving the opposite effect. The diagonal elements of the traffic matrix T_{ii} are usually zero, because the purpose of the matrix is to characterise traffic between nodes. Some nodes may have no subscribers and carry only transit traffic. For these a row and column of the matrix will be zero.

To complicate the picture in actual networks, both flow levels and flow patterns change during the day, and so different parts of the network could limit the overall capacity at different times. But a simplification is possible by considering only the flow pattern of the two main traffic peaks, in the morning and afternoon.

These factors are known for working networks, but some problems of optimization arise in planning completely new networks, and here the traffic pattern is rarely known. One approach is to estimate the traffic and then apply a scaling factor to all the elements of the matrix so that the main performance figures such as delay can be plotted against a single flow variable.

Optimization of flow patterns by calculation is a useful technique because it can form part of the overall network layout optimization, as we shall see later, but the actual routes taken by calls or packets are the result of adaptive measures taken when the network is running. Fortunately the traffic usually builds up slowly and experience can be gained with light loads.

12.4   NETWORK RELIABILITY

A tree network is the most economical way to connect a set of nodes together, if there is no need to guard against the disconnection of some nodes from the network by a link failure. Tree networks are adopted for the pipelines which collect gas from a gas field, because a single breakdown, even though it disconnects several wells, is not serious. But in telecommunication networks any disconnection of a part of the system from another is a serious loss of service, so we generally use mesh structures which are intermediate between trees and complete graphs.

Failures will happen both in nodes and links. Careful design and duplication of equipment can largely eliminate failure in the nodes, if the cost is warranted. Failure of individual links is more difficult to avoid, for example, cables can be damaged by digging operations. Networks are usually designed on the assumption that link failures will occasionally happen. The attitude to node failure depends on whether a node is the only means of access to the network for a group of subscribers. In general, the alternative routing feature should be continued down the network hierarchy as far as possible towards the subscriber. Node failures enter into our present calculations because certain combinations of node failures can disconnect other nodes from the network. Calculations of network reliability should distinguish between node and link failures and be based on different failure probabilities for these two equipments.

Probability of Disconnection

When we are comparing network topologies for their effect on network reliability it is useful to have a numerical measure of reliability of the whole network. One such measure is the probability that *any* kind of disconnection will occur, another measure is the average number of node pairs which are still capable of communication. The first measure is more appropriate when any kind of disconnection is serious and its probability will be kept low. The second measure is more appropriate in military situations where the extent of disconnection may be large and should be estimated.

Consider now the network example in Figure 12.4(a) and the probability that S and T will become disconnected when each link has a probability p of failure and all the failure mechanisms are independent. The assumption of independent failures is important because links that are topologically separated might nevertheless share a common duct in the ground for part of their extent, and this would conflict with the assumption.

A particular failure pattern might, for example, have four links failed and five still in operation. The probability of precisely this pattern happening is $p^4(1-p)^5$. If expressions like this were summed over all relevant disconnection patterns the total would give the disconnection probability for source S and terminal T. In all, it would be necessary to examine the 512 subsets of the nine links to determine whether a failure of a particular subset would disconnect S and T.

More generally, for a network of m links and the subsets which contain i links, the number of subsets to be examined is ^mC_i and let us denote by A_i the number of these subsets which would disconnect S and T. These are not just the S-T cut sets, but all those sets which contain such cut sets. Then the probability of disconnection is

$$P(S, T) = \sum_{i=1}^{m} A_i p^i (1 - p)^{m-i} \qquad (12.1)$$

A similar expression could be written down for the probability of *any* disconnection, simply by counting in A_i the number of link sets which cause any disconnection. Because these expressions are non-linear in p, a given network can be better than another for small p and worse for large p. This has been shown to be the case for the two networks of Figure 12.6. Both have eight nodes and 12 links. Graph (a) is likely to disconnect more often than (b) if p, the failure probability of links, is low. So graph (b) is better. But when the link failure probability is high it is graph (a) which gives the more reliable network.

Concentrating our attention on very reliable networks, we are interested in the case of very small values of p, and this means that the first non-zero term in equation (12.1) is dominant. Suppose that the S-T link cut set with the smallest number of links has just $\theta(S, T)$ links, then the first non-zero term in the equation has $i = \theta(S, T)$.

For simple networks it is easy to determine $\theta(S, T)$ by inspection, but

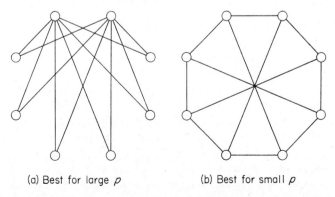

(a) Best for large p (b) Best for small p

Figure 12.6.   Two networks with different reliability characteristics

this is not so for large and heavily connected ones. The Ford-Fulkerson algorithm can be used to calculate its value. The method used is to assign a flow capacity of 1 to all the links of the network. We know by the max-flow min-cut theorem that the maximum flow from S to T equals the capacity of the minimum cut, which equals the number of links in the minimum cut, $\theta(S, T)$. This provides a good way to calculate $\theta(S, T)$ by the flow calculation algorithm already established.

The probability of disconnection of S and T is proportional to $p^{\theta(S,T)}$, and if p is small, as we have assumed, the smallest of the $\theta(S, T)$ values for all node pairs is a measure of the network's vulnerability to any kind of disconnection by link failure. This quantity θ is the smallest number of links that must be removed in order to disconnect some part of the network.

The quantity $\theta(S, T)$ has a different interpretation which comes from the theorem that the maximum number of *link-disjoint* paths between S and T is $\theta(S, T)$. A path between S and T is a set of links connected end-to-end between these nodes, and two paths are link-disjoint if they have no links in common, though they could meet somewhere at a node. This theorem is a close relative of the max-flow min-cut theorem, for each of these link-disjoint paths could carry a unit flow if all the capacities were unity and $\theta(S, T)$ the minimum cut capacity.

The remark that these paths could have a node in common draws our attention to the vulnerability of the network to node failure, which could be serious (even with node failure less probable) if very few node failures were able to disconnect the network.

Node Failures

The theory of disconnection due to link failure is based on the concept of a link cut set, and it led us to the definition of $\theta(S, T)$ the minimum number of links that must be removed to disconnect S from T and θ, the minimum number of links that must be removed to disconnect any set of nodes from the rest.

Node failures need a slightly different treatment, and we shall find it convenient to combine the theory with that of mixed failures—those involving either nodes or links.

A node cut set is a minimal set of nodes which, when they are removed, disconnect the nodes that remain. In a similar way, disconnection by node failure means disconnection of nodes other than those which fail. Therefore it is only the effect on transit traffic which is being calculated in what follows. The possibility that node failure will disconnect local subscribers must be taken into account separately.

The minimum number of nodes which must be removed to disconnect S from T is called $v(S, T)$. The node cut sets that are considered here do not include nodes S and T themselves. If there is a direct S-T link, S and T cannot be disconnected by node failure, so $v(S, T)$ is not defined. The probability that S and T will be disconnected by node failures when these have a small probability q is proportional to $q^{v(S, T)}$.

It can be shown that, when S and T are not connected by a link

$$v(S, T) \leqslant \theta(S, T) \tag{12.2}$$

and this corresponds to the intuitive idea that node failures are more serious in their effect on network topology than are link failures.

To prove the result, consider a particular link cut set which has exactly $\theta(S, T)$ members. For each link, take one of its ends, other than S or T, to represent the link and consider the set of nodes thus obtained. For example in Figure 12.3(b) links 4-6 and 5-6 must be represented by nodes 4 and 5 respectively if node 6 is T. Links 3-5 can be represented by 3 or 5 and link 1-3 must be represented by node 3 if node 1 is S. The set of nodes produced in our example is 3, 4 and 5. This leads to the node cut set shown in Figure 12.3(c) which disconnects S (node 1) from T (node 6) as effectively as the link cut set in Figure 12.3(b), but with less elements. In general, starting with a smallest link cut set of $\theta(S, T)$ components, each link can be replaced by a node, but not all these nodes need be different, so we obtain a node cut set having $\theta(S, T)$ nodes or less. This proves the inequality (12.2).

The node cut sets, and the connectivity measures $v(S, T)$ which they produce, suffer from the disadvantage that nodes which are directly linked cannot be disconnected by node failures, so for these pairs $v(S, T)$ is undefined. For the network as a whole a measure of its vulnerability is the minimum value of the $v(S, T)$ over all the pairs for which this number is defined, and this quantity v is the size of the smallest set of nodes which, if removed, would disconnect the network. For a fully connected network none of the $v(S, T)$ is defined, so v is not defined, but there is a useful convention that $v = N - 1$ for a fully connected network of N nodes.

In addition to $v(S, T)$ and $\theta(S, T)$ which are defined for nodes and links respectively, we can define a connectivity measure $\mu(S, T)$ for *mixed* cut sets. It is the number of elements in the smallest mixed cut set which disconnects S and T. This number is defined for any pair of nodes, and it tells us more about the network than $v(S, T)$ because wherever the latter is defined it can easily be shown that

$$v(S, T) = \mu(S, T) \tag{12.3}$$

The proof follows the same lines as the proof of the relation (12.2). Consider a smallest mixed cut set having $\mu(S, T)$ elements and replace each link in the set by a node at one of its ends, excluding S and T. The result is a node cut set with $\mu(S, T)$ nodes or less. Therefore $v(S, T) \leqslant \mu(S, T)$. But the node cut set is a special case of a mixed cut set so it could not have less than $\mu(S, T)$ members and the equation (12.3) follows. If μ is the minimum of

$\mu(S, T)$ for all node pairs it can be proved that

$$\mu = \nu \tag{12.4}$$

The result does not follow straightforwardly from equation (12.3) because ν is not defined for all node pairs. Equation (12.4) is also true for fully connected networks, where $\nu = N - 1$.

Recalling that $\theta(S, T)$ equals the maximum number of link-disjoint paths between S and T, a similar relationship can be proved between $\mu(S, T)$ and the minimum number of *node-disjoint* paths between S and T. Two paths are node-disjoint if they have no nodes in common other than S and T. Clearly the $\mu(S, T)$ node-disjoint paths are also link-disjoint and may be counted among the $\theta(S, T)$ link-disjoint paths between S and T. From this it follows that

$$\mu(S, T) \leqslant \theta(S, T) \tag{12.5}$$

This relationship is more general than (12.2) because it applies whether or not S and T have a direct connecting link.

The numbers $\mu(S, T)$ form the best method of specifying the connectivity properties of a network which are needed to ensure its resilience to node and link failures. To specify only $\theta(S, T)$ might leave open the possibility of a single node failure disconnecting a large part of the network. Even with the greatest attention to node reliability this risk is not likely to be accepted. So $\mu(S, T)$ can be specified for each node pair, or else the value of μ can be specified, say $\mu = x$.

Algorithms like the Ford-Fulkerson algorithm can be applied to determine $\mu(S, T)$ by maximizing the flow in a network with a capacity of 1 for each link and node, but a complete study of disconnection in a large network would be a big task. For example, a 1000-node network has 500,000 S-T pairs, and a flow maximization calculation would be needed for each pair. To determine that $\mu = x$ we must show that $\mu(S, T) \geqslant x$ for all pairs S, T. There is a method due to Kleitman[6] for doing this economically.

First we take one node S_1 and determine whether $\mu(S_1, T) \geqslant x$ for all other nodes T. Having done this (and assuming success) node S_1 is deleted and so are all the attached links. Then a second node S_2 is chosen and the condition $\mu(S_2, T) \geqslant x - 1$ is tested for all remaining nodes. Then S_2 is deleted, with its attached links, and for a third node S_3 the condition $\mu(S_3, T) \geqslant x - 2$ is tested, and so forth. Since x is usually a small integer, the process will soon stop. To test, at the last stage, that $\mu(S, T) \geqslant 0$ simply means testing that the remaining network is connected. For example, a test for a 1000-node network to determine if $\mu \geqslant 3$ would require 999 tests for $\mu \geqslant 3$, 998 tests for $\mu \geqslant 2$ and 997 tests for $\mu \geqslant 1$; less than 3000 flow maximizations in all. With the aid of Kleitman's method, reliability calculations for very large networks are possible.

12.5   ROUTING METHODS

In a data network which handles packets or messages, there must be some algorithm which at each node determines the link on which a packet or message should be forwarded if it is not already at its destination. The operation of the routing algorithm depends on the network geography, and how well it operates will affect the average delays in transit. Because this delay is important in packet switching, most of the recent study of routing has been applied to this type of network. More elaborate routing methods can be applied to packet networks because such networks provide the means for rapid exchange of control information.

Routing does not only affect average delays. It can change the flow capacity of the network, because a poor algorithm uses more links to move a packet to its destination. The behaviour of the network near congestion is very much affected, and in practice routing methods are linked to methods of flow control.

Flooding and Random Routing

There are two very simple routing strategies which are theoretically interesting, and may have applications to special kinds of network.

In *flooding* the packet is sent by the originating node to each of its neighbours. Packets are uniquely identified, such as by their source node and a serial number. Each node which receives a packet determines whether it has been received already and if it has, discards it. When it receives a packet for the first time it forwards it to all the neighbours except the one it arrived from. In this way a packet arrives at all the nodes of the network. Apart from the possible delay in checking and replication, it arrives at each node as fast as it could come by any route. But this speed is achieved at the cost of extra traffic, which is increased by approximately the number of links in the network divided by the average number of links in a good route. This factor increases with network size. In favour of the method is its great resilience to node and link failures. In a network which is very lightly loaded, flooding would be a practical method.

Flooding could also be used as a path finding method. Suppose that a route was to be established from S to T and then used for very many packets. A short 'path finder' packet would be sent from S by flooding, and each packet generated in the 'flood' would record the route it took. Then the first packet to reach the destination T would have in its record an optimum route under the traffic conditions then prevailing. This route could be returned to the source S to control the path of all the subsequent data packets. Flooding might therefore have an application, at least in smaller networks.

The second simple strategy is random routing which uses only one copy of the packet. Each node that receives it sends it forward on a link chosen at random. The packet makes a 'Brownian motion' or 'drunkard's walk' round the network and eventually arrives at the destination. Instead of a completely random choice of link, the probabilities could be chosen to guide packets in roughly the right direction, but leaving a substantial random element to cope with the possibility of link or node failure. A bias of this kind would reduce the otherwise very long delay. The increase of traffic due to unnecessary journeys would be greater in random routing than in flooding. The method is simple, but has no attractions for routing data-carrying packets. It does appear later as a method for distributing 'permits' in the 'isarithmic' network.

Directory Routing

We have described two kinds of 'unintelligent' routing which make no use of information about network topology. The more 'intelligent' methods of routing employ tables at each node which are consulted to decide, for a given destination of packet, on which link it should leave. Figure 12.7 gives an example of these routing tables or directories. At each node the routing table is just one column of the array given in the figure. Take, for example, node 1 for which the table consists of the first column. For destinations 2, 3 and 4 there is a direct link so the preferred route is obvious. To indicate the outgoing link in this table, we use the number of the node to which it goes. If a packet arrives at node 1 destined for node 5, row 5 of the table is consulted,

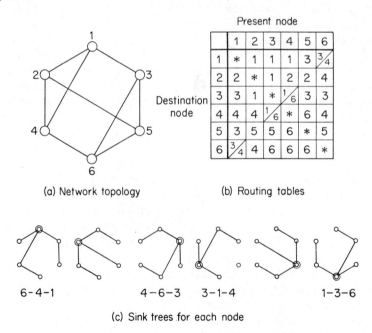

(a) Network topology   (b) Routing tables

Present node

Destination node	1	2	3	4	5	6
1	*	1	1	1	3	$3/4$
2	2	*	1	2	2	4
3	3	1	*	$1/6$	3	3
4	4	4	$1/6$	*	6	4
5	3	5	5	6	*	5
6	$3/4$	4	6	6	6	*

6-4-1   4-6-3   3-1-4   1-3-6

(c) Sink trees for each node

Figure 12.7. Example of routing tables and sink trees

and it states that the link leading to node 3 should be taken. The network used in the example is simple in that no route has more than two links. In the general case, a table may have to be consulted at each intermediate node en route to the destination.

The symmetry of the network shown in the figure leads to four cases where the choice of shortest route is undecided because there are two routes of equal length. These are for the journeys 1-6, 6-1, 3-4 and 4-3 which use the four links 1-3, 3-6, 6-4 and 4-1. The choice of one of the route possibilities in each case should take account of the traffic in each of the links concerned. Supposing that all the S-T pairs had equal flows then a symmetric arrangement is probably the best solution, and one possibility is

$$\left.\begin{pmatrix}1\text{--}3\text{--}6\\6\text{--}4\text{--}1\end{pmatrix}\right\} \text{ clockwise}$$

$$\left.\begin{pmatrix}3\text{--}1\text{--}4\\4\text{--}6\text{--}3\end{pmatrix}\right\} \text{ anticlockwise}$$

For a uniform traffic matrix this arrangement loads each link of the rectangle equally in both directions. But such routing choices are more difficult to decide in complex networks with unequal flows.

Suppose that the choices have been made and in the routing tables each entry shows a unique exit link, then the significance of the table is that for a given destination a packet's route is determined by where it is, not by how it got there. This condition has been called the *Markov constraint*[4] because of its similarity to a Markov process. Because of this constraint, the routes from all other nodes to a given destination node form a *tree*, which has been called the *sink tree* of that node. The sink trees for the example are shown in the figure, using the choices given above. It is not necessarily true that the routes from a given *source* to all other nodes must form a tree. Routes from a single source could diverge, converge to a common node and then diverge again to different destinations within the Markov constraint implied by the directory routing tables.

Minimum Weight Routing

When fixed directory routing is used the network designer is faced with the problem of constructing the routing tables. Among the different criteria that could be used to guide the construction of the tables are:

1. The best use of links at busy periods by spreading the traffic.
2. Minimizing the transit delay.
3. Minimizing the route-miles travelled by packets.
4. Minimizing the number of nodes visited in transit.

All except the first of these criteria can be expressed by assigning a 'weight' to each link, namely the delay, the link length and 1, respectively, for the three cases listed. Then the routing criterion is to minimize the weight when this is summed over the links comprising the route. The general name for this method is 'minimum weight routing'.

It might be considered useful to attach a weight to each node visited by a packet and to add the weights over the nodes and links. For example delay in a node should add to link delay. No change is needed in the formalism to achieve this, because the node's contribution can be added to the weight of each outgoing link.

Suppose now that a route has been found by this method which starts at S, calls at I en route and ends at T. Let us call the route chosen S-a-I-b-T where *a* and *b* are two sections of the chosen route. Now consider a packet which starts its journey at I and is destined for T. If there was a better route I-*b'*-T then S-a-I-*b'*-T would be better than the route chosen according to the minimum weight criterion, and this contradicts our assumption. Therefore I-*b*-T is the best route for any packet starting at I. The routing method therefore satisfies the Markov constraint, in other words it is a 'directory routing' method and therefore each destination has a sink tree.

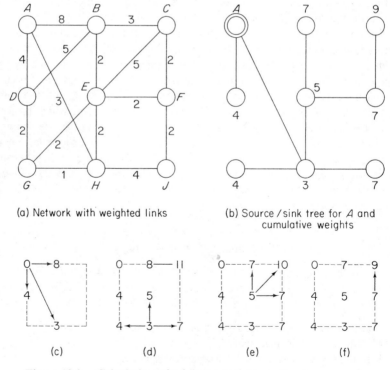

(a) Network with weighted links

(b) Source/sink tree for *A* and cumulative weights

(c)   (d)   (e)   (f)

Figure 12.8.   Calculation of minimum weight routing for one node

A similar argument shows that S-a-I is the best route for packets originated at S and destined for I. Therefore there is also a *source tree* for each source, such that all routes for packets originating from that source are part of the source tree. There is a complication if the minimum weight criterion does not give a unique best route, where there is more than one route of equal minimum weight. To meet the source tree and sink tree conditions it would be necessary to make consistent choices among equal alternatives. One way to achieve this is to perturb the weights slightly so that there is no exact equality.

A method of deciding the minimum weight routes and thus constructing the routing tables is shown in Figure 12.8. This nine-node network has the weights shown by labels on the links, and the nodes have been called A to J. The links are bidirectional with equal weights for the two directions, from which it follows that the best route from S to T is in reverse the best route from T to S. Part (b) of the figure shows a source tree for node A, and the bidirectionality with equal weights implies that this is also the sink tree for node A.

The method of calculating the best routes associates with each node a cumulative weight formed by adding the link weights along the various routes. With A as source and using the best routes shown in (b) the cumulative weights are shown at each node. Parts (c) to (f) show successive steps in deriving the weights, from which the routes are deduced. This is a labelling algorithm in which the cumulative weights are gradually improved, i.e. decreased. The convention is made that any unlabelled node has a weight greater than any labelled node. The starting point is to label the source, A, with zero cumulative weight. Ignore the arrows for the present.

At the first step (c) each node which is directly linked to A is labelled with the weight of the connecting link. This is a special case of a general rule which calculates the weight at each node by reference to the previous step. Thus in (d) each node j is considered in turn and for each link (i, j) arriving at that node from i the sum $W_i + W_{ij}$ is formed where W_{ij} is the weight of the link and W_i is the weight previously attached to node i. If this new sum is less than the previous weight at node j, it replaces that weight and becomes W_j. This calculation is carried out for each node at each step and produces parts (d), (e) and (f) of the figure in turn. The process then terminates because the cumulative weights no longer change. They have reached the values shown in (b) which are the cumulative weights of the best routes.

To obtain the routes and the source/sink tree there are two methods which give similar results. One is to mark all those links for which the difference of the cumulative weights of the two connected nodes equals the link's weight. Making an arbitrary choice where there are alternative routes with equal weight these marked links form the source or sink tree. The other method, while carrying out the labelling algorithm, makes a note at each node whenever its weight changes, of the node which caused the change. These changes are shown in parts (c)-(f) of the figure by the arrows showing how a change at one node is caused by another node. The last arrow towards any given node is the one that remains in the data stored at the end of the process. For example, node C is affected first by B, then by E and finally by F. At the end of the process there is a note at C that F caused its last change of weight. The link C-F is therefore part of the source/sink tree. This method of finding routes already makes the arbitrary choice where there are alternatives and yields a simple tree.

The process shown in Figure 12.8 refers only to node A, and must be repeated for each node in turn to obtain their trees. From these trees the routing tables can be constructed.

Instead of scanning all the nodes at one stage and using as data the cumulative weights from the previous stage, the process could be simplified computationally by the successive updating of a single set of cumulative weight data. It is important to observe that the precise sequence of the operations, and the separation into stages, is immaterial. The termination of the process and the optimality of the result can be proved. Its insensitivity to the sequence in which the nodes are processed will be exploited later in methods of adaptive routing.

12.6 ADAPTIVE ROUTING

A packet routing scheme should be able to adapt itself to link or node failures and to local congestion by finding alternative routes around the trouble spots. There are two special methods of routing that are designed to be adaptive, and these will be described, but first let us look at the possibilities for introducing adaption into the basic directory method.

The routing table can show, for each destination, not just one outgoing link but several possibilities in order of preference. The failure of the first preference outgoing link or of the far node on that link would immediately bring into operation the second choice. But this mechanism is purely local, and it is sometimes better to redirect packets before they reach a node which is directly affected. The occurrence of congestion is one way to detect trouble ahead, and congestion, shown by a queue length above a certain level, could also be used as an indicator for the use of lower preference links.

The routing table can list all the outgoing links in order of preference for a given destination, then a packet will be sent out from a node on the highest preference link that is not out of action or congested. Since for any node there is a total outgoing link capacity equal to the incoming link capacity a packet will always get away along some link, but in extreme cases it may be the link on which it arrived. This philosophy that a packet must be kept moving at all costs is called 'hot potato routing'. It has been found that it can sometimes result in oscillatory effects. A packet may 'ping-pong' between two nodes or it may cycle indefinitely round the node it is aiming for. In one simulation carried out at NPL a considerable improvement in traffic handling capacity was obtained by 'cooling' the hot potato as soon as it was one link away from its destination. Where there was a direct link to a destination, no alternative route was allowed, unless the direct link was out of order. Small changes in routing rules, like this, can have a dramatic effect on network performance.

Congestion is liable to spread because routes intersect and therefore a warning of trouble should move ahead of the congestion. This can be done by using special control packets. In the SITA high level network, routing tables have been calculated for the intact network and for a large number of failure situations. Failure of a link or node is detected by the adjacent nodes and signalled to all the others. These nodes then amend their tables in ways that have previously been agreed. A given node has in practice to react to only a certain number of the possible failures, because distant failures can often be ignored.

The aim of routing systems is to manage all the network's properties, not just the delay. It is probably a better formulation of the problem to require that the transit delay be within some specified limit and, under this constraint, to choose routes in such a way that the maximum amount of traffic is carried. Beyond a certain level it is better to refuse extra traffic *at the point of entry to the network* rather than allow all the traffic to be delayed.

Directory routing, even with the refinement of multiple entries, is probably not the best way to spread the traffic over the alternative routes. It seems likely that a random element in the choice of routes would improve the flow pattern whenever there are several paths that meet the delay criterion. This technique does not seem to have been attempted yet as part of a directory system. The methods to be described below use a measurement of the delays actually experienced in operation to amend their tables. They can spread the traffic, but only by frequent changes of routing tables.

Baran's Heuristic Routing Method

In the series of reports 'on distributed communications'[7] Paul Baran introduced an ingenious adaptive routing technique. He was concerned with a military network which would quickly amend its routing tables after the loss of many links and nodes. Since in this method the information on which the choice of routes is based is carried by the data packets themselves, the exact behaviour during the process of recovery after an attack is affected by chance. Baran called his method 'heuristic routing', but most adaptive methods are, in a sense, heuristic and there is a need for a more descriptive title. It has also been called 'backwards learning'.

Suppose that minimum delay is the routing criterion and that the delay in transit from X to Y by a given route is roughly equal to the delay in transit from Y to X by the reverse route. When a packet is at an intermediate node I and its destination is T, a useful measure of the delay from I to T is the delay from T to I. Any packets making the journey from T to I can report this delay at I while passing through. This is, of course, the way in which travellers usually find out what is ahead; they ask those who have come the other way.

The form taken by the routing table at I is a matrix giving the estimated delays for travelling to each other node on the network, when leaving by each of the possible outgoing links. When a packet arrives, its source and the link on which it arrives is noted. These two items identify one of the entries in the routing table. The delay it has suffered can be determined by recording in the packet its time of origin and subtracting this from the current time, but there are other approximate ways to estimate delays such as adding together the lengths of queues. Now that a packet has arrived at I its estimate of the delay is combined with the existing estimate for this route in order to keep a running average. For example, if the average is to be taken over about ten events and e was the previous estimate, the new estimate after a delay d has been derived is $0.9e + 0.1d$. Such a running average as this gives a weight to past delays which falls off exponentially.

For any packet now about to depart to destination T, there is a delay estimate for each outgoing link for journeys to T (the estimate is based on journeys *from* T) and the link with smallest delay is chosen. But if the link has just failed or its queue is full, the next preference is taken. This, of course, is a 'hot potato' method.

A theoretical objection to the method is that its delay estimates are based on the opposite journey to the one being taken. In principle, however, when a packet arrives on link l at node n it could be told about the estimated delay for departure *from* n on link l, as measured by the queue lengths.

A second objection is that the method depends on the accident of traffic density to get sufficient delay data. Baran proposed that after a severe change to the network, enquiry packets should be sent out to stimulate traffic from a good variety of sources and help to correct the delay estimates.

In simulation, the method has been found to show, on occasion, the continuous looping of a packet around a congested or failed destination or the ping-ponging of a packet between two nodes. To avoid filling the network by such frustrated packets a 'handover number' was included in the packet format which recorded how many times it had been 'handed over' from node to node. When this number reached a value which was too high to be reasonable for the size of the network, the packet was destroyed. To send it back to its source would probably not ease the congestion. Because the communicating devices of Baran's network could deal with a small loss of packets, a separate notification to the sender was unnecessary.

Although Baran's heuristic routing has received a lot of theoretical attention, and is attractively simple, the method next described seems more likely to be used in practice. It is based on the labelling algorithm for minimum weight routing which was described on page 441.

Adaptive Routing by Exchanging Delay Vectors

In Baran's method the delay data which comes into a node to update its routing tables are part of the process of transmitting packets. Earlier in the chapter we dealt with a static situation in which link delays (in the guise of weights) were known and, by using a labelling algorithm, an exact solution for the routing tables could be found. In this algorithm, delay data were transferred only between adjacent nodes. We shall now develop this labelling algorithm to adapt to a changing situation by sending delay data in special messages.

To do this, consider the network of Figure 12.8(a) which has a weight attached to each link. To be more specific, these weights will be taken to be the delays involved in passage from node to node, including any queuing delay in the source node. As traffic builds up, the queues increase, and so do the delays, and we no longer have the simple condition that the delay in a link is the same in both directions.

The routing tables of the original network, in the lightly loaded condition of Figure 12.8, had the form shown in Figure 12.9(a) for the nodes A, B, D and H. In the table, for each node the computed delays to each destination (the delay vector) are shown, and the outgoing links (OL) which achieve this delay are also shown. The OL part of the table gives the routes, and the *delay vectors* for each node are used in the adaptive technique.

Now the network has changed and the new link delays, affected by queuing, are shown in part (b) of the figure. The figure shows just one step of the algorithm, which has not yet resulted in correct delay data. The algorithm as applied to node A is shown, and it uses the (previously calculated) delay vectors of nodes B, D and H, which are the nodes attached to A through its three links. In practical terms this means that the three delay vectors V_B, V_D and V_H must be sent as messages in packets to node A. Here, each vector has added to all its elements the delay estimated over the corresponding *outgoing* link, a delay which node A is able to deduce from its queues and is 8, 5 and 6·5 respectively. The results are the three vectors d_B, d_D and d_H shown in the table in Figure 12.9(c). Each item here represents the computed delay to the destination *via* the node shown by the suffix. Clearly, the best choice of route is to take the minimum delay for each row of the table—the element which is ringed in the table. From this value the *new* routing table at A is formed as shown in the last two columns of the table, with V_A, the new delay vector and the corresponding outgoing links. The V_A value for the node itself, destination A, is always set at zero.

The method employed in the algorithm for minimum weight routing was that *each* node did the calculation just described at the same time, using the transmitted *old* delay vectors from its neighbours. This method is called *synchronous updating* and in the ARPA network it was done at $\frac{1}{2}$ second intervals. Given a new delay situation the routing tables will clearly settle to a new 'minimum delay' optimum, but the changes of route which occur, as in our example, before the optimum is reached, will soon change the lengths of queues and therefore the link delays. There is evidently a possibility

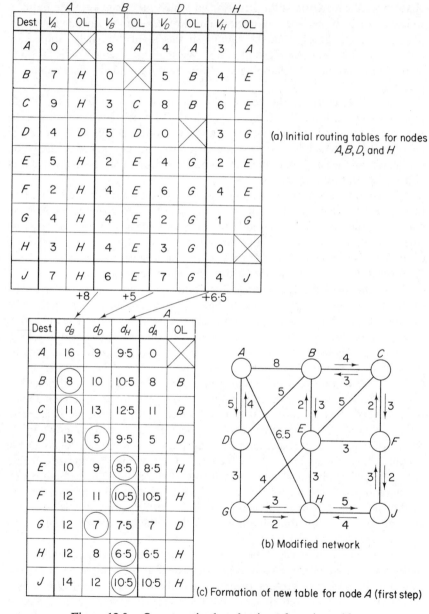

Dest.	V_A	OL	V_B	OL	V_D	OL	V_H	OL
A	0	✕	8	A	4	A	3	A
B	7	H	0	✕	5	B	4	E
C	9	H	3	C	8	B	6	E
D	4	D	5	D	0	✕	3	G
E	5	H	2	E	4	G	2	E
F	2	H	4	E	6	G	4	E
G	4	H	4	E	2	G	1	G
H	3	H	4	E	3	G	0	✕
J	7	H	6	E	7	G	4	J

(a) Initial routing tables for nodes A, B, D, and H

+8   +5   +6·5

Dest.	d_B	d_D	d_H	d_A	OL
A	16	9	9·5	0	✕
B	8	10	10·5	8	B
C	11	13	12·5	11	B
D	13	5	9·5	5	D
E	10	9	8·5	8·5	H
F	12	11	10·5	10·5	H
G	12	7	7·5	7	D
H	12	8	6·5	6·5	H
J	14	12	10·5	10·5	H

(c) Formation of new table for node A (first step)

(b) Modified network

Figure 12.9. One stage in the adaption of routing tables

of oscillatory behaviour and this has been observed in practice. It need not be harmful, because it spreads the traffic over more than one alternative route, but it is not necessary to update the table in these regular steps. Indeed, if updating continues at regular intervals when the routes have settled down, the work will be superfluous. It is possible, therefore, to recast the operation of the algorithm so that updating only happens when it matters. Suppose, for example, that all delay differences less than Δt are to be ignored. A node will receive new delay vectors from its neighbours at irregular intervals. Often, these will not change its own delay vector and routing table. Only when its own delay vector is changed by Δt or more does the node transmit its new delay vector to its neighbours. This event could be triggered off by incoming vectors or changes in queue lengths. It is easily seen that a small change may not propagate very far through the network. The updating will be asynchronous because the transmission of delay vectors depends on traffic conditions or failure incidents.

In simulation experiments for the ARPA network it has been shown that asynchronous updating is significantly better than synchronous. It is not yet certain whether there is much penalty, in the size of control program or the use of processor time, attached to asynchronous updating, nor is the reason for the improvement fully understood.

If, in the asynchronous method, the delay threshold Δt is set rather high, it is possible to make local changes of routing table as a result of changes in the queue lengths, which alter the transit delay estimates. Thus in Figure 12.9 no new delay vectors will have been received from the neighbours, but the values of d_B, d_D and d_H alter because of new estimates of outgoing link delays and so the routing table alters sufficiently to change the routes, but not sufficiently to be transmitted if Δt is large enough. This appears to be a useful operating regime. Updating traffic is low, but the updating mechanism is ready for use if there is a link failure, for example. Without updating, the locally decided changes of route operate on a short time scale and serve to spread the traffic over alternative routes.

12.7 OPTIMIZATION OF NETWORK DESIGN

Thus far, we have described methods for calculating or designing the performance of a network when the geography of the network has already been decided. The network planner would like to have methods for choosing the best network geography. For this problem there are few analytical tools but a number of heuristic methods have been shown to work.[5,6,8]

The network planner is rarely faced with the design of an entirely new network for a well determined traffic matrix. This may perhaps happen in the early history of a private network. Because the links are rented from the telephone company (or public network authority) at an advertised cost the designer is not constrained to choose the best layout to use existing links and can act as though he was creating the links afresh. But after the network has been in use, real traffic figures will replace the assumed ones, and traffic increase will probably require network enhancements. The changes to be made are then constrained by the existing layout because of the inconvenience and expense of a wholesale change of layout.

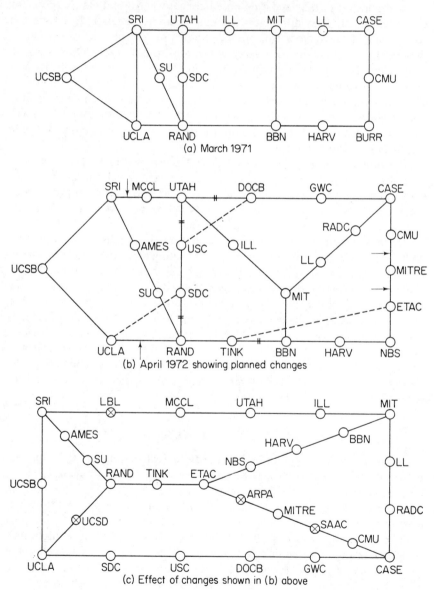

Figure 12.10.   Stages in the layout of the ARPA network

Figure 12.10 shows three stages described in the literature for the planned evolution of the ARPA network (the full names of the nodes are in Table 8.1 on page 307). From its early beginnings nodes and links were added without changing the previous network until the layout at (a) was reached. To progress to layout (b) the SRI-UCLA link was dropped, a new branch from Utah to Case Western Reserve added and nodes added in the middle of links. The Burroughs node at Paoli was dropped because the Illiac IV computer moved to Ames Airforce base. The development then planned from (b) to (c) was more drastic but it can be understood from the notation shown on layout (b) in which three added links are shown and four links are marked for deletion. In addition, the four nodes marked with a cross in (c) are added in the middle of existing links at the places shown by an arrow. In this way the considerable changes involved between stages (a) and (c) are actually made up from a collection of small changes. The investigation of layouts by heuristic procedures follows similar lines.

A public network is less likely to make drastic changes than a private one because it must take account of the existing routes of long lines and the real costs of changing links. The heuristic method of evaluating small changes to a network are therefore more useful in practice than a complete re-optimization.

The Link Capacity Assignment Problem

If the topology of the network is kept constant, an optimization problem can be formulated for the link capacities. Extra link capacity costs money, but too small a capacity causes congestion or delay to packets. In practice, link capacity is not infinitely variable and must be chosen from a discrete set of values such as 2,400 bit/s, 9,600 bit/s and 48,000 bit/s. Nevertheless, the solution of the problem with continuously variable link capacity gives interesting results and might be a pointer to the choice among the discrete values of capacity. Kleinrock[1] studied the question of assigning link capacities to minimise the average packet transit time T subject to a fixed cost.

We have to establish a relationship between the cost and the capacity of a link. The simplest relationship is the linear one

$$D = \sum_i d_i C_i \tag{12.6}$$

where D is the total link cost, d_i the cost parameter for the ith link and C_i the capacity of the ith link. The values of d_i are not all equal because the links have different lengths.

If the cost/capacity relationship for published tariffs is examined, it is found to fit better with a power law such as

$$D = \sum_i d_i C_i^{\alpha} \tag{12.7}$$

The value of α is in the region of $0 \cdot 3$ to $0 \cdot 45$, but the result of the optimization was found to be little affected by α in the range $0 \cdot 3$ to $1 \cdot 0$ so we use equation (12.6).

To obtain a tractable expression for T in terms of the capacities C_i it was necessary to make simplifying assumptions. Packet lengths were assumed to be exponentially distributed, and arrivals at each node to form a Poisson process. These assumptions made each queuing problem independent. In spite of this great simplification of the queuing problem, T derived in this way was shown to match the results of a more exact simulation over a wide range of traffic levels.

The average delay for the ith link is given by the waiting time in the queue as

$$T_i = \frac{1}{\mu C_i - \lambda_i} \qquad (12.8)$$

where λ_i is the packet traffic in the link and $1/\mu$ the mean packet size in bits. To form a suitable average over all the queuing processes, the T_i are weighted by λ_i/γ where γ is the total input packet rate. In this way, the total delay suffered by all packets per second of network operation $\sum_i \lambda_i T_i$ is divided by the total number of packets carried by the network per second. The mean delay T is then given by

$$T = \sum_i \frac{\mu_i}{\gamma} \left(\frac{1}{\mu C_i - \lambda_i} \right) \qquad (12.9)$$

A similar average for the number of times a given packet passes over a link during its transit is called $\bar{n}$ and formed as

$$\bar{n} = \sum_i \frac{\lambda_i}{\gamma} \qquad (12.10)$$

The expression for T can be improved by adding terms for packet handling time and transmission delay and taking account of a mixture of short and full-length packets. These refinements produce a good match with the results of detailed simulations of the ARPA network, showing that the general form of the expression for T is correct. We shall use the simplified expression in equation (12.9).

The capacity assignment which minimizes T at constant D is derived by the method of Lagrangian undetermined multipliers and is given by the equations

$$C_i = \frac{\lambda_i}{\mu} + \frac{D_e}{d_i} \frac{\sqrt{\lambda_i d_i}}{\sum \sqrt{\lambda_j d_j}} \qquad (12.11)$$

where D_e is given by

$$D_e = D - \sum \frac{\lambda_i d_i}{\mu} \qquad (12.12)$$

The value λ_i/μ is the link capacity to carry the traffic of the ith link at saturation level, the 'bare' capacity, so the term on the right of equation (12.11) can be regarded as the 'excess capacity' assigned to the link. The bare capacities would give rise to a total cost $\sum_i (\lambda_i d_i)/\mu$ so that D_e in equation (12.12) is the money left after paying for the bare capacity. Equation (12.11) is called the 'square root excess capacity assignment' because it shows that the excess capacity available should be shared according to the square root of the traffic on the link. The value of the resultant transit delay using the choice of assignments given in equation (12.11) is given by

$$T_{min} = \frac{\bar{n}}{\mu D_e}\left(\sum_i \sqrt{\frac{\lambda_i d_i}{\lambda}}\right)^2 \qquad (12.13)$$

In this expression λ is the sum of the traffic values λ_i over all the links. Since $\bar{n}$ is the mean value of the number of link transits experienced by a packet, the expression depends in a simple and understandable way on packet transmission time and the number of transmissions. The average transit time is seen to be inversely related to the money D_e which remains after the bare capacity of all the links has been paid for.

Optimization of Network Geography

The more difficult problems of network design optimization concern network geography in all its aspects and in particular the choice of links when the number and position of the nodes has been decided, in other words the topology of the network. The methods used to study the topology of the ARPA network[5,8] will illustrate the nature of the problem.

Fortunately it is usually possible, when optimizing topology, to fix the number of nodes and their positions. This is obviously true for a private network which is built to serve certain known sites. For public networks, the concentration of the subscribers in towns and the existing terminations of long lines tend to fix the position of switching centres.

Given the position of the nodes, the essential task is to evaluate the performance of networks with many different topologies, that is, many choices of sets of links. Suppose for the moment that one particular topology is being tested, then the steps in evaluation might be as follows:

1. Test the topology for its effect on reliability under link and node failure.
2. Find suitable routes for the traffic specified by the traffic matrix.
3. Calculate the traffic in each link.
4. Choose link capacities and calculate the total cost of links.
5. Calculate transit delays for all source/terminal pairs and check their acceptability.

Since this entire process must be repeated for a very large number of topologies, there is a great need for economy of computational method. Some of the steps can be simplified.

In step 1 the reliability criterion can be stated simply as a requirement for the value of v for the network and in the ARPA case the value 2 was chosen, which is easy to test.

In step 2, a simple method can be applied to the routing of traffic. It is not necessary to use the same rules as are actually used in the network. The routing method can depend on a global knowledge of the flows, which would not be possible in a real network. A method was used which was quick to carry out and gave close to the best flow pattern.

Steps 4 and 5 could have been replaced by a link capacity optimization

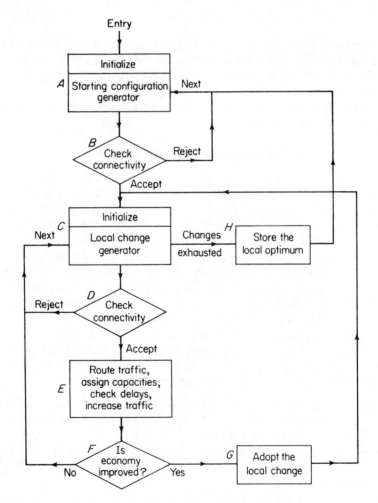

Figure 12.11.   Exploration of network layouts

of the kind that Kleinrock investigated, but the choice of link capacities was rather sparse. In practice it was found to be sufficient to choose the smaller one of the four available capacities (50, 108, 230·4 and 460 kbit/s) which exceeded the link traffic, and the delay was then almost always small enough. Because this method often gave excess capacity everywhere, a step was added to the calculation in which the traffic matrix was increased proportionately until the delay reached 0·2 seconds, and the total traffic then flowing was used to measure the network's economy in terms of the cost per megabit of transmitted data.

The network configurations to be tested were not chosen at random, but produced by a series of local changes from various starting configurations. Figure 12.11 is a block diagram of the procedure. In box A initial configurations are generated. Those that pass the topological check at B (which checks the value of μ) are accepted for local amendment to see if they can be improved. The local changes follow a definite sequence, and when this is exhausted the best configuration that has been found is recorded as the *local optimum* and a new starting configuration is tried. After each change, the value of μ is tested, then the traffic is routed, capacities are assigned to the links, the transit delays are checked and the traffic increased proportionately until the worst delay is 0·2 seconds. The test in box F uses the annual link cost divided by total traffic carried as a measure of economy which can be compared with the best value yet obtained from the current starting configuration.

The generator of starting configurations is devised to have a high probability of producing a topologically acceptable network. For example a generator used to produce survivable networks[6] worked in the following way. First the nodes were numbered at random. Then links were added one by one. The survivability was specified as a matrix of $\mu(S, T)$ and this gave a minimum number of links that must connect to each node S, i.e. the greatest of the integers $\mu(S, T)$ for all T. While links were being added the *deficit* in this link count at each node was recorded to guide the process.

A link was added between nodes X and Y, chosen according to these rules:

1. To find X, all the nodes with the largest deficit value were considered. The lowest numbered node among these was chosen.
2. To find Y, all the remaining nodes with the highest deficit value and no existing connection to X were considered. Of these, those with the lowest link cost, judged by length, were considered. If there were still candidates of equal merit, the lowest numbered node was chosen.

The operation of this set of rules is shown more clearly by an example in Figure 12.12. In this example $\mu(S, T)$ is required to be at least 3 for all node pairs, i.e. $\mu = 3$. In the generator algorithm we aim to have at least three links attached to each node, therefore the initial deficit at each node is 3. The nine nodes are numbered arbitrarily, and it is this numbering, produced by a pseudorandom process, which ensures that a rich variety of starting

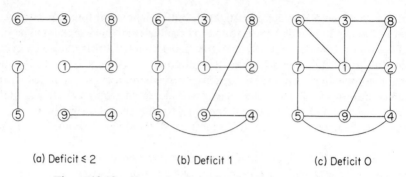

(a) Deficit ≤ 2   (b) Deficit 1   (c) Deficit O

Figure 12.12.   Example of starting configuration generator

configurations is generated. By applying the rules, the links 1-2, 3-6, 4-9 and 5-7 are added in this order leaving node 8 still with a deficit of 3 and all the others with deficit 2. The next link, 8-2, reduces all nodes to a deficit of 2 or less and gives the configuration shown at (a). The next links to be added were 1-3, 4-5, 6-7 and 8-9 which produce the circuit shown at (b) and a uniform deficit of 1. Finally links 1-7, 2-4, 3-8, 5-9 and 7-1 reduce all deficits to zero, node 1 having, as it happens, 4 links. In this case the value $\mu = 3$ is successfully achieved and the configuration goes forward to have local changes tested and produce a local optimum.

The block diagram of Figure 12.11 does not show how the process terminates. In practice the end point is determined by the amount of time that can be devoted to the calculation. Though there is a finite number of starting configurations these are too numerous to be exhausted.

In the ARPA investigation a scatter diagram was made by plotting cost

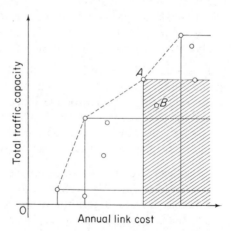

Figure 12.13.   Cost/performance of locally optimal networks

against total traffic for each local optimum and the best solutions emerged in the form of the dominant points shown in the (fictitious) example of Figure 12.13. Point A is said to *dominate* point B because the cost of A is not greater than that of B, the performance is not less than that of B (and they are not identical). The region of the plane dominated by A is shown shaded. Local optima which are not dominated are those linked by the broken line. These optima provide the best topologies for each traffic level that might be required.

The local changes made to a topology during the optimization process follow rules which yield only a finite number of possible changes and yet they must allow complex changes to be built up from a succession of smaller changes which themselves are also network improvements. As well as adding a link and deleting a link, there must at least be the possibility of moving a link to a new position. The changes used have to be fitted to the problem. When modifying trees, for example, the number of links is fixed, and the only change needed is that of moving one link. This is illustrated in Figure 12.14. First, a link (AD) is added, then the cycle is found which results from adding the new link. Any of the other links in the cycle is a candidate for deletion, namely AB, BC or CD. In the example, CD is deleted to give a new tree. By systematic changes of this kind, all possible trees can be explored. In some techniques of topology optimization it has been found necessary to remove one or two links and add one or two new ones. Figure 12.15 shows the kind of local transformation used to improve the reliability of networks. These various procedures are known as *link exchange*. The quality of the optimum

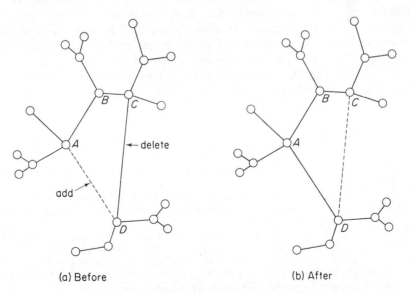

(a) Before   (b) After

Figure 12.14.   Application of link exchange to a tree

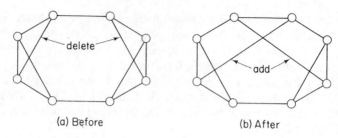

(a) Before   (b) After

Figure 12.15.   Application of link exchange to a network

has been found not to depend much on the heuristic used for choosing which links to change, so it is best to use rules which are simple to implement.

When a small change is made to a network, it is not necessary to recheck the reliability for all S-T pairs or to recalculate the traffic routing throughout. There are short cuts which greatly reduce the computation needed, by using much of the labelling which was produced for the earlier topology.

In the studies of the ARPA network[8] it was found that the exact form of the traffic matrix did not greatly affect the traffic carried at the delay limit of 0·2 seconds. As an experiment 300 'random' traffic matrices were produced, with their elements in the range 1,000 to 38,000 bit/s, and for each case the flow was optimized, with a fixed topology. A uniform traffic matrix produced only 10-13% more total traffic than the average for the 'random' matrices. For the whole set of examples the standard deviation of total traffic was only 10% of the mean. Evidently the total traffic is more important than its precise distribution. It was also observed that layouts obtained by making only small changes to an existing network (to avoid the practical problems of a complete reconstruction) had a performance within a few per cent of the optimum topology. The optimization of topology for packet networks is therefore not a critical problem, but the possible gains in economy make these elaborate calculations worthwhile for an extensive network.

References

1. Kleinrock, L., *Communication nets; stochastic message flow and delay*, McGraw-Hill (1964).
2. Ford, L. R., and Fulkerson, D. R., *Flows in networks*, Princeton, (1962).
3. Frank, H., and Frisch, I. T., *Communication, transmission, and transportation networks*, Addison-Wesley (1971).
4. Silk, D. J., 'Routing doctrines and their implementation in message switching networks', *Proc. Inst. Elect. Engrs.*, **116**, No. 10, 1631 (October 1969).
5. Frank, H., Frisch, I. T., and Chou, W., 'Topological considerations in the design of the ARPA computer network', *AFIPS Conference Proceedings Spring Joint Computer Conference*, **36**, 581 (May 1970).
6. Steiglitz, K., Weiner, P., and Kleitman, D. J., 'The design of minimum-cost

survivable networks', IEE Trans. Circuit Theory, CT-16, No. 4, 455 (November 1969).
7. Baran, P., Boehm, S., and Smith, P., *On distributed communications*, series of 11 reports by Rand Corporation (August 1964).
8. Frank, H., and Chou, W., 'Routing in computer networks', *Networks*, **1**, No.1, 99 (1972).

Chapter 13

The Software of Packet Switching Systems

13.1 INTRODUCTION

The operation of a communications network has been described in terms of procedures for flow control, routing of packets, acknowledgement of messages, allocation of buffers, and so forth, all of which clearly need to be administered by stored program computers. In this chapter we consider the software organization needed in the 'control' computers which run the network.

At the same time, the existence of effective communication networks requires new software in the computers that will use the networks. There will be a whole new range of computer applications, based on networks, and the cooperation between a group of computers attached to a network raises new organizational problems. But our concern in this chapter is more with the software in the network itself.

The chapter begins with a discussion on some of the features of communications systems which impinge upon the control software of the component computers. One of the key features of this software is its multi-task and, to a lesser extent, its real-time nature, and the next part of the chapter is concerned with some of the concepts underlying this form of programming. The basic ideas of one particular approach are described. This approach, which is gaining increased acceptance, is based on the notion of independently-executing, cooperating processes. The ideas developed are given more explicit form later in the chapter where a simple multi-task executive for a single-processor system is described in some detail. Finally, we turn back to packet switching systems and develop a hypothetical network design to a level of detail sufficient to describe the structure and operation of the communications control program for a node of this network. This software makes use of the multi-task executive described earlier in the chapter.

For anyone who is familiar with software used to control a typical telephone central office, the comparative simplicity of the scheme described in this chapter may be a surprise. The main difference lies in the nature of the control task. A telephone central office contains a large quantity of equipment (arrays of crosspoints, line equipment, junctions, registers) which it must treat as external and capable of interrupting it in an uncontrolled fashion. It needs to hold a perpetually maintained map of the state of this equipment, and to be very conscious of priorities in meeting its demands. On the other hand, in the kind of data switching node we shall describe the computer *is* almost the whole switch. Outside it are only the link control equipments, and these are designed specifically to ease its task.

The central office must perform a task defined by the existing telephone network. The control signalling methods of that network are, we can now see, completely wrong for the stored program era, but they must be used, and not just one but a variety of signalling methods must be accommodated. The data network can be designed to simplify the nodes. For example we shall find that a good choice of link protocol can simplify the real-time considerations. It is not surprising that the software problem is much simpler. We could epitomise the situation by remarking that, if just the signalling component of the telephone system were allowed to be redesigned and built in a modern fashion, this would be like a packet switched network.

In some respects, however, the comparison is unfair. The switching node which we have chosen as the example to be worked through in this chapter is the simplest component of the network because it is separated from the network's terminals by a second kind of switch that handles network processes. Experience already shows that the complexity of the latter is greater. It must handle large numbers and variety of terminals and it requires more store and bigger programs.

A more important source of extra complication in a data network is the need for a multiprocessor system in the switch and for recovery after the failure of a subunit, such as a processor or store. We have not attempted to explore this aspect fully. Clearly it chiefly complicates the local switch which handles terminals. Multiprocessor systems are also needed in transit nodes when they must handle total data rates in the megabit region.

The value of the concepts described below is in no way reduced by the fact that the example is simplified. They are very general and can be applied in every kind of control computer. The example is described in considerable detail so that the concepts, such as the levels of 'virtual machine', are made explicit to an extent that is not possible with a general description.

Hardware-software Tradeoffs

In a general-purpose network, each communications control computer will be linked to neighbouring control centres and some of them will be linked to subscribers' terminals. The variety of terminal equipments will be large, ranging from simple data logging devices to powerful multi-access computers. The types of communications hardware which have to be managed by the control centres will also be quite diverse. Clearly, the efficient operation of this hardware is one of the prime considerations in the design of communications software. The nature and complexity of the hardware, and the way in which it interacts with the software are important factors determining the performance of the system as a whole.

The simplest possible type of communications hardware requires the control computer to scan all the lines, picking out the bit-transitions and building up the incoming data a bit at a time in its store. The state of the line may, in such cases, have to be sampled several times per bit period in order to locate accurately the centre of each bit-signal in the line, thereby minimizing errors that might be caused by distortion. The output of data to line would similarly take place in a bitwise fashion in such systems. It is obvious that the data rate through the control computer must be low when it is operating in this way and that a large proportion of the processing power can be saved if these simple communications functions are performed by special hardware.

There are many tasks of a simple repetitive nature such as the formation and validation of sum checks, which are very time-consuming when done by program but to which hardware is ideally suited. Where fast links, in the kbit/s to Mbit/s range are handled, the use of these more complex controllers is essential. It is possible to go further and envisage more functions that could be delegated to special hardware, for example, the generation and recognition of special kinds of packets such as acknowledgements. Cost and performance play a part in determining the optimum balance between hardware and software in a practical system. With present-day trends it is also quite feasible to consider the use of fast, microprogrammable processors in place of the special hardware units, thus introducing a greater degree of parallelism into each communications centre. This last step takes us back to base in the sense that these microprogram processors have themselves to be microprogrammed.

The architecture of the control processor is also a significant factor. Should it be a machine with a highly tailored structure and order code, or will a general-purpose computer perform these tasks adequately? It seems that small general-purpose machines currently being produced are able to meet the performance and reliability requirements for fast communications systems. There are many advantages in the use of such computers, not least is that established programming techniques and existing tools such as compilers, loaders, debugging programs and editors can be used so reducing the problem of programmer training and the cost of the programming. The necessary specialization of the hardware to match the application is more easily achieved by developing units, such as the link controllers discussed above and interfacing them to an existing processor, rather than trying to develop a totally new computer system.

Among the (so-called) general purpose computers, there are many kinds of machine optimized for different areas of application. In communication systems very little numerical computation is involved. The emphasis is on control, and in particular on efficient interaction with the machine's external environment. Thus, the type of computer we are concerned with is a fast machine with good input/output and interrupt facilities, but which may be quite simple in other respects.

Data coming into or out of the control computer on high speed lines will usually be transferred directly between the main store and the link controllers without the intervention of the CPU, which will only be involved at the beginning and end of the transfer of a block of data (e.g. a packet). Direct store access mechanisms of this type share the computer's main store between the CPU and the link units on an equal basis. A high data transfer rate will mean that the computer programs execute more slowly because of the reduced availability of the store (a phenomenon sometimes referred to as channel interference). This effect can be reduced on machines which can have independent store modules, by using different modules for program (with its working data) and for communications traffic, because access by the program to the data in transit is relatively infrequent.

In packet switched communication systems the target we are aiming for is an across-network delay of the order of tens of milliseconds for individual packets. To achieve this level of performance, the bit rates of the transmission lines must be in the Mbit/s region and the switching centres must have a high throughput and impose only small delays. Their control computers must be fast and the programs must respond rapidly to each new demand created by the communications hardware. This aspect of the software is an important one; the system and its program must effectively be 'event-organized' and will frequently be required to operate in a real-time manner.

The Need for Real-time Operation and Critical Timing

The term 'real-time' encompasses many types of application; it applies to any computer system which interacts with its environment in a time-scale dictated by the needs of that environment. Usually, the term is applied to those systems in which the computer is closely connected to the environment by means of hardware and communications devices, and where the response time requirements lie in the range from milliseconds to a few seconds at most.

The real-time aspects of packet switching systems come from the need to control various types of communications hardware, and to operate control procedures which may have critical timing constraints. Thus, failure to respond to a particular hardware signal within a specified time may lead to irrecoverable loss of information or some other type of system malfunction. This is another area in which the detailed nature of the hardware and of system operation as a whole can have a significant effect upon the performance of the control software.

In Chapter 3 we referred to the way that the crisis times of a system could be completely altered or even eliminated by redesign of the hardware. It is also possible to avoid critical timing problems by a suitable design of protocol. A good example is provided by the way in which the links between IMPS were controlled in the first version of the ARPA network. In that system the IMP which is sending a packet always retains a copy and does not destroy that copy until an acknowledgement of correct receipt has been obtained. If such an acknowledgement does not arrive within a set time, the packet is retransmitted. Eventually, after several tries on one link, the IMP may use an alternative route for the packet. It is now possible to take advantage of this design to ensure that no critical timing problems can arise at the receiving end of a link. When the receiving IMP has accepted one packet, the receiving link hardware unit is put into a disabled state in which it will ignore any further incoming packets. It is re-enabled when the IMP control program has the time and the other necessary resources are available (for example, an empty buffer). Any packet received while the IMP was in its 'deaf' state will not be acknowledged and will therefore eventually be retransmitted. Thus, the receiver control programs are able to accept packets according to current availability of CPU time and other resources in a very natural manner. All communications system software must be time-conscious in some way, but approximate timeouts of the type needed in the ARPA network are far less demanding on the programs than critical timing constraints.

It might be argued that if a system is designed so as to avoid critical timing problems the control software is no longer real-time in the strictest sense. In this sense, designs which avoid real-time operation are to be preferred. Nevertheless there is still a prime need for efficiency and speed of response to externally originated events. Such systems, which do not have a definite real-time emphasis, can best be described as 'event-driven', or 'multi-task' systems.

Multi-task Systems

An external event, such as the completion of packet input, may be regarded as giving rise to a 'task', such as analysing the control information of an input packet, routing the packet to an appropriate output queue and handling its subsequent output. These separate aspects of the overall task can be carried out by a number of task handlers or *processes* which pass tasks from one to another as each stage of processing is completed. This use of the word 'task' is different from its use in programming languages and is similar to the notion of a 'transaction' in other systems.

In general, these control computers handle many communication links and, since the programs have no direct control over the timing of external events, the computer will have to be capable of handling a number of tasks simultaneously, sharing its resources efficiently amongst them. This is perhaps the most characteristic structural feature of data communications software.

The software, therefore, may be regarded as composed of a number of processes, perhaps two or three per full duplex link of a packet switching node. The activity of a process can be triggered off externally by the occurrence of a particular interrupt, or internally by means of a command issued by another process. At any instant there may be several processes which require to execute, so a 'process scheduler' is needed to decide which shall proceed. In a multiprocessor computer, there can be several processes executing at once. The processes must be provided with a means to synchronize their operations; for example, where two or more processes share common data, only one of these can actually be allowed to alter its contents at any instant, or inconsistencies will arise. Similarly, the sharing of common resources, such as a pool of free packet buffers, must be disciplined to prevent clashes.

In a single-processor system it is only possible to run one process at a time. In this case the synchronization facilities are easier to provide, but still essential because it is not in general possible to ensure that one process will complete all its activities before it becomes suspended and another process runs. Process scheduling, synchronization and so forth can be built into the communications software in an ad-hoc manner, or they can be provided in the form of a general-purpose multi-task executive which supports the applications-specific software. The concepts underlying this type of software organization, and the structure of multi-task executives are felt to be of such central importance that a large part of the chapter is devoted to them.

Other Aspects of Communication Software

The software of packet switching systems must also be considered from the point of view of the resources that have to be managed, such as the buffer space and CPU time that have to be shared out between contending communication links. Whether this type of management is a 'localized' problem for the software depends on the overall system design. Thus it may be possible to construct the system in such a way that there is a known limit to the number of packets (say) that may require storage in the node, in the worst case. Provided that this number of packet buffers is available, no contention problem arises.

The various control procedures used in communications networks may be regarded as mechanisms for achieving global management of resources, for example the isarithmic scheme discussed in Chapter 11. When these aspects are being considered, such networks must be viewed as special-purpose 'distributed multiprocessing' systems. The control procedures operated by the software of each control centre are designed so that the overall resources of the system are correctly managed. Traffic then flows smoothly between the nodes and there is no congestion or lock up.

Another aspect of communications systems which can have a considerable impact upon the control software is that of reliability. Good reliability is essential in any communications network and the requirement can be met in two ways. In the first approach, the system can be designed assuming that each component is itself highly reliable, building the necessary reliability into the individual components. Then each node must have redundant modules such as extra CPU's and stores so that failure in one module does not imply failure of the entire node. There are various methods for achieving this, which can be quite complex from the software point of view. Probably the simplest is the 'fully duplexed' system (sometimes known as the 'hot stand-by' method) in which one set of hardware (the standby) carries out all the functions of the active hardware in synchronism. The results of every operation are compared by an extra hardware unit (which must itself be very reliable). Should one system fail, the other automatically continues to carry the traffic. The main problem with this type of approach is that of determining which component has failed when there is a discrepancy.

The second approach is to design the overall system assuming that each component is inherently unreliable. Thus in the case of packet switching networks, the nodes are connected in a redundant fashion so that there is more than one route between any two points. Should one link or node fail, the system as a whole can continue to function, possibly with the loss, at the instant of failure, of a few packets, which will generally be tolerable. This method is equivalent to the first, in that redundancy is provided, but at a 'higher level'. While the second method is probably preferable for the trunk network of a communication system, the control centres which connect to the subscriber terminals are still vulnerable, because for cost reasons most subscriber lines will terminate at one control centre only. Should such a local centre fail, all subscribers connected to it would lose service. Consequently, it is necessary to provide some low-level redundancy for the local centres.

We have suggested that the control centre software for packet switching networks must be of the type to respond rapidly to the occurrence of external stimuli, and that it must operate in a multi-task manner. There are virtually no aspects of software organization or of particular programming technique which can be said to be unique to such systems. Many types of system have the same general requirements, in many different areas of application, for example process control.

All such control programs are required to be efficient and to interact closely with the hardware to which the computer is connected. These factors have often led to the use of low-level programming languages, such as assembly languages. High-level languages such as ALGOL 60 or FORTRAN are considered to be limited, in the efficiency of the programs generated. In particular, these languages do not usually offer adequate facilities for controlling hardware directly and are very restricted in the types of data structures which they manipulate efficiently. Languages have been developed which do offer the desired degree of control over code efficiency, input/output operations and data structure handling, combined with many of the more desirable features of high-level languages. Examples of these 'intermediate' languages

are PL 360[1], PL 516[2], CORAL 66[3], and BCPL[4], they are sometimes referred
to as 'implementation' or 'system programming' languages.

An aspect of communications software which has not always been given
the weight it deserves is maintenance. Any system in active use must be
expected to evolve as patterns of usage change and as new types of requirements arise. This evolution means that the systems programs have to be
amended, often by programmers who were not involved in the original
implementation. It is therefore important that the programs be very well
documented. For this, a considerable aid is an implementation language with
expressive power approaching that of a high-level language. The structure
of the software must also be clear, logical and modular. The concept of
modularity is difficult to define precisely, as there are many alternative
approaches to this objective. In essence, the program should be divided up
into units each of which conforms to a standard interface definition. Ideally,
each unit should correspond to a self-contained function of the software.
Programming language features such as the 'subroutine' or 'procedure' can
assist in building a modular system, but they are not by themselves sufficient
in a multi-task environment. A major problem with modular systems is loss
of efficiency. This could occur, for example, when the control program is
broken up into a large number of small processes and there are significant
overheads in the passing of control from one process to another. It is clearly
important that the software should be designed in such a way that the number
of distinct process executions, and hence of intermodule communication steps,
is minimized on the program paths which determine performance. Conversely,
away from the performance-limiting paths, modularity can be used more
generously. Unfortunately, it is not easy, at the design stage, to determine
which program paths are critical to overall performance.

The requirements of the basic executive are firstly that it should offer
a flexible and efficient framework upon which to base the rest of the software,
permitting a natural division of that software into processes and scheduling
their execution. Secondly, it should handle the basic hardware elements of the
system, in particular the interrupts, which are the primary means of coordinating the sequential processor with its asynchronous environment. Thirdly,
it must offer methods by which processes can synchronize their operations,
share the resources of the computer and communicate with each other in a
convenient and orderly manner.

An interrupt mechanism is the most widely used method of interaction
between control computers and their environment, but not the only one. There
is increasing interest in systems which employ more hardware to organize
their external interaction. For example, external events may be handled by
specialized processors in a multiprocess system, and they can be made to insert
messages directly into queues, so that their servicing is less critical. The
system of scanning or 'polling' by the computer to recognize external events
was rejected as inefficient in the early history of computers (see Chapter 3),

but when a computer's main job is to handle a steady stream of external stimuli it can become attractive again, particularly if there is some form of hardware queuing of the stimuli. Therefore, in some ways, the interrupt system is more difficult than it need be, but because it is so common, the examples used in this chapter assume the use of interrupts.

13.2 THE UNDERLYING CONCEPTS OF MULTI-TASK OPERATION

In order to introduce the basic concepts of multi-task systems, it is convenient to start with a discussion of multiprogramming. Consider a single program running on a computer which requires to perform input or output operations. Most peripheral devices are much slower than the computer. Take the example of a punched paper tape reader capable of reading 500 characters a second for a computer which can execute an instruction every 2 μs. There is a disparity in speed of 1000 to 1, so that while a program is reading data, the computer in fact spends the greater proportion of its time waiting for the reader to complete each operation. This time could usefully be spent executing another program.

Here we have the principle of multiprogramming in its simplest form: when the program currently being executed is held up awaiting the completion of an input or output operation, the execution of another program is begun. This program will continue to run until it, in turn, is held up by an input or output operation. At this point the execution of the first program may be continued, if the operation that originally caused it to become suspended is

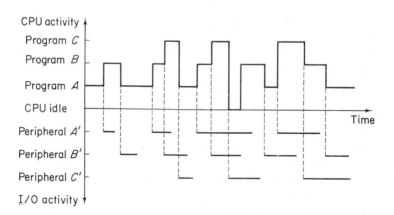

Solid horizontal line indicates program or peripheral activity
Solid vertical line indicates switch of program
Dotted vertical line indicates initiation of peripheral activity

Figure 13.1.   Idealized multiprogramming

now completed. If it is not, then the execution of a third program can begin, and so on. This state of affairs is illustrated in Figure 13.1 which shows three programs A, B, C, which may execute and perform I/O operations independently of each other using the three peripherals A', B', C', respectively. These programs are ranked in priority order $A > B > C$, so that the processor will always execute program A if it is able to continue, otherwise B, otherwise C. In this scheme, a program, once executing, will continue until it reaches a hold-up. If no program is able to continue then the processor idles. The peripheral devices operate independently of each other, and in parallel. It is assumed, for the sake of this example, that the I/O hold-ups experienced by each program are variable. From the figure it can be seen that the processor must always be busy provided that at least one of the peripherals used by the three programs is idle, so that its efficiency is considerably greater than it would be if each of these programs ran to completion in turn. The utilization of the computer's peripherals is also improved by this method of working.

Matters are not quite so simple because the computer hardware itself is not able to swap programs automatically. The conditions for choosing the next program to be run at a hold-up point may be quite complex, requiring yet another program to make the decisions. This program, which controls the multiprogramming system is often referred to as a 'supervisor' (or by several other names). The supervisor program itself needs processor time in order to carry out its functions, so that the vertical lines of Figure 13.1, which imply instantaneous program swapping, do not represent the true state of affairs; the lines should be sloped to make allowance for the overheads introduced by supervisor execution. These overheads offset the gain in efficiency made by the use of multiprogramming. In most practical systems, the user programs do not perform I/O operations directly but make calls on the supervisor program, which controls the peripheral devices itself. The supervisor detects the completion of each I/O operation and therefore is aware, at any stage, of the user programs that are able to continue execution.

Interrupts

In a multiprogramming system, the supervisor cannot scan peripheral devices directly to detect the completion of I/O transfers since this would require the supervisor to run for most of the time. Therefore some hardware must be provided to allow the supervisor to regain control from the running user program immediately an I/O operation terminates. In communications and real-time systems one of the principal requirements is a mechanism for synchronizing the computer with its asynchronous environment. The most widely used means of informing the control programs of some significant event in the external hardware is the *interrupt*, which was mentioned in Chapter 3 in connection with I/O. An interrupt is initiated by a signal sent by the asynchronous device to the processor, causing it literally to interrupt the execution of the current program and start running another program whose job it is to respond in some way to the interrupt—an interrupt service program.

The interrupt mechanisms of computers differ from one another in their details, and some examples of the methods used were described in Chapter 3. Here, we shall emphasise the software implications, but first recall the main features. In most cases an interrupt signal can be acted upon by the processor following the execution of any instruction. That is, the instruction's execution cycle includes a check to see that an interrupt has not occurred. If an interrupt has occurred, the action taken by the processor can be most simply described as an 'interpolated subroutine call'. A return address is stored (the address of the next instruction to be obeyed in the interrupted program) and execution of the interrupt service program is started, in much the same way that the subroutine call instruction works. Indeed, in most computers, the subroutine entry instruction is actually used by the processor to activate the interrupt program. The net effect is as though the interrupted program had an extra instruction temporarily inserted into it. When the service program terminates, it can return control to the interrupted program by means of a normal subroutine exit instruction. The original program then continues to run from the point of its interruption as though the interrupt had never occurred. In more complex systems, control may be returned to the interrupted program by the supervisor after other programs of higher priority have been executed.

Rather than force the interrupt service program to start from a fixed location (known to the hardware), most computers provide a 'signpost', a fixed location into which the starting address of the service program may be

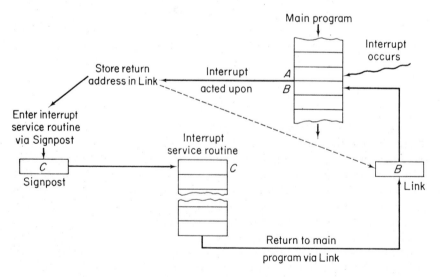

Figure 13.2. Schematic diagram of interrupt handling

placed. Figure 13.2 illustrates the sequence of events following an interrupt. An interrupt is assumed to occur some time during the execution of the instruction in store location 'A', in the main program. It will not be acted upon until the execution of that instruction has been completed, whereupon the address of the next instruction to be obeyed in the main program, B (which may not equal $A+1$), is placed in a special return link location and a branch made to the start of the interrupt service program via the special signpost location. When this program terminates, a branch back to the next instruction of the interrupted program, in location B, is made via the return link location.

In most systems there are several different sources of interrupts. The computers will have several peripheral devices each of which may generate an interrupt signal and one device may have several different reasons for interrupting. The computer must provide a means for the interrupt program to determine the reason for the interrupt. In some computers this is achieved by giving the programmer the ability to scan the devices one at a time, interrogating their current state, until the reason for the interrupt is discovered. With more elaborate systems there are several, distinct, interrupt signals and each has a special signpost location pointing to the associated interrupt program. In this way the scanning needed to determine the cause of an interrupt is reduced or eliminated.

The possibility of several interrupt service programs forces us to consider what happens if one such program is interrupted by another. If all interrupt signals are regarded as being of equal priority then it is not necessary to permit this to happen. But, if a priority structure is required, the processor must provide some additional facilities. In the simplest case these consist of a means for selectively enabling and disabling each interrupt source. Using these instructions an interrupt program can disable all lower priority sources of interrupts as soon as it starts to execute, enabling them again before returning control to the point of interruption. The program thus remains interruptible only by higher priority signals. An interrupt which occurs on a disabled line will not be acted upon by the processor until the line is enabled once more (i.e. the interrupt is 'queued' by the hardware). Some more sophisticated computers provide by hardware a priority structure for interrupts. The occurrence of any interrupt prevents lower priority signals from seizing the processor and pending interrupts are acted upon in the correct order when higher priority programs terminate.

Since a program may in general be interrupted at any stage of its execution, it is essential that there be absolutely no unintentional interaction between it and any interrupt service program. If there is, the program will fail; indeed, its behaviour will change on different occasions according to the particular pattern and timing of interrupts. To avoid unintentional interaction the computer must protect all information that may be altered by an interrupt service program, including all processor registers, such as 'accumulators', 'index registers', 'condition registers' and the various other pieces of information that are alterable by program but which do not reside in the machine's main store. The extent to which such protection is automatically provided depends on the particular computer. In some cases only the address of the next instruction of the interrupted program is automatically retained and it is left to the interrupt service program to preserve the contents of the other processor registers that it uses. In other cases some or all special machine registers are preserved automatically so that the interrupt program is immediately free to use them. The information may be dumped in a special area of main store or held in another set of processor registers.

Computers which have storage protection mechanisms may in some cases automatically restrict the store references of the interrupt service program to certain allowed regions which would normally be disjoint from those available to the interrupted program. In other cases the storage protection is lifted for interrupt service programs, taking the risk that these can be trusted completely.

There are a number of potential problems if the computer hardware permits an interrupt service program to interrupt itself, as may happen when a number of independent peripherals share a single interrupt line, for example. The interrupt program may preserve the contents of a processor register in a specific location, restoring the original value immediately before exit. If it is allowed to interrupt itself, it will use the same store location to preserve the contents of the register again, losing the original value. These problems are usually overcome by the processor locking out further interrupts automatically as soon as it acts upon an interrupt; in some cases only the specific interrupt line is locked out, since the interruption of one interrupt program by another causes no such difficulties.

The problem of insulating the main programs from the interrupt service programs is one both of considerable importance and some difficulty. A program which may be interrupted at any point cannot give consistent results if its working quantities are altered in an indeterminate manner by the interrupt programs. On the other hand, some communication between main and interrupt programs is essential. The difficulties of arranging for controlled interaction between such programs, which give consistent results for all possible combinations and timings of interrupt activities, is one of the major causes of software unreliability.

Consider two programs sharing a single main store variable at location L, the interrupt service program adding one to its value each time it is activated, the 'main' program subtracting one from it at various points of its execution. If the computer being used is capable of decreasing the value of a store location by one in a single instruction then there is no problem, since an interrupt cannot be acted upon *during* the execution of an instruction. But in some computers, this operation would need a sequence of instructions, for example using the processor register R:

$$R := L$$
$$R := R - 1$$
$$L := R$$

The servicing of an interrupt after the first or second of these instructions would result in the value of the variable (initially x) becoming $x - 1$ after execution of the main program sequence is completed; but, if the interrupt was acted upon at any other time, the result would be the original value x, which is the correct result. Computers designed for multiprocessor situations usually have read-alter-write instructions to deal with the case we have just described.

In general, then, controlled interaction is not achievable when critical sequences of more than one instruction are involved, unless their interruption is prevented (so that the critical sequences effectively behave as single instructions). For this purpose, the selective 'interrupt disable' and 'enable' instructions may be used to bracket the critical sequences. In addition, most computers provide an instruction to lock out all interrupts, and a converse 'unlock' instruction.

Processes

The interrupt is a means of synchronizing the serial computer (serial in the sense that a single-processor system can only perform one operation at a time) with its asynchronous environment. Thus peripheral devices operate in parallel with the computer (and with each other) and independently of it in the sense that the computer cannot usually control the timing of their operations. Even where it is possible to predict the time of occurrence of some particular event, such as the completion of a printing operation, it is generally much simpler to use an interrupt to signal its occurrence. However, consideration of the relationship between an interrupting and an interruptable program shows that the occurrence of interrupts leads in fact to asynchronous program executions within the computer itself, since an interrupt program may execute at any time in relation to the program it interrupts.

Programs that could execute simultaneously (given more than one processor) we term *parallel programs*. Where such independent programs are obliged to share a single processor, they are termed *pseudo-parallel*. Thus we see that the occurrence of interrupts can lead to pseudo-parallel program activity. In general, a system having N distinct sources of interrupts may be regarded as consisting of N pseudo-parallel programs plus a background program which executes when there is no interrupt activity.

Strictly speaking, pseudo-parallel programs are synchronized at the instruction level, and asynchronous above that level, since any program can only be interrupted following the execution of one of its instructions. This means that controlled interaction can be achieved between such programs by means of the interrupt manipulation instructions, and this is how synchronization between the operations of the computer and its external environment is ultimately achieved. However, the ad-hoc use of these 'synchronizing primitives' in complex systems is difficult and can lead to software which is hard to debug and inherently unreliable because it may be dependent upon the timing of interrupts. We require a conceptual framework which will extend the meaning of 'pseudo-parallel program', give it a more precise definition and provide a better method of controlling the interactions of such programs.

Such a framework has been constructed by Dijkstra and others [5,6,7,8,9]. A complex software system can be regarded, in general, as consisting of a set of cooperating *processes*. A process is an activity whose function is determined by the program which it executes at any time. We must carefully distinguish the notion of a process from that of a program. A set of instructions held in a computer's store is a completely static entity which may be executed at any time by a processor. Indeed, if such a program is fully re-entrant it may be executed simultaneously by any number of processors. A process will frequently be dedicated to a particular task, such as handling input from a teletype. Where there are a number of teletypes, we may have a process for each, using a common (re-entrant) program. It is most helpful to view a process as a 'pseudo-processor' which may execute a particular program or may be *idle* and waiting for a task to perform. Consider a system of N processes and M processors. If $M > N$ then there will always be some idle processors. If $N > M$ however, there will always be some processes which are either idle or waiting for a processor in order to execute their associated programs. Thus it is necessary for each process to have states, such as 'waiting for work' or 'waiting for a processor', relating to its overall operation, in addition to the states arising from its execution of a particular program.

The temporal independence of one process from another is of central importance to the notion of a process. A set of processes is regarded as being completely asynchronous, that is, nothing can be assumed about the relative rates at which different processes execute their programs. On the other hand, each process is strictly sequential in that the order in which the process executes instructions is determined by the program and by the data on which the program operates. In other words, the order of instruction execution by any one process is determinate, but the relative order of execution of instructions belonging to different processes is indeterminate. This view of a set of processes applies whether their operation is truly parallel or pseudo-parallel.

Semaphores

It will now be clear that the problem of synchronizing the operation of a set of asynchronous processes so that they can cooperate in the performance of some overall system function is similar to the problem already encountered with interrupts. Indeed, the idea of the pseudo-parallel program introduced in

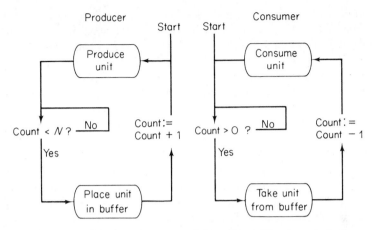

Figure 13.3.   Producer/consumer interaction without semaphores

the context of interrupts is essentially the same as that of the process. However, we are seeking a more general synchronizing primitive than that provided by interrupt lockout, and one which will be effective in the multiprocessor environment.

A simple example which nicely illustrates the problem is provided by two cooperating processes, one of which (the Producer) produces units of information, the other (the Consumer) consuming these units. A similar problem was considered in Chapter 6 from a hardware viewpoint. The processes share a buffer which can hold up to N units of information. The Producer consists of a cycle in which it first generates a unit and then places it in the buffer, returning to repeat the operation. In a similar cycle, the Consumer obtains a unit from the buffer, consumes it and then returns to get the next one. Whenever the buffer becomes full, the Producer must wait until a space becomes available and the Consumer must wait whenever it finds the buffer empty. Let us introduce a common variable, 'Count', giving at any instant the number of units in the buffer ($0 \leqslant$ Count $\leqslant N$, and initially Count $= 0$). The programs for these processes are shown in Figure 13.3. This solution is unsatisfactory in that each process *actively* waits for the required condition to be fulfilled, wasting processor time and blocking other processes that might usefully run. In addition, the alteration of the value of 'Count' by both processes can lead to erroneous results.

These problems can be solved by using Dijkstra's *semaphore* concept. In its simplest form, a semaphore is a two-valued quantity which is operated upon by the two functions 'P' and 'V'. P(S) attempts to reduce by 1 the value of the sempahore S. If the value was already zero, the operation cannot be completed and the process which attempted the operation is prevented from continuing to execute its program. At this point it is worthwhile defining the possible process states. A process that is executing its program (i.e. has a processor 'assigned' to it) we will call *running*. One which is logically able to run but is waiting for a processor we will call *active*. One which is waiting for the completion of a P operation we will call *waiting*. When a process is caused to wait by a P operation, the processor that was assigned to it becomes free for another process, so that the wasteful 'active waiting' is avoided. It is also necessary to arrange that when the semaphore resumes a positive value the P operation is carried out and the process returns to the active or running state.

The V(S) operation is the converse of the P operation, adding 1 to the value of the semaphore S, but, if the value of S was already 1, the V operation has no effect and the process which attempted the V operation continues running. If more than one process is waiting on the semaphore which has S = 0 then the end result of a V operation will be S = 0 again and *only one* of the waiting processes will cease waiting. Which one of several waiting processes is released by this operation we need not define for the moment, but clearly it must not be possible for a process to be held in the waiting state indefinitely. For the semaphore mechanism to function correctly it is essential that P and V are the only operations that can be applied to a semaphore.

The use of the simple semaphore will be illustrated by considering a system of several processes, which operate on common data. While one process is working on the data the other processes must be prevented from doing so as the results may be incorrect. The processes can be protected from mutual interference (and the execution of their so-called 'critical sections' restricted to one process at a time) by the use of a semaphore. The critical sections of all the processes are preceded by a P operation on a semaphore LOCK and followed by a V operation on that same semaphore. Initially, the value of LOCK will be 1, signifying that no process is executing its critical section. The first process requiring to enter its critical section and operate on the common data will perform its P operation and continue. Other processes attempting to enter their critical sections will be held in the waiting state, the value of LOCK being zero, until the first process has performed its V operation on LOCK. This event will permit just one of the waiting processes to enter its critical section. Thus, at any time there can be at most one process operating on the common data, and the remainder are either performing other computations or being held in the waiting state.

A semaphore can be allowed to take values greater than 1, to some advantage. The application of this kind of semaphore will be illustrated by the Producer-Consumer problem. We introduce two multivalued semaphores, UNITS and SPACES. The former gives the number of information units in the buffer at any time and is initially zero. The latter gives the number of vacant places in the buffer and is initially N. In addition we will assume that the two operations of putting an information unit into the buffer and taking one out should not be performed simultaneously, so these two operations are protected

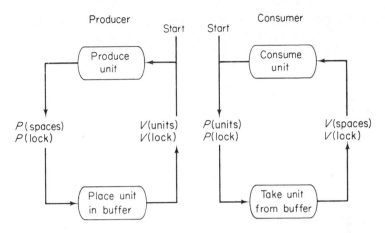

Figure 13.4.   Producer/consumer interaction using semaphores

from mutual interference by the use of a two-valued semaphore LOCK (initial value 1). The form of the programs for the two processes are shown in Figure 13.4. Evidently the producer will be held up when the buffer is full and will wait for the consumer to make a space. Similarly, the Consumer will be held up when the buffer is empty and will wait for the Producer to make a new unit available. This solution is satisfactory in every respect, and the two processes will operate correctly whatever the relative speeds of the individual operations. For example, the Producer and Consumer operations could entail input/output. In fact the processes are forced by this mechanism to produce and consume at the same average rate, assuming that a large number of units are processed in relation to the buffer size. Precisely the same mechanism was described in Chapter 6 (page 196) in relation to elastic buffering. An indication of buffer content at the receiving end of a data link was sent back to the sending end to control the data sending rate.

The order in which both processes perform their P operations is significant. If these operations were reversed in the Producer program, for example, the solution would no longer be satisfactory. To show this, suppose that the buffer is full when the Producer successfully enters its critical section. Since we can make no assumptions about the relative rates of the two processes, it is logically possible for this situation to arise. Because the buffer is full, the Producer will be held on the SPACES semaphore with LOCK = 0 and is unable to complete the execution of its critical section and perform a V operation on LOCK until the Consumer makes a space available in the buffer. However, the Consumer is equally prevented from doing so because it may not enter its critical section until the Producer performs the V operation on LOCK. So we have a stalemate situation, which is often referred to as a 'deadly embrace'. A deadly embrace, in this context, is a state into which a group of cooperating processes can get, in which it is logically impossible for some of the processes to continue. Such situations result from design errors in the programs. They occur in many guises[10] and are in no way peculiar to systems which are constructed using the explicit notions of process and semaphore.

As well as providing for the mutual synchronization of processes, semaphores can be used to control the sharing of any system resources, for example, peripheral devices. A unique resource such a single lineprinter can be managed by means of a two-valued semaphore. The process which successfully performs a P operation on that semaphore has the line printer allocated to it until it performs the V operation, which releases the peripheral.

Groups of resources such as pools of buffers or spaces in queues (as in the Producer-Consumer example) can be managed by using multi-valued semaphores. In such cases the resources must be equivalent to each other as far as the processes are concerned, since it is not then possible to request a particular one of these resources. Semaphores can be used in other situations, for example, to ensure that a routine which is called by the programs of a number of processes is used by only one process at a time. This is a particular example of a 'critical section'.

Multi-task Systems

The principal purpose of multi-task systems is to respond in some way to the occurrence of external events, whose sequence and timing are outside the direct control of the computer. It is consequently impossible to build the control software as one sequential program. However, an organization into processes allows the software to reflect the asynchronous character of the computer's environment in a very natural manner. So we may regard the software as composed of a set of asynchronous processes whose cooperation achieves the overall system function.

This is an essential difference between multiprogramming systems discussed at the beginning of this section, and multi-task systems. In the former, the user programs are completely independent of each other and it is the function of these systems to execute programs which are of this nature. User programs will in general interact with the multiprogramming supervisor to obtain the use of system resources like main store, backing store and peripherals. Each program is regarded as being completely unknown to the system as regards the effects which it might have on the system, and hence on other programs sharing the computer. Therefore it is essential that the supervisor provides complete protection of one program from another (and its own protection). For example, each program will only be permitted to access those areas of main store which belong to it. The provision of these facilities depends upon adequate protection features in the computer hardware.

In contrast, multi-task systems are often dedicated to a single application such as the switching node function in a packet switching network. The various activities which make up the overall function could be allowed to cooperate with each other in an informal, ad-hoc, manner so that the notion of a process is not clearly defined. Alternatively, the processes making up the applications-dependent software could run under the control of a multi-task executive which provides the necessary semaphore mechanism to allow processes to synchronize their activities.

Multi-task executives are usually simpler than the supervisors of multi-programming systems. The supervisors provide a wide range of facilities for the user programs, such as a 'job control language', and a filing system, and handle a considerable diversity of peripheral devices. The multi-task executives usually give only basic facilities and may not even provide for peripheral device support, since this could be the function of the applications software. It is interesting to note that the type of executive we are considering here is usually to be found at the 'kernel' of the more powerful supervisory systems of large computers. Multi-task executive design has been described well by D. L. Mills.[11]

13.3 THE FUNCTIONS OF A MULTI-TASK EXECUTIVE

The concept of a 'process' and the 'semaphore' mechanism have been described in general terms, and we now intend to demonstrate their use in a multi-task executive. First we shall describe the function which the executive has to perform, leading up to the design of a particular example of multi-task executive.

A process may be regarded as an environment in which a program is executed. This environment includes the various processor registers, such as the 'next instruction address' register. In addition, we need in the environment a state variable which describes the condition of the process and there may be other information depending on the precise way in which the process notion is implemented. Some of this information will be kept in processor registers when the process is in the running state and some in main store locations belonging to each process. When a process is not in the running state, the processor register information must be dumped into special store locations associated with the process. We refer to the block of store holding information unique to a process as its *process control block* (pcb for short). Since there is a distinct pcb for every process, we can say that a process is defined by the information held in its pcb. Indeed, it is very convenient in practice to use the 'address of the pcb' to identify a process.

Since there will in general be a greater number of active processes than available processors, the first requirement of any multi-task executive is process scheduling; that is, choosing the next active process to transfer to the running state, when a processor becomes free, and setting up the correct environment for the process program to be executed. There are many strategies that could be employed for choosing the active process. For example, the identities of the active processes could be held in an 'active queue' where the scheduler chooses the top process in this queue to go to the running state. A scheme offering greater flexibility has a number of priority levels and an 'active queue' for each level. The scheduler services each queue on a first-come, first-served basis, as before, but operates on the highest priority non-empty queue.

The facilities of the multi-task executive might be made available as subroutines that can be called by the user programs. A process may leave the *running* state voluntarily as the result of calling one of these 'executive subroutines' or involuntarily as the result of an interrupt. The handling of interrupts by multi-task executives will be considered later; for the time being we can regard an interrupt as an 'enforced' call on an executive procedure. The executive procedure may, depending on its purpose, return control to the calling program, in which case we may simply regard it as having been executed by the running process, or it may terminate that process, storing away the process environment in the pcb and thus making the processor available to another process by passing control to the scheduler.

It can now be seen that the familiar 'critical section' problem is present within the executive itself. Thus consider a multiprocessor computer in which the scheduler may be executed by any processor when the process currently assigned to that processor is terminated. The scheduler assigns the processor which is executing it to the next *active* process to be run. We will assume for the sake of simplicity that there is one active queue and that all processors use this queue. Evidently the scheduler must be re-entrant, but it will have at least one critical section in which the active queue is being manipulated, so that we need the P and V operators at the executive level. In most computers there are no instructions that, by themselves, provide all the required features of these two operators. But for multiprocessor systems an 'exchange register with store' instruction is adequate, operating on a two-valued semaphore held in a store location accessible to all the processors. This semaphore will be reserved for use by the multi-task executive and there could be other similar semaphores for other critical sections of the executive.

The way in which this semaphore mechanism works is shown in Figure 13.5; its operation may be clearer if we substitute the terms *busy* and *free* for the values 0 and 1. The processor register is set *busy* initially, so that the exchange operation sets the semaphore *busy* and simultaneously picks up the original value in the register. If the semaphore was *free* originally, the processor may continue with the execution of the critical section, otherwise it must repeat the exchange instruction until it is eventually able to 'book' the semaphore. The V operation is simply effected by setting the register *free* and storing its value in the semaphore location. It is important to realize that the mechanism described here will only work correctly if the exchange instruction 'locks out' the store location while the exchange takes place. It must not be possible for another processor to access that location during the execution of the exchange instruction—it is a 'hardware critical section'. The critical section problems found within the executive are solved more easily for single processor systems since it is then only necessary to prevent the occurrence of pseudo-parallel program execution (resulting from interrupts) during these phases of executive operation. This can be done by the interrupt enable/disable instructions.

The simple synchronizing mechanism suggested above does not have all the properties required of the Dijkstra P and V operators. For example, the method shown in Figure 13.5 uses an 'active wait'. However, these primitives are needed only within the executive; they are for the use of *processors*, not *processes*, and therefore are sufficient. Thus, if a processor executing the scheduler is locked out temporarily from the *active* queue, there is nothing it can do but wait 'actively'.

True P and V operators, for the use of *processes*, must be provided by the executive, possibly in the form of procedures. One particularly simple method of forming the necessary association between a semaphore and a waiting process is to construct each semaphore from two elements, the semaphore value itself and a 'queue control' element (e.g. head and tail pointers) which is used to queue the identitities of waiting processes. The

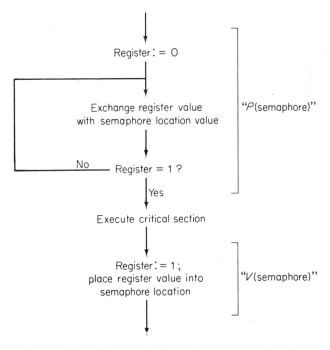

Figure 13.5.   The use of the exchange instruction to implement P and V

organization of the semaphore queues resolves the question of which process shall resume the active state when a V operation is performed on a semaphore having several waiting processes. As with the active queue and the scheduler, the semaphore queues could be operated on a first-come, first-served basis. This simple approach will be considered in more detail later.

We must now consider how interrupts are to be dealt with in the *process* framework. Let us assume that interrupts are to be serviced by processes. The semaphore now appears to be a very natural way of dealing with interrupts, since we may imagine that a process waiting for a particular interrupt has performed a P operation on a semaphore permanently linked with that interrupt. The occurrence of an interrupt will then be interpreted as a V operation on the associated semaphore. It is straightforward in most machines to arrange that the executive traps all interrupts and performs V operations on the appropriate semaphores, so that the occurrence of an interrupt causes a V operation to be interpolated into the executing program, as though it had been performed directly by the running process. Thus the notion of the interrupt can be removed from the view of the programmer in favour of the more general one of the semaphore.[12]

Single Processor Systems

The executive functions that have so far been considered may be implemented equally well for multiprocessor or single-processor systems. In the case of single-processor systems there can, of course, be only one process in the running state at any instant. In this case the rules which determine when a process shall be removed from the running state are important. The executive could be arranged so that the execution of a process only terminates when it performs a P operation which forces it into the waiting state. With this strategy the state changes of a process must always follow the paths shown in Figure 13.6(a). An alternative strategy would be to return the running process to the active state whenever another process becomes active for the first time as the result of a V operation either performed voluntarily by the running process or interpolated by an interrupt. Such a strategy would be suggested when multi-level priority operation is required since by this means the executive can ensure that the running process is always the one of highest priority. If the running process executes a V operation which causes a process of *higher* priority to become active, the running process will be switched to the active state, its identifier being placed at the end of the appropriate active queue and the scheduler entered to run the new process. But, if the newly activated process was of *equal* or *lower* priority then the running process will not be changed. The possible state changes under this scheme are shown in Figure 13.6(b).

With the method of Figure 13.6(b) processes run in a pseudo-parallel fashion, their executions being asynchronous (if interrupts are being used).

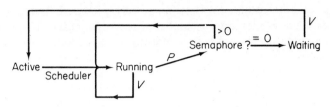

(a) Simple pseudo–asynchronous operation

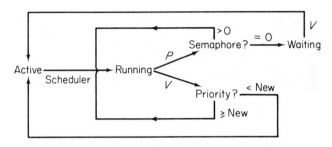

(b) Asynchronous operation with priority rules

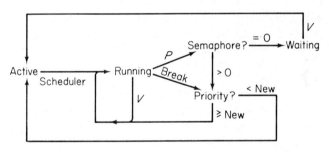

(c) Pseudo–asynchronous operation with priority rules

Figure 13.6.   Process state changes under different executive strategies

With the method of Figure 13.6(a) the programmer knows the points at which any process may terminate execution, since this can only result from a programmed P operation. This strategy is termed *pseudo-asynchronous* because of the greater degree of control over process operation afforded to the programmer. The approach can only be used in single processor systems. It allows a significant simplification of the software and a corresponding improvement in the efficiency of multi-task systems. Any critical section, which is completely enclosed within an execution of a process (i.e. which contains no P operations and whose execution therefore cannot be interleaved with that of other processes) is automatically protected. For example, any procedure which is shared by a number of processes, but which contains no P operations, need not be written re-entrantly since it can only be executed by one process at a time.

Of necessity, the pseudo-asynchronous approach is only applicable to systems in which the processes are well behaved, because the executive has no means of regaining control from a running process. This type of executive can be kept very simple, so that the overheads involved in process swapping are minimal. In addition the amount of process swapping will generally be reduced. For example, the processor information that must be preserved and restored by the executive could in the simplest case be restricted to just the 'next instruction address', it being left to the programmer to ensure that the process is in a 'tidy' state on termination, with significant working variables stored away in the pcb. With truly asynchronous working it is essential that the executive preserves and restores the complete processor environment in the pcb. In the same way, the overheads involved in re-entrancy can be reduced.

Under the pseudo-asynchronous strategy, a process which is activated (as the result of an interrupt or a programmed V operation) cannot immediately enter the running state but must wait at least until the current process has terminated. Thus the utility of this approach for true real-time working would seem to be limited. However, this limitation need not be too great, since in many dedicated systems the process execution times are short. In order to ensure that response-time deadlines are met it is possible to introduce a *break* procedure into the executive, whose function is to switch the running process into the active state if there are active processes of higher priority. The break procedure would be used by the programmer to break up the execution of long-running sections of programs. This method of operation is illustrated in Figure 13.6(c). Since the break procedure would be called very frequently in systems requiring a rapid response, it is essential that it should add very little overhead when no process swapping results.

For the kind of dedicated, multi-task system exemplified by communications control, efficiency is of prime importance. This search for efficiency has led us to propose, in single processor systems of moderate complexity, that the pseudo-asynchronous strategy should be used. The price paid for this simplicity is that the functions provided by the executive, while being considerably more powerful than those available on the 'bare' computer, are still primitive in some respects, leaving many tasks to the programmer and demanding a disciplined approach to programming.

This kind of tradeoff, between simplicity and efficiency of the executive on the one hand and ease of use on the other, appears in other areas. Suppose we wish to associate priority values with semaphores. Any process using a resource will be given a temporary priority value at least equal to that of the associated semaphore. The priority will apply from the successful execution of a P operation until the V operation. This scheme ensures that processes will be executed promptly while they are in possession of vital resources, but it necessarily involves a greater overhead than a simple, fixed-priority scheme. In a dedicated system it is often possible to obtain the advantages of a priority scheme by appropriate organization of the processes without complicating the executive. Again, consider the problem of deadly embraces. It is possible for an executive to schedule the execution of processes so that simple types of deadly embrace cannot occur, given certain prior information as to the resource requirements of each process. To do so, however, is a complex matter and involves considerable overhead at run time. In any dedicated multi-task system the possibilities for deadly embraces can better be removed by careful design of the process programs.

Appearance and Structure of the Executive

The way in which the executive appears to the programmer is important. If its functions appear simply as a set of procedures which may be called by the programmer then we have a situation similar to the use of assembly languages. The computer's capabilities have been extended in certain directions, but no syntactic or semantic discipline has been imposed on their use. The situation can be improved considerably by incorporating the executive functions into a programming language such as one of the 'systems programming languages'. It would then be possible to perform various checks on program correctness at compile time. For example, the language could include the *semaphore* as one of its *types*, when it would be a simple matter for the compiler to check that the operands of the P and V functions were always semaphores and that no operation other than P or V was applied to a semaphore. Such a problem-oriented programming language could go a long way toward removing the constraints under which a programmer must otherwise operate, simplifying his tasks and improving software reliability, yet permitting the run time executive to be kept simple. This idea is not developed here and for the remainder of the chapter it will be assumed that executive functions are made available to the applications programmer in the form of procedures.

The type of executive that we have been considering can be regarded as being an extension of the computer, implementing a *virtual machine* which is highly adapted for multi-task programming. This virtual machine allows the program designer to think in terms of processes, whose scheduling it controls. Additional operations, such as P and V, are provided, while some of the basic computer instructions, such as those controlling the interrupt system, are hidden from the programmer. (If the programmer were allowed to use these 'hidden' facilities, he might prevent the executive from functioning correctly.) It is quite conceivable that this type of executive could be embodied in the hardware or 'firmware' of future computers; in fact this objective could be achieved in a computer with an alterable microprogram.

In practical multi-task applications such as communications control, executive functions will be required in addition to the basic facilities which have already been considered. For example, it will usually be necessary to provide other mechanisms for process synchronization, formal methods of interprocess communication, some form of store management and timing information for processes. These extra facilities should be added to the executive as a series of 'virtual machine layers', each virtual machine being implemented in terms of the functions of the preceding ones.[13] Such an approach simplifies the construction of the executive and makes debugging easier. For example, store management programs will require semaphores to control the use of store by processes. If the store management program is implemented in terms of the basic virtual machine, then the semaphore mechanism is directly available to it.

The hierarchical organization also improves the flexibility of the executive and allows it to be tailored somewhat to the application. Take the example of store management. In a communications application of the packet store-and-forward type a very simple method will suffice, based on the use of a single size of store unit, large enough to hold the largest packet. For this purpose the store management layer of an existing executive could be replaced by the simpler version and the change would affect only some of the 'higher' virtual machine layers. A change to any layer will affect higher layers, but only if the change affects the functions provided by that layer, that is, changes purely internal to a layer can have no effect elsewhere.

13.4   DESIGN OF A MULTI-TASK EXECUTIVE

It is important to know the principles underlying the design of a multi-task executive, but the only way to understand what is actually involved in the design is to work through an example in detail. This we now intend to do. The example is simplified to bring out the essentials, but it is a fully practical design, very similar to an executive which is in operation. It is a pseudo-asynchronous, multi-task executive, constructed using the hierarchy principle. After some details have been covered, we shall describe it level by level.

In the descriptions of programs which follow, formal names of entities such as procedures, pointers and addresses are printed in small capitals. An example is SCHEDULER, which is the name of a procedure.

The executive includes, as well as the basic *process* and *semaphore* mechanisms, facilities sufficient to support some simple types of communications software; its functions will be made use of later in the chapter to describe the software of a packet handling node. The 'virtual machine' levels of the executive are:

1. Processes, semaphores, scheduling and interrupt handling.
2. Simple facilities for re-entrancy.

3. Storage allocation.
4. Timing facilities.

This executive would run in a typical control computer and where assumptions about specific features of machine architecture are necessary, this will be pointed out. The programs are defined in general terms using flowcharts with a notation based on ALGOL 60 and a few informal variations which are self-explanatory.

The Process Control Block

All the information about a process needed by the executive is held in a block of consecutive store locations, the *process control block*, whose format is shown in Figure 13.7. Levels 1, 2 and 4 require fields in the pcb. The applications programs executed by processes may also make use of the pcb for information storage. The size of the stack area in each pcb is determined by factors such as the maximum depth of procedure nesting and the amount of space required for stacking and unstacking local variables of re-entrant procedures. Because its size is dependent on the application program requirements, the stack is placed at the end of the executive's area in the pcb. The other pcb fields are arranged in order of executive level to which they relate. The first field, called LINK, is used to hold a pointer to another pcb when the process is held in one of the queues managed by the executive.

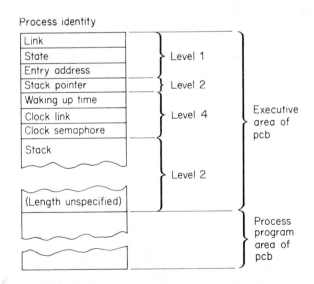

Figure 13.7.   The process control block layout

Queue Management

Queues consist simply of one-way chained lists, since this structure is sufficient for the purpose. Each queue is defined by a 'queue control element' made up of head and tail pointers, as shown in Figure 13.8. A queue control element is referred to by the address of the HEAD POINTER field. Each item held on a queue contains a pointer word used to link successive items together, as shown. The HEAD POINTER field contains the address of the first item in the queue and the TAIL POINTER field contains the address of the last item. In addition, the pointer word of the last item in a queue is set to zero. When a queue is empty, the value of HEAD POINTER is zero (and that of TAIL POINTER is undefined).

Two procedures, QUEUE and DEQUEUE are provided for queue manipulation. Both procedures are passed the address of the queue control element as a parameter. In addition, QUEUE is passed another parameter, which is the address of the pointer word of a new item. The function of QUEUE is to link the given item onto the tail of the specified queue while the function of DEQUEUE is to unlink an item from the head of the specified queue and return the address of its pointer word to the calling program. The result of DEQUEUE will be zero if the queue was empty. The operation of these two procedures is shown in the flowcharts of Figures 13.9 and 13.10. In these flowcharts, the brackets {} indicate that the value of the enclosed expression is to be used as the address of a location, whose contents are thereby referenced. Thus {QUEUE ELEMENT ADDRESS + 1} refers to the TAIL POINTER of the control element and it follows that {{QUEUE ELEMENT ADDRESS + 1}} is the pointer word of the last item in a queue.

The advantage of this technique for queue handling is that any address

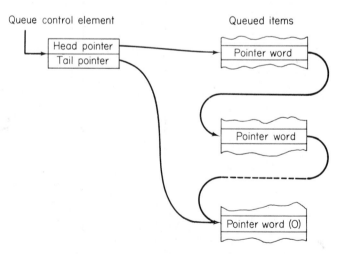

Figure 13.8. The queue organization used by the executive

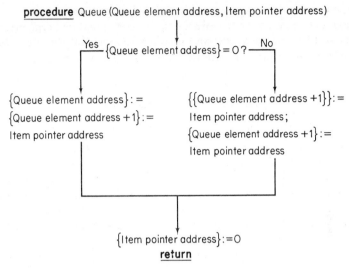

Figure 13.9.   Flowchart of procedure Queue

can be used for a queue control element and it becomes possible to build up more complex data structures which use these control elements as components. Also, the size and format of items held on queues is immaterial to these procedures since they operate only on the pointer fields. Queued items may therefore be complex data structures possibly containing other pointer fields. This is the case with the pcb, which has two pointer fields (LINK and CLOCK LINK) and a queue control element within the executive area.

In some executives more complex queue organizations may be required. If a dynamic priority scheme is employed, for example, it may be necessary

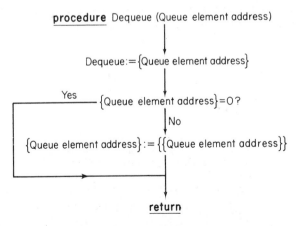

Figure 13.10.   Flowchart of procedure Dequeue

to move pcbs from one queue to another when process priorities change. Such an executive may have to extract items from the middle of queues, which is facilitated by using backward and forward pointers for each item, but for our purposes the simple structure we have described is sufficient.

Level 1 — Process Scheduling

The first layer of the executive handles the process scheduling, semaphore operations and interrupt handling. The pcb fields STATE and ENTRY ADDRESS are used directly by the procedures of this level. STATE may take one of the values running, active or waiting (which will be represented by suitable constant values). ENTRY ADDRESS is only meaningful when the process is active or waiting, and then it contains the address of the instruction at which execution of the process program is to be resumed when the process returns to the running state.

The environment of a process program consists of 'locations' belonging to one of two categories. Locations may be unique to a process, such as those kept permanently in the pcb or they may be shared with other processes and their contents must then be preserved when execution of the program terminates. Into the latter category falls the 'processor environment' and the 'global' locations shared by different process programs. For our simple executive it is assumed that any significant processor and global quantities will be saved by the programmer before termination of the program.

Two items are automatically preserved and restored by the executive itself: the next instruction address and the identity of the running process. The latter is needed so that the process program and the executive can refer to the pcb of the process. The address of the pcb LINK field is used to identify each process, so that the process identity can be used simply in queues.

A global variable RUNNING PROCESS is used to hold the identity of the process which is running. In the flowcharts, RUNNING PROCESS is treated as

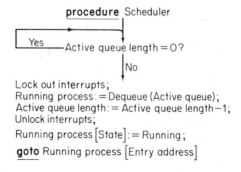

Figure 13.11. Flowchart of procedure Scheduler

an ALGOL 60 *array*, so that the state field of the pcb of the running process can be referred to as RUNNING PROCESS [STATE] for example.

Process scheduling is a straightforward first-come, first-served matter so a single queue is needed, the active queue, containing those processes that are in the active state. The variable ACTIVE QUEUE points to the queue control element of the active queue, and ACTIVE QUEUE LENGTH is, of course, the length of this queue. The pcbs of active processes are chained together on the queue by means of the LINK field. Processes are placed at the tail of ACTIVE QUEUE as the result of V operations (under certain circumstances) and they are taken from the head of the queue by the scheduler.

The SCHEDULER procedure is shown in Figure 13.11 and is called when the running process terminates as the result of an unsatisfied P operation.

The SCHEDULER first checks the length of ACTIVE QUEUE. If the queue is empty then the processor must idle, there being no processes ready to run (under these circumstances a process can only become active as the result of an interrupt-originated V operation). When the queue is found to have entries, a process is removed from its head and its process identity is assigned to RUNNING PROCESS. ACTIVE QUEUE LENGTH is decremented. These two operations must take place with all interrupts locked out, since interrupt handling can affect the state of ACTIVE QUEUE. Finally, the process is set into the running state and control transferred to the next instruction of its program. Thus SCHEDULER, although it is called as a procedure, does not return control to the calling program.

Level 1 — Semaphores

A semaphore in this system is composed of a semaphore count and a queue control element, upon which are queued the pcbs of processes that are waiting for the resources it controls. A semaphore is identified by the address of the count field, as Figure 13.12 shows. As with queue control elements, semaphores are freely located and may be incorporated into more complex structures. Multi-valued semaphores are provided and the count field is

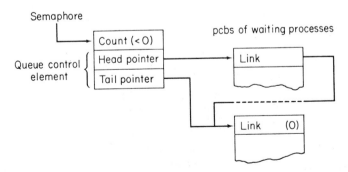

Figure 13.12. The semaphore data structure

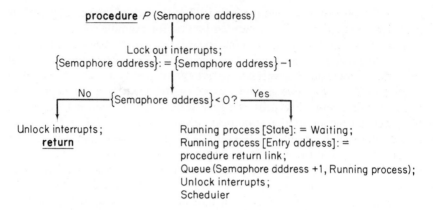

Figure 13.13.   Flowchart of procedure P

allowed to take both positive and negative values. A positive value indicates that there are resources available, and gives their number. A negative value, $-s$, indicates that there are s processes waiting on this semaphore.

A flowchart of the P procedure is shown in Figure 13.13. P (SEMAPHORE ADDRESS) causes one to be subtracted from the semaphore count field. If the result is positive then control is returned immediately to the calling program, the required resource having been 'booked' on its behalf. Otherwise, the resource is not available, the running process must be put into the waiting state and its pcb linked onto the tail of the semaphore queue (SEMAPHORE ADDRESS +1 signifies the address of the queue control element).

The STATE field of the running process is set to waiting. In the ENTRY ADDRESS field is placed the address to which the P procedure would return

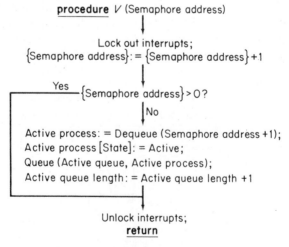

Figure 13.14.   Flowchart of procedure V

control, i.e. the contents of the procedure return link. This approach means that the P procedure does not need to be re-entrantly coded, and it can be applied in simple computers. Thus when the waiting process eventually resumes the running state, execution will commence as though by a direct return of control from the P procedure, whose call had stopped the running of the process program. After queueing the waiting process on the semaphore, the P procedure calls SCHEDULER to start the execution of the next active process. Interrupts are locked out during the execution of P to prevent interference which may arise from manipulation of the same semaphore by an interrupt-handling program.

The V procedure shown in Figure 13.14 begins by adding one to the count field of the semaphore. If the resulting value is greater than zero, there are no processes waiting for the freed resource and the operation simply causes another member of the group of resources to be marked as available. But if there are processes waiting for the resources, the V procedure removes the waiting process at the head of the semaphore queue, marks it as active and queues it into the tail of the ACTIVE QUEUE. For these operations, the flowchart of Figure 13.14 uses the local array identifier ACTIVE PROCESS. Interrupts must be locked out during the execution of the V procedure to prevent interference from operations on the semaphore queue or ACTIVE QUEUE by interrupt handling programs.

Level 1 — Interrupt Handling

Interrupts are treated as interpolated V operations (see p. 480). A semaphore is associated with each distinct source of interrupts and the occurrence of a particular interrupt results in a V operation on the appropriate semaphore by the interrupt-handling program. We need at this point to know something about the computer's interrupt mechanism and will assume that it has a single interrupt 'signpost' and a set of instructions for scanning the various interrupt sources to determine which ones are active. A possible organization of the INTERRUPT TRAP procedure (assumed to be called by a hardware-interpolated subroutine entry instruction) is shown in the flowchart of Figure 13.15. The procedure preserves the operating environment of the processor (if that is not done automatically) and then scans the interrupt sources until an active one is found. A V operation is performed on the corresponding semaphore and the procedure returns to scan for other active sources. Finally, the processor environment is restored and control is returned to the running process program.

There are two important points concerning possible interference. Firstly, INTERRUPT TRAP, as it is organized, must not itself be interrupted. It is assumed that the processor hardware locks out all interrupts upon entry to the interrupt procedure, so the procedure merely has to unlock interrupts before returning control. Secondly, a slightly modified version of the V

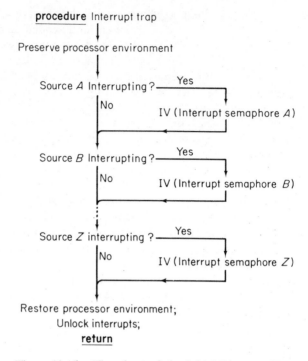

Figure 13.15.   Flowchart of the initial Interrupt Trap
procedure

procedure, called IV, is needed for use by INTERRUPT TRAP. The difference is simply that the interrupt lock and unlock instructions are omitted because the former is redundant while the latter would cause interrupts to be unlocked prematurely.

The use of a separate procedure at this point sidesteps the problem of re-entrancy at Level 1 on machines whose hardware does not lend itself readily to this method of operation. For the same reason it may be necessary to have distinct but identical procedures to QUEUE and DEQUEUE (IQUEUE and IDEQUEUE, say) for use within IV.

It has been assumed in the flowchart of Figure 13.15 that the interrupt signal is cancelled as a side-effect of the instructions 'source x interrupting?' If a separate instruction is required to cancel the signal, this should precede the call on IV.

Level 2 — Re-entrancy

The programs executed by processes in most practical, multi-task systems will have sections in common, usually represented by procedures which may be used by a number of process programs. In fully asynchronous systems, these common procedures can be in simultaneous (or arbitrarily interleaved) execution by different processes. Some special provision is required if the procedures are to operate satisfactorily. The problem may be avoided, as we have already observed, by making common procedures 'serially reusable' and ensuring by the use of semaphores that each one may only be executed by one process at a time. But this approach cannot always be adopted because it could lead to the possibility of deadly embraces. Therefore it will usually be necessary to allow some procedures to be used simultaneously by making them re-entrant.

A re-entrant section of program must consist of instructions, which are not modified by the program, and program constants. All data accessed by the program must be unique to each execution of the program, and in the case of procedures this includes the return link to the calling program. In elaborate computers, all data accesses are made via processor registers, which are preserved automatically. Procedure return links are stacked and unstacked by hardware. The stack, or 'first-in, last-out' mechanism (see p. 494) ensures that the return links for a set of nested procedure calls are used in the reverse order on return. In simpler computers these operations must be provided by program. In any case, each process must have its own stack for procedure return links because the sequence of procedure entry and exit for different processes is completely unrelated.

With the pseudo-asynchronous type of organization a common procedure need be made re-entrant only if it contains a call on the P procedure either directly or via a call on a procedure which is itself re-entrant. Since the point of potential suspension of the procedure is known to the programmer, it is possible to relax the rules for re-entrant programming considerably. It is no longer necessary to ensure that all data accesses are unique to each execution of the procedure. Local variables can be used, if their significance does not extend over a potential point of suspension of the procedure. Where they do extend over a suspension point, the programmer must preserve their values in an area of store unique to the process, and subsequently restore them. In simple machines, it is convenient to use the pcb for this purpose. The programmer works with 'pcb variables' for all items of long-term significance, using the local variables of procedures only on a temporary basis. Thus the overheads of re-entrant programming, which can be appreciable on some computers, are reduced.

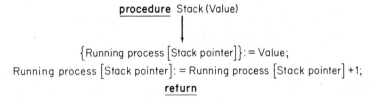

$$\textbf{procedure } \text{Stack (Value)}$$

$$\{\text{Running process } [\text{Stack pointer}]\} := \text{Value};$$
$$\text{Running process } [\text{Stack pointer}] := \text{Running process } [\text{Stack pointer}] + 1;$$
$$\textbf{return}$$

Figure 13.16.   Flowchart of procedure Stack

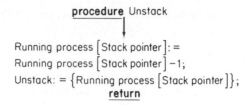

Figure 13.17. Flowchart of procedure Unstack

For each process, it is necessary to provide a stack for the return links of re-entrant procedures. This stack is located in the pcb and is controlled by the STACKPOINTER field (see Figure 13.7). 'STACKPOINTER' contains the address of the location that is currently at the top of the stack. Level 2 provides two procedures STACK and UNSTACK, which operate upon the pcb stack of the running process. The flowcharts of these procedures are given in Figures 13.16 and 13.17. The function of STACK is to place the value which is passed to it as parameter into the top location of the stack and to step on STACKPOINTER so that it points to the next free location at the top of the stack. UNSTACK has the reverse function, stepping back the STACKPOINTER so that it points to the item currently at the top of the stack, picking up the value of this item and returning it to the calling program.

These two procedures are used by the programmer to obtain the necessary stacking and unstacking of re-entrant procedure return links. STACK would be called upon entry to such a procedure, UNSTACK immediately before return to the calling program. These operations could be performed implicitly if a suitable programming language interface was available. The procedures could also be used to save and restore the values of local variables, but direct use of the pcb would be more efficient.

For machines which provide hardware link stacking these procedures are not needed. In this case the level 1 procedures SCHEDULER and P would be modified so that they preserved and restored the value of the processor stack pointer register at process swapping, using the STACKPOINTER pcb field.

Above level 2 we may distinguish two types of procedure, *re-entrant*, and *serially reusable*. They are shown as such in the flowcharts. Even where link stacking and unstacking is automatic, the programmer must be aware of the distinction between these two types of procedure so that local variables will be treated correctly.

Level 3 — Storage Allocation

This level of the executive is concerned with a form of store allocation suitable for use in a packet switching application, where the use of fixed-size buffers is all that is required. The available main store is divided into fixed-length blocks which are linked onto a queue by means of a pointer word (the first word of each block, say). The address of the queue control element for the free blocks is held in the variable FREE BLOCK QUEUE and this queue is associated with a BLOCK SEMAPHORE, whose count field (when positive) gives the number of store blocks in the FREE BLOCK QUEUE. All free blocks are equivalent as far as the applications programs are concerned; the use of the queue mechanism for handling this 'pool' of blocks is not essential but is adopted as a matter of expediency.

A store block is obtained by calling the re-entrant procedure GET BLOCK, which returns the address of a free block's pointer word to the calling program. The flowchart of this procedure is shown in Figure 13.18. The

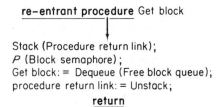

re-entrant procedure Get block

Stack (Procedure return link);
P (Block semaphore);
Get block: = Dequeue (Free block queue);
procedure return link: = Unstack;

return

Figure 13.18.   Flowchart of procedure Get Block

procedure preserves its return link and executes a P operation on BLOCK SEMAPHORE. On continuation from the P operation a block will have been reserved for the program. The procedure can then take a free block from the head of the queue and return its pointer word address to the calling program (after unstacking the return link from the pcb). The given block may be used in any way by the process program.

When the block is no longer required and all references to it by the programs have been removed, it can be returned to the pool by passing its pointer word address as parameter to the serially reusable procedure PUT BLOCK, whose flowchart is given in Figure 13.19. PUT BLOCK simply links the freed block to the tail of FREE BLOCK QUEUE and executes a V operation on BLOCK SEMAPHORE.

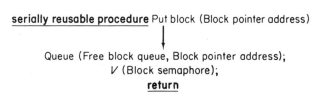

serially reusable procedure Put block (Block pointer address)

Queue (Free block queue, Block pointer address);
V (Block semaphore);
return

Figure 13.19.   Flowchart of procedure Put Block

Level 4 — Timing Facilities

The facility incorporated into the simple executive at level 4 is a timing mechanism for use by processes. The method employed illustrates very well the use of some of the features already developed. The normal way of introducing timing information is to have a periodic clock interrupt. This defines a basic time interval in terms of which all timeouts will be measured. A process in the executive handles the clock interrupt, and a procedure called DELAY is provided so that a process can ask to be suspended for a specified time interval, measured in units of the basic time interval, after which it becomes active again.

The executive maintains a queue of delayed processes in time sequence with the earliest process to be re-activated at its head. The queue control element address is held in the variable CLOCK QUEUE. The pcbs in this queue are chained not by the normal LINK field, but by another field known as CLOCK LINK (see Figure 13.7). Also held in the pcb for the use of level 4 are the fields WAKING UP TIME and CLOCK SEMAPHORE. When a process is delayed WAKING UP TIME holds the time value at which the process is to be re-activated. The CLOCK SEMAPHORE field is a normal semaphore which is incorporated into the pcb and is used to put the process in the waiting state while it is being delayed. Its count value at other times is zero, so that a P operation upon it will always cause the process to be placed in the waiting state. CLOCK SEMAPHORE is, of course, reserved for the sole use of level 4. The state of the pcb while a process is being delayed is shown in Figure 13.20. As can be seen, the pcb has to be linked into two queues, the CLOCK QUEUE and the CLOCK SEMAPHORE's queue, which has only one item. The return link for the DELAY procedure occupies the top entry of the stack. While this method may at first seem over-elaborate it is essential to a strictly hierarchical executive structure. Adding new states to the process, for example, would have reflected back on the procedures of lower levels. The facilities of level 4 can be provided very simply by using the procedures of the lower levels in this way.

Flowcharts of the CLOCK PROCESS program and the re-entrant procedure

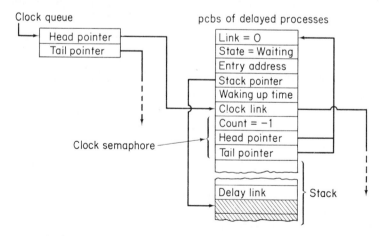

Figure 13.20. The Clock Queue and the layout of a delayed process pcb

DELAY are shown in Figures 13.21 and 13.22. DELAY is called with the required delay as its parameter. The procedure return link is stacked away, then the absolute time at which the process is to be 'woken up' is formed and stored in the WAKING UP TIME field of the pcb. The current time is maintained by the CLOCK PROCESS in the global variable TIME NOW. In the body of DELAY the correct place for insertion in the CLOCK QUEUE is found. The CLOCK QUEUE is scanned from the head item downwards until a pcb is found which has a WAKING UP TIME later than that of the process now being delayed. If such a pcb is found, the running process pcb is inserted immediately above it. Otherwise the pcb is linked onto the tail of CLOCK QUEUE by calling QUEUE in the normal manner. These operations involve the use of pcb field addresses other than LINK itself. For example, the address of the CLOCK LINK field is given by the expression 'RUNNING PROCESS + CLOCK LINK'. At any stage, {POINTER} contains the address of the CLOCK LINK field of a pcb, POINTER being a local variable of DELAY. The construct {{POINTER} − CLOCK LINK + WAKING UP TIME} therefore yields the value of the WAKING UP TIME field of that pcb.

After the pcb of the running process has been inserted into CLOCK QUEUE at the appropriate place, the procedure executes a P operation on the private CLOCK SEMAPHORE to cause the process to enter the waiting state for the required length of time. Control then passes via the P procedure to the SCHEDULER. Eventually, the CLOCK PROCESS will activate the delayed process, which will then resume execution at the next instruction of the DELAY procedure. This simply unstacks the procedure return link and passes control back to the calling program, its task having been completed.

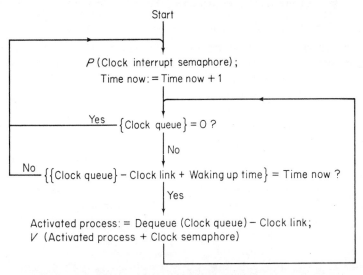

Figure 13.21.   Flowchart of the Clock Process program

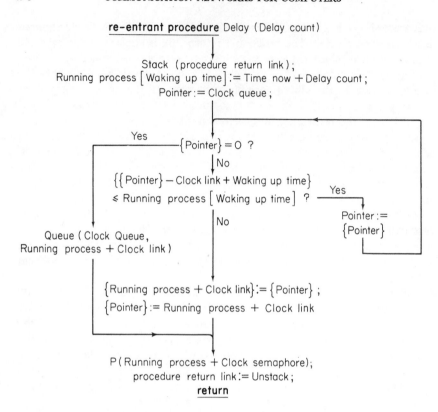

Figure 13.22.   Flowchart of the procedure Delay

The CLOCK PROCESS itself starts off by waiting for a clock interrupt on the system semaphore CLOCK INTERRUPT SEMAPHORE. On resumption, the software clock TIME NOW is incremented and the CLOCK QUEUE examined. If this queue is empty nothing more needs to be done at this time, so that the process returns to await the next clock interrupt. If not, the WAKING UP TIME value of the head pcb in the CLOCK QUEUE is checked. If its time value has not yet been reached, nothing further needs to be done. If it has, the pcb is removed from the head of CLOCK QUEUE and the delayed process is activated by means of a V operation on its private CLOCK SEMAPHORE. In this case the process program also checks to see whether there are further delayed processes to be 'woken up' at the same time and when none are found it returns to the start.

Figure 13.21 shows that the CLOCK PROCESS program is written as a continuously running loop. Upon initial entry (at the label START), the program may have to perform some initializing actions, such as setting the hardware clock running. Its subsequent execution is broken each time it executes the P procedure, since the CLOCK INTERRUPT SEMAPHORE will be zero until the interrupt. Thus, in practice, the amount of processor time actually consumed will be small if the basic time interval is not too short. The pseudo-asynchronous nature of the executive prevents any interference between CLOCK PROCESS and DELAY, both of which operate upon CLOCK QUEUE, because the DELAY procedure executes as part of the currently running process.

The Executive as a Whole

To summarize the features of this multi-task executive, seven procedures are available for the use of the applications programmer (P, V, STACK, UNSTACK, GET BLOCK, PUT BLOCK and DELAY) in addition to the two basic procedures QUEUE and DEQUEUE. In addition, there will be a system semaphore for each distinct interrupt source and a 'clock' which can be read by the program. The procedures SCHEDULER, INTERRUPT TRAP and IV and the CLOCK PROCESS program are internal to the executive. The executive programs operate upon data structures which can be constructed by the programmer with some degree of freedom.

This philosophy has the disadvantage that run time checking of correct use of the executive facilities can at best be very limited. But this is tolerable in dedicated software systems. It could be improved by incorporating the executive features into a 'systems programming language'.

The P and V functions are logically sufficient for synchronizing a set of cooperating, asynchronous or pseudo-asynchronous processes. Some existing multi-task and real-time executives provide various other mechanisms for synchronizing processes and organising interprocess communication. In particular, some executives allow a process to wait for a number of different events at the same time. It is possible to achieve the AND function of a number of semaphore-controlled conditions or events by using a sequence of P operations (taking care to avoid deadly embraces). The OR function is not possible within one process, with the form of P operation described, since a process can only be waiting on one semaphore at a time. But it is possible to simulate this function in a fairly straightforward manner. Clearly, applications programs must incur an overhead when making use of the executive. For example, the process swapping resulting from an unsatisfied P operation involves the immediate overhead of executing the P procedure followed by the SCHEDULER. The amount of processor time consumed by these procedures is strongly dependent on the computer's architecture. Some computers provide operations, such as environment changing and stack management, which fit very closely with the requirements of the type of multi-task executive discussed here. In microprogrammable computers it might even be possible to build some of the executive layers into the hardware so that the overheads could become very small.

Efficiency is of prime importance in applications such as high-speed communications control, so that it is vital to design multi-task software in such a way that it makes effective use of the facilities provided by the executive. One of the primary rules is that run time optimization should be sought on those program paths which are critical to system performance, while space optimization can be sought in the other parts of the program.

The number of distinct process executions lying on each critical path should be minimized so that the executive overhead from process swapping is reduced. This consideration is made all the more important by the fact that in many multi-task systems the amount of processing needed for most of the events which are handled is quite small. Therefore, if a key event involves a number of processing stages, it will be better to incorporate all these into a single process rather than use several separate processes. Away from these performance-limiting paths, it is best to make fuller use of the executive facilities and achieve a more natural structure for the applications software.

13.5 SOFTWARE EXAMPLE — A PACKET SWITCHING NODE

The purpose of the multi-task executive which we have been describing is to allow the 'communications programs' to be written conveniently in terms of a number of pseudo-asynchronous processes. In the last part of this chapter we shall follow through an example of the design of the communications program. As with the executive itself, it is necessary to treat an example in some detail to show the kind of problems which this software poses to the designer.

The chosen example is the so-called 'node' of a packet switching network. This node, which is part of the trunk network shown in Figure 10.9, handles only fully-formed packets and is not responsible for the 'interface computer' functions, and this simplifies its design, as befits an example meant for exposition. But the system and its design considerations are typical of packet switching systems. In some respects the link between the nodes in our example functions like the link in the ARPA network.

The purpose of the example is to demonstrate the software design, but first we need to say enough about the hardware, the packet format and the link protocol to set the scene for the software.

The Link Hardware

A node is connected to its neighbours by means of full duplex communications links. Each end of a link is terminated in a communications controller consisting of independent *send* and *receive* units as illustrated in Figure 13.23. The link hardware may therefore be considered as two independent simplex channels, send to receive, receive to send. The job of the send unit is to extract a packet from the store of the node computer when instructed to do so, and control its transmission to the receive unit of the adjacent node. When this operation is complete, an interrupt is given to the node computer to inform

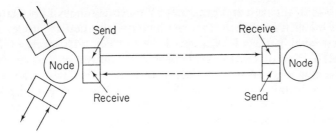

Figure 13.23. Node-Node connections

the program that the packet has been dispatched and that the link is free to handle the next packet out on that link.

The receive unit monitors the communication line for the start of a new packet, putting the packet into the store of its node computer and informing the program by means of an interrupt when this operation has been completed. The unit does not monitor the line for the start of a new packet until instructed to do so, so that if a packet starts to arrive while the unit is in this *deaf* state, it will be completely ignored. When the receive unit gives the 'packet input complete' interrupt, it immediately reverts to its deaf state. Each packet carries a sum check, generated by the send unit and verified by the receive unit. If the receive unit detects an error in an incoming packet, this will be indicated to the node program by an error flag which may be read by the program when the 'packet input complete' interrupt is being dealt with, and is then reset. When the send unit is instructed to initiate packet output, it will be given the core store addresses of the first and last packet locations. The receive unit will similarly be given the first and last addresses of a core buffer large enough to hold the longest possible packet. Packets have a variable length up to some specified maximum.

Other details of the link hardware operation are not essential to this exposition, but for the sake of completeness, Figure 13.24 illustrates the envelope of a packet as it might appear on the communication lines. Between

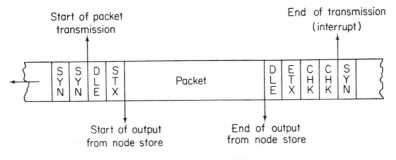

Figure 13.24. Format of transmitted packet

transmissions, the send unit generates SYN (Synchronous Idle) characters on the line. The hardware frames or envelops the packet proper with the character combinations DLE (Data Link Escape), STX (Start of Text) and DLE, ETX (End of Text) so that the receive unit can unambiguously detect the beginning and end of each packet. In order to maintain transparency to information within the packet proper, the send unit checks each character before transmission, and prefixes any DLE character in the packet proper by an extra DLE. The receive unit correspondingly reduces any double DLE combination to a single DLE, which is treated as a continuation of the packet. The final two characters, shown as CHK, are the 'check' field for error detection. These conventions are the customary ones, but here they only concern the hardware designer.

Packet Format

The layout of packets sent from or received into the store of each node is shown in Figure 13.25. Normal traffic packets which pass through the trunk network (DATA packets) consist of the fixed length 'header' and a variable length 'text' body shown in part (a) of the figure. Control information of significance to the nodes is contained in the header. The text body contains user's data and is never examined or altered by the trunk net. In our example, the packet header consists simply of a type code, a link sequence number, source and destination address fields. The addresses identify the source subscriber and the destination of the packet, but only a part of the address field, specifying the destination node, will be of significance to the node programs we shall describe. The destination address determines the route through the trunk network to be taken by a packet, while the source address is needed by the destination subscriber or interface computer which receives the packet.

The only other type of packet which concerns us here is the Acknowledgement or ACK packet which has no text section and an abbreviated

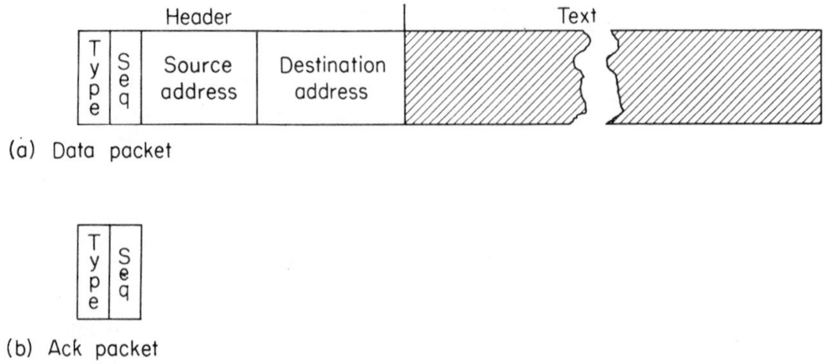

(a) Data packet

(b) Ack packet

Figure 13.25.   Format of the stored parts of DATA and ACK packets

header, as shown in Figure 13.25 (b). The ACK packet is sent from one node to a neighbour to acknowledge a DATA packet received. The link sequence number field is used in the node-node control procedure which is described below.

The Link Control Procedure

A simple but reliable procedure will be adopted to control the flow of packets from one node to the next. Whenever a DATA packet is accepted by the receiving node, an ACK packet is returned to the sender. The sending node is in general allowed to transmit DATA packets without having received acknowledgements for earlier ones. A one-packet-at-a-time method of operation is not imposed because, although it is simple to implement, it is also inefficient on long lines. The link sequence number field must be used to relate acknowledgements to the originally transmitted DATA packets, and a fail-safe procedure must be designed on the assumption that some of the DATA and ACK packets will be corrupted, lost or ignored.

Having transmitted a DATA packet, the sending node retains a 'security' copy. If an ACK packet is received which has a sequence number tallying with that in the header of a DATA packet security copy, that copy may be deleted in the sending node and the space it occupied may be re-used, acting on the assumption that the packet has been safely accepted by the receiving node, which now assumes full responsibility for it. But if a security copy remains unacknowledged for more than a predetermined length of time, it can be assumed that either it has not been accepted by the receiving node or the acknowledgement has been lost. Under these circumstances the 'timed-out' DATA packet is again transmitted, but its security copy is not destroyed. A retransmitted DATA packet carries its original link sequence number so that the recipient, if the packet had been accepted earlier, recognizes that it is not a new packet. After a number of retries, without success, a sending node takes other action, such as choosing an alternative route for the blocked packet, but we shall not cover this point in our outline program.

This packet transmission procedure allows a receiver to ignore packets by simply making no acknowledgement, because the packets will eventually be sent again. In this way, the receiver can control the flow of packets on an incoming link according to its operational needs. If the receive unit is in its deaf state when a packet starts to arrive, the receiving node will never be made aware of its appearance. If the packet is stored but a checksum error is detected by the hardware, or if the packet is successfully received but cannot be accepted by the node control programs for internal reasons, then no acknowledgement will be generated.

A more detailed description of the link control procedure is necessary for a full understanding of the programs given in the next section. We assume that the link sequence number field consists of eight bits, so that these numbers must lie in the range 0 to 255 inclusive. They are used in a cyclic manner, 0 following immediately on 255. Let us introduce the notation that if x is any integer, Rem (x) is the integer in the range 0 to 255 which differs from x by a multiple of 256. For each of its links, a node maintains a *current output sequence number* (COSN), the sequence number value that will be assigned to the next new packet to be transmitted along the link. Having transmitted a new packet, therefore, the next value of COSN is given by Rem $(COSN + 1)$. It is clearly not possible to allow new packets to be transmitted indefinitely without the receipt of acknowledgements for the earlier ones, because the use of a cyclic sequence number means that ambiguities will arise. Therefore, a node must associate another number with each link, the sequence number of the oldest unacknowledged packet copy, which is termed the *expected acknowledgement sequence number* (EASN). The rule is imposed that a new packet may be sent on any link only if the inequality Rem $(COSN - EASN) \leqslant L$ holds for that link. L is a parameter of the system which determines how far the sending and receiving ends of a link can get 'out of step'. Clearly, L must be less than 256. This parameter also represents the maximum number of packet security copies that a node must be prepared to hold for each of its links.

At the receiving end of a link, DATA packets are accepted only in strict sequence according to their sequence numbers. One missing packet in the sequence holds up all the following ones. This procedure is very simple to operate and has the useful side-effect that the order of packets sent on a fixed route through the network is preserved. Associated with each incoming link is the sequence number of the next new DATA packet to be accepted, the *expected packet sequence number* (EPSN). If the sequence number, S, of an incoming packet is such that Rem $(S - EPSN) < L$ then we know, by the rule given in the preceding paragraph, that this packet must be a new one, not previously accepted. If $S = EPSN$ the packet is accepted and acknowledged with an ACK packet carrying sequence number S, since it is the next DATA packet in sequence. The value of EPSN is then stepped on to Rem $(EPSN + 1)$. Otherwise, the packet is ignored and no acknowledgement issued. A timeout eventually causes retransmission.

If Rem $(S - EPSN) \geqslant L$, the packet must be one that has previously been accepted and acknowledged. The retransmission would be the result of a lost or badly delayed acknowledgement. In this case the repeated packet must be ignored by the receiver but acknowledged so that the sender can delete its security copy.

The sequence number of the security copies held for each link run from EASN (the oldest) up to but not including COSN (the next to be used). The sequence number, S, on a received ACK must therefore be compared with EASN and COSN to determine whether a security copy is to be deleted. Because of the cyclic nature of the sequence numbers there are two cases, depending on whether EASN $\leqslant$ COSN. This is illustrated in Figure 13.26

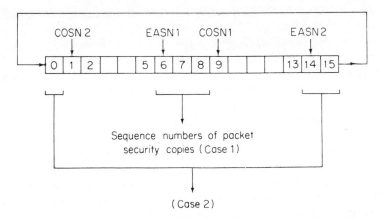

Figure 13.26. Cyclic sequence number operation

for a sequence length of 16. With EASN = 6 and COSN = 9, S can only be valid if *both* S < COSN and S ≥ EASN. However, when COSN has recycled, so that EASN = 14 and COSN = 1 for example, then S must satisfy only *one* of the conditions S < COSN or S ≥ EASN. Values of S not satisfying these inequalities are ignored, being repetitions of previously received acknowledgements. Normally, an acknowledgement will refer to the oldest security copy, however, the loss of ACK packets can lead to successfully received acknowledgements referring to newer security copies. In such cases, since the preceding DATA packets must have been accepted and acknowledged by the receiving node according to our procedural rules, all *older* security copies may be deleted at the same time as the one with the given sequence number. The value of EASN is updated to Rem (EASN + 1) for every security copy deleted.

When a DATA packet has been transmitted, a timer is started up for the security copy retained in the sending node's store and if the packet has not been acknowledged before the timer expires, its retransmission is initiated. The copy having a sequence number S = EASN must clearly be the first to time-expire, either because the transmitted DATA packets was lost or ignored, or because the returned ACK was lost or delayed. In either of these cases, it is sufficient just to retransmit the timed-out packet, but in the case of the lost DATA packet, which is perhaps the more probable of the two, our procedural rules tell us that eventually all the succeeding DATA packet copies will have to be retransmitted as well. Therefore, the approach adopted in the program described below is to retransmit *all* security copies immediately upon time-expiry of the first.

These link protocol rules may seem complex, but a careful study will show that they provide a secure system. No system, however, can be proof against any sequence of faults. At best, the probability of actual errors can be kept low.

13.6 THE SOFTWARE DESIGN FOR A NODE COMPUTER

Having described the link protocol, we are now able to specify, in outline, the principal part of the control software for a store-and-forward node of a trunk data network. We are concerned with the programs responsible for controlling the transmission of packets between adjacent nodes, and shall ignore some of the software functions such as generation of statistics, handling of node-to-node messages for the updating of routing tables and so on, which are important in practical systems but not essential to an understanding of the software organization. This software is based upon the multi-task executive described earlier and operates in a pseudo-asynchronous manner. The node computer in this example must therefore consist only of a single processor. It is also assumed that the input of data from the receive hardware is autonomous and so is the output to the send hardware. Each significant external event, such as completion of a packet input or a packet output, is signalled by means of a distinct interrupt leading to a V operation on a semaphore unique to this kind of event. No further assumptions need be made about the features of the node computer, which could be any control computer.

We shall commence by describing a particular node software design in reasonable detail, leaving to the end a more general discussion of the design criteria. With each link from a node there is associated a send and a receive interrupt. Each link has three queues, a queue of DATA packets awaiting output to the neighbouring node, a queue of ACK packets awaiting output and a queue of packet security copies awaiting acknowledgement from the neighbouring node. These queues are referred to as DATA QUEUE, ACK QUEUE and RETRANSMIT QUEUE respectively. When a node is ready to accept a new packet from a neighbour via the receive hardware, it allocates a buffer to that link. The arrival of an ACK packet may cause one or more of the security copies held in the RETRANSMIT QUEUE to be deleted and the buffer space occupied to be returned to the pool. The arrival of an acceptable DATA packet results in the packet buffer being placed at the tail of a DATA QUEUE for another link, as determined by an unspecified routing algorithm, using the destination address in the packet header. Once a DATA packet has been accepted by a node, it stays in the same buffer until it is deleted from the RETRANSMIT QUEUE. The movement of packets from one queue to another is achieved by the manipulation of pointers.

Incoming ACK packets are dealt with directly, and their buffer space re-used immediately. Outgoing acknowledgements occupy a buffer while they are being queued, but when their output is complete the space is re-used. (ACK packets do not have to wait for acknowledgement.) It might be more efficient in practical systems to use separate short buffers to hold ACK packets awaiting output, but for simplicity we assume that all packet buffers are of the same size. The DATA and ACK QUEUES have to share the use of the outgoing links. When the output of one packet is complete, the control pro-

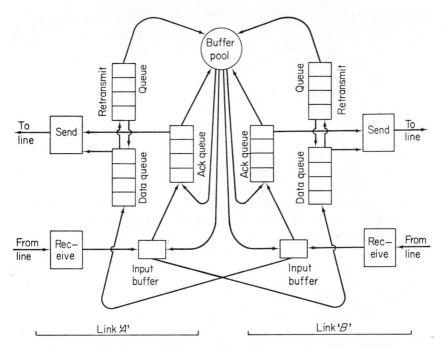

Figure 13.27. Packet buffer and I/O paths in a node with two links

gram must initiate the transmission of the next packet from the head of one of these queues. When a DATA packet is sent out, its buffer is removed from the head of the DATA QUEUE and placed at the tail of the RETRANSMIT QUEUE to await acknowledgement or eventual retransmission. The movement of packet buffers between the queues and the packet buffer pool is shown in Figure 13.27. For clarity, only two links are shown. The figure also indicates the I/O paths of the two send and receive units.

The node software organization adopted makes use of three processes for each link. One, the Input Process, deals with incoming DATA and ACK packets from the receive unit, servicing the receive interrupt semaphore. The second, the Output Process, services the DATA QUEUE, while the third, the Ack Process, services the ACK QUEUE. The latter two processes share the outgoing link and the servicing of the send interrupt semaphore. Time checking and initiation of output from the retransmit queues is performed by a single retransmit process which serves all the links of the node. Later in the chapter, some alternatives to this form of process organization are considered.

The Link Record

The node processes synchronize their activities by means of four semaphores for each link (in addition to the interrupt semaphores). Three of these semaphores, DATA QUEUE ENTRIES, ACK QUEUE ENTRIES and RETRANSMIT QUEUE SPACES, control operations on the corresponding queues, while the fourth, OUTPUT LINK, is used to ensure disjoint use of the outgoing link by the Output Process and the Ack Process.

The four types of processes act upon common data. Because of this, it seems best to hold the shared data in a contiguous record for each link, called the LINK RECORD.

One copy of the program will serve the Input Processes for all the links, and similarly for the other two types of repeated process. These programs use local variables on a temporary basis, but operate for the most part on the data held in the appropriate link record. To achieve the required process program re-entrancy, the link record identity could be held in a processor register or common global location, so that the value is preserved and restored as each process leaves and enters the running state. However, we assume here that the link record address is held in a user pcb location of each of the three repeated processes, the location being identified as LINK RECORD. Therefore a process program actually refers to a link record variable such as COSN by a chain of record-accesses which could be written CURRENT PROCESS [LINK RECORD [COSN]]. But for clarity these references will simply be written as [COSN] in the flowcharts whenever a process is referring to an item in its own link record. Table 13.1 shows the link record items required by the four process programs.

Link Record Item	Significance
COSN	Current output sequence number
EASN	Expected acknowledgement sequence number
EPSN	Expected packet sequence number
DATA QUEUE	Address of the Data Queue control element
ACK QUEUE	Address of the Ack Queue control element
RETRANSMIT QUEUE	Address of the Retransmit Queue control element
DATA QUEUE ENTRIES	Address of the semaphore controlling the data queue
ACK QUEUE ENTRIES	Address of the semaphore controlling the ack queue
RETRANSMIT QUEUE SPACES	Address of the semaphore controlling the retransmit queue
RECEIVER INTERRUPT	Address of the receiver interrupt semaphore
SENDER INTERRUPT	Address of the sender interrupt semaphore
OUTPUT LINK	Address of the semaphore controlling use of the output link
INPUT PACKET	Address of the packet buffer currently being used for input from the link
RETRANSMIT	Boolean used when a timeout-initiated retransmission of packets is required
SENDER	Address permitting the programs to issue control instructions to the correct link hardware peripheral
RECEIVER	As for sender

Table 13.1   The link record items

Packet buffer

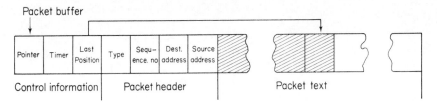

Figure 13.28.   The packet buffer format

The format of a packet buffer and the names of the data fields in it are shown in Figure 13.28. Packet buffers are always manipulated by means of the address of the first (pointer) field, which is used here to access the other fields (as in a pcb and link record). We thus find expressions such as [INPUT PACKET] [TYPE] used in the program flowcharts, in this case to refer to the TYPE field of a packet header as it is held in the packet buffer. The TIMER field is used while the buffer is held in the RETRANSMIT QUEUE and the LAST POSITION field indicates the last text character of the packet.

Flowcharts of the programs for the four types of process are shown in Figures 13.29 to 13.32. References in the text to lines of the program are given by numbers in brackets.

The Input Process

Referring to Figure 13.29, the Input Process begins (1) by requesting a free packet buffer, whose address it assigns to the link record variable INPUT PACKET. The appropriate commands, and the start and finish addressses of the packet area of the buffer are then issued (2, 3) to the receive unit defined by the address RECEIVER. The hardware then starts monitoring the incoming line for the beginning of a new packet which it stores in the buffer allocated to it.

The program then, by a P operation on a semaphore (4), causes the Input Process to wait for the interrupt which signifies that this operation has been completed. When this happens, and the process continues, the receive unit's error flag is read (5) and, if a sum check error is found, the program returns to re-use the existing input buffer, overwriting the erroneous packet with the next input. If the packet is acceptable the LAST POSITION field of the buffer must be loaded from data read back from the receive unit. This is needed to ensure that the correct length of the packet field will be sent out when the packet is forwarded. This operation precedes line 6 of the flowchart.

The next phase of the Input Process acts on the data in the packet header. First (6) the packet sequence number is placed in a local variable S and a branch (7) made depending on whether the packet is of type ACK or DATA.

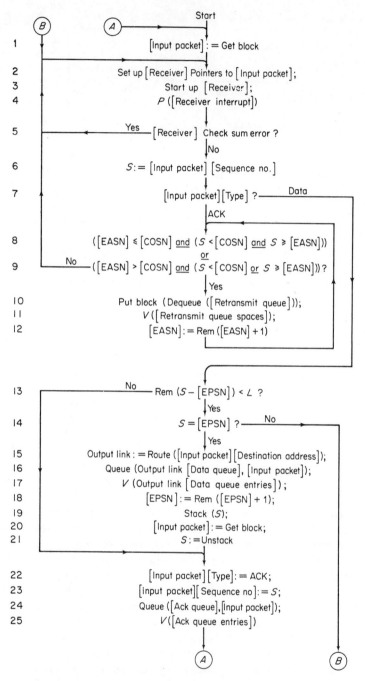

Figure 13.29   Flowchart of the Input Process program

Consider first the case of an acknowledgement. The sequence number is checked (8, 9) to see that it satisfies the inequality relationships explained earlier which verify that it refers to a packet security copy held in the RETRANSMIT QUEUE. If the sequence number is not in the expected range, the acknowledgement is ignored and the program returns to re-use the buffer for the next input.

If the sequence number lies within the current range of the RETRANSMIT QUEUE the buffer at the head of this queue is removed (10) and returned to the pool of free buffers, because the security copy it contains is no longer required. A V operation (11) is performed on the semaphore controlling the RETRANSMIT QUEUE in order to update the space in the queue and EASN is incremented (12). These operations are repeated as long as S remains within the current range of the retransmit queue, that is until all packet buffers up to and including the one with sequence number S have been deleted from the head of the queue and their space returned to the pool. EASN now indicates the sequence number of the next expected acknowledgement. After these operations have been completed, the program returns to use the current packet buffer for the next input.

On the other branch of the program a DATA packet has been received. The program checks (13) to see whether the sequence number lies within L of the expected value EPSN. If not, the packet is treated as a repeat of a previously accepted one and acknowledged (re-using the packet buffer for the acknowledgement; this involves lines 22 to 25 of the program which are described below). A repeat packet is otherwise ignored. If the sequence number indicates that the packet is a new one, not previously accepted, it will nevertheless be completely ignored (not acknowledged) unless it is the next in sequence (14). If it is ignored, its retransmission will eventually be caused by timeout. If it can be accepted, then the destination address contained in its header is passed to a routing procedure (15) whose job it is to determine the best outgoing link for the packet according to the prevailing network conditions. Routing methods were treated in Chapter 12. The routing procedure returns as its value the address of the link record for the chosen destination link, and the program assigns this address to the local variable OUTPUT LINK.

When the output link identity has been established, the program places the packet it is handling on the tail of its DATA QUEUE (16) and executes a V operation (17) on its DATA QUEUE ENTRIES semaphore to signify the presence of the packet. The expected packet sequence number, EPSN, is then updated (18). The next task of the Input Process is to acknowledge the DATA packet, for which it must first obtain (20) a free packet buffer. Since this operation may cause the process to be put into the wait state, the value of the local variable S, which is required later, must be preserved in the pcb stack (19) and then restored after the buffer is obtained (21). This is necessary because the same program may be executed in the meantime by another Input Process which would change the value of S. These operations could have been avoided by making S a Link Record variable.

To complete the acknowledgement, when a new buffer is available, the TYPE field in the packet heading is changed to ACK (22) and the sequence number S inserted (23). The buffer is then queued (24) at the tail of the ACK QUEUE and the queue control semaphore stepped by means of a V operation (25). Finally, the program recycles to the point where it obtains a new packet buffer ready for the next packet input.

The Input Process program has the appearance of a continuously running program whose execution is suspended only while the process awaits a new packet buffer it has requested or the arrival of the next packet on its communication link. But when the process is activated after suspension in the wait state, it cannot necessarily enter the running state immediately, because it shares the node processor with the other processes. Therefore the packet arrival interrupt on any link does not always get immediate attention. This is the reason for choosing the link hardware design outlined earlier. The interaction of the Input Processes with the other node processes is very straightforward and takes place through the medium of the three types of queue, their controlling semaphores and the variables COSN and EASN. An Input Process operates on the link record belonging to a *different* link only when it accepts a new DATA packet.

The Ack Process

The Ack Process, shown in Figure 13.30, is very simple. It waits (1) for an entry to appear in the ACK QUEUE, so it is set in motion by the Input Process of

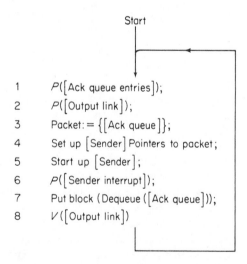

Start

1	$P([\text{Ack queue entries}])$;
2	$P([\text{Output link}])$;
3	Packet: $= \{[\text{Ack queue}]\}$;
4	Set up $[\text{Sender}]$ Pointers to packet;
5	Start up $[\text{Sender}]$;
6	$P([\text{Sender interrupt}])$;
7	Put block (Dequeue $([\text{Ack queue}]))$;
8	$V([\text{Output link}])$

Figure 13.30. Flowchart of the Ack Process
program

the link. When there is work for it to do, it waits for the outgoing link to become available and reserves it for its own use (2). The start and finish addresses of the packet at the head of the queue are then passed to the appropriate send unit (3, 4) and a start command is issued to the send hardware (5). The process then waits for the completion of the output operation (6). Finally, the packet buffer is deleted from the head of the ACK QUEUE and returned to the pool (7) and the OUTPUT LINK is released (8).

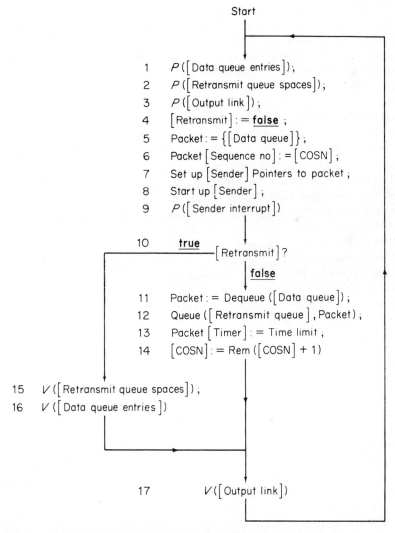

Figure 13.31. Flowchart of the Output Process program

The Output Process

The Output Process shown in Figure 13.31 operates in a similar way to the Ack Process. The process starts the output of a DATA packet from the head of the DATA QUEUE when three conditions are met. There must be (1) at least one packet in the DATA QUEUE, (2) space for the packet security copy in the RETRANSMIT QUEUE and (3) the OUTPUT LINK should be available. The requirement that there should be space in the RETRANSMIT QUEUE is the reason for operating the queue control semaphore according to the amount of space *remaining* in this queue. The maximum permitted length of the queue is given by the parameter L (which is the initial value of RETRANSMIT QUEUE SPACES). Holding up transmitting whenever the RETRANSMIT QUEUE is full ensures that COSN and EASN never differ by more than L, as required by the link procedure.

Line (4) of the program is explained later. The current output sequence number, COSN, is placed (5, 6) in the sequence number field of the packet to be transmitted. Then the send hardware is prepared and started up (7, 8). When the output operation is completed (9) and the program resumes its operation, a test (10) is made that will be explained later. The packet buffer at the head of the DATA QUEUE is moved to the tail of the RETRANSMIT QUEUE (11,12) and the packet TIMER field initialized (13). Finally (14) the output sequence number is stepped on and the OUTPUT LINK released (17).

The interaction of the Output Process with the Ack Process and the Input Process is very simple and causes no problem. A more complex situation arises with the (common) Retransmit Process, and this is the reason for the parts of the program we have not yet explained. We shall return to it after describing the retransmit process.

The method of sharing the output link between the Output Process and the Ack Process means that, whenever there are entries in both the DATA QUEUE and the ACK QUEUE, the output of DATA and ACK packets will alternate because each time that one process gives up the output link, the other is ready to take it. It may be thought desirable to give higher priority to the output of acknowledgements, but this cannot be achieved by reversing the order of the two P operations at the start of the Ack Process. Such a change could lead to the situation where the Ack Process has seized the output link but then has no work to do so that the Output Process is blocked. (Though bad for efficiency, this is not a deadly embrace situation, because ACK packets can still be placed in the queue by the Input Process.) One way to give acknowledgements priority is to examine the ACK QUEUE ENTRIES semaphore after the output of every packet. If the semaphore is greater than zero a P operation will not cause the process to wait, so that it may safely be allowed to make another ACK packet output without releasing and reclaiming the use of the output link. This approach is possible with pseudo-asynchronous operation but would not be possible with asynchronous operation. In that case, it would be necessary to include a 'conditional P' operation in the multi-task executive.

The Retransmit Process

The function of the Retransmit Process shown in Figure 13.32 is to scan all the RETRANSMIT QUEUES and whenever a time-expired entry is found resend that packet. The program comprises a main cycle which starts off (1) with a call on DELAY. Therefore the main cycle of the program is executed periodically, the period being determined by the value of TIMESTEP. It must be noted that the pseudo-asynchronous strategy does not allow exact timing. In this instance, the delay of TIMESTEP is increased by the time the retransmit process

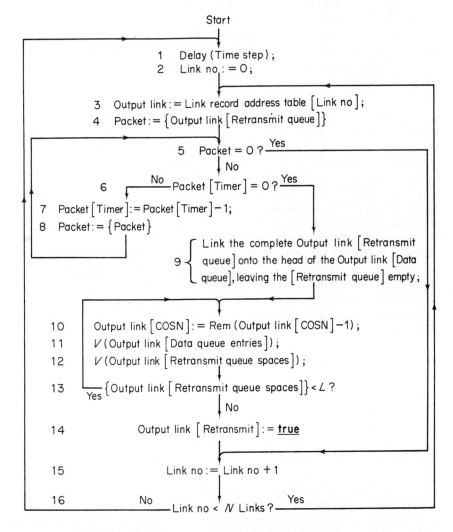

Figure 13.32. Flowchart of the Retransmit Process program

spends in the active state. Our method of node operation does not require accurate time-outs so the fluctuations in the delay period are immaterial.

When the process runs, the outer loop (2, 15, 16) causes it to operate on each of the links in turn, the total number being defined by the parameter NLINKS. The link record address is assumed to be held in the array LINK RECORD ADDRESS TABLE, indexed by the link number (3, 4). For each link, the process steps down the RETRANSMIT QUEUE (8) from the head element, using the pointers which indicate the next queue item. For each item in the queue it reduces the TIMER field of the packet by 1 (7) and checks (6) for a zero result. The scan ends either (5) when the end of the queue has been reached (pointer value 0) or a zero TIMER field is found (6). Because of the link procedure employed, a zero TIMER field will always be found, if at all, in the head item of the queue (this being the *oldest* unacknowledged packet). The longest time that a packet can remain on the RETRANSMIT QUEUE is TIMESTEP × TIME LIMIT where TIME LIMIT is the initial value of the packet TIMER field set by the Output Process (the unit of time is fixed by the hardware timer's period).

If the current RETRANSMIT QUEUE is found to be time-expired the link procedure requires that the entire queue shall be retransmitted. This is done by linking (9) the RETRANSMIT QUEUE onto the head of the DATA QUEUE. The Output Process then carries out the retransmission. The semaphores for the two queues are updated (11, 12) and the current output sequence number stepped back (10) by the loop which ends (13) when there are L retransmit queue spaces. COSN is then equal to the sequence number of the head packet in the expanded output queue.

Synchronization between the several Output Processes and the single Retransmit Process is a problem because of the possibility that the Retransmit Process will run while packet output is taking place on one of the links and the Output Process is waiting for its send interrupt. When the Output Process resumes, it attempts to transfer the output packet from the head of the DATA QUEUE to the end of the RETRANSMIT QUEUE. But if in the meantime a retransmission has been put into operation, the packet which has just been sent will not be at the head of the DATA QUEUE any more. Under these circumstances, we can put matters right by ignoring the fact that the packet has been sent (it will be sent again) and refraining from updating COSN. We must also ensure that the entry in the DATA QUEUE and the space in the RETRANSMIT QUEUE which have been reserved for the program's use by P operations, before the start up of the send unit, are released by performing V operations. These are the operations carried out by the side branch in Figure 13.31, lines (15, 16). The information that a retransmission has been started is contained in the link record flag RETRANSMIT. The value of this flag is set to *false* by the Output Process (4) before packet output and its value is tested (10) when output is completed. The flag is set *true* by the Retransmit Process (14) if it initiates a retransmission and therefore changes the state of the DATA QUEUE.

13.7 SOME SOFTWARE DESIGN CONSIDERATIONS

The structure of the node software is determined to a considerable extent by the nature of the underlying multi-task executive and by the functional specification of the node's operation. Nevertheless there remains some degree of choice, and we shall devote the remainder of this chapter to the consideration of a few alternatives and the criteria that a designer can apply when deciding between them.

The principal design criteria are efficiency and clarity. The designer must adopt a software structure which gives the best overall node performance, in particular, maximizing the throughput of packets. In this respect there is a strong dependence between 'systems design' and 'software design' and the boundary between the two is undefined. It is difficult to predict the effect of the various design decisions on performance in such complex systems; the obvious design may well prove to be inefficient when the system is operational, and such mistakes are costly. Simulation can be a very powerful aid to the designer, allowing the performance of a proposed system and software design to be studied before the detailed implementation.

An Example of Design Changes to Promote Efficiency

The performance of the system described earlier in the chapter is very dependent upon the number of packet retransmissions that take place. Every 'refusal' of a packet by a receiving node delays the progress of the packet through the trunk network. Furthermore, while the packet is being delayed in a node, it is occupying a buffer and increasing the probability that this node will refuse incoming packets. A packet may be refused either because the input hardware is not ready or because it is not the next in sequence. The second of these causes is a consequence of the link control procedure and it could be removed (or at least, reduced in probability) by using a more complex procedure.

As we have already explained, if the input hardware is allowed to ignore packets, the node software has to meet no deadlines. It has no strict crisis times and its operation is greatly simplified. But even with this feature the system and software design should be such that there is a very low probability of the input hardware not being ready to receive a packet.

The interval after the receipt of a packet before the Input Process issues the *ready* command to its receive unit, arises for two reasons. The Input Process may be delayed in the active state by the execution of other processes or it may be delayed in the waiting state because no packet buffer is available. The first source of delay could be reduced by introducing a priority scheduling mechanism into the executive. With such a scheme there would still be contention between the Input Processes for each link since these would have the same priority.

Schemes for process priorities must be considered rather carefully.

Thus, we might equally argue that the Output and Ack Processes should have higher priority than the Input Processes to ensure that a node can get rid of packets as quickly as possible, and make the storage space they occupy available to receive new packets. Taking all these considerations into account, it would seem best to make no priority distinctions between the node's main processes. But a priority scheduling mechanism would probably be useful in a complete, practical system to give these main processes preference over 'ancilliary' or 'support' processes.

The second reason for delay to the Input Process could be reduced by decreasing or eliminating the possibility that there are no available packet buffers. This can be done by imposing a limit, D, on the lengths of the data queues so that the maximum number of packet buffers associated with each link is $D + L + 1$. L is the maximum length of the retransmit queue and the extra buffer is the one assigned for input. If the packet buffer pool starts with $N(D + L + 1)$ entries where N is the number of links serviced by a node, an Input Process will never be held up for lack of buffers. A sufficient pool of short buffers is also maintained for use by ACK packets queued for output.

The data queue limitation implies that an incoming DATA packet, even if it is in the correct sequence, must be refused if there is no space in the data queue it is destined for. So we have exchanged one reason for refusal for another. But it might well prove that the new scheme gives a better overall performance. Simulation could be used to explore this alternative.

Software Clarity

Software should be clear and simple in structure so that it can be implemented and tested quickly. Clarity also eases the task of software maintenance and improvement. The task of proving the correct operation of the node programs is made more tractable, and a reliable system is produced more quickly, if the programmer is relieved of the burden of taking into account detailed timing in the software-hardware interaction. In this respect, we have already emphasized the value of process-organized software with explicit process synchronisation by means of semaphores. It is much easier to guard against subtle design errors when processes operate on shared data if a pseudo-asynchronous approach is employed.

The interaction between processes in the main example of this chapter can be seen to be very simple and the main reason for this is the virtual disappearance of critical sections, achieved by pseudo-asynchronous operation. With a truly *asynchronous* system it would have been necessary to protect all operations on common data that could give rise to inconsistencies. For example, all queue manipulations would have had to be done within critical sections since they involve several operations. In practice, therefore, interrupt response times in pseudo-asynchronous systems will not necessarily be significantly longer than those in asynchronous systems.

The only problem of the critical-section kind in our example involves the operation by the Output and Retransmit Processes on the shared data queue. This queue must remain in a consistent state until the output of a DATA packet is complete. If this section of the Output Process program (lines 5 to 14 of Figure 13.31) had been protected by means of P and V operations, the Retransmit Process would have been blocked whenever it attempted to push the retransmit queue back onto the head of a data queue whose head packet was currently undergoing output. The Retransmit Process would therefore have been delayed until the output had been completed and the Output Process had finally terminated its critical section. This would in turn have delayed the checking of the retransmit queues for other links, since the Retransmit Process is common to them all. The approach adopted in Figures 13.31 and 13.32 avoids the use of a critical section and makes use of the rule that if a packet has to be retransmitted all the following packets that have already been transmitted will have to be retransmitted.

The use of a straightforward critical section in each Output Process would be perfectly acceptable if we had taken the decision to have a Retransmit Process for every link, and this software structure might perhaps be regarded as superior in clarity.

Choice of Processes

One may query some early design decisions in our example. For instance, why use separate Ack and Data queues, and why not have a single Output Process for each link? Is it necessary to have separate processes for each link?

As a first step towards answering these questions, we can determine that it is simpler to have a separate process for each autonomous hardware function in the node. Each send and receive unit is independent in operation and best served by (at least) one independent process. If we had, for example, a single Input Process to serve all the receive units, it would be necessary for this process to wait for the *next* receiver interrupt. We would run into new problems when the Input Process requires a free packet buffer to assign to one of its links. In waiting on the control semaphore, it blocks *all* further link activity. This problem is surmountable by having a new process, which is woken up whenever the Input Process needs a new buffer (and the buffer is not immediately available). This buffer allocation process has the task of waiting for the resource and restarting the *appropriate* link when it becomes available. Such an approach involves greater overheads and is less natural for our typical node application but when a communications control computer has to serve a very large number of links (as may be the case for a local switch with a large number of terminal devices) the alternative approach is better. Excessive storage requirements for pcbs are avoided by allocating processes on a *functional* rather than a per-terminal basis.

Combining the Ack and Output Processes to form a single Output Process for each link is also feasible and produces an alternative design of the software which is worth exploring. First, it allows us to dispense with the OUTPUT LINK semaphore. The new combined Output Process is responsible for output of both DATA and ACK packets and it must not be blocked unless *neither* of these activities is possible. The output of acknowledgements must therefore be allowed to proceed even when the output of DATA packets is not possible, as for example when the retransmit queue is full. Because of this feature it is best to keep the data and ack queues separate.

The interaction between the Input and Output Processes now needs revision because the condition for continuation of the Output Process is a complex one, namely: ack queue length >0 *or* (data queue length >0 *and* retransmit queue length $<L$). The three queue control semaphores DATA QUEUE ENTRIES, ACK QUEUE ENTRIES and RETRANSMIT QUEUE SPACES are replaced by simple count variables held in the link record and a new semaphore OUTPUT POSSIBLE is introduced. This semaphore, as its name implies, will be stepped by a V operation whenever the Input or Retransmit Processes detect that an output operation *might* be possible; for example, whenever receipt of acknowledgements makes space available in the retransmit queue. To detect these possibilities, V ([OUTPUT POSSIBLE]) replaces the V operations found on lines 11, 17 and 25 of Figure 13.29 and the two V operations on lines 11 and 12 of Figure 13.32 are together replaced by V ([OUTPUT POSSIBLE]). In addition, the queue counts have to be amended at these points in the programs.

The new combined Output Process is shown in Figure 13.33. When (1) output is possible, the process must check to see whether it is an acknowledgement output or a DATA packet output (lines 2 or 9 and 10 respectively). Following output of an ACK packet (lines 3 to 8) or a DATA packet (11 to 23), the program returns to check for another possible output. Since ACK output is always attempted first, this activity is given higher priority. Note that DATA output is protected by P and V operations on the new semaphore RETRANSMIT, which replaces the old flag of the same name. We are assuming that there is a Retransmit Process for each link. Line 9 of Figure 13.32 is preceded by a P operation on RETRANSMIT and line 14 is replaced by the converse V operation.

This alternative strategy is perhaps less clear than the one we described at first. It is also slightly less efficient because the Output Process will on occasion be activated unnecessarily. Consider for example the arrival of a new DATA packet when the retransmit queue is full. This will cause OUTPUT POSSIBLE to be stepped by the Input Process and will activate the Output Process, but the latter will find that it cannot continue and will return to the P ([OUTPUT POSSIBLE]) operation. The deletion of entries in the retransmit queue will cause a similar, redundant operation if the data queue is empty. The defects could be eliminated by more extensive checking within the Input Process program.

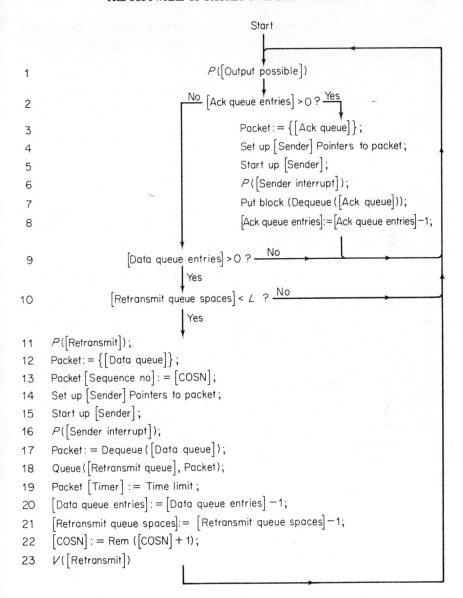

Figure 13.33.   Flowchart of the alternative Output Process program

Design Methods

The worked example which has formed the main part of the chapter is intended as a concrete example of design method. The most important feature of the software design has been the use of processes which have a certain degree of conceptual independence, for it enables the design of the software to take place in two stages, the first concentrating on individual processes and the second on their interaction.

Division of the node's operation into component processes is necessarily an early design decision but it may be questioned at a later stage. It is probably best to design the process programs at first in outline only, in the kind of detail shown in the figures of this chapter, then to consider carefully their interaction and the design alternatives before proceeding to detailed programming. Such an approach lengthens the design phase but greatly shortens the program writing. Properly carried out it can almost eliminate those timing or interaction bugs which are difficult and costly to find.

The pseudo-asynchronous approach, and the concentration of the process-to-process and process-to-hardware interactions into a well defined mechanism like the semaphore are important aids to clear and simple software. Since the interrupt mechanism is replaced by a different mechanism for the programmer it is possible that radical change in the hardware could take place without too much disturbance and that a better mechanism than the interrupt could be devised.

Although formal design methods are being explored[14] the current practice still uses heuristic or intuitive methods for finding and controlling process interaction. As our example showed, the majority of interactions need no more than a simple semaphore to control them. But it also showed that some interactions need individual attention to find all the critical sections and avoid deadly embraces. Simple precautions, such as listing all uses by processes of common data, will throw up most cases, but there seems, nevertheless, to be no substitute for an intuitive understanding of the process mechanisms. The interaction between system design and software design implies that the solution of interaction problems that have become intractable is possibly to be found somewhere else in the overall system.

It is not sufficient to produce a structure of 'executive' and 'process programs' which is logically impeccable; there must also be a reasonable operating efficiency. But it is extremely difficult to determine, except by actually running the program, what the efficiency will be. Simulations have removed detail (in order to be worth doing in advance of the actual program they must be greatly simplified) and this prevents them giving accurate timings. Nevertheless, it is possible to compare design alternatives and get rough ideas of program efficiency.

When all the formal tools and methods have been exploited, the design of software for data communication systems remains an intuitive process, and the design decisions which interact with the software—in the hardware and the overall system—can seldom be revised at a late stage of design. It is, therefore, extremely important that system and hardware designs should anticipate software problems, for example in the reduction or removal of crisis time situations. Software design, although it often comes late in the design process, is vital because it puts into exact terms the formats and rules of protocol which the system designers have produced. It also determines some of the basic performance parameters. All this argues for the consideration of software organization as early as possible and the adoption of system designs which, like packet switching, are describable in terms which are easily translated into software.

References

1. Wirth, N., 'PL 360—A programming language for the 360 computers', *J. ACM*, **15**, No. 1, 37 (Jan. 1968).
2. Bell, D. A., and Wichmann, B. A. 'An ALGOL-like assembly language for a small computer', *Software Practice and Experience*, **1**, 61-72 (1970).
3. *Official definition of CORAL* 66, London, H.M.S.O. (May 1970).
4. Richards, M., 'BCPL: A tool for compiler writing and system programming', *AFIPS Conference Proceedings Spring Joint Computer Conference*, **34**, 557 (1969).
5. Dijkstra, E. W., 'Co-operating Sequential Processes', *Programming Languages* (Ed. Genuys, F.), Academic Press (1968).
6. Lampson, B. W., 'A scheduling philosophy for multiprocessing systems', *Comm. ACM*, **11**, No. 5, 347 (May 1968).
7. Dennis, J. B., and Van Horn, E. C., 'Programming semantics for multiprogrammed computations', *Comm. ACM*, **9**, No. 3, 143 (March 1966).
8. Gosden, J. A., 'Explicit parallel processing description and control in programs for multi- and uni-processor computers', *AFIPS Conference Proceedings Fall Joint Computer Conference*, **29**, 651, (1966).
9. Habermann, A. N., 'Synchronisation of communicating processes', *Comm. ACM*, **15**, No. 3, 171 (March 1972).
10. Coffman, E. G., Elphick, M. J. and Shoshani, A., 'System deadlocks', *Computing Surveys*, **3**, No. 2, 68 (June 1971).
11. Mills, D. L., 'Multiprogramming in a small systems environment', *Second International Seminar on Advanced Programming Systems*, Jerusalem, 227 (1969).
12. Wirth, N., 'On multiprogramming, machine coding and computer organisation', *Comm. ACM*, **12**, No. 9, 489 (September 1969).
13. Dijkstra, E. W., 'The structure of the "THE"—multi programming system', *Comm. ACM*, **11**, No. 5, 341 (May 1968).
14. Gilbert, P., and Chandler, W. J., 'Interference between communicating parallel processes', *Comm. ACM*, **15**, No. 6, 427 (June 1972).

Chapter 14

Review of the Design Principles of Data Networks

14.1 INTRODUCTION

Each chapter of this book has described some part of a data communication network and the whole adds up to a system of considerable complexity. But certain principles of design have reappeared several times. In this final chapter these principles are reviewed.

The primitive idea of a telephone connection was extremely simple; it consisted of two telephone sets joined by a pair of wires. The introduction of switching in the telephone network began with a manual switchboard handling only local lines and was also extremely simple. In the same way, the primitive idea of data communication was extremely simple; it consisted of a pair of modems and a telephone network.

The telephone network is now a very complex system which is still developing. Indeed its future development is supported by some of the best research in the world. The complexity comes partly from the increasing size of the system, which grew from local networks of thousands to national networks of millions of telephones. Without big changes of technology the cost per subscriber would have increased enormously. The system also provides new services, of course, which accounts for some of the added complexity.

In the similar fashion, a data network (like some of our private networks) which serves a thousand or so terminals, all of one kind, joined by a star-network, remains basically very simple. Some of the extra complexity will be needed to bring it economically to the size of public network expected in the 1980s, with tens of millions of subscribers. The addition of new services, such as higher speeds will add extra complexity.

When it is remembered that data communication networks will have to evolve much further than the systems described in this book, their ultimate complexity seems likely to exceed that of the already highly developed telephone system. For example, we have written little in this book about the replication and redundancy needed to maintain reliable service, and the subjects of network maintenance, monitoring and call accounting have had scant attention. In addition, the extension of network-wide protocols to cover more aspects of the users' activities (files, jobs etc.) will complicate them further.

Let us recall the various levels at which data network design has been described. They group into two sections, the lower levels describing hardware functions and the higher ones software functions.

The lowest level regards the design of data transmission as the choice of waveform, regeneration, equalisation, discrimination etc. to get the best out of the transmission medium. This was the principal subject of Chapters 2 and 5.

The second level concerns the coding of bits on the channel to provide bit transparency which is only a small step from the lowest level.

The third level employs a unit of data, such as a byte contained in an envelope, as the transmission unit—a technique introduced in Chapter 7 for efficient multiplexing and developed further in Chapter 9 for switching.

The fourth level takes us out of the hardware-operated network functions and is the introduction of formats and procedures *inside* the network.

The fifth level brings us to user-protocols—all those protocols which involve more that the network itself. Chapter 11 described some of these protocols.

So there are many different levels at which a network can be described. If, for example, we are engaged in describing a computer-computer protocol for exchange of files we want to use facilities provided by lower protocols at all the other lower levels down to the pair of wires, but without the need to understand any of their details.

This kind of organization we have sometimes described as 'hierarchical'. The concept has arisen in more than one context, and to show the usefulness of the concept (and the differences between hierarchies) two of the uses of this concept will be reviewed.

14.2   THE NETWORK CONNECTION HIERARCHY

Any kind of mesh network, whether for data or telephones, can be conceived as an homogenous network covering, let us say, one country. But, beyond a certain size a homogenous, one-level system is usually replaced by something more complex.

For example a mesh of considerable density (in which all the connections lie between neighbouring nodes) has the effect that long distance calls employ a large number of nodes. In the telephone network this would lead to a slow call set-up and (in an analogue network) degraded speech quality. To avoid this, we use long-distance links, but to do this in a disorganized way would not minimize the number of links used in a call.

Therefore the network is constructed in the form of a long-distance network 'laid over' the more closely spaced mesh. This begins to form a 'network connection hierarchy'. As we described it in Chapter 2 there can be several levels in the telephone network, starting at the bottom with the local network. At the top level is the transit network and possibly a fully-connected subset which is the highest level of all.

It is a characteristic of this connection hierarchy that the part of the network nearest the user, the local network, is the *lowest* level of the network. It is for this reason that the trunk network in data systems (possibly following the example of the SITA network) is sometimes called the 'high level network'.

The hierarchical form of a network's connection pattern is essential for economy, and it will need to be imposed on data networks when they exceed a certain size. When the ARPA network was at the 20-node level, studies were already under way to find the limits of the 'homogenous' mesh, and ideas were being formed for a 'super-node'. Not only do the performance requirements impose this kind of structure but economy demands it. It is only by concentrating long distance traffic onto a few routes that the economies of multiplexing onto high-rate lines can be obtained.

To summarize, the network connection hierarchy has its 'low' levels near the user's terminal and basically it is a network-centred concept aimed at improving the communication network's performance and economy.

14.3   THE NETWORK PROTOCOL HIERARCHY

The protocol structure of packet switching networks was described at length in Chapter 11. It is apparently at this point that much of the conceptual difficulty arises in modern data networks. One of the figures of that chapter is redrawn in Figure 14.1 to show the 'higher-lower' relationships of these protocols.

The lowest levels are those concerned with transmission of packets over the physical link between adjacent switching nodes. The next level is that of communication between the distant nodes of the network that are concerned with a particular call. Clearly, this protocol must invoke the 'link protocol' but it does so through the medium of the various activities in the nodes themselves which provide a packet-carrying facility.

The next higher level is the one called in the ARPA network project the HOST-to-HOST protocol. It is on the HOST-to-HOST protocol that all the higher levels are built.

The higher levels of this hierarchy are the ones presented to the users. This is because the protocols are basically user-centred and not network-centred. This is no criticism of network connection hierarchy—it simply serves a different purpose. This apparent inversion of the high-low relationship could be confusing, except that there is really little connection between the two hierarchies, which concern different aspects of network design.

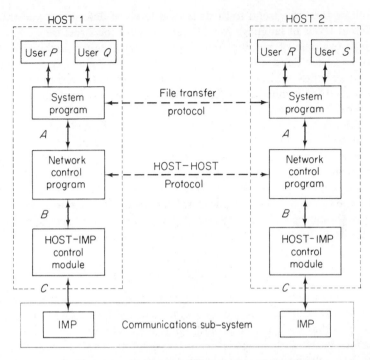

Figure 14.1.   Examples of protocols and interfaces

We must question the need for such complexity, and ask the reason for this hierarchy of protocols.

Thinking back to the telephone network, we find a similar situation in the protocols employed there, but on a simpler scale. For example the setting up of a call in a modern signalling system requires exchanges of many short messages between one switching centre and several others, and these exchanges are governed by strict protocol. The simplicity was necessary because these protocols were designed before stored program control was widely used. The designers were forced to use simple and economical means, and to avoid any duplication of functions at different levels. The same discipline might have produced simpler data networks but stored-program control imposes few constraints.

The hierarchy itself is needed for two reasons: ease of design and ease of modification. It would be possible, in principle, to devise one set of rules defining all the actions that could take place in a network. It would be extremely difficult to make it work, because of the errors caused by having no understandable overall concepts, and it could never be modified because the effects of a modification would ramify in an unknown manner.

The situation parallels the early development of computer programming, and follows the same trend towards several levels of description and the use of different levels of language for different parts of the structure.

As an example of modification, suppose that a better method of error control had been devised for the physical node-node connection. This could be introduced into one link at a time without disturbing the rest of the system, if it provided (as it must) the right facilities for the next level above. At the same time, higher levels of protocol could be developed experimentally without damaging the substructure. In fact, because the higher levels are still being defined it is almost certain that changes are taking place at these levels. It is also most important that the structure that exists should allow experimental protocols to be built up and tested.

The concept of a 'protocol' has been widely used and yet is really defined only by the examples we have given. It is characteristic of rather basic ideas that they should be difficult to explain, particularly those that are related to language itself. Protocol is such an idea, and so is the concept of an interface.

14.4   THE INTERFACE CONCEPT

The concept of an interface was introduced to enable modular hardware to be specified accurately. A complex system would be divided into separate modules, so that design teams could work in parallel on the modules. This need arose particularly when different contractors where working on one system. Exact definition of the function of each module was very necessary in this situation.

The residual design problems in these modular systems were found, of course, to lie in the exact interplay between connected modules, that is, in their interfaces. It was found that a well-defined interface was necessary for successful design, and that the details of the interface were often difficult to define exactly. The interface was often evolved as the detailed design continued. Early highway interfaces for computer input/output showed all the signs of untidy evolution, particularly in the way that actions across the interface could be carried out in more than one fashion. An example of an accurate (and successful) interface definition is given in the Appendix, p. 531.

An interface is physically a boundary across which signals are exchanged. Because the purpose is to assist the design process, the essence of the interface is the exact definition of what signals can be passed across the boundary and what their significance is. This is exactly like the definition of a language, which has two parts: syntax and semantics.

The syntax of an interface definition defines what signals across the boundary are valid, and by inference most of the possible sequences of signals are declared to be invalid. For example, in the BS 4421 interface the sequence of control signal changes is defined.

The semantics must refer to concepts beyond the interface itself—such things as the '0' and '1' states and the 'most significant bit' are semantic concepts which concern the modules that employ the interface. It is also important that the interface should retain a good deal of transparency. For example any sequence of bytes can be transferred—or any stream of bits. Thus the interface definition is also characterized by what it does *not* say about the signals. It is the transparency of the interface which allows higher-level processes to use it. The analogy in a language is the ability to define new words and, indeed, new procedures.

Interfaces were originally defined between two modules only, and these are still the most satisfactory interfaces because exact definition is more easily obtained. If the 'syntax' rules are broken by the modules there must be some means of recovery. No interface definition can cope with all the possible sequences of syntax errors, but some recovery from simple errors is possible. If more than one module contributes to an interface the complexity is greatly increased, and so are the possibilities for one of the units not obeying the rules. It is, indeed, doubtful whether highway interface definitions are ever fully understood, even by their designers.

In a network there are many modules of hardware and software, all capable of interaction, but the interfaces need be defined only between pairs of modules.

Essentially, therefore, a protocol and an interface are the same thing when they are defined between two modules that directly exchange messages. The similarity between the BS 4421 interface and a message exchange protocol was pointed out in Chapter 6.

Figure 14.1 shows direct interfaces labelled A, B and C between modules of program in a 'HOST' computer and it also shows that these modules carry out a 'protocol' at their own level with modules in other HOSTS. These protocols are like interfaces, but are conceptual, in that no messages are exchanged directly. The messages pass across the actual interfaces at A, B and C. So Figure 14.1 shows the distinction we propose to make between a protocol and an interface.

14.5   HIGHER LEVEL PROTOCOLS

Higher level protocols are built up from the facilities provided by the HOST-to-HOST protocol. Users could communicate (i.e. processes could communicate) without them, but only by bilateral agreements in each case.

It is clearly better to make conventions to govern all the kinds of inter-action which are network-wide. This avoids the need to develop new protocols where they already exist and it allows new users to communicate with all existing users by means of one set of system programs. But agreement on these higher level protocols may be difficult to obtain.

Network-wide functions must relate to common features of operating systems, such as their file structures. The file transfer protocol, for example, must declare in the 'heading' of any file enough about its structure to ensure that it can be consulted remotely with some efficiency and with no danger of damaging it by accident.

Another function at the same level is the transfer of jobs from one computer to another. At present this is difficult to achieve because of the wide variations in operating systems, but it must be made possible (by means of new standards) if the load-sharing properties of networks are to be achieved other than on a parochial scale.

For terminal users, not only is there a need for a 'virtual terminal' to which their terminals can be matched, they also need standard methods to begin an interaction by identifying themselves to the distant computer. After the 'logging on', the operation of the terminal can, to a large extent, be taught by the computer itself.

Therefore, the use of higher level protocols which characterize modern data networks is designed to meet the need for data sharing, computer power sharing, terminal sharing and so forth, which is the declared purpose of computer networks. This is the reason why the apparent complexities of protocols were not found in the earlier use of the telephone network to carry data for private networks with limited functions. The protocols are part of the computer network, not the communication subsystem. Worldwide agreement on these protocols will be needed to obtain the full benefit of computer interaction.

Appendix

British Standard Specification Number 4421

A.1 INTRODUCTION

The standard was published in April 1969 and is entitled 'A digital input-output interface for use in data collection systems'. It comprises three main parts: a functional specification which describes the interface lines and the meaning of the signals they carry; an electrical specification, which details the nature of the signals used to exchange information across the interface; and a physical specification covering the connectors and cables to be employed. The interface is illustrated by Figure A.1.

A.2 THE FUNCTIONAL SPECIFICATION

The functional specification is based on principles which apply generally to a wide range of applications. No particular types of equipment were considered in formulating the specification which is intended to give a device independent method transferring information between a source of data and an acceptor of data. No restrictions are placed on the content of the data which passes from source to acceptor, and a minimum number of control signals is provided to govern the transfer of data and to signal the status of one device to the other.

With this approach to defining an interface it is essential to agree upon procedures for the exchange of information between particular devices. Such information exchange procedures do not form part of the Interface Specification, which is concerned merely with the passage of signals across the boundary between the devices. The same approach was adopted in the V24 Recommendations made by the CCITT for interface connections between modems and customers data terminal equipment, where the interface covers the serial transmission of information on a pair of wires, and has no regard for the content of the transmitted information.

The British Standard Interface is intended for the parallel transmission of information, and is also transparent to the data passing across it. Only one acceptor interface may be connected to a source interface (highway operation

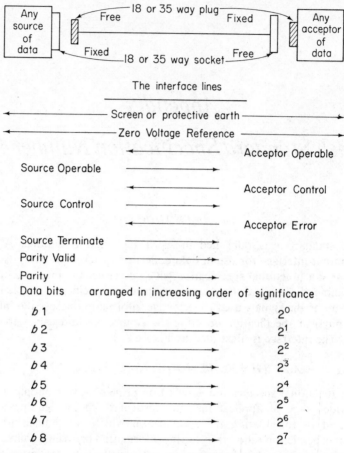

Figure A.1.   British Standard Interface No. 4421

is not envisaged) and for bidirectional data flow two interfaces are required, one in each direction.

The specification defines eighteen lines which are listed in Figure A.2. The first two lines are passive, the remainder carry binary signals. Eight of these represent data, one optionally may carry parity, and the rest may be regarded as control signals. These effect the transfer of data in the form of characters of up to eight parallel binary digits or as blocks of such characters.

The data signals and some of the control signals originate in the source and are defined at the source socket. The remaining signals originate in the acceptor and are defined at the acceptor plug.

The logic states zero and one are represented by the steady state values of the signals defined in the electrical specification. The precise meaning attached to these logic states for the signals of each interface circuit is given below.

CIRCUIT NUMBER	CIRCUIT DESIGNATION	ABBREVIATION	DIRECTION	PIN CONNECTIONS			CLASS OF CIRCUIT
				CATEGORY 1 (UNBALANCED) 18-way Connector	CATEGORY 2 (BALANCED) 34-way Connector		
					wire 'a'	wire 'b'	
1	Screen	S	Passive link	A	A	–	EARTHS
2	Zero Voltage Reference	Z	Passive link	B	–	B	
3	Acceptor Operable	AO	Acceptor to Source	C	C	D	
4	Source Operable	SO	Source to Acceptor	D	E	F	CONTROL CIRCUITS
5	Acceptor Control	AC	Acceptor to Source	E	H	J	
6	Source Control	SC	Source to Acceptor	F	K	L	
7	Acceptor Error	AE	Acceptor to Source	H	M	N	
8	Source Terminate	ST	Source to Acceptor	J	P	R	
9	Parity Valid	PV	Source to Acceptor	K	S	T	
10	Parity Bit	P	Source to Acceptor	L	U	V	SIGNAL CIRCUITS
11	Data Bit $b1$	2^0	Source to Acceptor	M	W	X	
12	Data Bit $b2$	2^1	Source to Acceptor	N	Y	Z	
13	Data Bit $b3$	2^2	Source to Acceptor	P	AA	BB	
14	Data Bit $b4$	2^3	Source to Acceptor	R	CC	DD	
15	Data Bit $b5$	2^4	Source to Acceptor	S	EE	FF	
16	Data Bit $b6$	2^5	Source to Acceptor	T	HH	JJ	
17	Data Bit $b7$	2^6	Source to Acceptor	U	KK	LL	
18	Data Bit $b8$	2^7	Source to Acceptor	V	MM	NN	

Figure A.2.　Interface lines

Screen or Protective Earth (S)

This line is intended to maintain the continuity of protective earths throughout a series of interconnected devices; it must normally be electrically connected to the chassis or frame of each device.

However, there may be situations where equipment must conform with special safety regulations requiring the chassis or frame to be joined to a local earth such as a mains earth. If this is the case, an earth loop with undesirably high circulating currents may be formed. Exceptionally therefore, the specification allows a resistor, of not more than one hundred ohms, to be used for connecting the Protective Earth line to the chassis or frame of a device in place of a direct connection.

Zero Voltage Reference (Z)

As its name implies, this establishes the common reference potential for all other lines except line 1 (Screen or Protective Earth). It will connect together the zero voltage points of the power supplies in the two devices joined by the interface. In each device there must be provision for a wire strap to be fitted between this line and Protective Earth. This enables the earthing arrangements to be chosen to suit particular circumstances. A common requirement will be the use of a single connection between the two passive lines. For this reason the wire strap should normally be omitted.

Acceptor Operable (AO) and Source Operable (SO)

The most important information required from a device is whether it is able to operate correctly. The Operable signal provides this information; it is logic one while the device is operable, and logic zero when it is not.

Strictly, no cognizance should be taken on any other active interface signals while the Operable signal is at logic zero; the correct interpretation is that outside attention is required. But it is sometimes convenient to make simple devices assume a standby state when the incoming Operable signal becomes logic zero. This is an example of a procedural matter to be agreed between users of the Interface.

It is, however, vital to ensure that the logic state of an out-going Operable signal does not depend on that of the incoming Operable signal. For example, if a tape punch acceptor and tape reader source were both designed to start their motors upon receipt of an incoming Operable signal, and were additionally made to signal an inoperable state when their motors were stationary, they would not operate when joined together.

Acceptor Control (AC) and Source Control (SC)

The two control lines carry signals which cooperate in a 'handshake' fashion to effect the transfer of information from the source to the acceptor.

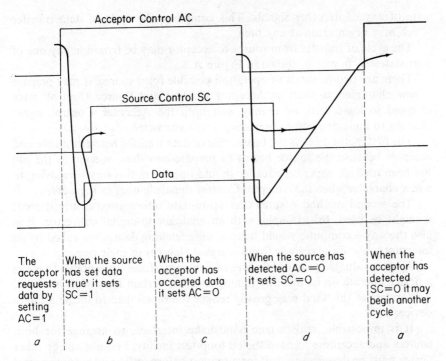

The acceptor requests data by setting AC=1	When the source has set data 'true' it sets SC=1	When the acceptor has accepted data it sets AC=0	When the source has detected AC=0 it sets SC=0	When the acceptor has detected SC=0 it may begin another cycle
a	b	c	d	a

Figure A.3. The handshake method of controlling data transfer

The transfer of each character requires the occurrence of a cycle of signal states; a change in one signal must be followed by a change in the other as shown in Figure A.3. This method of controlling transfers places no timing restriction on the two devices, and the rate of transfer depends solely on the characteristics of the two devices and on the intervening cable delays.

The cycle of signals on the control lines begins with both control signals at logic zero. When the acceptor is ready for data it sets Acceptor Control to logic one. When the source has detected the logic one state of the Acceptor Control signal and has set its data and other output signals appropriately it sets the Source Control signal to logic one. (Once the Source Control signal has been set, the state of all the signals from the source must remain unchanged until it detects that the Acceptor Control signal has changed to logic zero. This will occur only after the acceptor has made use of the source signals.)

The acceptor may make use of the information presented by the source as soon as the Source Control signal logic one condition has been detected; immediately it has done so it indicates that the information may change by setting the Acceptor control signal to logic zero.

When the source has detected the logic zero state of the Acceptor Control signal, it may set the Source Control signal to logic zero and may change the state of any of its other signals. This completes the cycle of data transfer which may begin again at any time.

The cycle of transfer from source to acceptor may be frozen in any one of four states: a, b, c or d, shown in Figure A.3.

There are two methods of operation possible for a source: it may prepare a new character as soon as Acceptor Control and Source Control have changed to logic zero, or it may wait until the Acceptor Control signal changes to logic one before preparing a new character.

The first method offers the fastest rate of data transfer between source and acceptor because the source begins to prepare new data as soon as the old has been used. A paper tape reader should operate in this way by moving to a new character when the Acceptor Control signal changes to logic zero.

The second method ensures that up-to-date information is transferred; it might be used, for example, with an analogue-to-digital convertor. It is also the way a computer would behave: only fetching data when called by an interrupt when the Acceptor Control signal changes to logic one.

A most valuable practical feature of some interfaces is the ability to make a device operate on its own, by joining together certain lines of its interface. A loop test of this kind may greatly reduce the time taken to locate a faulty device.

It is impossible, with a true handshake interface, to arrange for both sources and acceptors to have such a loop test facility, because one or other device must be designed to wait for a request before setting its output control signal to logic one.

In the British Standard Interface, it is a source that waits for a logic one input before presenting a logic one output; it, therefore, cannot be made to

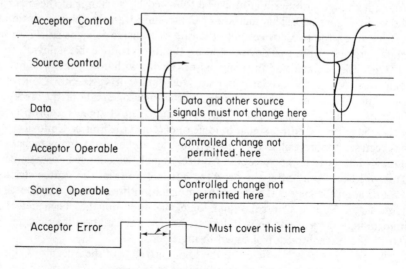

Figure A.4. Character transfer

self-operate by connecting together its input and output control circuits. However, if the Source Control signal from a source is inverted and is applied to its Acceptor Control input circuit, self-operation of the source will occur.

An acceptor sets its Acceptor Control signal to logic one when it is ready for data, and is stimulated by a change to logic one of the Source Control input signal. A loop between the input and output control circuits will, therefore, cause self-operation of an accepter.

For both source and acceptor it is also necessary to join together the two operable lines during a control loop test. In each case, the outgoing Operable signal simulates the incoming Operable signal normally provided by the other device.

The loop test facility emphasizes a point which is not specifically made by the specification, i.e. that a source or acceptor must be ready to receive replies to its signals, however quickly they come back. The specification deliberately avoids setting any upper limits on operating speed; therefore any device must be designed to work with another device which responds immediately.

Acceptor Error (AE)

Some acceptors may be capable of testing the validity of data presented to them. This might be done by checking character parity or block parity, by inspecting a sum check, or perhaps, by estimating the likely value from past experience. Whatever the method, a means of informing the Source is required, and is provided by the Acceptor Error signal.

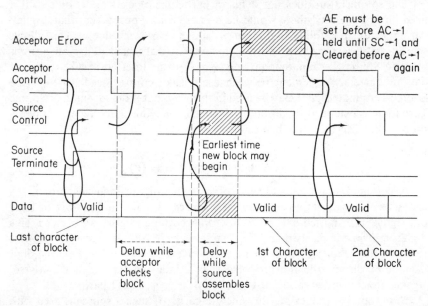

Figure A.5. Block transfer

The precise behaviour of sources and acceptors using Acceptor Error is a procedural matter not defined in the specification which merely states that, when an error is to be indicated, the Acceptor Error signal must be set to logic one before the Acceptor Control signal is set to logic one and must remain at logic one at least until the Source Control signal change to logic one is detected (see Figures A.4 and A.5).

Source Terminate (ST)

This signal provides the facility for transferring blocks of characters which may be pure binary, i.e. there are no code combinations which may be used for indicating control or status information. The specification states that the Source Terminate signal must be set to logic one to signal the presence of the last character of a block. It is set at the same time as the last character, and is maintained until the Acceptor Control signal change to logic zero is detected. Effectively, therefore, it behaves as an extra data digit. The process of block transfer is illustrated in Figure A.5. The last character of the block is accompanied by a Source Terminate logic one signal. It is accepted as another character by the acceptor and the Acceptor Control signal is set to logic zero. The acceptor now carries out the appropriate block acceptance procedure prior to setting the Acceptor Control signal to logic one. Depending on whether an error has also been signalled, the source repeats the previous block or presents a new one.

The specification does not define a particular block length; indeed, if a fixed block were used there would be no need for a Source Terminate signal. An important possibility is the use of 'single character' blocks. This allows special status, control or address characters, (distinguished by an accompanying Source Terminate logic one signal), to be inserted in a sequence of data characters. Agreement between users is, of course, needed before the Source Terminate signal may be used in this way, but if the meaning of Source Terminate is extended by decoding the accompanying character the applications of the interface may be usefully widened.

Parity Valid (PV) and Parity (P)

A common practice is the use of an extra digit which accompanies a character, its logic state is chosen by a source to make the number of logic one signals transmitted either odd or even according to prior agreement. This digit is known as a parity digit (See Chapter 6, page 206); it allows an acceptor to check the validity of each character received. Provision for a parity digit is made by the specification; it behaves as a data signal as far as the control signals are concerned, and must be chosen to given ODD parity.

Many simple sources do not generate parity. If such a source is used with an acceptor which is able to check parity it is necessary to disable the parity checking circuits. To allow this to be done automatically so that characters with, and without, parity may be intermixed, a Parity Valid signal accompanies a character and behaves like an extra data signal as far as the control signals are concerned. It is set to logic one if the parity signal is in use, and to logic zero if it is not.

Data (D)

The information to be transferred by the source to the acceptor is carried by the signals on lines 11 to 18. The least significant digit is assigned to line 11, and the other lines carry the remaining digits in ascending order of significance.

The specification permits up to eight digits to be used, stating that unused digit signals above the most significant must be set to logic zero. It further suggests the preferred code used should be the ISO 7-bit Code (see Chapter 6, page 224) transmitted on circuits 11 to 17 with the least significant digit assigned to circuit 11. The transfer of each set of data signals is achieved by the interaction of the Acceptor and Source Control signals, as described above.

A.3 THE ELECTRICAL SPECIFICATION

It is unfortunate that no obviously 'correct' solution exists to the problem of specifying an electrical specification. It is desirable to combine a high speed of data transfer with a high tolerance to ambient noise; but a specification satisfying these criteria is likely to lead to expensive circuits. Clearly, no one specification could satisfy efficiently all requirements, and any 'best' compromise solution will alter with changes in technology.

Fortunately, if there is common agreement on a functional specification it is relatively easy to convert from one electrical specification to another.

Indeed, in different organizations the British Standard 4421 Functional Specification has been implemented using TTL (transistor-transistor logic) signals within systems; using twisted pair cables—with balanced transmitters and receivers—for coupling high speed systems, and using opto-electronic convertors where common-mode noise is excessive. In all these cases the use of the Functional Specification has brought a common understanding to the discussion and analysis of problems and has allowed the exchange of ideas and equipment between organizations with very little difficulty.

Nevertheless, it is necessary to chose a compromise Electrical Specification which will serve as a 'reference' standard to join different systems; so that each system can be converted to the reference standard at the point of interconnection. The 'reference' Electrical Specification adopted was based on the following criteria:

1. Compatability with existing standards.
2. Effect of different cable delays on relative timing of parallel signals (skew).
3. Effect of system noise, i.e. cross-talk in cables.

4. Effect of external noise, i.e. signals induced in cables by external electrical interference.

The only internationally accepted interfaces are described in the CCITT recommendation V24 for data transmission equipment. This recommendation advises the use of a positive voltage to represent one logic state and a negative voltage to represent the other. These voltages are generated and detected with respect to a zero voltage reference wire joining two devices. The advantage of

OUTPUT CHARACTERISTICS

Open circuit voltage must not exceed +12·5 v

Output impedance must lie between 100 Ω and 1kΩ

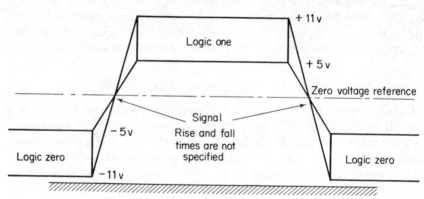

Open circuit voltage must not exceed −12·5 v

INPUT CHARACTERISTICS

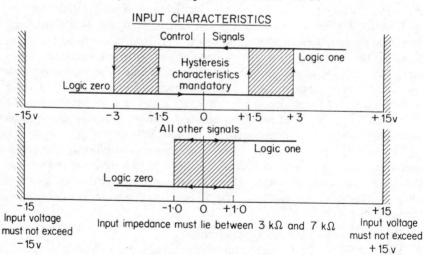

Figure A.6. Electrical parameters

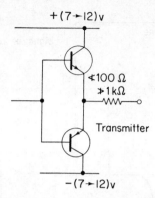

Figute A.7. The transmitter

this arrangement over the use of, say, a positive voltage for one state and zero voltage for the other are:

1. The reference voltage is zero rather than must being midway between the two logic-level voltages, i.e. it does not have to be generated locally.
2. A power failure is distinguishable from both signal states.

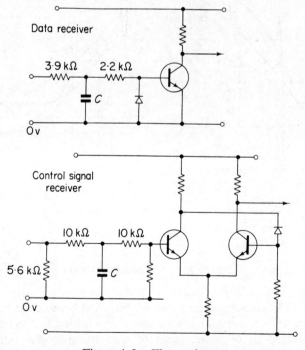

Figure A.8. The receivers

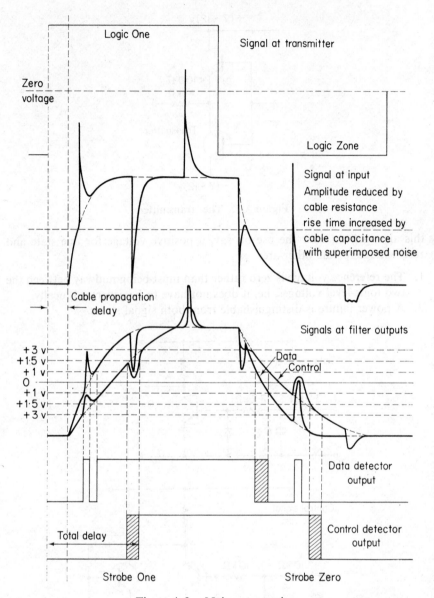

Figure A.9.   Noise suppression

The CCITT scheme was therefore adopted, but because the interface has several parallel digit lines, a more stringent specification had to be devised to meet considerations of noise, speed of data transfer, and extra distance between devices.

The remaining criteria were satisfied by specifying:

1. The use of detectors with hysteresis input characteristics for control signals.
2. The use of more sensitive detectors for all other signals.
3. The use of noise rejection circuitry in the input of all detectors.

The important parameters fixed by the specification are summarized in Figure A.6, with illustrative circuits for a transmitter in Figure A.7 and for receivers in Figure A.8. The circuits demonstrate the subsidiary requirements of the specification for symmetry of output impedance and voltage in the two logic states, and provide noise rejection by the use of smoothing circuits with exponential time constants. The time constant of the data signal filters is roughly half that of the control signal filters. Note that the control signal detector uses a Schmitt trigger circuit to provide the required hysteresis characteristics. The circuits shown are to aid this explanation, they are not part of the Standard and should not be used without consulting the full Specification published by the British Standards Institution.

Figure A.9 shows how noise and skew are overcome by the above illustrative circuits. The top waveform is the output from a transmitter. It rests at a positive potential in the logic one state, and at a negative potential in the logic zero state; there is no upper or lower limit set on the time of transition between the two logic states. The next waveform is that appearing at an input to a receiver. Compared with the top waveform the amplitude is reduced due to cable resistance and the rise time is increased due to cable capacitance. Noise pulses are shown superimposed on this waveform; their origin might be cross-talk or external interference or a mixture of both.

The third diagram shows two waveforms drawn together for comparison. One is the signal appearing at the output from a control-signal filter, the other is the output from a data-signal filter. The shorter time constant of the latter allows a faster output voltage rise and causes less attenuation of the noise pulses. Also drawn on the diagram are the threshold levels specified for the detector.

The last two waveforms are the output signals from the data and control signal detectors. The transitions in these waveforms are shown to correspond with the times at which the filter output signals cross the detector threshold levels. The shaded areas indicate the timing variations covered by the tolerance allowed on threshold levels.

Note that by using the control-signal detector output waveform transitions to strobe or inspect the data-signal detector output waveform, a correct noise-free signal is obtained. However bad the noise interference may be, the filter time constants can be increased until a reliable data transfer is obtained. This is, of course, at the expense of operating speed.

Another important factor covered by the specification is the variation of the interface signals caused by the resistance of the connecting cable. For a cable composed of single wires, the voltage drop along the Zero Voltage

Reference circuit shall not exceed 2 volts. This limit has been set for the Zero Voltage Reference because all the signal return currents flow in it, and in the worst case this current may be the sum of the currents in all sixteen active circuits.

The Electrical Specification described above offers a method of transferring characters from a source to an acceptor in the presence of electrical interference induced in the coupling cable. Any degree of interference may be tolerated, but at the expense of speed of transfer.

Alternative Electrical Specification

Since British Standard No. 4421 was published an alternative electrical specification has been prepared based on the use of balanced-pair cables. This allows much higher data transfer rates to be achieved and is particularly suited to connections between computers that are adjacent to each other.

A.4   THE PHYSICAL SPECIFICATION

This specification requires each source of data to be fitted with a fixed socket, and each acceptor of data with a fixed plug. The fixed connectors are joined by a cable with a free plug at one end and a free socket at the other (see Figure A.1). This scheme was adopted because:

1. The two devices may readily be joined by any type of cable. For example, light multi-core unscreened cable for short distances or heavy, individually screened, cores for maximum noise tolerance.
2. It is impossible, by mistake, to join two sources or two acceptors to each other.
3. It is easy to join cables together to form long cables because a free plug will mate with a free socket.

The type of connector chosen has several optional features. Some, the use of soldered or crimped connections, may be chosen by the user, but others affecting how connectors mate are arbitrarily defined in the specification.

A.5   INITIAL CONDITIONS

British Standard No. 4421 contains rules governing the behaviour of sources and acceptors when they are switched on, or become operable after being inoperable. These rules are intended to ensure that, no matter whether a device is isolated or connected to another device (which may be on or off) no loss or replication of data will occur if the device is switched on, or becomes operable in a controlled manner.

A.6 DEVICE MARKING

The Specification requires each device fitted with the Interface to indicate what data codes are used, and to state certain operating times. The indication of data codes used is clearly of value to the user, while the operate times should enable an estimate to be made of the probable performance of a collection of devices.

Figure A.10 illustrates the relationship of the various operating times which are described below, with some discussion of how they are affected by the design of devices.

There is no limit on the operating times of devices, the specification merely requires them to be stated. This is important to the user because, depending on whether devices incorporate buffer stores, the times may vary in ways that may affect the usefulness of a particular device for a given application. The operate times of a device may be checked using the loop test facility (See page 537).

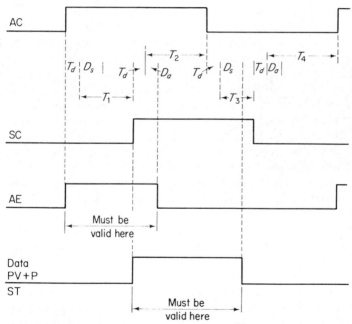

T_d = Cable delay

T_1, T_3 operate times of source

T_2, T_4 operate times of acceptor

D_a = Time to detect signal (SC) in acceptor

D_s = Time to detect signal (AC) in source

Figure A.10. Transfer times

The operate time T_1 of a source is defined as the time between the Acceptor Control signal changing to logic one, indicating it is ready to accept data, and the Source Control signal changing to logic one indicating that data has been presented. As discussed earlier, some sources may start to prepare data when the Acceptor Control signal changes to logic zero. A high speed source of this type may have data ready before the Acceptor Control signal changes to logic one. So, when this change occurs, the data will be presented immediately and operate time T_1 will be small. But with sources that wait for the Acceptor Control signal to become logic one before preparing data, the operate time T_1 will inevitably be longer.

The operate time T_2 of an acceptor is defined as the time between the Source Control signal changing to logic one, to indicate data has been presented and the Acceptor Control signal changing to logic zero indicating the data has been accepted. Operate time T_2 may be very short if the acceptor incorporates a buffer store, or may be indefinitely long.

An interesting situation arises with an acceptor that is synchronous by nature and does not include a buffer store. According to the specification an acceptor should set its Acceptor Control signal to logic one when it is ready for new data; but a synchronous acceptor without a store cannot strictly obey this rule. As an example, consider a Teletype paper tape which can perforate tape only during one particular part of its cycle of operation, as determined by an internally generated synchronizing pulse. If this pulse is used to set a punch Acceptor Control signal to logic one, but an associated source does not provide a character within a few hundred microseconds, the available time for punching passes, and it becomes necessary to wait for the next synchronizing pulse. Externally this type of acceptor appears to have a time to accept data—operate time T_2—which varies from the actual punching time, up to a cycle plus the actual punching time.

It is not very satisfactory to use such an acceptor with a computer which has no output buffer, because it would regard the change of the Acceptor Control signal to logic one as an 'interrupt' calling for data, and would expect the data to be accepted quickly whenever it answered the 'interrupt'. As each device has to be designed independently, and a synchronous acceptor may be used with any kind of source, it should really be considered essential to employ an input buffer store.

A synchronous punch incorporating a buffer store has a fixed value for T_2 if the Acceptor Control signal is set to logic one as soon as punching is completed. The store will be waiting for the next character from the source and, as soon as the Source Control signal is detected at logic one, the data may be stored and the Acceptor Control signal set to logic zero. The operate time T_2 will, of course, be the interface delay time plus the time to fill the store, i.e. a few microseconds; it will not depend on relative timing of source and acceptor.

The operate time T_3 of a source is the time between the Acceptor Control signal changing from logic one to logic zero to indicate the data has been accepted, and the Source Control signal changing from logic to logic zero indicating the Acceptor Control signal change has been detected. This time interval will normally be short.

The operate time T_4 of an acceptor is the time between the Source Control signal changing from logic one to logic zero indicating the acceptor may request new data, and the change of the Acceptor Control signal to logic one to request data. There may be wide variations in operate time T_4. Some acceptors, for example a core store with autonomous data transfer properties, could be ready for each character as soon as the previous one had been accepted; others might accept data and present it for human appraisal and acknowledgment before calling for another character. In such a case operate time T_4 could be indefinitely long.

Although it is usually easy to determine the character transfer rate in specific cases, there is no simple general formula covering the many different types of source and acceptor, particularly if several Interfaces interact with one another. This could occur in multiplexers or similar devices having several sources and acceptors. The Specification merely says that the upper and lower limits to the character transfer rate may be obtained by inserting the appropriate values in the expression

$$T_1 + T_2 + T_3 + T_4 + 4T_d$$

where T_d is defined as the cable delay under the worst conditions. When the cable delay makes a significant contribution to the total delay, i.e. for long cables or high character transfer rates, it is necessary to note that the cable delay can be highly dependent on the signals carried by other wires in the cable, and so the worst case value must be used.

It should also be noted that the operate time T_4 may be dependent on T_1 and that the operate time T_2 may be dependent on T_1, but only in the special, and undesirable, case of a synchronous acceptor without a buffer store discussed above. If a source takes a long time to provide the next character the acceptor will be ready and waiting, and T_2 and T_4 will be functions only of the acceptor itself.

However, any acceptor will have a minimum cycle time, i.e. a minimum time between being able to take successive characters and, if the source it is used with starts to fetch the next character when Acceptor Control changes to logic zero, the apparent operate time T_1 may be dependent on the acceptor operate times.

A.7 APPLICATIONS OF THE STANDARD

To bring out further aspects of British Standard Specification No. 4421 the following illustrative applications to a Paper Tape Reader source and Paper Tape Punch Acceptor are described.

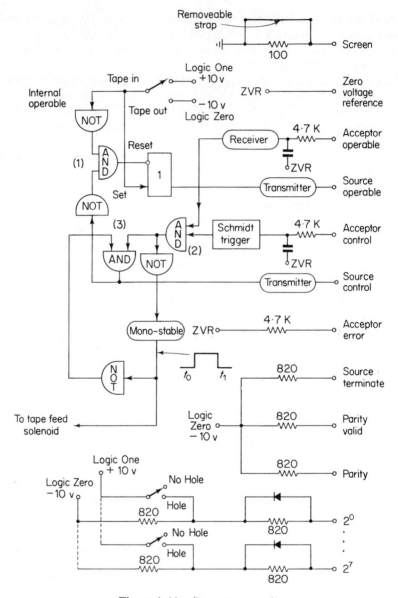

Figure A.11.   Paper tape reader

A schematic diagram of a simple mechanical tape reader fitted with Source Interface is shown in Figure A.11. The reader has 'sensing' contacts operated by the holes in the tape and a solenoid which is energized to advance the tape between characters. The following features of the Interface are illustrated:

1. Screen or Protective Earth must be connected to chassis or a local earth through a resistor and a parallel shorting strap. The strap may be removed in situations where undue earth-loop currents are experienced.

2. Except through malfunction, an Operable signal may change to logic zero only while the corresponding Control signal is logic zero. This requirement is met in Figure A.11 by including bistable 1 and gate 1; the bistable may change state to make Source Operable logic zero only when the internal Operable signal *and* Source Control are both logic zero.

3. If an input line to a device is not employed it must be terminated with the specified receiver input impedance; unused lines from a device must be connected to the appropriate logic voltage by a resistor equal to the specified transmitter output impedance. (See Acceptor Error; Source Terminate, Parity Valid and Parity.)

The cycle of operation of the tape reader when connected to an acceptor begins when Acceptor Control is detected at one by the Schmidt Trigger. Noise pulses induced in the coupling cable are prevented from affecting the Schmidt Trigger by the associated input smoothing filter, which has a time constant chosen to reduce the noise amplitude to less than the hysteresis zone of the trigger). If Acceptor Operable is one, the output signal from the Schmidt Trigger will open gate 2. This causes gate 3 to open because its other input, the inverted output of the inactive monostable, is also one. Source Control is set to one via gate 3 indicating that the first character is ready.

When the character has been accepted, the acceptor indicates that the data may be changed by setting Acceptor Control to zero. The resulting change of the Schmidt Trigger output signal to zero closes gate 2 (and consequently gate 3) and triggers the monostable. The pulse from the monostable operates the tape advance solenoid while holding the second input of gate 3 at zero. Thus, Source Control changes to zero when Acceptor Control changes to zero and remains at zero while the tape is moving, even if Acceptor Control returns to one before the tape has come to rest. When the monostable pulse ends, *and* Acceptor Control has been detected at one again, the cycle is repeated with the next character on the tape.

It is worth noting that if Source and Acceptor Operable are shorted, and Source Control connected to Acceptor Control via an inverter, self-operation of the reader occurs. This is a useful test feature of a Source Interface.

The schematic diagram of a simple paper tape punch fitted with the Acceptor Interface is shown in Figure A.12. The punch has eight solenoids for operating the punch knives and a further solenoid for feeding the tape.

The screen and unused lines are treated in accordance with the specification, as described for the tape reader. Acceptor Operable is prevented from changing to zero (unless Acceptor Control is zero) by bistable 1 and gate 1, again as described for the tape reader.

It is convenient to describe the action of the punch when connected to a

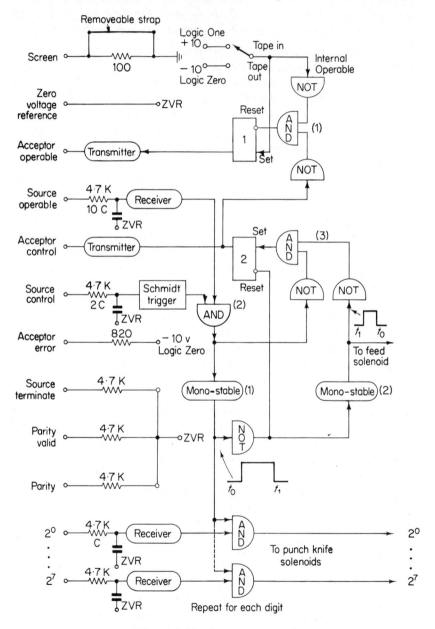

Figure A.12. Paper tape punch

source by assuming that Acceptor Control has just become one. The source will duly present data and set Source Control to one. The Schmidt Trigger will operate and, if Source Operable is one, gate 2 will open and monostable 1 will be triggered: the resulting pulse strobes the data onto the punch knife solenoids. At the end of the pulse, bistable 2 and monostable 2 are set; bistable 2 makes Acceptor Control zero—indicating the data may be changed —and the feed solenoid is energized by a pulse from monostable 2. When this pulse is ended, *and* Source Control has become zero, gate 3 will open and bistable 2 will be reset. This restores Acceptor Control to one and completes the cycle.

If Acceptor Control is joined to Source Control, and Acceptor Operable to Source Operable (thus simulating the connection of a high-speed Source) self-operation of the punch will occur. This is a useful test feature of an Acceptor Interface.

Reader to Punch Connection

By following the descriptions given above for the operation of the reader and punch it will be apparent that, when they are connected together, a continuous transfer of data will occur. The reader will be stationary while punching takes place, then both devices will advance their tape, the slower device determining the delay before the next punching operation occurs.

Glossary of Terms

Acceptor of Data (Acceptor)

A term used to describe any device capable of accepting data in a controlled manner; it is used in British Standard Interface Specifications to refer to devices which take data from a source.

Adaptive Equalisation

Equalisation which is adjusted during the transmission of data so that it adapts to changing line characteristics. See also automatic equalisation.

Adaptive Routing

Routing in which the behaviour adapts to network changes such as changes of traffic pattern or failures. The 'experience' used for adaption comes from the data traffic being carried. The term 'alternate routing' is sometimes used to cover failure situations.

Alphabet

An agreed set of characters used to store or transmit data.

Amplitude Modulation

Modulation method in which the amplitude of a carrier waveform is varied according to the baseband signal.

Anisochronous signal

A signal which is not related to any clock, and in which transitions could occur at any time.

ARPA

Advanced Research Projects Agency of the U.S. Department of Defence, which supports the ARPA resource-sharing computer network.

Automatic Equalisation

Equalisation of a transmission channel which is adjusted automatically while sending special signals. See also adaptive equalisation.

Baseband or Basic Signal

The original signal from which a transmission waveform is produced by modulation. In telephony it is the speech waveform. In data transmission many forms are used, and the basic signal is usually made of successive signal elements.

Baud

The unit of signalling speed. The speed in bauds is the number of signal elements per second. Since a signal element can represent more than one bit the term baud is not synonymous with bits per second.

Bipolar Coding

A method of transmitting a binary stream in which binary 0 is sent as no pulse and binary 1 is sent as a pulse which alternates in sign for each 1 that is sent. The signal is therefore ternary.

Bipolar Violation

In a waveform which is mainly bipolar, there may be violations of the bipolar rule, i.e. a '1' pulse that has the same sign as the preceding '1' pulse. A violation may be used deliberately to carry information outside the binary stream.

Bit Stuffing

Insertion into a binary stream of an occasional 'dummy' bit so that the mean data rate is slightly less than the bit signalling rate of the channel. The position of the stuffed bits must be signalled on a supplementary channel. Also called pulse stuffing.

Buffer

A store, usually associated with a peripheral device or communication link, which accommodates changes or differences of data rate.

Bulk Redundancy

A method of coding an anisochronous channel on a synchronous stream of bits in which a 1 state is represented by a string of 1s while it lasts, and an 0 state by a string of 0s. It is a redundant method because the strings must be long ones to reduce telegraph distortion when the anisochronous signal is reconstructed.

Burst Isochronous

A burst isochronous signal consists of bursts of digits synchronized to a clock, interspersed by 'silent' periods when no bits are presented. To indicate the bursts and silence a special clock may be provided which operates only when bits are present. This is called a 'stuttering clock'.

Byte

A small group of bits of data that is handled on a unit. In most cases it is an 8-bit byte and for this unit an alternative word is octet.

Byte Multiplexing

In this form of time-division multiplexing, the whole of a byte from one sub-channel is sent as a unit, and bytes from different sub-channels follow in successive time slots.

Byte Stuffing

Insertion into a byte stream of some 'dummy' bytes so that the mean data rate is less than the rate of the channel. The qualifying bit, if used, can distinguish the dummy bytes, which then appear as a species of control signal.

CCITT

The International Consultative Committee for Telephones and Telegraphs, part of the International Telecommunications Union (UIT) which is an organ of the UN. CCITT is the forum for international agreement on recommendations for international communication systems, including data.

Chaining of I/O Commands

The linking together (in a chain) of the commands which initiate Input-Output operations. When one command is finished the next one in the chain begins operation.

Channel

A path along which signals or data can be sent. Unless otherwise stated, the term implies one-way communication, whereas the term 'circuit' generally implies two-way communication.

Circuit Switching

Switching as performed in the telephone network where a call is set up by establishing a circuit from one subscriber to another, the circuit being held for the duration of the call. Contrasts with message switching and packet switching (q.v.).

Circular Buffer

A form of queue in which items are placed in successive locations in a store, and are later taken from these locations in the same sequence. Two pointers keep track of the head and tail of the queue. When a pointer reaches the end of the available store it returns to the start. The items in the circular buffer may themselves be pointers to the items in the queue.

Clock

A repetitive signal used to control a synchronous process such as logic or transmission.

Clock Interrupt

A type of interrupt which occurs at regular intervals and is used to initiate processes such as polling, which must happen regularly.

Clock Recovery

The extraction, from the signal received on a synchronous channel, of the clock which accompanies the data.

Cohesion

The cohesion of a connected network is the minimum number of links which, if they were removed, could disconnect the network i.e. divide it into at least two parts which are not joined by any links.

Command

A term used in several ways. An I/O command is an instruction to initiate an input/output operation (by a channel, or an I/O processor). Otherwise, a command can be an instruction to the operating system, or to software systems such as an editor or file-store

Compander

A device which applies a variable gain to a transmitted analogue signal and also to the received signal in such a way that the gain overall is roughly constant. This is used to reduce the amplitude range of signals on the line.

Concentrator

Usually means a line-concentrator in which a number of circuits (or lines) which are not all used at once are switched into a smaller group of circuits for economical transmission. A different concept is that of 'message concentrator', which stores and forwards messages and also serves to concentrate the traffic from under-used circuits into fewer channels for transmission.

Congestion

Any communication network has a limit to the traffic it can carry. Beyond that limit the network must somehow restrict traffic. Congestion means the condition in which traffic is thus restricted.

Contention

A 'dispute' between several devices for the use of common equipment. Examples are : contention for access to a store, contention by two terminals for the use of a half duplex circuit and contention by many peripherals on a highway interface.

Control Character

A character which, in certain circumstances, alters the interpretation or handling of other characters. For example a separator or delimiter.

Control Signals

Digital signals which pass between one part of communication system and another as part of the mechanism of controlling the system.

Critical Section

An element of a process (q.v.) that interacts in some way with elements of other processes; for example, the execution of a piece of program code which operates upon shared data. The execution of corresponding critical sections of processes must be disjoint in time.

Cut Set

A minimal set of elements of a connected graph (nodes, links, or both) which, when removed from the graph, disconnects it. It must be a minimal set, which means that any proper subset of the cut set does not disconnect the graph. The graph is 'disconnected' when it is separated into at least 2 parts without connecting links between them.

Cyclic Access to Store

Access to a store (for reading or writing) in which successive addresses are accessed in turn returning eventually to the first address.

Data

Numbers, facts, instructions, etc. which are represented in a formalized manner for processing, storage or transmission. By contrast, 'information' is the significance attached to the data by people, but the distinction is not always recognized.

Dataset

See 'modem'. (Dataset is a registered trade mark of AT and T Corporation.)

Data Structure

A system of relationships between items of data. To express these relationships when a data structure is stored, lists may be used, or other systems using pointers etc.

Data Terminal Equipment

In the context of a data network it is the equipment which is attached to the network to send or receive data, or both.

Data Rate

The rate at which a channel carries data, measured in bits per second (bit/s). If a binary stream is unrestricted, it can be synonymous with 'bit rate'. An alternative term is data signalling with rate.

Deadly Embrace

A state of a system of cooperating processes in which it is logically impossible for the activity of some or all of these processes to continue. A deadly embrace may result, for example, when the existence of a critical section (q.v.) is not recognized.

Delay Vector

Associated with one node of a packet switching network, the delay vector has as its elements the estimated transit times of packets destined for each other node in the net work. Nodes send copies of the delay vector to their neighbours as part of an adaptive routing scheme.

Delta Modulation

Method of representing a speech waveform (or other analogue signal) in which successive bits represent increments of the waveform. The increment size is not necessarily constant.

Directory Routing

A message or packet routing system which uses a directory at each node which states, for each destination, the preferred outgoing link. The directory may also show second preferences.

Duobinary Signalling

A method of transmitting a synchronous binary waveform in which neighbouring signal elements influence one another in a controlled manner. The resultant signal is, as a consequence ternary.

Duplex circuit

A circuit used for transmission in both directions at the same time. It may be called 'full duplex' to distinguish it from 'half duplex' (q.v.).

Dynamic Multiplexing

A form of time-division multiplexing in which the allocation of time to constituent channels is made according to the demands of these channels.

Echo Modulation

A method of producing a shaped pulse in which a main pulse with 'echoes' is generated, then put through a simple band-limiting filter. The 'echoes' are pulses of controlled amplitude occurring both before and after the main pulse.

Echoplex

A method of operating a terminal in which each character sent out is returned (echoed) from some distant point for local printing. The echoing point can be in a number of different places, but traditionally it has been at a computer centre or its F.E.P.

Elastic Store (or Buffer)

A store or buffer which can hold a variable amount of data. It behaves like a queue, sending the data out in the same sequence as it receives it, but able to vary the rate of output somewhat, subject to the limits of 'full' and 'empty'. The units of data held might typically be bits or bytes.

Envelope Delay

See 'group delay'.

Envelope (in the Analogue Context)

In an amplitude modulated signal the waveform has maxima and minima at almost exactly the carrier frequency. The location of these maxima and minima can be joined by two smooth curves which form the envelope of the waveform.

Envelope (in the Digital Context)

A group of bits in a specific format which usually has a data field as well as qualifiers or addresses etc.

Equalisation

The use of a filter which can be adjusted to counteract the (linear) distortion caused in a transmission line. See also adaptive and automatic equalisation. When a line is equalised to meet a certain standard, this is sometimes called 'conditioning' the line.

Eye Diagram

The diagram produced by superimposing many received waveforms, taken with a wide range of bit patterns (e.g. a pseudo-random bit sequence). A useful eye diagram shows the waveforms at the point at which regeneration takes place. The 'eye' is the hole in the pattern which is necessary for successful regeneration.

Flag

An indicator that an equipment or a program has reached a certain state. Often it is one bit, and it may be set or read by hardware or software.

Flooding

A packet routing method which replicates packets and sends them to all nodes, thus ensuring that the actual destination is reached.

Flow Control

In data communication networks which employ storage there is a possibility of congestion if more data flows into a node than flows out of it. To remove this possibility, flow control is needed.

Four Wire Circuit

A telephone circuit is basically duplex (it carries voice signals both ways). In the local network this is achieved over two wires because the waveforms, travelling each way can be distinguished. In the trunk network, where amplifiers are needed at intervals and multiplexing is common, it is easier to separate the two directions of transmission and use (effectively) a pair of wires for each direction. At this point it is a four wire circuit.

Frame

One complete cycle of events in time-division multiplexing. The frame usually includes a sequence of time slots for the various sub-channels and extra bits for control, framing etc.

Framing

Synchronizing of the equipment at the receiving end of a TDM channel so that it correctly recognizes the frame.

Free List

A list structure holding all the units of store which are not currently in use. It may be operted as a kind of queue so that store units which become free are added to the tail, while new requests for store are met from the head of the queue, but other regimes are possible.

Frequency Division Multiplexing (FDM)

A multiplexing method in which each constituent channel is shifted in frequency (by modulation) so that the different channels all use different sections of the spectrum. They can be separated by filtering and demodulation.

Frequency Modulation

Modulation method in which the frequency of a carrier is varied according to the baseband signal.

Group Delay or Envelope Delay

If a complex signal with a narrow bandwidth is sent down a transmission path, at the receiving end the envelope of the signal will appear to have suffered a delay, called the group or envelope delay.

Half Duplex Operation

The use of a bidirectional circuit only in one direction at a time. This method of operation is also sometimes called simplex, but that word is used in two different senses.

Hamming Distance

The Hamming distance between two binary words (of the same length) is the number of corresponding bit positions in which the two words have different bit values. Also known as 'signal distance'.

Handshaking

Operation of signals across an interface in which each signal is followed by a response in the other direction. Both sides of the interface therefore control the rate of operation.

Heuristic Routing

A routing method proposed by Baran in which delay data produced by normal data-carrying packets coming in on different links from a given source node are used to guide the outgoing packets as to the best link for getting to that node.

High Density Bipolar (HDB)

A modified bipolar code which avoids the long absence of pulses and thus eases clock recovery. There are many versions. Bipolar violations are used to signal strings of zeros.

HOST Computer

A computer which (in addition to providing a local service) acts as 'host' to a communication computer (IMP) that gives it access to many other 'hosts' via the network. Term used in the ARPA network.

Hot Potato Routing

Packet routing which sends a packet out from a node as soon as possible, even though this may mean a poor choice of outgoing link.

IMP

Interface Message Processor or IMP is the name of a data switching centre of the ARPA network. The network was built for the Advanced Research Project Agency of the U.S. Department of Defence.

Intelligent Terminal

A terminal that is programmable and can process its messages, for example to check validity.

Interface

A boundary between two pieces of equipment across which all the signals which pass are carefully defined. The definition includes the connector signal levels, impedance, timing, sequence of operation and the meaning of signals. The term has been extended to include the idea of a software interface. The essence of an interface is its accurate definition.

Interface Computer

Part of a packet switching network which mediates between network subscriber and the high-level or trunk network. It can be regarded as containing a local area switch and terminal processors.

Interrupt

A jump out of one program into another due to an external event. A mechanism is usually provided to store the information needed for a return to the interrupted program. In addition to external events in the I-O system, interrupts are sometimes allowed from clocks and timers and for various malfunctions.

Inter-symbol Interference

An (analogue) waveform which carries binary data is generally transmitted as a number of separate signal elements. When received, the signal elements may be influenced by neighbouring elements. This is called inter-symbol interference.

Interval Timer

A timer can be set by a program to produce an interrupt after a specified interval.

I-O Channel

An equipment forming part of the input-output system of a computer. Under the control of I-O commands the 'channel' transfers blocks of data between the main store and peripherals.

Isarithmic Control

The control of flow in a packet switching in such a way that the number of packets in transit is held constant.

Jump

Also known as a control jump or control transfer. It is a change in the normal sequence of obeying instructions in a computer. A conditional jump is a jump which happens only if a certain criterion is met.

Junctor

Part of a circuit-switching exchange. The switching matrix brings to the junctor the two lines which are to be connected. In the junctor there is the common equipment needed in the circuit during the call.

Leased Circuit

A telecommunication circuit leased by the user for his exclusive use between certain locations. No switching is employed, so the circuit is ready for immediate use. It may be point-to-point or multidrop.

Link

In one sense it is the physical communication path between two 'nodes' or switching centres. In a different sense it means a conceptual link between two parties in a packet switching network, signifying that they are in communication with each other. The 'parties' may be subscribers, or processes within the subscribers computers.

Link Exchange

A technique for improving network topology by trying the effect of substituting one link for another.

List

A data structure in which each item of data can contain pointers to other items. Any data structure can be represented in this way, which allows the structure to be independent of the storage of the items.

Markov Constraint

A constraint on the routing method according to which the future route of a packet is independent of its past history, such as its source or its route so far. This constraint is implied by directory routing.

Message

A sequence of characters used to convey information or data. In data communication, messages are usually in an agreed format with a 'heading', which controls the destiny of the message and 'text' which consists of the data being carried.

Message Switching

The switching method in which messages find their way through a network by being handled as separate entities, without having a circuit established in advance. The network's switches must be able to store a received message but it is not essential that each message be completely received before transmission begins.

Minimum Weight Routing

A routing scheme which minimizes the sum of the weights of the links employed in the route. These 'weights' could be link delays, cost or error rate — anything which adds together in transit and should be minimized.

Modem

The device which accepts a digital waveform and adapts it for transmission over an analogue channel, such as a telephone circuit provides, and also receives signals from the distant modem and converts them back to digital form. A contraction of 'modulator-demodulator', but a modem contains more than this.

Modulation

The process of shifting a basic or baseband signal to a higher part of the spectrum. The de-modulator reverses the process.

Modulo 2 Addition

A method of adding binary digits which gives

$$0+0 = 0$$
$$0+1 = 1$$
$$1+0 = 1$$
$$1+1 = 0$$

Other names for the operator are 'not equivalent' and 'exclusive OR'.

Multi-access

The ability for several users to communicate with the computer at the same time, each working independently on his own job.

Multi-drop Line

See Multipoint line.

Multiplexer

Equipment which takes a number of communication channels and combines the signals into one common channel (of greater bandwidth or data rate) in such a way that the original signals can be extracted again by a demultiplexer. In a slightly different sense the term has been used for equipment which combines digital channels for access to a computer.

Multipoint Line

A four-wire circuit which is connected by branching points to several terminals distributed along its length. Known as a Multi-drop line in the U.S.A.

Multiprocessing

Strictly, this term refers to the simultaneous application of more than one processor in a multi-CPU computer system to the execution of a single 'user job', which is only possible if the job can be effectively defined in terms of a number of independently executable components. The term is more often used to denote multiprogramming operation of multi-CPU computer systems.

Multiprogramming

A method of operation of a computer system whereby a number of independent 'user jobs' are processed together. Rather than allow each job to run to completion in turn, the computer switches between them so as to improve the utilization of the system hardware components.

Multithreading

Concurrent processing of more than one message (or similar service-request) by an application program.

Negative Acknowledge (NAK)

In the method of error control which relies on repeating any message received with (detectable) errors, the return signal which reports an error is NAK, the opposite to ACK, or acknowledge. May be written 'NACK'. NAK is the correct spelling for this control symbol in CCITT alphabet No. 5.

Network Terminating Unit (NTU)

The part of the network equipment which connects directly to the data terminal equipment. The NTU operates between the local transmission lines and the subscriber's interface.

Node

In a topological description of a network a node is a point of junction of the links. The word has also come to mean a switching centre in the context of data networks, particularly in the context of packet switching.

Non-blocking Switch

A circuit switch can connect together any free pair of lines, whatever existing connections it is also carrying.

On-line

Connected to a computer so that data can pass to or from the computer without human intervention.

Packet

A block of data handled by a network in a well-defined format including a heading. A maximum size of packet is set, and messages longer than that size have to be carried as several packets.

Packet Interleaving

Where packet interleaving is used on a line, each packet is completed before the next one is sent. This contrasts with the interleaving of bytes belonging to different packets, which is also sometimes used. Packet interleaving is appropriate at a computer's interface with the network.

Packet Switching Network

A network designed to carry data in the form of packets. The packet and its format is internal to that network. The external interfaces may handle data in different formats, for example byte by byte.

Pair-selected Ternary (PST)

A pseudo-ternary code in which pairs of binary digits are coded together in such a way that the resultant signal has no long strings of zeros.

Parallel Transmission

The simultaneous transmission of a number of signal elements belonging to the same stream of data. The elements might be sent over separate lines in parallel, or be combined on one channel by using different frequencies.

Parity

The property of being odd or even. The parity count of a binary sequence is the parity of the number of ones it contains. It can also be regarded as the modulo 2 sum of the bits themselves.

Peripheral Device or Equipment

A peripheral device of a computer is typically an input or output device, but the term is used also to include those kinds or store (drums, discs etc) which are handled like external devices.

Peripheral Interface

A standard interface used between a computer and its peripherals so that new peripherals may be added or old ones changed without special hardware adaption.

Phase Modulation

Modulation method in which the phase of a carrier is varied according to the baseband signal. For digital transmission, 2, 4 or sometimes 8 different phases are used. Bits are signalled by changes of phase, to avoid phase ambiguity.

Pointer

A word in a computer's store containing the address of another item of data. It is said to 'point' to that item. The manipulation of pointers may save many operations by avoiding the movement of larger items to which they point.

Polling

Inviting a station to transmit data. When many stations are connected to the same circuit, polling from the centre is used to ensure an orderly flow of data to the central location.

Primary Group

A group of basic signals which are combined by multiplexing. It is the lowest level of the multiplexing heirarchy. The term is also used for the signal obtained by multiplexing these basic signals or for the transmission channel which carries it. In FDM it usually comprises 12 voice channels. PCM speech channels are usually combined in 'primary groups' of 24 or 30.

Private Wire

See leased circuit.

Process

An activity in a software system organised as a set of self-contained but interacting activities. A process is most simply regarded as a 'pseudo-processor' which may possess certain states such as 'active' or 'dormant' and which may execute a piece of program code.

Protocol

A strict procedure required to initiate and maintain communication. Protocols may exist at many levels in one network such as link-by-link, end-to-end and subscriber-to-switch.

Pulse Code Modulation (PCM)

Representation of a speech signal (or other analogue signal) by sampling at a regular rate and converting each sample to a binary number. 8000 samples per second is standard for telephone speech.

Pulse Stuffing

See 'bit stuffing'.

Pure Code

A program written so that none of the program (code) is altered during execution. All data and working storage is outside the program area. A process using the pure code can be stopped at any point and the program re-entered with a different process. Also called reentrant code.

Qualifier or Qualifying Bit

When a data field is used for more than one purpose, a qualifier can be added to denote which purpose is being served. An example is the qualifying bit attached to a byte of data to distinguish between customers' data and control signals.

Quantization Error (or Noise)

When an analogue signal is represented digitally, the various samples can be numerically specified with only a certain accuracy. Quantization error is the difference between the signal as specified digitally and its true (analogue) value.

Queue

A collection of items which can be thought of as arranged in sequence, the two ends being the head and tail. New items are added to the tail and items are removed at the head. A queue can be stored as a list or in a circular buffer.

Real-time

A real-time computer interacts with external events and must respond fast enough to meet certain timing requirements of the overall system. The term has meaning only if the response time requirements of the system are known. Typically they range from milliseconds to seconds. For longer times the term is not used.

Rearrangeable Switch

A circuit switch wich accommodates extra connections by rearrangement of some of the connections it already carries, so that they follow different paths through the switch. By such rearrangement a switch may become non-blocking.

Re-entrant Code or Program

See 'pure code'.

Regenerator

Equipment which takes a digital signal that has been distorted by transmission and produces from it a new signal in which the shape, timing and amplitude of pulses has been restored.

Response Time

The time between the last key depression by an operator and the receipt of the first character of the computer response. Applied to a data communication network it is the time between the completion of message input at the source and the start of message output at the destination.

Routing Table

A table associated with a node which states for each packet destination the preferred outgoing link that the packet should use. Synonymous with 'directory'.

Scrambler

Coding device applied to a digital channel which produces an apparently random bit sequence. A corresponding device is used to decode the channel, i.e. the coding is reversible. By this means, harmful repetitive patterns in the data sent over a transmission line are avoided. They could still occur, but with low probability.

Selection

The process of indicating the number of the terminal being called. In the telephone case this would be termed 'dialling'. The term 'selection' is now preferred because the number may not come from a dial, but from push buttons, a keyboard or a computer, for example. 'Selection' has other meanings as in the selection of a peripheral on a highway interface.

Semaphore

A mechanism for the synchronization of a set of cooperating processes. It is used to prevent two or more processes from entering mutually critical sections (q.v.) at the same time.

Signal

The physical process used to carry information from one place to another. Often the signal is an electrical waveform, but it can be a radio or optical signal, for example.

Signal Distance

See 'Hamming distance'.

Simplex Circuit

May mean either:
(a) a circuit used in one direction only
(b) a circuit used in either direction, but not at the same time.
It is perhaps best not to use the term. Case (a) is rare and the word 'channel' is available. Case (b) is called 'half duplex' in this book.

Single Threading

A program which completes the processing of one message before starting another message is called 'single threading'. See also multi-threading.

Sink Tree

For a given node T, the links employed by packets destined for T (wherever they start) form a tree if directory routing is employed. This is the 'sink tree' of node T.

SITA

Societe Internationale de Télécommunications Aéronautiques, which operates a message and data network for a large group of airline companies.

Source of Data (Source)

A term used to describe any device capable of supplying data in a controlled manner; it is used in British Standard Interface Specifications to refer to devices which provide data to an Acceptor.

Space-division Switching

Method for switching of circuits in which each connection through the switch takes a physically separate path.

Spectrum Roll-off

Applied to the frequency response of a transmission line, or a filter, it is the attenuation characteristic at the edge of the band.

Stack

A collection of items which can be thought of as arranged in sequence. One end of the sequence is the 'top' of the stack. New items are added at the top, and items are also read or removed from the top of the stack. A stack can be stored as a list. Sometimes pointers to parts of the stack other than the top are retained.

Start-stop Envelopes

A type of anisochronous signal which is widely used. It employs a string of signal elements, the first of which is a start element, followed by elements representing the binary data, and finally stop elements. The number and length of the elements is fixed, and the whole unit, called a start-stop envelope. can begin at any time.

Status Information

Information about the logical state of a piece of equipment. Examples are:
(a) A peripheral device reporting its status to the computer.
(b) A network terminating unit reporting status to a network switch.
Status information is one kind of control signal.

Store-and-forward

The handling of messages or packets in a network by accepting the messages or packets completely into storage then sending them forward to the next centre.

Synchronous Network

A network in which all the communication links are synchronized to a common clock.

Telegraph Distortion

Distortion which alters the duration of signal elements.

Telex Network

The switched public telegraph network. Telex is also the name of a U.S. corporation, but in this book the technical meaning is implied.

Terminal Processor

In a packet switching network it is convenient to treat terminals like other processors needing communication. To this end, each terminal has a process looking after it. This can be regarded as residing in a terminal processor (a separate processor is not essential — it could be part of an interface computer, for example).

Ternary

Having three possible values. There are ternary number representations using, for example, the digits 0, 1, 2 and there are ternary signals which nominally take 3 possible values, for example $+1$ volt, 0, -1 volt.

Time-division Multiplexing (TDM)

A multiplexing method in which the time on the multiplexed channel is allocated at different times to different constituent channels. The allocation may be repeated regularly (fixed cycle) or may be made according to demand (dynamic).

Time-division Switching

Switching method for a TDM channel requiring the shifting of data from one slot to another in the TDM frame. The slot in question may carry a bit or byte (or, in principle, any other unit of data).

Time-out

In a communication procedure, one party may have to take action it if gets no response from the other within a specified time. This occurrence (exceeding the allowed time) is called a time-out.

Time Sharing

The sharing of an equipment between several processes by giving the processes access to the equipment in turn, i.e. sharing out its time. Usually applied to processor time, but TDM is also a form of time sharing.

Trace Packet

A special kind of packet in the ARPA network which functions as a normal packet but because its 'trace' bit is set causes a report of each stage of its progress to be sent to the network control centre.

Traffic Matrix

A matrix of which the (i, j) element contains the amount of traffic originated at node i and destined for node j. The unit of measurement could be calls, or packets per second, for example, depending on the kind of network.

Transit Network

The highest level of a switched network. The transit network is well provided with links between its switching centres so that it rarely needs intermediate switching.

Transparency

A transmission path that passes a signal through unchanged is said to be transparent to it. But it is usually some particular feature of the signal to which the path is transparent, for example the sequence of bits. The term should therefore always be qualified, for example 'bit-sequence transparency'.

Transversal Filter

In this filter the input is passed through a delay network and delayed versions of the signal, through suitable attenuators, are added to generate the output. The attenuators must be able to invert the signal.

Virtual Terminal (or Terminal Image)

An ideal terminal which is defined as a standard for the purpose of uniform handling of a variety of actual terminals. The terminal processor is given the job of 'mapping' or 'conversion' between the virtual terminal and actual terminals.

Watch Dog Timer

A form of interval timer which is used to guard against malfunction. By repeatedly resetting this timer, an interrupt is prevented. If the program gets into a loop or something stops normal operation, the resetting will be missed and the interrupt will start a program for recovery.

Index

Glossary entries and References at the end of chapters are shown in italic